Special Edition

Using

Linux
System
Admin-
istration

Arman Danesh

Gautam Das

Ram Samudrala

A Division of Macmillan Publishing USA
201 W. 103rd Street
Indianapolis, Indiana 46290

SPECIAL EDITION USING LINUX SYSTEM ADMINISTRATION

Copyright © 2000 by Que

All rights reserved. No part of this book shall be reproduced, stored in a retrieval system, or transmitted by any means, electronic, mechanical, photocopying, recording, or otherwise, without written permission from the publisher. No patent liability is assumed with respect to the use of the information contained herein. Although every precaution has been taken in the preparation of this book, the publisher and author assume no responsibility for errors or omissions. Nor is any liability assumed for damages resulting from the use of the information contained herein.

International Standard Book Number: 0-7897-2352-2

Library of Congress Catalog Card Number: 00-100144

Printed in the United States of America

First Printing: June 2000

02   01   00   4   3   2   1

Trademarks

All terms mentioned in this book that are known to be trademarks or service marks have been appropriately capitalized. Que cannot attest to the accuracy of this information. Use of a term in this book should not be regarded as affecting the validity of any trademark or service mark.

This publication was produced using the Advent **3B2** Publishing System.

Warning and Disclaimer

Every effort has been made to make this book as complete and as accurate as possible, but no warranty or fitness is implied. The information provided is on an "as is" basis. The authors and the publisher shall have neither liability nor responsibility to any person or entity with respect to any loss or damages arising from the information contained in this book.

Associate Publisher
Tracy Dunkelberger

Acquisitions Editor
Gretchen Ganser

Development Editor
Maureen A. McDaniel

Technical Editor
Brian Walters

Managing Editor
Matt Purcell

Project Editor
Natalie F. Harris

Copy Editor
Cynthia Fields

Indexer
Tina Trettin

Proofreaders
Juli Cook
Maribeth Echard

Team Coordinator
Cindy Teeters

Interior Designer
Ruth Harvey

Cover Designers
Dan Armstrong
Ruth Harvey

Production
Brandon Allen
Susan Geiselman
Cheryl Lynch

TABLE OF CONTENTS

ABOUT THE AUTHORS

Arman Danesh is pursuing an advanced degree in Computer Science at Simon Fraser University in Vancouver, British Columbia. Formerly the MIS Manager at Landegg Academy (www.landegg.edu), a private international university in Switzerland, Arman managed a network of Linux desktops and servers. He spent almost seven years as a technology journalist writing for newspapers in the Far East. He worked on staff for the South China *Morning Post* and currently freelances for them, contributing regular Internet and shareware columns as well as product reviews and how-to articles. Arman is also editorial director of Juxta Publishing (www.juxta.com), a Hong Kong-based print and Web publisher. He manages several Web sites for nongovernmental organizations including The Baha'i World (www.bahai.org), the official Web site of the Baha'i International Community. Arman has written, contributed to, and revised several books, including *Mastering Red Hat Linux 6.0*, *Mastering Linux, Mastering Linux Premium Edition, Sams Teach Yourself JavaScript in a Week*, *JavaScript 1.1 Developer's Guide, JavaScript Interactive Course*, and *Sams Teach Yourself Web Publishing with HTML in 14 Days*. Arman lives with his wife Tahirih in Vancouver.

Gautam Das works as a Systems and Network Administrator at the Baha'i World Centre, Haifa, Israel. He holds a bachelor's degree in Chemical Engineering from the Indian Institute of Technology, Kharagpur, India, and has spent more than 14 years working with and managing UNIX systems and networks. Before moving to Israel, he was a Member of Technical Staff at Tellabs, Inc., in Lisle, Illinois, writing software for data communication systems. He also spent a few years designing microphones at Shure, Inc., in Evanston, Illinois.

Ram Samudrala is post-doctoral fellow at Stanford University, researching protein folding, structure, function, and evolution using computational approaches. His work has led to several journal publications and to freely copiable software for molecular modeling (used on a cluster of machines running Linux that will shortly be expanded to include more than 300 processors, which he manages). In addition to his scientific interests, Ram is a musician and has released an album under the pseudonym Twisted Helices; the complete album is published online free of any intellectual property restrictions (a second album is in progress). He is the author of "Free Music Philosophy" and other texts regarding intellectual property, which have been referenced in *Forbes, Hot Wired*, and *The New York Times*. As with free software, these philosophies have heralded a new paradigm for the distribution of music and other forms of creative expression over the Internet. Ram's Web page is accessible at http://www.ram.org.

DEDICATION

To my grandmother, Khadijeh. May your eyes keep their light forever.

-Arman Danesh

To my mother, Sheela Das, and father, the late Jyotish Chandra Das, for their encouragement to never stop seeking knowledge and truth. To my wife, Carolyn, and our sons, Jyoti and Christopher, for bringing much joy to my life.

-Gautam Das

ACKNOWLEDGMENTS

The number of people who contribute to a book of this breadth are numerous and all deserve recognition. Most notably, the staff at Que—Gretchen Ganser, Maureen McDaniel, Natalie Harris, and Brian Walters—and other contributors have given extensively to the project. I am indebted, also, to my co-author, Gautam Das, who brought the necessary expertise to the book and helped make the book the advanced reference that it is.

As always, my wife, Tahirih, is owed my gratitude. She tolerated the insufferably long hours I had to commit to this project and helped me bear the pressure. Without her, none of my books would have been possible.

-Arman Danesh

I want to thank Arman Danesh for asking me to co-author this book with him. I have worked with Linux since its inception, and was happy to have the opportunity to write about it. My sincere gratitude goes out to Linus Torvalds for creating this great operating system, Linux, and making it freely available to everyone. I am grateful to George Thiruvathukal of DePaul University, Chicago, Illinois, for introducing me to Linux in its early days.

I want to express my heartfelt appreciation to the editors at Macmillan—Maureen McDaniel, Brian Walters, Mandie Rowell, Cynthia Fields, and Katie Robinson—for closely working with me in preparing the manuscript, getting all the details right, and suggesting many improvements to the original work.

I am also indebted to my colleagues at the Baha'i World Centre—Stephen Gouthro, Robert Francis, and Shoa Aminpour for their continued encouragement, support, and understanding while I was striving to get the chapters written and delivered on time to the publisher.

-Gautam Das

TELL US WHAT YOU THINK!

As the reader of this book, *you* are our most important critic and commentator. We value your opinion and want to know what we're doing right, what we could do better, what areas you'd like to see us publish in, and any other words of wisdom you're willing to pass our way.

As an Associate Publisher for Que, I welcome your comments. You can fax, email, or write me directly to let me know what you did or didn't like about this book—as well as what we can do to make our books stronger.

Please note that I cannot help you with technical problems related to the topic of this book, and that due to the high volume of mail I receive, I might not be able to reply to every message.

When you write, please be sure to include this book's title and author as well as your name and phone or fax number. I will carefully review your comments and share them with the author and editors who worked on the book.

Fax:	317-581-4666
Email:	quetechnical@macmillanusa.com
Mail:	Tracy Dunkelberger
	Associate Publisher
	Que
	201 West 103rd Street
	Indianapolis, IN 46290 USA

INTRODUCTION

As one of the most rapidly growing contenders in the operating system market, Linux has come from a hacker's toy and a student's inexpensive alternative to UNIX to a respectable player in a market largely dominated by Microsoft.

In fact, Linux has been so successful in the server arena and has proven reliable and stable enough to be accepted in corporate information systems environments that numerous organizations now have Linux servers acting as Web servers, mail servers, file servers, and database servers. Where once Linux suffered from a lack of commercial, enterprise-class software, it now faces a rush to port and release commercial applications from sources as diverse as Adobe, Corel, Sun, Oracle, and Allaire. In fact, it is now possible to deploy a Linux-based system as an Intranet server running the same commercial tools that normally run on expensive commercial UNIX systems.

This book focuses on installing, configuring, and administering Linux as an operating system for organizational information systems. It covers all the major roles Linux can play in the enterprise and looks at advanced topics such as compiling the kernel and managing RAID disk arrays.

Linux is a freely redistributable UNIX-like operating system and, as such, offers most of the benefits of a UNIX environment at a fraction of the cost. These benefits include the following:

- **Multitasking:** Linux is a multitasking operating system capable of running a large number of simultaneous applications in an ideal way for corporate servers and high-end workstations.

- **Multiuser:** Linux is a true multiuser operating system that multiple users can simultaneously log in to and use; this allows Linux to be used as an applications server for users on desktop computers or terminals.

- **Stable:** Linux has shown itself to be extremely stable. Linux systems are known to run for weeks or months at a time without requiring system reboots and it is rare for a single, poorly written application to crash an entire Linux system.

- **Manageable:** Like UNIX systems, Linux can be entirely controlled and managed from a command-prompt without resorting to less-than-efficient graphical tools; accordingly, a Linux system can be fully managed remotely through a simple serial or Telnet connection.

WHO SHOULD USE THIS BOOK?

This book is targeted at individuals faced with the task of administering Linux systems as part of their work, including the following:

- System administrators for UNIX and Windows NT networks who are now faced with supporting Linux systems being added to their environment

- Power users tasked with managing a small Linux-based workgroup server in their offices or small businesses
- Administrators of Linux systems who need a guide and a reference for their work

Because this is a book about systems administration it is not designed for the first-time Linux user or for readers simply interested in learning how to install and use Linux for personal use. It presumes sufficient understanding of computing and networking to be able to manage a system or small network, and it introduces Linux administration within the context of this pre-existing knowledge.

Accordingly, this book presumes that the reader has the following:

- Familiarity with computers and their basic hardware
- A basic understanding of networking
- Familiarity with the fundamental issues in system and network administration, including security, stability, and robustness
- Enough confidence in his skills to experiment and learn by trying new tasks without fear

WHO SHOULD NOT USE THIS BOOK?

By its nature, this book targets an advanced audience. Accordingly, it dispenses with many discussions of basic topics or only treats them in a cursory manner in order to focus on the advanced skills and knowledge that are required to administer Linux systems and networks.

If you are a regular computer user curious to learn to use Linux because of the media attention it has garnered, this book is probably not for you. In this case, consider referring to *Special Edition Using Linux* from Que or *Mastering Linux Premium Edition* by the author from Sybex.

Similarly, if you are an advanced user more interested in Linux as a powerful workstation operating system or development platform rather than a corporate information systems platform, this book's focus might be ill suited to your needs.

HARDWARE REQUIREMENTS

The topic of hardware requirements for Linux is not a simple subject. The selection of suitable hardware depends entirely on how you will be using Linux in your environment and the number of users who will be using it. These details are addressed in Chapter 12, "Capacity Planning."

Linux is available for multiple hardware platforms, including Intel x86 systems, Compaq Alpha-based systems, Sun Sparc platforms, PowerPC-based computers, MIPS environments, and numerous others.

While there are subtle differences in the installation and configuration of Linux in these different environments, in this book we will focus on Linux in the Intel x86 environment. This is the most common Linux platform, and the vast majority of enterprise-class commercial software is available only for Linux on Intel x86 hardware.

HOW THIS BOOK IS ORGANIZED

This book is organized in five parts:

- **Part I—Linux Deployment and Installation:** This part covers a range of hardware, naming, and configuration issues related to installing Linux and addresses remote and automated installation of Linux.

- **Part II—General System Administration:** This part covers fundamental administration topics including user management, the Linux boot process, X Windows applications servers, distributed network user authentication, task scheduling, and backup and restore procedures.

- **Part III—Network Management:** This part covers network-specific issues including network configuration with TCP/IP, printer and file sharing with UNIX and Windows networks, routing, and Linux email services.

- **Part IV—Security and Stability:** This part covers security issues and topics including physical security, network security, firewalls, and log management and analysis.

- **Part V—The Internet and the Intranet:** This part covers the use of Internet technology with Linux, including the deployment of Linux as a DNS, Web, FTP, database, and News server.

In addition, two appendixes provide a Linux command reference and a copy of the Linux Hardware Compatibility HOWTO.

PART I

LINUX DEPLOYMENT AND INSTALLATION

## CHAPTER 1

ISSUES IN LINUX INSTALLATION

In this chapter

INSTALLATION AND THE DISTRIBUTIONS

Unlike Windows, there are numerous flavors of Linux known as *distributions*. Each distribution consists of a unique collection of Linux applications sitting on top of a specific version of the Linux kernel—the core of the operating system.

In addition, each distribution has its own installation program and methodology. Accordingly, there is no standardized methodology for installing Linux. The way in which each installation program runs is different and each program performs basic steps in different orders. For this reason, we will not attempt to provide a step-by-step guide to the installation process. The documentation with each distribution usually provides sufficient guidance in this regard. Instead we will consider broader installation-related issues.

This is not to say there aren't commonalties. First, most distributions of Linux can be installed by booting from a floppy disk or from the distribution's CD-ROM. In addition, you have a choice of installation media:

- CD-ROM
- Hard disk image
- NFS-mounted network directory
- Remote FTP server

Several common issues arise during installation of all versions of Linux:

- Hardware and hardware compatibility questions
- Linux device naming
- Disk partitioning schemes
- Selecting the size of the swap partition

These issues will be discussed in the rest of this chapter.

HARDWARE CONCERNS

Before attempting to install Linux, it is essential that you have a comprehensive list of the hardware in the target system. Knowing this information makes the process of installing and configuring Linux quicker and easier. You want to create as precise a list as possible, including the following information about all hardware where relevant:

- Brand name
- Model name or number
- IRQ setting
- I/O address
- Attached port

- Available memory
- Any other relevant hardware settings

The Linux Installation and Getting Started Guide by Matt Welsh, et al., suggests using the following worksheet to summarize your system's hardware before installation:

```
General

Processor:          Type:          386 486 Pentium PPro

Speed (optional):

Mfg:

Intel AMD Cyrix

Motherboard:              Make:              Chip Set:

Example:          Make:  unknown      Chip Set: triton II

Mouse:           Mfg:              Type: bus  PS/2  serial port

If serial:          COM1 (ttyS0)       COM2 (ttyS1)

Hard disk drive(s):       Type:          IDE/MFM/RLL/ESDI    SCSI

Size (list each drive):

If SCSI Controller:      Make:        Model:

Example:       Make: BusLogic      Model: 948

Boot:           Linux          DOS/Windows        OS/2        Other

Disk:          Partition:          Size:              Boot:

Disk:          Partition:          Size:              Boot:

Disk:          Partition:          Size:              Boot:

Disk:          Partition:          Size:              Boot:

CD-ROM:          IDE/ATAPI  SCSI  Proprietary

Mfg:           Model:

(Proprietary only):

X-Windows:

Video Card:          Mfg:          Model:

RAM:          1Mb      2Mb      4Mb      8Mb      16Mb

Monitor:          Mfg:          Model:          Max scan rate:
```

```
Networking:

Modem:            Mfg:              Model:

Serial port:           COM1        COM2         COM3        COM4

      (ttyS0)          (ttyS1)            (ttyS2)          (ttyS3)

Computer hostname:                  Example: rainier

NIC Type:         ethernet          token ring        FDDI          other

NIC Mfg:          Model:

Network domain name:               (Example: mountains.net)

IP Address:            (Ex: 192.168.1.2)

Network address:            (Ex: 192.168.1.0)

Netmask:          (Ex: 255.255.255.0)

Broadcast address:          (Ex: 192.168.1.255)

Gateway(s):            (Ex: none or 192.168.1.1)

DNS(s):           (Ex: 192.168.1.2)
```

Having determined your hardware inventory, it is advisable to take the time to consult the Hardware Compatibility HOWTO (reproduced in Appendix A) to ensure that Linux is compatible with all the hardware on your system. In this way, you can replace incompatible hardware before attempting to install Linux. Otherwise you will have trouble installing and using Linux.

Among the types of hardware likely to cause problems are:

- USB devices (which Linux does not support)
- Some plug-and-play devices
- Windows-only modems known as Winmodems (which Linux does not support)
- Windows-driven printers known as GDI printers (which Linux does not support)
- Some types of video cards

LINUX DEVICE NAMING

Linux uses a special file system for accessing devices. All devices are accessed through device files in the /dev directory. These device files contain information about a device's permissions, its type, and a unique identifier.

Table 1.1 outlines some of the more common Linux device files and the devices they are associated with. To see a list of all device file names, view a listing of the /dev directory.

TABLE 1.1 SOME COMMON LINUX DEVICES

Linux Device File	Typical DOS Device Name	Description
/dev/ttyS0	COM1:	Serial port
/dev/ttyS1	COM2:	Serial port
/dev/ttyS2	COM3:	Serial port
/dev/ttyS3	COM4:	Serial port
/dev/lp0	LPT1:	Parallel port
/dev/lp1	LPT2:	Parallel port
/dev/lp2	LPT3:	Parallel port
/dev/psaux		PS 2 Mouse port
/dev/fd0	A:	Primary Floppy drive
/dev/fd1	B:	Secondary Floppy drive
/dev/hda		First IDE hard disk or CD-ROM drive on the primary IDE chain
/dev/hda1		First primary partition on the first IDE hard disk on the primary IDE chain
/dev/hda2		Second primary partition on the first IDE hard disk on the primary IDE chain
/dev/hda3		Third primary partition on the first IDE hard disk on the primary IDE chain
/dev/hda4		Fourth primary partition on the first IDE hard disk on the primary IDE chain
/dev/hda5 and up		Logical partitions on the first IDE hard disk on the primary IDE chain
/dev/hdb		Second IDE hard disk or CD-ROM drive on the primary IDE chain
/dev/hdb1		First primary partition on the second IDE hard disk on the primary IDE chain
/dev/hdb2		Second primary partition on the second IDE hard disk on the primary IDE chain
/dev/hdb3		Third primary partition on the second IDE hard disk on the primary IDE chain
/dev/hdb4		Fourth primary partition on the second IDE hard disk on the primary IDE chain
/dev/hdb5 and up		Logical partitions on the second IDE hard disk on the primary IDE chain
/dev/hdc		First IDE hard disk or CD-ROM drive on the secondary IDE chain

TABLE 1.1   CONTINUED

Linux Device File	Typical DOS Device Name	Description
/dev/hdc1		First primary partition on the first IDE hard disk on the secondary IDE chain
/dev/hdc2		Second primary partition on the first IDE hard disk on the secondary IDE chain
/dev/hdc3		Third primary partition on the first IDE hard disk on the secondary IDE chain
/dev/hdc4		Fourth primary partition on the first IDE hard disk on the secondary IDE chain
/dev/hdc5 and up		Logical partitions on the first IDE hard disk on the secondary IDE chain
/dev/hdd		Second IDE hard disk or CD-ROM drive on the secondary IDE chain
/dev/hdd1		First primary partition on the second IDE hard disk on the secondary IDE chain
/dev/hdd2		Second primary partition on the second IDE hard disk on the secondary IDE chain
/dev/hdd3		Third primary partition on the second IDE hard disk on the secondary IDE chain
/dev/hdd4		Fourth primary partition on the second IDE hard disk on the secondary IDE chain
/dev/hdd5 and up		Logical partitions on the second IDE hard disk on the secondary IDE chain
/dev/sda		First SCSI hard disk
/dev/sda1		First primary partition on the first SCSI hard disk
/dev/sda2		Second primary partition on the first SCSI hard disk
/dev/sda3		Third primary partition on the first SCSI hard disk
/dev/sda4		Fourth primary partition on the first SCSI hard disk
/dev/sda5 and up		Logical partitions on the first SCSI hard disk
/dev/sdb		Second SCSI hard disk
/dev/sdb1		First primary partition on the second SCSI hard disk
/dev/sdb2		Second primary partition on the second SCSI hard disk

TABLE 1.1   CONTINUED

Linux Device File	Typical DOS Device Name	Description
/dev/sdb3		Third primary partition on the second SCSI hard disk
/dev/sdb4		Fourth primary partition on the second SCSI hard disk
/dev/sdb5 and up		Logical partitions on the second SCSI hard disk
/dev/sdc		Third SCSI hard disk
/dev/sdc1		First primary partition on the third SCSI hard disk
/dev/sdc2		Second primary partition on the third SCSI hard disk
/dev/sdc3		Third primary partition on the third SCSI hard disk
/dev/sdc4		Fourth primary partition on the third SCSI hard disk
/dev/sdc5 and up		Logical partitions on the third SCSI hard disk
/dev/sdd		Fourth SCSI hard disk
/dev/sdd1		First primary partition on the fourth SCSI hard disk
/dev/sdd2		Second primary partition on the fourth SCSI hard disk
/dev/sdd3		Third primary partition on the fourth SCSI hard disk
/dev/sdd4		Fourth primary partition on the fourth SCSI hard disk
/dev/sdd5 and up		Logical partitions on the fourth SCSI hard disk
/dev/st0		First SCSI tape drive
/dev/st1		Second SCSI tape drive
/dev/st2		Third SCSI tape drive
/dev/scd0		First SCSI CD-ROM drive
/dev/scd1		Second SCSI CD-ROM drive
/dev/scd2		Third SCSI CD-ROM drive
/dev/sonycd		Sony CD-ROM drive on a proprietary controller

TABLE 1.1 CONTINUED

Linux Device File	Typical DOS Device Name	Description
/dev/sbpcd0		First CD-ROM drive connected to a SoundBlaster controller
/dev/sbpcd1		Second CD-ROM drive connected to a SoundBlaster controller
/dev/sbpcd2		Third CD-ROM drive connected to a SoundBlaster controller

Note

The DOS devices listed in Table 1.1 are not in a fixed relationship to the Linux device files. Instead they are typical correspondences. For instance, in DOS, LPT1: specifies a particular parallel port whereas /dev/lp0 specifies the first available parallel port in Linux. Therefore, LPT1: normally corresponds to /dev/lp0. However, if LPT1: doesn't exist on your system and you only have LPT2:, then LPT2: corresponds to /dev/lp0.

Typically, common devices such as mouse devices and CD-ROM drives have special links in the /dev/ directory for easy access. For instance, most Linux distributions create /dev/cdrom as a link to the correct device file for your particular CD-ROM drive so that you can easily access your CD-ROM drive as /dev/cdrom on all systems regardless of the particular hardware being used as a CD-ROM drive. Similarly, a /dev/mouse link is created for your mouse in most Linux distributions.

LINUX PARTITIONING SCHEMES

During the Linux installation process you will need to determine how to partition your hard drives in the best manner possible. Linux systems can be installed as the sole operating system on a computer or in a dual-boot situation with Windows or other operating systems. We will consider the installation of Linux as the sole operating system on a computer because this is typical of the environment found on Linux-based servers and workstations in a corporate or institutional network.

Note

In this section, the term *partition* is used to refer to any partition on your system. This can be a single partition that spans an entire hard drive or one of many partitions on a single hard drive.

In order to understand possible partitioning strategies, it is necessary to understand how Linux handles multiple partitions. In DOS and Windows, each partition is assigned a separate drive letter through which it is accessed. Each drive letter has a separate root directory and all other directories are subdirectories in the drive's individual tree structure.

In Linux, however, all partitions are accessible through a single file system hierarchy starting at the root directory (/) and continuing through a tree of subdirectories. Each partition is mounted at a given location in the tree to make it accessible. At a minimum, you must have one Linux partition mounted as the root directory. Ideally, you will have more than one Linux partition mounted.

The simplest partitioning strategy for Linux is to have two partitions: a Linux partition mounted as the root directory and a swap partition that is used to provide virtual memory and swap space. Although it is possible to run Linux without a swap partition, it is unadvisable and rarely done.

However, this simple strategy is rarely used in practice except on the most basic installations. There are several reasons why this two-partition approach is less than ideal:

- It makes upgrades difficult.
- It makes additional disk space difficult.
- It creates a severe bottleneck because all disk traffic for the operating system, applications, and user data happens on one partition.

For most users, you should split your Linux installation across two or three partitions plus the swap partition. For instance, on a system with a large number of users, it is a good idea to place user home directories (typically under the /home directory) on a separate partition. This means you would mount the partition at /home.

In this way, as user data grows you can upgrade the user home directories to larger partitions as demand for disk space grows without affecting your core operating system or application files.

In addition, if the home directory partition is on a separate physical disk, you will distribute the workload of the disks and improve performance.

Similarly, if you find that applications are typically launching and stopping on a regular basis, you might want to store most of your installed applications on a separate physical partition, preferably on a separate physical disk. Typically, Linux applications are either stored under the /usr or /opt branch of the file system hierarchy. Depending on your system configuration and preferences, you would mount a separate partition at one of these locations.

Caution

Not all directories can be placed on mounted partitions other than the partition mounted as the root partition. Any directory containing files needed to boot the system and mount the other partitions must be on the root-mounted partition. In particular `/bin`, `/dev`, `/etc`, `/lib`, `/lost+found`, `/proc`, `/root`, and `/sbin` must be on the root partition and not mounted from other partitions.

Generally, the following directories are good candidates for mounting from separate partitions:

- `/home`
- `/opt`
- `/usr`
- `/var`

SWAP PARTITIONS

The question of how to size a swap partition is one that is unclear. The swap partition is used as virtual memory into which memory pages will be swapped as physical memory fills up.

Advice about sizing your swap partition can come from two camps. Low-end advocates say that if you have plenty of RAM you don't need much swap space. They claim that most systems can get away with 16MB of swap space. Others recommend that you should match your physical memory with swap space so that a system with 64MB of RAM should have 64MB of memory.

Because disk space is cheap, it doesn't hurt to have more swap space rather than less so that if it is needed, it is available. A couple of swap space limitations should be kept in mind:

- You can't have more than eight swap partitions.
- Some versions of Linux limit the size of swap partitions to 128MB.
- Some old versions of Linux limit the size of swap partitions to 16MB. If they are larger, only the first 16MB are used.

On a heavily used server, placing the swap partition on a separate physical disk can help improve performance of the system significantly.

USING `fdisk`

Historically, most Linux distributions have used the `fdisk` program during installation to provide disk-partitioning capabilities. Although some distributions now have their own partitioning tools for the installation process (for instance, Red Hat Linux has Disk Druid), `fdisk` is still the de facto standard partitioning tool and is available in all distributions for use post-installation. Also, by understanding `fdisk` you can quickly and easily use any other partitioning tool made available during installation of your selected distribution.

`fdisk` enables you to create, delete, and modify partitions. `fdisk` uses a simple menu-based interface to enable you to perform all actions.

Although `fdisk` can be used for numerous purposes, the following are the most common actions:

- Creating a primary partition
- Creating a logical partition
- Setting a partition type
- Displaying existing partitions
- Deleting an existing partition
- Writing changes to disk

CREATING A PRIMARY PARTITION

To create a primary partition with `fdisk`, follow these steps:

1. Use the `n` menu option to create a new partition.
2. When prompted, enter `p` to indicate you want to create a primary partition.
3. When prompted, enter a number from 1-4 to indicate which primary partition you want to create.
4. When prompted, enter the cylinder where the partition should start.
5. When prompted, enter the cylinder where the partition should end or enter the size (for instance, `+32M` for a 32MB partition).

A typical `fdisk` dialog for creating a primary partition is as follows:

```
Command (m for help): m
Command action
   e   extended
   p   primary partition (1-4)
p
Partition number (1-4): 1
First cylinder (1-810, default 1): 1
Last cylinder or +size or +sizeM or +sizeK (1-810, default 810): +32M

Command (m for help):
```

CREATING A LOGICAL PARTITION

In order to create a logical partition with `fdisk`, you first need to create an extended partition to contain one or more logical partitions. To do this, use the follow these steps:

1. Use the `n` menu option to create a new partition.
2. When prompted, enter `e` to indicate you want to create an extended partition.
3. When prompted, enter a number from 1-4 to indicate which extended partition you wish to create.
4. When prompted, enter the cylinder where the partition should start.
5. When prompted, enter the cylinder where the partition should end or enter the size (for instance, `+3200M` for a 3200MB partition).

> **Note**
>
> Keep in mind that the extended partition you create must be large enough to contain all logical partitions you plan to create in it.

To create a logical partition with `fdisk` in the extended partition, follow these steps:

1. Use the `n` menu option to create a new partition.
2. When prompted, enter `l` to indicate you want to create a logical partition.
3. When prompted, enter the cylinder where the partition should start.
4. When prompted, enter the cylinder where the partition should end or enter the size (for instance, `+3200M` for a 3200MB partition).

> **Note**
>
> Keep in mind that the logical partitions you create cannot be larger than the remaining available space in the extended partition in which they are created.

A typical `fdisk` dialog for creating a logical partition is as follows:

```
Command (m for help): m
Command action
   l   logical (5 or over)
   p   primary partition (1-4)
l
First cylinder (262-522, default 262): 262
Last cylinder or +size or +sizeM or +sizeK (1-810, default 810): +16M

Command (m for help):
```

SETTING A PARTITION TYPE

Each partition must have a type associated with it. By default, all partitions are created as Linux partitions. However, if you want to use a partition as a swap partition or as a DOS/Windows partition, you must change the partition type. To change the partition type, follow these steps:

1. Use the `t` menu option to create a new partition.
2. When prompted, enter the number of the partition you want to change the type of.
3. When prompted, enter the hexadecimal code of the partition type for the selected partition.

When prompted to enter the hexadecimal code of the partition type, you can enter `L` to display all partition types and their codes:

```
Command (m for help): t
Partition number (1-5): 1
Hex code (type L to list codes): L
```

```
0  Empty              17 Hidden HPFS/NTF 5c Priam Edisk     a6 OpenBSD
1  FAT12              18 AST Windows swa 61 SpeedStor       a7 NeXTSTEP
2  XENIX root         1b Hidden Win95 FA 63 GNU HURD or Sys b7 BSDI fs
3  XENIX usr          1c Hidden Win95 FA 64 Novell Netware  b8 BSDI swap
4  FAT16 <32M         1e Hidden Win95 FA 65 Novell Netware  c1 DRDOS/sec (FAT-
5  Extended           24 NEC DOS         70 DiskSecure Mult c4 DRDOS/sec (FAT-
6  FAT16              3c PartitionMagic  75 PC/IX           c6 DRDOS/sec (FAT-
7  HPFS/NTFS          40 Venix 80286     80 Old Minix       c7 Syrinx
8  AIX                41 PPC PReP Boot   81 Minix / old Lin db CP/M / CTOS / .
9  AIX bootable       42 SFS             82 Linux swap      e1 DOS access
a  OS/2 Boot Manag    4d QNX4.x          83 Linux           e3 DOS R/O
b  Win95 FAT32        4e QNX4.x 2nd part 84 OS/2 hidden C:  e4 SpeedStor
c  Win95 FAT32 (LB    4f QNX4.x 3rd part 85 Linux extended  eb BeOS fs
e  Win95 FAT16 (LB    50 OnTrack DM      86 NTFS volume set f1 SpeedStor
f  Win95 Ext'd (LB    51 OnTrack DM6 Aux 87 NTFS volume set f4 SpeedStor
10 OPUS               52 CP/M            93 Amoeba          f2 DOS secondary
11 Hidden FAT12       53 OnTrack DM6 Aux 94 Amoeba BBT      fd Linux raid auto
12 Compaq diagnost 54 OnTrackDM6         a0 IBM Thinkpad hi fe LANstep
14 Hidden FAT16 <3 55 EZ-Drive          a5 BSD/386         ff BBT
16 Hidden FAT16       56 Golden Bow
```

Table 1.2 lists common partition types and their codes.

TABLE 1.2   COMMON fdisk PARTITION TYPE CODES

Type	Hexadecimal Code
FAT 16	6
NTFS	7
Windows 95 FAT 32	b
Linux Swap	82
Linux	83

DISPLAYING EXISTING PARTITIONS

You can display existing partitions with fdisk using the p menu option:

```
Command (m for help): p

Disk /dev/hdb: 4 heads, 63 sectors, 810 cylinders
Units = cylinders of 252 * 512 bytes

    Device Boot    Start      End    Blocks   Id  System
/dev/hdb1             1       261    32854+   83  Linux
/dev/hdb2           262       782    65646     5  Extended
/dev/hdb5           262       505    30712+   83  Linux

Command (m for help):
```

DELETING AN EXISTING PARTITION

To delete an existing partition, use the d menu option:

```
Command (m for help): p
Partition number (1-5): 5

Command (m for help):
```

Caution

> If you delete an extended partition containing any logical partitions, the logical partitions will be deleted as well.

WRITING CHANGES TO DISK

After you have finished editing the partition table of a disk, you must write the table to disk. To do this, use the w menu option. fdisk will apply the changes and then exit:

```
Command (m for help): w
The partition table has been altered!

Calling ioctl() to re-read partition table.
Syncing disks.

WARNING: If you have created or modified any DOS 6.x
partitions, please see the fdisk manual page for additional
information.
```

Note

> If you are making changes to a live system, it is usually advisable to reboot your system after editing the partition table with fdisk. This enables all applications to be aware of the changes. During installation, it is generally not necessary to reboot after editing the partition table with fdisk.

Tip

> Because fdisk manipulates your hard disk at a low level, it is always wise to have a backup of your disk before using fdisk.

## CHAPTER 2

AUTOMATED INSTALLATION

In this chapter

ISSUES IN AUTOMATED INSTALLATION

Although Linux installation has become quite simple, there are still cases where it can be too cumbersome or time-consuming. In particular, the following issues exist:

- When faced with installing a large number of similar systems, manually installing each system is too time-consuming.
- If you want to allow users to install their own systems, the typical Linux installation process can be too complex.

In both these situations, system administrators need an automated installation process that will answer all the prompts that arise when installing Linux. It is desirable to devise a method for unattended installation, and completely remove or minimize the human intervention that is necessary to initiate the installation process.

Most Linux systems cannot be automatically installed. However, Red Hat Linux provides an automated installation method known as *Kickstart*.

AUTOMATED INSTALLATION WITH RED HAT'S KICKSTART

Automated installation is useful when you need to build a large number of Linux workstations with identical hardware and software. The Kickstart installation process can save you substantial time when you need to install a large number of identical or similar systems.

THE KICKSTART CONCEPT

The Kickstart method uses a text configuration file that supplies answers to all Red Hat installation questions and allows for automated system install. The Kickstart configuration file can be placed either on the boot floppy or on a DHCP server on the network.

When placed on a boot floppy, the installation process is as simple as putting the floppy in and turning on the machine. After 15 or 20 minutes the installation will be complete on an average system. With the boot floppy method you will need an up-to-date boot floppy, the Kickstart configuration file, and an installation CD-ROM.

Network installation using Kickstart is more suitable when you want to install Red Hat Linux on a large number of machines. This method requires a DHCP or BOOTP server, an NFS server, and a DNS server. You can of course combine all of these services on a single installation server.

BUILDING A KICKSTART CONFIGURATION FILE

Red Hat Linux 6.2 comes with a utility called `mkkickstart`. If this is not installed on your system you can add the package from the Red Hat CD-ROM by mounting the Red Hat Linux CD-ROM and then using a command such as the following:

```
# rpm -i /mnt/cdrom/mkkickstart-1.2-1.i386.rpm
```

To build a sample Kickstart configuration with `mkkickstart`, use the following command:

`# mkkickstart > ks.cfg`

You can then edit the sample Kickstart configuration file to meet your specific needs. The Kickstart configuration file consists of three main sections:

- The pre-installation section
- The packages section
- The post-installation section

THE PRE-INSTALLATION SECTION

The pre-installation section is used to answer questions about the system configuration. This section describes the language of the installation, the installation media source (which can be a CD-ROM drive or the network), and the keyboard type. The pre-installation section also describes partitioning information, the installation type (an update or new installation), the mouse type, the time zone information, the X Server parameters, the `root` account password, the authentication scheme, and the `lilo` parameters. The following is a typical pre-installation section of a Kickstart configuration file:

```
lang en
network -ip 10.2.0.101 -netmask 255.255.0.0 -gateway 10.2.0.254 -nameserver
10.2.0.1
cdrom
device ethernet 3c59x
keyboard us
zerombr yes
clearpart --linux
part /boot --size 10
part swap --size 128
part / --size 1000
part /home --size 500
install
mouse ps/2
timezone Israel
xconfig --server "Mach64" --monitor "Sony uuu-15uu2"
rootpw --iscrypted $1$b4Psev3d$YZ4kPMhvi6ni0wQ8fm6QF0
auth --nisdomain bwc --useshadow
lilo --location mbr
```

You can adjust these entries as needed. For instance, you can change the installation language to French by changing the `lang en` entry to `lang fr`. Table 2.1 outlines the meaning of the critical entries from the pre-installation section of the Kickstart configuration file.

TABLE 2.1　THE PRE-INSTALLATION SECTION OF THE KICKSTART CONFIGURATION FILE

Entry	Description
lang <*language code*>	Specifies the language to use during installation as a two-letter ISO country code.
network <*network definition*>	Specifies how Kickstart should option its network configuration information. This can be --bootproto dhcp or --bootproto bootp for dynamic assignment of network configuration information or a combination of IP address, network mask, default gateway, and name server IP address.
nfs	Specifies the NFS installation method.
cdrom	Specifies the CD-ROM installation method.
device <*device definition*>	Specifies optional device information such as Ethernet cards, SCSI cards, and non-SCSI, non-IDE CD-ROM drives. This is generally not necessary for PCI devices.
keyboard <*language code*>	Specifies the keyboard layout to use in Linux as a two-letter language code.
zerombr <*yes or no*>	Indicates whether the installation should clear the current partition table on the target system.
clearpart <*options*>	Indicates whether you want to remove Linux-related partitions (with the --linux option) or all partitions (with the --all option).
part <*mount point*> --size <*size*>	Specifies partitions you want to create, their mount points, and their sizes in megabytes.
install	Specifies a new installation of Linux.
upgrade	Specifies an upgrade installation of Linux.
mouse <*mouse type*>	Specifies your system's mouse type.
timezone <*timezone*>	Specifies your time zone.
xconfig <*X Windows configuration options*>	Specifies the configuration of X for your system.

TABLE 2.1   CONTINUED

Entry	Description
`rootpw -iscrypted <encrypted password>`	Specifies the encrypted form of the root password for the new installation.
`lilo -location <location>`	Indicates where to install LILO.

PART

I

CH

2

> **Note**
>
> Complete details of the pre-installation entries can be found in the "Kickstart Installations" chapter of the Red Hat Linux Installation Guide provided with the commercial version of Red Hat Linux.

THE PACKAGES SECTION

The packages section starts with the keyword %packages and is followed by a list of all the packages you want installed. There are two ways of defining packages. One way is to use one of the predefined groups similar to those listed during the manual installation. The names of these groups are prefixed with the @ sign. Typical examples of predefined package groups are @Base and @C-Development. An alternative to using pre-defined package groups is to list each package by name. The following is a typical packages section:

```
%packages
@Networked Workstation
@Kernel Development
bind-utils
dhcpcd
```

In this example, both pre-defined groups and individual package names have been used. In Red Hat Linux 6.2, the following are possible groups:

```
@Base

@Printer Support

@X Window System

@GNOME

@KDE  @Mail/WWW/News Tools

@DOS/Windows Connectivity

@Graphics Manipulation

@Games

@Multimedia Support

@Networked Workstation

@Dialup Workstation

@SMB (Samba) Server

@IPX/Netware(tm) Connectivity
```

```
@Anonymous FTP Server
@Web Server
@Development
@Kernel Development
@Utilities
```

A complete list of groups and individual packages is in the file `RedHat/base/comps` on the Red Hat Linux installation CD-ROM.

POST-INSTALLATION SECTION

The post-installation section starts with the keyword `%post`. You can add any post installation tasks here, including additional packages to be added with the `rpm`, custom startup scripts to be run, `crontab` entries to be added, and any other necessary tasks.

A sample post-installation section is shown here. It shows how startup commands can be added to the `/etc/rc.local` file and how to add a new entry to `root` account's `crontab`:

```
%post
cat <<EOF >>/etc/rc.local
echo 8192 > /proc/sys/kernel/file-max
echo 32768 > /proc/sys/kernel/inode-max
EOF
cat <<EOF >/tmp/crontab.root
# Keep the time up to date
0,15,30,45 * * * * /usr/sbin/ntpdate -s eggtimer 2>&1 >/dev/null
```

Basically, the post-installation section consists of a shell script to be executed after the system is installed and functional. Commands here should be specified as they would be in a shell script. Be aware, it is not possible to have any interactive installation actions in the post-installation section of Kickstart.

INSTALLING CUSTOM PACKAGES   You can install your own RPM packages by adding `rpm` install commands in the post-installation section of the Kickstart configuration file. For instance, suppose that you have two custom packages called `sudo.rpm` and `ssh.rpm` placed in the `/kickstart/RPMS` directory on the NFS server you are using for network installation of the Linux software. You can arrange for these packages to be automatically installed by adding directives in the post-installation section of the configuration file as follows:

```
%post
rpm -i /kickstart/RPMS/sudo.rpm
rpm -i /kickstart/RPMS/ssh.rpm
```

The post-installation commands are executed after the operating system is completely installed and the system is fully functional. The two `rpm` commands shown will execute and the `sudo` and `ssh` packages will be automatically installed.

KICKSTART USING A BOOT FLOPPY DISK

To run a Kickstart installation from the boot floppy disk requires copying the Kickstart configuration file to the boot floppy. This can be done using the following command from the system where you created the Kickstart configuration file:

```
# mcopy ks.cfg a:
```

If the Red Hat boot floppy is very full and you don't have room to add the `ks.cfg` file, you can delete the message files from the boot floppy using the following command:

```
# mdel a:\*.msg
```

PART

1

CH

2

To start a Kickstart installation from the boot floppy, enter the following command at the boot prompt when the system boots from the installation floppy disk:

```
LILO boot: linux ks=floppy
```

You can edit the file `syslinux.cfg` on the boot floppy to automatically enter Kickstart installation mode when booting from the floppy. For automatic Kickstart installation, edit the `syslinux.cfg` file to have the following contents:

```
default ks
      prompt 0
      label ks
          kernel vmlinuz
          append ks=floppy initrd=initrd.img
```

KICKSTART USING A DHCP SERVER

The Kickstart configuration file can be fetched from the network. This requires setting up a DHCP server, an NFS server, and a DNS server.

The Kickstart configuration file must be modified for network installation. DHCP and NFS options must be configured to boot using DHCP and to receive the Linux distribution from an NFS server. A sample pre-installation section of the Kickstart configuration file for a network installation is shown in the following table:

```
lang en
network --bootoption dhcp
nfs --server linux.bwc.org -dir /redhat/i386
device ethernet 3c59x
keyboard us
zerombr yes
clearpart -linux
part /boot --size 10
part swap --size 128
part / --size 1000
install
mouse microsoft --emulthree
timezone Israel
xconfig --server "SVGA" --monitor "Sony CPD100SF"
rootpw --iscrypted $1$lS1zGXZz$yL5tB2qwsJzzNBla9kt5A0
auth -useshadow --enablemd5
lilo --location mbr
```

DHCP SERVER SETUP

The DHCP server supplies the IP address, network mask, gateway, DNS domain name, and DNS server addresses of the client on which Linux will be installed. The following listing shows a sample dhcpd.conf file suitable for Kickstart installations:

```
subnet 10.2.0.0 netmask 255.255.0.0 {
        range 10.2.0.101 10.2.0.110;
        default-lease-time 600;
     max-lease-time 7200;
        option subnet-mask 255.255.0.0;
        option broadcast-address 10.2.255.255;
        option routers 10.2.0.254;
        option domain-name-servers 10.2.0.252;
        option domain-name "bwc.org";
}
# Work stations can be assigned fixed IP addresses matching the
# hardware Ethernet addresses.
host ws1 {
    hardware ethernet 00:c0:4f:a9:f9:26;
    fixed-address 10.2.0.101;
     filename "/kickstart/ks.cfg";
}
host ws2 {
    hardware Ethernet 00:c0:4f:a9:f9:10;
    fixed-address 10.2.0.102;
    filename "/kickstart/ks.cfg";
}
```

In this sample DHCP configuration file, the target workstations ws1 and ws2 receive IP addresses of 10.2.0.101 and 10.2.0.102 respectively and fetch the Kickstart configuration file /kickstart/ks.cfg from the DHCP server, which is also setup as an NFS server. The /kickstart directory must be exported to allow client workstations to mount it using NFS as outlined in Chapter 14, "Printer and File Sharing with NFS and Samba." The next section describes the specific configuration of the NFS server for a Kickstart installation.

NFS SERVER SETUP

The NFS server provides both the Kickstart configuration file and the Linux software distribution.

In our sample configuration, the ks.cfg file is placed in the directory /kickstart. Next symbolic links are created to the ks.cfg file. The names of the symbolic links must be of the form IPAddress-kickstart. This is because Kickstart expects to find the configuration files named /kickstart/<IP Address>-kickstart on the DHCP server. The following commands will set up the /kickstart directory on the DHCP/NFS server:

```
# cp ks.cfg /kickstart
# cd /kickstart
# ln -s ks.cfg 10.2.0.101-kickstart
# ln -s ks.cfg 10.2.0.102-kickstart
...
# ln -s ks.cfg 10.2.0.110-kickstart
...
```

Now you must set up the Red Hat distribution directory. For instance, you can mount the Linux distribution CD-ROM on /mnt/cdrom.

Both the Red Hat distribution directory and the /kickstart directory must be exported so that the client workstations can mount them using NFS. Add the following directory entries to the /etc/exports file on the DHCP/NFS server to achieve this:

```
# Contents of /etc/exports file
/kickstart
/mnt/cdrom
```

PART

I

CH

2

Next, restart NFS:

```
# killall -HUP /usr/sbin/mountd
# killall -HUP /usr/sbin/nfsd
```

DNS Server Setup

The DNS server provides forward and reverse name lookups for the IP addresses handed out by the DHCP server. DNS records must be added to the DNS server or Kickstart will pause and prompt for the system name, domain name, and other DNS-related information. Add entries in DNS for ws1 = 10.2.0.101, ws2 = 10.2.0.102, and so on for the number of systems on which you are going to run Kickstart installation.

Do not forget to send a SIGHUP signal (HUP) to the DNS server after adding the DNS entries as outlined in Chapter 22, "DNS."

Kickstart Installation Process

To start the Kickstart installation, boot from the Red Hat boot floppy and at the LILO prompt enter linux ks as follows:

```
LILO boot: linux ks
```

This specifies a Kickstart installation from the network as opposed to using linux ks=floppy, which reads the Kickstart configuration file from the floppy.

You can check the progress of the installation, or gain root shell access, by switching virtual terminals on the console. To do so, use the following key combinations:

- Alt+F1: Installation screen
- Alt+F2: Root shell
- Alt+F3: Install log
- Alt+F4: System log
- Alt+F5: Other messages

TROUBLESHOOTING

Whenever Kickstart encounters a problem of some sort it will pause and ask for input from the console.

A common error is to overlook setting up DNS for the workstations prior to starting the Kickstart installation. The outcome of this is that the installation pauses and prompts for domain name and system name. Here are several possible reasons for this, and suggested fixes:

- DNS has not been set up properly; fix DNS and try again.
- You are using a fixed IP address for the client; use DHCP instead.
- Check the `dhcpd.conf` file on the DHCP server to make sure that the information about the DNS server and the domain name is being handed out correctly to the clients.

In addition, Kickstart installation sometimes does not recognize a PS/2 mouse, and installation pauses. This appears to be the result of a bug in the Kickstart software. To pass this problem, use the Tab key to select the Retry button and press the Enter key. Installation should proceed smoothly from that point on.

GENERAL SYSTEM ADMINISTRATION

## CHAPTER 3

USER AND GROUP ADMINISTRATION

In this chapter

USERS AND GROUPS IN LINUX

Users and groups form the basis of security and system access in Linux. Each user of a system has an account that has a home directory, a password, and a default group associated with it. The creation of user accounts allows the differentiation of users on a multiuser system. Without user accounts, the system would have no way of determining which files belong to which user or to what resources a user should be granted access.

Users in Linux are identified by numeric user IDs, or *UIDs*. A UID is used by the kernel to identify each user. UIDs are mapped to text-based usernames that are used by users to gain access to the system and to provide a human-friendly way to identify system users.

User accounts are stored in a user database file at `/etc/passwd`. This file contains one entry for each user on the system and each entry identifies the user's UID, username, password, default group ID, full name, home directory and default shell.

Accounts can belong to groups that allow easy application of security restrictions and permissions for files, directories, and services without having to define these security settings individually for each member of a group.

THE `/etc/passwd` FILE

The `/etc/passwd` file is a text database of user accounts. It contains one entry for each account on the system with each entry on a separate line. Each entry contains a series of fields separated by colons:

```
<username>:<password>:<UID>:<GID>:<full name>:<home directory>:<default shell>
```

The fields have the following meanings:

- **Username**: The username that the user uses to log in to the system and by which humans can identify the user's account. Usernames should not contain spaces and they must start with a letter or number.

- **Password**: This field will contain an encoded version of the user's password. Normally, these encoded passwords are generated using the `passwd` command and are not directly edited in the `/etc/passwd` file.

- **UID**: Every user on the system must have a unique UID that is a numeric identifier used by the system and kernel to identify the user account. You can define any scheme for assigning UIDs as discussed below in the section "Selecting UIDs."

- **GID**: Every user on the system must belong to a default group. The group must be a valid group in the `/etc/group` file which is discussed in the section "The `/etc/group` File." The group is identified in the `/etc/passwd` file by its numeric GID.

- **Full Name**: For each user account you can provide a full name for the user. This full name is used in situations where an application wants to identify a user fully such as on the From line of outgoing email messages where both the full name and username are used.

- **Home Directory**: Every account needs a home directory, which is the default location where the user can store files and create directories. The location of home directories is entirely arbitrary and should follow some consistent policy as outlined in the following section "Where to Locate Home Directories."

- **Default Shell**: When a user logs in, his default shell is launched to provide him with a command-line environment. Typically, Linux systems use Bash as the default shell for accounts but you can use any valid shell available on your system. Valid shells are those which are installed on the system and are listed in the `/etc/shells` file, which contains a list of all valid shells. In this field, you need to provide the full path and filename of the shell's executable binary file.

Although the `/etc/passwd` file is a plain text file, you should not edit it directly with your preferred text editor. Instead, edit it with the `vipw` command as outlined in the section "Editing the `/etc/passwd` File."

Selecting UIDs

Choose a policy for assigning UIDs that guarantees unique ID numbers for each user as well as keeping your user accounts organized in a logical fashion.

UIDs are integer values in the range from 0-65,534; UIDs do not need to appear in sequence and you can create your scheme for using these numbers.

Generally, the UIDs below 100 are reserved for system accounts such as `root` and `bin` and accounts created by applications for their use such as `ftp` and `gdm`.

By default, most Linux distributions use a simple numbering scheme for other accounts that works well for workstations or small servers. For instance, Red Hat Linux starts assigning user accounts at UID 500 and increments the number by one for each new account.

For small sites, this type of simple incrementing of UID is sufficient. However, if you manage large numbers of user accounts, it is useful to segment the available range of UIDs into logical groups based on some organizational principle. For instance, you can segment the UID number space into discrete groups of 1,000 or 10,000 based on geographical location of users, organizational division or department of users, or even by last name.

This type of segmentation of UIDs makes UID assignment less arbitrary and makes it easier to find user accounts in a large database of users.

This type of grouping of UIDs can also be linked to the default group of users. For instance, if you create a group for each department in an organization you might want to segment the UID range into sections for each group so that users in a specific group have UIDs reflecting this group membership as well.

WHERE TO LOCATE HOME DIRECTORIES

Typically, Linux systems place home directories as subdirectories of the /home directory. Each home directory is named after the account's username so that the account user1 will have its home directory at /home/user1/.

As with UIDs, this is a simple organizational scheme that works well for a small system with a limited number of users. However, on a system with a large number of users, this scheme is problematic. Not only is it hard to keep track of a large number of subdirectories in /home, but all the subdirectories will exist on a single hard disk partition. This immediately creates a problem because the home directories will need to have severe storage limitations placed on them even with the largest available hard disks. For instance, if a single 20GB hard disk is allocated to the /home directory but you have 1,000 home directories, each home directory is restricted to an average disk consumption of roughly 20MB of disk space.

Accordingly, with a large site, you need to segment your home directories into a logical structure. Generally, you will want to create several directories that in turn contain home directories. For instance, you might want to further subdivide /home into subdirectories reflecting some logical structure such as geographic location of users or organizational departments.

For instance, if an organization has users in Canada, Switzerland, Israel, Hong Kong, and the United States, you might want to create the following directories to hold home directories:

- /home/ca
- /home/ch
- /home/il
- /home/hk
- /home/us

Then, user1 in Hong Kong would have its home directory at /home/hk/user1 and user2 in Canada would have its home directory at /home/ca/user2.

EDITING THE /etc/passwd FILE

Never edit the /etc/passwd file directly. Instead, use the vipw command to set the necessary locks to enable safe editing of the passwd file and then open the file in an editor.

The vipw command uses your default editor as indicated by the EDITOR environment variable and if none is set, defaults to the vi editor. If you have a preferred editor, set the EDITOR environment variable and then launch vipw to edit the /etc/passwd file:

```
# export EDITOR=emacs
# /usr/sbin/vipw
```

Note

If you are using the C Shell instead of Bash, set the EDITOR environment variable with the command setenv EDITOR emacs.

The /etc/group File

The /etc/group file defines user groups on a Linux system. It contains a series of entries of the form:

`<group name>:<password>:<GID>:<user list>`

The fields in each entry have the following meanings:

- **Group Name**: The name by which humans can identify the group. Group names should not contain spaces and they must start with a letter or number.
- **Password**: This field will contain an encoded version of the group's password. Generally, groups do not require passwords.
- **GID**: Every group on the system must have a unique GID that is a numeric identifier used by the system and kernel to identify the group. You can define any scheme for assigning GIDs as discussed in the section "Selecting Groups and GIDs."
- **User List**: A comma-separated list of usernames indicating the users who are members of the group.

You can edit the group file directly with your preferred text editor.

Selecting Groups and GIDs

GIDs are numeric values in the range from 0-65534. Each group should have a unique GID in this range. You are free to segment this range in any way that makes sense for your site and it is not necessary to assign GIDs in consecutive order.

Current Linux distributions take one of two approaches to the assigning of groups. Some distributions, such as Red Hat Linux, create a separate group for each user to serve as the default group for that user. For instance, if user1 has a UID of 550, they will have as their default group user1 with the GID 550.

This provides for a strong security mechanism because no other users will belong to a user's default group, which means that the group ownership permissions on their home directory don't expose their data to access by other users.

However, this approach provides no flexibility in terms of using groups to assign permissions to broad ranges of users.

By contrast, other distributions create a single users group and make all new users members of that group. This makes it possible to easily grant permissions to access a file or directory to all users by making the users group the group owner of a file or directory. However, this approach does not offer fine-grained access control and, depending on permissions on a user's home directory, can expose all of their data to viewing by all users on the system.

If you have a complex organizational structure or a large number of users, neither of these schemes is ideal. For instance, if you have a large user base, the scheme of creating a separate default group for each user means that you need to manage both a large user database in /etc/passwd as well as a large group database in /etc/group. By contrast, if you take the approach of placing all users in a single users group you have a single, hard-to-edit group that provides no value in terms of granting permissions to organizational divisions.

Generally, you will want to create a set of groups mapping to a logical division within your organization. That division can be departmental or geographic, for instance. Then, it is possible to give users one of these groups by default so that it is easy to grant large groups of users access to resources in some logical manner. For instance, all users in a given department should logically be able to share a printer but users in another department probably do not need access to that printer. By dividing groups on a department line it is possible to grant permissions in this way.

Often, you need multiple group schemes where you can have geographic and departmental groups and users belong to one or both with one serving as their default group. Then, it is possible to grant users permissions based on different criteria by granting access to the correct group.

CREATING USERS

The creation of user accounts for new users is a task normally undertaken by the root user. A standard system user does not have the permission necessary to create new user accounts.

The process of creating a user account has several basic steps:

- Select a UID for the user
- Select a group for the user
- Create an entry in the /etc/passwd file
- Set the password for the user
- Create a home directory for the user
- Populate the home directory for the user

These processes can be executed manually or automatically using a system utility such as adduser or useradd.

CREATING USERS MANUALLY

The manual creation of user accounts, although not difficult, is cumbersome and not ideally suited to sites where user accounts must be created frequently. Nonetheless, understanding the process of manual account creation enables you to better use the automated tools available and to create customized automated tools suited to your needs.

First you need to select the basic account information:

- **Username**: Each user needs a unique username on the system for easy identification of the account. Follow the rules for selecting valid usernames as outlined earlier in the section "The /etc/passwd File."

- **UID**: Each user needs a unique UID on the system. Select the UID for the new account using the policies you have defined for UID assignment as suggested earlier in the section "Selecting UIDs."

- **GID**: Each user needs a default group as specified by a GID. Select the default group's GID for the new account using the policies you have defined for group assignment as suggested earlier in the section "Selecting Groups."

- **Full Name**: Each account can have a full name specified.

- **Home Directory**: Each account on the system needs a home directory. This is the default location where the user can create files and directories and keep personalized configuration files. Select a home directory for the account using the policies you defined as suggested earlier in the section "Where to Locate Home Directories."

- **Default Shell**: Each account needs a default shell. The default shell indicates the command-line shell that will be launched when a user logs in. On most Linux systems the default shell is Bash but you can choose any valid shell available on your system. You will need to specify the complete path of the shell's binary executable file such as `/bin/bash` for Bash.

Using this information, you need to create a new entry for the account in the `/etc/passwd` file. As outlined earlier in the section "The `/etc/passwd` File," entries in the password file take the following form:

```
<username>:<password>:<UID>:<GID>:<full name>:<home directory>:<default shell>
```

Leave the password field blank so a typical entry for a new account might look like the following:

```
someuser::501:501:A new user account:/home/someuser:/bin/bash
```

> **Caution**
>
> It is crucial that you do not edit the `/etc/passwd` file directly. As outlined earlier in the section "The `/etc/passwd` File," use the `vipw` command to edit the `/etc/passwd` file.

After the entry is added to the account, assign an initial password to the account with the `passwd` command. For instance, to assign a password to the `someuser` account, use the following command:

```
# passwd someuser
Changing password for user someuser
New UNIX password:
Retype new UNIX password:
passwd: all authentication tokens updated successfully
```

The `passwd` command will encrypt the password and add it to the appropriate field in the account's entry in the `/etc/passwd` file:

```
someuser:fog4fihy6UjJI:501:501:A new user account:/home/someuser:/bin/bash
```

After the password is assigned, you need to create the home directory for the account at the location specified in the account's entry in the /etc/passwd file. In the case of the someuser account, this directory is /home/someuser. Create the directory with the mkdir command:

```
# mkdir /home/someuser
```

This creates an empty home directory with no default resource or configuration files. This is fine unless you need a default set of files designed for your system. Generally, default files for new home directories are kept in the /etc/skel directory. Most Linux distributions place a set of default files in this directory such as shell resource files and X Windows and window manager or desktop environment configuration files.

To create a new home directory populated with files from the /etc/skel directory, create the home directory by copying the /etc/skel directory instead of using the mkdir command:

```
# cp -R /etc/skel /home/someuser
```

After the home directory is created, make the new account the owner and the account's group the group for the directory. For instance, if someuser's default group is somegroup, use the following command:

```
# chown -R someuser:somegroup /home/someuser
```

You also must assign appropriate permissions to the directory. These permissions are largely dependent on the level of access other users require to the directory. By default, the user should have full access to the directory. You can assign these permissions to the directory with the command:

```
# chmod 700 /home/someuser
```

If you want to extend permission so that members of the user's default group have read access to the account's home directory, use the command:

```
# chmod 750 /home/someuser
```

Note

The chmod command enables you to set file and directory permissions. The chmod command is described in detail in the chmod manual page, which you can read with the command man chmod. This manual page can be found in Appendix A, "Linux Command Reference."

CREATING USERS WITH A SYSTEM UTILITY

Creating users manually, as outlined in the last section, is not a difficult task. However, it is clear that the process is time-consuming and human resource-intensive.

To ease this process, Linux provides the useradd command, which enables you to add an account to the system with a single command. In its simplest form, you simply provide useradd with a username:

```
# useradd newuser
```

On most Linux systems, this command will create the account `newuser` as follows:

- An entry for the user will be created in the `/etc/passwd` file without a password.
- A UID will be automatically assigned to the account using the default scheme for the distribution being used.
- A default group will be assigned to the account using the default scheme for the distribution being used.
- A home directory will be created for the user by copying the contents of the `/etc/skel` directory.

You can override the default settings of `useradd` using the arguments outlined in Table 3.1.

TABLE 3.1   ARGUMENTS OF THE `useradd` COMMAND FOR OVERRIDING DEFAULT SETTINGS

Argument	Description
`-c <comment>`	Use the specified comment as the full name for the account.
`-d <directory>`	Use the specified directory as the home directory for the account.
`-g <Group name or GID>`	Use the specified group as the default group for the account.
`-m`	Force creation of the user's home directory even if the default is to not create a home directory.
`-s <shell>`	Use the specified shell as the default shell for the account.
`-u <UID>`	Use the specified UID as the UID for the account.

For instance, to add the account `someuser` with the UID `11202` and the default group support with the home directory `/home/ca/someuser`, use the following command:

```
# useradd -u 11202 -g someuser -d /home/ca/someuser someuser
```

Note When you create an account with `useradd` you still must assign it a password with the `passwd` command. This is not done automatically by `useradd`.

CHANGING DEFAULT SETTINGS FOR NEW USERS

When you create a new user using the `useradd` command, it will use default settings unless you specify otherwise with command-line arguments. You can display the default settings using the `-D` argument of the `useradd` command:

```
# /usr/sbin/useradd -D
GROUP=100
HOME=/home
INACTIVE=-1
EXPIRE=
```

```
SHELL=/bin/bash
SKEL=/etc/skel
```

This example shows that new accounts will be assigned to groups with the GID 100 by default and will have their home directories created as subdirectories of the /home directory by default. They will use Bash as their default shell if none is specified and will copy their home directory contents from /etc/skel.

You can change these settings by using the -D argument of the useradd command followed by one or more of the arguments outlined in Table 3.2.

TABLE 3.2   ARGUMENTS OF THE useradd COMMAND FOR CHANGING DEFAULT SETTINGS

Argument	Description
-b <directory>	Use the specified directory as the prefix for home directories for accounts where no home directory is specified at time of creation.
-g <Group name or GID>	Use the specified group as the default group for accounts where no group is specified at time of creation.
-s <shell>	Use the specified shell as the default shell for accounts where no shell is specified at time of creation.

For instance, your site can have the following special requirements:

- All user's home directories should be of the form /u/<username> instead of /home/<username>.
- All users should use the C shell instead of Bash.

In this case, you could change the default settings for useradd with the following command so you do not need to list these special requirements every time you create an account:

```
# useradd -D -b /u -s /bin/csh
```

After doing this, using useradd -D will display the default settings of useradd, which should reflect these changes:

```
# /usr/sbin/useradd -D
GROUP=100
HOME=/u
INACTIVE=-1
EXPIRE=
SHELL=/bin/csh
SKEL=/etc/skel
```

CHANGING USER INFORMATION (NAME, DEFAULT SHELL, AND SO FORTH)

You can change a user's information in several ways depending on the information you want to change as follows:

- **Username**: Edit the /etc/passwd file and, if needed, change the name of the home directory.

- **Password**: Use the passwd command.

- **UID**: Ideally, you do not want to change a user's UID but if you do need to change a user's UID, edit the /etc/passwd file and then change the ownership of all files owned by the user with the find and chown commands.

- **GID**: Edit the /etc/passwd and /etc/group files.

- **Full Name**: Edit the /etc/passwd file.

- **Home Directory**: If necessary, move the user's home directory to the new location and then edit the /etc/passwd file.

- **Default Shell**: Use the chsh command or edit the /etc/passwd file manually.

CHANGING AN ACCOUNT'S USERNAME

To change an account's username, simply edit the /etc/passwd file using the vipw command as outlined earlier in the "Editing the /etc/passwd File." Because the kernel uses the UID to identify a user, all references to the username, such as in ownership indications in directory listings, will reflect the change to the username because the UID has not changed.

For instance, if you change an account's username from user1 to user2, before the change, the file owned by the account will appear in a directory listing as:

```
-rw-rw-r--  1 user1   somegrp     12 Jan 28 18:31 foo
```

After editing the username in the /etc/passwd file, the same file will appear in directory listings as:

```
-rw-rw-r--  1 user2   somegrp     12 Jan 28 18:31 foo
```

In addition to editing the /etc/passwd file, you will need to edit the /etc/group file and change any references to user1 to user2.

If you want to keep your home directories in synchronization with account's usernames, you will need to move the home directory and edit the account's entry in the /etc/passwd file to reflect the change. For instance, if the user's home directory is /home/user1 before the change, you will probably want to change it to /home/user2.

First, move the home directory to its new location with the command:

```
# mv /home/user1 /home/user2
```

Next, edit the /etc/passwd file to reflect the change using the vipw command.

CHANGING AN ACCOUNT'S PASSWORD

The root user can change any user's password using the password command as follows: passwd <*username*>. As the root user, changing a user's password does not require knowledge of the user's existing password. For instance, to change user1's password, use the following command:

```
# passwd user1
Changing password for user user1
New UNIX password:
Retype new UNIX password:
passwd: all authentication tokens updated successfully
```

CHANGING AN ACCOUNT'S UID

Changing an account's UID is a drastic measure that should be avoided at all costs. It changes an account's identifier, effectively causing the kernel to treat it as a different account. If you change an account's UID, it immediately ceases to own any files or directories it previously owned and if applications are configured to identify the account by its UID instead of its username, they will cease to recognize the account.

To change an account's UID, first edit the /etc/passwd to change the UID in the account's entry using the vipw command as outlined earlier in the "Editing the /etc/passwd File" section. Make sure to note the account's original UID because you will need this to change the ownership of all files owned by the account.

After the UID is changed in the /etc/passwd file, the account will no longer own its files. For instance, if you are changing user1's UID from 500 to 999, before the change, files and directories owned by the account will appear in directory listings as follows:

```
-rw-rw-r-- 1 user1    somegrp    12 Jan 28 18:31 foo
```

After the change, the file will appear as follows in the following in directory listings:

```
-rw-rw-r-- 1 500      somegrp    12 Jan 28 18:31 foo
```

Notice that the account is no longer owned by user1 but continues to be owned by the UID 500.

Once the UID has been changed in the /etc/passwd file, you will need to find all files owned by the UID 500 and change the ownership to the user1 account. To do this, use the find command to find all files and directories owned by UID 500 and then use the -exec option to invoke the chown command to change the file's ownership:

```
# find / -uid 500 -print -exec chown user1 {}\;
```

CHANGING AN ACCOUNT'S GID

To change an account's default group, edit the /etc/passwd file using vipw as outlined earlier in the "Editing the /etc/passwd File" section and change the account's GID field to the GID of the new default group.

Next, edit the /etc/group file and remove the user from the list of user's in the original default group. Add the user to the list of users in the new default group.

CHANGING AN ACCOUNT'S FULL NAME

To change an account's full name, simply make the necessary changes in the /etc/passwd file by editing it with the vipw command as outlined earlier in the "Editing the /etc/passwd File" section. Changing the full name of an account has no impact on the account's operation because it is not used in any way to identify the account by the system or its applications. The full name simply serves a descriptive purpose and in no way affects the operation of the system or any applications.

CHANGING AN ACCOUNT'S HOME DIRECTORY

To change an account's home directory, you will need to move the home directory and then edit the account's entry in the /etc/passwd file to reflect the change. First, move the home directory to its new location with the mv command:

```
# mv <old location> <new location>
```

Next, edit the /etc/passwd file to reflect the change using the vipw command.

CHANGING AN ACCOUNT'S DEFAULT SHELL

You can change an account's default shell to any valid shell listed in the /etc/shells file using the chsh command. In its simplest form, specify the account's username to the chsh command and chsh will prompt you to enter the new default shell:

```
# chsh user1
Changing shell for user1.
New shell [/bin/bash]: /bin/csh
Shell changed.
```

If you enter a shell not listed in the /etc/shells file, chsh will warn you that the shell is not valid but will still change the account's default shell:

```
# chsh user1
Changing shell for user1.
New shell [/bin/csh]: /bin/false
Warning: "/bin/false" is not listed in /etc/shells
Shell changed.
```

You can also specify a shell on the command line with the -s option of the chsh command:

```
# chsh -s /bin/bash user1
Changing shell for user1.
Shell changed.
```

DELETING AND DISABLING USERS

If a user should no longer have access to the system or must be temporarily disallowed from using a system, it is necessary to either disable or delete the account. Disabling an account makes it impossible for a user to log in to their account while deleting an account removes the account from the system. It is necessary to create a new account for a user if their account has been deleted and they need to be granted access to the system again.

DISABLING USERS

To disable a user's account, you want to make it impossible for that user to log in. There are several reasons why you might want to disable a user's account:

- You limit use of the system by time, disk space, or CPU usage, and the user has exceeded their threshold.
- You limit access to the system when users violate usage policies of your organization.
- A user is away from work for an extended period of time and it is safer not to leave the account open to unauthorized login attempts.

To disable an account, you must make it impossible to log in to the account with any password, including the user's actual password. If you want to re-enable the account with the user's original password, disable the account by editing the user's entry in /etc/passwd and adding an asterisk (*) at the start of the password field. Make sure you use vipw to edit the passwd file as outlined earlier in the "Editing the /etc/passwd File" section.

The asterisk at the start of the password field changes the password field so that it represents no possible encoded password but keeps the original encoded password intact so that the account can be re-enabled by simply editing the passwd file and removing the asterisk.

By way of example, say a user's entry in the passwd file is the following:

```
someuser:fog4fihy6UjJI:501:501:A new user account:/home/someuser:/bin/bash
```

Then after disabling, the entry will be this:

```
someuser:*fog4fihy6UjJI:501:501:A new user account:/home/someuser:/bin/bash
```

An alternative method for disabling a user's account is to change the default shell of the account to a special script which displays a message to the user and then exits without ever providing a command prompt. You can do this with a tail script.

To do this, first create a script to display the message in a logical location such as /usr/local/bin/disabled. The script should be similar to the following:

```
#!/usr/bin/tail +2
This account has been disabled by the system administrator.
Contact the administrator at root@localhost for more information.
```

You can place any text message in this file so long as the first line starts with #!/usr/bin/tail and you change the +2 to reflect the number of lines in the message.

After the file is created, make it executable with the command:

```
# chmod +x /usr/local/bin/disabled
```

Then, to disable an account, change the account's default shell to this script. For instance, to disable the someuser account, use the following command:

```
# chsh -s /usr/local/bin/disabled someuser
Changing shell for someuser.
Warning: "/usr/local/bin/disabled" is not listed in /etc/shells
Shell changed.
```

To re-enable the account, simply change the shell back to a standard shell such as bash:

```
# chsh -s /bin/bash someuser
Changing shell for someuser.
Shell changed.
```

DELETING USER ACCOUNTS

Deleting a user's account is a more drastic, permanent action that is often irreversible. Reasons for deleting an account include the following:

- Users leaving an organization
- Signs that an account is being used to attack your system or other systems

Many organizations do not delete a user's account immediately upon their leaving the organization but instead do so after a delay of days, weeks, or months so that the user's data is still accessible in case it is needed after the user leaves. In this case, it is not uncommon to disable the account in the period between a user's departure and an account's deletion.

PART

II

CH

3

Deletion of an account is a multistep process:

1. Edit the /etc/passwd file and remove the user's entry. Be sure to use the vipw program to edit the passwd file as outlined earlier in the "Editing the /etc/passwd File" section. Make a note of the user's UID for reference later.

2. Edit the /etc/group file and remove all references to the user from user lists in that file. If you have a separate default group associated with each user, remove that user's group from the group file.

3. If you want to retain an archive of all data in the user's home directory, use the tar command to create an archive of the user's directory. For instance, if you are deleting the user someuser, you might use the command:
   ```
   # tar czvf someuser.tar.gz /home/someuser/
   ```

4. Delete the user's home directory with the command:
   ```
   # rm -rf /home/someuser
   ```

> **Caution**
>
> Keep in mind that this rm command is final. After it is executed you will only be able to re-create the user's home directory from backup tapes or an archive of the home directory.

> **Caution**
>
> Using the rm -rf command is powerful because it removes entire directories recursively without prompting you for confirmation for every file. However, when used as the root user, it is also dangerous because if the command is mistyped, it can potentially delete your file system. For instance, if you accidentally have a space

before the final slash (`rm -rf /home/someuser /`) you are actually deleting two directories recursively: the `/home/someuser` directory and your system's root (`/`) directory.

5. If the user has a mail spool file on the system, delete the file with a command such as:

    ```
    # rm /var/spool/mail/someuser
    ```

    Mail spools are discussed in Chapter 16, "Linux Mail Services with sendmail."

6. If you want to search the system for other files owned by the user and delete them, you can do so with the `find` command. For instance, if `someuser`'s UID is 900, use the following command to delete any files owned by that user:

    ```
    # find / -uid 900 -type f -print -exec rm {}\;
    # find / -uid 900 -type d -print -exec rmdir {}\;
    ```

PASSWORD SECURITY AND SHADOW PASSWORDS

The standard UNIX and Linux model of storing encoded passwords in `/etc/passwd` suffers from two serious shortcomings:

- The passwords stored in the `passwd` file are normally encoded with the UNIX crypt command, which simply requires time and a computer to decode. This is not a highly secure format.

- The `passwd` file contains information such as UIDs, GIDs, and home directories, which must be readable by all users on the system. Therefore, although a regular user cannot directly alter the `passwd` file they can copy its contents and proceed to decode the passwords it contains at their leisure.

Fully securing your password database requires two steps:

- Use a more powerful encryption scheme such as MD5 encryption to store user passwords instead of standard UNIX crypt.

- Use the Shadow Password suite to move the encrypted password to a file not readable by all users.

USING MD5 ENCRYPTION

Some Linux distributions offer the alternative of encrypting passwords with MD5 encryption. Red Hat is an example of such a distribution that, during installation, allows you to enable or disable MD5 encryption for user passwords.

MD5 encryption comes as part of the Shadow Password Suite, which is discussed in the next section. With MD5 encryption, passwords are made safer because they can be longer than eight characters (a limitation with standard Linux passwords) and because they use an encryption scheme which does not allow for quick and easy cracking of passwords.

USING THE SHADOW PASSWORD SUITE

The Shadow Password Suite is an attempt to eliminate the risk of an unauthorized or malicious user copying the contents of the /etc/passwd file, including any encrypted or encoded passwords, and cracking them at his or her own leisure.

This is done by splitting information from the /etc/passwd into two files:

- **/etc/passwd**: Contains the same fields as a standard passwd file except that passwords are replaced by a place holder (x). The file is readable by all users.

- **/etc/shadow**: Contains the username, password and additional password-related information for each account that appears in the /etc/passwd file. The file is only accessible to the root user.

The Shadow Password Suite also provides password expiry mechanisms, which allow you to define when a password will need to be changed and to forcibly deny users access to the system if they do not change their passwords when they expire.

The Shadow Password Suite is included with most distributions and you should install the version that comes with your system if it is not installed by default. Many leading distributions, including Red Hat Linux 6.2, install the Shadow Password Suite by default.

If your distribution does not include the Shadow Password Suite you will need to install it from ftp://ftp.icm.edu.pl/pub/Linux/shadow/shadow-current.tar.gz. Consult the documentation included with the file as well as the Shadow Password HOWTO at http://www.linuxdoc.org/HOWTO/Shadow-Password-HOWTO.html before installing the Suite. Many applications that rely on the password verification mechanism, such as IMAP, Samba, FTPD, and xlock, can break when you install the Suite and will need to be patched and rebuilt after installing support for shadow passwords.

The /etc/shadow file contains entries in the following format:

`<username>:<password>:<last change>:<allow changes>:<require change>:<warning>:`
`<expiry>:<days disabled>:<reserved>`

The fields have the following meanings:

- **Username**: A username corresponding to a username in the /etc/passwd file.
- **Password**: The account's encrypted or encoded password.
- **Last Change**: The number of days since January 1, 1970, when the password was last changed.
- **Allow Changes**: The number of days before the user can change the password. If you want to allow changes at any time, set this value to -1.
- **Require Change**: The number of days before the user must change the password. If you want to prevent expiry of passwords, set this value to an arbitrarily large value such as 99,999.
- **Warning**: The number of days before the require change day that the user should be warned that the password will expire.

- **Expiry**: The number of days after the require change day that the user's account should be disabled if the password has not been changed.
- **Days Disabled**: The number of days since January 1, 1970, when the account was disabled.
- **Reserved**: Reserved for use by the shadow password software.

The Shadow Password Suite includes altered versions of system tools such as passwd and useradd, which support the shadow password software. In addition, the system /bin/login program is replaced with a shadow password-capable version so that users can log in after shadow password support is installed.

A couple of extra arguments to the useradd program enable you to specify the date-related information for the /etc/shadow file:

- **-e** *<date>*: Specifies the date on which the account's password will expire in the form MM/DD/YYYY.
- **-f** *<days>*: Specifies the number of days after expiry of the password when the account should be disabled if the password is not changed.

In addition, the passwd command has extra arguments that the root user can use to control password expiration:

- **-x** *<days>*: Specifies the maximum number of days that the password should remain valid before expiring.
- **-n** *<days>*: Specifies the minimum number of days between password changes (to prevent users changing their passwords and immediately changing them back to their previous value).
- **-w** *<days>*: Specifies the number of days before expiry when a user should be warned.
- **-i** *<days>*: Specifies the number of days after expiry before an account should be disabled if the password has not been changed.

TROUBLESHOOTING

Several common problems occur when managing accounts, including the following:

- **You are denied permission to add new users or change user passwords**: This normally happens because you attempt either action as a normal user instead of the root user. Become the root user and then try adding new users or changing users' passwords.
- **The vipw program opens in a strange editor**: By default, vipw uses the vi editor, which many newer Linux users and administrators are not comfortable with. To override this editor, set the EDITOR environment variable to your preferred editor using the export EDITOR=*<editor>* (Bash) or setenv EDITOR *<editor>* (C Shell) command before running vipw.

- **When you change a user's shell to a newly installed shell you are warned that the shell is not valid**: This occurs because the `/etc/shells` file must contain a list of valid shells. Add the new shell to the end of the list in this file.

- **After installing the shadow password suite, system services such as FTPD, IMAP, and Samba no longer allow users to log in**: This occurs because the Shadow Password Suite changes the password verification program and these applications must be rebuilt to support shadow passwords. Consult the Shadow Password HOWTO at `http://www.linuxdoc.org/HOWTO/Shadow-Password-HOWTO.html` for more details.

USEFUL SCRIPTS

If you perform much user management, you should consider creating scripts to automate some of the more common processes. In this section we present two scripts as examples of user management scripts you might want to create for your system:

PART

II

CH

3

- `disableuser`
- `enableuser`

disableuser

As discussed earlier in the "Disabling Users" section, you can disable a user by changing their shell to a `tail` script. The following script, `disableuser`, disables users in this way assuming you have a `tail` script with an appropriate message at `/usr/local/bin/disabled` as outlined in the "Disabling Users" section.

The following is the source code for the script:

```
#!/bin/sh

/usr/bin/chsh -s /usr/local/bin/disabled $1
echo User $1 is disabled.
```

Create this script as the file `/usr/local/bin/disableuser` and make it executable:

```
# chmod o+x /usr/local/bin/disableuser
```

You can disable users with the script as follows:

```
# disableuser <username>
```

enableuser

As discussed earlier in the "Disabling Users" section, you can disable a user by changing their shell to a `tail` script. The following script, `enableuser`, enables users that have been disabled in this way.

The following is the source code for the script:

```
#!/bin/sh

/usr/bin/chsh -s /bin/bash $1
echo User $1 is enabled.
```

Create this script as the file /usr/local/bin/enableuser and make it executable:

```
# chmod o+x /usr/local/bin/enableuser
```

You can enable users with the script as follows:

```
# enableuser <username>
```

CHAPTER **4**

BOOTING UP AND SHUTTING DOWN

In this chapter

BOOTING UP

Linux is a complex operating system and starting up or shutting down Linux is more than just flipping a power switch. Booting up and shutting down the system must be performed correctly to maintain a properly functioning system.

Booting is the process of starting a system from a halted or powered-down state. During boot up the operating system loads into memory and starts executing. The system goes through a series of initialization phases before it is ready for users to log in.

It is very important for system administrators to understand the boot up sequence. Several reasons are possible for the system not to boot properly, but if you have a clear understanding of this process, you will be able to troubleshoot and fix such problems. The booting process is hardware dependent and will be not be the same on all systems, but the general principles will apply to all Linux systems.

Under normal conditions, a system boot-up sequence will continue until the system is ready for multiuser operation. This is the default behavior. There are times, however, when you will need to boot the system into single-user mode. This is done by manually issuing specific commands to the boot loader program. Booting in to single-user mode becomes necessary when you need to repair the file system after a system crash, when you are adding new hardware or replacing old hardware, or for other administrative functions.

The various steps involved in the boot process are the following:

- Loading Linux into memory
- Kernel initialization and hardware configuration
- Startup of special kernel threads
- Running initialization scripts in the /etc/rc.d directory
- Entering the optional single-user mode for system maintenance
- Entering multiuser operating mode

LOADING LINUX INTO MEMORY

The first boot task is to load the Linux operating system into memory and start executing it. The operating system is a program called vmlinux or vmlinuz. The latter is the compressed version of the operating system kernel, which is more commonly used. The name vmlinuz stands for "Virtual memory Linux kernel", and the z at the end differentiates it as a compressed kernel image. Depending on the particular distribution of Linux you are running, the pathname of the kernel file can be /vmlinuz or /boot/vmlinuz. The filename can also specify the kernel version number such as /boot/vmlinuz-2.2.15smp, which indicates a compressed Linux kernel image of version number 2.2.15, which is suitable for symmetric multi-processor machines.

The operating system is loaded as a two-step process:

1. A small boot program called LILO (Linux Loader) is loaded by your system's BIOS.
2. LILO loads the Linux kernel file.

LILO

LILO is a boot loader program for x86-based Linux systems. It can boot Linux kernel images from floppy disks and hard disks. It can also be used to boot other operating systems such as DOS, OS/2, Windows 9x, and Windows NT.

LILO is a collection of programs, data files, and a configuration file. It consists of the map installer /sbin/lilo, a configuration file at /etc/lilo.conf, several data files, and the boot loader program. These data files and the boot loader program typically reside in the /boot directory, and are called boot.b, map, and chain.b. The boot loader part of LILO is loaded by the BIOS and in turn loads the Linux kernel or the boot sectors of other operating systems.

The LILO boot loader itself is divided into two parts. The first part, which is very small, is stored in the boot sector of a floppy or hard disk. This part of the boot loader knows from where to load the second-stage boot loader. Both parts of the boot loader are usually stored in the file /boot/boot.b.

When LILO is installed by running the map installer /sbin/lilo it writes the first part of the boot loader into the boot sector of a floppy disk or the master boot record of the primary hard disk. Parameters are generally passed to LILO through the configuration file /etc/lilo.conf. A typical lilo.conf file is shown here:

```
boot=/dev/sda
map=/boot/map
install=/boot/boot.b
prompt
timeout=50
delay=100
image=/boot/vmlinuz-2.2.12smp
        label=linux
        root=/dev/sda1
        initrd=/boot/initrd-2.2.12smp.img
        read-only
image=/boot/vmlinuz-2.2.5-15smp
        label=linux.old
        root=/dev/sda1
        initrd=/boot/initrd-2.2.5-15.smp.img
        read-only
```

This configuration will install the LILO boot loader on the master boot record of the primary hard disk /dev/sda. LILO will use the boot loader program /boot/boot.b and the map file /boot/map. The root=/dev/sda1 line tells LILO the Linux root file system is on the partition /dev/sda1. The line image=/boot/vmlinuz-2.2.12smp specifies the name of the Linux kernel. The second image=/boot/vmlinuz-2.2.5-15smp line tells LILO that an alternate older Linux kernel image /boot/vmlinuz-2.2.5-15smp is available for booting and

PART
II
CH
4

can be specified by command line options to `LILO`. The `initrd=` lines specify the RAM disk images that are available if you need to boot an alternate root file system in a RAM disk for system maintenance purposes. These kernel image names and locations are stored in the LILO map file.

The `prompt` option instructs the boot loader to always prompt for command-line options that can be entered at boot time. The `timeout=50` option sets a timeout of five seconds for the prompt. If no command-line options are entered, the system will continue booting after waiting for five seconds.

The `delay=100` instructs the boot loader to wait ten seconds if the Shift key is pressed during booting. Otherwise the first kernel image mentioned is booted. If the Shift key is pressed, the boot loader prompts for the name of the kernel image to boot. This option is very useful when you install a new kernel. LILO provides a method to boot the older kernel, just in case there are problems with the new one.

Many possibilities and options are available with LILO. To learn about LILO, read the documentation—`Technical_Guide.ps` and `User_Guide.ps` typically found in the directory `/usr/doc/lilo-0.21`.

KERNEL INITIALIZATION AND HARDWARE CONFIGURATION

In this phase of booting the kernel has been loaded by LILO and starts executing and initializing itself. One of the first things the kernel does is to check the available memory on the system. The kernel reserves a fixed amount of memory for itself, its internal data stores, and buffers. A message to this effect is printed on the system console and also recorded in `/var/log/dmesg`. For example, a message such as the following is printed about the available system memory and how much of it is reserved by the kernel.

```
Memory: 387200k/393216k available (1044k kernel code, 416k reserved,
\
 4184k data, 68k init)
```

After the kernel has initialized itself it starts probing the system to see what devices are present. When a custom kernel is built it is usually configured to include a set of drivers for devices that are expected to be on the system. A generic kernel can contain support for many more devices than you actually have on your system. As the kernel detects these devices it prints very brief messages about them. The following is sample output of boot up messages on a dual CPU machine that shows the various devices the kernel has detected and configured. The output messages on your system will vary depending on the type of hardware and peripherals installed:

```
Linux version 2.2.5-15smp (root@porky.devel.redhat.com) (gcc version egcs-2.91.66
\
 19990314/Linux (egcs-1.1.2 release)) #1 SMP Mon Apr 19 22:43:28 EDT 1999
Intel MultiProcessor Specification v1.4
    Virtual Wire compatibility mode.
OEM ID: COMPAQ   Product ID: PROLIANT    APIC at: 0xFEE00000
Processor #1 Pentium(tm) Pro APIC version 16
Processor #0 Pentium(tm) Pro APIC version 16
```

```
I/O APIC #2 Version 1 at 0xFEC00000.
Processors: 2
mapped APIC to ffffe000 (fee00000)
mapped IOAPIC to ffffd000 (fec00000)
Detected 199434877 Hz processor.
Console: colour VGA+ 80x25
Calibrating delay loop... 199.07 BogoMIPS
Memory: 387200k/393216k available (1044k kernel code, 416k reserved,\
  4184k data, 68k init)
VFS: Diskquotas version dquot_6.4.0 initialized
Checking 386/387 coupling... OK, FPU using exception 16 error reporting.
Checking 'hlt' instruction... OK.
POSIX conformance testing by UNIFIX
mtrr: v1.26 (19981001) Richard Gooch (rgooch@atnf.csiro.au)
per-CPU timeslice cutoff: 50.10 usecs.
CPU1: Intel Pentium Pro stepping 09
calibrating APIC timer ...
..... CPU clock speed is 199.4250 MHz.
..... system bus clock speed is 66.4747 MHz.
Booting processor 0 eip 2000
Calibrating delay loop... 199.07 BogoMIPS
OK.
CPU0: Intel Pentium Pro stepping 09
Total of 2 processors activated (398.13 BogoMIPS).
enabling symmetric IO mode... ...done.
ENABLING IO-APIC IRQs
init IO_APIC IRQs
 IO-APIC pin 0, 16, 17, 18, 19, 20, 21, 22, 23 not connected.
..MP-BIOS bug: 8254 timer not connected to IO-APIC
...trying to set up timer as ExtINT... .. (found pin 0) ... works.
number of MP IRQ sources: 16.
number of IO-APIC registers: 24.
testing the IO APIC......................
.... register #00: 02000000
.......    : physical APIC id: 02
.... register #01: 00170011
.......     : max redirection entries: 0017
.......     : IO APIC version: 0011
.... register #02: 00000000
.......     : arbitration: 00
.... IRQ redirection table:
NR Log Phy Mask Trig IRR Pol Stat Dest Deli Vect:
00 001 01  0    0    0   0   0    0    7    51
01 000 00  0    0    0   0   0    1    1    59
02 000 00  0    0    0   0   0    1    1    51
03 000 00  0    0    0   0   0    1    1    61
04 000 00  0    0    0   0   0    1    1    69
05 0FF 0F  1    1    0   1   0    1    1    71
06 000 00  0    0    0   0   0    1    1    79
07 000 00  0    0    0   0   0    1    1    81
08 000 00  0    0    0   0   0    1    1    89
09 0FF 0F  1    1    0   1   0    1    1    91
0a 000 00  0    0    0   0   0    1    1    99
0b 000 00  0    0    0   0   0    1    1    A1
0c 000 00  0    0    0   0   0    1    1    A9
0d 000 00  1    0    0   0   0    0    0    00
0e 000 00  0    0    0   0   0    1    1    B1
```

```
0f 000 00   0     0     0   0   0     1   1   B9
10 000 00   1     0     0   0   0     0   0   00
11 000 00   1     0     0   0   0     0   0   00
12 000 00   1     0     0   0   0     0   0   00
13 000 00   1     0     0   0   0     0   0   00
14 000 00   1     0     0   0   0     0   0   00
15 000 00   1     0     0   0   0     0   0   00
16 000 00   1     0     0   0   0     0   0   00
17 000 00   1     0     0   0   0     0   0   00
IRQ to pin mappings:
IRQ0 -> 2
IRQ1 -> 1
IRQ3 -> 3
IRQ4 -> 4
IRQ5 -> 5
IRQ6 -> 6
IRQ7 -> 7
IRQ8 -> 8
IRQ9 -> 9
IRQ10 -> 10
IRQ11 -> 11
IRQ12 -> 12
IRQ13 -> 13
IRQ14 -> 14
IRQ15 -> 15
................................... done.
PCI: PCI BIOS revision 2.10 entry at 0xf005e
PCI: Using configuration type 1
PCI: Probing PCI hardware
PCI: Device 00:00 not found by BIOS
PCI: BIOS reporting unknown device 00:a2
PCI: 00:00 [8086/1237]: Passive release enable (00)
PIIX3: Enabling Passive Release
Linux NET4.0 for Linux 2.2
Based upon Swansea University Computer Society NET3.039
NET4: Unix domain sockets 1.0 for Linux NET4.0.
NET4: Linux TCP/IP 1.0 for NET4.0
IP Protocols: ICMP, UDP, TCP, IGMP
Initializing RT netlink socket
Starting kswapd v 1.5
Detected PS/2 Mouse Port.
Serial driver version 4.27 with MANY_PORTS MULTIPORT SHARE_IRQ enabled
ttyS00 at 0x03f8 (irq = 4) is a 16550A
ttyS01 at 0x02f8 (irq = 3) is a 16550A
pty: 256 Unix98 ptys configured
Real Time Clock Driver v1.09
RAM disk driver initialized:  16 RAM disks of 4096K size
PIIX3: IDE controller on PCI bus 00 dev a1
PIIX3: not 100% native mode: will probe irqs later
    ide0: BM-DMA at 0x1000-0x1007, BIOS settings: hda:pio, hdb:pio
hda: HITACHI CDR-7930, ATAPI CDROM drive
ide0 at 0x1f0-0x1f7,0x3f6 on irq 14
hda: ATAPI 8X CD-ROM drive, 128kB Cache
Uniform CDROM driver Revision: 2.54
Floppy drive(s): fd0 is 1.44M
FDC 0 is a National Semiconductor PC87306
md driver 0.90.0 MAX_MD_DEVS=256, MAX_REAL=12
```

```
raid5: measuring checksumming speed
   8regs     :    337.947 MB/sec
   32regs    :    242.316 MB/sec
using fastest function: 8regs (337.947 MB/sec)
scsi : 0 hosts.
scsi : detected total.
md.c: sizeof(mdp_super_t) = 4096
Partition check:
RAMDISK: Compressed image found at block 0
autodetecting RAID arrays
autorun ...
... autorun DONE.
VFS: Mounted root (ext2 filesystem).
ncr53c8xx: at PCI bus 1, device 4, function 0
ncr53c8xx: 53c875 detected
ncr53c875-0: rev=0x03, base=0x40101000, io_port=0x7000, irq=9
ncr53c875-0: ID 7, Fast-20, Parity Checking
ncr53c875-0: on-chip RAM at 0x40100000
ncr53c875-0: restart (scsi reset).
ncr53c875-0: Downloading SCSI SCRIPTS.
scsi0 : ncr53c8xx - revision 3.1h
scsi : 1 host.
   Vendor: FUJITSU    Model: M2954Q-512      Rev: 0153
   Type:    Direct-Access                    ANSI SCSI revision: 02
Detected scsi disk sda at scsi0, channel 0, id 0, lun 0
   Vendor: FUJITSU    Model: M2954Q-512      Rev: 0153
   Type:    Direct-Access                    ANSI SCSI revision: 02
Detected scsi disk sdb at scsi0, channel 0, id 1, lun 0
   Vendor: FUJITSU    Model: M2954Q-512      Rev: 0153
   Type:    Direct-Access                    ANSI SCSI revision: 02
Detected scsi disk sdc at scsi0, channel 0, id 2, lun 0
   Vendor: SONY       Model: SDX-300C        Rev: 0400
   Type:    Sequential-Access                ANSI SCSI revision: 02
Detected scsi tape st0 at scsi0, channel 0, id 6, lun 0
ncr53c875-0-<0,0>: tagged command queue depth set to 8
ncr53c875-0-<1,0>: tagged command queue depth set to 8
ncr53c875-0-<2,0>: tagged command queue depth set to 8
ncr53c875-0-<0,*>: FAST-20 WIDE SCSI 40.0 MB/s (50 ns, offset 15)
SCSI device sda: hdwr sector= 512 bytes. Sectors= 8498506 [4149 MB] [4.1 GB]
 sda: sda1 sda2 < sda5 sda6 sda7 sda8 >
ncr53c875-0-<1,*>: FAST-20 WIDE SCSI 40.0 MB/s (50 ns, offset 15)
SCSI device sdb: hdwr sector= 512 bytes. Sectors= 8498506 [4149 MB] [4.1 GB]
 sdb: sdb1 sdb2
ncr53c875-0-<2,*>: FAST-20 WIDE SCSI 40.0 MB/s (50 ns, offset 15)
SCSI device sdc: hdwr sector= 512 bytes. Sectors= 8498506 [4149 MB] [4.1 GB]
 sdc: sdc1 sdc2
autodetecting RAID arrays
autorun ...
... autorun DONE.
VFS: Mounted root (ext2 filesystem) readonly.
change_root: old root has d_count=1
Trying to unmount old root ... okay
Freeing unused kernel memory: 68k freed
Adding Swap: 530108k swap-space (priority -1)
```

PART

II

CH

4

STARTUP OF SPECIAL KERNEL THREADS

The first process started by the kernel is init. init has the process ID of 1. The kernel itself has the process ID of 0, which is not visible with the ps command. This is indirectly inferred by running the ps command and looking for the parent process ID (PPID) of init as shown here:

```
UID        PID  PPID  C STIME TTY        TIME CMD
root         1     0  2 17:38 ?      00:00:03 init [S]
```

The init process starts a few special system processes: kflushd, kpiod, kswapd, and mdrecoveryd. All these are kernel threads. kflushd is a kernel thread that replaced the older user space process called bdflush. It flushes dirty buffers back to disk. kpiod is a kernel thread that performs page input and output. kswapd is the kernel swap daemon, which frees memory when it gets fragmented or full. mdrecoveryd is a kernel thread that monitors RAID meta devices.

At this stage the booting of the kernel itself is complete. However the processes that accept user login and other daemons have not been started.

LINUX RUN LEVELS

The booting process of Linux is complicated by the fact that it can boot in to numerous different states. These modes of operation are known as init states or run levels, and are maintained by the init program. Table 4.1 summarizes the different run levels of Linux.

TABLE 4.1   LINUX RUN LEVELS

Run Level	Description
0	Power Down the machine
1 or S	Single-user mode
2	Multiuser mode without NFS
3	Full multiuser mode
4	Not Used
5	Full multiuser mode with X-Windows
6	Shutdown and reboot

Note

The run levels shown in Table 4.1 are generally accepted as standard in most UNIX systems, including Linux. For run levels 2-5, it is possible to arbitrarily pick and choose the services that run at these init states. The above mentioned init states are a good rule of thumb.

The run levels are controlled by a configuration file that `init` reads called `/etc/inittab`. The default run level is always the full multiuser mode of operation, which is either run level 3 or 5. A sample `/etc/inittab` file is shown here:

```
#
# inittab        This file describes how the INIT process should set up
#                the system in a certain run-level.
#
# Author:        Miquel van Smoorenburg, <miquels@drinkel.nl.mugnet.org>
#                Modified for RHS Linux by Marc Ewing and Donnie Barnes
#
# Default runlevel. The runlevels used by RHS are:
#   0 - halt (Do NOT set initdefault to this)
#   1 - Single user mode
#   2 - Multiuser, without NFS (The same as 3, if you do not have networking)
#   3 - Full multiuser mode
#   4 - unused
#   5 - X11
#   6 - reboot (Do NOT set initdefault to this)
#
id:3:initdefault:
# System initialization.
si::sysinit:/etc/rc.d/rc.sysinit
l0:0:wait:/etc/rc.d/rc 0
l1:1:wait:/etc/rc.d/rc 1
l2:2:wait:/etc/rc.d/rc 2
l3:3:wait:/etc/rc.d/rc 3
l4:4:wait:/etc/rc.d/rc 4
l5:5:wait:/etc/rc.d/rc 5
l6:6:wait:/etc/rc.d/rc 6
# Things to run in every runlevel.
ud::once:/sbin/update
# Trap CTRL-ALT-DELETE
ca::ctrlaltdel:/sbin/shutdown -t3 -r now
# When our UPS tells us power has failed, assume we have a few minutes
# of power left.  Schedule a shutdown for 2 minutes from now.
# This does, of course, assume you have powerd installed and your
# UPS connected and working correctly.
pf::powerfail:/sbin/shutdown -f -h +2 "Power Failure; System Shutting Down'"
# If power was restored before the shutdown kicked in, cancel it.
pr:12345:powerokwait:/sbin/shutdown -c "Power Restored; Shutdown Cancelled"
# Run gettys in standard runlevels
1:2345:respawn:/sbin/mingetty tty1
2:2345:respawn:/sbin/mingetty tty2
3:2345:respawn:/sbin/mingetty tty3
4:2345:respawn:/sbin/mingetty tty4
5:2345:respawn:/sbin/mingetty tty5
6:2345:respawn:/sbin/mingetty tty6
# Run xdm in runlevel 5
# xdm is now a separate service
x:5:respawn:/etc/X11/prefdm -nodaemon
```

The `init` process remains active for as long as the system is running. It makes sure all the daemons are started. For example, when you log in, the getty process (`/sbin/mingetty` in Linux), which monitors the terminal, is replaced by your login shell. As a result the getty process no longer exists for that terminal. However when you log out, the shell exits, leaving a dead terminal port that cannot be used. The init process detects when the shell dies and spawns another getty process for that terminal port. This provides the Login: prompt at the terminal.

As we have stated earlier, the init process takes the instructions regarding which daemons need to be running from the file /etc/inittab. The inittab file is a typical line-oriented UNIX control file with several entries consisting of four fields separated by colons. Lines starting with the # symbol are comment lines and are ignored. The fields are used as follows:

- The first field of each line is an identifier that effectively names the line, and must be unique.

- The second field defines the run levels for which the line is active. This can specify several run levels such as 2345, which indicates that the entry is active for run levels 2, 3, 4, and 5. If this field has no contents, it will be active in all run levels. For example, the si (system initialization), ud (update), ca (control-alt-delete), and pf (powerfail) lines in the sample inittab file all have empty run level lists and will apply in all run levels.

- The third field describes the action that init should take when it is in one of the run levels specified in the second field. Some typical values of this field are once, respawn, wait, and initdefault. once tells init to execute the program when it enters the specified run level but not to wait for it to complete. waiton the other hand, tells init to wait until execution of the specified program is completed, before continuing. respawn instructs init to start the specified program when init enters the pertinent run level and to restart the program whenever init detects that the program is not running. Finally, the initdefaultvalue has special meaning and entries containing this value in the third field do not include the fourth field. It specifies the system default run level and instructs init to enter this run level when the system is first booted.

- The last field specifies a command line to be executed by init when the system is in the run levels named in the second field. This can be a shell script or an executable program, and command-line arguments and shell redirection are supported.

In the sample inittab file shown above, the default run level is specified as 3. This instructs init to take the system to run level 3 when it first boots unless overridden by commands passed to LILO requesting that the system boot to single-user mode.

RUNNING INITIALIZATION SCRIPTS IN /etc/rc.d DIRECTORY

The system initialization scripts are found in the /etc/rc.d directory. The init program first runs the script called rc.sysinit. rc.sysinit sets various system variables and performs other startup initialization functions. Next init runs all the scripts specified for the default run level. Finally init runs the script called rc.local.

The following is a typical listing of the contents of the /etc/rc.d directory:

```
# ls -l
total 25
drwxr-xr-x   2 root     root        1024 Nov 30 19:14 init.d
-rwxr-xr-x   1 root     root        2722 Apr 15  1999 rc
```

```
-rwxr-xr-x  1 root      root          693 Aug 17  1998 rc.local
-rwxr-xr-x  1 root      root         9822 Apr 14  1999 rc.sysinit
drwxr-xr-x  2 root      root         1024 Nov 30 19:14 rc0.d
drwxr-xr-x  2 root      root         1024 Nov 30 19:14 rc1.d
drwxr-xr-x  2 root      root         1024 Nov 30 19:14 rc2.d
drwxr-xr-x  2 root      root         1024 Dec 26 12:46 rc3.d
drwxr-xr-x  2 root      root         1024 Nov 30 19:17 rc4.d
drwxr-xr-x  2 root      root         1024 Nov 30 19:17 rc5.d
drwxr-xr-x  2 root      root         1024 Nov 30 19:14 rc6.d
```

The /etc/rc.d/init.d contains initialization and termination scripts for changing run levels. These scripts are linked as appropriate to files in the /etc/rc.d/rc[0-6].d directories.

Files in the rc[0-6].d directories have names of the form [SK]nn<init.d filename> where S indicates that the program should be started at this run level, and K indicates that the program should be killed at this run level. The number nn is the relative sequence number for killing or starting the program.

When entering a run level (0,1,2,3,and so forth) the scripts in /etc/rc.d/rc[0-6].d that are prefixed with K are executed followed by those scripts prefixed with S. When executing each script in one of the rc[0-6].d directories, a single argument is passed to the script. The argument stop is passed to scripts prefixed with K and the argument start to scripts prefixed with S. There is no harm in applying the same sequence number to multiple scripts. In this case both scripts will be executed but the order of execution is unpredictable.

The K and S scripts are links to the real scripts in the init.d directory. When init calls rc0.d/K30sendmail, for example, it is equivalent to running the following command:

```
# /etc/rc.d/init.d/sendmail stop
```

Similarly when init runs rc3.d/S80sendmail it translates to running the following command:

```
# /etc/rc.d/init.d/sendmail start
```

Note

As an administrator, there will be times when you must run startup scripts by hand to reconfigure a service. When you run these scripts manually remember to use the actual script in the /etc/rc.d/init.d directory with the stop, start, and restart arguments.

By way of example, the following table lists scripts that are executed when the system enters run level 3, which is one of the full multiuser states:

```
# ls /etc/rc.d/rc3.d
K05innd          K20rwhod        K45named       K96pcmcia      S40crond      S85httpd
K08autofs        K25squid        K50snmpd       S10network     S50inet       S86squid
K15postgresql    K28amd          K55routed      S11portmap     S55xntpd      S90xfs
K15sound         K30mcserv       K60mars-nwe    S13ypbind      S60lpd        S99linuxconf
K20bootparamd    K34yppasswdd    K75gated       S15netfs       S60nfs        S99local
K20rstatd        K35dhcpd        K80nscd        S20random      S75keytable
```

```
K20rusersd     K35smb          K88ypserv      S30syslog      S80sendmail
K20rwalld      K45arpwatch     K92apmd        S40atd         S85gpm
```

In the preceding listing all the K and S scripts are links to files in the /etc/rc.d/init.d directory, with the exception of S99local which is a link to rc.local in the /etc/rc.d directory. First the K scripts are executed and then the S scripts, starting with the lowest numbers working up to the highest ones. As you can see in the preceding listing the script S99local, which points to ../rc.local, is executed last.

Note

> There is one other script called rc in the /etc/rc.d directory. This script is used to change run levels. This script takes one argument, which is a number corresponding to the new run level.

SINGLE-USER MODE

The single-user mode of operation can be invoked at boot time by issuing a special directive to the boot loader LILO. The command entered at the LILO: prompt to boot the system to single-user mode is shown below:

```
LILO: linux single
```

Note

> The above assumes you are booting the default kernel image labeled linux in /etc/lilo.conf to single-user mode. If, for example, you want to boot a different kernel image labeled linux-new to single-user mode, the command entered at the LILO: prompt would be linux-new single.

When this command is issued the kernel notifies init to enter single-user mode of operation. Startup scripts in rc1.d are executed. init then starts a shell on the system console and waits for it to terminate before continuing with the rest of the system startup process. When you leave single-user mode by exiting the shell, the system moves on to the default multiuser state. In Linux, the single-user shell is bash and runs as the super-user root.

Certain system maintenance tasks, such as file system repair, can be performed when the system is in single-user mode.

A sample ps output when the system is in single-user mode is shown here:

```
# ps -aef
UID        PID  PPID  C STIME TTY          TIME CMD
root         1     0  2 17:38 ?        00:00:03 init [S]
root         2     1  0 17:38 ?        00:00:00 [kflushd]
root         3     1  0 17:38 ?        00:00:00 [kpiod]
root         4     1  0 17:38 ?        00:00:00 [kswapd]
root         5     1  0 17:38 ?        00:00:00 [mdrecoveryd]
root        90     1  0 17:38 tty1     00:00:00 init [S]
```

```
root        91    90    0 17:38 tty1      00:00:00 /bin/sh
root        93    91    0 17:40 tty1      00:00:00 ps -aef
```

MULTIUSER OPERATING MODE

To enter multiuser mode, the initialization scripts of run level 3 or 5 are executed. After all initialization scripts are run, the system is fully operational. Once the getty processes are spawned, users will be able to log in. When the /etc/rc.d scripts have all completed, init starts the getty processes.

SHUTTING DOWN

Unlike booting up a system, which can essentially be done only one way, there are several different ways of shutting down a Linux system. In principle, a correct shutdown will notify system users to log off before the system goes down and should properly terminate the non-essential processes, update system files and logs, synchronize the disk with contents of in-memory buffers, and finally kill the remaining processes and halt the system.

The following commands can all be used to shut down a Linux system in different ways:

- shutdown
- telinit and init
- reboot
- halt
- Ctrl+Alt+Del (For x86 machines only)

The recommended command to use for a typical system shutdown is the shutdown command.

shutdown

The shutdown command is the one most recommended because it is the safest and most thorough way to initiate a halt, reboot, or bring the system down to single-user mode. However, because of its thoroughness it is also the slowest.

shutdown brings the system down in a secure way, all logged-in users are notified that the system is going down, and shutdown creates the /etc/nologin file that blocks new login attempts. The syntax of the command is

/sbin/shutdown -t <seconds> -r -k -h -n -c -f -F <time> <warning-message>

The options are used as follows:

- The -t flag specifies the number of seconds to wait before the system shuts down by sending the SIGTERM signal to all processes. This flag is optional and if omitted, the shutdown will begin immediately.
- The -r and -h flags are used to reboot (run level 6) and halt (run level 0) the system, respectively. If neither is specified, shutdown switches to single-user mode (run level 1).

- The -k option sends out a fake shutdown message and does not really shut down the machine.
- The -n option causes shutdown to kill processes itself and not by calling init. It turns off quota, accounts, and swapping, and unmounts all file systems. The use of this option is not recommended because it might not behave exactly as expected.
- The -f option instructs init to skip running fsck on reboot. shutdown creates a file /fastboot which is checked at boot time, and if found, the file is removed and fsck is skipped.
- The -F option forces fsck to run on reboot. shutdown creates a file /forcefsck which is checked at boot time, and if found, the file is removed and fsck is run.
- The -c option is used to cancel an already running shutdown command.
- The time argument specifies when to shut down the machine. It can be specified in an absolute time format (hh:mm), or a relative "minutes from now" format. The relative format uses a plus sign; for instance, +5 means shutdown in five minutes from now. The special time now can be used to initiate an immediate system shutdown.
- The warning message is the message sent to all logged-in users.

The following is a typical shutdown:

```
shutdown -h +5 "System maintenance shutdown - Please log out now"
```

This command indicates that the system should be halted in five minutes and that the message System maintenance shutdown-Please log out now will be sent to all logged-in users.

telinit AND init

The programs telinit and init can be used to shut down a machine. When these methods of shutdown are used, no message is sent to logged-in users. These commands are useful when broadcasting of shutdown messages to all users is not desired, such as when rebooting a special-purpose server that does not have logged-on users (a DNS or DHCP server, for instance). Examples of using telinit and init to shut down a machine are

```
# telinit 0
```

or

```
# init 0
```

These commands instruct init to switch to run level 0, the halt state. Similarly, telinit 1 or init 1 place the system in single-user mode and telinit 6 and init 6 reboot the system by changing to run level 6.

halt

Running halt causes the shutdown -h command to be executed. haltlogs the shutdown, kills the system processes, executes a sync system call to write the data in memory buffers to disk, waits for the write to complete, and then halts the processor.

The `halt` command has several flags: `-n`, `-w`, `-d`, `-f`, `-i`, and `-p`. The `-n` flag prevents the `sync` call. It is sometimes necessary to halt the system in this way after repairing the root file system with `fsck`. The `-f` flag is used to bring the system down in a hurry. It does an immediate halt without syncing the file system, killing processes, or writing logs. This is not a recommended way to shut down a machine.

The `-w` flag does not halt the machine but only writes a `wtmp` entry. The `-d` flag prevents writing of the `wtmp` entry when halting the machine. The `-i` flag causes all network interfaces to shut down just before the halt. The `-p` flag tells `halt` to power off the machine after the halt.

reboot

`reboot` is similar to `halt`, except that it causes the machine to reboot from scratch after halting. Using the `reboot` command is similar to running `shutdown -r`. The `reboot` command has the same flags as the `halt` command.

CTRL+ALT+DEL

Another easy and safe way to shutdown or reboot an x86 based Linux machine is to use the all too familiar Ctrl+Alt+Del key combination. This causes the following line in the `/etc/inittab` file to be processed by `init`:

```
ca::ctrlaltdel:/sbin/shutdown -t3 -r now
```

When you press Ctrl+Alt+Del, `init` runs the command `/sbin/shutdown -t3 -r now`. The shutdown starts immediately, as specified by the argument `now`. The `-t3` argument tells init to wait three seconds before sending the terminate signal to all processes. The `-r` argument tells the system to reboot after the shutdown.

> **Note**
>
> Sometimes it is desirable to disable the Ctrl+Alt+Del command to prevent accidental reboot of machines by novice users. To disable this command, change the line in the `/etc/inittab` file starting with the `ca:` entry to the following:
>
> After editing the `/etc/inittab` file, signal init to reread its configuration file with the `telinit` command as follows:
>
> `# telinit q`

TROUBLESHOOTING

You might be faced with situations when a system will not boot successfully. This can be caused by hardware problems, file system corruption, an improperly configured newly built kernel, or by errors in startup scripts.

HARDWARE PROBLEMS

If a certain piece of hardware has failed, it must be replaced. If the failed hardware is a disk drive, you will need to replace the disk, build a new file system, and then restore the files from backup tapes.

Bad memory chips are another possible cause of booting failure. In this case the task is to identify the bad chips, replace them, and then proceed to boot the machine.

Faulty power supplies can cause system failures. It is good to check the power supplies of each individual piece of equipment. Make sure cooling fans are working. Also check loose network cables, SCSI cables, and SCSI terminators. Make sure all disk drives are online. These things can seem obvious but are easy to overlook.

Sometimes just power cycling all the equipment will clear up boot problems. Turn power off to all equipment. Power up all peripherals and external disk drives first, and power up the CPU at the very end.

Finally, run hardware diagnostics programs that are suitable for your hardware to isolate problem areas.

Sometimes it is possible to avoid a catastrophic system failure by regularly checking system logs. Often a failing piece of hardware will start logging errors and if caught early, you can schedule a system downtime and replace it, thereby avoiding a major system crash and subsequent rebuild.

FILE SYSTEM CORRUPTION

If a system goes down because of a sudden power failure, it can cause the file system to be corrupted. This can generally be corrected by booting the system in single-user mode and running `fsck` on all file systems.

You need to pay close attention to the boot-up messages. Any messages about inodes, superblocks or other disk-related subjects suggest file system problems, and running `fsck` is the way to fix them. This of course assumes that you do not have a physically failing disk, in which case you must replace the disk and restore files from backup tapes.

NEWLY BUILT KERNEL WON'T BOOT

When you build a new kernel you can run into problems if the kernel was misconfigured and the system can refuse to boot. When building new kernels, always make sure you create a backup LILO entry to boot the older kernel. An example of how you can specify alternate Linux boot images in `lilo.conf` was discussed in the LILO section earlier on in this chapter.

Another way would be to boot using an emergency boot disk, mount the root partition on the hard disk, reconfigure and rebuild the kernel properly, and reboot using the newer fixed kernel.

ERRORS IN STARTUP SCRIPTS

This is a common problem that is fortunately not hard to fix. What typically happens is that you add or make changes to startup scripts in /etc/rc.d and then when you reboot, the system refuses to come up in multiuser mode.

The solution is to boot the system in single-user mode and look for the changes last made to the startup scripts, identify and fix any errors, and reboot your system.

## CHAPTER 5

USING xdm TO CREATE AN X WINDOWS APPLICATION SERVER

In this chapter

WHAT IS AN X APPLICATION SERVER?

The X Windows System, the graphical environment for UNIX and Linux, offers the capability to display applications on remote hosts on the network. This means an application running on one host can be displayed and used interactively on another. The capability to distribute X applications, effectively separating the user interface from the processing, makes it possible to deploy X application servers.

An X Windows System application server is a system that accepts logins from X desktops (which can be special hardware X terminals) and then runs applications that are displayed on these desktops. Using this mechanism, you can deploy X applications on centrally managed servers and focus the hardware power for processing and running these applications in a few servers. This limits the need for powerful, complex hardware on the desktop.

This type of centrally managed application environment offers the promise of reduced total cost of ownership because desktops become essentially dumb graphical terminals which do not need individual configuration and can easily be replaced when they fail.

UNDERSTANDING THE RELATIONSHIP BETWEEN CLIENT AND SERVER IN THE X WINDOWS SYSTEM

When X applications are run remotely in the fashion just described, a strange thing happens: The terms client and server become confused and unclear. A distinction is made between the X application program and the X Windows System.

In the context of requesting and running an application, the user sits at a workstation that is the client from which a request is made to run an X application on a remote X application server. The application executes on the remote X application server but its input is received from, and its output displayed on, the client workstation. This is quite straightforward because the client and server terms apply as they are normally understood.

However, in the context of the X Windows System environment itself, the terms are reversed. X consists of two components: the X server and the X client. The X server program runs on the client workstation, and renders the graphic display of the application. The X application program is the client, issuing rendering commands to the X server program running on the client workstation. The X client program can be running on the local workstation, or on a remote X application server. Notice how the client and server roles are reversed in the X Windows System context.

In the distributed X environment of an X Windows System application server, the X server runs on the client desktops and the applications, which are clients to these X servers, run on the X application server.

Therefore, the client terminal runs an X server and the X application server runs X applications, which are clients of the X server. The fact that the applications running on the X application servers are X clients actually is logical: The applications request the service of the

X server to render their graphical displays. Without the service of the X server, these clients could not operate.

USING xdm TO CREATE LINUX-BASED LOGINS FOR X WORKSTATIONS AND TERMINALS

Typically, Linux distributions install the X Windows System as part of the installation process. When X is run locally on a Linux system, both the X server and the X applications acting as clients to the X server run on the same local system. However, for all practical purposes the client/server environment described previously in the remote scenario exists: The X applications and the X server really don't care or behave differently because they are running on the same system.

This means you log in to your local system using Linux's standard login prompt and then start X Windows locally. However, in the distributed scenario, your client desktops should simply start an X server and then allow an X application server to display a graphical login prompt instead of providing a local login prompt. This enables users to log directly in to the X application server they will work with instead of logging in to a local system and then connecting to a remote X application server.

In this way, it is possible to build hardware-based X terminals that embed the X server and networking capability in hardware and have no other real functionality. When these terminals are turned on, the X server starts and the network is polled for an X application server which can display a login prompt.

For an X application server to display a login prompt on an X terminal, it must use the X display manager control protocol (XDMCP). Support for this protocol is provided by the xdm daemon. xdm can be used to display a graphical login prompt on the local system in place of the standard text-based Linux login or it can display a login prompt on a remote system allowing users on the remote system to log in to the system running xdm. It is this latter approach which is used by an X application server to display a login prompt on terminals.

For an X application server to be created using xdm to provide the login prompt, several things must be in place, including the following:

- **The X Windows System should be installed and functioning on the server**: The X Windows System should be included with your Linux distribution and should install by default during the installation process. If not, consult your distribution's documentation for guidance on installing the necessary packages.

- **Any X applications that should be made available to users of the X application server should be installed and functional**.

- **xdm should be installed**: xdm should be included with your Linux distribution and installed by default during the installation process. If not, consult your distribution's documentation for guidance on installing the necessary packages.

PART

II

CH

5

After this is in place, you are ready to configure your X application server to use xdm. xdm uses the Xsession or .xsession file to determine how the X Windows System should behave. Typically, the file /etc/X11/xdm/Xsession or /etc/X11R6/xdm/Xsession is the global file which is overridden by an .xsession file in a user's home directory, should the file exist.

The Xsession script determines what applications should be launched after a user successfully logs in through an xdm login prompt. Typically, Xsession is configured to first try a user's personal .Xclients file. If that doesn't exist, the global /etc/X11/xinit/Xclients or /etc/X11R6/xinit/Xclients file is executed. These are the same files that determine the applications that run when X is manually started on the local system.

The following is a typical Xsession file (taken from Red Hat 6.2):

```
#!/bin/bash -login
#  1999 Red Hat Software, Inc.

# redirect errors to a file in user's home directory if we can
for errfile in "$HOME/.xsession-errors"
        ➥"${TMPDIR-/tmp}/xses-$USER" "/tmp/xses-$USER"
do
    if ( cp /dev/null "$errfile" 2> /dev/null )
    then
        chmod 600 "$errfile"
        exec > "$errfile" 2>&1
        break
    fi
done

xsetroot -solid '#356390'

# clean up after xbanner
if [ -x /usr/X11R6/bin/freetemp ]; then
    /usr/X11R6/bin/freetemp
fi

userresources=$HOME/.Xresources
usermodmap=$HOME/.Xmodmap
sysresources=/usr/X11R6/lib/X11/xinit/.Xresources
sysmodmap=/usr/X11R6/lib/X11/xinit/.Xmodmap

# merge in defaults and keymaps
if [ -f $sysresources ]; then
    xrdb -merge $sysresources
fi

if [ -f $sysmodmap ]; then
    xmodmap $sysmodmap
fi

if [ -f $userresources ]; then
    xrdb -merge $userresources
fi
```

```
if [ -f $usermodmap ]; then
    xmodmap $usermodmap
fi

we see if xdm/gdm/kdm has asked for a specific environment
case $# in
1)
    case $1 in
    failsafe)
        exec xterm -geometry 80x24-0-0
        ;;
    gnome)
        exec gnome-session
        ;;
    kde)
        exec startkde
        ;;
    anotherlevel)
        # we assume that switchdesk is installed.
        exec /usr/share/apps/switchdesk/Xclients.anotherlevel
        ;;
    esac
esac

# otherwise, take default action
if [ -x "$HOME/.xsession" ]; then
    exec "$HOME/.xsession"
elif [ -x "$HOME/.Xclients" ]; then
    exec "$HOME/.Xclients"
elif [ -x /etc/X11/xinit/Xclients ]; then
    exec /etc/X11/xinit/Xclients
else
    exec xsm
fi
```

Normally, if you launch the xdm program, it starts X Windows on the local system where it is running and displays a graphical login prompt. When a user logs in, xdm uses the Xsession file to determine which applications to run in the local X Windows session.

However, on an X application server you do not want xdm to run X locally and display a login prompt. Instead you want it to wait for remote requests for a login prompt through XDMCP and then display the prompt on those remote systems. This behavior is controlled by the /etc/X11/xdm/Xaccess or /etc/X11R6/xdm/Xaccess file. This file controls access to the xdm server through XDMCP. Four types of entries can be used in the Xaccess file:

- **Entries to control access from direct queries**: Direct queries are those queries received from a desktop which xdm should respond to by displaying a login prompt. Entries take the form:

  ```
  <host name or host name pattern>
  ```

  Any desktop that matches the hostname or pattern will be handled directly by xdm. A hostname pattern can include an asterisk (*) to match zero or more characters or a question mark (?) to match any single character.

- **Entries to control access from indirect queries**: Indirect queries are those queries received from a desktop which xdm should redirect to another xdm system to handle. Entries take the form:

  `<host name or host name pattern> <list of alternate xdm hosts>`

  Any desktop that matches the hostname or pattern will be redirected to one of the alternate xdm hosts. The list of alternate xdm hosts is separated by spaces.

- **Entries to display a chooser to desktops**: The chooser allows desktops to select from a list of available xdm servers and then log in to one of the servers. Entries take the form:

  `<host name or host name pattern> CHOOSER <list of xdm hosts>`

  Any desktop that matches the hostname or pattern will be presented with the chooser. The list of xdm hosts will be listed in the chooser. In place of a list of xdm hosts, you can use the keyword BROADCAST, which will cause xdm to broadcast on the network to discover all available xdm servers which will handle requests from the connecting desktop and present those in the chooser's list.

- **Entries to define macros**: Macros allow you to define a name for a list of hosts and then use that macro name anywhere a list of hosts is required in other Xaccess entries. Entries take the form:

  `%<macro name> <list of hosts>`

  For instance, if you define a macro named %mymacro and assign it the list of hosts host1 host2 host3 then you can use %macro in other Xaccess entries to indicate the three hosts.

This means that the simplest Xaccess file contains a single entry:

```
*
```

With this entry, any host requesting service through XDMCP will be presented with a login window and users can proceed to log in and use the server. In an environment with a single X application server, this will be sufficient because users only have the choice to log in to one server.

You might have more than one X application server and might want to allow users the choice to log in to any of the servers. To do so, use the following two entries in your Xaccess file to cause xdm to display a chooser list with all xdm servers to the user:

```
*
* CHOOSER BROADCAST
```

A more complex Xaccess file might look like the following:

```
fin*
per* per-xserver
mis* CHOOSER BROADCAST
```

This `Xaccess` file controls `xdm` access for three groups of terminals: those with hostnames starting with `fin` (the finance department's terminals), those starting with `per` (the personnel department's terminals), and those starting with `mis` (the information system department's terminals).

Finance department terminals are handled directly by `xdm`. Personnel department terminals are redirected to `xdm` running on the X application server `per-xserver`. Information system terminals are presented with a chooser enabling them to log in to any valid X application server running `xdm`.

For `xdm` to start at boot time so that your X application server is always ready to respond to XDMCP queries, you must change your default run level from 3 to 5. Run levels are discussed in more detail in Chapter 4, "Booting Up and Shutting Down."

To change your default run level file, edit the file `/etc/inittab` and change the line:

```
id:3:initdefault:
```

to the following:

```
id:5:initdefault:
```

You also must make sure that `xdm` will enter run level 5. Check the `inittab` file for an entry similar to the following:

```
x:5:respawn:/usr/bin/X11/xdm -nodaemon
```

If the line is missing, add it to the file.

> **Note**
>
> Red Hat Linux 6.2 uses the `prefdm` script to launch `xdm` in run level 5. This means the relevant entry is `x:5:respawn:/etc/X11/prefdm -nodaemon`. To ensure that `xdm` will be launched by `prefdm` (instead of an alternate login manager such as `kdm` or `gdm`), edit the file `/etc/X11/prefdm` and set the `preferred` variable on line 6 to `preferred=xdm`.

By default, when `xdm` starts on your X application server, it will also start X on the local system and display a login prompt there. This creates an unnecessary draw on the resources of the application server which really doesn't need to be running X Windows on the console. The `/etc/X11/xdm/Xservers` or `/etc/X11R6/xdm/Xservers` file contains a list of local X servers which should be managed by `xdm`. To prevent `xdm` from starting a local X server, comment out all entries in the file by placing a hash mark (#) at the start of all lines in the file. In most default installations, there will be one entry you need to comment out:

```
:0 local /usr/X11R6/bin/X
```

CUSTOMIZING THE xdm LOGIN PROMPT

The /etc/X11/xdm/Xresources or /etc/X11R6/xdm/Xresources file controls the appearance of the xdm Login window. The file contains a series of X resource entries defining the appearance and behavior of xdm. The following is a typical Xresources file:

```
! $XConsortium: Xresources /main/8 1996/11/11 09:24:46 swick $
xlogin*login.translations: #override\
        Ctrl<Key>R: abort-display()\n\
        <Key>F1: set-session-argument(failsafe) finish-field()\n\
        Ctrl<Key>Return: set-session-argument(failsafe) finish-field()\n\
        <Key>Return: set-session-argument() finish-field()
xlogin*borderWidth: 3
xlogin*greeting: CLIENTHOST
xlogin*namePrompt: login:\040
xlogin*fail: Login incorrect
#ifdef COLOR
xlogin*greetColor: CadetBlue
xlogin*failColor: red
*Foreground: black
*Background: #fffff0
#else
xlogin*Foreground: black
xlogin*Background: white
#endif

XConsole.text.geometry: 480x130
XConsole.verbose:        true
XConsole*iconic:         true
XConsole*font:           fixed

Chooser*geometry:               700x500+300+200
Chooser*allowShellResize:       false
Chooser*viewport.forceBars:     true
Chooser*label.font:             *-new century schoolbook-bold-i-normal-*-240-*
Chooser*label.label:            XDMCP Host Menu  from CLIENTHOST
Chooser*list.font:              -*-*-medium-r-normal-*-*-230-*-*-c-*-iso8859-1
Chooser*Command.font:           *-new century schoolbook-bold-r-normal-*-180-*
```

X resource entries are grouped into classes where, typically, a single application or resource has its own class. For instance, in the Xresources file, the xlogin class controls the appearance and behavior of the xdm login window and the chooser class handles the appearance and behavior of the chooser.

Resource entries take the following standard form:

```
<class name>*<resource name> : <value>
```

In the sample Xresources file above, several key entries control the appearance of the xdm login window:

- **xlogin*borderWidth**: Specifies the width of login window's border in pixels.
- **xlogin*greeting**: Specifies the greeting title to display at the top of the xdm login window. The special keyword CLIENTHOST will be replaced with the hostname of the xdm system.

- **xlogin*namePrompt**: Specifies the prompt to display asking for the user's account name.

- **xlogin*fail**: Specifies the text to display if the user fails to authenticate.

- **xlogin*greetColor**: Specifies the color of the greeting title displayed at the top of the xdm login window.

- **xlogin*failColor**: Specifies the color of the text to display if the user fails to authenticate.

- **xlogin*Foreground**: Specifies the foreground color of the xdm login window.

- **xlogin*Background**: Specifies the background color of the xdm login window.

In the sample Xresources file, the following key entries control the appearance of the xdm chooser:

- **Chooser*geometry**: Specifies the location and dimensions of the chooser window.

- **Chooser*label.font**: Specifies the font for the chooser's label.

- **Chooser*label.label**: Specifies the label text to display in the chooser's window.

- **Chooser*list.font**: Specifies the font for displaying the list of available xdm hosts.

CONFIGURING A LINUX CLIENT TO OBTAIN ITS LOGIN PROMPT FROM A REMOTE xdm SERVER

If you want to use a Linux system as a terminal that connects to an X application server and runs applications remotely, you must configure the Linux terminal system to obtain an xdm login prompt from an application server when X starts on the terminal system.

To do this, you have two choices:

- Cause the X server to broadcast on the network for an available xdm server.

- Cause the X server to query a specific xdm server for a login window.

To broadcast for an xdm server, pass the -broadcast argument to the X server by using startx as follows:

```
# startx -- -broadcast
```

To query a specific xdm server for a login window, use the -query argument to the X server:

```
# startx -- -query <xdm server host name>
```

To start X Windows when the terminal system boots, edit the /etc/inittab on the terminal system by following these steps:

1. Set the default run level to 5 by changing the line:

    ```
    id:3:initdefault:
    ```

    to the following:

    ```
    id:5:initdefault:
    ```

PART

II

CH

5

2. Find one of the following lines:

```
x:5:respawn:/etc/X11/xdm -nodaemon
```

```
x:5:respawn:/etc/X11/prefdm -nodaemon
```

Change it to either of the following:

```
x:5:respawn:/usr/X11R6/bin/startx -- -broadcast
```

```
x:5:respawn:/usr/X11R6/bin/startx -- -query <xdm server host name>
```

Note

If you have a large number of X clients in a network, it is strongly advised that you allocate specific X application servers to service specific X clients, by using the -query option as previously shown. This ensures X client queries are directed to pre-defined X application servers and avoids broadcast traffic. In large networks, creating additional broadcast traffic is not a good idea because it can seriously impact network performance.

TROUBLESHOOTING

If an X server is not displaying a login window as expected, first make sure the X server process is running on the client workstation by moving the mouse and verifying that the cursor moves.

If the client is configured to log in to an xdm login server, make sure the client has been granted proper access to connect to the xdm process on the X application server. Access is provided by adding the client's name or a matching wildcard pattern in the /etc/X11/xdm/Xaccess, /etc/X11R6/xdm/Xaccess, or /usr/lib/X11/xdm/Xaccess file. After you edit the Xaccess file don't forget to send a SIGHUP signal to the xdm process. When the xdm process receives the SIGHUP signal it rescans its configuration files.

Tip

Never kill and restart the parent xdm process on an xdm login server. This will cause all the xdm child processes that are servicing X client workstations to die. Identify the parent xdm process and send it a SIGHUP signal. On Red Hat Linux systems the PID of the parent xdm process is logged in the /var/run/xdm.pid file. Check the /etc/X11/xdm/xdm-config file to learn where the xdm.pid file is being written on your system.

On the X application server make sure the proper number of xdm processes are running. There should be one parent xdm process and a number of xdm child processes. There is one xdm child process for each X server requiring a login window. If you do a process listing of all the xdm processes with the ps command, you will see the names of the various displays being managed by each xdm process. xdm modifies its command-line argument to show the name of the display it is managing. This is an excellent debugging aid.

If a client workstation is having problems connecting to xdm, or dying mysteriously, an error log is written to the xdm's error log file. The location of the error log file is specified in the xdm-config file, which is usually in the /etc/X11/xdm or /etc/X11R6/xdm directory. The default location of the xdm error log file in Red Hat Linux is /var/log/xdm-error.log. Check the contents of the xdm-error.log file for clues. Resource problems, such as not being able to find a font, will also show up in this log file.

If the login process appears to be failing, you can try using the failsafe option. This usually involves pressing the F1 key instead of the Enter key at the time of logging in, after the username and password have been entered. The failsafe option provides a minimal session for debugging. By default a single xterm application is launched for this option.

If none of the X clients are able to get the xdm login prompt, barring network connectivity problems, the problem is almost certainly a dead xdm parent process on the xdm login server. Determine the process ID of the parent xdm process by examining the contents of the /var/run/xdm.pid file. Verify that this process is dead, and start up a new xdm parent process. X clients should now be able to get xdm login windows. You will notice child xdm processes starting up as client workstations start connecting to the xdm login server.

A common problem with the Xaccess file is when it contains names of retired hosts whose IP addresses can no longer be resolved. Any valid hostnames that appear after this invalid hostname are not recognized by xdm, and these hosts are unable to receive xdm login windows. The fix is to remove the invalid hostnames from the Xaccess file and issue a SIGHUP signal to the parent xdm process.

If everything fails, you can run xdm in debug mode with the -debug command-line option. However this is not very useful from the X Windows System administration point of view. This option is intended for X Windows System developers.

PART

II

CH

5

## CHAPTER 6

AUTHENTICATING USERS AND NETWORK RESOURCES

In this chapter

NETWORK AUTHENTICATION IN UNIX AND LINUX

Unix and Unix-like operating systems in a networked environment often use a form of centralized user authentication and distribution of resource information (such as user databases or host tables).

Often, these services are provided using the Network Information Service (NIS). NIS was originally designed by Sun Microsystems and was formerly known as Yellow Pages, a name that turned out to be a registered trademark owned by British Telecom. As a result, the name was changed to NIS.

The purpose of NIS is to place network information in a centralized database that can be used by any machine on the network. The following is the information most commonly distributed with NIS:

- hosts maps (/etc/hosts)
- passwd maps (/etc/passwd)
- group maps (/etc/group)
- netgroup maps (/etc/netgroup)
- services maps (/etc/services)

By running NIS, system administration demands can be eased. For instance, changing a password entry in the NIS database reflects the change to all systems on the network running NIS client programs. There is no need to maintain individual password entries on each machine on the network and make changes to all these databases each time a password changes.

NIS operates using a client/server architecture. NIS databases are replicated across one or more servers. Generally, a network will have one NIS master server along with one or more optional NIS slave servers. The master server holds the read-write NIS database. Read-only copies of this database are replicated to slave servers. The slave servers provide load balancing and answer client broadcast queries. Changes to database contents are made on the master server.

NIS NETWORK CONFIGURATIONS

The simplest NIS network configuration is to create a network with a master NIS server and one or more NIS client systems, as illustrated in Figure 6.1.

However, most networks are more complicated than this simple example. For instance, on a large network that requires high-availability, having slave servers can be a good idea. These servers not only help minimize the load on any one NIS server, thus improving responsiveness, but they also provide redundancy so that if one NIS server is not functioning, another can answer requests for NIS services.

Figure 6.1
A simple NIS network with a single NIS master server.

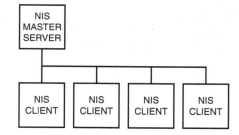

A typical network with an NIS master server and two slave servers is shown in Figure 6.2.

Figure 6.2
An NIS network with a single NIS master server and two slave servers.

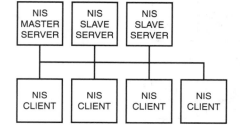

ROUTED NETWORK

Both examples of simple single and multiple NIS server networks shown previously have one thing in common: All the client and server machines are on the same single network. However, the typical corporate network will have more than one network connected through routers. These separate physical networks may reflect geographic distribution of the organization or simple workgroup distinctions.

Often on these networks, the same user database needs to be accessible throughout all the organization's networks. However, NIS uses broadcasting for the client systems to find a server to service requests. Because an NIS master server can only exist on one physical network, slave servers are needed to play the role of duplicating the NIS databases on each physical network and answering requests for service on those networks.

In Figure 6.3, the entire organizational infrastructure consists of two physical networks connected by a router. The NIS master server is on network A. However, NIS clients on network B won't be able to find the master server because their broadcast requests searching for the server won't cross the router. By placing a slave server on network B, the clients on network B will talk to the slave server to service all their NIS requests. The slave and master servers then communicate across the router for the purpose of synchronizing changes from the master NIS server to the slave.

PART
II

CH
6

Note

While NIS clients often broadcast to find a server to handle their requests, you can configure an NIS client to use a specific host as its NIS server. In this case, an NIS client can communicate with an NIS server across a router because the hostname and IP address of the server are hard-coded in the client's configuration. In this case, the name and IP address of the NIS server needs to be contained in the /etc/hosts file on the client system.

Figure 6.3
A routed network configuration with master and slave NIS servers on separate physical networks.

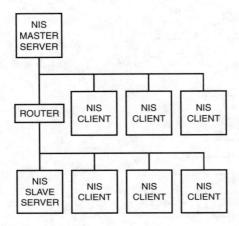

NIS MAPS

NIS was designed to provide a centralized location for a large number of standard Unix configuration files, generally stored in the /etc directory. As a result, NIS has available a large number of tables, known as *maps*, as outlined in Table 6.1.

TABLE 6.1   NIS MAPS

Map Name	Description
bootparams	Lists diskless clients and location of files needed for booting
ethers.byaddr	Lists the Ethernet addresses of hosts and their corresponding names
ethers.byname	Lists names of hosts and their corresponding Ethernet addresses
groups.bygid	Lists membership information about groups using group id as the key
groups.byname	Lists membership information about groups using group name as the key
hosts.byaddr	Lists names and IP address of hosts using IP addresses as the key
hosts.byname	Lists names and IP addresses of hosts using hostnames as the key
mailaliases	Lists all mail aliases

TABLE 6.1 CONTINUED

Map Name	Description
netgroup	Contains netgroup information using group name as the key
netgroup.byhost	Contains netgroup information using hostnames as the key
netgroup.byuser	Contains netgroup information using usernames as the key
netid.byname	Contains secure RPC netname of hosts and users, along with their UIDs and GIDs
netmasks.byaddr	Contains network masks used with IP subnetting using address as the key
networks.byaddr	Contains names and address of networks in the name space using address as the key
networks.byname	Contains names and addresses of networks in the namespace using network names as the key
passwd.byname	Contains password information using username as the key
passwd.byuid	Contains password information using userid as the key
protocols.byname	Lists the network protocols used
proctocols.bynumber	Lists the network protocols using protocol numbers as the key
publickey.byname	Contains public and secret keys for secure RPC
rpc.bynumber	Lists known program names and numbers of RPCs
services.byname	Lists the available internet services
ypservers	Lists all NIS servers in the namespace along with their IP addresses

SETTING UP AN NIS MASTER SERVER

Setting up an NIS master server consists of three basic steps:

1. Setting an NIS domain name.
2. Populating configuration files for the NIS maps.
3. Running ypinit.

SETTING AN NIS DOMAIN NAME

NIS networks are identified by domain name. An NIS server serves a particular domain, and a client is configured to belong to a specific domain and use the server or servers for that domain to handle any NIS requests it makes.

It is possible for different NIS domains to exist on the same physical network: Each domain will have its own master NIS server and one or more slave servers and individual client systems will be configured to belong to one of the domains on the network.

Each domain is identified by a name. Generally, the NIS domain is distinct from a DNS domain name. The domain name is set with the `domainname` command. This command takes the NIS domain name that a system should join. For instance, if you want to call your NIS domain `mydomain`, you need to issue the following command to make your master server the server of the `mydomain` domain:

```
# /bin/domainname mydomain
```

POPULATING CONFIGURATION FILES FOR THE NIS MAPS

On the NIS master server, the NIS maps are built from the standard Linux configuration files in the `/etc` directory.

- `/etc/passwd`: user database
- `/etc/group`: groups database
- `/etc/hosts`: host to IP address table
- `/etc/networks`: network addresses
- `/etc/services`: network port numbers and service names
- `/etc/protocols`: network protocol names and numbers
- `/etc/netgroup`: netgroup definitions
- `/etc/rpc`: remote procedure call program numbers

Configure these files in the normal fashion with any data you want propagated to the entire network through NIS.

RUNNING ypinit

Once you have populated the configuration files in `/etc`, use the `ypinit` command to generate the necessary NIS maps from these files. Using the following command:

```
# /usr/lib/yp/ypinit -m
```

This will create the directory `/var/yp/<domainname>` and generate dbm-type database files using `makedbm`. A pair of dbm files are created for each NIS map. For example, for the `hosts.byname` map there will be two files: `hosts.byname.dir` and `hosts.byname.pag`. Also, hosts can be looked up by addresses instead of names and there will be a `hosts.byaddr` map consisting of `hosts.byaddr.dir` and `hosts.byaddr.pag`. Likewise, there will be other dbm files created for various NIS maps in a `/var/yp/<domainname>` directory.

MAKING SURE EVERYTHING IS RUNNING

After setting up NIS on your Master Server, you will need to start up the following programs:

- `ypserv`
- `ypbind`

- rpc.yppasswdd
- rpc.ypxfrd

Note

rpc.yppasswdd is a program that runs only on the NIS master and allows users to change their NIS passwords. rpc.ypxfrd also only runs on the NIS master and speeds up map transfers to NIS slave servers.

To start ypserv and ypbind use the following commands:

```
# /etc/rc.d/init.d/ypserv start
# /etc/rc.d/init.d/ypbind start
```

To start rpc.yppasswdd, use this command:

```
# /etc/rc.d/init.d/yppasswd start
```

To start rpc.ypxfrd, use this command:

```
# /usr/sbin/rpc.ypxfrd
```

When the system is rebooted, these programs will start automatically. On some Linux systems, rpc.ypxfrd will not be configured to start at boot time and you will need to edit the scripts in /etc/rc.d/init.d/ to make sure the program starts when the system boots. Consult Chapter 4, "Booting Up and Shutting Down Linux," for details of the boot process and the scripts in /etc/rc.d/init.d/.

SETTING UP AN NIS CLIENT

Once you have set up your NIS master server, you can configure your NIS clients to use the master server to handle NIS service requests. The following three steps are required to configure an NIS client:

1. Setting the NIS domain name in the /etc/yp.conf file
2. Running ypbind
3. Editing the /etc/passwd file

SETTING THE NIS DOMAIN NAME IN THE /etc/yp.conf FILE

On the NIS client, you set the NIS domain name in the /etc/yp.conf file. This file is read by the ypbind daemon, which connects your NIS client to the appropriate NIS domain.

PART

II

CH

6

- You have two choices in the yp.conf file:
  - **Configure the ypbind daemon to broadcast for an NIS server for the correct domain:** Include the directive domain *domainname* broadcast. This directive indicates that the client should connect to the specified domain name and broadcast for a server to handle requests.
  - **Configure the ypbind daemon to connect to a specific NIS server:** Include the directive ypserver *hostname*. This directive is to use a specific host as the NIS server. The hostname and its IP address must be listed in /etc/hosts on the client.

RUNNING ypbind

After the correct configuration has been entered in /etc/yp.conf, you need to run ypbind to bind your client to the NIS domain. Do so with the following command:

```
# /etc/rc.d/init.d/ypbind start
```

If ypbind were already running on your system, you would first stop ypbind and then restart it with the above command. To stop ypbind, use the following command:

```
# /etc/rc.d/init.d/ypbind stop
```

EDITING THE /etc/passwd FILE

Once your system is a client on an NIS network, you need to configure it to perform user authentication against your NIS maps. To do this, add the following line to the end of the /etc/passwd file:

```
+::::::
```

The plus sign tells the system to look up usernames not defined in the local /etc/passwd file through NIS.

However, if a user already has an entry in the local /etc/passwd file that appears before the + entry, and the /etc/nsswitch.conf file is configured to consult the local password file first before consulting the NIS database, this password entry will override the NIS password entry. Refer to the section "Understanding the Name Server Switch" for an explanation of how the nsswitch.conf file is used.

Password file overrides should be avoided in general, unless there is a very good reason for a user to have a different UID, GID, home directory, or local password on a specific machine. Maintaining local user accounts on individual machines creates the same administrative overhead that NIS is designed to avoid.

ADDING AN NIS SLAVE SERVER

Configuring a system as an NIS Slave Server requires two steps:

1. Setting the NIS domain name
2. Runing `ypinit`

SETTING THE NIS DOMAIN NAME

The domain name is set with the `domainname` command. This command takes the NIS domain name that a system should join. For instance, if your master server has been configured with the NIS domain `mydomain`, you need to issue the following command to make your slave server part of the `mydomain` domain:

```
# /bin/domainname mydomain
```

RUNNING `ypinit`

As with a master server, `ypinit` is used to initialize all the necessary files on As with a master server, `ypinit` is used to initialize all the necessary files on your NIS slave server. The format of the command on the NIS slave server is:

```
# /usr/lib/yp/ypinit -s masterhostname
```

where `masterhostname` is the hostname of the master NIS server. This hostname and its IP address must be in the `/etc/hosts` file on the NIS slave server.

As when `ypinit` was used to create a master server, on the slave server the directory `/var/yp/<domainname>` will be created. The NIS maps will then be copied from the master server into this directory on the slave server.

MOVING NIS MASTER FUNCTIONS TO ANOTHER MACHINE

Once you have configured machines in the role of master and slave NIS servers, there is no straightforward and easy way to change these roles. However, there are times when it is necessary to change the master server system.

For instance, if your NIS master server runs on an old system which you need to upgrade or retire, you will need to move the master services to a new system.

The brute force approach says to build a new master server from scratch and then rebuild all the slave servers. However, this is a time-consuming and unnecessary process. The process can be made simpler.

Still, it is not as simple as promoting a slave server to the role of master or building a new master server and then asking all the slaves to start accepting NIS maps from the new master.

The difficulty lies in the fact that slave servers, once configured, expect to receive map updates from a specific master server and will reject maps pushed to them from other systems. This serves as a form of security and prevents unauthorized systems and users from setting up alternate master servers for a domain and attempting to push invalid map data to all the slaves.

To get around this problem, several steps are involved:

1. Creating the new master server as a slave server
2. Adding the new master server to the ypservers database
3. Copying the /etc configuration files from the old master to the new master
4. Copying the NIS Makefile in /var/yp from the old master to the new master
5. Deleting the time stamp files from /var/yp on the new master
6. Running make with the NOPUSH=1 option
7. Transferring the new NIS maps from the new master server to the old master server
8. Pushing the new maps from the old master server to all slave servers
9. Retiring the old master server

CREATING THE NEW MASTER SERVER AS A SLAVE SERVER

Follow the instructions in the section "Adding an NIS Slave Server" earlier in this chapter to set up your new master server machine as a slave in the NIS domain. In summary, the relevant steps are as follows:

1. Set the NIS domain name.
2. Run ypinit -s masterhostname.

ADDING THE NEW MASTER SERVER TO THE ypservers DATABASE

The ypservers database is the NIS map that contains the hostnames of all NIS servers in the NIS domain. The new master server's name must be added to the ypservers database. This is done by performing the following steps on the old NIS master server:

1. Take a snapshot of the database in a text file.
2. Edit the text file.
3. Regenerate the ypservers database from the file.
4. Push the new database to all slaves.

TAKE A SNAPSHOT OF THE ypservers DATABASE

You can take a snapshot of any NIS database and save it to a file using the ypcat command. The ypcat command is discussed in detail later in this chapter.

The following command will dump a copy of the ypservers NIS map to the file /etc/ypservers:

```
# /usr/lib/yp/makedbm -u ypservers > /etc/ypservers
```

EDIT THE FILE /etc/ypservers

Once the contents of the ypservers NIS database is saved in text form in the file /etc/ypservers, you need to edit the file. The file typically has the following format:

```
foo foo
YP_MASTER_NAME linux
YP_LAST_MODIFIED 942365535
linux linux
```

This file contains entries for two NIS servers (foo and linux) and indicates that linux is the master NIS server for the domain.

To add the new master server to the file, delete the first two lines containing YP_MASTER_NAME and YP_LAST_MODIFIED, and append a line at the end of the file with the server's hostname repeated twice and separated by a space:

```
newhostname newhostname
```

REGENERATE THE ypservers DATABASE

Once the new master server's hostname is in the file /etc/ypservers, you need to regenerate the ypservers NIS map from this file. This is done by passing the contents of the text file through the makedbm program that generates an NIS map file.

This requires the following two steps:

1. Change your working directory to the directory containing the NIS maps for your domain with the following command:

    ```
    # cd /var/yp/<domainname>
    ```

2. Use cat to display the contents of /etc/ypservers to the standard output and pipe this through makedbm to create the resulting NIS map:

    ```
    # cat /etc/ypservers ¦ /usr/lib/yp/makedbm - ypservers
    ```

PUSH THE NEW DATABASE TO THE SLAVE SERVERS

Using the yppush command you can push the ypservers map to all slave servers in the domain:

```
# yppush ypservers
```

COPYING THE /etc CONFIGURATION FILES

Several configuration files in /etc on the master NIS server are used to generate NIS maps:

- /etc/passwd: user database
- /etc/group: groups database
- /etc/hosts: host to IP address table
- /etc/networks: network addresses
- /etc/services: network port numbers and service names

- `/etc/protocols`: network protocol names and numbers
- `/etc/netgroup`: netgroup definitions
- `/etc/rpc`: remote procedure call program numbers
- Any other `/etc` files for which NIS maps are created.

For this reason, you need to copy these files from the old NIS master to the new one. Several options are available to do this, depending on your system and network configuration.

- Use FTP to transfer the files from one system to the other.
- Use NFS to mount `/etc` from one system to the other and then use the `cp` command to copy the files.
- Use the `rcp` or `rdist` command to copy the files between systems.
- Use the `tar` command to write the files to a floppy and transfer them to the new master.

DELETING TIME STAMP FILES FROM `/var/yp` ON THE NEW MASTER

NIS generates timestamp files in `/var/yp` which are used to determine when data has changed. You need to delete any such files from the new master in order to force a database rebuild. These files all have `.time` extensions and can be deleted with the following `rm` command:

```
# rm -f /var/yp/*.time
```

RUNNING make WITH THE NOPUSH=1 OPTION

Once the time stamp files have been deleted, you need to rebuild the NIS maps on the new master server. This will re-create the maps with the name of the new master server in them. The NOPUSH=1 option is used when generating these new maps so that the maps are not pushed out to the slaves automatically. This is necessary because the slave servers are still not ready to accept NIS maps from the new master server. To build the maps, change your current working directory to `/var/yp` and issue the following `make` command:

```
# cd /var/yp
# make NOPUSH=1
```

TRANSFERING THE NEW NIS MAPS FROM THE NEW MASTER SERVER TO THE OLD MASTER SERVER

You can force the transfer of NIS maps from the new master to the old master by using the `ypxfr` command on the old master server. If the hostname of your new NIS master server is newmaster, then the form of the `ypxfr` command is the following:

```
# ypxfr -h newmaster -f mapname
```

You will need to issue this command once for each NIS map. The complete list of NIS maps is outlined earlier in this chapter. If custom maps have been added at the local site, these will need to be transferred also. You can list the contents of /var/yp/<domainname> to find all NIS maps used at the site.

PUSHING THE NEW MAPS FROM THE OLD MASTER SERVER TO ALL SLAVE SERVERS

Once the old master server has the new maps, you can push them to the slaves who still only accept maps from the old master server. Once the new maps are received from the old master server, they will begin treating the new master server as the NIS master server because the new maps contain pointers to the new master server.

To push the maps to the slave servers, change your working directory to /var/yp/<domainname> and then use the following yppush command:

```
# yppush mapname
```

As with the transfer of the new maps to the old master server in the previous step, you need to use the yppush command once for each NIS map.

RETIRING THE OLD MASTER SERVER

The transfer is now complete and the new master server has replaced the old one for the NIS domain. It is wise now to edit the ypservers NIS map on the new master server to remove the entry for the old master. This is similar to the process used to add the new master server to the ypservers map in a previous step:

1. Dump ypservers map to a text file with the following command:

   ```
   # ypcat -k > /etc/ypservers
   ```

2. Delete the line containing the hostname of the old master from /etc/ypservers text file.

3. Regenerate the ypservers database from the text file with the following commands:

   ```
   # cd /var/yp/<domainname>
   # cat /etc/ypservers ¦ /usr/lib/makedbm - ypservers
   ```

4. Push the new database to all slaves with the following command:

   ```
   # yppush ypservers
   ```

REMOVING AN NIS SLAVE SERVER

Sometimes it is necessary to remove an NIS slave server from the network. This can be for any number of reasons, such as the current slave server being retired or moved to a new location, or being assigned a new function to perform.

You can simply remove an NIS slave server from a network and NIS will continue to function; however, future NIS updates will take longer because the master server will attempt to push updated databases to the non-existent slave server. The master server will have to wait for a timeout to occur before failing and moving on to the next slave server. This can be very annoying.

To prevent this from happening, you need to remove the retired slave server's entry from the ypservers database.

The method used to edit the ypservers map has been already explained in detail earlier in this chapter.

AN ALTERNATE APPROACH TO EDITING ypservers

The four-step approach to editing the ypservers file is flexible and general purpose. It can be used to remove entries, add entries, and edit entries. However, it is possible to remove a server with a single command. For instance, if you want to remove the server named foo from the ypservers database for the NIS domain mydomain, change your current working directory to /var/yp/mydomain/ and then use the following command on the master NIS server:

```
# ypcat -k ypservers ¦ grep -v '^foo foo$' ¦ /usr/lib/yp/makedbm - ypservers; yppush
ypservers
```

This command is actually two commands separated by a semicolon. The commands will be executed in sequence. The first command is a compound command built by piping data through three commands. The output of ypcat -k ypservers (in other words, the contents of the ypservers database) is piped through grep, which uses the -v option to display any line not containing foo foo. The caret (^) and the dollar sign ($) are meta-characters, that respectively match the beginning and end of a line. The output of this grep command is then passed through makedbm to regenerate ypservers. The second command pushes the new database out to the slave servers on the network.

> **Caution**
>
> Do not use grep -v foo instead, as it would match all server names that contain the string foo and delete them from the ypservers database.

MAINTAINING NIS MAPS

NIS maps generally require little care or attention. However, some work is needed to keep everything in perfect working order. In particular, any changes to the NIS maps need to be made on the master server and the NIS maps need to be rebuilt after changes are made. In addition, several scripts should be scheduled to run automatically to ensure that NIS maps are kept synchronized on all NIS servers.

EDITING NIS MAPS

In general, if you want to change NIS maps, you should change the source files in /etc on the master server and then rebuild your NIS maps. For instance, to add users, you should add them to the /etc/passwd file on the master server. Similarly, new hosts should be added to the hosts table, /etc/hosts, on the master NIS server.

After changes of this sort are made, you need to remake your NIS maps. To do this, change your current directory to /var/yp and then issue the following command:

```
# make
```

The NIS maps will be rebuilt and pushed to the slave servers. You can refer to the contents of /var/yp/Makefile for a more detailed understanding of how the maps are built and pushed to the slave servers.

SYNCHRONIZING NIS MAPS ON A SCHEDULE

Three scripts are provided with the NIS server packages to ensure that the NIS maps on all servers are synchronized. These scripts are as follows:

- **/usr/lib/yp/ypxfr_1perday**: This script needs to run automatically once per day.
- **/usr/lib/yp/ypxfr_1perhour**: This script needs to run automatically once per hour.
- **/usr/lib/yp/ypxfr_2perday**: This script needs to run automatically twice per day.

Decide when you want to run these scripts and then add them to the root user's crontab file as outlined in Chapter 7, "Scheduling Tasks."

OTHER NIS PROGRAMS

The following three NIS programs are useful for managing and working with NIS maps:

- **ypwhich**: This returns the name of the NIS server providing services to the NIS client where the command is used.
- **ypcat**: This displays the values of all keys of a specific NIS map.
- **ypmatch**: This displays the value of one or more specified keys in a specific NIS map.

THE ypwhich COMMAND

The ypwhich command is used to display the name of the NIS server the current client is using to service its NIS requests. In its most simple form, the command is used without arguments, as follows:

```
# ypwhich
```

You can also use ypwhich to display the master server for a particular NIS map using the -m argument. For instance, to display the master server for the ypservers map, use the following command:

```
# ypwhich -m ypservers
```

Similarly, you can display the NIS server servicing requests for another host using ypwhich by specifying the hostname. For instance, to display the server servicing the host foo, use the following command:

```
# ypwhich foo
```

PART II
CH 6

THE ypcat COMMAND

The ypcat command lets you display the values of all the keys in a specified NIS map. For instance, to display the values in the ypservers map, use the following command:

```
# ypcat ypservers
```

In addition, you can use ypcat to display both the key and the value, with each key-value pair on a separate line using the following -k argument:

```
# ypcat -k ypservers
```

THE ypmatch COMMAND

The ypmatch command lets you display the values of one or more specific keys in a specified NIS map. The basic form of the command follows:

```
ypmatch <key list> <map name>
```

The key list is a space-separated list of key names. For instance, to display the values of the user1 entry in the passwd.byname map, use the following command:

```
# ypmatch user1 passwd.byname
```

To display the values for more than one user, such as user1 and user2, list them all in the following command:

```
# ypmatch user1 user2 passwd.byname
```

If you want to display the key name with each value displayed, add the -k argument as follows:

```
# ypmatch -k user1 user2 passwd.byname
```

UNDERSTANDING THE NAME SERVER SWITCH

Using NIS can introduce the potential for confusion. Consider a simple example: On an NIS client you also maintain a local user database in /etc/passwd to allow limited local logins. How does the system know whether to attempt authentication against the local user database of the NIS user database?

This is done with a name server switch file stored at /etc/nsswitch.conf. This file specifies the order in which data should be obtained out of the three following possible sources:

- Local /etc files
- NIS maps
- A DNS server for host-specific data

Consider the following sample nsswitch.conf file:

```
passwd:    files nis
group:     files nis
```

```
shadow:      files nis
hosts:       nis files dns

services:    nis [NOTFOUND=return] files
networks:    nis [NOTFOUND=return] files
protocols:   nis [NOTFOUND=return] files
rpc:         nis [NOTFOUND=return] files
ethers:      nis [NOTFOUND=return] files
netmasks:    nis [NOTFOUND=return] files
netgroup:    nis
bootparams:  nis [NOTFOUND=return] files
publickey:   nis [NOTFOUND=return] files
automount:   files
aliases:     nis [NOTFOUND=return] files
```

In this file, several entries deserve attention to highlight the way the file works. Consider the following entry:

```
passwd:    files nis
```

This entry says that user lookup should first be performed against the local /etc/passwd file and, if the user is not found, then user lookup should be performed against the NIS user database. By contrast, consider the following entry:

```
hosts:    nis files dns
```

This entry indicates that hostname lookups should first be done against the NIS host database. If a matching entry is not found, then the local /etc/hosts file should be consulted. If a host match is still not found, then a DNS query should be attempted to resolve the hostname into an address.

The following entry

```
services: nis [NOTFOUND=return] files
```

is an example of several entries containing [NOTFOUND=return]. This indicates that the lookup should only continue from the relevant NIS database map to the relevant file in /etc when the NIS lookup fails for a reason other than a lack of a match in the database.

For instance, if you attempt a lookup and a matching entry is not found in the NIS database, then the lookup fails and stops. But if you attempt a lookup and the request to the NIS server times out, then the lookup continues with the local file in /etc.

USEFUL SCRIPTS

NIS management can be eased by the creation of several administrative scripts. In particular, it is useful to use a script for adding and removing servers from an NIS domain. The following script, add-rm-ypservers, eases this management task.

add-rm-ypservers

The following script can be used to add or remove an entry from the ypservers NIS map. Create this script in the file /usr/local/bin/add-rm-ypserver on your master NIS server and make the file executable:

```
# chmod 755 /usr/local/bin/add-rm-ypserver
```

To add a server to the map, use the script as follows:

```
# add-rm-ypserver add hostname
```

Similarly, to delete a server from the map, use the script as follows:

```
# add-rm-ypserver remove hostname
```

The logic of the script is simple:

- On lines 13-16, a check is made to see if two arguments have been provided. If not, the usage message is displayed and the script exits.
- On line 18, the hostname of the system where the script is being executed is stored for future use.
- On line 19, the hostname of the system providing the master of the ypservers database is obtained with ypwhich and stored for future use.
- On lines 21-25, a check is made to see if the current hostname and the name of the master for the ypservers database are the same. If not, the script is not being executed on the NIS master server. An error message is displayed and the script exits.
- On line 18, the hostname of the system where the script is being executed is stored for future use.
- On lines 27-42, a decision is made about what action to perform. If the user has indicated that a record should be added, the contents of ypservers are stored in a temporary text file, a new entry is added to the file, and the ypservers database is regenerated and pushed to the slave servers. If the user has indicated that a record should be removed, the entry is removed as outlined earlier in this chapter and the database is regenerated and pushed to the slave servers. If neither option is specified on the command line, a usage message is displayed.

SOURCE CODE

The following is the source code for the add-rm-ypservers script:

> **Note**
> Line numbers are provided for reference purpose only.

```
01: #!/bin/sh
02: # File: add-rm-ypserver
03: # Description: Add or remove a ypserver from the yservers NIS map
```

```
04: # This script needs to execute on NIS master only
05:
06: PATH=/bin:/usr/bin:/usr/lib/yp
07: export PATH
08:
09: usage(){
10:         echo "Usage: $0 [add ¦ remove] [ypserver]"
11: }
12:
13: if [ $# -ne 2 ]; then
14:         usage
15:         exit 0
16: fi
17:
18: thishost=`#180;hostnamè
19: ypmaster=`ypwhich -m ypserverso`
20:
21: if [ "$thishost" != "$ypmaster" ]; then
22:     echo "This script needs to run on ypmaster only"
23:     echo "This host does not appear to be the ypmaster --- exiting"
24:     exit 0
25: fi
26:
27: case $1 in add)
28:                 ypcat -k ypservers > /tmp/ypservers
29:                 echo "$2 $2" >> /tmp/ypservers
30:                 cd /var/yp/`domainname`
31:                 cat /tmp/ypservers ¦ makedbm - ypservers
32:                 rm -f /tmp/ypservers
33:                 yppush ypservers
34:                 ;;
35:         remove)
36:                 cd /var/yp/`domainname`     ypcat -k ypservers ¦ grep -v $2 ¦
    ➥makedbm - ypservers
38:                 yppush ypservers
39:                 ;;
40:         default)
41:                 usage
42:                 ;;
43: esac
```

TROUBLESHOOTING

Generally, NIS works smoothly, especially where your distribution installs and performs the initial NIS setup (as is done with Red Hat 6.0). Still, there are some problems related to NIS that you may encounter; the following are among them:

■ If you use ypbind earlier than version 3.3, and if your NIS stops and then restarts, ypbind may generate an error message such as yp_match: clnt_call: RPC: Unable to receive; errno = Connection refused. After this, logins are refused. To solve the problem, log in as root on the server and kill and restart ypbind. Alternately, upgrade to ypbind version 3.3 or newer.

PART
II

CH
6

- You cannot access the shadow passwords map with ypcat shadow. The correct map name is shadow.byname so the correct command should be ypcat shadow.byname.

- Library versions of libc are crucial to the correct functioning of NIS. Specifically, libc version 4.5.19 doesn't work with NIS. Library versions greater than 5.4.20 or glibc 2.x require the use of yp-clients version 2.2 and yp-tools version 2.x. Even so, for libc version 5.4.21 through 5.4.35, yp_maplist will not work, so you require a higher version of the libraries to ensure that ypwhich will work. If NIS is part of your distribution, you should have the correct libraries for the version of NIS that is installed. If you are installing NIS yourself, you should double-check your library version and then ensure that the version of NIS you are installing will work.

## CHAPTER 7

SCHEDULING TASKS

In this chapter

SCHEDULING TASKS IN LINUX

A multitasking operating system only fulfils its full purpose when it is engaged in processing jobs other than those being used interactively by users. That is, multitasking operating systems generally process background jobs which users do not see or interact with while users continue their interactive tasks.

While some of these background tasks will consist of server processes to handle FTP, HTTP, and other network requests, others will be tasks which launch and run automatically on a schedule to handle routine maintenance tasks, perform regular backups, or carry out any other periodic jobs.

Unix systems, from their early days, have been designed to operate all the time, shutting down only when maintenance tasks require it. On these types of systems, routine administrative tasks are generally scheduled to run late at night when the least numbers of users can be expected to be using the system. Linux is no exception: Any Linux server or workstation will likely need to be configured to handle some routine tasks during times of low usage, which are generally at night.

USING THE crond DAEMON

The crond daemon is the daemon responsible for running scheduled tasks. In Chapter 8, "Linux Process Management and Daemons," we discuss daemons in detail. Generally, daemons are processes that answer network requests from clients or wake up periodically to perform a specific task. For example, the server processes that answer HTTP requests from Web browsers or handle delivery of emails are daemons.

crond is actually a simple application: It reads configuration files containing lists of commands and the times at which to run them. The configuration files also specify the user identifier (UID) under which to run these commands. crond then launches the specified commands at the specified times as the specified user. Any application or script you can execute by hand can be scheduled with crond.

At system boot up, crond is started from a script in the /etc/rc.d directory. When crond starts, it scans the /var/spool/cron/crontabs directory (this directory is /var/spool/cron/ on some Linux systems, including Red Hat 6.2) for crontab files. On Red Hat Linux 6.2 the /etc/crontab file is also scanned. This file schedules execution of /etc/cron.hourly, /etc/cron.daily, /etc/cron.weekly, and /etc/cron.monthly scripts. crontab files are organized by username and list all scheduled tasks for a particular user. Each individual crontab file is named after the login name of the user it is associated with.

In addition, in Linux, crond also looks at the /etc/cron.d directory for scheduled tasks. This directory is used to store tasks scheduled by the system. All crontab files are read and loaded into memory. crond then wakes up every minute and checks if it has any jobs to run, and if so, runs them. In addition, on Linux systems crond checks the modified time of the /var/spool/cron/crontabs directory when it wakes up every minute. If it detects an updated time stamp, then it looks for modified time stamps of all crontab entries and reloads the changed or new entries in any altered files into memory.

> **Note**
>
> crond does not remember scheduled tasks which failed to run while the system was down. If you have to shutdown the system to perform maintenance, hardware upgrades, or recover from the rare system crash, keep in mind that any jobs scheduled to run during this downtime will not have run and will not be launched by crond after the system reboots. If these scheduled tasks are essential, launch the jobs manually. Alternately, you can wait for the tasks to run at their next scheduled occurrence.

THE crontab CONFIGURATION FILE

crond configuration files are known as crontab files. The format of crontab files is fairly straightforward. These files contain a series of entries, one per line. Comment lines start with a hash mark and continue to the end of the line. Each entry schedules particular tasks to run at particular times.

Each entry scheduling a job takes the following format:

```
<minute> <hour> <day> <month> <weekday> <command>
```

The particular format and restrictions of the six fields that make up each crontab entry are described in Table 7.1.

TABLE 7.1   FIELDS OF crontab ENTRIES

Entry	Description and Usage
Minute	Indicates the minutes portion of the time of a scheduled job. Possible values are from 0 to 59.
Hour	Indicates the hour portion of the time of a scheduled job. Possible values are from 0 to 23 (using a 24-hour clock).
Day	Indicates the day of the month on which to run a scheduled job. Possible values are from 0 to 31.
Month	Indicates the month in which to run a scheduled job. Possible values are from 0 to 12 or the first three letters of a given month's name. Both 0 and 12 are January.
Weekday	Indicates the particular day of the week on which to run a scheduled task. Possible values are from 0 to 7 or the first three letters of a given day's name. Both 0 and 7 represent Sunday.
Command	The command to execute at the scheduled time.

For all these fields except the last (the command field), there is flexibility about how you express these values:

PART

II

CH

7

- Multiple values can be separated by commas. For instance, to schedule a task on the 1st and the 15th day of the month, use `1,15` in the day field.

- Ranges of numbers of the form `a-b` can be used. For instance, to schedule a task to run at 4:00 p.m., 5:00 p.m., and 6:00 p.m., you could use `16-18` in the hour field.

- Ranges of numbers can be stepped through in increments using the form `a-b/c` where `a-b` is the range and `c` is the increment. For instance, to schedule a task to run every other hour between 10:00 a.m. and 10:00 p.m. you could use `10-22/2` in the hour field.

- An asterisk can be used to indicate the entire range of possible values in a field. For instance, to schedule a task to run every day of the month, put an asterisk in the day field.

Consider the following examples of the time and date fields from `crontab` entries:

- `0 4 * * *`: A job scheduled to run every day at 4:00 a.m.

- `30 4 * * 1`: A job scheduled to run every Monday at 4:30 a.m.

- `0 2,4,6 * * 1`: A job scheduled to run every Monday at 2:00 a.m., 4:00 a.m., and 6:00 a.m.

- `0 16 2 * *`: A job scheduled to run at 4:00 p.m. on the second day of every month.

- `30 16 * 3 thu`: A job scheduled to run at 4:30 p.m. on every Thursday in March.

- `0 12 4 jun *`: A job scheduled to run at noon on the June 4th of every year.

The command field bears some special attention. In particular, it is worth noting that commands scheduled to run are run by `crontab` by processing them through the `/bin/sh` shell.

However, the non-interactive nature of commands run through `crontab` is problematic when an application expects interactive input through the standard input. You can pass data to a command through the standard input by using percent signs. The first percent sign following the command marks the start of data considered to be standard input, and each subsequent percent sign serves as a new line character in the standard input sent to the command when it runs. For instance, consider the following command in the command field:

```
0 8 * * 5 /bin/mail -s ''Friday!'' user@some.host%It's Friday%%Thank God%%Me.
```

This command will send the email message:

```
It's Friday

Thank God

Me.
```

to `user@some.host` each Friday afternoon at 8:00 a.m.

The following examples illustrate how to interpret complete `crontab` entries:

- `15 3 * * * find / -fstype ext2 -name .nfs\* -mtime +7 -exec rm -f {} \;`: This `crontab` entry states that at 3:15 a.m. every day `crond` should run the `find` command to clean the file system of temporary `.nfs*` files that are more than 7 days old.

- `0,5,10,15,20,25,30,35,40,45,50,55 * * * * /usr/local/mrtg/mrtg -C \ /usr/local/mrtg/mrtg.cfg`: This `crontab` entry indicates that `crond` should run the program `/usr/local/mrtg/mrtg` every 5 minutes.

- `*/5 * * * /usr/local/mrtg/mrtg -C \ /usr/local/mrtg/mrtg.cfg`: This entry illustrates another way to indicate that `crond` should run the program `/usr/local/mrtg/mrtg` every 5 minutes, but using the extended step syntax.

- `10 7-18 * * 1-5 /usr/local/bin/syscheck`: This `crontab` entry indicates that `crond` should run the `/usr/local/bin/syscheck` program from Monday through Friday, once per hour for every hour between 7 a.m. and 6 p.m. at 10 minutes past the hour.

- `5 4 * * 6 /usr/lib/newsyslog >/dev/null 2>&1`: This `crontab` entry indicates that `crond` should run the `/usr/lib/newsyslog` program at 4:05 a.m. on Saturdays only.

- `0 4 28 * * /usr/local/arbitron/arbitron.bwc`: This `crontab` entry indicates that `crond` should run the `/usr/local/arbitron/arbitron.bwc` program once a month on the 28th day at 4:00 a.m.

In addition to containing entries for each scheduled job, a `crontab` file can contain definition of two environment variables: `SHELL` and `MAILTO`. The `SHELL` variable indicates which shell should be used to run jobs (the default is `/bin/sh`). The `MAIL` variable indicates which user should receive the output of any jobs run by `crond` (the default is the user for which a given job is being run).

EDITING USERS' crontab FILES

Normally, you won't directly edit the contents of users' `crontab` files but instead will manipulate the contents of these files using the `crontab` command.

With the `crontab` command, you can view the contents of a `crontab` file, replace the contents of a `crontab` file with the contents of another file, or edit a `crontab` file.

VIEWING THE CONTENTS OF crontab FILES

Users can view the contents of their own `crontab` file using the `crontab` command with the `-l` flag:

```
$ crontab -l
# daily job
5 0 * * *        $HOME/bin/daily.job >> $HOME/daily.out 2>&1
# monthly job -- output mailed to gautam
15 14 1 * *      $HOME/bin/monthly
```

The root user can view the contents of any user's `crontab` file by adding the `-u` flag:

```
# crontab -u <username> -l
```

CREATING THE crontab FILE

The simplest way for a user to create a new crontab file or replace the contents of an existing crontab file is to create a file in his home directory containing the desired contents of his crontab file and then load this data into his crontab file by using the crontab command:

```
$ crontab cronjobs
```

This command overwrites the current contents of the user's crontab file with the contents of the cronjobs file.

The root user can load the contents of a file into any user's crontab file by adding the -u flag:

```
# crontab -u <username> cronjobs
```

EDITING THE crontab FILE

Users can directly edit their crontab files using the -e flag of the crontab command. crontab will use a user's default editor as specified by the EDITOR environment variable to open the crontab file for editing. If no EDITOR environment variable exists, then the vi editor will be used by crontab to edit the file.

If you want to use a specific editor for editing your crontab file, first set the EDITOR environment variable. For instance, if you want to use the pico editor to edit your crontab file, use the following command to set the EDITOR environment variable:

```
$ export EDITOR=pico
```

Once your EDITOR environment variable is set, users can use the following command to open their crontab file in the specified editor:

```
$ crontab -e
```

The root user can edit any user's crontab file by adding the -u flag of the crontab command:

```
# crontab -u <username> -e
```

REMOVING THE crontab FILE

A user can erase the contents of his crontab file using the -r flag of the crontab command:

```
$ crontab -r
```

The root user can erase the contents of any user's crontab file by adding the -u flag of the crontab command:

```
# crontab -u <username> -r
```

CONTROLLING USE OF crontab WITH cron.allow AND cron.deny

By default, all users can use the crontab command and, therefore, can schedule tasks by editing their personal crontab files. However, this is not always wise. A regular user can easily schedule tasks to run overnight. This can either consume excess system resources or make use of system resources to run processes at night which attempt to crack password databases or perform other undesirable activity.

Because most regular users do not need to be able to run scheduled tasks, it is wise to restrict the use of the `crontab` command to those users who must run scheduled tasks as part of their jobs.

If the file `/etc/cron.allow` exists, then only users listed in this file are allowed to run the `crontab` command. This provides a way to restrict usage by indicating who can use `crontab` and is effective where the list of users who can use the command is small and manageable and where most users are denied access.

By contrast, if the file `/etc/cron.deny` exists, then users listed in this file are denied access to `crontab` but all other users can use `crontab`. If the list of users who should be denied access to `crontab` is small and manageable, then the `cron.deny` file is an effective way to control access to the `crontab` command.

USING THE at DAEMON

The at daemon, `atd`, runs scheduled jobs created by the `at` command. `atd` provides the capability to schedule jobs for later execution. In contrast to `crond`, which is used to schedule jobs to run repeatedly at set times, `atd` is normally used to schedule tasks to execute once at a specific time in the future.

Tip

> While it is possible to create recurring scheduled tasks with `atd` by including an `at` command to reschedule a task within a script which has been scheduled, it is advisable to use `crond` to schedule these tasks. `crond` provides superior scheduling control.

Any command or shell script which can be executed interactively at your shell's prompt can be queued for scheduled execution by `atd` with the `at` command. When scheduling a task, the at command takes the following form:

```
# at <time>
```

The at command will then prompt you to enter the commands to be scheduled. Commands can be entered on multiple lines. The Ctrl-D sequence is used to indicate the end of the series of commands being scheduled.

```
# at 12:30
at> mail -s "This is a test" user@some.host
at>
```

Alternatively, you can prepare a script file containing the series of commands to be scheduled with at and then load the contents of the file for scheduling using the -f flag of the at command:

```
# at <time> -f <script file name>
```

When a job is scheduled with at, the at command displays a job ID and the time the job will be executed. Jobs scheduled with at are run even if the user who scheduled the jobs is logged out. If the system is shut down at the time a job has been scheduled to run, the job will not run.

At the time you schedule a task using the at command, at records the current environment variables, current directory, the umask, and the ulimit; this information will be used by atd to create an operating environment when the job is run at the scheduled time. Any output or errors generated by a scheduled task are mailed by atd to the user who scheduled the job.

TIME FORMATS FOR THE at COMMAND

Many different formats are used for specifying times with the at command. The following examples illustrate these formats:

- at 16: Schedules a task for 4:00 p.m.
- at 4pm: Schedules a task for 4:00 p.m.
- at 8:00 January 1, 2000: Schedules a task for 8:00 a.m. on January 1, 2000.
- at now + 30 minutes: Schedules a task to run after a delay of 30 minutes.
- at midnight December 31, 1999: Schedules a task to run at midnight on the night of December 31, 1999.
- at noon: Schedules a task to run at noon.

Most standard variations on these date formats are accepted by at, including abbreviations for month names and days of the week. If you attempt to specify a date in a format not understood by at, it will return a "bad date specification" error message.

CHECKING THE atd QUEUE

Users can check their atd queue using the atq command or the -l flag of the at command. The following command:

```
$ atq
```

has the same effect as this:

```
$ at -l
```

Both display a list of all jobs scheduled by the user issuing the commands along with the job IDs and the time at which the jobs are scheduled to run. If the root user uses one of these commands, all jobs scheduled by all users are displayed.

REMOVING A JOB FROM THE atd QUEUE

Users can delete previously scheduled jobs from their atd queue using the -r option of the at command in the following format:

```
$ at -r <jobid>
```

Users can only remove jobs that they have scheduled. The root user can remove jobs from any users atd queue.

RESTRICTING ACCESS TO at WITH at.allow AND at.deny

By default, all users can use the at command and, therefore, can schedule tasks. However, this is not always wise. A regular user can easily schedule tasks to run overnight. This can either consume excess system resources or make use of your system resources to run processes that attempt to crack password databases or perform other undesirable activity.

Because most regular users do not need to be able to run scheduled tasks, it is wise to restrict the use of the at command to those users who must schedule tasks as part of their jobs.

If the file /etc/at.allow exists, then only users listed in this file are allowed to run the at command. This provides a way to restrict usage by indicating who can use at and is effective where the list of users who can use the command is small and manageable and where most users are denied access.

By contrast, if the file /etc/at.deny exists, then users listed in this file are denied access to at but all other users can use at. If the list of users who should be denied access to at is small and manageable, then the at.deny file is an effective way to control access to the at command.

USEFUL SCRIPTS

The ability to schedule tasks is extremely useful for system administration because it allows administrators to schedule regular checks of the state of their systems. This section discusses two system administration scripts that, once scheduled with crond, help administrators monitor the health of their systems:

- fschecker: Checks if file systems are getting full and also informs the system administrator of new error messages in the error logs.
- syscheck: Monitors system load and swap space.

fschecker

The following script can be used to check for file systems which are over 90% full and to inform the system administrator by email of any file systems which exceed this threshold, as well as to send the administrator a list of new error messages in the system logs. Create this script in the file /usr/local/sbin/fschecker and make the file executable:

```
# chmod 755 /usr/local/sbin/fschecker
```

The script should be scheduled in the root user's crontab with an entry similar to the following:

```
30 4 * * * /usr/local/sbin/fschecker
```

PART

II

CH

7

This entry schedules `fschecker` to run at 4:30 a.m. every morning.

The logic of the script is simple:

- On lines 19-21, the hostname of the system being checked and the current date and time are stored in a report file.

- On line 29, the `df` command is used to append a list of file systems which are more than 90% full to the report file.

- On lines 37-40, the `grep` command is used to add all new error messages during the past two days to the end of the report file.

- On line 42, the `mail` command is used to mail the contents of the report file to the administrator.

- On line 45, the report file is deleted.

SOURCE CODE

Note

The line numbers are provided for reference purpose only.

```
01: #!/bin/sh
02: #
03: # Name: fschecker - Run once a day from root's crontab
04: # Description: 1. Check if any (local) filesystems are getting full
05: #                 and mail warning message if necessary.
06: #              2. Check for new error messages since yesterday and today
07: #                 in /var/log/messages and mail warning message
08: #
09: # Add to root's crontab as follows:
10: # 30 4 * * * /usr/local/sbin/fschecker
11: PATH=/bin:/usr/bin:/sbin:/usr/sbin:/usr/ucb:/usr/local/bin:.
12: export PATH
13: MAILTO=root
14: progname=`basename $0`
15: thishost=`hostname`
16: fsreport=/tmp/fsreport.$$
17: # write the header for our logfile
18: #
19: cat <<EOF > $fsreport
20: `hostname`: File system report:`date`
21: EOF
22: #
23: # Check local file systems and report those that are over 90% full
24: #
25: # Print a header line
26: cat <<EOF >> $fsreport
27: Filesystems over 90% full:
28: EOF
```

```
29: df ¦ tr -d % \
        ¦ awk '/\/dev/ { if($5 > 90) print "Over 90%: " $0 }' >> $fsreport
30: #
31: # Check for errors in /var/log/messages dated today and yesterday
32: #
33: # Print a header line
34: cat <<EOF >> $fsreport
35: Errors reported in /var/log/messages:
36: EOF
37: today=date¦ awk '{printf "%s %s\n", $2, $3}'
38: yesterday=date ¦ awk '{printf "%s %s\n", $2, $3-1}'
39: grep "$yesterday" /var/log/messages ¦ grep -i error >> $fsreport
40: grep "$today" /var/log/messages ¦ grep -i error >> $fsreport
41:
42: Mail -n -s "$progname@$thishost: File system report:`date`" \
        $MAILTO < $fsreport
43:
44: #clean up temp files
45: rm -f /tmp/fsreport.$$
```

syscheck

The following script can be used to check whether the average system load exceeds a specific value and if free swap space is less than a specified number of megabytes. If either case is true, a warning email is sent to the system administrator. Create this script in the file `/usr/local/sbin/syscheck` and make the file executable:

`# chmod 755 /usr/local/sbin/syscheck`

The script should be scheduled in the root user's `crontab` with an entry similar to the following:

`0,10,20,30,40,50 * * * * /usr/local/sbin/syscheck 3 10`

This entry schedules `syscheck` to run every 10 minutes. The arguments 3 and 10 indicate that a warning should be sent if the average system load exceeds 3 or the available swap space is less than 10MB. If the load and swap limits are not specified, the script uses a system load of 3 and 10MB of swap space as default thresholds.

The logic of the script is simple:

- On lines 32-36, the system load is checked using the kernel's /proc/loadstat pseudo file system. If it exceeds the threshold, then the output of ps is mailed to the system administrator with a warning.

- On lines 48-54, the `free` command is used to determine the current free swap space. If this is less than the specified threshold, a warning message including the output of the `free` command is mailed to the system administrator.

SOURCE CODE

Note The line numbers are provided for reference purpose only.

```
01: #!/bin/sh
02: # Script name: /usr/local/sbin/syscheck
03: # Description: A system maintenance script, runs out of cron every hour.
04: #               It checks the system load and swap space and send warning
    #               messages
05: #               if a) system load exceeds a specified value
06: #               or b) system swap space drops below a specified value.
07: #
08: # Usage: syscheck loadlimit swaplimit
09: #
10: # Create an entry in root's crontab as follows:
11: # 1 * * * * /usr/local/sbin/syscheck 3 10
12: #
13: # Set the load limit and minimum swap space in megabytes per your needs.
14: #
15: # To run script in debug mode uncomment the next line
16: #set -x
17: PATH=/bin:/usr/bin:/sbin:/usr/sbin:/usr/ucb:/usr/local/bin:.
18: export PATH
19: MAILTO=root
20: progname=`basename $0`
21: thishost=`hostname`
22: # set default load limit to 3 unless passed in argv
23: if [ "$1" = "" ]; then
24:     loadlimit=3;
25: else
26:     loadlimit=$1;
27: fi
28: #
29: # Check the load average using uptime. If load limit exceeds $loadlimit
30: # send a warning message.
31: #
32:    load=`cat /proc/loadavg | awk -F"." '{print $1}'`
33: if [ `expr $load` -ge `expr $loadlimit` ]; then
34:     ps augx > /tmp/load.log$$
35:     Mail -n -s "Warning from $progname@$thishost" \
             $MAILTO  < /tmp/load.log$$
36: fi
37: #
38: #
39: # Set default free swap to 10M, unless passed in argv
40: #
41: if [ "" = "$2" ]; then
42:     SWAPLO=10
43: else
44:     SWAPLO=$2
45: fi
46: # Check the Swap space usage, if less than 10M is left send
47: # a message. The number 10M may need to be adjusted.
```

```
48: swapfree=`free -m¦grep Swap¦awk -F" " '{print $4}`
49: if [ `expr $swapfree` -le `expr $SWAPLO`]; then
50:     date > /tmp/swap.log$$
51:     echo "Swap space less than $SWAPLO" Megs >> /tmp/swap.log$$
52:     free >> /tmp/swap.log$$
53:     Mail -n -s "Warning from $progname@$thishost" \
            $MAILTO < /tmp/swap.log$$
54: fi
55:
56: #
57: # Clean up temp files
58: #
59: rm -f /tmp/load.log$$ /tmp/swap.log$$
60: exit 0
```

TROUBLESHOOTING

The most common problem faced by users and administrators when scheduling jobs with crond is that the jobs fail to run. For instance, consider the situation where a user has a script called testjob on their normal path and they have scheduled it to run using crond. However, every time crond attempts to run the script it fails and instead generates an email message back to the user who scheduled the task similar to the following:

```
Date: Sun, 23 Jan 2000 09:16:01 -0800
From: Some User <someuser@linux.juxta.com>
To: someuser@linux.juxta.com

/usr/bin:/bin
```

The problem here is that processes run from a crontab file are run in a highly restrictive environment in which the path will not be the user's typical complete path. For instance, on Red Hat 6.2, jobs run from crond have the following path: /usr/bin:/bin

In order to resolve the problem, you need to adhere to two rules when scheduling programs and scripts to run through crond:

- In your crontab file, specify the full path of the program or script you are scheduling.
- If you are scheduling a script, specify the full path to any external programs invoked by the script.

PART

II

CH

7

## CHAPTER 8

LINUX PROCESS MANAGEMENT AND DAEMONS

In this chapter

LINUX PROCESSES AND DAEMONS

Linux is a multiuser, multitasking operating system. As a result, at any given time more than one program will be running on a Linux system. These running programs are called *processes*. While the operating system makes it appear that all the processes are executing simultaneously, the reality is far from that. Instead, complex management and scheduling takes place to allocate sufficient resources to each process so that Linux can get its work done while still providing a responsive, usable system to the user.

Related to process management are daemons. *Daemons* refer to programs that run in the background on a system answering requests for particular types of services. For instance, an FTP daemon answers requests for FTP connections while a line printer daemon answers request for printer services.

With all these background daemons running, the average Linux system has a large mix of processes running even if the system appears idle. For this reason a strong grasp of processes and the tools available for managing them is essential to proper system management.

UNDERSTANDING PROCESSES

At any given time, only one process can be executing on a CPU. This means that on a typical single-processor desktop PC only one process is executing at a time. On a multiple-processor system one process can be executing on each available CPU at any given time.

The operating system might give the impression that all these programs are running at the same time, but that is not true. For multiprocessor systems you can have multiple processes running at the same time equal to the number of processors the system has. This chapter focuses on single-processor systems; the concepts will also apply to multi-processor systems.

The apparent impression of many processes executing simultaneously is achieved by using a technique called *time-slicing* (also known as time-sharing). The operating system kernel uses time-slicing to switch quickly between active processes, giving each in turn a slice of processor time. The result is the impression of multiple processes executing simultaneously.

The concept of a process can be somewhat vague. The best way to look at a process is as an instance of a running program. This means if you run a program such as `ls`, you actually launch a process that is an instance of the `ls` program. If multiple people run the `ls` program, then multiple processes as instances of `ls` are created and run.

It is important to remember that you cannot simply equate a process to execution of a specific command. For instance, consider the following command:

```
$ ls -l
```

This command causes a single process to come into existence and execute. However, the following command does more:

```
$ ls -ls | sort -n
```

Here two processes are created, one for the ls program and one for the sort program. The pipe in the command indicates the mechanism through which the sort and ls processes communicate.

Properties and Attributes of Processes

The following attributes characterize all processes:

- **Process Address Space:** A section of virtual memory allocated by the kernel to a particular process. Generally, each process has a unique address space that is protected from use by other processes. The process address space consists of three sub-spaces: code space, data space, and stack space.

- **Internal Data Structures:** The kernel maintains a set of internal data structures for each process. The internal data structure tracks a broad range of information about a process and its current state, including:

  - Process Owner
  - Address space map
  - Current status
  - Priority
  - Memory usage
  - Signal mask

Table 8.1 describes the most important attributes of processes.

TABLE 8.1	PROCESS ATTRIBUTES
Attribute Name	**Description**
PID	PID stands for Process Identification number. The kernel assigns a new PID to every new process. The purpose of the PID is to uniquely identify a process. PIDs are assigned in increasing order as new processes are created. If the kernel runs out of PIDs it simply restarts the numbering process and skips over PIDs that are still in use.
PPID	PPID is the parent process's PID. The parent process is the process that created the current process, which is called its child. A child process can continue running even after the parent has exited.
UID	UID stands for User Identification number. The UID of a process is the user who created the process. UIDs of users are set in the /etc/passwd file. This user is the owner of this process and can change certain operational parameters of the process. In addition to this user the only other user who can do that is the super-user or root.
EUID	EUID stands for the Effective User Identification number. The EUID is used to determine what resources the process has permissions to access. In general the UID and EUID are the same, except for setuid programs.

TABLE 8.1 CONTINUED

Attribute Name	Description
GID	GID is Group Identification number. GIDs are set in the /etc/group file. When a process is started it normally inherits the GID of its parent.
EGID	EGID relates to GID the same way as EUID relates to UID. EGID stands for the Effective Group Identification. If the process cannot access a resource due to lack of ownership permissions, the kernel will check if the permission may be granted based on the EGID of the process.

PROCESS PRIORITY

The priority of a process determines how much CPU time it gets. When the current process has used up its time-slice and the kernel picks the next process to run, it chooses the process with the highest priority. When assigning priorities in Unix, the lower the number the higher its priority.

A newly created process will inherit the priority of its parent process. Most processes will start with a system-wide default value when started from an interactive shell. The owner of a process can lower its priority, but cannot raise it. Only the superuser can raise the priority of a process.

The priority of a process is not the only factor the scheduler takes into account to grant it CPU time. If that were the case then low priority processes might never get to run. The kernel uses specialized algorithms to make sure all processes get a sufficient share of the CPU given the number of processes demanding CPU resources. A higher priority simply means that the share received by a process will be larger than those with lower priorities.

PROCESS CREATION

Soon after the kernel boots, it starts the first process. On Linux systems, this initial process is the init program and always will have a PID of 1. The init process is the great ancestor of all processes on a system, in that it starts all other crucial system processes. Some of these system processes run as daemons that usually live forever until the system is shut down or rebooted.

Note

In order to know which processes to start at boot time, the init program reads the /etc/inittab file and takes the system to the specified default run level. At a specified run level, the init process will launch child processes to set up critical system services. The init program is discussed in more depth in Chapter 4, "Booting Up and Shutting Down."

MONITORING PROCESSES WITH THE ps COMMAND

The ps utility is used to display information about processes running on the system. Using this tool, it is possible to display the UID, PID, PPID, priority, controlling terminal (TTY), current status, percentage of CPU usage, percentage memory usage, start time, CPU time, and other information about current processes. The ps man page provides complete details of all the information about processes that can be displayed using the ps command.

PROCESS STATES

The ps program can be used to learn the current state of a process. At any given time, a process can be in one of five states as outlined in Table 8.2.

TABLE 8.2   PROCESS STATES

State	Description
Runnable	A runnable process is a process waiting in the scheduler's run queue. It has all the resources it needs and is just waiting for CPU time.
Sleeping	A sleeping process is waiting for something to occur. An interactive shell sleeps waiting for terminal input. A process might be sleeping waiting for a file read or write to complete. A daemon might be sleeping till someone needs service and the kernel wakes it up. A sleeping process is woken up by a signal. Signals are discussed later in this chapter.
Swapped	A swapped process is one that has been completely removed from the computer's main memory and been written out to disk.
Zombie	A zombie process is one that has died but did not exit cleanly and some shreds of information about this dead process are still lurking around in the kernel's data structures. For all practical purposes, zombies can be safely ignored. Sometimes a zombie disappears after its parent process exits. In most cases, though, the only way to clean up zombies is to reboot the system.
Stopped	A stopped process is one that is marked as not runnable by the kernel. The best example of a stopped process is when you press Ctrl+Z during an interactive process running in bash or csh. The process stops running until you put it in the background using the shell's bg (for background) command, at which time the process resumes in the background and you can proceed to use the shell interactively for another purpose. This process of stopping a program (and later resuming it) is discussed later in this chapter, in the section "Linux Signals."

SAMPLE ps OUTPUT

The ps program can display process information in a highly variable fashion depending on the arguments used with the command. In its most basic form, the ps command displays a simple list of processes which the user executing the command has running in the current terminal (tty). It doesn't display processes owned by any other user.

```
$ ps
  PID TTY          TIME CMD
  411 tty2     00:00:00 login
  440 tty2     00:00:00 bash
  459 tty2     00:00:00 grep
  460 tty2     00:00:00 ps
```

Several extensions make it possible to display more information with the ps command. For instance, generally users will want to view all processes they own rather than just those on the current terminal where the ps command is issued. This is done with the x flag of the ps command:

```
# ps x
  PID TTY       STAT    TIME COMMAND
    1 ?         S       0:05 init[3]
    2 ?         SW      0:00 [kflushd]
    3 ?         SW      0:00 [kpiod]
    4 ?         SW      0:00 [kswapd]
    5 ?         SW<     0:00 [mdrecoveryd]
  299 ?         S       0:00 syslogd -m 0
  310 ?         S       0:00 klogd
  342 ?         S       0:00 inetd
  410 tty1      S       0:01 login -- root
  411 tty2      S       0:00 login -- root
  413 ?         S       0:00 update (bdflush)
  414 tty1      S       0:00 -bash
  440 tty2      S       0:01 -bash
  459 tty2      T       0:00 grep foo
  460 tty2      R       0:00 ps x
```

There are two important points to note about this output:

- **Processes appear for more than one terminal:** A terminal can be associated with more than one process. And some processes are not associated with any terminal (as indicated by the question mark in the TTY column); these processes are daemons. Kernel processes and background daemons have no controlling TTY associated with them.

- **The state of each process is displayed:** Process states are indicated in the STAT column with a one-letter code followed by optional additional one-letter codes. The initial one-letter code is one of the following: D for uninterruptible sleep, R for runnable (waiting on the run queue), S for sleeping, T for traced or stopped, and Z for a zombie process. The additional possible letters are: W for processes with no resident pages, < for a high-priority process, N for a low-priority process, and L for processes with pages locked into memory.

Another useful application of the ps command is to view processes owned by all users in the current terminal using the a flag of the ps command: ps a. Combined with the x flag, you can view all processes owned by all users on any terminal, as shown in the following example:

```
# ps ax
  PID TTY       STAT    TIME COMMAND
    1 ?         S       0:05 init[3]
    2 ?         SW      0:00 [kflushd]
```

```
    3 ?        SW      0:00 [kpiod]
    4 ?        SW      0:00 [kswapd]
    5 ?        SW<     0:00 [mdrecoveryd]
  252 ?        S       0:00 portmap
  299 ?        S       0:00 syslogd -m 0
  310 ?        S       0:00 klogd
  324 ?        S       0:00 /usr/sbin/atd
  342 ?        S       0:00 inetd
  371 ?        S       0:00 xfs
  410 tty1     S       0:01 login -- root
  411 tty2     S       0:00 login -- root
  413 ?        S       0:00 update (bdflush)
  414 tty1     S       0:00 -bash
  440 tty2     S       0:01 -bash
  459 tty2     T       0:00 grep foo
  475 tty2     R       0:00 ps ax
```

The output here is much the same as when the x flag is used on its own, except that now processes owned by all system users are displayed. The difficulty is that there is no indication of what users own which processes. By adding the u flag, this information is displayed along with additional information about the process:

```
# ps aux
USER      PID   %CPU %MEM  VSZ   RSS TTY   STAT START  TIME COMMAND
root        1   0.1  3.2  1096   472 ?     S    19:39  0:05 init[3]
root        2   0.0  0.0     0     0 ?     SW   19:39  0:00 [kflushd]
root        3   0.0  0.0     0     0 ?     SW   19:39  0:00 [kpiod]
root        4   0.0  0.0     0     0 ?     SW   19:39  0:00 [kswapd]
root        5   0.0  0.0     0     0 ?     SW<  19:39  0:00 [mdrecoveryd]
bin       252   0.0  2.5  1084   354 ?     S    19:40  0:00 portmap
root      299   0.0  4.0  1264   592 ?     S    19:40  0:00 syslogd -m 0
root      310   0.0  4.8  1372   708 ?     S    19:40  0:00 klogd
daemon    324   0.0  3.2  1112   472 ?     S    19:40  0:00 /usr/sbin/atd
root      342   0.0  3.8  1236   556 ?     S    19:40  0:00 inetd
xfs       371   0.0  6.6  1988   968 ?     S    19:40  0:00 xfs
root      410   0.0  8.0  2136  1178 tty1  S    19:41  0:01 login -- root
root      411   0.0  8.0  2136  1178 tty2  S    19:41  0:00 login -- root
root      413   0.0  1.9  1052   280 ?     S    19:41  0:00 update (bdflush)
root      414   0.0  6.7  1732   976 tty1  S    20:19  0:00 -bash
root      440   0.0  7.4  1832  1080 tty2  S    20:20  0:01 -bash
root      459   0.0  2.6  1148   392 tty2  T    20:22  0:00 grep foo
root      480   0.0  5.8  2472   878 tty2  R    21:01  0:00 ps aux
```

Notice that this output has several more columns than the previous examples:

- **%CPU**: Percentage of CPU resources being used by the process at the time of display.

- **%MEM**: Percentage of system memory being used by the process at the time of display.

- **VSZ**: Total virtual memory being used by the process in bytes.

- **RSS**: Total physical memory being used by the process in bytes.

- **START**: The time at which the process started.

Tip

An alternative to the ps aux command which provides similar output is the ps -aef commandps aux is BSD Unix style ps, whereas ps -aef is System V style ps; Linux ps supports both flavors). This command selects all processes (the -e flag) associated with a tty terminal except session leaders (the -a flag; note that this is different from the a flag without the dash) and displays a full listing (the -f flag). The resulting output looks like the following:

```
# ps -aef
UID        PID PPID C STIME TTY      TIME CMD
root         1    0 0 19:39 ?        00:00:03 [init] 3
root         2    1 0 19:39 ?        00:00:00 [kflushd]
root         3    1 0 19:39 ?        00:00:00 [kpiod]
root         4    1 0 19:39 ?        00:00:00 [kswapd]
root         5    1 0 19:39 ?        00:00:00 [mdrecoveryd]
bin        252    1 0 19:40 ?        00:00:00 portmap
root       299    1 0 19:40 ?        00:00:00 syslogd -m 0
root       310    1 0 19:40 ?        00:00:00 klogd
daemon     324    1 0 19:40 ?        00:00:00 /usr/sbin/atd
root       342    1 0 19:40 ?        00:00:00 inetd
xfs        371    1 0 19:40 ?        00:00:00 xfs
root       410    1 0 19:41 tty1     00:00:01 login -- root
root       411    1 0 19:41 tty2     00:00:00 login -- root
root       413    1 0 19:41 ?        00:00:00 update (bdflush)
root       414  410 0 20:19 tty1     00:00:00 -bash
root       440  411 0 20:20 tty2     00:00:01 -bash
root       459  440 0 20:22 tty2     00:00:00 grep foo
root       527  440 0 21:55 tty2     00:00:00 ps -aef
```

This output provides a comprehensive list of processes similar to the ps aux command but in a different format. In particular, a different layout of columns and information presented is displayed. Some columns are the same, including UID (presenting the same username information as the USER column), PID, STIME (presenting the same start time information as the START column), TTY, TIME, and CMD (presenting the same command information as the COMMAND column). In addition to these common columns, the parent process; PID is displayed in the PPID column.

MONITORING PROCESSES WITH THE top COMMAND

Another useful tool for monitoring processes is the top program. This program is a full-screen application that presents a periodically updated display of process information. Normally, the top command is used without any flags and displays a regularly updated list of processes with the processes displayed in reverse order by the percentage of CPU resources being used by each process:

```
10:26pm  up  2:39,  3 users,  load average: 0.07, 0.03, 0.00
44 processes: 42 sleeping, 2 running, 0 zombie, 0 stopped
CPU states:  1.3% user,  0.7% system,  0.1% ps, 97.7% idle
Mem:    30736K av,  29868K used,    868K free,  30700K shrd,     660K buff
Swap:   72288K av,   5900K used,  66388K free                  13228K cached
  PID USER       PRI  NI  SIZE  RSS SHARE STAT   LIB %CPU %MEM   TIME COMMAND
  661 root        16   0   944  944   772 R        0  3.8  3.0   0:00 top
  383 root        18   0  8484 7876  1144 R        0  1.9 25.6   2:04 X
    1 root         0   0    64    0     0 SW       0  0.0  0.0   0:03 init
    2 root         0   0     0    0     0 SW       0  0.0  0.0   0:00 kflushd
    3 root         0   0     0    0     0 SW       0  0.0  0.0   0:00 kupdate
    4 root         0   0     0    0     0 SW       0  0.0  0.0   0:00 kpiod
    5 root         0   0     0    0     0 SW       0  0.0  0.0   0:00 kswapd
  163 bin          0   0    64    0     0 SW       0  0.0  0.0   0:00 portmap
  186 root         0   0   224  160   120 S        0  0.0  0.5   0:00 syslogd
  197 root         0   0   244    0     0 SW       0  0.0  0.0   0:00 klogd
  211 daemon       0   0   136  104    64 S        0  0.0  0.3   0:00 atd
  225 root         0   0   236  188   152 S        0  0.0  0.6   0:00 crond
  239 root         0   0   216  172   148 S        0  0.0  0.5   0:00 inetd
  267 root         0   0    96   56    36 S        0  0.0  0.1   0:00 gpm
  290 xfs          0   0  1684 1488  1040 S        0  0.0  4.8   0:00 xfs
  312 uucp         0   0   672    4     0 SW       0  0.0  0.0   0:00 faxq
  314 uucp         0   0   440    0     0 SW       0  0.0  0.0   0:00 hfaxd
  323 root         0   0   136    0     0 SW       0  0.0  0.0   0:00 dhcpd
  355 root         0   0   244    0     0 SW       0  0.0  0.0   0:00 login
  356 root         0   0    60    0     0 SW       0  0.0  0.0   0:00 mingetty
  357 root         0   0    60    0     0 SW       0  0.0  0.0   0:00 mingetty
  358 root         0   0    60    0     0 SW       0  0.0  0.0   0:00 mingetty
  359 root         0   0    60    0     0 SW       0  0.0  0.0   0:00 mingetty
  360 root         0   0    60    0     0 SW       0  0.0  0.0   0:00 mingetty
  363 root         0   0   204    0     0 SW       0  0.0  0.0   0:00 bash
  375 root         0   0   124    0     0 SW       0  0.0  0.0   0:00 startx
  382 root         0   0   124    0     0 SW       0  0.0  0.0   0:00 xinit
  386 root         0   0  1532 1376  1208 S        0  0.0  4.4   0:00 gnome-session
  395 root         0   0   488  236   156 S        0  0.0  0.7   0:00 gnome-smproxy
  401 root         2   0  1820 1700  1252 S        0  0.0  5.5   0:02 enlightenment
  414 root         0   0   780  688   588 S        0  0.0  2.2   0:03 xscreensaver
  416 root         0   0  3388 3388  2688 S        0  0.0 11.0   0:00 panel
  418 root         0   0  4620 4616  3328 S        0  0.0 15.0   0:01 gmc
  420 root         0   0  4784 4784  3276 S        0  0.0 15.5   0:00 gnome-help-brow
  428 root         0   0  1176 1176   976 S        0  0.0  3.8   0:00 gnome-name-serv
  434 root         1   0  2988 2988  2456 S        0  0.0  9.7   0:01 gnomepager_appl
  436 root         0   0  2808 2808  2300 S        0  0.0  9.1   0:00 gen_util_applet
  440 root         0   0  3112 3112  2436 S        0  0.0 10.1   0:02 gnome-terminal
  441 root         0   0   552  552   464 S        0  0.0  1.7   0:00 gnome-pty-helpe
  442 root         0   0   984  984   772 S        0  0.0  3.2   0:00 bash
  445 root         0   0  3820 3504  1672 S        0  0.0 11.4   0:23 emacs
  592 root         1   0  3060 3060  2436 S        0  0.0  9.9   0:01 gnome-terminal
```

At the beginning of the top display are five lines of special information:

- The first line displays the output of the uptime command. This line indicates the amount of time the system has been running (since the last reboot), the number of users logged in, and the load on the system.

- The second line indicates the total number of processes plus the number sleeping, running, in a zombie state, and stopped.

- The third line indicates the percentage of CPU time spent in user mode, system mode, on tasks with a negative priority, and in an idle state.

- The fourth line displays memory usage information including total available memory, memory used, memory free, the amount of shared memory, and the amount of memory allocated to buffers.

- The fifth line displays information about swap space including total swap space, the amount of swap in use, and the amount of swap still available for use.

THE ROLE OF DAEMONS

Daemons are special kinds of processes as explained earlier in the chapter. Unlike normal processes that are almost always associated with a controlling terminal, daemons do not have a controlling terminal. Look at the TTY column of the ps output shown earlier in the chapter for daemons such as inetd or init, and you will see there is no tty terminal associated with them.

In UNIX, daemons are a collection of specialized programs that perform particular system tasks. The following table lists common Linux daemons.

TABLE 8.3   COMMON LINUX DAEMONS

Daemon	Description
init	This is the great ancestor of all processes in the system. If init is killed or stops running for any reason, the system will reboot.
kupdate	This is the kernel updater process. It executes the sync system call every 30 seconds and writes current versions of all super blocks to disk. Keeping super blocks on disks up to date is very important, as it reduces the risk of file system damage in the event of a crash.
kswapd	This process is responsible for swapping pages out of main memory to disk and loading them back to memory when needed.
inetd	This is the Internet super-daemon. It starts up by reading its configuration file /etc/inetd.conf. This file tells it which ports inetd should listen to. It monitors these ports for incoming network connection requests. When a request arrives it spawns an instance of the appropriate daemon to handle that request. A more detailed discussion of this daemon can be found in Chapter 18, "General Security Issues."
crond	This is the cron daemon. It wakes up periodically and runs jobs listed in /var/spool/cron/crontab directory. A detailed discussion of this daemon can be found in Chapter 7, "Scheduling Tasks."
named	This is the internet name server daemon. It maps hostnames and IP addresses. A full discussion of this daemon is covered in Chapter 22, "DNS."

TABLE 8.3	CONTINUED
Daemon	**Description**
dhcpd	This is the Dynamic Host Configuration Protocol daemon. This daemon manages leasing of IP addresses to DHCP hosts from a predefined pool of addresses. A full discussion of this daemon is covered in Chapter 13, "Linux Network Configuration and TCP/IP."
gated	This is a routing daemon and it understands various routing protocols like OSPF, RIP, and BGP. A discussion of gated is covered in Chapter 15, "Routing with Linux."
innd	This is the Internet Network News daemon. It provides for Usenet News transport, reading and posting. A complete discussion of this daemon can be found in Chapter 26, "News Services."
syslogd	This is the system logger daemon. It writes log files for all programs that use its service. A full discussion of this daemon can be found in Chapter 20, "Log Management and Analysis."
ftpd	This daemon handles FTP (File Transfer Protocol) requests. See Chapter 27, "FTP Servers," for a full discussion of this daemon.
httpd	This daemon handles HTTP (Hyper Text Transfer Protocol) requests. See Chapter 23, "Apache and the World Wide Web," for a detailed discussion of the Apache HTTP daemon.
sendmail	This daemon is responsible for sending and receiving mail between systems across the internet. See Chapter 16, "Linux Mail Services with sendmail," for a detailed discussion of sendmail.
lpd	This daemon is the line printer daemon. It handles print requests from user programs. More details on this can be found in Chapter 14, "Printer and File Sharing with NFS and Samba."

STOPPING PROCESSES WITH THE kill COMMAND

The kill program is used to send signals to processes. These signals can stop a running process, continue a stopped process, or tell the process any number of other things. However, as the name of the command suggests, the kill program is most often used to stop, or kill, a running process.

Users can use the kill program to send signals to processes that they own while the root user can send a signal to any process on the system. The syntax for the command is the following:

```
$ kill -signal PID
```

In this case, the specified signal is sent to the processes indicated by the specified PID. In its simplest form, a default signal is assumed and the command can simply be

```
$ kill PID
```

The default signal is the SIGTERM signal (signal number 15). The complete list of Linux signals is outlined later in this chapter in the section "Linux Signals." As the name suggests, the SIGTERM signal is a process termination signal and it asks processes to terminate and exit.

Signals are indicated by their number or name. For instance, to explicitly specify the SIGTERM signal and send it to the process with PID 459, you could use one of the following commands:

```
$ kill -15 459
```

```
$ kill -TERM 459
```

When the symbolic names of signals are passed to the kill command, they are specified without the initial SIG part for brevity. For example, to issue the SIGQUIT signal to a process with PID 123, the kill command will take the following form:

```
$ kill -QUIT 123
```

At times, processes might not respond to the SIGTERM signal. Processes can, in fact, choose to ignore this signal. In this case, issuing a standard kill PID command will not kill a process. Instead, you need to use the SIGKILL signal (signal number 9). Processes cannot choose to ignore this signal. In this case, one of the following two commands should kill a process which is ignoring the SIGTERM signal:

```
$ kill -9 PID
```

```
$ kill -KILL PID
```

Another common use of the kill command is to send a hang-up signal (SIGHUP; signal number 1). Some daemons are designed to reread their configuration files when they receive the SIGHUP signal. This makes it possible to change the configuration of a running daemon without stopping it and restarting it. For instance, the SIGHUP signal is commonly used with the inetd and named daemons to update their configurations while leaving them running. To send the SIGHUP signal to a process, use one of the following commands:

```
# kill -HUP PID
```

```
# kill -1 PID
```

Caution

It is important to pay close attention to the processes you kill with signals such as SIGKILL and SIGTERM. Not only can you cause users to lose data by killing open, active applications, but if you kill critical system processes such as inetd or init, important system services may stop working or the system may stop functioning completely.

LINUX SIGNALS

A *signal* is a way of interrupting a process from whatever it is doing and telling it to stop and handle the signal. When a signal is sent to a process, it can choose to either handle the signal or ignore it. This depends on who has sent the signal and what kind of signal it is.

Linux supports a large number of signals that can be sent to processes. Normally, the three signals mentioned in the previous discussion of the `kill` command are the only ones you will need to use on a regular basis. At times, though, it is necessary to use a more obscure signal. Table 8.4 outlines available signals for Linux. The information is taken from section 7 of the Linux Programmer's Manual, which is available online on all Linux systems. To view this manual page, issue the following command:

```
% man 7 signal
```

TABLE 8.4   LINUX SIGNALS

Sbignal	Flag for kill Command	Value (Intel Platform)	Default Action	Comment
SIGHUP	-HUP	1	Terminate	Hangup from controlling terminal or death of controlling process
SIGINT	-INT	2	Terminate	Interrupt from the keyboard
SIGQUIT	-QUIT	3	Terminate	Quit from the keyboard
SIGILL	-ILL	4	Terminate	Illegal Instruction
SIGTRAP	-TRAP	5	Dump Core; not POSIX.1 conformant	Trace or breakpoint trap
SIGABRT	-ABRT	6	Dump core	Abort signal from the abort system call
SIGIOT	-IOT	6	Dump Core; not POSIX.1 conformant	Abort signal from the abort system call
SIGBUS	-BUS	7	Terminate; not POSIX.1 conformant	Bus error
SIGFPE	-FPE	8	Dump core	Floating point exception
SIGKILL	-KILL	9	Terminate; cannot be caught or ignored	Kill signal
SIGUSR1	-USR1	10	Terminate	User-defined signal 1
SIGSEGV	-SEGV	11	Dump Core	Invalid memory reference

TABLE 8.4 CONTINUED

Sbignal	Flag for kill Command	Value (Intel Platform)	Default Action	Comment
SIGUSR2	-USR2	12	Terminate	User-defined signal 2
SIGPIPE	-PIPE	13	Terminate	Broken pipe (write to pipe with no readers)
SIGALRM	-ALRM	14	Terminate	Timer signal from the alarm system call
SIGTERM	-TERM	15	Terminate	Termination signal
SIGSTKFLT	-STKFLT	16	Terminate; not POSIX.1 conformant	Stack fault on co-processor
SIGCHLD	-CHLD	17	Ignore	Child stopped or terminated
SIGCONT	-CONT	18		Continue if stopped
SIGSTOP	-STOP	19	Stop; cannot be caught or ignored	Stop the process
SIGTSTP	-TSTP	20	Stop	Stop issued at the tty terminal
SIGTTIN	-TTIN	21	Stop	Tty input received for a background process
SIGTTOW	-TTOW	22	Stop	Tty output generated for a background process
SIGURG	-URG	23	Ignore; not POSIX.1 conformant	Urgent condition on a socket
SIGXCPU	-XCPU	24	Terminate; not POSIX.1 conformant	CPU time limit exceeded
SIGXFSZ	-XFSZ	25	Terminate; not POSIX.1 conformant	File size limit exceeded
SIGVTALRM	-VTALRM	26	Terminate; not POSIX.1 conformant	Virtual alarm clock
SIGPROF	-PROF	27	Terminate; not POSIX.1 conformant	Profile alarm clock
SIGWINCH	-WINCH	28	Ignore; not POSIX.1 conformant	Window resize signal

TABLE 8.4   CONTINUED

Sbignal	Flag for kill Command	Value (Intel Platform)	Default Action	Comment
SIGIO	-IO	29	Terminate; not POSIX.1 conformant	I/O is now possible
SIGPWR	-PWR	30	Terminate; not POSIX.1 conformant	Power failure
SIGUNUSED	-UNUSED	31	Terminate; not POSIX.1 conformant	Unused

CHANGING PROCESS PRIORITIES

Processes have priorities associated with them which govern the amount of CPU resources they get when attempting to share the CPU with other processes. Fortunately, the priority of processes is not fixed. The norm is that new processes inherit the priority-level of the parent process. However, using the nice command, it is possible to specify a different priority level at the time of launching a program.

As a normal user you can only lower the priority of a process you are starting. As the super-user, or root user, you can raise or lower the priority level of a process. Generally, priorities are specified numerically in the range of -20-19, where lower values signify higher priorities. Therefore a process with a priority of -5 has a higher priority than one with a priority of 5.

The nice command takes the following form:

```
# nice -adjustment command
```

For instance, to start a new bash shell with a priority lowered by 5, use the following command:

```
$ nice -5 /bin/bash
```

Similarly, you can start the same shell with a priority adjusted (raised) by -10 using the following command:

```
# nice --10 /bin/bash
```

Notice here the use of the double dash: The first is the required dash for the flag and the second is part of the negative priority value.

While it useful to be able to alter the priority of a process at the time a program is launched, it is also important to be able to adjust the priority of running processes. This is especially important when you are trying to control the load of a running machine, especially if that machine is a heavily used server that has to provide optimal performance.

Consider an example: You administer an application server into which multiple users can telnet and run interactive or background processes. One user logs in and starts a computationally intensive statistical analysis of a large data set. This can easily have a negative impact on all other user's processes and, in particular, interactive performance on the system. In this situation you have two choices as the administrator:

- Kill the user's computationally demanding process.
- Change the process to a lower priority.

Your choice of action depends on the context. If the user is not following your usage policies by running the demanding task, you probably will want to kill the process. But, if the task being performed by the process is legitimate, you can allow it to continue running but provide more CPU resources to other users' processes by lowering the priority of the process. The end result will be better performance for other processes at the expense of the longer time it will take to finish the CPU-intensive statistical analysis.

To change the priority of a process, you use the `renice` command. Regular users can use this command to lower the priority of processes that they own. The root user can raise or lower the priority of any process with the `renice` command.

In its most simple form, the `renice` command takes the following form:

```
# renice priority -p PID
```

For instance, you can lower the priority of a running process, say the process with PID 459, by 5 with the command:

```
# renice 5 -p 459
```

Similarly, you can raise the priority of the same process by -10 with the command:

```
# renice -10 -p 459
```

You can also change priority of multiple processes by providing the PIDs of the processes as a space-separate list:

```
# renice -10 -p 459 623 720
```

This command raises the priority of the processes identified by the PIDs 459, 623, and 720 by -10.

In addition to setting the priority of running processes by specifying their PIDs, you can change the priority of processes owned by a given user, using the following form of the `renice` command:

```
# renice priority -u username
```

For instance, to lower the priority of all processes owned by the user someuser by 15, use the command:

```
# renice 15 -u someuser
```

As with PIDs, you can specify multiple users' names in a space-separated list:

```
# renice 15 -u user1 user2 user3
```

TRACKING SYSTEM LOAD AND PERFORMANCE WITH vmstat

Another useful tool for gathering information about processes, memory, paging, and CPU activity is vmstat. This tool is used to produce periodically updated reports of the number of processes, memory usage, CPU usage, and more.

A typical run of vmstat looks like the following:

```
# vmstat 5 50
     procs                memory    swap       io      system       cpu
 r  b  w   swpd  free  buff cache  si  so   bi   bo   in   cs  us sy  id
 1  0  0  11588   644   656 11260   2  26   98   12  130  237   7  2  91
 2  0  0  13788   540   652 10864  46 447  557  116  187  320  52  5  44
 1  2  0  14516   492   660 11500 394 202 1020   55  178  222   4  2  94
 2  1  0  15964  1016   656 12160 125 315  834   81  218  323   6  2  92
 1  4  0  16628   336   656 12940 147 143  560   51  222  306   5  3  93
 1  1  0  17100   544   660 12344 152 114 1093   37  219  514   8  3  89
 2  1  1  17680   348   660 12400 110 122  626   37  184  467   9  3  88
 2  2  0  21228   852   652 11940  61 714  763  187  189  458  35  6  59
 2  1  0  21088   784   652 15116 114   0  726    8  205  551  37  8  55
 2  0  0  21556   696   652 11620   0 118  285   30  155  248  47  4  49
 4  0  0  22396   688   652 12256   0 168  267   68  165  247  38  5  57
 3  0  0  22396  1084   680 12124   0   0   19    0  105  203  91  6   3
 2  0  0  22396  1300   696 12160   0   0    5   15  109  274  89 11   1
 2  0  0  22364  1376   716 12172  20   0   16   28  114  351  90  9   1
 2  0  0  22364  1368   732 12200   0   0    4    0  102  339  90 10   0
 3  0  0  22364  2928   748 12292   0   0   17   20  111  224  85 13   2
 3  0  0  22364  4660   864 12596   0   0   77    3  116  221  85  8   7
 2  0  0  22344   292   840 12656 313   0  153   47  204  450  83 10   7
 2  0  0  22808   824   652 10788  21  98   23   29  161  423  94  4   1
 3  0  0  22832  2320   688 11288  56  11  181   23  183  313  83  6  12
 3  0  0  23196   772   652 11576 344  74  128   19  150  287  92  5   3
 5  0  0  23148   756   652 10684  62   0   91   25  118  176  99  0   0
 2  0  0  23148  4008   732 12064   0   0  267    1  145  240  60  3  37
 2  0  0  23496  3368   668 12412   0  70   38   48  124  245  88  9   3
 3  0  0  23496  1460   688 12448   0   0    8    0  107  243  90 10   0
 3  0  0  23496  1304   672 12280   0   0   10   26  116  241  92  8   0
 3  0  0  23868   820   652 12172   0  74   28   19  106  196  95  4   0
 4  0  0  23860  5356   912 12480  34   0   76   19  123  198  86  4  10
 3  0  0  23444  1396   964 13596 126   0  179    2  144  302  74 12  14
11  0  0  23928   624   764 12468  89 119   96  108  195  336  91  5   4
 2  0  0  23928  5028   696 12048  24   0   66    0  140  349  85  3  12
 2  0  0  23928  1064   708 12292   0   0   39    0  108  226  85 10   6
 2  0  0  23920  1796   740 12504  11   0   34   24  112  198  94  5   1
 2  0  0  23920   808   740 12464   0   0   13   26  111  203  92  7   1
 2  0  0  23920  1756   768 12504   0   0    8    0  102  194  96  4   0
 2  0  0  23920  4040   800 12704   0   0   37   21  113  229  87 11   2
 2  0  0  23920  1472   660 12376   0   0    7   24  110  214  95  5   0
 2  0  0  23920  4280   680 12408   0   0    6    0  102  192  93  7   0
 2  0  0  23920  3512   888 13172   0   0  155   16  139  258  64  7  29
```

```
3  0  0  23920   528   992  13408   0    0    97    6  117  236  80  11   9
3  0  0  23920  1568   900  11724   0    0     3   91  124  185  98   2   0
3  0  0  24452  6636   832  11436   0  106    35   50  120  219  84   6  10
4  0  0  24452  2876   848  11564   0    0    21    0  131  268  83  14   4
3  0  0  24452  5032   968  12064   0    0    91   18  209  428  75  11  14
5  0  0  24448  2124   984  12612  18    0    97    4  206  451  82  15   3
7  0  0  24420  1668  1000  13128  76    0    50   38  194  442  78  14   9
3  0  0  24096   380   652  13220 428    0   508   26  202  387  88  11   1
3  0  0  23928  4340   676  12408  73    0    47    0  130  264  93   7   0
3  0  1  23764  3096   696  12348  18    0     8   16  144  327  92   7   0
3  0  0  23760  3712   712  12464   0    0    22    5  115  260  91   9   1
```

This example uses the vmstat with two arguments. The first indicates the delay between generating each report line and the second indicates how many reports to generate before exiting. In this case a report line is generated every 5 seconds and 50 reports are generated (hence, vmstat 5 50).

Both arguments are not required. If you omit the second argument, vmstat runs indefinitely or until stopped (for instance by canceling it with Ctrl+C). If you omit the first argument as well, vmstat generates a single report and exits:

```
# vmstat
   procs                      memory      swap          io     system          cpu
 r  b  w   swpd    free   buff  cache   si  so    bi    bo   in   cs  us  sy  id
 1  0  0  11588    644    656  11260    2  26    98    12  130  237   7   2  91
```

The values displayed by vmstat are average values from the last reboot until the time of each report, with the exception of the process and memory columns, which reflect the current state of the system.

To fully understand the output, you need to learn about each section of the output in turn.

THE Procs SECTION

The Procs section displays information about processes on the system and their current states. This information is displayed in three columns:

- **r:** The number of runnable processes waiting for the CPU
- **b:** The number of blocked processes (waiting for some I/O to complete; these processes are in a state of uninterruptible sleep)
- **w:** The number of runnable processes swapped out

THE Memory SECTION

The Memory section displays information about memory usage at the time of the report. This information is broken down into four items:

- **swpd:** The amount of virtual memory used
- **free:** The amount of free memory

- **buff**: The amount of memory used as buffers
- **cache**: The amount of memory used for cache

All values are in kilobytes.

THE Swap SECTION

The Swap section displays information about swapped memory broken down into two subcategories:

- **si**: The amount of memory swapped in from disk
- **so**: The amount of memory swapped out to disk

These values are displayed in kilobytes per second as averages since the last system reboot.

THE Io SECTION

The Io section displays information about blocks of data sent to and from I/O devices broken down into two values:

- **bi**: Number of blocks sent to a block device
- **bo**: Number of blocks received from a block device

These values are displayed in blocks per second as averages since the last system reboot.

THE System SECTION

The System section displays information about process switching displayed as two values:

- **in**: The number of interrupts per second, including the clock
- **cs**: The number of context switches per second

THE CPU SECTION

The CPU section displays information about the use of total CPU time as averages since the last reboot:

- **us**: User time (CPU time spent on user processes)
- **sy**: System time (CPU time spent on kernel processes)
- **id**: Idle time (CPU time spent in an idle state)

These values are represented as percentages of total available CPU time.

INTERPRETING vmstat OUTPUT

Armed with an understanding of the different columns in the vmstat output, you can learn how to interpret the data in useful ways.

Generally, vmstat is used as a tool to identify system bottlenecks. The simple rule of thumb is to watch the first three columns. If under normal operating load a system always shows a large number of processes in the r column of the Procs section, it means you have a CPU bottleneck. Changing to a faster CPU or adding more CPUs in the case of a multiprocessor machine will help. If the b column of the Procs section consistently shows many processes, it means the system is suffering from I/O bottlenecks. Changing to faster disks and I/O channels will help. Lastly too many processes in the w column of the Procs section is a clear sign of too much swapping of the system, and adding more memory will help.

For instance, consider the sample 50-line vmstat output shown earlier in this chapter. This output was generated during a kernel compilation on a relatively low-end Linux system. There are several interesting points to note in this output:

- At the start, the CPU idle value (the id column in the CPU section) was approximately 90%. As the compilation progressed, the idle value dropped until it reached roughly 1%. This signified the increasing CPU time usage of the compilation leaving less and less time for the CPU to idle.

- At the start, the process run queue (the r column in the Procs section) started out with 1 process waiting. As the compilation progressed, this number reached 5 processes waiting. This is because the compilation spawns a number of child processes that start contending for limited CPU resources. The CPU cannot service each request quickly enough and the run queue grows.

- During the period being displayed, at times, there were processes shown as blocked and waiting for I/O to complete (the b column in the Procs sections). In most cases, this represents processes waiting for file read or write operations to finish.

- The fact that processes were rarely swapped to disk (as shown in the w column in the Procs section) indicates that memory demands were not excessive.

Put together, this information can help identify bottlenecks to system performance. In the example in question, the compilation process has made the CPU into a bottleneck.

If you look at vmstat output from the same system after compilation is complete, you will see that the CPU idle time has risen to 99% (a big change from the low of 1% at the height of the compilation) which serves as a strong indication that the CPU is a bottleneck on the system in question:

```
# vmstat 5 5
   procs                    memory      swap        io     system        cpu
 r  b  w   swpd   free  buff  cache  si  so   bi   bo   in    cs  us sy  id
 2  0  0  24244   1404  2616  15956   8  11   41   10  122   225  25  3  71
 0  0  0  24244   1404  2616  15956   0   0    0    0  101   143   0  1  99
 0  0  0  24244   1404  2616  15956   0   0    0    1  101   139   0  0  99
 0  0  0  24244   1404  2616  15956   0   0    0    0  101   140   0  0  99
 0  0  0  24244   1404  2616  15956   0   0    0    0  101   140   0  0  99
```

USEFUL SCRIPTS

The following are three useful scripts for managing your system's processes and daemons:

- **chkdaemon**: Checks if a daemon is running and restarts it if it has stopped.
- **chkload**: Checks if the system load gets too high and if it crosses a threshold, alerts the administrator.
- **chkswap**: Checks the amount of swap space available and if it drops below a threshold, alerts the administrator.

chkdaemon

The following script can be used to check if a daemon is running; if it isn't it will restart the daemon. Create this script in the file /usr/local/bin/chkdaemon and make the file executable:

```
# chmod 755 /usr/local/bin/chkdaemon
```

To use the script, simply pass it the name of a daemon as an argument. For instance, to check whether dhcpd is running and, if it isn't, restart it, use the command:

```
# chkdaemon dhcp
```

The logic of the script is simple:

- On line 6 the path for the script it set. You can only check and restart daemons that exist on the path. Alter the path if you need to use the scripts for daemons that exist in other directories.
- On lines 11-14, a check is made to see if the specified daemon exists on the path and, if not, the script exists with an error.
- Line 16 determines the PID of the specified daemon using the pidof command.
- On line 17-21, the script first checks if a PID was found for the daemon. If not, a message is echoed to a log file, the script is started, and an email message is sent to the root user indicating that the daemon was started.

If you have critical system services, you can schedule this script to run on a regular basis as outlined in Chapter 7, "Scheduling Tasks."

SOURCE CODE

Note The line numbers are provided for reference purpose only.

```
01: #!/bin/sh
02: # Script to check if a daemon is running.
03: # If not start it and notify root
```

```
04: # Name of daemon is passed as a command line argument
05: #
06: # May be distributed under the terms of the GNU Public License
07:
08: PATH=/sbin:/usr/sbin:/bin:/usr/bin
09: export PATH
10:
11: if [ $# -ne 1 ]; then
12:         echo "$0 <name of daemon>"
13:         exit 0
14: fi
15:
16: pid=`pidof $1`
17: if [ "$pid" = "" ] ; then
18:   echo "`date`: Restarting $1" > /var/log/$1.restart.log
19:   $1 >> /var/log/$1.restart.log
20:   Mail -s "`hostname` : $1 restarted" root < /var/log/$1.restart.log
21: fi
```

chkload

The following script can be used to check current system load and alert the system administrator if it exceeds 3. Create this script in the file /usr/local/bin/chkload and make the file executable:

```
# chmod 755 /usr/local/bin/chkload
```

To use the script, simply use it with no arguments:

```
# chkload
```

The logic of the script is simple:

- On line 9 the output of the uptime program is parsed to extract the current system load.

- On lines 12-16, if the load exceeds 3 a message is written to a log file, the output of uptime is written to the log file, and an email message is sent to the root user.

Ideally, you will want to schedule this script to run on a regular basis as outlined in Chapter 7.

SOURCE CODE

Note The line numbers are provided for reference purpose only.

```
01: #!/bin/sh
02: # Description: Alert sysadmins if system load goes above 3
03: #
04: # May be distributed under the terms of the GNU Public License
05:
06: PATH=/sbin:/usr/sbin:/bin:/usr/bin
07: export PATH
```

```
08:
09: load=`uptime ¦ awk -F" " '{print $10}' ¦ awk -F"," '{print $1}' \¦ awk -F"."
10: '{print $1}'`
11:
12: if [ `expr $load  -ge 3 ]; then
13:         date > /var/log/chkload.log
14:         uptime >> /var/log/chkload.log
15:         Mail -s "`#180;hostname`: load > 3.0" root  < /var/log/chkload.log
16: fi
```

chkswap

The following script can be used to check current swap usage and alert the system administrator if less than 10MB is available. Create this script in the file /usr/local/bin/chkswap and make the file executable:

```
# chmod 755 /usr/local/bin/chkswap
```

To use the script, simply use it with no arguments:

```
# chkswap
```

The logic of the script is simple:

- On line 8 the output of the free program is parsed to extract the amount of swap space available.
- On line 9, the minimum available swap space threshold is set to 10MB.
- On lines 10-14, if the available swap space is less than the specified threshold a message is written to a log file, the output of free is written to the log file and an email message is sent to the root user.

Ideally, you will want to schedule this script to run on a regular basis as outlined in Chapter 7.

SOURCE CODE

> **Note** The line numbers are provided for reference purpose only.

```
01: #!/bin/sh
02: # Description: Alert sysadmins if less than 10 MB of swap space is available
03: #
04: # May be distributed under the terms of the GNU Public License
05: PATH=/sbin:/usr/sbin:/bin:/usr/bin
06: export PATH
07:
08: swapfree=`free -m¦grep Swap¦awk -F" " '{print $4}'
09: SWAPLO=10
10: if [ `expr $swapfree -le `expr $SWAPLO` ]; then
11:         date > /var/log/swap.log
12:         free -m >> /var/log/swap.log
```

```
13:              Mail -s "`hostname`: Less than 10m swap free" root < /var/log/
➥swap.log
14: fi
```

TROUBLESHOOTING

You can ascertain a lot about your system just by observing the processes that are running. It is not difficult to identify the processes that are consuming most of the system's memory and CPU resources. Here are some tips to deal with common process-related problems:

■ Sometimes you may find the system is loaded with many identical jobs created by the same user. Depending on the gravity of the situation you may need to kill these jobs. When you do this it is always a good idea to inform the user of your actions and provide reasons. This will help educate users so that the situation can be prevented in the future. Often a situation like this is caused by a novice programmer who has written a buggy shell script or C program.

■ Sometimes you may encounter a process that has been running for a very long time and has accumulated an unusually large amount of CPU time. It is likely the process is in an infinite loop and generally indicates that something is amiss. You should verify with the user if the process is still performing something useful, and if not you should terminate it.

■ Sometimes you may observe a process consuming a very large percentage of CPU over an extended period of time. If the CPU load incurred by the process is affecting other users, you can lower the jobs priority with the renice command and then inform the user.

■ Sometimes you will encounter a runaway process. A *runaway process* is a process that enters an infinite loop and spawns new processes. This can cause an overflow in the process table that will not allow any new processes to start. They will fail with the error messages such as "Cannot fork process" or "System temporarily out of resources." In this situation, you need to identify and stop the runaway process. This isn't always easy. Generally, you want to look for one program that is consuming more CPU time than is reasonable or a large number of processes which are all running the same program and have a common parent. Once you identify the runaway process, you should terminate it and then all of its children. The program pstree is useful in displaying processes in a tree format. It can be used to quickly identify parent and child processes.

> **Note**
>
> If you kill the children of a runaway process first, you may not succeed in terminating the runaway process. When the children are terminated, the parent may immediately spawn new children to replace the ones you killed. Sometimes, attempting to kill the children of a runaway process before killing the parent runaway process leads to rapid spawning of new children until the only way to solve the problem is to reboot the system because so many children have launched that the system becomes non-responsive.

■ Sometimes a process will refuse to stop with the standard `kill PID` command. As outlined earlier in this chapter, this can normally be handled by using the SIGKILL (9) signal with the `kill` command, as in either of the following examples:

```
# kill -9 PID
# kill -KILL PID
```

## CHAPTER 9

INSTALLING AND USING RAID

In this chapter

UNDERSTANDING RAID

RAID is an acronym for Redundant Array of Inexpensive (or Independent) Disks. The term was first coined by Patterson, Gibson, and Katz to describe how a number of inexpensive or independent disks could be combined into what appears as a single storage unit to the computer with performance similar to large disks (see Figure 9.1).

Figure 9.1
A single logical
storage unit
(RAID).

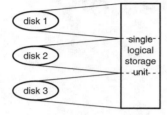

WHY YOU SHOULD USE RAID

The primary reasons to use RAID are increased storage capacity, fault tolerance during disk failure due to its redundancy, and speed. The economic costs of a disk failure can be extremely high (not just because of downtime, but also because of lost productivity and recovery costs). RAID systems generally enable one to recover from single disk failures quickly and transparently, without any downtime. Thus RAID is a good option for those who want an *additional* support layer to shore up a traditional backup system and do not want to always bother with restoring backups every time a disk fails.

STRIPING

Fundamental to understanding how RAID works is the concept of "data striping." Data striping involves splitting up the storage space of each drive into small chunks of data (or stripes) which are then interleaved across the different drives in the array (see Figure 9.2). The combined data is composed of stripes in succession from each drive. The stripes can be as small as one sector (512 bytes) or as large as several megabytes, depending on the environment in which the array is used.

Figure 9.2
Data striping
across several
disk drives.

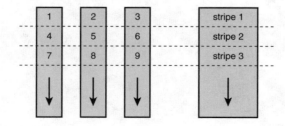

DIFFERENT RAID ARCHITECTURES

The six recognized types of RAID architectures are RAID-0 through RAID-5. Each provides a different type of disk fault tolerance and offers different trade-offs in features and performance. Fault tolerance is key to a RAID system because the average failure time of the array is equal to the average time between failures of each drive divided by the total number of drives. Therefore, some redundancy in the data storage to make up for the lower average time between disk failures for the array as a whole is essential. The level of fault tolerance also affects the performance and features of the array.

Each type of RAID is described here. Table 9.1 compares the different types of RAID and their features at a glance:

- RAID-0 arrays are sets of striped disk drives with no redundancy (thus it doesn't completely fit the RAID acronym) in the data storage, and consequently without any fault tolerance. These arrays are commonly configured with large stripes for applications requiring intensive I/O, because the splitting of data across drives results in higher throughput and data storage efficiency. However, a single drive failure will cause the entire array to crash. This level is also known as disk striping, and is the fastest and most efficient array type.

- RAID-1 arrays consist of pairs of disk drives that store duplicate data. Thus there is complete redundancy: If one drive fails, the other one of the pair is still available. Level 1 arrays tend to perform better on reads (because both drives can perform reads simultaneously) than on writes (because every write must be done on both drives of the pair). Striping is not used with a single pair of drives. This level offers decent performance and fault tolerance, but has the least storage efficiency of any RAID level. This level is also known as disk mirroring, and is most useful for performance-critical fault-tolerant environments.

- RAID-2 arrays are similar to RAID-0 arrays except that error correcting (ECC) information is stored to achieve disk fault tolerance. This level is seldom used today because modern disk drives have ECC information embedded within each sector.

- RAID-3 arrays are similar to RAID-2 arrays except that a single drive contains the parity information, and the data is striped at a byte level across several drives. As a consequence, RAID-3 can perform only one I/O operation at a time, limiting its use to single-user systems. However, it is good for data-intensive single-user environments where long sequential records are accessed.

- RAID-4 arrays are similar to RAID-3 arrays with the exception of large stripe sizes. The performance of this level is very good for reads (on the same level as for RAID-0), and not so good for writes (because the parity information must be updated each time). Large sequential writes are fairly fast, but slow random writes can be very slow. All the parity data is stored on a single drive and therefore this level is cost efficient.

■ RAID-5 arrays circumvent the bottleneck caused in RAID-4 due to storing parity in one drive by evenly distributing the parity information among all the drives in the array (see Figure 9.3). Thus multiple write operations can be processed simultaneously, resulting in improved performance. The equivalent of one drive's storage space is used to store the array's parity data. RAID-5 arrays are extremely flexible because they can be configured with either large stripes (for multitasking and multiuser environments) or small stripes (for maximizing transfer rates). The cost efficiency of this level is the same as for RAID-4. This level is one of the most commonly used levels today, and is the best choice in multiuser environments that are not write sensitive.

Note

It is important to remember that RAID generally requires that all disks in the array be the same size.

Figure 9.3
A RAID-5 array with the parity information distributed across all the drives.

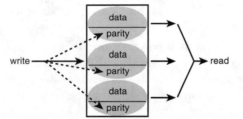

TABLE 9.1   COMPARISON OF FEATURES OF THE DIFFERENT RAID LEVELS

Feature	RAID-0	RAID-1	RAID-2	RAID-3	RAID-4	RAID-5
Fault tolerance	None	Best	Good	Good	Good	Good
Storage efficiency	Best	Worst	Good	Good	Good	Good
Read performance	Best	Good	Good	Good	Good	Good
Write performance	Best	Good	OK	OK	OK	OK

For more information on RAID, refer to the What is RAID? FAQ by Michael Neuffer at http://www.uni-mainz.de/~neuffer/scsi/what_is_raid.html and the DPT Understanding RAID primer at http://www.dpt.com/library/library.html.

RAID IMPLEMENTATIONS

RAID can be implemented in the hardware, in the form of specialized controllers that manage the array, or in software, as part of the kernel that is layered between the low-level disk driver and the file system above it.

HARDWARE RAID

Hardware-based RAID can take two forms:

- HOST-based controllers, where an adapter card plugs in to an ISA/EISA/PCI slot in your computer.
- SCSI-to-SCSI controllers, where an external "box" that is connected to the host with a normal SCSI controller appears to the host as a single disk.

In the former case, the adapter/controller card manages the RAID independently from the host. The primary advantage of using a controller card has to do with its capability to utilize multiple SCSI channels to read and write from the RAID array, thus increasing the transfer rate over the SCSI bus. In the latter case, a machine containing both a controller and an external disk subsystem accomplishes all the RAID handling. A single SCSI channel must be used to control the RAID and this can create a bottleneck. Thus host-based controllers are the preferred choice for a hardware RAID system.

SOFTWARE RAID

RAID can also be implemented purely in software, without any requirement of extra hardware, by a set of kernel modules and management utilities. The MD driver (multiple devices driver) under Linux is one example of such a RAID implementation (which implements levels 0, 1, 4, and 5). The Linux RAID driver is implemented as a kernel layer between the block-device interface (upon which the file system resides) and the low-level disk drivers (for IDE and SCSI drivers). For more information, see the Software-RAID HOWTO at http://www.linuxdoc.org/HOWTO/mini/Software-RAID.html.

HARDWARE VERSUS SOFTWARE RAID

Software-based arrays run like any other application on the system and therefore will consume many CPU cycles. They are also operating system-dependent. The performance of a software-based RAID is greatly affected by the other applications that are running concurrently on the system. In contrast, hardware-based arrays generally do not depend on the CPU performance and load of the host machine.

Hardware-based RAID schemes have little in common with software-based RAID systems except in terms of the array functionality. Hardware-based arrays have true multitasking, because the processor in the controller can execute multiple instructions independent of the operating system type and function. Hardware-based RAID controllers also have an on-board memory cache that can allow high transfer rates into the large controller cache. Hardware-based RAID systems are more reliable because special software is not required to boot the system.

Hardware-based RAID arrays are transparent to the operating system, which makes their management easier. Software RAID implementations have several configuration options, tending to complicate management.

In contrast, software-based RAID systems are extremely cost efficient (because cheaper IDE disks can be used without any need for additional hardware). With software-based systems, different partitions in a single disk can be grouped together to create redundancy and fault-tolerance, whereas hardware-based systems group together whole drives. Also, under Linux, software-based RAID management is completely possible within the operating system, whereas dedicated management tools under Linux for hardware implementations might not be available.

INSTALLING AND CONFIGURING RAID IN LINUX

In order to install and configure RAID on your Linux system, it is necessary first to decide what type of controller to use. Several types of controllers are available, including the following:

- DPT Controllers
- ICP Vortex Controllers
- Mylex Controllers

SUPPORTED CONTROLLERS

Currently a well-supported host-based hardware RAID controller (that is, a controller for which there exists one or more well-supported drivers under Linux) is one that is made by DPT (http://www.dpt.com). However, other host-based and SCSI-to-SCSI controllers exist that can work under Linux. These include the ones made by Syred (http://www.syred.com), ICP-Vortex (http://www.icp-vortex.com), and Mylex (http://www.mylex.com). See the RAID solutions for Linux page http://linas.org/linux/raid.html for more information.

DPT CONTROLLERS

Essentially all the SmartRAID IV and V controllers are supported. The installation and configuration section will focus on setting up SCSI-based hardware RAID, mainly on host-based adapters from DPT, although the principles applied here are fairly general. Specifically, the Smartcache IV PM2144UW and PM3334UW controllers have been tested, with DPT supplied enclosures, on Linux 2.0.3x and 2.2.x kernels. The SmartRAID V Decade cards require additional software. For additional detail and the latest information, consult the DPT Hardware RAID HOWTO at http://www.ram.org/computing/linux/dpt_raid.html.

ICP VORTEX CONTROLLERS

ICP vortex has a complete line of disk array controllers that support Linux. The ICP driver is in the Linux kernel since version 2.0.31. All major Linux Distributors—SuSE, LST Power Linux, Caldera, and Red Hat—support the ICP controllers as boot/installation controllers.

The RAID system can easily be configured with their `romsetup` program (you do not have to boot MS-DOS for configuration). With their monitoring utility, `gdtmon`, it is possible to manage the complete ICP RAID system during operation (check transfer rates, set parameters for the controller and hard disks, and exchange defective hard disks, and so forth).

MYLEX RAID CONTROLLERS

The DAC960 driver supports all of the current Mylex PCI RAID controllers, including the eXtremeRAID 1100 (DAC1164P), the AcceleRAID 150/200/250, and the older DAC960PJ/PG/PU/PD/PL models. Red Hat Linux 6.0+ and SuSE Linux 6.2 include support for these controllers. Besides installing the driver, a special set of utilities which provide source paths and statically linked executables of lilo and fidks are necessary to understand the DAC960 RAID devices. The driver, the utilities, and additional information are available via the Dandelion Digital's Linux DAC960 page: `http://www.dandelion.com/Linux/DAC960.html`.

This utility makes ICP Vortex controllers stand out with respect to Linux Hardware RAID controllers.

WHAT HARDWARE SHOULD BE USED?

In selecting your RAID hardware, you need to give consideration to two factors:

- The choice of controller type (such as SCSI-to-SCSI or host-based)
- The choice of enclosure type for your disks (which determines hot-swapping, warnings, and other features)

CONTROLLER TYPE

Given these options, if you're looking for a RAID solution, you need to think carefully about what you want. Depending on what you want to do, and which RAID level you want to use, some cards can be better than others. SCSI-to-SCSI adapters might not be as good as host-based adapters, for example. See the discussion by Michael Neuffer, the author of the EATA-DMA driver, on his Linux High Performance SCSI and RAID page: `http://www.uni-mainz.de/~neuffer/scsi/`.

ENCLOSURE TYPE

The enclosure type affects the hot swap feature of the drive, the warning systems (that is, whether there will be indication of failure, and whether you will know which drive has failed), and what kind of treatment your drive receives (for example, redundant cooling and power supplies). DPT-supplied enclosures worked extremely well, but they are expensive. Wetex (`http://www.wetex.com`) enclosures lack the hot swap capability of the DPT enclosures but otherwise work well.

INSTALLATION

There are two parts to installation: configuring the hardware, and configuring the kernel.

INSTALLING AND CONFIGURING THE HARDWARE

Refer to the instruction manual to install the controller and the drives. For DPT, because a storage manager for Linux doesn't exist yet, you must create an MS-DOS-formatted disk with the system on it (usually created with the command `format /s` at the MS-DOS prompt). You will also use the DPT storage manager for MS-DOS, which you should probably make a copy of for safety.

After the hardware is in place, boot using the DOS system disk. Replace the DOS disk with the storage manager, and invoke the storage manager using the following command:

```
a:\ dptmgr
```

Wait a minute or so, and you will get a menu of options. Configure the set of disks as a hardware RAID (single logical array). Choose "other" as the operating system.

The MS-DOS storage manager is much easier to use with a mouse, so you might want to have a mouse driver on the initial system disk you create.

Technically, it should be possible to run the SCO storage manager under Linux, but it might be more trouble than it's worth. It is probably easier to run the MS-DOS storage manager under Linux.

CONFIGURING THE KERNEL

You will need to configure the kernel with SCSI support and the appropriate low-level driver. Refer to Chapter 11, "Building the Linux Kernel" for guidance in compiling your kernel. Alternately, consult the Kernel HOWTO `http://sunsite.unc.edu/mdw/HOWTO/ Kernel-HOWTO.html` for information on how to compile the kernel. After you choose "yes" for SCSI support, in the low-level drivers section, select the driver of your choice (EATA DMA or EATA ISA/EISA/PCI for most EATA DMA-compliant (DPT) cards, EATA PIO for the very old PM2001 and PM2012A from DPT). Most drivers, including the EATA DMA and EATA ISA/EISA/PCI drivers, should be available in recent kernel versions.

After you have the kernel compiled, reboot; if you have set up everything correctly, you should see the driver recognizing the RAID as a single SCSI disk. If you use RAID-5, you will see the size of this disk to be two thirds of the actual disk space available.

BOOTUP MESSAGES

The messages you see upon bootup if you're using the EATA DMA driver should look something like this:

```
EATA (Extended Attachment) driver version: 2.59b
developed in co-operation with DPT
(c) 1993-96 Michael Neuffer, mike@i-Connect.Net
Registered HBAs:
```

```
HBA no. Boardtype      Revis  EATA Bus  BaseIO  IRQ DMA  Ch ID Pr QS  S/G IS
scsi0 : PM3334UW       v07L.0 2.0c PCI  0xef90  10  BMST 3  7  N  64  252 Y
scsi1 : PM2144UW       v07L.Y 2.0c PCI  0xef50   9  BMST 1  7  N  64  252 Y
scsi2 : PM2044U        v07K.V 2.0c PCI  0xef10  11  BMST 1  7  N  64  252 Y
scsi0 : EATA (Extended Attachment) HBA driver
scsi1 : EATA (Extended Attachment) HBA driver
scsi2 : EATA (Extended Attachment) HBA driver
scsi : 3 hosts.
   Vendor: DPT       Model: RAID-5           Rev: 07L0
   Type:   Direct-Access                     ANSI SCSI revision: 02
Detected scsi disk sda at scsi0, channel 0, id 0, lun 0
scsi0: queue depth for target 0 on channel 0 set to 64
   Vendor: DPT       Model: ATOS             Rev: 07LY
   Type:   Direct-Access                     ANSI SCSI revision: 02
Detected scsi disk sdb at scsi1, channel 0, id 8, lun 0
scsi1: queue depth for target 8 on channel 0 set to 64
   Vendor: SONY      Model: SDT-9000         Rev: 0200
   Type:   Sequential-Access                 ANSI SCSI revision: 02
scsi2: queue depth for target 0 on channel 0 set to 64
SCSI device sda: hdwr sector= 512 bytes. Sectors= 105676800 [51600 MB] [51.6 GB]
 sda: sda1
SCSI device sdb: hdwr sector= 512 bytes. Sectors= 35561984 [17364 MB] [17.4 GB]
 sdb: sdb1
```

The above display is for a setup with three DPT SCSI controllers with two RAID-5 arrays of size 51.6GB (seven 9GB disks) and 17.4GB (three 9GB disks).

The messages you see upon bootup if you're using the EATA ISA/EISA/PCI driver should look something like this:

```
EATA0: IRQ 11 mapped to IO-APIC IRQ 16.
EATA/DMA 2.0x: Copyright  1994-1999 Dario Ballabio.
EATA config options -> tc:y, lc:n, mq:16, eh:y, rs:y, et:n.
EATA0: 2.0C, PCI 0xef10, IRQ 16, BMST, SG 122, MB 64.
EATA0: SCSI channel 0 enabled, host target ID 7.
EATA1: IRQ 9 mapped to IO-APIC IRQ 18.
EATA1: 2.0C, PCI 0xef50, IRQ 18, BMST, SG 122, MB 64.
EATA1: wide SCSI support enabled, max_id 16, max_lun 8.
EATA1: SCSI channel 0 enabled, host target ID 7.
scsi0 : EATA/DMA 2.0x rev. 5.10.00
scsi1 : EATA/DMA 2.0x rev. 5.10.00
scsi : 2 hosts.
   Vendor: SONY      Model: SDT-9000         Rev: 0200
   Type:   Sequential-Access                 ANSI SCSI revision: 02
EATA0: scsi0, channel 0, id 0, lun 0, cmds/lun 2.
   Vendor: DPT       Model: ATOS             Rev: 07LY
   Type:   Direct-Access                     ANSI SCSI revision: 02
Detected scsi disk sda at scsi1, channel 0, id 8, lun 0
EATA1: scsi1, channel 0, id 8, lun 0, cmds/lun 16, unsorted, tagged.
SCSI device sda: hdwr sector= 512 bytes. Sectors= 35561984 [17364 MB] [17.4 GB]
 sda: sda1
```

The above display is for a setup with two DPT SCSI controllers, with one RAID-5 array of size 17.4GB (three 9GB disks).

CONFIGURING AND TESTING YOUR ARRAY

You can now start treating your RAID 5 array as a regular disk. The first thing you need to do is partition the disk (using `fdisk`). You then need to set up an ext2 file system. This can be accomplished by the following command:

```
# mke2fs/dev/sdxN
```

`/dev/sdxN` is the name of the SCSI partition. After you do this, you will be able to mount the partitions and use them as you would any other disk (including adding entries in `/etc/fstab`).

HOT SWAPPING

In order to test the hot swap feature on your array, simply remove one of the drives from the array while the system is running. If your RAID 5 array is configured and working correctly, the system should keep running with one disk removed. Performance will be degraded because the missing data must be rebuilt on-the-fly as you access the disks.

If you reinsert the removed disk or a new disk, the data for that disk will be rebuilt while the system continues to run. Performance will be affected during the rebuild, and if your array is used heavily, this will be noticeable to users.

Tip

Keep in mind that RAID 5 arrays offer limited redundancy. You cannot simultaneously remove two drives from the array. If you do this, the array will cease to work, data will be lost and you will need to recover from backups.

PERFORMANCE

You can test the performance of your RAID array using the bonnie program. `bonnie` is a file system benchmarking utility which is available from `http://www.textuality.com/bonnie/`.

`bonnie` is one of the best "open systems" benchmarks available that measures system I/O performance. It, along with other benchmarks, can be retrieved at the AC&NC RAID and Disk Storage Benchmarks page at `http://www.acnc.com/benchmarks.html`.

Tip

No matter what type of RAID you use, or what benchmark you use, make sure you test performance in a real application environment also. Don't just rely on benchmark results!

The following is an example of timings output from `bonnie` for an array using a 3344 UW controller:

```
-------Sequential Output-------- ---Sequential Input-- --Random--
      -Per Char- --Block-- -Rewrite-- -Per Char- --Block--- --Seeks---
   MB K/sec %CPU K/sec %CPU K/sec %CPU K/sec %CPU K/sec %CPU  /sec %CPU
 1000  1714 17.2  1689  6.0  1200  5.7  5263 40.2  7023 12.1  51.3 2.2
```

FEATURES IN THE EATA DMA DRIVER

This section describes some commands available under Linux to check on the RAID configuration. Again, although references to the eata_dma driver are made, this can be used to check on any SCSI driver.

To see the configuration for your driver, type the following:

cat /proc/scsi/eata_dma/*N*

N is the host ID for the controller. You should see something like this:

```
EATA (Extended Attachment) driver version: 2.59b
queued commands:         17664
processed interrupts:    17664

scsi0 : HBA PM3334UW
Firmware revision: v07L.0
Hardware Configuration:
IRQ:  0, edge triggered
DMA: BUSMASTER
CPU: MC68000 0MHz
Base IO : 0xef90
Host Bus: PCI
SCSI Bus: Speed: 5MB/sec.
SCSI channel expansion Module: not present
SmartRAID hardware: not present.
     Type: -
     Max array groups:            7
     Max drives per RAID 0 array:  7
     Max drives per RAID 3/5 array: 7
Cache Module: not present.
     Type: -
     Bank0: 0MB without ECC
     Bank1: 0MB without ECC
     Bank2: 0MB without ECC
     Bank3: 0MB without ECC
Timer Mod.: not present
NVRAM     : not present
SmartROM  : enabled
Alarm     : off
Host<->Disk command statistics:
        Reads:      Writes:
     1k:         0           0
     2k:         0           0
     4k:         0           0
     8k:         0           0
    16k:         0           0
    32k:         0           0
    64k:         0           0
   128k:         0           0
   256k:         0           0
```

```
  512k:              0              0
 1024k:              0              0
>1024k:              0              0
Sum    :              0              0
Attached devices:
Host: scsi0 Channel: 00 Id: 00 Lun: 00
  Vendor: DPT       Model: RAID-5          Rev: 07L0
  Type:   Direct-Access                    ANSI SCSI revision: 02
```

To get advanced command statistics, type this:

```
# echo "eata_dma latency" > /proc/scsi/eata_dma/N
```

Then you can enter the following command:

```
# cat /proc/scsi/eata_dma/N
```

To get more detailed statistics, use the following:

```
EATA (Extended Attachment) driver version: 2.59b
queued commands:          17737
processed interrupts:     17737


scsi0 : HBA PM3334UW
Firmware revision: v07L.0
Hardware Configuration:
IRQ:  0, edge triggered
DMA: BUSMASTER
CPU: MC68000 0MHz
Base IO : 0xef90
Host Bus: PCI
SCSI Bus: Speed: 5MB/sec.
SCSI channel expansion Module: not present
SmartRAID hardware: not present.
    Type: -
    Max array groups:              7
    Max drives per RAID 0 array:   7
    Max drives per RAID 3/5 array: 7
Cache Module: not present.
    Type: -
    Bank0: 0MB without ECC
    Bank1: 0MB without ECC
    Bank2: 0MB without ECC
    Bank3: 0MB without ECC
Timer Mod.: not present
NVRAM     : not present
SmartROM  : enabled
Alarm     : off
Host Latency Command Statistics:
Current timer resolution: 10ms
        Reads:      Min:(ms)    Max:(ms)    Ave:(ms)
   1k:     36          0          30           9
   2k:      0          0           0           0
   4k:      3          0          10           6
   8k:      0          0           0           0
  16k:      0          0           0           0
  32k:      0          0           0           0
  64k:      0          0           0           0
 128k:      0          0           0           0
```

```
   256k:           0              0              0              0
   512k:           0              0              0              0
  1024k:           0              0              0              0
 >1024k:           0              0              0              0
           Writes:       Min:(ms)       Max:(ms)       Ave:(ms)
     1k:          24              0              0              0
     2k:           0              0              0              0
     4k:           0              0              0              0
     8k:           0              0              0              0
    16k:           0              0              0              0
    32k:           0              0              0              0
    64k:           0              0              0              0
   128k:           0              0              0              0
   256k:           0              0              0              0
   512k:           0              0              0              0
  1024k:           0              0              0              0
 >1024k:           0              0              0              0
Attached devices:
Host: scsi0 Channel: 00 Id: 00 Lun: 00
  Vendor: DPT      Model: RAID-5         Rev: 07L0
  Type:   Direct-Access                  ANSI SCSI revision: 02
```

To turn off advanced command statistics, type the following:

```
# echo "eata_dma nolatency" > /proc/scsi/eata_dma/N
```

TROUBLESHOOTING

The following are several typical RAID problems that are discussed in this section:

- Upon Bootup, No SCSI Hosts are Detected
- RAID Configuration Shows Up as N Different Disks
- Machine or Controller is Shut Down in the Middle of a Format
- SCSI_ABORT_BUSY Errors Produced During Initial File System Format

UPON BOOTUP, NO SCSI HOSTS ARE DETECTED

Sometimes, when you boot your system no SCSI hosts will be detected. This can be the result of several things, but typically it indicates that the appropriate driver has not been configured. To resolve this, check and make sure the appropriate drive (such as EATA-DMA or EATA ISA/EISA/PCI for DPT cards) is installed and configured. You can use the lsmod command to see if the appropriate modules have been loaded and should refer to your system logs for boot-time errors regarding SCSI drivers.

> **Tip**
>
> In general, it is best to make complete backups of data before any troubleshooting operation is performed.

RAID CONFIGURATION SHOWS UP AS *N* DIFFERENT DISKS

If your RAID array has not been configured properly, it may indicate a different number of disks than are actually in place. In the case of a DPT storage manager, you must configure the RAID disks as a single logical array. When you configure the controller with the storage manager, start it with the parameter /FW0 or select Solaris as the operating system. This will cause the array setup to be managed internally by the controller.

MACHINE OR CONTROLLER IS SHUT DOWN IN THE MIDDLE OF A FORMAT

Serious problems can be introduced with some RAID controllers if you shut down the system or the controller during a disk format operation. Problems can be so severe that in some cases, disks have to be returned to the manufacturer.

If this occurs, you may be able to recover use of your disks by performing a low-level format on them. In the case of the DPT controllers, a special formatting program called clfmt is provided on their utilities Web page at http://www.dpt.com/techsup/. Read the instructions after unzipping the clfmt.zip file. After you do the low-level format, you might be able to treat the disks as if they were new.

SCSI_ABORT_BUSY ERRORS PRODUCED DURING INITIAL FILE SYSTEM FORMAT

When you do a mke2fs on the SCSI drive, you may see errors of the form:

```
scsi: aborting command due to timeout : pid xxx, scsi0, channel 0, id 2, lun 0
write (10) xx xx xx xx xx xx xx xx xx
eata_abort called pid xxx target: 2 lun: 0 reason: 3
Returning: SCSI_ABORT_BUSY
```

This may cause the machine to freeze. Often, you can fix this problem by reading 100 or 200 MB from the RAID array with the dd command as follows:

```
# dd if=/dev/sdX of=/dev/null bs=1024k count=128
```

During a format, a fast rush of requests for chunks of memory that is directly accessible is made, and sometimes the memory manager cannot service the requests in a reasonable amount of time. The dd solution outlined above is a workaround that will simply create the requests sequentially instead of in one huge heap (which is typical in the case of formatting).

CHAPTER **10**

BACK UP AND RESTORE

In this chapter

WHY BACKUP IS IMPORTANT

Backing up and restoring are extremely important system administration activities. Backing up file systems means copying them to removable media, of which tapes are the most common type. In most networks, the amount of data that needs backing up is generally so large that it is impractical to use other forms of removable media such as floppy disks or Jaz disks. These media can be used for quick backup and retrieval of smaller data sets such as critical system configuration files.

The importance of backups cannot be understated. They are the primary safeguard against accidental loss of data. A well-crafted backup plan that implements a systematic procedure of backing up critical file systems is essential to

- Guarantee that you can recover from a disk crash
- Ensure that you can restore accidentally deleted users' files
- Safeguard against a failed system upgrade, or application patch

In addition, backups are useful to transfer data from one system to another, or to reorganize the file system of an existing system and replace smaller capacity disk drives with larger ones.

No matter how carefully you maintain your systems, or how educated your users, sooner or later you will be faced with situations of lost files. This can range from a few files accidentally deleted by a user to an entire file system wiped out in an instant by a disk crash. Although backups are the norm for large systems, many small systems and networks fail to implement sufficient backup procedures. Backups are important for systems of all sizes.

PLANNING A BACKUP STRATEGY

The more frequently data is backed up, the safer it is from loss. This would suggest that the ideal backup plan implements frequent backups, even more than once per day.

However, the backup process itself is costly. In particular, backups use system resources and operator time and therefore cannot be performed too frequently. Instead, administrators must also analyze the data stored on a system to determine what data needs to be backed up and how often it should be backed up.

For instance, user files generally change frequently. Therefore, backing them up on a daily basis is a good policy. System files, by contrast, generally change less frequently and a weekly backup may be sufficient. Within the Linux context, the / and /usr file systems generally change infrequently and are good candidates for weekly backups. By contrast, the /home and /var directory trees contain data including user files in home directories and mail inboxes which change frequently. Ideally these should be backed up on a daily basis.

Because of the costs incurred in terms of network speed, disk usage, and CPU time, backups need to be run when other use of systems is at a minimum. Also, backups should be run when the data being backed up is least likely to change. Generally, this means that backups should be scheduled to run late at night or in the early morning hours for most networks and systems. In most environments, no users will be logged in at this time and data will be least volatile.

To conserve on tape media and backup time, a good backup strategy is to perform a full backup once per week (on the weekend, for instance) and incremental backups on a daily basis during the week. A full backup copies the entire file system to backup media while an incremental backup copies only files that have changed since the last full backup. This saves on tape media and also drastically shortens the backup times during the week.

This does not mean the strategy of combining weekly full backups with daily incremental backups is without flaws. In particular, this strategy means that restoring from backups requires the use at least two sets of backups: First the latest full backup must be restored and then changed files from more recent incremental backups must be restored on top of the restored full backup. In general, though, the overall savings of tape media cost and shorter backup times with this plan far outweigh the small inconvenience of handling multiple sets of tapes.

TAPE DRIVES

Several different types of tape drives are available. Drives are categorized into two major classes:

- SCSI drives
- IDE drives

In general, SCSI drives perform better and except in the smallest networks and systems, you should select a SCSI tape drive for your backups. Several different types of SCSI tape drives are available, including the following:

- **Advanced Intelligent Tape (AIT):** AIT is the premier tape technology for high-volume network and server backups. AIT technology was developed by Sony and uses an 8mm tape format. AIT-1 offers speeds up to 6.0Mbps, 35GB native capacity, and up to 70GB of compressed storage on a single tape. AIT-2 is backward compatible with AIT-1 and offers 50GB native capacity, and up to 100GB compressed storage per tape. This high speed and storage capacity makes the technology costly but ideal for high-demand backups.
- **Digital Linear Tape (DLT):** DLT is an extremely fast tape technology offering tape capacities of 35GB native, and up to 70GB compressed capacity per tape, and transfer rates of 5Mbps. High data reliability rates are reported with DLT tapes guaranteed for as many as 500,000 passes. With the high speed and reliability, DLT drives are generally a costly option.

- **Digital Audio Tape (DAT):** DAT originated as a format for audio recording but was adapted for computer backup. DAT tapes range in size from 2GB to 16GB and offer lower media costs in exchange for higher drive costs than some competing technologies such as QIC and Travan. DAT drives offer above average speed, making them suited to small workgroup and network backups.
- **Exabyte 8mm:** The Exabyte 8mm format is an adaptation of 8mm technology used in camcorders. Tapes range in size up to 7GB with transfer rates reported as high as 0.3MBps. Because of the low cost of the drives, 8mm drives are often used for network backup solutions.
- **Exabyte Mammoth:** The Exabyte Mammoth format is an 8mm technology which offers backward compatibility with other Exabyte 8mm technologies while offering compressed data storage of up to 43GB per tape with data transfer rates up to 3MBps.
- **Travan:** Travan drives are widely used as a backup technology for desktop computers because they offer a good price point for the home user and small business. Travan NS 8 offers a native capacity of 4GB, compressed capacities up to 8GB, and speed of 0.6Mbps. Travan NS 20 provides 10GB native, up to 20GB compressed capacity, and drive speed of 1.5Mbps. Travan NS 36 is about to hit the market. It has a native capacity of 18GB, up to 36GB compressed, with maximum speed capability of 4Mbps. Travan drives support both SCSI and EIDE interfaces.

Throughout this chapter, we have used a Sony AIT drive connected to a Linux system running the 2.2.15-smp Linux kernel. The examples all presume you are using a SCSI tape drive because these drives are the most common in network and server environments.

TESTING YOUR TAPE DRIVE

After you have a tape drive connected to your system, you should test it to ensure it is functioning properly. The mt command can be used to test the basic functionality of your drive.

First, check the /var/log/messages after rebooting to make sure your system detected and recognized your tape drive. You can do this using the dmesg command. If your drive was detected successfully, the output of the dmesg command should include an extract similar to the following, outlining the make and type of tape drive you have installed:

```
Vendor: SONY        Model: SDX-300C        Rev: 0400
  Type:   Sequential-Access                ANSI SCSI revision: 02
  Detected scsi tape st0 at scsi0, channel 0, id 6, lun 0
```

In this example, the drive has a SCSI ID of 6 and has been assigned to the device /dev/st0.

> **Note**
>
> If you have a single SCSI tape drive on your system, it will normally be assigned to the device /dev/st0. We presume this throughout this chapter.

Tip

If the output of `dmesg` indicates that your drive was not detected and recognized, check your hardware: Ensure all cables are tightly connected, double-check your SCSI chain's termination, and make sure the tape drive's SCSI ID is unique on the chain. After power-up you should see a SCSI card BIOS message printed by the adapter, followed by the SCSI devices that were detected.

When the drive has been recognized, insert a tape into the drive so that you can test basic tape operations using the `mt` command. The `mt` command can take many options, which are all listed in the mt manual page accessible with the command `man mt`.

To check the status of the tape drive and the inserted tape, use the `status` options of the `mt` command. The `-f` flag is used to specify the tape drive:

```
# mt -f /dev/nst0 status
SCSI 2 tape drive:
File number=0, block number=0, partition=0.
Tape block size 512 bytes. Density code 0x30 (unknown to this mt).
Soft error count since last status=0
General status bits on (81010000):
 EOF ONLINE IM_REP_EN
```

Note

In the above example `/dev/nst0` was used instead of `/dev/st0`. This refers to the same device as `/dev/st0` but as a non-rewinding tape device. When referenced as a non-rewinding tape device such as `/dev/nst0`, the tape will not rewind after a tape read or write operation.

Tip

It is generally preferable to use the non-rewinding tape device (`/dev/nst0` instead of `/dev/st0`, for example) in backup situations. This allows the backup software to determine how and when the tape is rewound.

In this example we used the `-f` option to specify the specific tape device to test. We can make a particular tape device the default tape device so that we do not need to specify it with the `-f` flag. This is useful because many systems only have a single tape drive and specifying this drive as the default makes it easier to work with the drive.

To make your drive the default drive, create a symbolic link `/dev/tape` to your tape device:

```
# ln -s /dev/nst0 /dev/tape
```

When the default tape device is specified in this manner, you only need to use the `-f` option of the `mt` command to work with a tape drive other than the specified default. Therefore, we can test the status of the default drive as follows:

```
# mt status
SCSI 2 tape drive:
File number=5, block number=0, partition=0.
Tape block size 512 bytes. Density code 0x30 (unknown to this mt).
Soft error count since last status=0
General status bits on (81010000):
 EOF ONLINE IM_REP_EN
```

After you have checked the status of your tape drive, erase the tape in the drive with the erase option of the mt command. This command should not generate any errors:

```
# mt erase
```

In addition to erasing your tape, you should be able to rewind and eject the tape. To rewind the tape, use the rewind option of the mt command:

```
# mt rewind
```

To eject the tape, take the drive offline with the offline option of the mt command:

```
# mt offline
```

Tip   You can rewind and eject the tape with one command: mt rewoffl.

WHAT BACKUP SOFTWARE TO USE

Linux distributions normally include some standard data archiving applications that can be used to perform backups and restore from backups. In particular, Linux distributions include the following:

- tar: a tape archiving program
- dump and restore: a pair of programs for creating and restoring from full and incremental backups

In addition, the freely available Amanda package provides a complete environment for creating a robust networked backup regime.

BACKING UP WITH tar

The name *tar* stands for *tape archiver*. tar is an archiving program which takes multiple files and directories and stores them in a single file, which can be written to a tape or to a file on a hard disk.

Linux includes the GNU version of tar that provides multi-volume support as well as incremental and full backup capabilities.

tar can be operated in three modes as indicated by the first flag:

- `tar c`: Create mode for creating and appending to an archive
- `tar x`: Extract mode for extracting files from the archive
- `tar t`: List mode for listing the table of contents of the archive

By combining the initial mode flag with the wide variety of other flags available for `tar`, you have fine-grained control over the way in which tar operates.

WRITING A `tar` FILE TO TAPE

To back up the entire directory hierarchy to tape, use tar as follows:

```
tar cvf <device or file for backup> <directory to backup>
```

For instance, to back up the `/usr` directory to your tape drive, use the following command:

```
# tar cvf /dev/tape /usr
```

The v flag indicates that `tar` should operate in verbose mode. This means that the complete pathname of each file written to the backup file will be displayed on the console. If you prefer silent operation, omit the v flag. The f flag should precede the file (or device) where the backup file should be stored. In this case it precedes `/dev/tape` indicating `/dev/tape` is the destination location for the backup file.

Note Without the f flag, `tar` will attempt to back up to its default device, which is `/dev/rmt0`. This is the typical default tape device on some Unix systems and normally is not available on Linux systems. For this reason, you will always need to use the f flag when using tar in Linux.

LISTING THE CONTENTS OF A `tar` FILE ON TAPE

To list in detail the contents of a `tar` file on tape, use the following steps:

1. Rewind the tape:
   ```
   # mt rewind
   ```

2. Position the head at the start of the desired file. For instance, to position the head at the start of the fifth file, use the following command:
   ```
   # mt fsf 5
   ```

3. Display a list of the table of contents of the file:
   ```
   # tar tf /dev/tape | more
   ```

Notice the use of the f flag of the `tar` command to indicate the device containing the backup file to list the contents of. The output is piped through more because backup files generally contain numerous files and it will be necessary to view the list one screen at a time.

RESTORING FILES FROM TAPE

If you want to extract everything from a `tar` file on tape to your current location in your Linux directory structure, you would use tar as follows:

```
tar xf <location of backup file>
```

Typically, you want to restore files to a different location than they were originally backed up from and then move them to the real location. This is safer than backing up over the existing files because it prevents the introduction of problems should backup fail before it is complete or if the data stored on the backup media is corrupt.

For instance, if you want to restore the `/usr` directory from its tape backup file to the `/restore` directory and then move the files to the `/usr` directory, use the following steps:

1. Change your current directory to `/restore`:
   ```
   # cd /restore
   ```

2. Make sure you have enough disk space available with the `df .` command.

3. Rewind the tape:
   ```
   # mt rewind
   ```

4. Extract the contents of the backup file with the command:
   ```
   # tar xf /dev/tape ./usr
   ```

5. Check the files and then move them to `/usr`.

If you want to specify files to extract from a backup file, specify them in the `tar` command:

```
tar xf <location of backup file> <filename to extract> <filename to extract>...
```

If you do not specify any filenames, then `tar` extracts the entire backup file.

Caution

> `tar` extracts files to the current working directory with the same names that files had when they were archived. Be careful not to overwrite existing files with the same names.

USING dump AND restore

With the `dump` program you can perform full or incremental backups. The `dump` command keeps track of the times of previous backups in a file called `/etc/dumpdates`. The program builds a list of files that have changed since the last backup and then can create one large archive constituting all these files and write it to tape or other media.

Depending on the needs of your site, you may decide to run full backups every day or you may run full backups once a week, or fortnight, or month, and then run incremental backups periodically between these full backups.

The type of backup to perform is specified using dump levels. Dump levels are specified numerically. Dump level zero indicates a full backup and dump levels 1-9 indicate that an incremental backup should be performed where all files modified since the last run with a level less than or equal to the specified dump level are archived.

To use dump to perform a backup, use the following syntax:

`dump <dump level>usf <tape length> <tape device> <partition to back up>`

The u flag indicates that dump should update /etc/dumpdates so that incremental backups are possible. Entries will be created in the /etc/dumpdates file of the form:

`<partition> <dump level> <date and time>`

For instance, the following entry indicates that the /dev/sdb2 partition was backed up on December 27 and a full backup (dump level zero) was performed:

`/dev/sdb2      0 Mon Dec 27 22:18:47 1999`

The s flag in combination with the tape length value specifies the length of the tape being used in feet. If you don't know the length of your tape, use an arbitrarily large number such as 650,000 because the default length is only 2,300 feet, which means that dump will prompt you to change your tape well before the tape is filled. Finally, the f flag in combination with the tape device indicates where the backup should be stored.

For instance, consider the following command:

`# dump 9usf 650000 /dev/tape /opt`

This command indicates that the partition mounted at /opt should be backed up to the tape device using a level 9 incremental backup.

The dump command generates output indicating the partition being backed up, the success of each stage of the backup, and the time taken to complete the backup, as illustrated in the following example:

```
# dump 0usf 650000 /dev/tape /opt
  DUMP: Date of this level 0 dump: Tue Dec 28 22:14:04 1999
  DUMP: Date of last level 0 dump: the epoch
  DUMP: Dumping /dev/sda6 (/opt) to /dev/tape
  DUMP: mapping (Pass I) [regular files]
  DUMP: mapping (Pass II) [directories]
  DUMP: estimated 14685 tape blocks on 0.34 tape(s).
  DUMP: dumping (Pass III) [directories]
  DUMP: dumping (Pass IV) [regular files]
  DUMP: DUMP: 14852 tape blocks on 1 volumes(s)
  DUMP: finished in 11 seconds, throughput 1350 KBytes/sec
  DUMP: Closing /dev/tape
  DUMP: DUMP IS DONE
```

RESTORING FILES AND FILE SYSTEMS

The restore command allows you to restore files and directories from backups created with the dump command. The restore command can be used to recover an entire file system hierarchy from a level 0 dump and incremental dumps that follow it or one or more files from one or more dump tapes. The restore command must be run by the root user, so that file ownerships, modes, and times can be restored to match the original files.

The following command will restore an entire file system hierarchy:

```
# restore rf /dev/tape
```

The r flag indicates that you want to restore an entire file system and the f flag along with /dev/tape specifies the source of the backup data.

The restore command can be used to restore files interactively using the i flag. When invoked with the i flag, the restore command provides an interactive shell where you can change directories within a backup set, list directory contents, and extract files.

Consider the following example where the file /opt/src/amanda-2.4.1p1.tar.gz is restored to the temporary /restore directory:

```
# cd /restore
# mt rewind
# restore if /dev/tape
restore > ls
.:
lost+found/ src/
restore > cd src
restore > ls
./src:
README                   amanda-2.4.1p1.tar.gz  glibc22.patch
amanda-2.4.1p1/          glibc21.patch
restore > add amanda-2.4.1p1.tar.gz
restore > extract
You have not read any tapes yet.
Unless you know which volume your file(s) are on you should start
with the last volume and work towards the first.
Specify next volume #: 1
set owner/mode for '.'? [yn] n
restore > quit
# ls
lost+found   src
# cd src
# ls -l
total 697
-rw-r--r--   1 root     root       709624 Nov 21  1998 amanda-2.4.1p1.tar.gz
```

Within the interactive restore shell, two commands are critical:

- add <filename>: Adds a file to the set of files to be restored
- extract: Restores the specified set of files from the backup to the current location

BACKING UP WITH AMANDA

Amanda is a freely available backup software program developed at the University of Maryland. The name AMANDA stands for Advanced Maryland Automated Network Disk Archiver. Its primary author is James da Silva of the University of Maryland.

Amanda is ideally suited to backing up medium and large networks. It allows you to perform network backup of multiple machines to a central backup server. Amanda uses GNU `tar` or the native dump program available with most Linux systems to perform backups. Used in conjunction with Samba, Amanda can also back up Windows 95 and NT machines.

The philosophy behind Amanda is to centralize backup of many machines onto a master tape server that has one or more tape drives and a large holding disk. Backup of many systems can be done over the network to the holding disk on the backup server. Several network backups can also be done in parallel. Once data has been backed up to the holding disk, it is written to a fast tape drive in a continuous streaming mode. This provides for efficient tape writing without tape interruption.

> **Note**
>
> Amanda can operate without a holding disk: Data from network clients can be written directly to tape but performance will be degraded and the total backup time can increase by several fold.

Amanda backup software is comprised of a suite of client and server software. Amanda provides its own networking protocols that run on top of standard UDP and TCP protocols. Currently Amanda uses UDP port 10080, and TCP ports 10082 and 10083 for communication between Amanda clients and servers. Amanda provides a very flexible data compression scheme that be configured to compress data on the tape server to reduce load on the client machines, or to compress data on the clients and reduce network traffic between the clients and the tape server.

Amanda is a powerful piece of software; to fully understand and master it requires time. Consider subscribing to the Amanda mailing list by sending a message to `amanda-users-request@amanda.org`. This is a good resource for learning more about Amanda and getting help from other administrators running Amanda.

BUILDING AMANDA FROM SOURCE

You can download the Amanda source code from `http://www.amanda.org`. The latest stable version at the time of this writing is 2.4.1p1. Amanda requires certain other software packages to be available on the system before compiling the software:

- GNU `tar` 1.12 or later version
- Perl 5.004 or later version
- GNU `readline` 2.2.1 or later version
- GNU `awk` 3.0.3 or later version
- Gnuplot 3.5 or later version

If you are going to back up Windows 95, 98, NT, or 2000 client systems using Amanda, you will also need to install Samba 1.9.18p10 or later version on the Amanda backup server.

THE BUILD PROCESS

Use the following steps to install Amanda from the source code:

1. Download the Amanda archive and save it in a convenient location such as `/usr/local/src`. At the time of writing, the current version of the source code archive was `amanda-2.4.1p1.tar.gz`.

2. Change your current directory to `/usr/local/src`:

   ```
   # cd /usr/local/src
   ```

3. Extract the source code archive:

   ```
   # tar xzf amanda-2.4.1p1.tar.gz
   ```

   The source code will be extracted into the subdirectory `amanda-2.4.1p1`.

4. Change your current directory to the new subdirectory:

   ```
   # cd amanda-2.4.1p1
   ```

5. Configure the software with the following command:

   ```
   # ./configure -with-user=bin -with-group=backup \
   --with-tape-device=/dev/nst0 --with-amandahosts
   ```

   The `with-user` option specifies which user the software will run as, the `with-group` option specifies which group the software will run as, the `with-tape-device` option indicates the default tape device, and the `with-amandahosts` option indicates that an `.amandahosts` file will be used instead of an `.rhosts` in configuring Amanda. The user that is to run Amanda needs to have sufficient privileges to read and write to any tape drives you will be using; typical choices are `bin`, `amanda`, or `backup` for this purpose. Common group choices include `backup`, `disk`, or `operator`.

   This command will configure Amanda with a default backup configuration named `Daily`. If you want to use a different configuration name, add `--with-config=<your configuration name>` to the `configure` command. If you are compiling Amanda only to run on a client without need to provide Amanda server capabilities, add the `--without-server` option to the `configure` command.

   By default, Amanda will be configured to install in the directories outlined in Table 10.1.

TABLE 10.1 AMANDA INSTALLATION DIRECTORIES

Directory	Description
`/usr/local/sbin`	Directory containing server-side binaries.
`/usr/local/libexec`	Directory containing client-side binaries.
`/usr/local/lib`	Directory containing Amanda (shared) libraries.
`/usr/local/man`	Directory containing the manual pages.
`/usr/local/etc/ amanda`	Directory where the runtime files are found. Amanda supports multiple configurations per site; these are contained in subdirectories of this directory.

TABLE 10.1   CONTINUED

Directory	Description
`/usr/local/var/ amanda/gnutar-lists`	This specifies the directory where gnutar should place the listed incremental directory lists it uses to do incremental backups.
`/tmp/amanda`	Directory where debug output of different Amanda programs are stored.

The `configure` command will build a `makefile` for your system.

6. Compile Amanda with the following command:

   `# make >& make.out`

7. Install the compiled software with this command:

   `# make install >& make.install.out`

8. Open the `/etc/services` file on your Amanda server and all Amanda clients in a text editor. If you are running NIS, open the file on your master NIS server.

9. Add the following lines to the `/etc/services` file:

   ```
   amanda    10080/udp
   amandaidx  10082/tcp
   amidxtape  10083/tcp
   ```

10. Save `/etc/services` and close your text editor.

11. If you are running NIS, rebuild your NIS maps on the master NIS server.

12. Open the `/etc/inetd.conf` file on your Amanda server in a text editor.

13. Add the following entries to the `/etc/inetd.conf` file:

    ```
    amanda   dgram  udp wait bin /usr/local/libexec/amandad   amandad
    amandaidx stream tcp nowait bin /usr/local/libexec/amindexd amindexd
    amidxtape stream tcp nowait bin /usr/local/libexec/amidxtaped amidxtaped
    ```

14. Save `/etc/inetd.conf` and close your text editor.

15. Open the `/etc/inetd.conf` file on all your Amanda clients in a text editor.

16. Add the following entry to these `/etc/inetd.conf` files:

    ```
    amanda   dgram  udp wait bin /usr/local/libexec/amandad   amandad
    ```

17. Save the files and close your text editor.

18. Send a SIGHUP signal to inetd on all systems where you edited `inetd.conf` with the command:

    `# kill -1 `cat /var/run/inetd.pid``

CONFIGURING AMANDA

On Amanda client machines as well as on the server, after installing the Amanda binaries and adding the required entries to `/etc/services` and `/etc/inetd.conf`, you need to create an `.amandahosts` file (`.rhosts` if you didn't use the `with-amandahosts` option of the `configure` command).

PART

II

CH

10

The `.amandahosts` or `.rhosts` file must be created in the Amanda user's home directory. The file needs to contain a single entry of the following form:

```
<Amanda server host name or IP address> <Amanda user name>
```

For instance, if your server is `tape.some.host` and the Amanda user is `bin`, the entry should be the following:

```
tape.some.host bin
```

In addition, on the Amanda server you need to create the `amanda.conf` and `disklist` files. Amanda includes default `amanda.conf` and `disklist` files that you can use as the basis of your configuration.

You can install these files as follows:

1. Select a name for your configuration.
2. Create a configuration directory with this name in `/usr/local/etc/Amanda/` as follows:
   ```
   # mkdir /usr/local/etc/Amanda/<configuration name>
   ```
3. Copy the `amanda.conf` and `disklist` files from the `examples` directory in your source distribution to this new directory:
   ```
   # cp /usr/local/src/amanda-2.4.1p1/examples/amanda.conf.in \
   /usr/local/etc/Amanda/<configuration name>
   # cp /usr/local/src/amanda-2.4.1p1/examples/disklist \
   /usr/local/etc/Amanda/<configuration name>
   ```
4. Edit the files to meet the needs of your site as outlined in the following section.

EDITING THE `amanda.conf` FILE Several pieces of information are needed to correctly edit the `amanda.conf` file for your site:

- The tape device you will use
- The names and sizes of holding disks
- Your dump cycle
- Your preferred backup program (`dump` or `tar`)
- Any partitions you want to compress

If you decide to use holding disks, the size of the holding disk should be large enough to hold at least the two largest backup images to achieve optimal performance. This allows one image to continue writing to the disk while another is being read from the disk and written to tape.

The dump cycle indicates how often you require full dumps. The shorter the dump cycle the easier it will be to restore, because there are fewer incremental tapes; longer dump cycles distribute load better and require fewer tapes.

A sample `amanda.conf` file is listed here. The comments next to each option explain briefly what that option means.

```
#
# amanda.conf - sample Amanda configuration file.
#

org "BWC"          # your organization name for reports
mailto "root"          # space separated list of operators at your site
dumpuser "bin"          # the user to run dumps under
inparallel 4          # maximum dumpers that will run in parallel
netusage  6000 Kbps      # maximum net bandwidth for Amanda, in KB/sec
dumpcycle 4 weeks      # the number of days in the normal dump cycle

runspercycle 20     # the number of amdump runs in dumpcycle days
# (4 weeks * 5 amdump runs per week -- just weekdays)

tapecycle 25 tapes     # the number of tapes in rotation
# 4 weeks (dumpcycle) times 5 tapes per week (just
# the weekdays) plus a few to handle errors that
# need amflush and so we do not overwrite the full
# backups performed at the beginning of the previous
# cycle
### ### ###
# WARNING: don't use `inf' for tapecycle, it's broken!
### ### ###

bumpsize 20 Mb          # minimum savings (threshold) to bump level 1 -> 2
bumpdays 1          # minimum days at each level
bumpmult 4          # threshold = bumpsize * bumpmult^(level-1)
etimeout 300      # number of seconds per filesystem for estimates.
#etimeout -600     # total number of seconds for estimates.
# a positive number will be multiplied by the number of filesystems
# on each host; a negative number will be taken as an absolute total
# time-out.
# The default is 5 minutes per filesystem.


# Specify tape device and/or tape changer.  If you don't have a tape
# changer, and you don't want to use more than one tape per run of
# amdump, just comment out the definition of tpchanger.
# Some tape changers require tapedev to be defined; others will use
# their own tape device selection mechanism. Some use a separate
# tape changer device (changerdev), others will simply ignore this
# parameter.  Some rely on a configuration file (changerfile) to
# obtain more information about tape devices, number of slots, etc;
# others just need to store some data in files, whose names will
# start with changerfile.  For more information about individual
# tape changers, read docs/TAPE.CHANGERS.
# At most one changerfile entry must be defined; select the most
# appropriate one for your configuration.  If you select
# man-changer, keep the first one; if you decide not to use a tape
# changer, you may comment them all out.
runtapes 1     # number of tapes to be used in a single run of amdump
#tpchanger "chg-manual"     # the tape-changer glue script
tapedev "/dev/nst0"     # the no-rewind tape device to be used
rawtapedev "/dev/null"          # the raw device to be used (ftape only)
#changerfile "/usr/adm/amanda/bwc/changer"
#changerfile ''/usr/adm/amanda/bwc/changer-status"
#changerfile "/usr/local/etc/amanda/bwc/changer.conf"
#changerdev "/dev/null"
```

```
tapetype SONY-AIT         # what kind of tape it is (see tapetypes below)
labelstr "^bwc[0-9][0-9]*$" # label constraint regex: all tapes must
#                    match
# Specify holding disks. These are used as a temporary staging area
# for dumps before they are written to tape and are recommended for
# most sites.
# The advantages include: tape drive is more likely to operate in
# streaming mode (which reduces tape and drive wear, reduces total
# dump time); multiple dumps can be done in parallel (which can
# dramatically # reduce total dump time.
# The main disadvantage is that dumps on the holding disk need to be
# flushed (with amflush) to tape after an operating system crash or
# a tape failure.
# If no holding disks are specified then all dumps will be written
# directly to tape.  If a dump is too big to fit on the holding disk
# than it will be written directly to tape.  If more than one
# holding disk is specified then they will all be used round-robin.
holdingdisk hd1 {
comment "main holding disk"
directory "/disk1"    # where the holding disk is
use 2 Gb              # how much space can we use on it
# a negative value mean:
#        use all space except that value
chunksize 1 Gb # size of chunk if you want big dump to be
# dumped on multiple files on holding disks
#   N Kb/Mb/Gb split disks in chunks of size N
#   0          split disks in INT_MAX/1024 Kb chunks
#  -1          same as -INT_MAX/1024 (see below)
# -N Kb/Mb/Gb dont split, dump larger
#             filesystems directly to tape
#             (example: -2 Gb)
}
holdingdisk hd2 {
directory "/disk2"
use 2 Gb
}
# If amanda cannot find a tape on which to store backups, it will
# run as many backups as it can to the holding disks.  In order to
# save space for unattended backups, by default, amanda will only
# perform incremental backups in this case, i.e., it will reserve
# 100% of the holding disk space for the so-called degraded mode
# backups.
# However, if you specify a different value for the `reserve'
# parameter, amanda will not degrade backups if they will fit in the
# non-reserved portion of the holding disk.
# reserve 30 # percent
# This means save at least 30% of the holding disk space for
# degraded mode backups.
# Amanda needs a few Mb of diskspace for the log and debug files,
# as well as a database.  This stuff can grow large, so the conf
# directory isn't usually appropriate.  Some sites use
# /usr/local/var and some /usr/adm.
# Create an amanda directory under there. You need a separate
# infofile and logdir for each configuration, so create
# subdirectories for each conf and put the files there.  Specify the
# locations below.
# Note that, although the keyword below is infofile, it is only so
```

```
# for historic reasons, since now it is supposed to be a directory
# (unless you have selected some database format other than the
# 'text' default)
infofile "/var/adm/amanda/bwc/curinfo"    # database DIRECTORY
logdir   "'/var/adm/amanda/bwc"           # log directory
indexdir "/var/adm/amanda/bwc/index"     # index directory
tapelist "/var/adm/amanda/bwc/tapelist"   # list of used tapes
# tapelist is stored, by default, in the directory that contains
# amanda.conf
# tapetypes
# Define the type of tape you use here, and use it in "tapetype"
# above.  Some typical types of tapes are included here.  The
# tapetype tells amanda how many MB will fit on the tape, how big
# the filemarks are, and how fast the tape device is.
# A filemark is the amount of wasted space every time a tape section
# ends.  If you run `make tapetype' in tape-src, you'll get a
# program that generates tapetype entries, but it is slow as hell,
# use it only if you really must and, if you do, make sure you post
# the data to the amanda mailing list, so that others can use what
# you found out by searching the archives.
# For completeness Amanda should calculate the inter-record gaps
# too, but it doesn't.  For EXABYTE and DAT tapes this is ok.
# Anyone using 9 tracks for amanda and need IRG calculations?  Drop
# me a note if so.
# If you want amanda to print postscript paper tape labels
# add a line after the comment in the tapetype of the form
# lbl-templ "/path/to/postscript/template/label.ps"
# if you want the label to go to a printer other than the default
# for your system, you can also add a line above for a different
# printer. (i usually add that line after the dumpuser
# specification)
# dumpuser "operator"    # the user to run dumps under
# printer "mypostscript" # printer to print paper label on
# here is an example of my definition for an EXB-8500
# define tapetype EXB-8500 {
# ...
#    lbl-templ "/usr/local/amanda/config/lbl.exabyte.ps"
# }
define tapetype SONY-AIT {
comment "Sony AIT "
length 51783 mbytes
filemark 772 kbytes
speed 6783 kbytes
}
define tapetype QIC-60 {
comment "Archive Viper"
length 60 mbytes
filemark 100 kbytes        # don't know a better value
speed 100 kbytes        # dito
}
define tapetype DEC-DLT2000 {
comment "DEC Differential Digital Linear Tape 2000"
length 15000 mbytes
filemark 8 kbytes
speed 1250 kbytes
}
# goluboff@butch.Colorado.EDU
```

```
# in amanda-users (Thu Dec 26 01:55:38 MEZ 1996)
define tapetype DLT {
comment "DLT tape drives"
length 20000 mbytes          # 20 Gig tapes
filemark 2000 kbytes             # I don't know what this means
speed 1536 kbytes          # 1.5 Mb/s
}
define tapetype SURESTORE-1200E {
comment "HP AutoLoader"
length 3900 mbytes
filemark 100 kbytes
speed 500 kbytes
}
define tapetype EXB-8500 {
comment "Exabyte EXB-8500 drive on decent machine"
length 4200 mbytes
filemark 48 kbytes
speed 474 kbytes
}
define tapetype EXB-8200 {
comment "Exabyte EXB-8200 drive on decent machine"
length 2200 mbytes
filemark 2130 kbytes
speed 240 kbytes
}
define tapetype HP-DAT {
comment "DAT tape drives"
# data provided by Rob Browning <rlb@cs.utexas.edu>
length 1930 mbytes
filemark 111 kbytes
speed 468 kbytes
}
define tapetype DAT {
comment "DAT tape drives"
length 1000 mbytes          # these numbers are not accurate
filemark 100 kbytes             # but you get the idea
speed 100 kbytes
}
define tapetype MIMSY-MEGATAPE {
comment "Megatape (Exabyte based) drive through Emulex on Vax 8600"
length 2200 mbytes
filemark 2130 kbytes
speed 170 kbytes          # limited by the Emulex bus interface
}

# dumptypes
#
# These are referred to by the disklist file.  The dumptype
# specifies certain parameters for dumping including:
#    auth    - authentication scheme to use between server and client.
#          Valid values are "bsd" and "krb4".  Default: [auth bsd]
#    comment    - just a comment string
#    comprate - set default compression rate.  Should be followed by
#          one or two numbers, optionally separated by a comma.
#          The 1st is the full compression rate; the 2nd is the
#          incremental rate. If the second is omitted, it is assumed
#          equal to the first.
```

```
#           The numbers represent the amount of the original file the
#           compressed file is expected to take up.
#           Default: [comprate 0.50, 0.50]
#   compress - specify compression of the backed up data. Valid
#           values are:
#           "none"      - don't compress the dump output.
#           "client best" - compress on the client using the best
#           (and probably slowest) algorithm.
#           "client fast" - compress on the client using fast
#           algorithm.
#           "server best" - compress on the tape host using the best
#           (and probably slowest) algorithm.
#            "server fast" - compress on the tape host using a fast
#                       algorithm.  This may be useful when a fast
#                       tape host is backing up slow clients.
#           Default: [compress client fast]
#   dumpcycle - set the number of days in the dump cycle, ie, set
#           how often a full dump should be performed.
#   Default: from DUMPCYCLE above
#   exclude     - specify files and directories to be excluded from
#           the dump. Useful with gnutar only; silently ignored by dump
#           and samba.
#           Valid values are:
#           "pattern"       - a shell glob pattern defining which files
#                       to exclude.
#                       gnutar gets --exclude="pattern"
#           list "filename" - a file (on the client!) containing
#           patterns
#                       re's (1 per line) defining which files to
#                       exclude.
#                       gnutar gets --exclude-from="filename"
#           Note that the `full pathname' of a file within its
#           filesystem starts with `./', because of the way amanda runs
#           gnutar: `tar -C $mountpoint -cf - --lots-of-options .'
#           (note the final dot!) Thus, if you're backing up`/usr'
#           with a diskfile entry like `host /usr gnutar-root', but
#           you don't want to backup /usr/tmp, your exclude list should
#           contain the pattern `./tmp', as this is relative to the
#           `/usr' above. Please refer to the man-page of gnutar for
#           more information.
#           Default: include all files
#
#   holdingdisk    - should the holding disk be used for this
#           dump.   Useful for dumping the holding disk itself.
#   Default: [holdingdisk yes]
#   ignore - do not back this filesystem up. Useful for sharing a
#           single disklist in several configurations.
#   index      - keep an index of the files backed up.
#   Default: [index no]
#   kencrypt - encrypt the data stream between the client and
#           server.
#   Default: [kencrypt no]
#   maxdumps - max number of concurrent dumps to run on the client.
#   Default: [maxdumps 1]
#   priority - priority level of the dump.  Valid levels are "low",
#           "medium", or "high".  These are really only used when
#           Amanda has no tape to write to because of some error. In
```

```
#           that "degraded mode", as many incrementals as will fit on
#           the holding disk are done, higher priority first, to insure
#           the important disks are at least dumped.
#   Default: [priority medium]
#   program   - specify the dump system to use.  Valid values are
#           "DUMP" and "GNUTAR".  Default: [program "DUMP"].
#   record    - record the dump in /etc/dumpdates.  Default:
#           [record yes]
#   skip-full - skip the disk when a level 0 is due, to allow full
#           backups outside Amanda, eg when the machine is in
#           single-user mode.
#   skip-incr - skip the disk when the level 0 is NOT due. This is
#           used in archive configurations, where only full dumps are
#           done and the tapes saved.
#   starttime - delay the start of the dump? Default: no delay
#   strategy  - set the dump strategy.  Valid strategies are
#           currently:
#           "standar" - the standard one.
#           "nofull"   - do level 1 dumps every time. This can be
#           used, for example, for small root filesystems that
#           only change slightly relative to a site-wide prototype.
#           Amanda then backs up just the changes.
#           "noinc" - do level 0 dumps every time.
#                   Unfortunately, this is not currently
#                   implemented.  Use `dumpcycle 0'
#                   instead.
#           "skip" - skip all dumps.  Useful for sharing a single
#                       disklist in several configurations.
#   Default: [strategy standard]
#
# Note that you may specify previously defined dumptypes as a
# shorthand way of defining parameters.
define dumptype global {
comment "Global definitions"
# This is quite useful for setting global parameters, so you don't
# have to type them everywhere.  All dumptype definitions in this
# sample file do include these definitions, either directly or
# indirectly.
# There's nothing special about the name `global'; if you create any
# dumptype that does not contain the word `global' or the name of
# any other dumptype that contains it, these definitions won't
# apply.
# Note that these definitions may be overridden in other
# dumptypes, if the redefinitions appear *after* the `global'
# dumptype name.
# You may want to use this for globally enabling or disabling
# indexing, recording, etc.  Some examples:
index yes
# record no
}
define dumptype always-full {
global
comment "Full dump of this filesystem always"
compress none
priority high
dumpcycle 0
}
```

```
define dumptype root-tar {
global
program "GNUTAR"
comment "root partitions dumped with tar"
compress none
index
exclude list "/usr/local/etc/amanda/bwc/exclude.gtar"
priority low
}
define dumptype user-tar {
root-tar
comment "user partitions dumped with tar"
priority medium
}
define dumptype high-tar {
root-tar
comment "partitions dumped with tar"
priority high
}
define dumptype comp-root-tar {
root-tar
comment "Root partitions with compression"
compress client fast
}
define dumptype comp-user-tar {
user-tar
compress client fast
}
define dumptype holding-disk {
global
comment "The master-host holding disk itself"
holdingdisk no # do not use the holding disk
priority medium
}
define dumptype comp-user {
global
comment "Non-root partitions on reasonably fast machines"
compress client fast
priority medium
}
define dumptype nocomp-user {
comp-user
comment "Non-root partitions on slow machines"
compress none
}
define dumptype comp-root {
global
comment "Root partitions with compression"
compress client fast
priority low
}
define dumptype nocomp-root {
comp-root
comment "Root partitions without compression"
compress none
}
define dumptype comp-high {
```

```
global
comment "very important partitions on fast machines"
compress client best
priority high
}
define dumptype nocomp-high {
comp-high
comment "very important partitions on slow machines"
compress none
}
define dumptype nocomp-test {
global
comment "test dump without compression, no /etc/dumpdates recording"
compress none
record no
priority medium
}
define dumptype comp-test {
nocomp-test
comment "test dump with compression, no /etc/dumpdates recording"
compress client fast
}
# network interfaces
#
# These are referred to by the disklist file.  They define the attributes
# of the network interface that the remote machine is accessed
# through.
# Notes: - netusage above defines the attributes that are used when
#          the disklist entry doesn't specify otherwise.
#        - the values below are only samples.
#        - specifying an interface does not force the traffic to
#          pass through that interface. Your OS routing tables do
#          that. This is just a mechanism to stop Amanda trashing your
#          network.
# Attributes are:
#    use        - bandwidth above which amanda won't start
#                 backups using this interface.  Note that if
#                 a single backup will take more than that,
#                 amanda won't try to make it run slower!
define interface local {
comment "a local disk"
use 1000 kbps
}
define interface le0 {
comment "10 Mbps ethernet"
use 400 kbps
}
# You may include other amanda configuration files, so you can share
# dumptypes, tapetypes and interface definitions among several
# configurations.
#includefile "/usr/local/amanda.conf.main"
```

Several entries in this file bear further analysis because you will need to customize them for your site. These are outlined in Table 10.2.

TABLE 10.2   CUSTOMIZING THE `amanda.conf` FILE

Entries	Description
`org "BWC"`	This entry specifies your organization name, which is used in reports generated by Amanda. In this case, the organization's name is `BWC`.
`mailto "root"`	This entry specifies a space-separated list of user accounts for operators of your backup system.
`dumpuser "bin"`	This entry specifies the Amanda user, in this case `bin`.
`inparallel 4`	This entry specifies the maximum number of dumps that can run in parallel.
`netusage 6000 Kbps`	This entry indicates the maximum bandwidth Amanda should be allowed to consume so that sufficient network bandwidth remains for other network activity.
`dumpcycle 4 weeks`	This entry specifies the length of the dump cycle you have selected for your site.
`runspercycle 20`	This entry specifies the number of dumps that will be executed during each cycle period. This determines the number of incremental backups between each full backup.
`tapespercycle 25 tapes`	This entry specifies the number of physical tapes available in your backup cycle.
`runtapes 1`	This entry specifies the number of tapes to use for each backup dump.
`tapedev "/dev/nst0"`	This entry specifies the tape device to use for backups, in this case `/dev/nst0`.
`tapetype SONY-AIT`	This entry specifies the name of the tape type used in the default tape device. The name specified refers to a `tapetype` definition later in the `amanda.conf` file.
`holdingdisk <holding disk name> ...`	This entry block defines the directory and size of a holding disk area. Multiple `holdingdisk` blocks can be used to define more than one holding disk area.
`define tapetype <tape type name> ...`	This entry block defines the length, file mark, and speed of a tape device type. The default `amanda.conf` file contains entry blocks of this type for most popular tape device types. You can define your own tape device type as well.
`define dumptype <dump type name> ...`	This entry block defines a dump type which can then be referred to in the `disklist` file. These blocks define particular methods for dumping a backup to tape including the program to use, if compression is necessary, and files and directories to exclude. The default `amanda.conf` file contains a predefined set of dump types. You can define additional types of your own.
`define interface <interface name> ...`	This entry block defines how to use a network interface, specifying how much bandwidth of an interface can be used by Amanda. These interfaces can then be referred to in the `disklist` file when defining actual backups. The default `amanda.conf` file contains a predefined set of interface definitions. You can define additional ones if you need to.

PART

II

CH

10

EDITING THE disklist FILE The disklist file specifies the partitions to back up and how to do so. It consists of a series of entries, one per line, taking the following form:

`<host name> <disk device> <dump type>`

Optionally, an entry can include a spindle and interface specification:

`<host name> <disk device> <dump type> <spindle> <interface>`

The hostname specifies the hostname of an Amanda client system from which to back up. The disk device is the mount point of a partition on that host to back up and the dump type indicates a dump type from the amanda.conf file, which indicates how to back up the partition. The interface field indicates an interface definition from amanda.conf that specifies how to use the network connection for the backup (such as limiting bandwidth consumption).

A typical entry would look like the following:

```
host.to.backup /directory dump-type
```

TESTING AMANDA

To test your Amanda configuration, use the following steps:

1. Insert a blank into the tape drive.

2. Label the tape with the amlabel command. Each tape needs a unique label and a common naming scheme is `<configuration name>-<tape number>` such as Daily-00 or mis-99. To label the Daily-00, use the following command:

   ```
   # /usr/local/sbin/amlabel Daily-00
   ```

3. Become the Amanda user. If bin is the Amanda user, use the following command:

   ```
   # su - bin
   ```

4. Test your Amanda setup with amcheck. If your configuration is named Daily, use the following command:

   ```
   $ /usr/local/sbin/amcheck Daily
   Amanda Tape Server Host Check
   -----------------------------
   /disk2: 1946168 KB disk space available, that's plenty.
   /disk1: 1940746 KB disk space available, that's plenty.
   NOTE: skipping tape-writable test.
   Tape Daily-00 label ok.
   Server check took 16.071 seconds.
   Amanda Backup Client Hosts Check
   --------------------------------
   Client check: 2 hosts checked in 0.209 seconds, 0 problems found.
   (brought to you by Amanda 2.4.1p1)
   ```

   This output reports the space available on the holding disks, indicates the tape label, reports the server check results, and reports the availability of the clients.

5. If amcheck runs without errors, perform a test dump with the amdump command:

   ```
   # amdump -m Daily
   ```

The -m flag causes a report of the results of the dump to be emailed to the operators specified in the amanda.conf file.

SETTING UP AMANDA TO RUN FROM cron

After you have successfully run some Amanda tests, you are ready to add Amanda-related crontab entries for unattended scheduled backups. Create the following two crontab entries listed in the Amanda user's crontab file:

```
0 16 * * 1-5 /usr/local/sbin/amcheck -m Daily
45 0 * * 2-6 /usr/local/sbin/amdump Daily
```

Replace Daily with the name of your backup configuration. Also change the times of the cron jobs to suit your site's needs. The amcheck job should run well in advance of the scheduled dump so that the email report which is generated can be reviewed by an operator, and if problems exist they can be addressed before the nightly backup.

RESTORING WITH AMANDA

Amanda provides two tools to perform data restore operations: amrecover and amrestore. In the following sections we will discuss both amrecover and amrestore.

amrecover   You can restore files backed up with Amanda by running the amrecover program on a backup client machine. The prerequisites for using amrecover are the following:

- The dumptype index parameter must be set to yes in amanda.conf on the Amanda server machine.

- The amindexd and amidxtaped services must be installed and enabled in inetd.conf on the Amanda server machine.

- The fully qualified name of the client machine and the root user must be added to the .amandahosts or .rhosts file on the Amanda server machine. This is necessary because amrecover needs to run as root on the client to be able to restore files. It also connects to the Amanda server machine to access the index databases and tape drives.

An index of backed up files in each dump image is generated as part of the dump process and stored in a database. With amrecover you can browse this database and select files and directories that you want to restore. After the selection is done you can start the restore operation, which reads the selected files from tape and writes it back to disk.

The syntax of the amrecover program is as follows:

```
amrecover -C <backup configuration> -s  <index server> \
-t <tape server>  -d <tape device>
```

The backup configuration is the name of the backup configuration specified on the Amanda server. The index server is the Amanda server that contains the backup index database. The tape server is the Amanda server containing the tape device and the tape device is the full

PART

II

CH

10

device name of the tape device on that tape server (such as /dev/nst0). Typically, the index server and the tape server are one and the same.

After the amrecover program has been invoked, it provides an interactive shell within which you can select and restore files. The following is a sample amrecover session:

```
# cd /
# amrecover -C Daily -s tapeserver -t tapeserver -d /dev/tape
AMRECOVER Version 2.4.1p1. Contacting server on tapeserver...
220 tapeserver AMANDA index server (2.4.1p1) ready.
200 Access OK
Setting restore date to today (2000-01-03)
200 Working date set to 2000-01-03.
200 Config set to Daily.
200 Dump host set to clientsystem.
$CWD '/' is on disk '/' mounted at '/'.
200 Disk set to /.
/
amrecover> ls
2000-01-01 .
2000-01-01 bin/
2000-01-01 boot/
2000-01-01 dev/
2000-01-01 etc/
2000-01-01 export/
2000-01-01 home/
2000-01-01 lib/
2000-01-01 lost+found/
2000-01-01 misc/
2000-01-01 mnt/
2000-01-01 opt/
2000-01-01 root/
2000-01-01 sbin/
2000-01-01 tmp/
2000-01-01 u/
2000-01-01 usr/
2000-01-01 var/
amrecover> cd /opt/src
/opt/src
amrecover> ls
2000-01-01 .
2000-01-01 amanda-2.4.1p1.tar.gz
2000-01-01 amanda-2.4.1p1/
2000-01-01 glibc21.patch
amrecover> add amanda-2.4.1p1.tar.gz glibc21.patch
Added /opt/src/amanda-2.4.1p1.tar.gz at date 2000-01-01
Added /opt/src/glibc21.patch
amrecover> lcd /var/tmp
amrecover> extract
Extracting files using tape drive /dev/tape on host cstlx001.
The following tapes are needed: BWC1Vol001
Restoring files into directory /var/tmp
Continue? [Y/n]: Y
Load tape BWC1Vol001 now
Continue? [Y/n]: Y
./opt/src/amanda-2.4.1p1.tar.gz
./opt/src/glibc21.patch
```

```
amrecover> quit
200 Good bye.
```

This `amrecover` session is quite simple:

- The `ls` command lists the contents of the current directory in the backup index.
- The `cd` command changes directory in the backup index.
- The `add` command adds a file in the index to the list of files to be restored.
- The `lcd` command changes the local directory to which the files will be restored. In this case the files will be recovered to a temporary directory `/var/tmp`.
- The `extract` command starts the restoration process. `amrecover` will prompt you for any tapes that need to be inserted on the Amanda tape server.
- The `quit` command ends the `amrecover` session.

`amrestore`   Although `amrecover` is very handy for interactive restore of individual files and directories, it is not ideally suited to recovering entire file systems. `amrestore` is better suited to this task.

The `amrestore` command restores whole backup images from tape. Before using `amrestore`, you must locate the tapes containing the backup images you wish to restore. There are several ways you can achieve this:

- After every run of `amdump`, a report of the dump is mailed to the backup administrator. As a backup administrator you should archive these messages. These reports tell you the hostnames of systems backed up, names of disks or file systems, backup levels (incremental or full), tape labels, and the status of the dump (success or failure). You can use these reports to find the tapes you need to restore a specific file system for a specific host.
- Using the `amadmin` utility provided with Amanda you can obtain a report of the tapes which contain a specific file system. The syntax of the command is `amadmin <configuration name> <host name> <partition>` such as `amadmin Daily clientsystem /directory`.
- You can generate a table of contents of a tape using the `amtoc` command after `amdump` has run.

When the tape is selected for restore, you should use the `mt rewind` and the `mt fsf <file number>` commands to pre-position the tape to the file of interest. This reduces considerably the time needed to do a restore.

`amrestore` extracts files from tape that match hostname, disk name and date stamp patterns given on the command line.

PART

II

CH

10

The amrestore command has several command line options:

- -p: The -p causes amrestore to return the restored content through the standard output for piping to another program instead of storing the files in the current directory.

- -c: The -c option allows you to restore files to a temporary area in a compressed format and later uncompress and move them to their proper locations.

- -r: The -r option writes out raw images exactly as they are on tape, including the amdump file headers. This option is useful for debugging purposes.

- -h: The -h option writes out the tape header block at the beginning of each file. The amrecover program uses information in the header block to determine which restore program to run.

To perform an interactive restore of the partition sdb2 on the host somesystem that was backed up with dump, use the following command:

```
$ amrestore -p /dev/tape somesystem sdb2 ¦ restore ivbf 2 -
```

The following command restores all files for host somesystem that are on a tape:

```
$ amrestore -p /dev/nst0 somesystem
```

DISASTER RECOVERY

The procedure described here is a general approach to disaster recovery and will work with any Linux distribution. *Disaster recovery* is the process of recovering from a disaster such as a system disk failure.

In the event of a system disk failure you will need to boot the affected system using an emergency root-boot floppy disk. Such a disk, due to obvious space limitations, will only hold the minimum set of tools necessary to boot the system, and recover files from a local tape device or a network file store. Therefore it is necessary to back up the operating system using native archiving tools such as tar or cpio.

In addition, you should back up the partition table data of the system separately on a network store or onto tape. This data will be necessary to partition the new disk to exactly match the failed system disk.

The steps involved in restoring the operating system to a new disk are the following:

1. Locate and mount the tape containing the most recent backup of the operating system on a networked tape system.

2. Restore the operating system and the partition table data to a file system where you have adequate free space. You may want to print a hardcopy of the partition table for later reference.

3. Export this file system to allow NFS mounting by client computers.

4. Replace the failed operating system disk with a new disk of the same capacity or larger.

5. Boot the new system using an emergency root-boot floppy.

6. Using the partition table printout, partition the new disk appropriately with the `fdisk` utility. Mark the root partition active. Create a swap partition. Create file systems as needed on the newly created partitions and prepare the swap partition.

7. NFS mount the network file system containing the restored operating system files.

8. Restore the operating system files onto the new disk using native tools such as `tar` or `cpio`, whichever you used when you created the backup image.

9. Install the boot block on the new system disk with `lilo`.

10. Reboot the system and you are all done.

It is generally more convenient to use tape drives attached to an existing networked backup server to perform restores than to attach a spare SCSI controller and a tape unit to the new system. But if you prefer to use a local tape drive instead, you can restore directly from the tape to the new disk rather than using an intermediate NFS mounted network file system. The ultimate goal is to restore the system quickly, and whatever method works better for a particular environment should be used.

RESTORING THE OPERATING SYSTEM TO A NEW DISK

The following example illustrates the steps in a system restoration. In this example, you will consider using an existing backup server and an intermediate network file system that can be accessed through NFS from the computer you are recovering to get at the backed up data.

For this example, use Tom's root-boot disk as the emergency repair disk. It can be downloaded from ftp://metalab.unc.edu/pub/Linux/system/recovery/tomsrtbt-1.7.185.tar.gz. Tom's root-boot disk comes with SCSI drivers for commonly used SCSI controllers, and Ethernet drivers for a variety of network adapters. It also contains all the utilities needed to perform the restoration, such as `ls`, `mount`, `umount`, `fdisk`, `mke2fs`, `mkswap`, `tar`, `cat`, `chroot`, and `lilo`.

Unpack the `tomsrtbt-1.7.185.tar.gz` archive and build the root-boot floppy based on instructions in the file `tomsrtbt.FAQ`. You will need a 1.44MB floppy disk with no bad blocks. After unpacking, the directory contents will look like the following:

```
$ ls tomsrtbt-1.7.185
buildit.s   fdflush   install.s   tomsrtbt.FAQ   unpack.s
clone.s     fdformat  settings.s  tomsrtbt.raw
```

Put the floppy disk into the floppy drive and run `install.s`. This will format the floppy to 1722KB capacity, write the `tomsrtbt.raw` image to the disk, and copy a few other files on to the floppy disk. Before we can use this floppy disk, some customization of the `settings.s` file will be necessary, as explained later in this section.

As mentioned earlier, you must save the partition table data somewhere on a network store or tape. In this example you will back up the system files and the partition table to a network file system, and later use it to rebuild the system. In a real situation, you will first need to restore these files from tape to this network store.

Assume your local system is called `client1`, and you have a server with a tape drive called `tapeserver`, which has a file system called `/backup` that is exported for NFS mounting. The following commands will write the partition table, copy the `/etc/fstab` file, and backup the operating system onto `tapeserver:/backup` using `tar` and `gzip`:

```
client1# mount tapeserver:/backup /mnt
client1# fdisk -l > /mnt/client1-partition-table
client1# cd /; tar cf - . | gzip -c > /mnt/client1-root.tar.gz
```

Now assume that the system disk has crashed and you need to restore the system from backup. For simplicity, consider a system that has a single `/` file system. If you have separate `/boot`, `/usr`, and `/var` file systems, you must back these up also using `tar` and `gzip`.

Before you can use the root-boot floppy you must edit the `settings.s` file. This is done by first mounting the floppy and then editing this file, and unmounting the floppy. The values that need changing are the IP address, DNS domain, network address, and network mask.

Mount the root-boot floppy using the following command:

```
# mount -o minix /dev/fd0u1722 /mnt/floppy
```

Note

The file system on the floppy disk is of type `minix`, and your kernel must support this file system type. If not, you must recompile the kernel adding `minix` file system support, or find another Linux system that supports it to mount and edit the files on the floppy.

An unedited listing of the first few lines of `settings.s` file can be displayed running the following commands:

```
# cd /mnt/floppy
# more settings.s
DOMAIN=rb.com
IF_PORT=10baseT
DNS_1=192.168.1.1
IPADDR=192.168.1.9
NETWORK=192.168.1.0
NETMASK=255.255.255.0
...
```

These default values must be edited to suit your network configuration. A sample edited `settings.s` file with values that suit our network is listed here:

```
DOMAIN=bwc.org
IF_PORT=100baseT
DNS_1=10.0.0.2
IPADDR=10.2.0.101
NETWORK=10.2.0.0
NETMASK=255.255.0.0
```

You must use values that fit the network settings for your system on the root-boot floppy disk. Save the edited file and unmount the root-boot floppy disk:

```
# cd /
# umount /mnt/floppy
```

Now you are ready to boot the system to be restored using this root-boot floppy disk.

BOOT THE SYSTEM

Insert the customized root-boot floppy disk into the floppy drive and boot the system. Make sure the system BIOS is set to boot from floppy disk first, and not from the hard disk or CD-ROM drive. At the boot prompt press Enter. Next you will be prompted for the keyboard type. Select the appropriate one and press Enter; to select the US type keyboard, simply press Enter. Next you will be prompted to log in. Log in as root and enter the default password xxxx. If you want to change this default password you can do so by editing the settings.s file discussed earlier.

CREATE PARTITIONS, FILE SYSTEMS, AND SWAP SPACE

Next you can partition the hard drive. Mount the NFS file system that contains the partition table and the backed-up operating system and check the directory listing:

```
# mount tapeserver:/backup /mnt
# ls /mnt
client1-partition-table          client1-root.tar.gz
```

Display the contents of the partition table of the client1 system:

```
# cat /mnt/client1-partition-table
Disk /dev/hda: 64 heads, 63 sectors, 1023 cylinders
Units = cylinders of 4032 * 512 bytes
   Device Boot    Start      End    Blocks   Id  System
/dev/hda1    *        1      900  1814368+   83  Linux
/dev/hda2           901     1023   247968     5  Extended
/dev/hda5           901     1023   247936+   83  Linux
```

Use this information to partition the disk exactly as the old system. This is done using the fdisk command. A sample partitioning session is shown here:

```
# fdisk /dev/hda
Command (m for help): p
Disk /dev/hda: 64 heads, 63 sectors, 1023 cylinders
Units = cylinders of 4032 * 512 bytes
 Device Boot Start End Blocks Id System
Command (m for help): n
Command action
 e extended
 p primary partition (1-4)
p
Partition number (1-4): 1
First cylinder (1-1023): 1
Last cylinder or +size or +sizeM or +sizeK ([1]-1023): 900
Command (m for help): n
Command action
 e extended
 p primary partition (1-4)
e'
```

```
Partition number (1-4): 2
First cylinder (901-1023): 901
Last cylinder or +size or +sizeM or +sizeK ([901]-1023): 1023
Command (m for help): n
Command action
 l logical (5 or over)
 p primary partition (1-4)
l
First cylinder (901-1023): 901
Last cylinder or +size or +sizeM or +sizeK ([901]-1023): 1023
Change the partition type to Linux swap
Command (m for help): t
Partition number (1-5): 5
Hex code (type L to list codes): 82
Changed system type of partition 5 to 82 (Linux swap)
```

Mark the root partition as active:

```
Command (m for help): a
Partition number (1-5): 1
```

Check the final state of the partition table, which should look like the following:

```
Command (m for help): p
Disk /dev/hda: 64 heads, 63 sectors, 1023 cylinders
Units = cylinders of 4032 * 512 bytes
   Device Boot    Start      End    Blocks   Id  System
/dev/hda1    *        1      900  1814368+   83  Linux
/dev/hda2            901     1023   247968    5  Extended
/dev/hda5            901     1023   247936+   83  Linux
```

Write the new partition table to disk and exit:

```
Command (m for help): w
The partition table has been altered!
Calling ioctl() to re-read partition table.
Syncing disks.
```

Now you must create a Linux file system on /dev/hda1 using the mke2fs command:

```
# mke2fs /dev/hda1
```

Next you must the swap space with the mkswap command:

```
# mkswap /dev/hda5
```

RESTORE THE DATA

At this point you are ready to restore the operating system onto the file system you just created on the new disk. Create a suitable mount point such as /restore, mount the new root file system on /restore and restore the operating system from the compressed tar image using the following commands:

```
# mkdir /restore
# mount /dev/hda1 /restore
# cd /restore
# gzip -dc /mnt/linux1-root.tar.gz ¦ tar xf -
```

INSTALL THE BOOT BLOCK

Install the boot block on the new disk by using LILO. Note that we need to run the `chroot` command to do this on the disk mounted on `/restore`. Just running LILO without `chroot` will cause the boot block of the root-boot floppy to get over-written, which is not what you want to do:

```
# chroot /restore /sbin/lilo
```

Now remove the floppy disk from the floppy drive and reboot the machine using the `init` command:

```
# init 6
```

Your system should be fully restored.

In this example, you have used a network file system as a staging area to get access to the operating system files and the partition table data of the backed-up system. This two-step approach is necessary because Tom's root-boot disk lacks the `rsh` and `rlogin` tools. If these tools were available, you could use them to directly access and restore from a tape drive mounted on a remote system. Maybe in future versions of Tom's root-boot floppy, the `rsh` tool will become available.

If you do not want to use an intermediate network file system to get to the backed-up data, you can install a SCSI card and attach a local SCSI tape drive. This will allow you to restore the backed-up files directly from tape on to the new disk.

TROUBLESHOOTING

New Amanda users frequently experience some common problems, such as the following:

- Amanda incorrectly reports the free space on the holding disk and `/tmp`.
- `amdump` reports all disks have failed.
- `amcheck` reports permissions problems.
- Amanda has problems writing to tape.

AMANDA INCORRECTLY REPORTS THE FREE SPACE ON THE HOLDING DISK AND /TMP

It is common for Amanda to report zero free space on the holding disk and `/tmp` on Linux systems using version 2.4.1p1 of Amanda. Amanda can compile and install correctly but `amcheck` will still report these errors:

```
Amanda Tape Server Host Check
-----------------------
WARNING: /holdingdisk2: only 0 KB free (1024000 KB requested).
WARNING: /holdingdisk1: only 0 KB free (1048576 KB requested).
.....
Amanda Backup Client Hosts Check
--------------------------------
```

```
ERROR: some.host: [dir /tmp needs 64KB, only has 0KB available.]
ERROR: some.host: [dir /tmp/amanda needs 64KB, only has 0KB available.]
```

The reason for this error is due to a header file introduced in GNU libc 2.1. This has broken the way Amanda computes file system sizes, causing it to always report zero. The fix is to apply the patch glibc21.patch, which is available from www.amanda.org.

amdump REPORTS ALL DISKS HAVE FAILED

The most likely reason for amdump to report that all disks have failed is an incorrectly configured Amanda client system. Make sure you run amcheck before your first attempt to run amdump and that amcheck is run as the same user that amdump runs as. The reports generated by amcheck will help you pinpoint the misconfigured client that you can then reconfigure.

amcheck REPORTS PERMISSIONS PROBLEMS

amcheck may report that a particular username is not allowed. This suggests a misconfigured .amandahosts or .rhosts file. Make sure the fully qualified hostnames and correct usernames appear in these files and correspond to those compiled into Amanda. Also, check your Amanda entries in /etc/inetd.conf to verify that the correct username is used there.

AMANDA HAS PROBLEMS WRITING TO TAPE

Sometimes Amanda can have problems writing to tape. The dump images are then held on the holding disk. Amanda provides a tool called amflush to manually write out these images to tape.

amflush is typically invoked with the config name as the argument as

```
$ amflush Daily
```

amflush looks in the holding disks specified in amanda.conf file in /usr/local/etc/amanda/ <configuration name> for non-empty Amanda work directories. You are then prompted to select a directory from these directories. The Amanda working directories on the holding disks are named by the date when amdump was run. For example if 20000105 is the name of the working directory, it is the year 2000, month 01, and day 05.

After amflush writes data to tape, it updates the databases and sends a mail report to the backup administrator, as happens with amdump.

Note

> Normally amflush will detach from the controlling TTY and run in background mode. If you want to force amflush to run in foreground mode you can specify the -f flag. This is useful if amflush runs as part of a script and you want to run mt fsf, mt rewind, or some other commands after amflush is finished running.

USING amstatus

A useful troubleshooting tool is amstatus, which is used to monitor amdump while it is running:

```
$ amstatus Daily
Using /var/adm/amanda/Daily/amdump
wagner:/m/wagner/2                          0  9617152k finished
bach:/m/bach/3                              0  9538816k finished
bach:/m/bach/6                             010547104k writing to tape
SUMMARY            part     real estimated
                            size      size
partition       :   3
estimated       :   3               29703383k
failed          :   0                     0k
wait for dumping:   0                     0k
dumping to tape :   0                     0k
dumping         :   0         0k          0k
dumped          :   3  29703072k   29703383k
wait for writing:   0         0k          0k
writing to tape :   1  10547104k   10547234k
failed to tape  :   0         0k          0k
taped           :   2  19155968k   19156149k
8 dumpers idle  : not-idle
taper writing, tapeq: 0
network free kps: 11400
holding space   : 34645138
```

You can monitor amdump to debug backup problems or to analyze performance bottlenecks.

CHAPTER **11**

BUILDING THE LINUX KERNEL

In this chapter

OVERVIEW OF THE KERNEL

The kernel is the innermost core of the operating system. The kernel can be described as the layer of software that sits in between the hardware and application programs. Table 11.1 provides a simplified view of the role the kernel plays and its relationship to the hardware, application programs, and system libraries.

TABLE 11.1 A SIMPLIFIED VIEW OF A SYSTEM KERNEL	
User Level	User and Application Programs *(vi, Emacs, cgcc, Netscape...)* System Libraries *(libc, libm, libresolv...)*
Kernel Level	System Call Interface *(fork, exec, open, close...)* File Subsystem Device Drivers Process Control Subsystem Scheduler memory management interprocess communication
Hardware Level	Hardware

The operating system kernel is a program similar to normal programs in some ways, and at the same time very different. In Linux the kernel is called vmlinux. Unlike normal programs, a ps listing does not show the kernel process, nor can you start the kernel from a command shell.

The kernel performs various primitive operations on behalf of user and system processes. The many services provided by the kernel can be broadly classified into the following categories:

- **Process control:** The kernel creates, terminates, suspends, and resumes processes, and it also provides a mechanism for inter-process communication.

- **Scheduling:** The kernel schedules processes for execution on the CPU in an equitable manner. When the time quota of one process is exhausted, the kernel schedules another process to run on the CPU. The suspended process is rescheduled to run again at a later time.

- **Memory management:** The kernel allocates memory for executing processes. When the system runs low on free memory, the kernel writes out memory pages of some suspended processes to swap devices. These swapped-out pages of a process are read back into memory when the process is ready to run again.

- **File system management:** The kernel performs file read/write operations, allocates and reclaims storage space, and provides access control.

- **Peripheral device management:** The kernel manages access to all peripheral devices, such as terminals, disk drives, CD-ROM drives, printers, modems, network devices, and tape devices.

The kernel hides the complexities of operating system functions behind simplified program interfaces. For example when a process wants to open a file, the kernel verifies the access rights, translates the filename into an *inode* number, finds its location on disk, reads it into memory, and then returns a handle to the file to the calling process. The process just makes a simple open() system call and all of the complex activity is transparently handled by the kernel.

The kernel uses device drivers to perform most of its tasks. For example, when opening a file, the kernel translates the file open request into a sequence of I/O requests, such as reading block 12345 from device number 5, and hands that task to the disk device driver to execute.

The kernel provides its services transparently. On behalf of user processes it performs a host of functions such as reading terminal input, spawning processes, synchronizing process execution, reading and writing files, creating pipes, redirecting I/O, performing network operations, and many other tasks. If the kernel did not do all of these things then writing a program to do the simplest of jobs would be a Herculean task.

WHY REBUILD THE KERNEL?

There are several good reasons for reconfiguring and rebuilding the Linux kernel:

- When you install a new Linux system, a generic kernel provided with your distribution is installed. Normally, this generic kernel will operate with your hardware environment, but for efficiency reasons, you should consider recompiling your kernel. Generic kernels are built to support a wide range of devices so that they will work on most of the systems on which you will install Linux. Usually, these kernels include most of the kernel options enabled and a large set of device drivers. This results in a kernel that is versatile, but very large: It consumes more memory than it needs to, takes longer to load, and runs less efficiently. By recompiling your kernel to include only device drivers and options necessary for your system, you can produce a tighter and faster kernel.

- However this highly efficient smaller kernel comes at the expense of not having support for additional devices that you may need at a future time. Whenever possible you should build dynamically loadable kernel modules for infrequently used devices. This prevents unnecessary kernel bloating, and when required the rare device driver module is dynamically loaded. This method provides an optimal solution by keeping the kernel lean, while still providing for additional hardware device support. However, not all devices can be supported with loadable kernel modules. Refer to the section titled "Understanding Modules" for more details.

- If you add new hardware to your system for which the necessary support has not been compiled for your kernel, you will need to reconfigure and recompile your kernel to integrate the new device driver into your environment.

- As new kernel versions are released you will need to compile new kernels if you want to upgrade to these newer versions of the Linux kernel. Generally, it is a good idea to keep your kernel up-to-date with the latest stable releases. Newer versions not only offer new features, but also provide bug fixes, performance improvements, and fixes for security vulnerabilities.

- The kernel runs in a fixed memory space. This limits the maximum number of processes, file handles, and file system buffers to fixed values specified when you compile your kernel. If your system starts hitting these thresholds, erratic behavior will ensue. For instance, new processes may not be able to start or existing processes may fail when they try to open files. To solve this problem, you may need to recompile your kernel and increase the size of these tables.

OBTAINING NEW VERSIONS OF THE KERNEL

Kernel source code can be obtained through anonymous ftp from `ftp.kernel.org` in the `/pub/linux/kernel` directory or any of its other mirror sites. To conserve Internet bandwidth, it is advisable to download from a mirror site close to you. The files are distributed as compressed tar archives. The naming convention used is `linux-n.n.n.tar.gz`, when `n.n.n` is the `major.minor.patch` number. For example, the current stable release of the kernel at the time of this writing is `linux.2.2.13.tar.gz`. The archives are also available in `.bz2` compression format. The Linux kernel development team follows a version naming convention where if the minor version is odd, the kernel in question is a development release, while the even numbered minor versions are production releases. For example version 2.3.x kernels are development releases, and 2.2.x kernels are production releases. Unless you are planning on kernel hacking, it is recommended that you only use production releases.

After downloading the archive you will need to unpack it. Make sure you have sufficient free space in `/usr/src` before unpacking the archive. `/usr/src` is the standard location for storing kernel source code. At the present time, the source code files are about 14MB in size and you will need an additional 70MB of disk space to successfully compile the kernel.

Source trees for each version of the Linux kernel which you keep on your system will be stored in subdirectories of `/usr/src`. Typically, the source code for the kernel currently in use on your system should be stored in `/usr/src/linux`. Assuming you want to upgrade from version 2.2.5 of the kernel to version 2.2.13 and have downloaded the new source code archive to `/tmp`, use the following steps to install the new kernel's source code:

```
# cd /usr/src
# mv linux linux.2.2.5
# tar xzvf /tmp/linux.2.2.13.tar.gz
# mv linux linux.2.2.13
# ln -s linux.2.2.13 linux
```

CONFIGURING THE KERNEL

To configure your kernel for compilation, you need to have all the details of the hardware on your system available. You should prepare an inventory of your hardware including, at a minimum, the details of the following devices:

- Disk drives
- Disk controllers
- Floppy drives
- Co-processors
- Network adapters
- Tape drives and controllers
- Raid controllers and arrays
- Graphic adapters
- Mouse
- Terminal interfaces
- Modems
- Printers
- Scanners
- Sound cards
- Other special purpose devices

With this information in hand, you need to configure the kernel for compilation, a process that will result in a customized `makefile`.

You can do this with one of three commands:

- **make config**: This command runs a command-line program through which you can choose your kernel options and hardware drivers.
- **make menuconfig**: This command runs a console-based, menu-driven application through which you can choose your kernel options and hardware drivers from a hierarchical structure.
- **make xconfig**: This command runs an X Windows program through which you can choose your kernel options and hardware drivers from a hierarchical structure.

`make menuconfig` and `make xconfig` are easier to use because they display kernel options and drivers in context, which makes it easier to locate, identify, and select them. Using `make xconfig`, you can also view detailed explanations of each option as well as suggested default values for those options. With the X Windows option you can also backtrack as you make choices and only commit to selections after completing your entire configuration. The X Windows approach also allows you to complete your configuration over multiple sessions:

Your choices are remembered between invocations of make xconfig. When you finally complete your configuration in X Windows and save your changes, the resulting configuration information is stored in a file named .config.

With all three configuration methods, each option can be enabled or disabled by selecting y for yes or n for no. Device drivers have a third option: m for module. This option is available for device drivers that are compiled as dynamically loadable modules that can be selectively loaded and unloaded at boot time. These can be loaded after the system has started as needed.

It is important to correctly select several key kernel options:

- **Processor family:** A set of processor family options allows for the selection of your processor type to ensure optimal performance on the target system where the kernel will be used. If you want to build a kernel that will run on any Intel x86 class processor, then you should choose the 386 option.

- **Kernel math emulation:** The math co-processor is built into the 486 and Pentium class processors. If you have one of these then you should not enable this option. If your system CPU type is 386 or 486SX, and the motherboard does not have a 387 or 487 math coprocessor chip, then you need math emulation, and the option should be enabled.

- **Enhanced (MFM/RLL) disk and IDE disk/CD-ROM support:** Unless your disks are all SCSI, you will need to enable this option. If you do so, you have to choose between new IDE drivers and old IDE drivers. The new IDE drivers can support 4 IDE devices (disk and CD-ROM) on a single interface, compared to the old ones that only support two. The new drivers also provide better performance on newer EIDE-type hardware.

- **Networking support:** In almost every instance, you need to enable networking support. Even a home system which connects to the Internet through a dial-up connection requires networking to be enabled. In addition, a standalone system without any form of networking will still require this support to be enabled in the kernel for many applications to work properly.

- **System V IPC:** IPC stands for Inter-process communication. Many programs need this feature to communicate with other processes, so this option should be enabled.

- **SCSI support:** If you have any SCSI hardware you must enable this option. If you do so, you will need to select among several sub-options as outlined in the kernel configuration help files.

- **Network device support:** If the system has a network card, or will participate in dial-up networking, this option should be enabled. If you enable network device support, you will be prompted to select the type of network devices to enable and the protocols for which you need support.

- **File systems:** Linux supports a variety of file systems. The second extended (ext2) file system is mandatory and must be enabled because it is the standard Linux file system.

In addition, if you need to access CD-ROMs you should enable the ISO9660 file system and if you have MS-DOS partitions or use MS-DOS floppies, the MSDOS or VFAT file system should be enabled. The VFAT file system supports long file names where the MSDOS option does not. If you will be accessing shared directories from other Unix or Linux systems on the network, the NFS file system should be enabled. Other common file systems include: UFS (Solaris), NTFS (Windows NT), and HPFS (OS/2). The /proc pseudo file system should be enabled because many important Linux tools depend on it for an interface to the kernel and processes.

- **Character devices:** These options provide support for printers, mice, and other devices. Read the help topics and answer appropriately.

- **Sound:** If you have a sound card then you should enable this option, and proceed to the sub-options. Read the help files and the Sound HOWTO file to learn more about your particular sound card before completing these options.

- **Kernel hacking:** If you are not a kernel developer and use your Linux system for production work, you should disable this option.

COMPILING THE KERNEL

PART
II
CH
11

Once the kernel configuration is finished, you can prepare it for configuration with the following two commands:

```
# cd /usr/src/linux
# make dep
# make clean
```

The make dep command, short for make depend, prepares all the dependencies for the configured kernel. It makes sure that all the necessary include files are available. The make clean command ensures that all old object files are removed before compiling. This is essential to ensure that all newly selected options are compiled into your new kernel.

Before compiling you should also verify that your version of gcc, the GNU C compiler, is at least the version specified in your version of the kernel's README file. At the time of writing, gcc version 2.7.2 was required to compile the latest kernel.

If you have the correct version of gcc available, you can compile the new kernel with the following commands:

```
# cd /usr/src/linux
# make bzImage 2]]>
```

In the make command, the tee command sends all status and errors messages both to the screen and to the file make.out. This way you can analyze these messages if your kernel fails to compile successfully. The compilation process can take anywhere from a few minutes to hours depending on the speed of your system. You should try to watch for errors during the compilation. If any errors are detected, make will abort. If you can't monitor the compilation while it is occurring, you can review the output later by viewing the contents of the make.out file.

If the compilation aborts, you may have made mistakes in your configuration or you may have the wrong version of gcc. You should double-check your configuration and gcc version and then compile again. Generally, however, a stable release should compile successfully.

> **Note**
>
> It may help to run `make mrproper` immediately after extracting the source archive. This ensures the source tree is in the cleanest possible state before you begin configuration and installation.

After successful completion of the compilation process you will have a newly built compressed image of the kernel called `bzImage` in the `/usr/src/linux/arch/i386/boot` directory.

If you opted to configure some of your device drivers as modules, it is now time to build the modules. To do this, use the following command:

```
# make modules 2>&1 ¦ tee make_modules.out
```

TESTING YOUR NEW KERNEL

Once you have compiled your new kernel, you need to test it before installing in order to ensure that your system will run using the kernel.

The safest way to test the new kernel, without replacing your current kernel, is to install it onto a floppy disk. To do this place a 1.44MB floppy disk in the floppy drive and issue the following commands:

```
# cd /usr/src/linux
# fdformat /dev/fd0H1440
# make bzdisk
```

The `fdformat` command will format the floppy disk. If it reports any bad blocks, replace the floppy disk with one that has no defects. The `make bzdisk` command will write the compressed kernel image onto the floppy disk.

You can now try to boot your system using the newly created boot floppy. If the new kernel does not boot, you can remove the floppy and just boot from your system's existing kernel. If you can boot the new kernel successfully it is time to install the modules and then the new kernel. If you have configured some drivers to be loaded as modules, you may see some errors about modules not being found when you boot from the floppy. This is understandable because you have not installed the new modules in `/lib/modules` yet.

TESTING THE KERNEL WITHOUT USING A BOOT FLOPPY

You can test the newly built kernel without first installing it onto a floppy disk. This can be done using LILO because you can configure LILO to provide booting from alternate kernel images. For instance, if your new kernel is stored at /usr/src/linux/arch/i386/boot/bzImage, copy the kernel image to /boot with a name such as vmlinuz-2.2.14, and append the following lines to the /etc/lilo.conf file:

```
image = /boot/vmlinuz-2.2.14
label = linux.new
root = /dev/hda1
```

The image statement specifies the location of the new kernel image. The label statement gives a new name to this image, and the root statement specifies the hard drive partition where the root file system resides. Make sure the root partition you specify correctly matches your system configuration.

> **Tip**
>
> Make sure you copy the new kernel image to /boot or / with an alternate name like /boot/vmlinuz-2.2.13 before testing it. If the kernel image is placed in a partition that falls beyond 1023 cylinders, you will not be able to boot the system. This is a limitation of the PC's BIOS, which cannot access disk cylinders beyond 1023 at boot time.

PART
II

CH
11

Once the lilo.conf file has been edited, run lilo:

```
# /sbin/lilo
```

When you reboot your system, press Shift when LILO starts and you will see the LILO prompt where you can enter linux.new to boot from the new kernel.

INSTALLING MODULES

After you have successfully booted up the new kernel either using a boot floppy or using LILO to boot an alternate kernel image, you are ready to install any newly compiled modules.

To install the modules, use the following commands:

```
# cd /usr/src/linux
# mv /lib/modules /lib/modules.old
# make modules_install
```

This will install the module binaries in the /lib/modules directory. Note that we have saved our old modules as /lib/modules.old. If we discover problems with the new modules we will be able to backtrack to the old kernel and the old modules.

After installing the modules, reboot the system again using the boot floppy containing the new kernel image, or by telling LILO to boot the new image. Now the system should boot cleanly and you should not see any `module not found` errors.

INSTALLING THE NEW KERNEL

After you are happy with the new kernel and it works the way you want it to, it is time to install it as the default system kernel.

First, save your existing kernel and install the new kernel as follows:

```
# cp /vmlinuz /vmlinuz.old
# cd /usr/src/linux
# make install 2>&1¦ tee make.install.out
```

Notice that these commands save your existing kernel as `/vmlinux.old` and then install your new kernel (which will be `/vmlinuz`). The `vmlinuz.old` kernel file can be used to backtrack to your previous kernel if needed.

Next, you need to configure LILO to boot the new kernel by default. To do this you need to edit the `/etc/lilo.conf` file.

Typically, your existing `lilo.conf` file should look like the following:

```
prompt
delay = 300
image = /vmlinuz
    label = linux
    root = /dev/hda1
```

Edit this file to add entries for your older kernel. After editing, the `lilo.conf` file will look like the following:

```
prompt
delay = 300
image = /vmlinuz
    label = linux
    root = /dev/hda1
image  = /vmlinuz.old
    label = linux.old
    root =  /dev/hda1
```

This file tells `lilo` to wait 30 seconds before booting the default kernel image (`/vmlinuz`). The file also allows for booting the old kernel using the `linux.old` label. This provides a mechanism by which you can boot back to your previous kernel if needed.

Once you have edited `lilo.conf`, run `lilo` to pick up the changes:

```
# /sbin/lilo
```

When you reboot your system, the new kernel will be used. If there is any kind of trouble, we have taken the necessary precautions to still boot the older kernel. Reboot the system again, and this time at the boot prompt, enter `linux.old`. This will cause the old kernel called `/vmlinuz.old` to be booted.

After successfully running the new kernel for a few days you can delete the old kernel and old modules by executing the following commands:

```
# rm  -f /vmlinuz.old
# rm -rf /lib/modules.old
```

PATCHING THE KERNEL

As bugs in the kernel are fixed, kernel patches are released. The kernel naming convention is of the type `kernel-name-major.minor.patch-level`. For instance, the kernel `linux-2.2.12` is named `linux`, has a major release number of 2, a minor release number of 2, and a patch level of 12. When a patch for this kernel is released it will be become available at the `kernel.org` and other mirror sites as `patch-2.2.13.gz`.

Download the patch from `ftp.kernel.org` or a mirror site and change to the directory `/pub/linux/kernel`. Depending on what version of kernel you are running, change to that directory; for instance, if you are running version 2.2, change to the directory `v2.2`. Listing of this directory will show the various kernel packages and patch files. Download the particular patch file you are interested in, such as `patch-2.2.13.gz`.

Copy the patch file to `/usr/src`. Before applying the patches it is advisable to save a copy of source tree, in case something goes wrong and you need to start over. First run `make clean` and then save the source tree as a compressed tar archive:

```
# cd /usr/src/linux
# make clean
# tar czvf linux.old.tar.gz linux
```

Next, apply the patches to the source tree using the following commands:

```
# cd /usr/src/linux
# zcat patch-2.2.13.gz ¦ patch -p0 2&1¦ tee patch.out
```

The patches will be applied to the source tree, a process that will generate considerable output to the screen reporting on all the patches that are being applied. If you want less voluminous output you can add a `-s` flag to the `patch` command which tells the `patch` program to only report errors. With the `tee` command we can send the output to a file as well as to the screen. If `patch` encounters errors it will create reject files that are files named with `.rej` extensions. You can find all of them by running the following command:

```
# find . -name '*.rej' -print
```

If `patch` produces errors, one of the likely causes is that it found a `config.in` file that is not exactly as `patch` expected it to be. This is because possible customizations have been done to this file during an earlier kernel build process. To fix this problem, take a look at the `config.in.rej` file. The `.rej` file indicates what part of the patch remains to be applied. The changes are typically marked with + and - at the beginning of the line. If you are familiar with how the UNIX program `diff` works, this will not seem unfamiliar.

The + symbol indicates the line should be added to the `config.in` file and the - indicates that the line should be deleted from `config.in`. Edit the `config.in` file accordingly and reapply the remainder of the `config.in.rej` file with the following command:

```
# patch -p0 > config.in.rej
```

If there are no errors reported, you can delete the `config.in.rej` file. It is not deleted automatically by patch. Next you can proceed with the configuration and compilation steps, as we have discussed in the "Configuring the Kernel" and "Compiling the Kernel" sections earlier in the chapter.

Installing patches out of order or applying non-standard patches is another reason for errors. If you continue to get more errors, it is better to start from scratch with a clean source tree that you have not modified in any way. For example, unpack the original `linux-2.2.12.tar.gz` that you used to build your current version. Run `make mrproper` to clean up the source tree and then apply `patch-2.2.13`.

CLEANING UP AFTER PATCHING

After patching source trees a few times, you will notice file names with `.orig` extensions starting to accumulate. You can remove these out by running a `find` command as follows:

```
# cd /usr/src/linux
# find . -name '*.orig' -exec rm -f {} \;
```

An earlier version of patch created tilde files instead of `.orig` files. To remove these you can run the following `find` command instead:

```
# find . -name '*~' -exec rm -f {} \;
```

UNDERSTANDING MODULES

Since Linux 2.0.x, modules have been introduced. These change the way kernels are built. In the past, any device driver or file system type that you needed access to had to be compiled into the kernel. For certain system configurations where the kernel had to occasionally support a lot of different devices, the kernel size would get very big, demanding a lot of system resources and resulting in performance degradation. To remedy this situation, modularized kernels were designed. This allows for building modules for infrequently used drivers or file systems. These modules can be loaded on demand, and later unloaded when they are no longer needed.

Good candidates for modules are a variety of Ethernet drivers, CD-ROM drivers, certain file system support drivers, and miscellaneous other modules.

Some changes in how modules are supported by the kernel have been made. In earlier kernels, a `kerneld` daemon would load and unload modules on demand. In current modules, `kerneld` has been replaced by `kmod`. `kmod` also loads and unloads modules on demand but does not require an external program to be running; it runs as a thread within the kernel. When the kernel needs a module to be loaded, kmod wakes up and spawns a modprobe process that actually loads the module.

kmod offers several advantages over kerneld, including the following:

- kmod does not require Sys V IPC support unlike kerneld. This allows Sys V IPC itself to become a module.

- Removing kerneld from Sys V IPC made it 40% smaller.

- kmod runs as a kernel thread unlike kerneld, which ran as a separate daemon.

- kmod reports errors using the normal kernel mechanisms, unlike kerneld which needed Unix domain sockets and thus could not be modularized.

To periodically unload unused modules, you can create a crontab entry for the root user as follows:

```
0-59/5 * * * * /sbin/rmmod -a
```

Add this line to the root user's crontab file as outlined in Chapter 7, "Scheduling Tasks."

In order for kmod to be able to spawn modprobe, the kernel must know the path to modpobe. This can be set using the /proc pseudo file system as follows:

```
# echo "/sbin/modprobe" > /proc/sys/kernel/modprobe
```

UNDERSTANDING THE /proc File System

The /proc file system is a pseudo file system which acts as a window into the internal data structures of the kernel. It can be used to collect information about the kernel and also to modify certain kernel parameters at run time. If you change directory into /proc and do a directory listing, you will find one sub-directory per running process. To get information about a specific process you can list its various attributes, which appear as sub-directories and files within the process directory. Consider the following sample listing of the /proc file system.

```
# ls /proc
1    304  421  441  476  bus          interrupts  misc        slabinfo
2    332  422  460  481  cmdline      ioports     modules     sound
228  355  423  467  482  cpuinfo      kcore       mounts      stat
251  377  424  468  5    devices      kmsg        net         swaps
262  379  425  469  540  dma          ksyms       partitions  sys
276  388  426  470  541  filesystems  loadavg     pci         tty
290  4    430  471  543  fs           locks       scsi        uptime
3    420  431  472  545  ide          meminfo     self        version
```

To look at information pertaining to the process with PID 1, list the contents of /proc/1:

```
# ls /proc/1
cmdline  cwd  environ  exe  fd  maps  mem  root  stat  statm  status
```

If you want to view the status information for the init process (PID 1), view the contents of /proc/1/status:

```
# cat /proc/1/status
Name:    init
State:   S (sleeping)
Pid:     1
PPid:    0
Uid:     0        0        0        0
Gid:     0        0        0        0
Groups:
VmSize:      1096 kB
VmLck:          0 kB
VmRSS:          0 kB
VmData:        32 kB
VmStk:          8 kB
VmExe:         24 kB
VmLib:       1000 kB
SigPnd: 0000000000000000
SigBlk: 0000000000000000
SigIgn: 7fffffffd7f0d8fc
SigCgt: 00000000280b2603
CapInh: 00000000fffffeff
CapPrm: 00000000ffffffff
CapEff: 00000000fffffeff
```

The information generated by /proc file and directory listings and file contents is generated using ps and is similar to the types of data which can be reported with the ps command.

You can obtain a lot of information about your kernel by listing various subdirectories of the /proc file system. For example, to list the modules currently loaded by your system you view the contents of /proc/modules:

```
# cat /proc/modules
ppp_deflate         40536    0 (unused)
bsd_comp             3620    0 (unused)
```

TUNING KERNEL PARAMETERS WITH /proc

A very useful feature of /proc is the capability to change kernel parameters. Of course, this can also be a dangerous privilege if not used with care.

To change a value you simply write the new value into the appropriate pseudo file in the /proc hierarchy. To make the change permanent you add this action to your system startup scripts so that every time the system reboots the kernel reinitializes with the new values you have supplied.

The files in /proc/sys can be used to tune certain kernel parameters. For instance, you can increase the size of the file table in the kernel by altering the contents of /proc/sys/fs/ file-max and /proc/sys/fs/inode-max. As the following commands show, these files each contain a single integer number:

```
# cd /proc/sys/fs
# ls
binfmt_misc   dquot-max   file-max   inode-max   inode-state   super-nr
dentry-state  dquot-nr    file-nr    inode-nr    super-max
```

```
# cat file-max
4096
# cat inode-max
4096
```

To double the size of the file table, we simply need to double both these values:

```
# cat 8192 > /proc/sys/fs/file-max
# cat 8192 > /proc/sys/fs/inode-max
```

SYMMETRIC MULTIPROCESSING

Symmetric multiprocessing is a specialized computer architecture that provides significant performance enhancement by making multiple processors available to run processes. Symmetric multiprocessing is based on shared memory architecture. All processors access the same physical memory, through the same system bus. This architecture imposes some practical limits on the number of CPUs that can be effectively put into parallel operation. Most SMP systems scale well using between two and sixteen processors. After that the rate of performance improvement drops with the addition of more processors. One of the principal bottlenecks of the SMP architecture is the shared bus. However, the advent of newer technologies and higher bus speeds make it possible to effectively utilize a larger number of processors.

The fundamental concept is simple. Multiple processors work together to share the workload of the system. The actual implementation, however, is quite complex and scalability is not linear, which means you do not get double performance by doubling the number of CPUs.

An operating system must be specifically designed to take advantage of the SMP architecture. Effective and intelligent task scheduling is at the core of a symmetric multiprocessing system. Scheduling is the mechanism that selects processes to run on different CPUs. In a symmetric multiprocessing operating system there is only one run queue. Processes are taken off the run queue and assigned to different CPUs based on different algorithms. An entire process may be mapped to a CPU, or different threads may be mapped on to different CPUs. Multithreaded processes benefit the most in a symmetric multiprocessing environment.

SMP was introduced to Linux with the version 2.0 kernel. The code has been steadily refined and finer grained locking mechanisms have been introduced in version 2.2.x kernels. This enables better performance when processes are accessing the kernel.

To build a kernel to support SMP, all you need to do is answer Yes to the Symmetric Multiprocessing Support option when configuring the kernel. The rest of the kernel build process is the same as in the case of single processor kernels.

When compiling kernels on SMP machines, you can run parallel compilation processes by invoking make with the -jX option, where X is the maximum number of compile processes.

After you have built the SMP kernel and installed it, you can verify that all CPUs are being used by querying the value of cpuinfo in the /proc file system. A typical output on a dual Pentium system is as follows:

```
# cat /proc/cpuinfo
processor       : 0
vendor_id       : GenuineIntel
cpu family      : 6
model           : 1
model name      : Pentium Pro
stepping        : 9
cpu MHz         : 199.434636
cache size      : 256 KB
fdiv_bug        : no
hlt_bug         : no
sep_bug         : no
f00f_bug        : no
fpu             : yes
fpu_exception   : yes
cpuid level     : 2
wp              : yes
flags           : fpu vme de pse tsc msr pae mce cx8 apic sep mtrr pge mca cmov
bogomips        : 199.07
processor       : 1
vendor_id       : GenuineIntel
cpu family      : 6
model           : 1
model name      : Pentium Pro
stepping        : 9
cpu MHz         : 199.434636
cache size      : 256 KB
fdiv_bug        : no
hlt_bug         : no
sep_bug         : no
f00f_bug        : no
fpu             : yes
fpu_exception   : yes
cpuid level     : 2
wp              : yes
flags           : fpu vme de pse tsc msr pae mce cx8 apic sep mtrr pge mca cmov
bogomips        : 199.07
```

You can also examine your system's boot messages using the dmesg command. A typical dmesg output for a dual-CPU system is as follows:

```
# dmesg
Linux version 2.2.5-15smp (root@porky.devel.redhat.com) (gcc version egcs-2.91.66\
  19990314/Linux (egcs-1.1.2 release)) #1 SMP Mon Apr 19 22:43:28 EDT 1999
Intel MultiProcessor Specification v1.4
    Virtual Wire compatibility mode.
OEM ID: COMPAQ   Product ID: PROLIANT      APIC at: 0xFEE00000
Processor #1 Pentium(tm) Pro APIC version 16
Processor #0 Pentium(tm) Pro APIC version 16
I/O APIC #2 Version 1 at 0xFEC00000.
Processors: 2
mapped APIC to ffffe000 (fee00000)
mapped IOAPIC to ffffd000 (fec00000)
Detected 199434636 Hz processor.
Console: colour VGA+ 80x25
Calibrating delay loop... 199.07 BogoMIPS
```

```
Memory: 387200k/393216k available (1044k kernel code, 416k reserved, 4184k data,
  68k init)
VFS: Diskquotas version dquot_6.4.0 initialized
Checking 386/387 coupling... OK, FPU using exception 16 error reporting.
Checking 'hlt' instruction... OK.
POSIX conformance testing by UNIFIX
mtrr: v1.26 (19981001) Richard Gooch (rgooch@atnf.csiro.au)
per-CPU timeslice cutoff: 50.10 usecs.
CPU1: Intel Pentium Pro stepping 09
calibrating APIC timer ...
..... CPU clock speed is 199.4418 MHz.
..... system bus clock speed is 66.4804 MHz.
Booting processor 0 eip 2000
Calibrating delay loop... 199.07 BogoMIPS
OK.
CPU0: Intel Pentium Pro stepping 09
Total of 2 processors activated (398.13 BogoMIPS).
enabling symmetric IO mode... ...done.
ENABLING IO-APIC IRQs
init IO_APIC IRQs
 IO-APIC pin 0, 16, 17, 18, 19, 20, 21, 22, 23 not connected.
..MP-BIOS bug: 8254 timer not connected to IO-APIC
...trying to set up timer as ExtINT... .. (found pin 0) ... works.
number of MP IRQ sources: 16.
number of IO-APIC registers: 24.
testing the IO APIC.......................
.... register #00: 02000000
.......       : physical APIC id: 02
.... register #01: 00170011
.......       : max redirection entries: 0017
.......       : IO APIC version: 0011
.... register #02: 00000000
.......       : arbitration: 00
```

TROUBLESHOOTING

A large number of problems can potentially occur in building, installing, and using a new kernel. These include the following:

- Your kernel doesn't compile.

- Your new kernel doesn't boot.

- Your system won't boot.

- Your system can't find a compressed kernel image file.

- You cannot compile other programs after a kernel upgrade.

- Your kernel is too large and too slow.

- You have problems with your parallel port or printer.

- You have problems with your CD-ROM drive.

YOUR KERNEL DOESN'T COMPILE

There are several reasons why your new kernel might not compile:

- An attempt at patching failed.
- Your kernel source tree is corrupted.
- Your version of gcc is too old.
- Your links to /usr/include/linux may be wrong or missing; consult your kernel's README file for guidance on setting these links correctly.

If a standard, stable, clean kernel source tree doesn't compile, this means something is seriously wrong with the system and many tools may need reinstalling. Hardware problems should not be ruled out, including faulty memory.

YOUR NEW KERNEL DOESN'T BOOT

The following are among the possible reasons why your system may not boot with a new, tested kernel:

- You forgot to run lilo.
- LILO is not configured correctly; for instance a small error in the boot entry can prevent LILO from booting your new kernel.
- You forgot to add ext2fs file system support. This is essential for Linux systems.

YOUR SYSTEM WON'T BOOT

If your system can't boot even with LILO properly configured and installed, then boot your system from a floppy disk or CD-ROM and prepare another bootable floppy disk.

To build a bootable floppy disk, follow these steps:

1. Boot from a boot/root combination floppy such as those available from ftp:// metalab.unc.edu/pub/linux/recovery.
2. Identify the location where you have a working kernel image. This will generally be one of the following:
   - /vmlinuz
   - /boot/vmlinuz
   - /usr/src/linux/arch/i386/boot/bzImage
3. Identify the disk partition which holds your root (/) and /usr file systems. For instance, your /dev/hda1 may include both / and /usr on a simple system.
4. Your boot/root combination floppy disk should have booted with a ram disk. If a /mnt directory doesn't exist on the ram disk, create one:
   ```
   # mkdir /mnt
   ```

5. Mount your root partition to `/mnt`:

    ```
    # mount -t ext2 /dev/hda1 /mnt
    ```

6. Change directory to the location where your working kernel image is located. For instance, if you want the `/usr/src/linux/arch/i386/boot/bzImage` kernel image, change your directory to `/mnt/usr/src/linux/arch/i386/boot`:

    ```
    # cd /mnt/usr/src/linux/arch/i386/boot
    ```

7. Remove the boot/root floppy disk and insert a blank floppy disk for creating a new bootable floppy disk for your system.

8. Format the floppy disk:

    ```
    # fdformat /dev/fd0H1440
    ```

9. Write the `bzImage` file to the floppy disk:

    ```
    # dd if=/mnt/usr/src/linux/arch/i386/boot/bzImage of=/dev/fd0
    ```

10. Configure the boot floppy to know where your root file system is with the command:

    ```
    # rdev /dev/fd0 /dev/hda1
    ```

11. Unmount `/mnt`:

    ```
    # cd /
    # umount /mnt
    ```

You should be able to boot your system using this newly built boot floppy.

YOUR SYSTEM CAN'T FIND A COMPRESSED KERNEL IMAGE FILE

If you see the error message `Not a compressed kernel Image file` when booting, you are using the uncompressed kernel image, `vmlinux`, in `/usr/src/linux`. Use the compressed kernel image in `/usr/src/linux/arch/i386/boot/bzImage` instead.

YOU CANNOT COMPILE OTHER PROGRAMS AFTER A KERNEL UPGRADE

If you cannot compile programs after installing a new kernel, you have problems with your include files. The Linux kernel source tree provides a number of include files referenced by the standard `/usr/include/` tree of a Linux system. Normally, a link exists from `/usr/include/linux` to `/usr/src/linux/include`. If this link is broken, points to a different location, or is missing, most programs will not compile.

To solve this problem, reinstall the Linux `include` files in the proper location with the proper permissions:

```
# cd /usr/src
# tar xzpvf linux.2.2.13.tar.gz  linux/include
```

The p flag of the `tar` command causes tar to preserve file permissions when expanding the archive.

PART

II

CH

11

YOUR KERNEL IS TOO LARGE AND TOO SLOW

If your kernel is too large and too slow, you probably have compiled too many options and drivers into your kernel. To solve this problem, you need to reconfigure your kernel to include the minimum options and drivers needed. You can check memory and swap usage by your kernel by viewing the contents of /proc/meminfo.

YOU HAVE PROBLEMS WITH YOUR PARALLEL PORT OR PRINTER

Printer device naming was changed in kernel 2.1. What used to be lp1 is now lp0 under the new kernel. Looking through system logs will help you track down what device names are being used.

When configuring the kernel, make sure you configured parallel port support and PC style hardware under General Setup. You must also configure parallel printer support under Character devices.

YOU HAVE PROBLEMS WITH YOUR CD-ROM DRIVE

Many people have problems with IDE/ATAPI CD-ROM drives. If your CD-ROM drive is the only drive on an IDE interface, be sure that it is jumpered to be the master drive.

If your CD-ROM drive is connected to your sound card's IDE interface, you may have trouble and may find that the drive will work better when connected to your computer's main IDE interface.

## CHAPTER 12

CAPACITY PLANNING

In this chapter

PLANNING FOR GROWTH

Capacity planning is the process of predicting the future capacity requirements of your workstations, servers, storage devices, network, backup devices, and so on. It is an attempt to predict when saturation of information system resources will occur. The more accurately you can make such predictions, the better prepared you are as an Information Technology manager to deploy sufficient computing resources to meet the constantly changing and ever-growing needs of your user community. It is a tightrope balancing act to match user expectations and system and network response times against finite IT budgets. To stay ahead in this game is no trivial task.

Capacity planning falls under the larger umbrella of capacity management. It is not possible to adequately plan for capacity without an understanding of user expectations and performance measurements. A capacity management scheme addresses three major areas, namely service-level agreements, performance management, and capacity planning. Capacity management acquires credibility when it can successfully project future workload resource requirements based on well-defined service level agreements. The goal of service-level agreements is to quantify the level of service that must be provided to users in unambiguous terms. It is an attempt to remove guesswork in capacity assessments and commit the data center to a service standard agreed upon with the user community.

The goal of performance management is to measure the performance of information technology resources. It is an on-going activity of collecting performance data, evaluating it, and assessing whether the performance meets the published service level agreements. When performance problems are detected, such data provide a systematic way of identifying those system components that need upgrading or enhancing to meet the desired level of performance. Performance measurements help identify areas that can be improved upon to boost overall system throughput. Optimal efficiency is achieved when all service-level agreements are met using minimal system resources.

Capacity planning is a complex activity. It is the assessment of information system resources required to satisfy future information technology needs. Capacity planning is not an exact science. It uses historical and current system usage and workload data along with projected estimates for future growth and deployment of new applications. These provide the best estimate for the resources required to support future workloads. Keeping abreast of the current advances in different areas of information technology is necessary to reap the maximum benefit for every IT dollar spent.

We will now take a look at some specific areas of capacity planning as they apply to file, application, database, Web, proxy, mail servers, and capacity planning of the network infrastructure.

REASONS FOR CAPACITY PLANNING

The continuous trend toward less expensive hardware prices raises the question of whether it is worthwhile bothering with capacity planning at all. However, it is generally accepted that even in this environment, capacity planning is better than quick guesses at future needs.

Several reasons that capacity planning is critical exist. First, the rate at which hardware becomes obsolete is extreme. Newer, faster, and cheaper components become available almost every day. In the past the overall useful life of systems was longer, and new systems could be roughly estimated and rolled out. Later users would be gradually added, and the system upgraded to deal with any added workload. This process would often take several years.

By contrast, in today's environment after a system is in place it quickly becomes an integral part of the overall network. The life cycle of these systems is much shorter. Taking the system down to perform upgrades is consequently more expensive in terms of lost production time, taking into account the shorter life span of the system. These reasons make it critical that careful planning be done before putting a system into production.

In addition, proper capacity planning can significantly reduce the overall cost of ownership. Although there is some initial investment in terms of staff time and resources to perform formal capacity planning, the potential losses that can result if no planning were done is staggering. Financial losses as a result of system downtime, cost of upgrading, and cost of replacing inadequate hardware at a later date because of faulty initial estimates provide more than enough reasons to justify the cost of capacity planning.

SERVER SIZING

Sizing a Linux or UNIX server is not a trivial activity. Underestimating the capacity of a server translates to poor performance and frustrated users. Overestimating on the other hand results in a machine that is too big for the job. The end result is an under-utilized server, and wasted IT dollars. The optimal goal of server sizing is to specify just the right amount of resources to deliver the required server performance and to handle both peak and average load at acceptable service levels.

First of all it is necessary to clearly define the performance objective. Most users care about fast response times for the applications they use. They are not interested whether batch jobs suffer or other users' applications perform poorly. Generally, servers are tuned to give higher priority to interactive sessions, at the expense of batch jobs running at much slower speeds. However, someone running large financial batch processes will not be pleased when the system delivers the results several hours too late. Often computer systems are sized based on peak load only, which results in a system that is optimally used for a few hours, and remains grossly under utilized for the rest of the day. However the overall gain in productivity can well justify the cost of implementing such a system.

A computer system consists of several components such as the CPU, main memory, cache memory, network interfaces, and disk subsystems. The overall performance of the system is determined by the slowest link in this chain. Most often the slowest component is the I/O subsystem. There is a big difference in speed between solid-state components, such as processors and memory, and mechanical devices, such as disk drives. Therefore it is necessary to understand how to speed up the slowest link in the chain to gain effective performance improvements. For example, a SCSI disk will give much better performance compared to an IDE disk. Significant performance gain can also be achieved by distributing the I/O load between several disks instead of on one large disk. This principle is utilized in RAID systems as discussed in Chapter 9, "Installing and Using RAID." For example, if you need 20GB of storage, you will get significantly faster performance if you build an array of several smaller-capacity disks instead of using a single 20GB disk.

Network interfaces usually are also prime sources of performance bottlenecks. When the network becomes the bottleneck, adding multiple network cards or using faster network technology such as newer gigabit Ethernet environments can deliver the required network throughput and increase overall system performance. Needless to say, to improve network throughput the entire network speed must be increased. Just making localized improvements will not yield the desired results. Shared media Ethernets should give way to switched Ethernets. The switches and various network segments must in turn be connected through high-bandwidth backbone networks. Fortunately, fast Ethernet switches and gigabit Ethernet routers and routing switches are becoming more affordable and more common-place.

ESTIMATING THE WORKLOAD

The importance of an accurate estimate of the workload prior to any capacity planning cannot be over-emphasized. Workloads can vary greatly between different applications. For example a database server will have a completely different workload compared to a file or Web server. In addition, even for the same server the workload will differ based on the number of client connections. In the case of database servers, the types of queries performed, and the amount of reporting and analysis done, are added variables to consider. For Web servers, the percentage of dynamic content, server-side CGI and Java processing, and database queries must all be considered to estimate the workload. Moreover, all these conditions will vary widely between one organization and another, and no single magic configuration can satisfy all of the varying needs.

The performance expectations must also be reasonable. No matter how many resources you throw at a database server, certain operations will still take a minimum amount of time, which should not be misinterpreted as poor response time.

UNDERSTANDING PERFORMANCE MEASUREMENT

Before delving into measuring server performance, it is first necessary to understand what metrics will be used, and the values that are acceptable for these metrics. Some of the common metrics used to measure performance are listed here:

- **Bandwidth:** Bandwidth is a measure of network capacity. It is the amount of data that can be transmitted over a network interface per unit of time. For example a T1 connection provides a bandwidth of 1.544 Mbps. In other words, one and a half million bits of data can be transmitted per second over a T1 connection. This can be the limiting factor when calculating the capacity of an Internet Web server.

- **Transactions Per Minute:** Transactions per minute is a measure of the number of transactions of a certain type hat can be executed in one minute. This metric is generally used to measure database and Web performance. For example, if you size a database server and you know that an average user issues 3 transactions a minute, to support 100 concurrent users your server must be equipped to handle 300 transactions per minute. This is your average workload. You can use this workload definition to decide on the number of CPUs, amount of memory, and types of RAID and network I/O channels for the database server.

- **Response Time:** Response time is a measure of the amount of time it takes to process a transaction from the time it is issued until results start flowing back to the source of the transaction request. Response times can vary greatly depending on the type of transaction. For example, it can be perfectly acceptable for a database transaction to take several minutes to compute and return a monthly financial report, whereas that would be too long a wait for a Web server to start returning a page. In other words, acceptable response times are not absolute values; they depend on the application context. Also response times are of more interest when looked at in terms of minimum, average, and maximum values.

- **Retrieval Time:** Retrieval time is a measure of the amount of time it takes a server to return all the results from the time it commenced returning the results. Retrieval times vary depending on the type of transaction. Similar to response time, minimum, average, and maximum values of retrieval times are useful in specifying performance requirements.

We will now look at some specific factors that govern the overall performance of various types of application servers. This knowledge will assist in planning capacities for servers. Table 12.1 outlines the general factors influencing the performance of different types of servers, although you will need to consider each situation individually, considering in particular the number of clients accessing the server.

TABLE 12.1   FACTORS INFLUENCING SERVER PERFORMANCE

Server Type	Disk	CPU	Memory	Network	Comments
Database	X	X	X	X	Databases push all hardware to the limit.
News	X	X	X	X	News servers are very demanding but place particularly high demand on disks and network bandwidth.

TABLE 12.1 CONTINUED

Server Type	Disk	CPU	Memory	Network	Comments
DNS					DNS servers require little in the way of hardware resources.
FTP			X	X	Generally, FTP servers do not require large systems except in the most extreme situations and place small demands on hardware.
X Application		X	X	X	X is CPU, memory, network bound.
Server Mail	X		X		`sendmail` makes extensive use of disks for writing temporary files and requires considerable memory to handle open connections.
Web (Static Files)			X	X	Serving static files places little pressure on disk and CPU. Memory and network bandwidth are the primary bottlenecks.
Web (Dynamic Content)			X	X	Memory and CPU critical for good dynamic content performance on a Web server.
Web (Search Engine)	X		X	X	Web search require considerable disk performance.

DATABASE SERVER CONSIDERATIONS

Before trying to estimate the capacity of a database server, you must understand the variables that govern a database application. When these variables and their relationships to each other are better understood, it is easier to arrive at capacity numbers.

In order to optimize the performance of a database application such as Oracle on a Linux system, three areas need attention:

- The proper choice of hardware
- Tweaking of operating system parameters by the UNIX system administrator
- Fine tuning of specific database parameters by the database administrator

Database applications are generally CPU, memory, and I/O bound. All these areas are important. Because memory access is much faster than disk access, databases perform better if data requests are satisfied by access to memory rather than to disk. When there is a memory shortage on UNIX and Linux systems, paging starts. *Paging* is a mechanism for managing memory limitations. Paging moves individual process pages from memory to disk, thereby reclaiming their memory for other waiting processes. Although some level of paging is bound to happen at some stage, excessive paging activity can rapidly degrade system performance, and must be corrected. Adding more physical memory is usually the easiest way to remedy this problem. Therefore, when capacity planning for a database server, it is better to add excess memory than be faced with constrained memory availability.

It is not difficult to roughly estimate the memory requirements of a database server. Generally database documentation provides a formula to arrive at the total memory requirement of the system. For example, the operating system itself needs memory to run, usually at least 16MB, and the memory footprint of the database engine will have its own requirements, often as much as 512MB. For each user, connection memory is needed. To support for instance 50 concurrent users, each requiring 10MB, you need 500MB. Finally, you will want to have some memory available for buffering activity, often as much as 256MB. Thus, the total memory requirement for this example is about 1.3GB.

Next you must assess the storage requirements. For example the database can require an initial storage capacity of 50GB, and must have room to grow. In such a case it can be wise to plan on a 90-120GB RAID system. In addition, you must plan on one or more separate disks for log files. Most databases write large log files, which are written first before any updates are made to the actual database tables. After a log file is successfully written, the transaction is considered complete. These log files are used to recover a database in the event of a system crash. Separate disks for the operating system, swap files, temporary files, and log files will distribute the I/O operations among multiple disks, and result in the best performance.

Finally, the network capacity must be adequately designed. In a client/server environment, the importance of a fast network cannot be overlooked if you want to assure good performance to database client systems. A fast database server on a slow network would defeat the whole purpose of effectively sizing server requirements.

EMAIL SERVER CONSIDERATIONS

The Simple Message Transfer Protocol (SMTP) is the most widely used mail protocol on the Internet. SMTP makes very heavy use of temporary files in UNIX and Linux systems. This is necessary so that mail files can be recovered in case of some sort of failure during message transmission. Busy mail servers process millions of messages each day. Therefore a very large number of files are created and deleted continuously on these servers.

The mail transport daemon, sendmail runs better if the system has adequate memory; therefore do not economize on memory for a mail server. In addition it is recommended to put /tmp, /var, and swap on separate disks. These file systems are heavily used by sendmail, and it is a good idea to distribute the I/O across multiple disks. For very large mail servers the mail spool should be on a RAID system, both for performance and reliability reasons.

WEB SERVER CONSIDERATIONS

Unless you are a very big site with high bandwidth connections to the Internet, you will not need a large system to run as a Web server. A Linux Apache Web server running on a standard Pentium II 300Mhz PC can saturate a T1 line, delivering over 100,000 transactions per hour, assuming static pages of an average 5KB document size. This translates to about 2 million transactions per day. For dynamic content you might need extra CPU power and memory.

Useful server metrics to design Web servers are the total data rate the server must support and the number of transactions the server must handle. If the server cannot handle transactions quickly enough, the number of concurrent transactions will rise. At some point the scheduling overhead of too many simultaneous connections can become an issue. The system must be configured to limit the number of concurrent transactions and process transactions as quickly as possible.

Search engines can add significant load to a Web server. In addition to CPU needs, search engines consume significant amounts of memory. Searches can be disk intensive if the search criteria does not match well with the indexing strategy. Therefore Web servers that perform many search functions should be designed around the search activity and not around the number of hits.

Server-side Java and CGI script processing adds more workload on the Web server. If your Web content is dynamically generated you must consider adding more CPU power and extra memory because this processing will be the primary bound on performance, not the number of hits.

CASE STUDY: PRACTICAL TIPS ON DATA COLLECTION AND ANALYSIS

So far in this chapter we have looked at the theoretical side of capacity planning. Now we will examine some practical methods for collecting data from your existing servers and analyzing it to assist you in sizing new systems. Although the overall task can seem quite overwhelming, once broken down into smaller components, you can apply simple tools and obtain good results.

One of the tasks that all system managers face is estimating future storage needs. Using a simple Linux tool such as df, it is possible to study disk space usage and project future needs. You can write a daily cron task to record the disk space usage on all your servers. After you have collected a month's worth of data you can total the disk usage for all systems and plot the data on a graph. This will give you the growth rate over a period of one month. Repeat this task to get quarterly, semi-annual, and annual reports of disk space usage and growth rates. With one year's worth of data, you are well equipped to project the needs for the next fiscal year.

A similar approach can be taken to study the performance of Web, database, or mail servers. Linux tools such as uptime, top, ps, and vmstat are very useful in analyzing CPU, memory, and I/O performance of systems. Databases such as Oracle provide their own tools to analyze database performance. Consult the database documentation to learn about these tools.

You can collect system load data by running uptime from cron every five minutes. Plot the results into a graph. This will provide a 24-hour picture of system load. You can extend this method to visualize your weekly load pattern. If you discover times of day when the load reaches unacceptable limits, run vmstat at these times and collect data that can be analyzed to pinpoint system bottlenecks. Using vmstat output, you can identify whether the system is low in memory, or whether it needs more CPU cycles; check if the system is lacking in disk or network I/O performance. A detailed discussion on how to interpret vmstat output is covered in Chapter 8, "Linux Process Management and Daemons." Use the capacities and performance of existing systems as a basis to size new systems.

To study network bandwidth usage, you should consider using the Multi-Router Traffic Grapher (MRTG). MRTG is useful for monitoring bandwidth on leased connections to your Internet provider and provides valuable data to assist you in sizing your Internet connection.

USING MRTG TO SIZE THE INTERNET CONNECTION

PART
II
CH
12

MRTG is a tool that monitors the traffic load on network links. It is freely available under the GNU General Public License. This tool is particularly useful for monitoring the Internet link to your ISP. The data collected and graphed by MRTG can be used to plan the capacity of your Internet connection.

MRTG allows for real time monitoring of network traffic. It converts the traffic reports into HTML pages and image files that can be viewed with any Web browser. MRTG is a collection of programs written in Perl and C. It uses the Simple Network Management Protocol (SNMP) to read the traffic counters from routers and logs the traffic data. The logs are used to create graphs for both inbound and outbound traffic.

A typical MRTG report showing traffic on a 256KBps-network link is shown in Figure 12.1.

The solid part on each graph shows the traffic coming into the site. The line traveling through the graph represents the outbound traffic. The left edge of the graph represents the current time. The maximum, average, and current traffic rates for both inbound and outbound traffic are numerically displayed below the graph.

Figure 12.1
A typical MRTG
graph report.

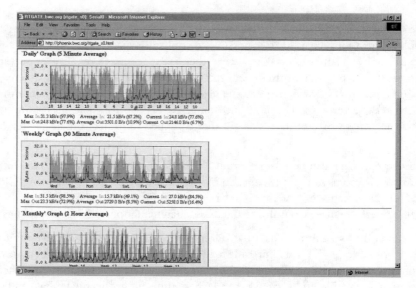

In addition to the daily graph, MRTG creates weekly, monthly, and yearly graphs that are very useful in monitoring the traffic patterns over a larger time window.

MRTG is not limited to monitoring network traffic. It can monitor any SNMP variable. You can get creative and monitor disk usage, system load, modem availability and other data with MRTG. If you wish to do these kinds of things, it is recommended that you join the MRTG mailing list, where you can share ideas with other MRTG users. Visit the MRTG Web site at http://www.mrtg.org/ to learn how to join the mailing list or search the list archives for contributed solutions.

RUNNING MRTG ON A LINUX SYSTEM

You can download the latest version of MRTG from http://ee-staff.ethz.ch/~oetiker/ webtools/mrtg/pub/. The distribution file is called mrtg.tar.gz. After downloading, unpack the archive in a suitable place such as /usr/local/src. The MRTG program requires Perl verion 5.004 or later installed on the system. Perl is installed by default on all Linux systems. If the version of Perl on your system is older than 5.004, you are probably running a very old version of Linux and should consider upgrading your Linux distribution.

To install MRTG, run the configure script to create a Makefile suitable for your Linux system, and run make to compile the MRTG programs. The latest version of MRTG at the time of this writing is 2.8.12. You should create a link at /usr/local/mrtg to point to the MRTG source tree at /usr/local/src/mrtg-2.8.12 as follows:

```
# ln -s /usr/local/src/mrtg-2.8.12 /usr/local/mrtg
```

In addition to installing MRTG, you must have a Web server such as Apache running on the system. The graphs and HTML pages created by MRTG must be placed within the document tree of the Web server to allow viewing of these pages using a Web browser.

After MRTG is built and installed, it must be configured to collect data from the router or routers of interest. MRTG uses SNMP to collect traffic data from the router. A utility called cfgmaker is provided with MRTG that can be used to create the MRTG configuration file. To run the cfgmaker tool you must know the SNMP read community name of the target router. Assuming the read community name is public you can run the following commands to create a MRTG configuration file for this router:

```
# cd /usr/local/mrtg/run
# ./cfgmaker public@router.do.main > mrtg.cfg
```

Replace the SNMP read community name public with the read community name you have set on your router. Replace the hostname router.do.main with the correct hostname of the router in the command. cfgmaker saves the configuration file as mrtg.cfg.

A sample output of the cfgmaker command is shown below:

```
# Add a WorkDir: /some/path line to this file


##################################################################
# Description: Cisco Internetwork Operating System Software IOS (tm) 2500
# Software (C2500-I-L), Version 11.2(7a), RELEASE SOFTWARE (fc1) Copyright
# 1986-1997 by cisco Systems, Inc. Compiled Tue 01-Jul-97 14:53 by kuong
# Contact: Gautam Das <gautam@bwc.org>
# System Name: RTGATE.bwc.org
# Location: Arc and Terraces Communication Centre
#......................................................................
.........
Target[rtgate_s0]: 3:public@rtgate
MaxBytes[rtgate_s0]: 32000
Title[rtgate_s0]: RTGATE.bwc.org (rtgate_s0): Serial0
PageTop[rtgate_s0]: <H1>Traffic Analysis for Serial0
  </H1>
  <TABLE>
    <TR><TD>System:</TD><TD>RTGATE.bwc.org in ATCC</TD></TR>
    <TR><TD>Maintainer:</TD><TD>Computer Technology Group <ctg@bwc.org></TD></TR>
    <TR><TD>Interface:</TD><TD>Serial0 (3)</TD></TR>
    <TR><TD>IP:</TD><TD>rtgate_s0 (194.90.88.213)</TD></TR>
    <TR><TD>Max Speed:</TD>
        <TD>32.0 kBytes/s (propPointToPointSerial)</TD></TR>
  </TABLE>
```

As is evident in the sample mrtg.cfg file shown above, the cfgmaker utility generates an HTML page. In this example the target router is a Cisco 2500. cfgmaker detects each interface of the router and creates an HTML section for that interface. Only the serial interface of interest, serial 0 is shown the example above. The other interfaces detected by cfgmaker are not included in the sample mrtg.cfg file.

The first line in the mrtg.cfg file instructs you to add a work directory specification to this file. The directory you specify is where MRTG will write the HTML pages and image files it creates. A good location for Workdir on a Red Hat Linux system is /home/httpd/html/mrtg, assuming you have an Apache server running on this server and are using Red Hat's default document root directory (/home/httpd/html).

To specify the working directory, edit the mrtg.cfg file and add a line similar to the following:

```
WorkDir: /home/httpd/html/mrtg
```

The Workdir should be the first directive in the mrtg.cfg file. The specified directory must exist. If it doesn't, create it as follows:

```
# mkdir /home/httpd/html/mrtg
```

Next, run mrtg manually to verify that mrtg can read its configuration file and write to the HTML document directory. The command to run mrtg and the sample output from the command are shown below:

```
# /usr/local/mrtg/run/mrtg /usr/local/mrtg/run/mrtg.cfg
Rateup WARNING: rateup could not read the primary log file for rtgate_s0
Rateup WARNING: rateup The backup log file for rtgate_s0 was invalid as well
Rateup WARNING: rateup Can't remove rtgate_s0.old updating log file
Rateup WARNING: rateup Can't rename rtgate_s0.log to rtgate_s0.old updating log file
```

These warnings are harmless and can be ignored.

Check the data files that are created by mrtg in the /home/httpd/html/mrtg directory. There should be one or more HTML files, log files, and image files present in this directory.

MRTG requires certain image files to be present in the HTML document directory. Copy the *.png files in the images subdirectory of the MRTG distribution into the Web document directory by using a command similar to the following:

```
# cp /usr/local/mrtg/images/*.png /home/httpd/html/mrtg
```

Now you are ready to run mrtg from cron every five minutes to collect traffic data from the desired router. You must create a root crontab entry for mrtg as follows:

```
0,5,10,15,20,25,30,35,40,45,50,55 * * * *
➥/usr/local/mrtg/run/mrtg /usr/local/mrtg/run/mrtg.cfg > /dev/null 2>&1
```

How to add crontab entries is discussed in detail in Chapter 7, "Scheduling Tasks." The MRTG distribution comes with a utility called indexmaker that will create an index.html file for you. You can run the indexmaker command as follows:

```
# cd /usr/local/mrtg/run
# ./indexmaker -t 'Router Stats' -r . *.cfg
➥>  /home/httpd/html/grtg/index.html
```

You can use a Web browser to view the HTML pages generated by MRTG by opening the URL http://mrtg-server.do.main/mrtg. Change the server name to the appropriate name of the Web server that is serving the MRTG pages.

The log files and image files MRTG creates are consolidated to keep a two-year record of the data, are self-limiting, and require no maintenance.

The MRTG graphs will let you monitor Internet bandwidth usage in real time. If you notice persistent link saturation over long periods of time, it is clear that you either must buy more Internet bandwidth, or tighten firewall rules and/or proxy rules to discourage use of the Internet for non-business-related activities.

NETWORK MANAGEMENT

## CHAPTER 13

LINUX NETWORK CONFIGURATION AND TCP/IP

In this chapter

UNDERSTANDING TCP/IP NETWORKING

TCP/IP is a suite of data communication protocols that are at the heart of networking on the Internet and many organizational networks.

The term *TCP/IP* is derived from the names of two key protocols: Transmission Control Protocol (TCP) and Internet Protocol (IP). In this combination, IP acts as the mechanism for directing TCP packets to and from their destinations while TCP is utilized by higher-level applications such as FTP and HTTP to construct data packets to be delivered on the network.

The foundation of TCP/IP originated in 1969 when Defense Advanced Research Projects Agency (DARPA) initiated a project to create an experimental packet-switching network. This network was called ARPANET and it provided the foundation for the Internet as we know it today.

By 1975 this experimental network was converted to an operational network. ARPANET continued to grow and evolve, and the basic TCP/IP protocols were developed within ARPANET. Later in 1983, TCP/IP was implemented in Berkeley Unix. As the Internet grew in popularity, so did TCP/IP, and other operating systems started adopting it as part of their supported networking protocols.

TCP/IP became popular and has retained its popularity for several reasons:

- It is an open protocol standard.
- It is independent of any specific vendor, computer hardware, or operating system.
- It is freely available.
- It is independent of any specific network hardware. TCP/IP networks can be implemented using Ethernet, token-ring, X.25, dial-up lines, fiber optics, radio, laser, infrared, and other as yet unknown transmission media.
- It offers standardized high-level protocols.
- It provides a common addressing scheme that allows all hosts connected to a worldwide network to be uniquely identified.

The success of TCP/IP can be attributed to the fact that it caters to a heterogeneous network with open protocols that are independent of operating systems and architectures. The protocols are freely available to everyone and evolve and develop through consensus. The current practice is to publish information about the protocols and standards as freely available documents on the Internet; these documents are known as Requests for Comments (RFCs).

THE OSI REFERENCE MODEL

The OSI Reference Model is a set of guidelines that provides a reference for discussing communication. While TCP/IP was developed before the advent of the OSI model, it has similar reference framework. Accordingly, familiarity with the OSI model is useful in looking at TCP/IP.

The OSI model defines the functions of data communication protocols by dividing protocols into seven layers as illustrated in Figure 13.1.

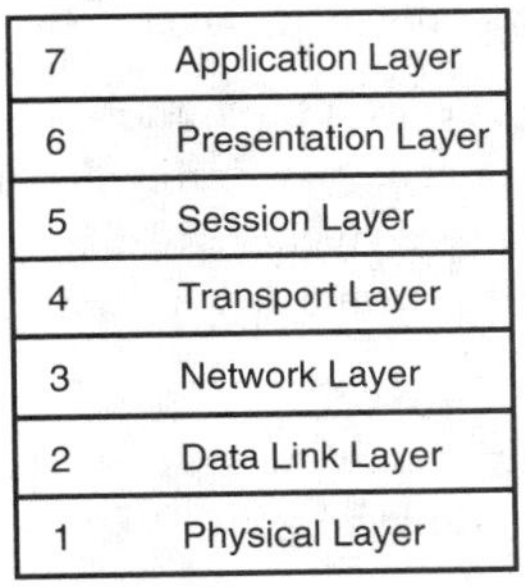

Figure 13.1
Protocol layers stack of the OSI reference model.

7	Application Layer
6	Presentation Layer
5	Session Layer
4	Transport Layer
3	Network Layer
2	Data Link Layer
1	Physical Layer

Table 13.1 outlines the definitions of each of the protocol layers in the OSI reference model.

TABLE 13.1 LAYERS OF THE OSI REFERENCE MODEL

Layer	Description
1 Physical Layer	Provides the physical connection between computers, for example, Ethernet Hardware Layer
2 Data Link Layer	Packs data into frames for communication, for example Ethernet frames
3 Network Layer	Provides for routing packets across the network, for example the Internet Protocol
4 Transport Layer	Performs end-to-end error checking and guarantees the receiver gets exactly the same data that was sent, for example the Transmission Control Protocol (TCP)
5 Session Layer	Establishes and terminates communication links; this layer does not exist in the TCP/IP hierarchy, which uses sockets and ports to establish connections with remote systems
6 Presentation Layer	Determines the data exchange format of participating application; in TCP/IP individual applications handle this task
7 Application Layer	Provides an interface between user programs and network protocols; in TCP/IP this layer falls within the network applications with which users interact

PART
III

CH
13

Each protocol layer on a local system communicates with its peer on a remote system. However, this is only a logical communication: There is no direct peer-to-peer communication between layers except at the physical layer level.

Consider the case of FTP. An FTP client passes data down the protocol stack from the application layer to the physical layer, at which point the data is transmitted across the physical network media to the FTP server, where it moves up the stack to the application layer.

While this is the physical path that the data packets take, the FTP client and FTP server are only aware of communicating with each other at the application layer.

In a way each protocol layer is only concerned with its peer on the remote system. It does not need to know anything about the other layers. The upper layers simply depend on the lower layers to transfer data to the network. Similarly the lower layers pass data up the protocol stack to the application. Therefore new network hardware and drivers can be added without having to rewrite application programs.

While the TCP/IP protocol suite does not precisely fit within the OSI reference, considering TCP/IP within this framework is useful for understanding how TCP/IP works.

TCP/IP PROTOCOL STACK

The TCP/IP Protocol Stack consists of four layers as illustrated in Figure 13.2.

Figure 13.2
Protocol layers
stack of the
TCP/IP suite.

4	Application Layer
3	Host-to-Host Transport Layer
2	Internet Layer
1	Network Access Layer

As in the OSI model, data is passed down the protocol stack to the physical network by the sending system and passed up the stack at the receiving end.

The Network Access Layer is the lowest layer of the TCP/IP protocol hierarchy. This layer provides the means to deliver data to other devices on a directly connected network. The Network Access Layer of TCP/IP encompasses the lower three layers of the OSI reference model.

The Internet Layer sits on top of the Network Access Layer in the TCP/IP protocol stack. The Internet Protocol (IP) is one of the basic building blocks of the Internet. IP is a connectionless protocol. This means it relies on higher-level protocols to establish the connection, if they require a connection-oriented service. The Internet Protocol does not do any error correction. Again it leaves this task to higher-level protocols to perform if they require error correction. The Internet Protocol defines the IP datagram and the Internet addressing scheme. It routes datagrams to remote hosts and performs fragmenting and re-assembly of datagrams.

The protocol layer above the Internet Layer is the Host-to-host Transport Layer. There are two protocols in this layer, User Datagram Protocol (UDP), and Transmission Control Protocol (TCP). UDP provides a connectionless datagram service. UDP is a low overhead protocol and it does not do any error correction. Applications using UDP need to devise their own error correction methods. TCP provides an end-to-end reliable data delivery service with error correction.

The Application Layer sits at the top of the TCP/IP protocol stack. Any process that uses the Transport Layer to deliver data is considered a TCP/IP application. Some of these applications use TCP, while others use UDP. Some examples of applications that use TCP are Telnet, FTP, and SMTP. Examples of applications using UDP are NFS, DNS, and RIP. Newer versions of NFS now use TCP instead of UDP.

Figure 13.3 illustrates two computers connected over Ethernet and running the tftp program. It summarizes with a simple example what we have covered so far about peer protocols and layers in TCP/IP communication.

Figure 13.3
Peer-to-Peer relationships in TCP/IP protocol layers.

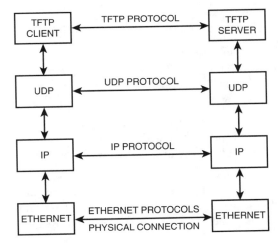

In Figure 13.3, the boxes at the lowest layer physically communicate with each other. The horizontal lines between boxes in each layer illustrate *peer-to-peer protocols*. The actual communication of data is from the tftp client box, down to the UDP box, down to the IP box, down to the Ethernet box, and then across through the physical link to the other system and up.

IP ADDRESSES

The Internet Protocol requires that each host connected to an IP-based network be assigned a unique 32-bit number, known as its IP address. Hosts that have more than one network interface are called routers or multi-homed hosts and are assigned more than one IP address—one per network interface at a minimum.

IP addresses are made up of two parts. The first part uniquely identifies the network in which the host resides, and the second part uniquely identifies the host on that network. The network section of an IP address precedes the host part; the size of the parts varies depending on the class of the network in which the IP address is being used. In any case, the total number of bits in the network and address part must be 32.

Three major classes of IP networks are known as Class A, Class B and Class C networks. Table 14.2 outlines the number of bits in the network and the host parts of an IP address for each of these three classes of networks.

TABLE 13.2   INTERNET ADDRESS CLASSES

Network Class	Network Part Size	Host Part Size
A	8 bits	24 bits
B	16 bits	16 bits
C	24 bits	8 bits

For each class of networks, the bits in the network parts are used in particular ways:

- With Class A networks, the left-most bit of the network bits is always 0, which serves to identify the network class. The remaining 7 bits in the network part identify the network address. The 24 bits in the host part allow for 16,777,214 host addresses in a Class A network.

- With Class B networks, the left-most two bits of the network part are always 10, which serves to identify the network class. The remaining 14 bits in the network part identify the network address. The 16 bits in the host part allow for 65,534 host addresses in a Class B network.

- With Class C networks, the left-most three bits of the network part are always 110, which serves to identify the network class. The remaining 21 bits in the network part identify the network address. The 8 bits in the host part allow for 254 host addresses in a Class C network.

In addition to these three major network classes, a fourth special-purpose network class exists: Class D networks. Class D networks are used for multicast addresses. Multicasting is used to group together machines that share a common protocol, unlike other network classes that share a common network. With Class D networks, the left-most three bits of the network part are always 111. However, the vast majority of network installations do not use Class D networks and they will not be considered in this book in any detail.

IP addresses are generally written in a dotted decimal format. The 32-bit address is split into four 8-bit (or 1 byte) numbers that are expressed as decimal numbers where each of the four sections of the address fall in the range of integers from 0 to 255. This representation makes the address representation quite easy to understand. Valid IP addresses include 194.148.43.193 and 204.50.107.151, but 192.115.144.294 would be invalid.

Using the standard assignments to the left-most bits for network classes outlined above, we can identify the network class of an IP address by the value of its first byte:

- The first byte of a Class A IP address will always be less than 128.
- The first byte of a Class B IP address will always be in the range from 128 to 191.
- The first byte of a Class C IP address will always be in the range from 192 to 223.

First byte values greater than 224 identify reserved networks such as multicasting Class D networks. In addition to these reserved networks, three other blocks of addresses are reserved for use on private intranets that are not directly connected to the Internet:

> 10.0.0.0 to 10.255.255.255
>
> 172.16.0.0 to 171.31.255.255
>
> 192.168.0.0 to 192.168.225.255

These reserved address blocks are not routed over the public Internet, which allows any organization to use any of these addresses without having to register them with an Internet registry. All other IP addresses need to be registered to ensure that there are no conflicts among assigned addresses on the public Internet.

SUBNETWORKS AND NETWORK MASKS

The process of dividing a network into smaller networks is called sub-netting or *subnetworking*. The motivation for dividing a network into smaller pieces is address conservation.

If every organization that required a single host to be connected to the Internet were assigned a Class C network (the smallest full network class) then available networks would quickly disappear. However, individual addresses from a Class C network cannot simply be assigned to hosts on the Internet because that would create routing problems.

To resolve this, we use subnetworking. In a subnetwork, the dividing line between the network address bits and host address bits is shifted, creating additional networks. The result of this is increasing the number of networks and reducing the number of hosts that belong to each network.

A subnetwork is defined by applying a mask, called a subnet mask, also known as a network mask or a *netmask*, to the IP address. In the subnet mask, if a bit is 1 it is interpreted as a network bit, and vice versa. If the bit is zero it belongs to the host part of the address.

The concept becomes easier to understand when we look at some examples. For a Class A network the subnet mask is 255.0.0.0. As explained earlier, the first byte of the subnet mask must be all ones (decimal value = 255) because the first byte of a Class A address is the network part; the bits are interpreted as 8 network bits. The other three bytes are all 0's. There are 24 host bits.

Similarly, the subnet mask for a Class B network is 255.255.0.0. This resolves to 2 bytes or 16 network bits, and 2 bytes or 16 host bits. Similarly the subnet mask for a Class C network is 255.255.255.0, which results in 24 network bits and 8 host bits.

Now consider a subnetworking example where you have one Class C network and would like to divide it into four subnetworks. To do this, you need to borrow some bits from the left end of the host part of the address and use them in the network part of the address.

With a normal class C network, the network mask is 255.255.255.0. Here, you have 24 bits set to 1 and eight set to 0, as illustrated in Figure 13.4.

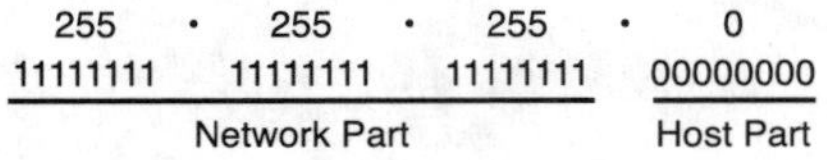

Figure 13.4
A Class C
network mask.

255	·	255	·	255	·	0
11111111		11111111		11111111		00000000

Network Part   Host Part

To subdivide a Class C network into four parts, you need to borrow enough bits from the host part of the address to represent the four subnetworks and add these to the network part of the address. In this case, two bits can be used to represent the four subnetworks, so these are added to the network, leading to a subnet mask of 255.255.255.192 (see Figure 13.5). Each subnet has 64 IP addresses defined by the 6 bits left in the host part of the address.

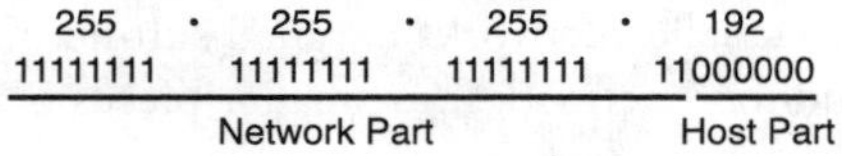

Figure 13.5
A network
mask for a
Class C
network
divided into
four subnets.

255	·	255	·	255	·	192
11111111		11111111		11111111		11000000

Network Part   Host Part

Note

The number of addresses available in a subnet or a network can be misleading. This is because the case where all host bits are 0 is the address of the network itself and the case where all host bits are 1 is reserved as a broadcast address. Therefore, for the Class C network 204.50.107.0, the IP address 204.50.107.0 is the network address and 204.50.107.255 is the broadcast address, leaving 254 available IP addresses, which can be assigned to actual hosts on the network.

Table 13.3 illustrates the effect of applying various subnet masks to IP addresses.

TABLE 13.3   APPLYING SUBNET MASKS TO IP ADDRESSES

IP Address	Subnet Mask	Interpretation
192.115.145.1	255.255.255.0	Host 1 on subnet 192.115.145.0
192.115.144.66	255.255.255.192	Host 2 on subnet 192.115.144.64
192.115.144.17	255.255.255.252	Host 1 on subnet 192.115.144.16

The first line in the above table is easy to understand, as there is no subnetting involved. It represents a full Class C network. The host address is 1 in the network starting at 192.115.145.0 and ending at 192.115.145.255.

The second and third lines are a bit more tricky. On the second line the mask 255.255.255.192 is used to represent a network of 64 addresses starting at 192.115.144.64 and ending at 192.115.144.127. The host address 192.115.144.66 effectively becomes host 2 in the network 192.115.144.64.

On the third line the mask of 255.255.255.252 is used to represent a network consisting of 4 addresses, starting at 192.115.144.16 and ending at 192.115.144.19. The host address 192.115.144.17 effectively becomes host 1 in the network 192.115.144.16.

LIMITATIONS OF CLASSFUL ADDRESSING

The exponential growth of the Internet was not envisioned by its original designers. In the early days of the Internet the IP address pool appeared as a seemingly unlimited resource. Addresses were allocated to organizations based on their request and not on their actual need. As a result large blocks of addresses were assigned without any concern that this resource would eventually be depleted.

IPv4 standardized on a 32-bit address space translates to 2^{32} or 4,294,967,296 addresses. Initially if a larger address space had been chosen we would not face the current address shortage problem.

Further, even though classful addressing of networks as Class A, B, C were easy to understand, it did not promote efficient allocation of blocks of addresses. The scheme of splitting networks on 8, 16, or 24 bit boundaries created either very large or very small networks. Thus in the past, sites requiring a few hundred hosts have been assigned a Class B network that can support 65,534 hosts, wasting most of those addresses in a network that couldn't use them all.

CLASSLESS INTER-DOMAIN ROUTING (CIDR)

CIDR was documented in Septemper 1993 in RFC 1517, 1518, 1519, and 1520. CIDR design goals were to address the following issues:

PART

III

CH

13

- Eventual exhaustion of the IPv4 32-bit address space
- The rapid growth in size of the Internet routing tables
- The near term exhaustion of the Class B network address space

The first issue of increasing the IP address pool is being worked on currently by the IPv6 working group of the Internet Engineering Task Force (IETF).

The concept of Supernetting or Classless Inter-Domain Routing (CIDR) covers the other two issues.

CIDR eliminates the traditional concept of Class A, Class B, and Class C networks. It enables more efficient allocation of the IPv4 address space and will allow for growth of the Internet until IPv6 is deployed.

CIDR supports route aggregation where a single routing table entry can represent thousands of traditional classful routes. Route aggregation helps the Internet's backbone routers, by reducing the amount of route information they have to maintain.

The concept of Supernetting is best explained by the following example. Consider an organization that has 8 consecutive Class C networks as follows:

- 192.115.144.0/24
- 192.115.145.0/24
- 192.115.146.0/24
- 192.115.147.0/24
- 192.115.148.0/24
- 192.115.149.0/24
- 192.115.150.0/24
- 192.115.151.0/24

Note

The syntax `<Network Start Address>/<network bits>` is commonly used to specify the range of a network.

These networks can be specified as a single super-network by removing 3 bits from the network part as follows:

`192.115.144.0/21`

Another way to arrive at the same result would require specifying a network mask of 255.255.248.0. For instance, a network address of 192.115.144.0 with a network mask of 255.255.248.0 would provide the address range from 192.115.144.0 to 192.115.151.255.

This is the method currently used to parcel out blocks of addresses to organizations that need more than one Class C address.

ROUTING

An inter-network or Internet connection is a connection of two or more distinct physical networks so that the hosts on one network can communicate with the hosts on other networks.

To enable these inter-network connections, specialized computers called gateways (or routers) are used to connect these distinct physical networks. Gateway computers have two or more network interfaces and run specialized software designed to route traffic correctly between the networks. Figure 13.6 shows two networks connected with a router.

Figure 13.6
Two networks connected with a router.

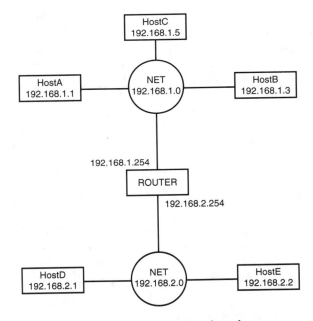

In this example, the network 192.168.1.0 has three hosts:

- **HostA**: 192.168.1.1
- **HostB**: 192.168.1.3
- **HostC**: 192.168.1.5

The network 192.168.2.0 has two hosts:

- **HostD**: 192.168.2.1
- **HostE**: 192.168.2.2

The router that connects the networks has two network interfaces: one connected to the 192.168.1.0 network with the IP address 192.168.1.254 and the other connected to the 192.168.2.0 network with the IP address 129.168.2.254. The router not only moves data from one network to another but it also decides which data packets are destined for which network.

When HostA wants to communicate with HostB or HostC it can send data packets directly to the hosts because they are on the same network. But if HostA wants to communicate with HostD or HostE it cannot do so directly because the hosts are on different networks. In this case, HostA sends data packets to the router, which looks at the destination address of the packets and forwards them to the other network through the appropriate network interface.

When a host must send a packet to another host, it must decide between two possible scenarios:

- If the packet is destined for a host on the same network it is sent directly to the destination host.
- If the packet is destined for a host on another network it will need to be routed. In this case the packet has to be sent to a gateway system for delivery. Generally, hosts are configured with a default router or gateway: Whenever a host has a packet destined for a host outside its own network it simply sends it to its default gateway, which then has the responsibility of figuring out how to deliver the packet.

In the latter case, the hosts on your LAN treat everything outside their network as a black box. They cannot directly see or communicate with any host outside their network; however, they know such a host exists when they give packets to the router for outside delivery and the packets somehow reach their destination.

Routers have a special task: When they receive a packet they must determine which network interface to send it through so that it reaches its destination. To do this, routers maintain routing tables that indicate which network interfaces can be used to reach which networks. Generally one of these network interfaces is designated as the default interface: If no interface is explicitly associated with a particular destination address of a packet it has to deliver, the router directs the packet to this interface. A router at the other end of the connection is then faced with the task of delivering the packet.

CONFIGURING LINUX NETWORKING

Two approaches are available for configuring Linux networking: using automated tools provided with your distribution or manually editing your configuration files.

CONFIGURING NETWORKING RED HAT LINUX 6.2

Red Hat Linux 6.2 provides a convenient network configuration tool called netconf. netconf provides a menu and form-driven interface for specifying network settings. You can launch netconf inside an xterm window or at the Linux console with the command:

```
# netconf
```

Note You need to run netconf as the root user in order to effect the necessary changes to the configuration files.

The main netconf will be displayed as illustrated in Figure 13.7.

Figure 13.7
The netconf main menu.

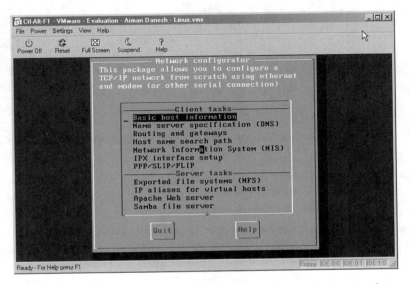

You can use the up and down arrow keys to choose menu entries and the enter key to open a selected menu entry.

To enable networking on your system, you only need to edit values in the Basic host information section. In addition, editing information in the Name Server Specification, Routing and Gateways, and Host Name Search path sections allows you to define extra features so that you can communicate with hosts outside the local LAN, resolving hostnames to IP addresses using DNS name servers and more.

SETTING BASIC HOST INFORMATION

At the very least, you need to edit data in the Basic Host Information section of netconf to enable networking on your Red Hat 6.2 Linux system. To edit basic host information, select the Basic Host Information entry in the Client Tasks section of the netconf main menu and press the Enter key. The Basic Host Information screen will be displayed as illustrated in Figure 13.8.

In this screen, you use the arrow key to move up and down between fields. You need to set the following information:

PART
III

CH
13

Figure 13.8
The Basic Host
Information
screen.

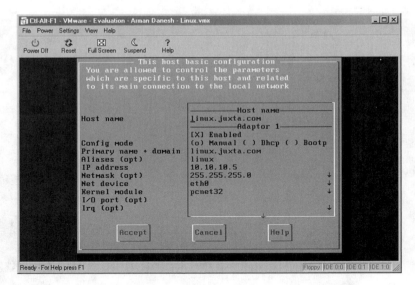

- **Hostname:** Enter the hostname for your system in the Host name field. If you initially installed your system without network support, this will likely be localhost. You should enter the host name assigned by your network administrator to your system.

- **Adapter 1**: You need at least one network adapter in your PC for networking to successfully work. With netconf, you can configure up to four network adapters. We will look at configuring only the first adapter; the principles are the same for each adapter. The first field in the Adapter 1 section is a check box allowing you to enable the adapter. Make sure the check box is selected; if it isn't toggle the check box with the spacebar.

- **Config Mode:** Your Red Hat Linux system can determine its network configuration in one of three ways:
  - **Manual:** You need to manually specify your IP address, name servers and gateway information.
  - **DHCP:** Your system automatically obtains its IP address and other network configuration information from a Dynamic Host Configuration Protocol server on your network.
  - **BOOTP:** Your system automatically obtains its network configuration information from a BOOTP server on your network.

    You will look at manual network configuration in this chapter. Use the left and right arrow keys to select Manual, DHCP, or BOOTP in the Config mode field.

- **Primary Name + Domain:** Many systems have multiple hostnames. You can specify the primary hostname and DNS domain name of your system in this field.

- **Aliases:** Any additional hostnames for your system can be specified in this field separated by spaces.

■ **IP Address:** The IP address you give your system should be specified in the IP address field.

■ **Netmask:** The netmask for your local LAN should be specified in this field.

■ **Net Device:** Each adapter configured with `netconf` needs to be associated with a device. Generally, Ethernet adapters on your system are named `ethX` where `X` is a number starting at zero. Therefore, if you have a single Ethernet adapter, it is likely to be `eth0` and this should be entered in the Net Device field. You can use your mouse to display a drop-down list of device names by clicking on the down arrow at the right end of the Net Device field.

■ **Kernel Module:** Every hardware device on your system must have a kernel module associated with it to work. The kernel module corresponds to a driver in Windows terminology. In the case of your network card, the choice of the correct module is highly specific to your card. If you are unsure which module is correct for your hardware, consult the Ethernet HOWTO at `http://www.linuxdoc.org/HOWTO/Ethernet-HOWTO.html` for details of selecting modules for your network hardware. You can use your mouse to display a drop-down list of kernel modules by clicking on the down arrow at the right end of the Kernel Module field.

■ **I/O Port:** Some kernel modules can automatically detect the I/O port of a card and others cannot. If you aren't sure if your module detects this information, enter the I/O port of your card in this field.

■ **Irq:** Some kernel modules can automatically detect the IRQ settings of a card and others cannot. If you aren't sure if your module detects this information, enter the IRQ of your card in this field. You can use your mouse to display a drop-down list of possible IRQs by clicking on the down arrow at the right end of the Irq field.

Once you have finished entering the relevant data for your system, press Tab to highlight the Accept button and press Enter to return to the main menu.

SETTING NAME SERVER INFORMATION

If your system is on a network connected to the Internet or if you use DNS on your LAN for distributing hostname to IP address mappings, then you need to specify this information using `netconf`. To edit DNS information, select the NameServer Specification entry in the Client Tasks section of the `netconf` main menu and press Enter. The NameServer Specification screen will be displayed (see Figure 13.9).

In this screen, use the arrow key to move up and down between fields. You need to set the following information:

■ **Default Domain:** The domain name you use most should be entered in this field. Generally, this will be the domain name of the LAN you are located on.

PART
III

CH
13

Figure 13.9
The Name
Server
Specification
screen.

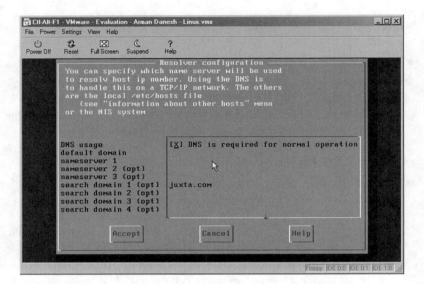

- **Nameserver 1:** The IP address of your primary name server should be entered here. Whenever your system attempts to resolve a name to an IP address using DNS, it will first attempt to query this server.

- **Nameserver 2:** The IP address of your secondary name server, if any, should be entered here. Whenever your system attempts to resolve a name to an IP address using DNS, it will first attempt your primary name server. If it fails to connect it will attempt to query the secondary name server.

- **Nameserver 3:** The IP address of a third name server, if any, should be entered here. Whenever your system attempts to resolve a name to an IP address using DNS, it will first attempt your primary and secondary name server and if it fails to connect to either of these servers it will attempt to query the third name server.

Once you have finished entering the relevant data for your system, press Tab to highlight the Accept button and press Enter to return to the main menu.

SETTING ROUTING AND GATEWAYS

If your system is on a network which is connected to other internal or external networks through routers then you need to specify this information using `netconf`. To edit routing information, select the Routing and Gateways entry in the Client Tasks section of the `netconf` main menu and press Enter. The Routing and Gateways menu will be displayed as shown in Figure 13.10.

In this screen, you use the arrow key to move up and down between entries in the menu and Enter to select a menu item. At a minimum you need to set a default route. Follow these steps:

Figure 13.10
The Routing
and Gateways
menu.

1. Select the Defaults entry from the Routing and Gateways menu. The Defaults screen will be displayed.

2. Enter the IP address of your network's default gateway in the Default Gateway field.

3. Press Tab to highlight the Accept button and press Return to return to the Routing and Gateways menu.

If you have alternate gateways to specific networks, you can specify these with the Other Routes to Networks entry and if you have alternate gateways to specific hosts you can specify these with the Other Routes to Hosts entry.

When you have finished configuring your routes, press Tab to highlight the Quit button and press Enter to return to the main menu.

SETTING YOUR HOSTNAME SEARCH PATH

Generally, there are three possible ways for your system to resolve host names into IP addresses:

- Using a local /etc/hosts file which contains entries mapping hosts to IP addresses
- Using an NIS server
- Using a DNS server

Depending on the services available to your system, you can specify the order in which your system attempts to resolve names to addresses. By default, Red Hat Linux 6.2 first attempts to resolve a name by checking the /etc/hosts file and if this fails, it attempts to resolve the name through DNS. NIS is not used. If this path is not suited to your network environment, you need to change it with netconf.

PART
III

CH
13

Note

While you can specify a search path containing any combination of one or more of the three available options listed above, it is generally wise to include the local hosts file in your path, preferably as the first option. You should include commonly looked-up names (including your own host) in this file so that these lookups don't require a network connection to a server for resolution. This will reduce network bandwidth requirements and speed up resolution of frequently used hostnames.

To edit your hostname search path, select the Host Name Search Path entry in the Client Tasks section of the netconf main menu and press Enter. The Host Name Search Path menu will be displayed (see Figure 13.11).

Figure 13.11
The Host Name Search Path screen.

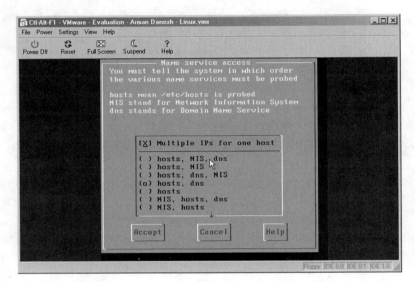

In this screen, you use the arrow key to move up and down between entries in the menu and Enter to select a menu item. This screen presents a pre-defined list of possible paths. Use the up and down arrow keys to highlight your preferred path and press the spacebar to choose this path. Press Tab to highlight the Accept key and press Enter to return to the main menu.

COMPLETING CONFIGURATION

To complete configuration of your network, save your changes. Follow these steps:

1. On the main menu, press Tab to highlight the Quit button and press Enter. The menu illustrated in Figure 13.12 will be presented.

2. Select the Activate the Changes entry, press Tab to highlight the Quit button and press Enter.

The changes will be applied and activated and netconf will quit and return you to the command line. If you entered your network settings correctly, your network should be active.

Figure 13.12
The status of
the System
menu.

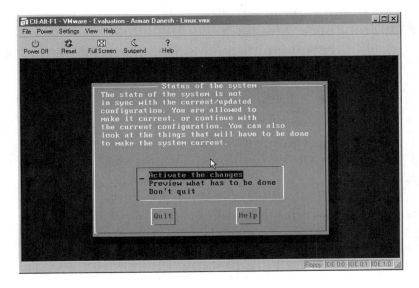

MANUAL LINUX NETWORK CONFIGURATION

While tools such as netconf are useful for quickly editing your network configuration, they hide the actual Linux tools and commands that are used to configure and enable your network. In this section, we consider the techniques for manually enabling your network.

Note

The examples here come from Red Hat Linux 6.2 but generalize to most versions of Linux. If you have problems using these techniques on a specific distribution, consult your distribution's documentation.

There are five key steps in manual network configuration:

- Configure your network interface
- Specify your name servers
- Edit your local hosts file
- Define your routes
- Automate your network setup

PART

III

CH

13

Note

This discussion assumes that the correct kernel module for your network card is already loading at boot time and is detected as /dev/eth0. If you are using a common card such a 3 COM card or an NE 2000-compatible card, this is a safe assumption with most modern distributions. Otherwise, consult Chapter 9, "Installing and Using RAID" for a discussion of installing the modules for your network adapter.

Tip

All the steps in this discussion should be performed as the root user. If you attempt to configure your network as a regular user, you are likely to encounter permissions problems at some point during the procedure.

CONFIGURE YOUR NETWORK INTERFACE

When configuring your Linux system's network support, the first step is to configure and enable your network interface. You do this with the `ifconfig` command.

Consider an example: Your network interface, eth0, is connected to the network 192.168.147.0 which has the network mask 255.255.255.0 and your system's IP address is 192.168.147.5. To configure your interface to connect to this network, use the following command:

```
# /sbin/ifconfig eth0 192.168.147.5 netmask 255.255.255.0 up
```

You can test if this configuration was successful. Use the `ifconfig` command without any arguments or flags to display the state of any currently enabled network interfaces.

```
# ifconfig
eth0      Link encap:Ethernet  HWaddr 00:20:AF:EB:41:69
          inet addr:192.168.147.5  Bcast:192.168.147.255  Mask:255.255.255.0
          UP BROADCAST RUNNING MULTICAST  MTU:1500  Metric:1
          RX packets:14583 errors:9 dropped:0 overruns:0 frame:9
          TX packets:521 errors:0 dropped:0 overruns:0 carrier:9
          collisions:6 txqueuelen:100
          Interrupt:10 Base address:0x300

lo        Link encap:Local Loopback
          inet addr:127.0.0.1  Mask:255.0.0.0
          UP LOOPBACK RUNNING  MTU:3924  Metric:1
          RX packets:8 errors:0 dropped:0 overruns:0 frame:0
          TX packets:8 errors:0 dropped:0 overruns:0 carrier:0
          collisions:0 txqueuelen:0
```

If you have used the `ifconfig` command correctly to enable your network interface then you should see an entry for eth0 like the one shown in this example. It is common as well to have a section for the local loopback device (lo); this is normally pre-configured by your distribution when you install Linux. The local loopback device provides the mechanism by which network applications can talk to the local host without using an external network interface. Because many applications in Linux presume the existence of a network, it is generally necessary to have a loopback device enabled.

Once you know that `ifconfig` is able to configure your network interface correctly, you can test that your system can actually talk to your LAN by using the `ping` command to test connectivity to another host on your LAN. For instance, if you want to ping a host with the IP address 192.168.147.1, use the following command:

```
# ping 192.168.147.1
```

SPECIFY YOUR NAME SERVERS

You can specify any DNS name servers you need to connect to the network or resolve names to IP addresses on your local network by creating entries in the `/etc/resolv.conf` file. Two key types of entries are needed in this file:

- **domain**: The `domain` entry specifies the domain name of your local network. For instance, if your local network has the domain name `juxta.com`, the first line of `resolv.conf` could be:

```
domain juxta.com
```

- **nameserver**: The `nameserver` entry specifies the name of a DNS server. You need one entry for each DNS server you have available to use in the order of preference. Therefore, your primary name server should be listed first, the secondary server listed second and so on. For instance, if you have two name servers, a primary at 192.168.147.200 and a secondary at 192.168.147.201, then you would have two `nameserver` entries:

```
nameserver 192.168.147.200
nameserver 192.168.147.201
```

EDIT YOUR LOCAL hosts FILE

As discussed earlier in this chapter when we covered configuring network in Red Hat Linux 6.2 using the `netconf` tool, most systems use a local `/etc/hosts` file as the first source of hostname to IP address mapping information.

To use this file, make sure that your name server search path is correctly configured. For instance, if you want name server lookups to first check your local `hosts` file and then attempt lookups against your DNS servers, then you need the following entry in the `/etc/host.conf` file:

```
order hosts,bind
```

This entry indicates that `hosts` lookups start with the hosts file and then move on to `bind`, the Berkeley Internet Name Daemon (or DNS).

Once the search path is defined, you need to create entries in the `/etc/hosts` file for those hosts which you frequently access. Each entry takes the following form:

```
<IP address> <hostname> <alias> <alias> ...
```

At a minimum, each entry needs the IP address and the primary hostname. In addition, you can specify one or more aliases which represent alternate names for the host in question. For instance, consider the following series of entries from an `/etc/hosts` file:

```
127.0.0.1        localhost.localdomain   localhost
192.168.147.30   linux.juxta.com         linux
192.168.147.50   foo.juxta.com
```

The first entry provides a mapping for the local loopback address. The second entry maps a host on the local domain with two names (linux.juxta.com and linux) pointing to 192.168.147.30. The final entry points the hostname foo.juxta.com to 192.168.147.50.

DEFINE YOUR ROUTES

To access hosts on your network, define the necessary routes so that your Linux system knows how to direct packets. At a minimum, you will want the following two routes defined for your system:

- A route specifying that your local machine is accessed through your loopback device.
- A route specifying that all packets destined for your local network need to be sent out through a particular network interface (eth0 in the examples in this chapter).

Routes are defined using the route command. To specify a route to a particular host, use the following syntax:

route add -host <IP Address or host name> <device>

For instance, to create a route to the local host (with the IP address 127.0.0.1) through the lo loopback network device, use the following command:

/sbin/route add -host 127.0.0.1 lo

Adding a route to a network uses a similar syntax:

route add -net <network address> netmask <network mask> <device>

For instance, in our manual configuration examples, your system is connected to the network 192.168.147.0 with the network mask 255.255.255.0. To define a route to this network through the device eth0, use the command:

/sbin/route add -net 192.168.147.0 netmask 255.255.255.0 eth0

Finally, if your LAN is connected through a router to an external network such as the Internet, you need to define your default gateway to this external network. To do this, use the route command with the following syntax:

route add default gw <IP address or host name> <device>

For instance, if your LAN's default gateway is 192.168.147.1 you would use the following command to direct packets for hosts on external networks to this host through the eth0 device:

/sbin/route add default gw 192.168.147.1 eth0

After configuring your routes, you can display a table of defined routes using the route command with no arguments or flags:

```
# /sbin/route
Kernel IP routing table
Destination     Gateway        Genmask         Flags Metric Ref    Use Iface
192.168.147.0   *              255.255.255.0   U     0      0        0 eth0
127.0.0.0       *              255.0.0.0       U     0      0        0 lo
default         192.168.147.1  0.0.0.0         UG    0      0        0 eth0
```

AUTOMATE YOUR NETWORK SETUP

You can automate the use of `ifconfig` and `route` to configure your network by editing two key system configuration files:

- `/etc/sysconfig/network`
- The configuration script for each network interface

The `/etc/sysconfig/network` file indicates if networking is enabled and whether it specifies key information such as your hostname, gateway, and gateway device. A typical Red Hat Linux `network` file looks like the following:

```
NETWORKING=yes
FORWARD_IPV4=no
HOSTNAME=linux
GATEWAY=192.168.147.1
GATEWAYDEV=eth0
```

Several critical entries are in this file:

- **NETWORKING**: Set to `yes` or `no`, this entry indicates if networking is enabled on your system.
- **HOSTNAME**: This entry indicates your system's hostname.
- **GATEWAY**: This entry indicates the IP address or hostname of your network's default gateway.
- **GATEWAYDEV**: This entry indicates the network interface your system should use to communicate with the default gateway.

In addition to this general `network` file, you need to indicate the specific network settings for each network interface on your system. One file will exist for each interface on your system in the directory `/etc/sysconfig/network-scripts/`. The files will be named after the network devices in the form `ifcfg-<device>`. For instance the configuration file for /dev/eth0 is `/etc/sysconfig/network-scripts/ifcfg-eth0`. A typical interface configuration file looks like the following:

```
DEVICE="eth0"
IPADDR="10.10.10.50"
NETMASK="255.255.255.0"
ONBOOT="yes"
BOOTPROTO="none"
IPXNETNUM_802_2=""
IPXPRIMARY_802_2="no"
IPXACTIVE_802_2="no"
IPXNETNUM_802_3=""
IPXPRIMARY_802_3="no"
IPXACTIVE_802_3="no"
IPXNETNUM_ETHERII=""
IPXPRIMARY_ETHERII="no"
IPXACTIVE_ETHERII="no"
IPXNETNUM_SNAP=""
IPXPRIMARY_SNAP="no"
IPXACTIVE_SNAP="no"
```

There are several key entries in this file related to TCP/IP networks:

- **DEVICE**: This entry indicates the device which the file applies to.
- **IPADDR**: This entry indicates the primary IP address associated with the interface.
- **NETMASK**: This entry indicates the network mask for the interface.
- **ONBOOT**: Set to yes or no, this entry indicates if the device should be activated at boot time or not.
- **BOOTPROTO**: Indicates the boot protocol, if any, which should be used to configure the network interface's settings. Possible values are none (network settings are defined manually), dhcp (a DHCP server should be used), and bootp (a BOOTP server should be used).

Once these files are edited, your system's network settings will be derived from these files at boot time.

CONFIGURING MULTI-HOMED HOSTS

Up to this point we have been discussing network configuration for hosts with a single network interface. Some consideration needs to be given to hosts with multiple network interfaces, also known as multi-homed hosts.

There are several reasons for a host to have multiple network interfaces, including the following:

- The host is acting as a router or gateway between two or more networks.
- The host needs to maximize its throughput on the network by using multiple network interfaces to effectively increase the speed with which it can communicate on the network.

Configuring multi-homed hosts is a simple extension of configuring a host with a single network interface:

- Each interface has associated with it a kernel module.
- Each interface has associated with it a device such as eth0, eth1, or eth2.
- For each interface, an appropriate ifconfig command needs to be issued to enable the interface and assign it an IP address. You can create a separate interface configuration file such as ifcfg-eth1 or ifcfg-eth2 to automate this process at boot time.
- Appropriate routes need to be set, including routes through the correct interface for each network to which the computer is connected.

> **Tip**
>
> Remember, no matter how many network interfaces a system has and how many networks a system is connected to, a system can only have a single default gateway through a single network interface.

Multi-homed hosts are discussed in more detail in Chapter 15, "Routing with Linux." For a Linux system to serve as a router it will require at least two network interfaces and routing is the most common reason for deploying a multi-homed server.

IMPLEMENTING MULTIPLE VIRTUAL IP ADDRESSES

Up to this point in the chapter, we have only discussed configuring your Linux systems with a single IP address for each network interface. At times, however, it is necessary to associate multiple IP addresses with a single network interface. These IP addresses are known as virtual IP addresses because there is no longer a one-to-one relationship between the IP addresses and the network hardware available.

There are several reasons to use multiple IP addresses:

- Your Linux system is providing Web hosting services for multiple Web sites. Ideally, each Web site's hostname should be associated with a unique IP address. For this to happen, your system must answer requests for all these IP addresses. This is typically done with virtual addresses.

- Your Linux system is providing mail services for multiple domains. You may want your server to be identified by a different hostname and IP address for each mail domain. Again, this is typically done with virtual addresses.

Assuming you have correctly configured your system to communicate with your local LAN, adding support for virtual addresses simply involved issuing an extra `ifconfig` command for each virtual address.

In the manual configuration examples earlier in this chapter, you looked at a system with a single Ethernet device (`eth0`) configured with IP address `192.168.147.5`:

```
# /sbin/ifconfig eth0 192.168.147.5 netmask 255.255.255.0 up
```

The only question is what Ethernet device to use. If you attempt to assign a second IP address to the device `eth0`, `ifconfig` will simply change the IP address associated with the device. Instead, virtual devices are used. Where `eth0` is associated with a particular physical network interface, `eth0:1`, `eth0:2`, `eth0:3`, and so on are virtual devices associated with the same physical network interface.

Therefore, if you want to assign a virtual IP address of `192.168.147.10` to `eth0`, use the following command:

```
# /sbin/ifconfig eth0:1 192.168.147.10 netmask 255.255.255.0 up
```

Similarly, to assign a third IP address of `192.168.147.15` to the same network interface, use this command:

```
# /sbin/ifconfig eth0:2 192.168.147.15 netmask 255.255.255.0 up
```

After doing this, using the `ifconfig` command to display the current status of your network devices will show each of these virtual devices separately:

```
# ifconfig
eth0        Link encap:Ethernet   HWaddr 00:20:AF:EB:41:69
            inet addr:192.168.147.5  Bcast:192.168.147.255   Mask:255.255.255.0
            UP BROADCAST RUNNING MULTICAST   MTU:1500  Metric:1
            RX packets:14583 errors:9 dropped:0 overruns:0 frame:9
            TX packets:521 errors:0 dropped:0 overruns:0 carrier:9
            collisions:6 txqueuelen:100
            Interrupt:10 Base address:0x300

eth0:1      Link encap:Ethernet   HWaddr 00:20:AF:EB:41:69
            inet addr:192.168.147.10  Bcast:192.168.147.255   Mask:255.255.255.0
            UP BROADCAST RUNNING MULTICAST   MTU:1500  Metric:1
            RX packets:14583 errors:9 dropped:0 overruns:0 frame:9
            TX packets:521 errors:0 dropped:0 overruns:0 carrier:9
            collisions:6 txqueuelen:100
            Interrupt:10 Base address:0x300

eth0:2       Link encap:Ethernet   HWaddr 00:20:AF:EB:41:69
            inet addr:192.168.147.15  Bcast:192.168.147.255   Mask:255.255.255.0
            UP BROADCAST RUNNING MULTICAST   MTU:1500  Metric:1
            RX packets:14583 errors:9 dropped:0 overruns:0 frame:9
            TX packets:521 errors:0 dropped:0 overruns:0 carrier:9
            collisions:6 txqueuelen:100
            Interrupt:10 Base address:0x300

lo          Link encap:Local Loopback
            inet addr:127.0.0.1  Mask:255.0.0.0
            UP LOOPBACK RUNNING   MTU:3924  Metric:1
            RX packets:8 errors:0 dropped:0 overruns:0 frame:0
            TX packets:8 errors:0 dropped:0 overruns:0 carrier:0
            collisions:0 txqueuelen:0
```

TROUBLESHOOTING

Because of the number of variables involved in a successful configuration (network interfaces, kernel modules, DNS servers, routing, network topology, and so forth), troubleshooting is a broad topic. It is difficult to give specific advice to address all possible problems.

Troubleshooting a TCP/IP network requires a good understanding of the basic networking principles, familiarity with the network, and proficiency with a set of diagnostic networking tools. It also requires a methodical approach to analyzing the problem at hand, and the ability to break down the problem into smaller pieces and home in to the root cause of the problem.

In analyzing a problem, the first step is to gather detailed information about what is happening. Some of the details will include the name of the application that is failing, the hostnames and IP addresses of the machines involved, and what error messages are being reported. Log in to the machine having the problem and try to duplicate it. Run the same application on a different system.

When a user reports a problem with running a particular network application, these possible scenarios need to be checked out:

- If all other network applications are running without problems, there is a possible misconfiguration of this particular application that needs to be discovered and fixed.

- Check if the problem with this application is occurring on all hosts. This may point to one of the remote hosts which is serving this particular application, and that may be where the problem lies.

- See if the remote host is on a different network than the application is trying to contact. If so, there may be a routing problem reaching this host.

In addition, there are some general tips to keep in mind when debugging network problems:

- Don't overlook the obvious. Check Ethernet cables, faulty hubs, misconfigured switch ports, bad connectors, and loose cables.

- Approach the problem methodically. Start testing from what is working and go toward what is not.

- Record the tests you have done and their results.

- Pay close attention to error messages. Error messages are recorded in system log files. Sometimes they do not tell you exactly what you are looking for, but often they provide clues that help you solve the problem.

- Do not take the problem description provided by a help desk staff or a user as definitive. Try and duplicate it yourself. Very often you will discover discrepancies in problem descriptions. After verifying and correcting the problem description you will often be able to find the solution.

- Do not rule out human errors. Sometimes problems are created by inexperienced IS staff members. Talk to them after you fix the problem to avoid similar mistakes being repeated in the future.

- Learn to use a few simple troubleshooting tools well. In TCP/IP you can diagnose networking problems with a handful of tools. We will look at some of these later in the next section.

- Make sure you test your end of things completely before you try to contact network administrators of remote systems. If all your tests indicate the source of the problem to be on a remote system that is not under your control, you should have collected enough test results to share with the remote administrator that would help his or her diagnostic efforts.

LINUX NETWORK TROUBLESHOOTING UTILITIES

Several useful tools for network troubleshooting are bundled with all Linux distributions. Using these tools, it is possible to diagnose and fix the vast majority of networking problems. While third-party commercial tools for network troubleshooting are available, they are usually not essential and are not discussed in this book.

Table 13.4 outlines the standard Linux TCP/IP tools which can be used for problem diagnosis and troubleshooting.

TABLE 13.4   LINUX TCP/IP UTILITIES

Utility	Description
ping	Tests basic network connectivity
traceroute	Traces the route packets are taking to travel from the source system to the destination system
netstat	Displays information about network connections; commonly used to check system routing tables
ifconfig	Displays information about network interfaces and sets an interface's IP address, network mask, and broadcast address
arp	Displays the IP addresses and corresponding Ethernet MAC addresses of hosts on the local network
nslookup	Looks up hostnames, IP addresses, and variety of other host and domain-related information stored in DNS databases
tcpdump	Displays packets on the network for analysis purposes

USING ping

ping stands for Packet Internet Groper. This utility is used to test accessibility of a remote host. The program works by sending an ICMP echo request to the remote host. This echo request requires a mandatory response from the remote system. If the system is operational and receives the echo request it must respond.

Generally, ping repeatedly issues echo requests until cancelled by the user. Each packet it transmits has associated with it a timestamp and a unique sequence number. This information can be used to determine if any packets have been dropped, duplicated, or reordered and can also be used to compute the round trip time (RTT) for packets to travel to the remote system and back again.

In addition to reporting this data, ping also reports any ICMP messages it receives from routers along the path to the remote system. Typical ICMP messages include "ICMP host unreachable" and "ICMP redirect," both of which indicate problems communicating with the destination system.

If you use the ping command without any flags or arguments except the address of the remote host, it will run forever, repeatedly sending echo requests to the remote host until the user cancels the command with Ctrl+C:

```
$ ping 10.10.10.1
64 bytes from 10.10.10.1: icmp_seq=0 ttl=253 time=0.8 ms
64 bytes from 10.10.10.1: icmp_seq=1 ttl=253 time=0.7 ms
64 bytes from 10.10.10.1: icmp_seq=2 ttl=253 time=0.8 ms
64 bytes from 10.10.10.1: icmp_seq=3 ttl=253 time=0.7 ms
64 bytes from 10.10.10.1: icmp_seq=4 ttl=253 time=0.7 ms
etc.
```

You can control how many echo requests `ping` sends to a remote host with the -c argument. For instance, to limit ping to five echo requests to the host 10.10.10.1, use the following command:

```
$ ping -c 5 10.10.10.1
64 bytes from 10.10.10.1: icmp_seq=0 ttl=253 time=0.8 ms
64 bytes from 10.10.10.1: icmp_seq=1 ttl=253 time=0.7 ms
64 bytes from 10.10.10.1: icmp_seq=2 ttl=253 time=0.8 ms
64 bytes from 10.10.10.1: icmp_seq=3 ttl=253 time=0.7 ms
64 bytes from 10.10.10.1: icmp_seq=4 ttl=253 time=0.7 ms
--- gatekeeper ping statistics ---
5 packets transmitted, 5 packets received, 0% packet loss
round-trip min/avg/max = 0.7/0.7/0.8 ms
```

The output above shows the IP address of the remote host, the ICMP sequence numbers, and the round trip travel times. Since it was invoked with the -c 5 option it runs five times and exits. It also prints a summary report of the number of packets transmitted, the number received, and the minimum, average, and round-trip travel times.

If `ping` cannot resolve a hostname to an IP address it displays an error message:

```
$ ping foo.bwc.org
ping: unknown host foo.bwc.org
```

When you receive an error like this, it means you have a problem with name resolution on your system. You should check your NIS and DNS servers and their databases and make sure the system in question can communicate with the necessary servers and that these servers can resolve the name in question.

If `ping` can resolve a hostname to an IP address but does not receive responses to its echo requests, then this is reflected in the summary statistics `ping` displays:

```
$ ping -c 5 www.juxta.com
PING www.juxta.com (204.50.107.151): 56 data bytes
--- www.juxta.com ping statistics ---
5 packets transmitted, 0 packets received, 100% packet loss
```

Notice that no packets were received and that 100% packet loss is reported. This indicates a possibility that the host www.juxta.com may be down or that some form of network failure prevents communication with the remote host. However many sites have firewalls configured to block ICMP traffic to protect themselves from Denial of Service attacks. `ping` cannot be used to conclusively test connectivity to such sites.

When you are trying to isolate a network fault with `ping`, it is advisable to start testing the local host with `ping` to make sure that the local network interface is up and running. After that, try hosts on your local network, then your network's default gateway, and then systems further and further away to determine the degree of network problems.

If ping works fine but you cannot telnet, or ftp, then you know the problem is not routing or ability to communicate with a remote system. Instead, you have identified an application level problem. At times a system responds to pings but nothing else works. This can happen if the Internet daemon (inetd) dies or some other higher-level system problem occurs. Often, restarting inetd will fix the problem. If that does not work, rebooting the affected system may be your only option.

USING traceroute

The traceroute utility traces the route of UDP packets from the local host to a remote destination. It prints the hostname (if it can be resolved) and the IP address of all routers between the local host and the remote host. If ping cannot reach a particular remote host, it is not always true that the remote host is down. The problem may exist at a gateway somewhere between your system and the remote host. The traceroute program can be used to locate such a problem.

traceroute uses two special techniques to force an error message to be sent back from each router in its path. It uses a small TTL value (time to live) and an invalid port number. When the packet reaches a router it sends back a "time exceeded" error message. traceroute uses this error message to identify the fact that a package has reached a particular router and to calculate roundtrip times. This enables traceroute to determine the time required for the hop to the first router. By increasing the time limit value, and re-sending the packet so that it will reach the second router in the path to the destination, which returns another "time exceeded" message, information can be calculated about the second router and so forth. Ultimately, traceroute determines when the packet has reached the destination if the destination can be reached. In this way traceroute constructs a list of the routers that are traversed to get to the destination host.

Consider the following sample output from a local host (cstlx001) to a remote host (www.bahai.org):

```
# traceroute www.bahai.org
traceroute to www.bahai.org (207.217.239.32), 30 hops max, 40 byte packets
cstrt001 (10.2.0.254)  1.840 ms  1.720 ms  1.657 ms
atcrt001-g2 (10.0.2.1)  1.702 ms  1.623 ms  1.606 ms
fw-nat (10.0.0.1)  0.987 ms * *
rtgate (192.115.144.18)  3.637 ms  3.102 ms  3.357 ms
tlv-fe110.netvision.net.il (199.203.4.200)  17.789 ms  16.479 ms  15.654 ms
nyc-s1-0-5-n011.netvision.net.il (194.90.0.54)  360.101 ms  360.117 ms 452.812 ms
nj-ny6t-H5-0-1.netvision.net.il (194.90.0.89)  367.297 ms  384.195 ms 466.206 ms
serial0-1-1.gw2.har1.alter.net (157.130.25.245)  371.438 ms  382.126 ms 372.043 ms
422.ATM9-0-0.GW1.HAR1.ALTER.NET (137.39.30.249)  365.694 ms  366.808 ms 377.897 ms
136.Hssi9-0.HR2.NYC2.ALTER.NET (137.39.69.49)  428.716 ms  384.896 ms  387.397 ms
142.ATM3-0.XR1.NYC1.ALTER.NET (146.188.177.34)  391.450 ms  398.219 ms  395.866 ms
195.ATM3-0.TR1.NYC1.ALTER.NET (146.188.178.182)  391.084 ms  382.795 ms 421.005 ms
104.ATM7-0.TR1.LAX2.ALTER.NET (146.188.137.129)  525.664 ms  448.192 ms 516.039 ms
299.ATM6-0.XR1.LAX4.ALTER.NET (146.188.248.249) 447.762 ms 451.041 ms 473.453 ms
193.ATM6-0.GW4.LAX4.ALTER.NET (152.63.113.89)  478.369 ms  486.643 ms  462.203 ms
earthlink-gw.customer.alter.net (157.130.231.222) 477.392 ms 534.410 ms 453.205 ms
18   f9-0-0-cr01-pas.neteng.itd.earthlink.net(207.217.1.107) \537.557 ms 458.573
➥ms449.132 ms
19   * f10-1-0-fr01-pas.neteng.itd.earthlink.net (207.217.2.106)  449.583 ms
➥ 518.765 ms
20  207.217.208.166 (207.217.208.166)  574.278 ms  514.836 ms  496.682 ms
21  207.217.239.32 (207.217.239.32)  516.840 ms  519.242 ms  526.422 ms
```

Here we see 20 routers between the local and remote hosts. Each line of the output represents one hop on the route to the remote host. For each hop we see the hostname (if available), the IP address of the gateway router, and three sample round trip times to reach the host. These three times are received by sending out three packets at each TTL value and reporting the time until the returned error packet is received. If no error packet comes back, an asterisk is displayed in place of a value:

```
# traceroute ftp.is.co.za
traceroute to ftp.is.co.za (196.4.160.12), 30 hops max, 40 byte packets
 1  cstrt001 (10.2.0.254)  1.906 ms  1.677 ms  1.657 ms
 2  atcrt001-g2 (10.0.2.1)  1.720 ms  1.644 ms  1.608 ms
 3  fw-nat (10.0.0.1)  1.014 ms * *
rtgate (192.115.144.18)  3.561 ms  3.327 ms  3.342 ms
tlv-fe110.netvision.net.il (199.203.4.200)  15.325 ms  19.331 ms  15.053 ms
nyc-s4-0-4-n002.netvision.net.il (194.90.0.185)  367.383 ms  366.807 ms 374.334 ms
nj-ny6t-H5-0-1.netvision.net.il (194.90.0.89)  387.460 ms  375.801 ms  369.297 ms
serial0-1-1.gw2.har1.alter.net (157.130.25.245)  374.683 ms  393.632 ms  374.661
➥ms
422.ATM9-0-0.GW1.HAR1.ALTER.NET (137.39.30.249)  377.170 ms  373.443 ms  448.300
➥ms
136.Hssi9-0.HR2.NYC2.ALTER.NET (137.39.69.49)  401.138 ms  392.110 ms  441.235 ms
442.ATM3-0.XR1.NYC1.ALTER.NET (146.188.177.34)  397.832 ms  391.710 ms  398.259 ms
195.ATM6-0.XR1.NYC4.ALTER.NET (146.188.178.82)  417.984 ms  394.524 ms  389.993 ms
189.ATM9-0-0.GW4.NYC4.ALTER.NET (146.188.179.161) \ 398.030 ms  399.579 ms
➥393.061 ms
iscoza-gw.customer.alter.net (157.130.22.182)  388.323 ms  399.139 ms  393.250 ms
168.209.0.129 (168.209.0.129)  956.494 ms  966.903 ms  969.841 ms
168.209.100.8 (168.209.100.8)  973.092 ms  963.411 ms  945.400 ms
* * *
* * *
* * *
* * *
```

This series of asterisks indicates failure to reach the remote host and that the trace has trailed off. This indicates a routing problem or network failure after the last gateway in the list of successful hops. If the last router is under your control, you have identified a problem location from which you can begin searching for the source of your communication problems.

USING netstat

The netstat command displays the current network status. It has many options that can be used to filter status data. The most useful netstat options are outlined in Table 13.5.

TABLE 13.5 SELECTED netstat OPTIONS

Option	Description
-a	Displays all active network connections and their statuses
-I	Displays summary information for each network interface
-s	Displays packet summaries sorted by protocol

PART
III

CH
13

Option	Description
-r	Displays information about routing tables and their statuses
-c	Displays continuous output updated every second
-N	Displays messages about the creation or deletion of interfaces or routes

TABLE 13.5 CONTINUED

The default operation of netstat is to display the status of network connections by listing open sockets. The following sample output displays the protocol, send and receive queues, local hostname or IP address, the remote hostname or IP address, and the state of each open connection:

```
# netstat
Active Internet connections (w/o servers)
Proto Recv-Q Send-Q Local Address           Foreign Address         State
tcp        0      0 cstlx001.bwc.org:8083   mcpws009.bwc.org:4185   TIME_WAIT
tcp        0      0 cstlx001.bwc.org:8083   allws025.bwc.org:3533   TIME_WAIT
tcp        0      0 cstlx001.bwc.org:8083   shjws159.bwc.org:1669   TIME_WAIT
tcp        0      0 cstlx001.bwc.org:8083   allws057.bwc.org:2542   TIME_WAIT
tcp        0      0 cstlx001.bwc.org:8083   allws057.bwc.org:2541   TIME_WAIT
tcp        0      0 cstlx001.bwc.org:8083   allws057.bwc.org:2540   TIME_WAIT
tcp        0      2 cstlx001.bwc.org:telnet 192.115.144.86:1034     ESTABLISHED
tcp        0      0 cstlx001.bwc.org:telnet 192.115.144.72:1030     ESTABLISHED
tcp        0      0 cstlx001.bwc.org:telnet 192.115.144.76:1028     ESTABLISHED
tcp        0      0 localhost:3410          localhost:3411          ESTABLISHED
tcp        0      0 localhost:3411          localhost:3410          ESTABLISHED
tcp        0      0 localhost:3408          localhost:3409          ESTABLISHED
tcp        0      0 localhost:3409          localhost:3408          ESTABLISHED
tcp        0      0 localhost:3406          localhost:3407          ESTABLISHED
tcp        0      0 localhost:3407          localhost:3406          ESTABLISHED
tcp        0      0 localhost:3404          localhost:3405          ESTABLISHED
tcp        0      0 localhost:3405          localhost:3404          ESTABLISHED
tcp        0      0 localhost:3402          localhost:3403          ESTABLISHED
tcp        0      0 localhost:3403          localhost:3402          ESTABLISHED
Active UNIX domain sockets (w/o servers)
Proto RefCnt Flags       Type       State         I-Node Path
unix  1      [ ]         STREAM     CONNECTED     606442 @000000dd
unix  1      [ ]         STREAM     CONNECTED     486    @0000001d
unix  1      [ ]         STREAM     CONNECTED     608660 @000000e7
unix  1      [ ]         STREAM     CONNECTED     566507 @000000da
unix  1      [ ]         STREAM     CONNECTED     606804 @000000e2
unix  1      [ ]         STREAM     CONNECTED     767    @00000030
unix  0      [ ]         STREAM     CONNECTED     134    @00000015
unix  1      [ ]         STREAM     CONNECTED     564    @00000023
unix  1      [ ]         STREAM     CONNECTED     608661 /dev/log
unix  1      [ ]         STREAM     CONNECTED     606805 /dev/log
unix  1      [ ]         STREAM     CONNECTED     606443 /dev/log
unix  1      [ ]         STREAM     CONNECTED     566508 /dev/log
unix  1      [ ]         STREAM     CONNECTED     768    /dev/log
unix  1      [ ]         STREAM     CONNECTED     623    /dev/log
unix  1      [ ]         STREAM     CONNECTED     487    /dev/log
```

The -i option can be used to provide useful diagnostic information about a local network:

```
# netstat -i
Kernel Interface table
Iface   MTU Met    RX-OK RX-ERR RX-DRP RX-OVR    TX-OK TX-ERR TX-DRP TX-OVR Flg
eth0   1500   0  4253182      0      0      0  4355313      0      0      0 BRU
lo     3924   0    48448      0      0      0    48448      0      0      0 LRU
```

In this example, output is displayed for each network interface. For each interface, the number of transmit and receive errors are displayed in the TX-ERR and RX-ERR columns. Normally, both of these values should be zero or close to zero. If you see large numbers or growing values in either column, this is a strong indication of a network problem such as a saturated local network, a faulty network interface or defective cabling.

On Linux and most other Unix systems, the -r option causes netstat to display information about routing tables:

```
$ netstat -r
Kernel IP routing table
Destination      Gateway        Genmask          Flags  MSS Window  irtt Iface
10.2.0.244       *              255.255.255.255  UH       0 0         0 eth0
10.2.0.0         *              255.255.0.0      U        0 0         0 eth0
127.0.0.0        *              255.0.0.0        U        0 0         0 lo
default          cstrt001       0.0.0.0          UG       0 0         0 eth0
```

In this sample output, the Destination column indicates the host or network for which the route is defined. The Gateway column indicates which gateway, if any, needs to be used for communicating with the host or network in question.

The last line shows the default route. The default route is a catchall. Whenever there is no specific route for a destination, the packets are sent to the default router or gateway. In the above example cstrt001 is the default router. Note the Flags column for this entry has the value UG. U means the route is up, or functional, and G means the route uses a gateway.

USING ifconfig

ifconfig is used to configure the network interfaces as discussed earlier in this chapter in the section on manual network configuration. At boot time ifconfig is invoked by the script /etc/rc.d/init.d/network to set up the interfaces as necessary. After that, it can be used for troubleshooting and debugging. It can also be used to tune certain network interface parameters.

When invoked with no arguments, ifconfig displays the status of the currently active network interfaces. If a single interface argument is given, it displays the status of that interface only. If invoked with the -a option, it displays the status of all interfaces, including those that are down.

A sample output of ifconfig -a is shown here:

```
# /sbin/ifconfig -a
eth0      Link encap:Ethernet  HWaddr 00:80:5F:6D:CF:C2
          inet addr:10.2.0.244  Bcast:10.2.255.255  Mask:255.255.0.0
          UP BROADCAST RUNNING MULTICAST  MTU:1500  Metric:1
          RX packets:4261292 errors:0 dropped:0 overruns:0 frame:0
          TX packets:4363313 errors:0 dropped:0 overruns:0 carrier:0
```

PART

III

CH

13

```
                       collisions:0 txqueuelen:100
                       Interrupt:5 Base address:0x6000
            lo         Link encap:Local Loopback
                       inet addr:127.0.0.1  Mask:255.0.0.0
                       UP LOOPBACK RUNNING  MTU:3924  Metric:1
                       RX packets:48474 errors:0 dropped:0 overruns:0 frame:0
                       TX packets:48474 errors:0 dropped:0 overruns:0 carrier:0
                       collisions:0 txqueuelen:0
```

The first line shows the interface name (eth0 in this case), the encapsulation method, and the Ethernet hardware address. The second line shows the IP address of the interface, the netmask, and the broadcast address. The third line shows the status of the interface (UP or DOWN). The lines after that give statistics on packets received and sent, and error counters.

Some common interface configuration problems are using the subnet mask or IP address. If two systems are accidentally configured with the same IP address, a very strange situation ensues. Packets intended for host A get stolen by the imposter B. Neither host can function properly. The situation worsens considerably if one of the hosts is a server of sorts to which many clients connect. In this case all applications that are trying to connect to this server will exhibit locking up behavior. To troubleshoot such a problem the most appropriate tool is the arp command, which we will look at in the next section.

One way to deal with a problem like this is to disconnect the network connection of the offending system immediately. This restores the network back to sanity and the larger problem is resolved. In addition you will have to delete the arp entry of the duplicate machine and temporarily add a static entry for the bona-fide system. Now you should be able to examine and correct the IP address of the offending system.

To change the IP address of eth0 to 10.1.0.5 and the netmask to 255.255.0.0, you can use the following steps:

```
# ifconfig eth0 down
# ifconfig eth0 address 10.1.0.5 netmask 255.255.0.0
# ifconfig eth0 up
```

In addition you should change the IP address in the local /etc/hosts file and correct the NIS and DNS databases.

USING arp

The arp command displays the translation of an IP address to an Ethernet MAC address. This makes it an excellent debugging tool because it allows you to track the relationship between IP addresses and particular network interfaces.

For example, in the previous section we looked at what happens when an IP address is accidentally assigned to two machines. If this happens a duplicate IP address error will be reported and logged. Checking /var/log/messages on the system whose IP address is stolen by some other system should include entries similar to the following:

```
Dec 6 14:42:56 saturn vmunix: duplicate IP address!!
      sent from ethernet address 00:C0:4F:A9:F9:26
```

From this information we can determine that the duplicate IP address is coming from a system whose Ethernet address is `00:C0:4F:A9:F9:26`.

Before attempting to physically locate the system with the culprit network interface, the first step is to remove `saturn`'s false arp entry containing the wrong Ethernet address and manually add a static arp entry with its correct Ethernet address. This static arp entry cannot be deleted and will prevent packets intended for `saturn` from being delivered to the offending host.

This will allow `saturn` to continue functioning normally while you identify the system which is attempting to use `saturn`'s IP address and fix the configuration problems on that system.

To remove `saturn`'s arp entry, use the `-d` option of the arp command:

```
# arp -d saturn
```

To add a static arp entry for `saturn`, use the `-s` flag of the arp command:

```
# arp -s saturn 00:03:E3:C0:05:07
```

Next, you can begin hunting down the offending system by obtaining a list of all systems in the arp cache with the `-a` flag of the arp command:

```
# arp -a
vered (10.2.0.100) at 08:00:20:07:55:CC [ether] on eth0
linux (10.2.0.252) at 00:C0:4F:A9:F9:11 [ether] on eth0
cstrt001 (10.2.0.254) at 00:E0:16:7E:F8:81 [ether] on eth0
saturn (10.2.0.248) at 00:03:E3:C0:05:07 [ether] on eth0
cronus (10.2.0.249) at 00:80:F1:00:0C:33 [ether] on eth0
```

USING `nslookup`

If you receive `unknown host` errors when using commands such as ping but are certain the hostnames you have used are correct, then you are faced with a name resolution problem and need to fix errors in the DNS database. DNS is discussed in detail in Chapter 22, "DNS."

The `nslookup` command allows you to query a DNS server and view the contents of its database. You can use this to check the values stored in the database for a particular host:

```
# nslookup cobra
Server:  bwcdc001.bwc.org
Address:  10.0.0.2
*** bwcdc001.bwc.org can't find cobra: Non-existent host/domain
```

In this sample output, `nslookup` failed to find an entry for the host cobra. The following output is an example of what happens when you use `nslookup` to look up a name successfully:

```
# nslookup saturn
Server:  bwcdc001.bwc.org
Address:  10.0.0.2
Name:    saturn.bwc.org
Address:  10.2.0.248
```

PART

III

CH

13

Note

If you are using NIS at your site in addition to DNS then you should check whether the hostname resolves properly through NIS also. To do that you will need to use the ypmatch command as outlined in Chapter 6, "Authenticating Users and Network Resources."

USING tcpdump

tcpdump is a powerful tool for network monitoring and data acquisition. This program allows you to generate reports about the traffic on a network. It can be used to examine the headers of packets on a network interface that match a given expression. However you should be aware that tcpdump can only sniff packets that reach its network interfaces. This is not a problem in networks using shared media or hubs. On switched Ethernet environments, its effectiveness is greatly minimized because you can only watch broadcast packets and other traffic that originate from or are destined to the host running tcpdump. In any case, the tool is still very useful.

You can use this tool to track down network problems, to detect "ping attacks," or to monitor network activities. To get a complete set of options refer to the tcpdump man pages.

Here, you will learn some examples of how tcpdump can be used to gather useful information about network traffic. In Linux you must be logged in as root to run this tcpdump.

Caution

If tcpdump is setuid root then it can be run by any user, but this is highly discouraged as this can pose a major security risk. The program can be misused to sniff clear text passwords on the network.

If you invoke tcpdump without any arguments it will capture all packets on the network and display them. A small sample output of tcpdump is shown here:

```
# tcpdump
23:39:41.638705 allws025.bwc.org.3743 > cstlx001.bwc.org.8083: . ack 2172208734
win 8760 (DF)
23:39:41.638835 cstlx001.bwc.org.8083 > allws025.bwc.org.3743: FP 1:187(186) ack
 0 win 32120 (DF)
23:39:41.642321 cstlx001.bwc.org.886 > saturn.bwc.org.657: udp 80
23:39:41.679044 allws025.bwc.org.3743 > cstlx001.bwc.org.8083: . ack 188 win 857
4 (DF)
23:39:41.690320 allws025.bwc.org.3743 > cstlx001.bwc.org.8083: F 0:0(0) ack 188
win 8574 (DF)
23:39:41.690424 cstlx001.bwc.org.8083 > allws025.bwc.org.3743: . ack 1 win 32119
 (DF)
23:39:41.696803 saturn.bwc.org.657 > cstlx001.bwc.org.886: udp 64
23:39:41.698009 cstlx001.bwc.org.887 > saturn.bwc.org.657: udp 80
23:39:41.700371 saturn.bwc.org.657 > cstlx001.bwc.org.887: udp 124
23:39:41.703604 shjws159.bwc.org.1879 > cstlx001.bwc.org.8083: S 43808644:438086
```

```
44(0) win 8192 <mss 1460> (DF)
23:39:41.703732 cstlx001.bwc.org.8083 > shjws159.bwc.org.1879: S 2162833501:2162
833501(0) ack 43808645 win 30660 <mss 1460> (DF)
23:39:41.704168 shjws159.bwc.org.1879 > cstlx001.bwc.org.8083: . ack 1 win 8760
(DF)
23:39:41.705443 cstlx001.bwc.org.888 > saturn.bwc.org.657: udp 80
23:39:41.706955 shjws159.bwc.org.1879 > cstlx001.bwc.org.8083: P 1:451(450) ack
 1 win 8760 (DF)
23:39:41.707061 cstlx001.bwc.org.8083 > shjws159.bwc.org.1879: . ack 451 win 306
60 (DF)
23:39:41.709400 cstlx001.bwc.org.8083 > shjws159.bwc.org.1879: . 1:1461(1460) ac
k 451 win 32120 (DF)
23:39:41.714870 saturn.bwc.org.657 > cstlx001.bwc.org.888: udp 60
23:39:41.826279 shjws159.bwc.org.1879 > cstlx001.bwc.org.8083: . ack 1461 win 87
60 (DF)
23:39:41.826379 cstlx001.bwc.org.8083 > shjws159.bwc.org.1879: FP 1461:1653(192)
 ack 451 win 32120 (DF)
23:39:41.826924 shjws159.bwc.org.1879 > cstlx001.bwc.org.8083: . ack 1654 win 85
68 (DF)
23:39:41.849289 shjws159.bwc.org.1879 > cstlx001.bwc.org.8083: F 451:451(0) ack
1654 win 8568 (DF)
23:39:41.849381 cstlx001.bwc.org.8083 > shjws159.bwc.org.1879: . ack 452 win 321
19 (DF)
23:39:41.853015 192.115.144.85.1037 > cstlx001.bwc.org.telnet: . ack 3722964229
win 8495 (DF)
23:39:41.853092 cstlx001.bwc.org.telnet > 192.115.144.85.1037: P 1:29(28) ack 0
win 32696 (DF)
23:39:41.853936 cstlx001.bwc.org.889 > saturn.bwc.org.657: udp 84
23:39:41.863642 saturn.bwc.org.657 > cstlx001.bwc.org.889: udp 32
23:39:41.865619 cstlx001.bwc.org.2178 > bwcdc001.domain: 9100+ (45)
23:39:41.867214 bwcdc001.domain > cstlx001.bwc.org.2178: 9100 NXDomain 0/1/0 (99
)
23:39:41.868653 cstlx001.bwc.org.890 > saturn.bwc.org.657: udp 76
23:39:41.870835 saturn.bwc.org.657 > cstlx001.bwc.org.890: udp 52
23:39:42.159239 192.115.144.85.1037 > cstlx001.bwc.org.telnet: . ack 29 win 8467
 (DF)
23:39:42.496991 cstrt001 > ospf-all.mcast.net: OSPFv2-hello 44: rtrid 22.98.192.
0 backbone [¦ospf] [tos 0xc0] [ttl 1]
23:39:42.497697 cstlx001.bwc.org.891 > saturn.bwc.org.657: udp 80
23:39:42.505288 saturn.bwc.org.657 > cstlx001.bwc.org.891: udp 64
23:39:42.505972 cstlx001.bwc.org.892 > saturn.bwc.org.657: udp 80
23:39:42.508210 saturn.bwc.org.657 > cstlx001.bwc.org.892: udp 72
23:39:42.508904 cstlx001.bwc.org.893 > saturn.bwc.org.657: udp 80
23:39:43.000856 saturn.bwc.org.657 > cstlx001.bwc.org.893: udp 32
23:39:43.001115 cstlx001.bwc.org.2178 > bwcdc001.domain: 9101+ (42)
23:39:43.001727 bwcdc001.domain > cstlx001.bwc.org.2178: 9101 NXDomain 0/1/0 (116)
```

As you can see above, each packet is time stamped. The fields in each entry vary depending on the protocol type (such as UDP or TCP).

For UDP packets, entries are of the following general format:

```
<time stamp> <source host>.<port> > <destination host>.<port>: \  <other optional
➥<fields> packet length>
```

For port numbers that have names associated with them, the names are printed instead. The following two lines show a domain name query and response:

```
23:39:43.001115 cstlx001.bwc.org.2178 > bwcdc001.domain: 9101+ (42)
23:39:43.001727 bwcdc001.domain > cstlx001.bwc.org.2178: 9101 NXDomain 0/1/0 (116)
```

The general format of a TCP packet is as follows:

```
<time stamp> <source host>.<port> <destination host>.<port>:\
  <flags> <data sequence number> <other fields>
```

Example TCP packets to and from a squid server running on port 8083 are shown here:

```
23:39:41.826279 shjws159.bwc.org.1879 > cstlx001.bwc.org.8083: . ack 1461 win 87
60 (DF)
23:39:41.826379 cstlx001.bwc.org.8083 > shjws159.bwc.org.1879: FP 1461:1653(192)
 ack 451 win 32120 (DF)
```

If you want to examine packets to and from a particular host you can invoke tcpdump with the host option as follows:

```
[root@cstlx001 /root]# tcpdump host saturn
tcpdump: listening on eth0
23:52:52.355364 arp who-has saturn.bwc.org tell cstws043.bwc.org
23:52:52.356495 cstlx001.bwc.org.909 > saturn.bwc.org.657: udp 80
23:52:52.367990 saturn.bwc.org.657 > cstlx001.bwc.org.909: udp 60
23:52:55.167137 arp who-has saturn.bwc.org tell cstlx001.bwc.org
23:52:55.167730 arp reply saturn.bwc.org is-at 0:3:e3:c0:5:7
5 packets received by filter
0 packets dropped by kernel
```

Here we can see the packets to and from the host saturn. This shows an interesting arp query and reply for the Ethernet address of saturn.

You can also monitor traffic on a particular port as shown by the following tcpdump output. The server in question is running the proxy server squid on port 8083:

```
[root@cstlx001 /root]# tcpdump port 8083
tcpdump: listening on eth0
23:55:26.067300 cstlx001.bwc.org.8083 > shjws100.bwc.org.2613: F 3141079005:3141
079005(0) ack 213785301 win 32120 (DF)
23:55:26.067691 shjws100.bwc.org.2613 > cstlx001.bwc.org.8083: . ack 1 win 8760
(DF)
23:55:26.880615 shjws100.bwc.org.2613 > cstlx001.bwc.org.8083: R 213785301:21378
5301(0) win 0 (DF)
```

tcpdump offers many other options. Depending on the problem that you are tackling you will need to decide which options best suit your needs. It is recommended that you read the tcpdump man page in detail with the following command:

```
$ man tcpdump
```

## CHAPTER 14

PRINTER AND FILE SHARING WITH NFS AND SAMBA

In this chapter

WHAT IS SAMBA?

Linux is ideally suited to act as a file and print server for Windows networks as well as a client on the same type of network. Windows networks generally use the Server Message Block protocol (or SMB) for file and printer sharing and the Samba package for Linux allows a Linux system to work as both a server and client with the SMB protocol.

Using the Samba package, a Linux system can perform many tasks on a Windows network, including the following:

- Serving files and printers
- Running as a NetBIOS name server, including playing the role of a master browser
- Accessing files on other SMB servers with an FTP-like interface
- Limiting Windows NT administrative capabilities from the Linux command line

With related packages, the following are also possible with Samba:

- Mounting SMB-shared file systems directly in Linux
- Viewing SMB activity with `tcpdump`
- Incorporating SMB functionality in any application with a set of libraries

Samba is included with most complete distributions of Linux and is installed by default. Some distributions, such as Corel Linux, have integrated SMB so tightly in their implementations of Linux that these Linux systems seamlessly operate on a Windows network immediately after installation.

If your distribution does not include Samba or you want to download the latest version of Samba, complete details and source code are available at the Samba Web site at `http://www.samba.org/`. In addition, the SMB HOWTO provides extensive guidance about installing and configuring Samba for different purposes. The SMB HOWTO is online at `http://www.linuxdoc.org/HOWTO/SMB-HOWTO.html`.

GETTING SAMBA UP AND RUNNING

Although most distributions perform the necessary initial configuration necessary to run Samba, it is worth checking this yourself before initially using Samba.

In order for Samba to run, several port definitions must appear in the `/etc/services` file. Check the `/etc/services` file for the following entries and if any of them are missing, add them to the file:

```
netbios-ns       137/tcp       nbns
netbios-ns       137/udp       nbns
netbios-dgm      138/tcp       nbdgm
netbios-dgm      138/udp       nbdgm
netbios-ssn      139/tcp       nbssn
```

If these entries are commented out (preceded with a hash mark), uncomment them by removing the hash mark (#) at the start of the line.

Next, decide whether you want to run Samba from `inetd` or run it directly as a standalone daemon. Samba will run slightly faster as a standalone daemon and if you plan to run a Linux system with Samba as a major file or print server for your network, you are better off running Samba as a standalone daemon.

If you typically run your network daemons through `inetd` and want to do so with Samba as well, add the following two lines to your `/etc/inetd.conf` file:

```
netbios-ssn stream tcp nowait root /usr/sbin/smbd smbd
netbios-ns dgram udp wait root /usr/sbin/nmbd nmbd
```

After editing the `/etc/inetd.conf` file, restart `inetd` with the command:

```
# kill -HUP `cat /var/run/inetd.pid`
```

Alternately, if your system has a start-up script for `inetd`, you can restart `inetd` with the following commands:

```
# /etc/rc.d/init.d/smb stop
# /etc/rc.d/init.d/smb start
```

Next, edit the Samba configuration file, `/etc/smb.conf`, as needed for your system. The particulars of the `smb.conf` file are discussed in context throughout the chapter as we discuss configuring Linux to play different roles on a Windows network. In general, though, the `smb.conf` file consists of a series of sections each with multiple entries:

```
[<section name>]
<entry>
<entry>
<entry>
...
```

Entries can either take the form of a single directive:

```
<directive>
```

Or as an assignment:

```
<setting name> = <value>
```

After the `samba.conf` file is written, you can start Samba manually with the following commands:

```
# /usr/sbin/smbd -D
# /usr/sbin/nmbd -D
```

Alternately, if your system has a startup script for Samba, you can start Samba with the following command:

```
# /etc/rc.d/init.d/smb start
```

PART

III

CH

14

THE smb.conf FILE

Samba is configured using the /etc/smb.conf file. Before looking at specific Samba configurations for different purposes, we need to consider the basic structure of the smb.conf file. The following is a typical smb.conf file:

```
#======================= Global Settings =========================================
[global]
    workgroup = MYGROUP
    server string = Samba Server
    printcap name = /etc/printcap
    load printers = yes
    log file = /var/log/samba/log.%m
    max log size = 50
    security = user
    socket options = TCP_NODELAY SO_RCVBUF=8192 SO_SNDBUF=8192
    dns proxy = no


#=========================== Share Definitions ===============================
[homes]
    comment = Home Directories
    browseable = no
    writable = yes

[printers]
    comment = All Printers
    path = /var/spool/samba
    browseable = no
    guest ok = no
    writable = no
    printable = yes

[mydir]
    comment = My Directory
    path = /usr/somewhere/private
    valid users = someuser
    public = no
    writable = yes
    printable = no
```

The smb.conf file is divided into sections. Each section starts with a section header such as [global] or [printers] that is followed by one or more directives, one per line. The header specifies the name of the section. Comments, which are ignored when in the smb.conf file, start at a hash mark (#) or a semicolon (;) and continue to the end of the line.

Directives in each section of the smb.conf file take one of two forms:

- A value assignment of the form:
  ```
  <directive name> = <value>
  ```

- A simple directive of the form:
  ```
  <directive name>
  ```

All `smb.conf` files contain a `global` section. This section contains any and all directives necessary to indicate how the particular Samba system should interact with the rest of the network, including specifying the workgroup or domain name, defining a security and authentication model, and setting other general settings.

In addition to the `global` section, a Samba server contains one or more share definition sections that define the resources on the system that need to be shared with the network and how to share them. A Samba client does not necessarily need to share resources on the network, although it can. The use of the share definition sections is discussed in more depth throughout this chapter as we consider various examples of Samba configuration.

A large number of directives can appear in the `global` section as outlined in the `smb.conf` manual page, which can be read with the command `man smb.conf`. Table 14.1 outlines some of the more commonly used directives for the `global` section.

TABLE 14.1 COMMON DIRECTIVES IN THE global SECTION OF THE smb.conf FILE

Directive	Description
`workgroup = <name>`	Specifies by name the workgroup or domain to which the system belongs.
`server string = <description>`	Provides a description of the Samba system which will appear when users browse the network.
`hosts allow = <host list>`	Specifies a list of IP addresses or network addresses, separated by spaces, which are allowed to access the Samba server; if not specified, no address-based restrictions will be enforced on the Samba server.
`printcap name = <printcap file>`	Specifies the location of the `printcap` file containing definitions of printers to share.
`load printers = <yes or no>`	Indicates whether the printers should be loaded from the `printcap` file so that they can be automatically shared rather than sharing each printer manually.
`guest account = <user name>`	Indicates which Linux user account to use when users attempt to access the Samba server as a guest user; by default, this will be the `nobody` account.
`log file = <log file name>`	Indicates where Samba should write its log files; the %m symbol indicates that a separate log file should be written for each client that connects and that the name of the file should be made unique using the hostname of each client.
`max log size = <size>`	Specifies the maximum log file size in kilobytes.
`security = <security level>`	Specifies the type of security to use; consult the `smb.conf` manual page for more details on security levels; generally you will want to use `user` security.
`password server = <host name>`	Specifies hostname of a password server for use when the security level is set to `server`.

TABLE 14.1   CONTINUED

Directive	Description
username map = *<map file>*	Specifies the name of a file containing a map associating Samba usernames with local Linux usernames.
domain controller = *<host name>*	Specifies the hostname of your domain's primary domain controller.
dns proxy = *<yes or no>*	Indicates whether Samba should use DNS to resolve NetBIOS hostnames.

The global section from the previous sample smb.conf file uses only some of these directives:

```
01: [global]
02:     workgroup = MYGROUP
03:     server string = Samba Server
04:     printcap name = /etc/printcap
05:     load printers = yes
06:     log file = /var/log/samba/log.%m
07:     max log size = 50
08:     security = user
09:     socket options = TCP_NODELAY SO_RCVBUF=8192 SO_SNDBUF=8192
10:     dns proxy = no
```

Note   Line numbers have been added to the above segment for reference purposes.

This global section can be broken down as follows:

- **Line 2**: Specifies that MYGROUP is the workgroup to which the Samba system belongs.
- **Line 3**: Specifies that the Samba system should be identified with the description Samba Server.
- **Lines 4 and 5**: Indicates that the printers in /etc/printcap should be automatically loaded for sharing purposes.
- **Line 6**: Indicates that a separate log file for each client should be created in /var/log/samba/.
- **Line 7**: Specifies that logs should be limited to 50KB in size.
- **Line 8**: Indicates that user-level security should used.
- **Line 9**: Creates settings to help improve the network performance of Samba.
- **Line 10**: Indicates that DNS should not be used to resolve NetBIOS hostnames.

TESTING YOUR `smb.conf` FILE

The Samba suite includes the `testparm` utility, which you can use to test the validity of your `smb.conf` file. To test your `smb.conf` file with this tool, use the following command:

```
# testparm /etc/smb.conf
```

`testparm` will report as it tests each section and if all sections appear correct and valid, will report successful analysis of the file:

```
Load smb config files from smb.conf
Processing section "[homes]"
Processing section "[printers]"
Processing section "[mydir]"
Loaded services file OK.
```

SHARING LINUX FILES WITH SAMBA

In order to share directories and the files they contain in your Samba server with the rest of the network, you must configure the global section of your `smb.conf` file as outlined in the previous section. Your Samba system must be properly connected to your network and you must create share definition sections for all the file systems you want to share. There are two main types of share definitions in the `smb.conf` file:

- The `homes` section to make user's home directories on the Samba system accessible as individual shares. The following is a typical `homes` section:

```
[homes]
  comment = Home Directories
  browseable = no
  writable = yes
```

- Individual share definition sections to share specific directories with specific parameters. For instance, the following section creates a share named `mydir` which shares the directory `/usr/somewhere/private` on the Samba system:

```
[mydir]
  comment = My Directory
  path = /usr/somewhere/private
  valid users = someuser
  public = no
  writable = yes
  printable = no
```

The `homes` section is usually quite simple. Typically, it contains two important directives. One is the `browseable` directive which, when set to `no`, ensures that all the home directory shares do not display in the list of shares available on the server when users browse the network. The second is the `writable` directive which, when set to `yes`, ensures that users have full read and write access to their home directories.

The `browseable` directive is especially important to set to `no` to prevent excessively long lists of shares when users browse the network and to keep user's home directory shares more secure because the names of their shares will not be made publicly available on the network.

Each user can access their home directory share with their username. For instance, if a user someuser's home directory is shared by the Samba server someserver then the share is accessible with the share path \\someserver\someuser.

Two other directives which are useful to have in the homes section are: preserve case and short preserve case. These make case important in name files, which can be essential in maintaining consistency between case-insensitive DOS and Windows systems and case-sensitive Linux systems. These directives also ensure that you do not end up with two files on the Linux system with different cases in their names but that are in fact the same file.

> **Note**
>
> Samba uses the user's account entry in the /etc/passwd file to determine their home directory for sharing purposes.

Individual share definition sections specify individual directories that must be shared on the network. Consider the sample share definition section above:

```
[mydir]
   comment = My Directory
   path = /usr/somewhere/private
   valid users = someuser
   public = no
   writable = yes
   printable = no
```

This section takes the directory /usr/somewhere/private and shares it on the network with the name mydir. If the Samba server is the host someserver then the complete path of the share on the network is \\someserver\mydir.

The valid users directive indicates which users are allowed to access the share and specifies a space-separated list of users. If not specified then the permissions of the directory in Linux will be the only source of access restrictions on the directory. The public directive, when set to no, makes sure that the directory is not publicly accessible (by guest users, for instance). The printable directory, when set to no, indicates that the resource is not a printer so that remote clients do not attempt to treat it as a printer.

Share definition sections can use several directives as outlined in the smb.conf manual page which can be viewed with the command man smb.conf. Common directives are outlined in Table 14.2.

TABLE 14.2　COMMON smb.conf SHARE DEFINITION SECTION DIRECTIVES

Directive	Description
comment = \<description\>	Specifies a descriptive comment for the share which is displayed to clients browsing the network to help them identify the share.
browseable = \<yes or no\>	Indicates whether the share appears in lists of available shares when a client browses the network.

TABLE 14.2   CONTINUED

Directive	Description
read only = <yes or no>	Indicates whether the share is accessible in read-only mode or, when set to no, read-write mode.
writable = <yes or no>	Indicates whether the share is accessible in read-write mode or, when set to no, read-only mode.
preserve case = <yes or no>	Indicates whether case is important in naming files.
short preserve case = <yes or no>	Indicates whether case is important in short format DOS filenames (commonly known as 8.3 format filenames).
create mode = <mode>	Specifies the file permissions mode for any files created in the shared directory. The file permissions should be specified numerically as they are with the chmod command. The default value is 750 if no creation mode is specified.
guest ok = <yes or no>	Indicates whether guests are allowed access to the directory.
public = <yes or no>	Indicates whether the directory is publicly accessible.
valid users = <user list>	Specifies a space-separated list of users who are allowed to access the share.
printable = <yes or no>	Indicates whether the shared resource is a printer.
only guest = <yes or no>	Indicates whether the shared directory should only be accessible to guest users.

SHARING LINUX PRINTERS WITH SAMBA

The easiest way to share Linux printers with your SMB network is to configure the global section of your smb.conf file as outlined previously in the "The smb.conf File" section. Your Samba system must be properly connected to your network and then you must create a printers section in the smb.conf file.

A typical printers section looks like the following:

```
[printers]
   comment = All Printers
   path = /var/spool/samba
   browseable = no
   guest ok = no
   writable = no
   printable = yes
```

Note several key points about this section:

■ The printers section automatically shares all printers listed in the printcap file specified with the printcap name defined in the global section of the smb.conf file.

PART

III

CH

14

- The `path` directive indicates which directory Samba should use to spool print jobs.
- The `writable` directive, when set to no, makes it impossible for clients to write directly to the printer through the share. This is advisable and forces printing to happen through the Samba spooling mechanism.

USING LINUX AS A SAMBA CLIENT

In order to access file systems shared by other SMB servers including Windows or Linux SMB servers, use either the `smbclient` or `smbmount` program to access the remote file system. The `smbclient` program uses an FTP-like interface to enable you to copy files to or from a remote file system on an SMB server. `smbmount` enables you to mount the file system to your Samba client system like any other mounted file system and access the contents of the remote SMB file system using standard Linux file system commands such as `ls`, `cp`, or `mv`.

With the `smbclient` program, you can list resources shared by a server using the `-L` flag:

```
# smbclient -L -I <host name>
```

The `-I` flag allows you to specify the hostname of the remote SMB system by using UNIX-style DNS hostname formats. For instance, if the remote SMB server is myhost.some.domain, the command would look like the following:

```
# smblient -L -I myhost.some.domain
```

After you identify a file system resource you want to access, you can connect to the resource with `smbclient` as follows:

```
# smbclient '<resource name>' -I <host name> -U <user name>
```

When connecting to a remote resource in this way, several things need to be considered:

- You must specify the complete resource name in standard UNC style of the form \\<NetBIOS host name>\<share name>.
- If the Linux client cannot resolve the NetBIOS hostname then you need to specify the DNS-style hostname of the SMB server using the `-I` flag.
- If you need to authenticate as a specific user to access the resource, use the `-U` flag to specify the username to use in accessing the resource. If a password is required, `smbclient` will prompt you for the password.

Like the Linux FTP client, `smbclient` provides its own command prompt where you can issue special commands to transfer and access files on the remote shared resource. The `smbclient` prompt looks like the following:

```
smb: \
```

The `smbclient` tool uses the commands in Table 14.3 to work with files on the remote shared resource.

TABLE 14.3   `smbclient` **COMMANDS**

Command	Description
`cd <directory>`	Change directory on the remote system.
`del <file>`	Delete a file on the remote system.
`dir`	Display the contents of the current directory on the remote system.
`exit`	Quit `smbclient`.
`get <file>`	Copy a file from the current directory on the remote system to the current directory on the local system.
`lcd <directory>`	Change directory on the local system.
`ls`	Display the contents of the current directory on the remote system.
`md <directory>`	Create a directory on the remote system.
`mkdir <directory>`	Create a directory on the remote system.
`mget <file list>`	Copy multiple files from the current directory on the remote system to the current directory on the local system.
`mput <file list>`	Copy multiple files from the current directory on the local system to the current directory on the remote system.
`put <file>`	Copy a file from the current directory on the local system to the current directory on the remote system.
`quit`	Quit `smbclient`.
`rd <directory>`	Remove a directory on the remote system.
`rmdir <directory>`	Remove a directory on the remote system.

An alternative approach to accessing files on an SMB-shared remote directory is using the `smbmount` command. With `smbmount`, you can mount a remote SMB directory to a mount point on your local system.

The syntax of the `smbmount` command is simple:

```
# smbmount "<resource name>" -c 'mount <mount point> \
-u <local user> -g <local group>'
```

For instance, if you want to mount the SMB resource \\someserver\somedir in your Linux system at the directory /sambamount (which must exist as an empty directory), you could use a command of the following form:

```
# smbmount \\someserver\somedir -c 'mount /sambamount \
-u <local user> -f <local group>'
```

This command tells `smbmount` to mount the specified directory using the specified mount command. In Linux, however, all files and directories must have an associated local user and local group. This is the role of the -u and -g flags. They specify the local user and group to be

PART

III

CH

14

treated as the owner of the mounted file system. The SMB server sharing the resource does not make this information available, therefore these flags are necessary.

For instance, if you want this shared resource to be owned by the user someuser and the group somegroup when mounted on the local Linux system, use the following smbmount command:

```
# smbmount \\someserver\somedir -c 'mount /sambamount -u someuser -f somegroup'
```

If your Linux system cannot identify the SMB server by its NetBIOS hostname (in this case, someserver) then you need to specify the actual IP address of the server with the -I flag. For instance, if the IP address of someserver is 10.20.30.40, your command would become:

```
# smbmount \\someserver\somedir -I 10.20.30.40 \
-c 'mount /sambamount -u someuser -f somegroup'
```

If you need to specify the NetBIOS username or workgroup for the shared resource, use the -U and -W flags. For instance, if you need to connect to the shared resource as the user sambauser in the workgroup mygroup, use the following command:

```
# smbmount \\someserver\somedir -I 10.20.30.40 -U sambauser -W mygroup -c 'mount
    /sambamount -u someuser -f somegroup'
```

ACCESSING SHARED PRINTERS WITH SAMBA

To print from Linux to printers shared by SMB servers you can use the smbprint script, which is included with the Samba source code distribution and with some binary Samba distributions. smbprint is a script which serves as an input filter for a printer queue managed by lpd.

In order to use this script correctly, several things are needed:

- You must be able to set up an entry in /etc/printcap for the destination printer. This includes using any necessary configuration for your target printer type if it is PostScript or PCL. Consult the lpd document for more details on configuring your /etc/printcap file.

- You must add the following if entry to the printer queue's entry in the /etc/printcap file:

  ```
  if=/usr/bin/smbprint
  ```

- For instance, a typical printer queue entry might be:

  ```
  myprinter:\
      :cm=Remote Samba Printer:\
      :lp=/dev/lp1:\
      :sd=myprinter:\
      :af=myprinter:\
      :mx#0:\
      :if=/usr/bin/smbprint:
  ```

Note The `lp=/dev/lp1` entry must point to a valid device even though the `smbprint` script will redirect print jobs to the remote printer instead of printing to the specified local printer.

The following is the source code of the `smbprint` script. If your Samba distribution doesn't exist, create this script at `/usr/bin/smbprint` and make it executable with the command `chmod +x /usr/bin/smbprint`:

```
#!/bin/sh

# This script is an input filter for printcap printing on a unix machine. It
# uses the smbclient program to print the file to the specified smb-based
# server and service.
# For example you could have a printcap entry like this
#
# smb:lp=/dev/null:sd=/usr/spool/smb:sh:if=/usr/local/samba/smbprint
#
# which would create a unix printer called "smb" that will print via this
# script. You will need to create the spool directory /usr/spool/smb with
# appropriate permissions and ownerships for your system.

# Set these to the server and service you wish to print to
# In this example I have a WfWg PC called "lapland" that has a printer
# exported called "printer" with no password.

#
# Script further altered by hamiltom@ecnz.co.nz (Michael Hamilton)
# so that the server, service, and password can be read from
# a /var/spool/lpd/PRINTNAME/.config file.
#
# In order for this to work the /etc/printcap entry must include an
# accounting file (af=...):
#
#   cdcolour:\
#     :cm=CD IBM Colorjet on 6th:\
#     :sd=/var/spool/lpd/cdcolour:\
#     :af=/var/spool/lpd/cdcolour/acct:\
#     :if=/usr/local/etc/smbprint:\
#     :mx=0:\
#     :lp=/dev/null:
#
# The /usr/var/spool/lpd/PRINTNAME/.config file should contain:
#   server=PC_SERVER
#   service=PR_SHARENAME
#   password="password"
#
# E.g.
#   server=PAULS_PC
#   service=CJET_371
#   password=""

#
# Debugging log file, change to /dev/null if you like.
```

```
#
# logfile=/tmp/smb-print.log
logfile=/dev/null


#
# The last parameter to the filter is the accounting file name.
#   Extract the directory name from the file name.
#   Concat this with /.config to get the config file.
#
eval acct_file=\${$#}
spool_dir=`dirname $acct_file`
config_file=$spool_dir/.config

# Should read the following variables set in the config file:
#   server
#   service
#   password
eval `cat $config_file`


#
# Some debugging help, change the >> to > if you want to save space.
#
echo "server $server, service $service" >> $logfile

(
# NOTE You may wish to add the line `echo translate' if you want automatic
# CR/LF translation when printing.
#        echo translate
    echo "print -"
    cat
) | /usr/bin/smbclient "\\\\$server\\$service" $password -U $server -N -P >>
➥ $logfile
```

| Note | Some Linux distributions such as Red Hat Linux and Corel Linux offer simple, graphical tools for setting up connections to shared SMB printers. |

WHAT IS NFS?

NFS stands for the *Network File System*. Originally developed by Sun Microsystems for their UNIX systems, NFS is now the de facto standard for file and directory sharing between UNIX and Linux systems over the TCP/IP network protocol. In addition to being used to share files and directories between Linux and UNIX systems, extensions are available for other operating system such as Windows and Novell NetWare to enable them to communicate with NFS servers and share their files and directories with NFS clients.

If you do not need to share files and directories with Windows SMB-based networks, consider using NFS for file and directory sharing because it is more tightly integrated into the core of Linux's networking environment and is easier to configure and keep running smoothly.

Caution	NFS has some well-know security problems and should be used carefully and only when necessary. Generally, you should only consider using NFS within protected intranets behind a firewall.

CONFIGURING NFS

Several programs are required to maintain a running NFS server. These include the following:

- **`portmap` or `rpc.portmap` depending on your distribution of Linux:** This program provides mapping of ports to remote procedure call (RPC) programs so that NFS can work. This program should be started at boot time if you plan to run an NFS server. Consult Chapter 4, "Booting Up and Shutting Down," for guidance in configuring your system to start `portmap` at boot time. You can check whether `portmap` is running using the following command:

```
# rpcinfo -p
  program vers proto  port
   100000   2  tcp   111 portmapper
   100000   2  udp   111 portmapper
```

- **`mountd` or `rpc.mountd` depending on your Linux distribution:** This program should start at boot time if you are running a Linux NFS server.

- **`nfsd` or `rpc.nfsd` depending on your Linux distribution:** This program should start at boot time if you are running a Linux NFS server.

After `mountd` and `nfsd` are running, `rpcinfo -p` should report their presence:

```
# rpcinfo -p
  program vers proto  port
   100000   2  tcp   111 portmapper
   100000   2  udp   111 portmapper
   100005   1  tcp   747 mountd
   100005   1  udp   745 mountd
   100003   2  tcp  2049 nfs
   100003   2  udp  2049 nfs
```

All configuration of exported directories is done in the `/etc/exports` file. The exports file contains a series of entries, one per line, of the general form:

```
<directory> <host name>(<permissions>) <host name>(<permissions>) \
<host name>(<permissions>) ...
```

The specified directory is the directory to share. Each hostname is the name of a host being given permission to access the shared directory and the permissions list is a comma-separated list of permissions granted to users on the specified host taken from the list of permissions that you see in Table 14.4.

TABLE 14.4 PERMISSIONS FOR THE /etc/exports FILE

Permission	Description
rw	Allow access to the directory in read-write mode
ro	Allow access to the directory in read-only mode
insecure	All non-authenticated access to the directory
kerberos	Use Kerberos authentication for access to the directory
link_absolute	Leave symbolic links unchanged
link_relative	Convert symbolic links to relative links as needed
root_squash	Deny root users on remote clients root access on the NFS server
secure-rpc	Use RPC authentication for access to the directory (on by default)

Typically, only one of rw or ro is needed with root_squash if the extra security it provides is required. For instance, to share the directory /somedir using NFS and allow users on host1 full read-write access and users on host2 limited read-only access with no root-account mapping, use the following entry in /etc/exports:

```
/somedir host1(rw) host2(ro,root_squash)
```

Hostnames in the /etc/exports file can also be specified with wildcards. For instance, to allow all hosts ending with mydomain.com to access the directory in question, use *.mydomain.com as the hostname in your entry in the /etc/exports file.

Whenever you change the /etc/exports file, force mountd and nfsd to reload the file by sending them the SIGHUP signal:

```
# killall -HUP /usr/sbin/mountd
# killall -HUP /usr/sbin/nfsd
```

USER PERMISSIONS AND NFS

When a user on a remote system attempts to access a shared directory through NFS, the NFS server first checks the /etc/exports file to see if users on the client host are allowed access to the directory. If they are, user and group mappings take place. If the NFS client and server share the same user and group ID numbers, the UID and GID of the user attempting to mount the directory are used to determine whether the user has sufficient access permissions to connect to the directory based on the directory's local Linux file permissions.

When the client and server have different UID and GID number spaces, the NFS daemon attempts to translate between the client's UID and GID space and the server's space to determine whether access should be granted.

ACCESSING REMOTE SHARED DIRECTORIES WITH NFS

In order to access directories shared by a remote NFS server, use the `mount` command on the client. The `mount` command is used to mount both local file systems as well as remote NFS file systems using the `nfs` file system type. To mount a remote file system, use the following syntax:

```
# mount -t nfs <host name>:<directory> <local mount point> -o <options>
```

The `<host name>:<directory>` combination is the hostname and directory of the remote shared directory. For instance, to access the directory `/somedir` on the remote NFS server `someserver`, you would be mounting `someserver:/somedir`. The local mount point is the path of a directory on the local system, preferably empty, through which the remote directory should be mounted and made accessible.

The series of options is optional and is a comma-separated list of options from the list given in Table 14.5.

TABLE 14.5   OPTIONS FOR MOUNTING NFS DIRECTORIES WITH mount

Option	Description
hard	Creates a hard mount. This is the default. When an attempt to hard mount a directory fails, it times out and generates an error message and then tries again with a larger timeout. This will continue repeatedly until a successful mount occurs.
intr	Allows interrupts to the NFS call. This is usually not necessary.
rsize=<datagram size>	Specifies the datagram size for read requests in bytes. The default of 1024 bytes is usually sufficient.
soft	Creates a soft mount. When an attempt to soft mount a directory fails, only major timeouts are generated and none are reported. You generally regain control of your system more quickly.
timeo=<time>	Specifies the timeout for NFS requests in tenths of a second. The default is 7/10 of a second.
wsize=<datagram size>	Specifies the datagram size for write requests in bytes. The default of 1024 bytes is usually sufficient.

For instance, to mount the `someserver:/somedir` directory locally at `/nfsmount` and specify a timeout of 1 second for a poor network connection, use the following command:

```
# mount -t nfs someserver:/somedir /nfsmount -o timeo=10
```

PART

III

CH

14

CONFIGURING lpd FOR REMOTE PRINTING

Linux typically uses the lpd daemon for printing. `lpd` can manage one or more printer queues for both local and remote printers. Earlier in this chapter when Samba was discussed, you saw an example of using lpd to configure a Linux system to print to a remote SMB-shared printer. For printer sharing between two Linux systems you only need to use lpd.

Linux printer sharing involves the following steps:

1. Configure the printer server for local printing with lpd.
2. Configure the printer server to allow remote systems to print to it.
3. Configure printer clients to print to the remote print server.

CONFIGURING A LOCAL PRINTER

In order to print to a local printer, several requirements must be met:

- The printer must be physically connected with a serial or parallel cable.
- An entry for the printer must be placed in the /etc/printcap file.
- The lpd daemon must be running.

The printcap file contains one entry for each printer queue lpd will be handling. Each entry takes a form similar to the following:

```
myprinter:\
        :lp=/dev/lp0:\
        :sd=/var/spool/lpd/myprinter:\
        :lf=/var/spool/lpd/myprinter/errors:\
        :sh:\
        :mx#0:\
        :sf:
```

This entry contains six fields defining a printer queue named myprinter:

- **lp**: Indicates the device the printer is attached to.
- **sd**: Indicates the directory where temporary files can be stored when printing; typically this is a subdirectory of /var/spool/lpd/.
- **lf**: Indicates a file to which error messages can be logged. Typically this file is located in the queue's spool directory (specified with sd).
- **sh**: Indicates that headers should be suppressed when printing to this printer; headers generate banner pages.
- **mx**: Indicates the maximum size of print jobs which can be sent to this printer; the size is specified in 1KB blocks. If the size is zero blocks, there is no size limit.
- **sf**: Indicates that end-of-job form feeds should be suppressed when printing to this printer. Generally, you only need these form feeds for older dot matrix printers.

Many other fields can be used in printcap entries. Consult the printcap manual page with the command man printcap for a full list of these fields.

After you have created an entry for a local printer in the printcap file, you should restart lpd with the following commands:

```
# /etc/rc.d/init.d/lpd stop
# /etc/rc.d/init.d/lpd start
```

After lpd restarts, you should be able to print to your printer with the lpr command:

```
# lpr -Pmyprinter <file name>
```

> **Tip**
>
> Typically, Linux applications generate PostScript or ASCII text data to be sent to a printer. This can be problematic. For instance, PostScript printers cannot print plain ASCII text files and printers using Hewlett Packard's Printer Control Language (PCL) cannot handle PostScript data. In addition, a Linux ASCII text file sent to a PCL printer will print with the incorrect formatting. To resolve this, you can use print filters which are special programs that lpd uses to preprocess data before it is sent to the printer. Many distributions come with printer filters. In addition, the popular APS Printer Filter System can be downloaded from ftp://metalab.unc.edu/pub/Linux/system/printing. APS is easy to install and configure by following the instructions contained in the distribution archive.

ALLOWING REMOTE PRINTER CONNECTIONS

In order to allow remote clients to print to a printer which you have configured for local printing as previously outlined, you must indicate which client systems are allowed to print to the printer. To do this, you must specify the hostname or IP address of each client in the /etc/hosts.lpd file. Each remote client name or address should appear on a separate line in the hosts.lpd file.

CONFIGURING A REMOTE CLIENT TO PRINT TO A LINUX PRINT SERVER

To configure a client system to print to a printer shared from another Linux system, you need to create an appropriate entry in the /etc/printcap file on the client system. The following is a typical printcap entry for printing to a remote printer:

```
myremoteprinter:\
        :lp=/dev/null:\
        :sd=/var/spool/lpd/myprinter:\
        :lf=/var/spool/lpd/myprinter/errors:\
        :sh:\
        :mx#0:\
        :sf:\
        :rm=someserver:\
        :rp=myprinter:
```

Three fields in this entry bear scrutiny:

- **lp:** All `printcap` entries must have a `lp` field. The device `/dev/null` is a device you can use in place of an actual physical device; because you are not printing to a locally connected printer, you should use `/dev/null` for remote printer entries.
- **rm:** Specifies the hostname of the remote printer server to which you want to print.
- **rp:** Specifies the printer queue name of the printer on the remote print server to which you want to print.

You need to restart `lpd` to force it to reread the `printcap` file:

```
# /etc/rc.d/init.d/lpd stop
# /etc/rc.d/init.d/lpd start
```

If you then print to the `myremoteprinter` queue on the printer client, the print job will be sent to the `myprinter` queue on the host named `someserver`.

TROUBLESHOOTING

If you have problems using NFS, you can check several things to see whether your system is working correctly:

- Check that `portmap`, `mountd`, and `nfsd` are still running. They can die and can need to be restarted.
- Check if `portmap` is not allowed to answer requests according to entries in `/etc/hosts.deny`.
- Check that the relevant entries in `/etc/exports` are correctly formatted and point to the correct directories.
- Check that hostnames in the `/etc/exports` file can be resolved by the NFS server system and match the correct clients trying to access the server.
- Check that the system clocks are in sync and have matching dates on the server and all client systems.
- Check that the user accessing the server is not in more than eight groups.

Another source of difficulty with NFS is problems with slow network connections. The default NFS settings presume a reasonable, fast connection which makes using NFS over slower connections unfeasible.

Clients attempting to mount remote NFS directories across slow connections can compensate for this by adjusting some of the options of the `mount` command:

- Never use `soft` mounts. Only use `hard` mounts.
- Increase the value of `timeo` until you can get a connection without numerous retries.

With Samba, after you have your installation configured correctly, the most common problem is that the `smbd` or `nmbd` daemons can become non-responsive or produce false authentication errors and need to be restarted.

PART
III

CH
14

CHAPTER **15**

ROUTING WITH LINUX

In this chapter

BASIC ROUTING PRINCIPLES

In a networked world, routing is an essential concept. Routing provides the capability to direct packets through a seemingly complex and chaotic maze of interconnected networks to their correct destinations.

To understand the need for routing, start by considering a basic LAN that is not connected to any other network. In this environment, it's simple for hosts on the network to direct their TCP/IP packets to the correct destination. They simply place the packet on the network through their network interface, and the destination host sees the packet addressed to it on the network and receives it.

However, things get complicated when two networks are connected. Consider the connected networks in Figure 15.1. Here, two class C networks that are part of the same organization are connected: the 10.10.10.0 network and the 10.10.20.0 network.

Figure 15.1
Two connected networks.

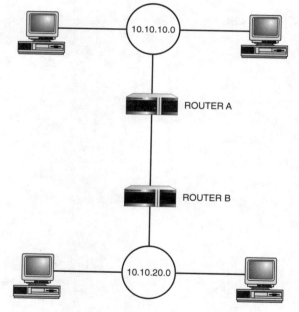

Now, a problem arises: If a host on the 10.10.10.0 network places a packet on the network addressed to another host on the 10.10.10.0 network, the receiving host sees the packet addressed to itself and collects it. Because both hosts are on the same network there is no routing involved, and the hosts can send packets to each other directly, without involving any intermediate routers.

However, if a host on the 10.10.10.0 network wants to send a packet to a host on the 10.10.20.0 network, it cannot simply place the packet on the network because hosts on the 10.10.20.0 network are not able to see the packet. This means the packet would never arrive.

This is where the routers come into play: The router is a computer or dedicated hardware device that is physically connected to both networks. It is configured to send packets from one network to another. In this example, when Router A receives a packet that is destined for the 10.10.10.0 network, it sends it out to the 10.10.10.0 network through the appropriate network interface. When it receives a packet for the 10.10.20.0 network, it sends it to Router B, which in turn routes the packet accordingly.

If hosts on both networks are configured to use their respective routers as their default gateway, the following happens: If a host on the 10.10.10.0 network wants to send a packet to a host on the 10.10.20.0 network, it does not simply place it on the 10.10.10.0 network. Instead, it places it on the network for delivery to the gateway instead of the actual destination, and Router A receives the packet and sends it to Router B, which places it on the 10.10.20.0 network for delivery to the final recipient.

Carry the situation one step further: The 10.10.10.0 network has a direct connection to the Internet as shown in Figure 15.2.

Here, the network 10.10.10.0 is connected both to the network 10.10.20.0 and the Internet through two different routers. This begs a question: How do hosts on the 10.10.10.0 network decide where to send packets destined for hosts on the 10.10.20.0 network?

Two possible approaches exist:

- Router C is designated the default gateway, the packets destined for the 10.10.20.0 network are sent there, and this router is configured to know that these packets should be rerouted to Router A for delivery to the 10.10.20.0 network.

- Each host on the 10.10.10.0 network is configured with two gateways: a hard-coded route to 10.10.20.0 through Router A and a default gateway for packets destined to all other networks that go through Router C.

Note

The concept introduced here is a static route; that is, it is a route that indicates that packets destined for a specific host, network, or group of networks should be routed through a particular gateway. This differs from the default gateway route, which is a catch-all router for all packets not covered by a static route.

Hosts on the 10.10.20.0 network also need to be able to communicate with the Internet and the 10.10.10.0 network. The task here is simpler because there is only one external connection from this network to the 10.10.10.0 network. Router B should be the default gateway for all hosts. When it receives packets for any external network, they are sent to Router A. Router A takes packets destined for the 10.10.10.0 network and places them on the network for delivery to their destination. It takes packets destined for the Internet and sends them to the default gateway, Router C, for delivery.

Figure 15.2
Two connected
networks with
a connection to
the Internet.

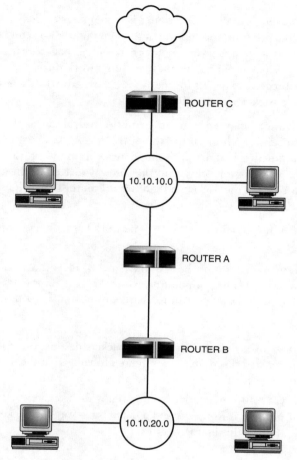

From the 10.10.20.0 network's perspective, the entire outside world, including the 10.10.10.0 network, is a black box; hosts on the 10.10.20.0 network do not need to know where different external hosts exist or the routes that packets take to reach those hosts. All packets destined for hosts other than those destined for the local network are delivered in the same way: They are sent to Router B.

LINUX SOFTWARE FOR ROUTING

Linux has several software components related to routing, including the following:

- Kernel modules that provide Linux with the capability to forward packets between networks.

- The route utility for defining and viewing routes on a host.

In addition, several specialized Linux distributions exist that make creation of Linux-based routers simpler than using full-blown distributions with a lot of extraneous software not needed on a router.

KERNEL MODULES FOR ROUTING

For a Linux system to route TCP/IP packets, you need to have the necessary IP forwarding kernel modules enabled in your kernel. IP forwarding is the process by which Linux can take packets it receives on one network interface and forward them out through another network interface.

You can check whether IP forwarding is enabled in your system by checking the ksyms file in the /proc file system:

```
# cat /proc/ksyms ¦ grep ip_forward
c00141364 ip_forward_Rf71ac834
```

If the command does not return an entry such as c00141364 ip_forward_Rf71ac834, IP forwarding is not enabled in your kernel. You need to recompile your kernel with support for the CONFIG_IP_ROUTER option. Consult Chapter 11, "Building the Linux Kernel," for guidance about compiling a new Linux kernel on your system.

THE route UTILITY

The route utility enables you to define the necessary routes for your router. You can use it to create static routes to particular hosts and networks as well as to define the route to the default gateway.

If you use the route command without any arguments, it displays existing routes defined on a host:

```
# /sbin/route
Kernel IP routing table
Destination     Gateway        Genmask           Flags Metric Ref   Use Iface
10.10.10.10     *              255.255.255.255   UH    0      0       0 eth0
10.10.10.0      *              255.255.255.0     U     0      0       0 eth0
127.0.0.0       *              255.0.0.0         U     0      0       0 lo
```

This output shows several static routes:

- The 10.10.10.0 network and the 10.10.10.10 host are accessible through the eth0 interface.
- The local loopback network 127.0.0.0 is accessible through the lo interface.

In addition, the fact that no address appears as a gateway address indicates that these routes are to the local network; in other words, packets for these destinations should not be sent to a gateway system but should simply be delivered onto the local network of the specified Ethernet interface.

To add a default gateway, use the route command as follows:

```
# /sbin/route add default gw <router IP address> dev <ethernet device>
```

For instance, to add the router with the IP address 10.10.10.1 as a default gateway and to tell a host to send packets to the router through the eth0 interface, use the following command:

```
# /sbin/route add default gw 10.10.10.1 dev eth0
# /sbin/route
Kernel IP routing table
Destination     Gateway      Genmask          Flags Metric Ref    Use Iface
10.10.10.10     *            255.255.255.255  UH    0      0        0 eth0
10.10.10.0      *            255.255.255.0    U     0      0        0 eth0
127.0.0.0       *            255.0.0.0        U     0      0        0 lo
default         10.10.10.1   0.0.0.0          UG    0      0        0 eth0
```

Notice that the output of the route command now includes a default destination through a gateway at 10.10.10.1.

If you want to add a static route to a network, use the command as follows:

```
# /sbin/route add -net <network address>/<network bits>
➥gw <router IP address> dev <ethernet device>
```

For instance, to create a static route to the class C network 10.10.20.0 through the router at IP address 10.10.10.2 and to send packets to the router through the eth0 interface, use the following command:

```
# /sbin/route add -net 10.10.20.0/24 gw 10.10.10.2 dev eth0
# /sbin/route
Kernel IP routing table
Destination     Gateway      Genmask          Flags Metric Ref    Use Iface
10.10.10.10     *            255.255.255.255  UH    0      0        0 eth0
10.10.20.0      10.10.10.2   255.255.255.0    UG    0      0        0 eth0
10.10.10.0      *            255.255.255.0    U     0      0        0 eth0
127.0.0.0       *            255.0.0.0        U     0      0        0 lo
default         10.10.10.1   0.0.0.0          UG    0      0        0 eth0
```

> **Note**
>
> Notice the use of the form 10.10.20.0/24 to specify the network address of the 10.10.20.0 class C network. This syntax is discussed in Chapter 13, "Linux Network Configuration and TCP/IP."

You can also add a static route to a particular host through a gateway using a similar command. For instance, to define a route to the host 10.10.30.100 through the router with the IP address 10.10.10.3 and using the eth0 device, use the following command:

```
# /sbin/route add -host 10.10.30.100 gw 10.10.10.3 dev eth0
# /sbin/route
Kernel IP routing table
Destination     Gateway      Genmask          Flags Metric Ref    Use Iface
10.10.10.10     *            255.255.255.255  UH    0      0        0 eth0
10.10.30.100    10.10.10.3   255.255.255.255  UG    0      0        0 eth0
10.10.20.0      10.10.10.2   255.255.255.0    UG    0      0        0 eth0
10.10.10.0      *            255.255.255.0    U     0      0        0 eth0
127.0.0.0       *            255.0.0.0        U     0      0        0 lo
default         10.10.10.1   0.0.0.0          UG    0      0        0 eth0
```

Notice the use of the -host option instead of -net when specifying a static route for a host. The route command is also discussed in Chapter 13.

PREPACKAGED ROUTING DISTRIBUTIONS

Although any Linux distribution can be used to create a Linux-based router, this is often inefficient. For instance, the complete Red Hat Linux distribution includes a large amount of extra software and kernel modules, which means it requires a larger memory and disk footprint than a Linux router necessarily requires. If you want to run a Linux system strictly as a router, distributions are available that even fit on a floppy disk that can create a Linux router with limited memory and no hard disk.

The advantages of a floppy-based approach to creating a Linux router include the following:

- No need to configure the router for additional security by turning off all the extra network services that typically run in a standard distribution.

- No need to recompile the Linux kernel with support for IP forwarding.

- Easy disaster recovery because you can keep multiple copies of the router diskette on hand and swap them if one fails.

- No need to perform backups. Everything is maintained on a single floppy disk that is easily duplicated and stored for future use.

Several single floppy disk distributions for creating a Linux-based router and firewall are available, including the following:

- **Linux Router Project (www.linuxrouter.org):** This is the leading single floppy disk router distribution. This distribution can be used to build Ethernet routers, ISDN routers, remote access servers, thin clients, firewalls, and network appliances.

- **floppyfw (http://www.zelow.no/floppyfw/):** floppyfw is a Linux-based static router with network address translation (IP Masquerading) and packet-filtering capabilities. It cannot be used for sophisticated firewalls but is perfect for a quick-and-dirty packet-filtering router and firewall.

- **MuLinux (http://sunsite.auc.dk/mulinux/):** MuLinux is a floppy disk-based Linux distribution that, although not specifically focused on router creation, is ideal for that purpose. Depending on how you configure it, MuLinux can include NFS booting for X-terminal clients, DHCP support, email processing and reading, Samba support, sound support, and X Windows capabilities.

- **DLX (http://www.wu-wien.ac.at/usr/h93/h9301726/dlx.html):** DLX is a single floppy disk distribution for general purpose use. It includes network support and parallel port zip drive support. It can be used for building a router and is ideal for network troubleshooting.

CREATING A LAN-TO-LAN ROUTER WITH LINUX

To illustrate the creation of a basic Linux router, implement a router for directly connecting two class C networks: 10.10.10.0 and 10.10.20.0. Figure 15.3 outlines the network configuration you want to implement.

Figure 15.3
Two networks connected by a router.

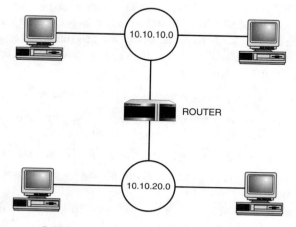

You can create a LAN-to-LAN router for this network topology using a standard Linux distribution as follows:

1. Check whether IP forwarding is compiled into your kernel, and if not, compile and install it. This process is described earlier in this chapter in the "Kernel Modules for Routing" section.

2. Install two network cards in your system and make sure they are running properly as outlined in Chapter 13 in the "Configuring Multi-Homed Hosts" section.

3. Configure eth0 to attach to the 10.10.10.0 network as outlined Chapter 13. Presume that the IP address of the router on the 10.10.10.0 network is 10.10.10.1.

4. Configure eth1 to attach to the 10.10.20.0 network as outlined Chapter 13. Presume that the IP address of the router on the 10.10.20.0 network is 10.10.20.1.

5. Check your routing table using the route command. You should have static routes to both networks through the appropriate interface as follows:

   ```
   10.10.10.0    *       255.255.255.0  U   0   0     0 eth0
   10.10.20.0    *       255.255.255.0  U   0   0     0 eth1
   ```

6. If the static route to the 10.10.10.0 network is missing, use the following command to create the route:

   ```
   # /sbin/route add -net 10.10.10.0/24 dev eth0
   ```

7. If the static route to the 10.10.20.0 network is missing, use the following command to create the route:

   ```
   # /sbin/route add -net 10.10.20.0/24 dev eth1
   ```

Hosts on the `10.10.10.0` network need to be configured to use the router at `10.10.10.1` as their default gateway:

```
# /sbin/route default gw 10.10.10.1 dev eth0
```

Similarly, hosts on the `10.10.20.0` network need to be configured to use the router at `10.10.20.1` as their default gateway:

```
# /sbin/route default gw 10.10.20.1 dev eth0
```

When your router is running, you need to consider security on the router:

- Should the router accept remote logins through `telnet` or `rsh` for remote management? If not, enable remote management with `ssh` or only allow management at the console.

- The router should not be part of your NIS domain to prevent regular user accounts from logging in to the router.

- Only the minimum number of user accounts in addition to system accounts and the root account should exist on the router.

- All unnecessary network services should be disabled on the router, including sendmail, FTP, Telnet, NFS, Samba, LPD. Not running unneeded services helps prevent unauthorized access to the router.

- Consult Chapter 18, "General Security Issues," and Chapter 19, "Linux and Firewalls," for guidance about securing your Linux router system. The same rules that apply to keeping a firewall secure apply to keeping a router secure.

DYNAMIC ROUTING

The preceding sections have discussed static routing. However, static routing suffers from a major drawback: the daunting task of maintaining routes in a changing network environment. Routing protocols provide a mechanism for handling both simple and complex routing environments.

There are a variety of routing protocols, and they all basically perform the same function: They determine the best route to a destination host or network. In this chapter, you will look at two such protocols: the Routing Information Protocol (RIP) and the Open Shortest Path First (OSPF) protocol. You will also consider two daemons used for deploying these protocols: `routed`, which implements RIP, and `gated`, which supports RIP, OSPF, and other routing protocols.

TYPES OF ROUTING PROTOCOLS

There are two types of routing protocols: interior protocols and exterior protocols. An interior routing protocol is used inside an independent network system. An independent network system is called an autonomous system (AS). RIP and OSPF are widely used interior routing protocols.

Exterior routing protocols are used to exchange routing information between independent networks or autonomous systems. The Border Gateway Protocol (BGP) and the Exterior Gateway Protocol (EGP) are examples of exterior routing protocols. Discussion of exterior routing protocols is beyond the scope of this book. BGP is the newer protocol that has evolved out of experience gained from EGP. For more information on BGP, refer to the following RFCs:

- RFC-1771, "A Border Gateway Protocol 4 (BGP-4)"
- RFC-1773, "Experience with the BGP-4 Protocol"
- RFC-1774, "BGP-4 Protocol Analysis"
- RFC-1965, "Autonomous System Confederations for BGP"
- RFC-1966, "BGP Route Reflection an alternative to full mesh IBGP"
- RFC-1997, "BGP Communities Attribute"
- RFC-1998, "An Application of the BGP Community Attribute"
- RFC-2283, "Multiprotocol Extensions for BGP-4"
- RFC-2385, "Protection of BGP Sessions via the TCP MD5 Signature Option"
- RFC-2439, "BGP Route Flap Damping"
- RFC-2545, "Use of BGP-4 Multiprotocol Extensions for IPv6 Inter-Domain"
- RFC-2547, "BGP/MPLS VPNs"

ROUTING INFORMATION PROTOCOL

The Routing Information Protocol (RIP) is one of the most commonly used interior gateway protocols. RIP classifies routers and hosts as active and passive. Active routers advertise their routes to others, whereas passive routers listen and update their routes based on advertisements but do not advertise their own routing tables to anyone. Typically, routers run RIP in active mode, whereas hosts run it in passive mode.

Active mode RIP routers broadcast updates at a set interval (normally every 30 seconds). RIP updates consist of a network IP address and an integer distance to that network. The distance to a network is based on the number of gateways that must be traversed to reach that network, and it is referred to as the *hop count*. Directly connected networks have a hop count of one, which is analogous to a RIP metric of one. Using hop counts to calculate the best route does not always produce the best result. For example, a route with a higher hop count crossing several fast-Ethernet segments might be much faster than a route with a lower hop count across a WAN connection over a slow-speed serial line.

To correct this situation, many RIP routers advertise artificially high hop counts for slow links. The maximum hop count is 15, beyond which the network is considered unreachable. In general, routing updates are sent out every 30 seconds. If a gateway is not heard from for more than 180 seconds, it is considered dead, and all routes using this gateway are deleted from the routing table. Many versions of UNIX run a RIP routing daemon called routed to implement RIP on their networks.

RIP version 2, which is more commonly known as RIP II, has added more capabilities to RIP. RIP II uses IP multicast to distribute route updates where RIP uses broadcast messages. RIP II uses IP multicast to prevent version 1 routers from getting confused with route information suitable only for version 2 routers. RIP II enhancements include support for next hop, network masks, and authentication.

routed

On many UNIX systems, including Linux, the Routing Information Protocol is run by a routing daemon, called routed. This daemon dynamically builds the routing table based on route information it receives via RIP updates. When routed starts, it broadcasts a request for route updates and then starts listening for replies to its request. Other hosts or routers that are configured to respond to RIP requests reply with an update packet. The update packets contain destination addresses from the routing table and the routing metric associated with each destination. In addition to responding to RIP requests, update packets are periodically issued to keep routing information current on all participating RIP routers and hosts.

When a RIP update is received, routed updates its own routing table with this information. If routes to new destinations are received, they are added to the routing table. If a route update is received with a lower metric for a route that already exists in the routing table, the new route is used. Routes are also deleted from the routing table if the route metric is greater than 15. If no updates are received from a gateway for a specified length of time, all routes to that gateway are deleted. Routing updates are generally issued every 30 seconds. In general, if updates are not received within 180 seconds from a gateway, the gateway is considered dead, and all routes through that gateway are deleted from the routing table.

To run RIP using the routed daemon, enter the following command:

```
# /sbin/routed
```

Another way of starting and stopping routed would be through the startup script in /etc/rc.d/init.d as follows:

```
# /etc/rc.d/init.d/routed start
# /etc/rc.d/init.d/routed stop
```

Generally, routed is started without any command-line arguments. However, if you want routed to never advertise its routes to other hosts and routers and only listen for routes advertised by other systems running routed, you can use the -q option.

THE /etc/gateways FILE

In most cases, routed can learn and build up its routing table by just listening to RIP updates coming from routers and hosts supplying RIP data. However, there might be times when you need to provide additional routing data to routed. For example, if you have a Cisco router on the network that is running the OSPF or EIGRP protocol and does not provide RIP updates, you need to provide this data to routed. To make routed aware of such a router, you need to add an entry in the /etc/gateways file, which is often used to define an entry for a default router. The syntax of entries in the /etc/gateways file is as follows:

```
net¦host <name or address> gateway <name or address> metric <number> active¦passive
```

An example entry for a default route would be the following:

```
net 0.0.0.0 gateway 10.2.0.254 metric 1 passive
```

The entry starts with the keyword `net` or `host`, indicating that the route is for a destination network or host. This is followed by the name or IP address of the network or host. In the example, `0.0.0.0` indicates the default route. Next comes the keyword `gateway`, which is followed by the name or IP address of the gateway. The keyword `metric` is followed by its numeric value. The use of metric is useful when there is more than one route to the same destination host or network. The lower metric value takes precedence in route selection because it should indicate a shorter route to the destination.

The last value in the route entry is the keyword `passive` or `active`. A route marked `passive` means the gateway does not need to provide RIP updates. This prevents the route from being deleted when no RIP updates are received from that gateway. A `passive` route is placed in the system's routing table and kept as long as the system is running. Functionally, this is the same as adding a static route to a system. A route marked `active`, however, is a route that is updated by RIP. `routed` expects to receive routing information from the active route's gateway and is deleted if updates do not arrive within a specified time.

OPEN SHORTEST PATH FIRST ROUTING PROTOCOL

Open Shortest Path First (OSPF) is a shortest path first or link-state protocol. OSPF is an interior gateway protocol that distributes routing information between routers within a single autonomous system. In OSPF, the least expensive path is considered the best path. OSPF is suitable for very complex networks and networks consisting of a large number of routers.

In OSPF, networks are grouped into areas. OSPF uses four types of routes. In order of preference, these are the following:

- **Intra-area routes:** Routes with destinations within the same area
- **Inter-area routes:** Routes with destinations in other OSPF areas
- **Type 1 external routes:** Routes to destinations outside the autonomous system
- **Type 2 external routes:** Routes to destinations outside the autonomous system

In a link-state protocol, each OSPF router maintains a database describing the entire autonomous system topology. This database is built out of the collected link-state advertisements of all routers. Each participating router advertises its local state, which is its operating interfaces and reachable neighbors, throughout the autonomous system. From the topology database, each router constructs a tree of the shortest paths with itself as the root of the tree. This shortest path tree gives the route to each destination within the autonomous system. When there are multiple OSPF routers in the same network backbone area, an election takes place, and one of the routers becomes the designated router. A second router becomes the backup designated router.

The designated router becomes responsible for collecting link-state updates from the other routers. A designated router keeps a lot of information about the link states of all the routers. If the designated router were to go down, it would take a long time to rebuild this link-state database. Therefore the link-state database is shared with the backup designated router, which can quickly assume the role of the designated router in case the designated router becomes suddenly unavailable.

OSPF uses the destination address and the type of service (TOS) information in a packet header to determine a route for the packet. In determining the shortest path route OSPF uses several cost metrics, such as route speed, traffic, reliability, and security. OSPF uses the HELLO protocol to pass state information between routers. The HELLO protocol uses time taken between hops to calculate optimum routes, instead of the number of hops, as RIP and most other protocols do.

Whenever packets are routed outside an autonomous system OSPF calls this external routing. As mentioned earlier, there are two types of external routing with OSPF, Type 1 and Type 2. For Type 1 external routes OSPF uses the same algorithms to calculate an external route as it would to derive an internal route. Type 2 external routes, however, are learned from external EGP or BGP routers.

OSPF allows a large network to be divided into smaller areas, each with its own routers and routing algorithms. Routing between areas is done using a backbone area. OSPF defines several types of routers that cater to the different OSPF areas. They are classified as follows:

- **An Internal Router**: A router in which all connections belong to a single area, or in which only backbone connections are made.
- **A Border Router**: A router that has connections outside its area.
- **A Backbone Router**: A router that has an interface to the backbone.
- **A Boundary Router**: A router that has a connection to another autonomous system.

OSPF routers send messages to each other about inter-network connections. These messages are known as route advertisements, and are sent using the HELLO protocol. There are four types of route advertisements in OSPF:

- **Router link advertisements**: These provide information about the local router's connections within an OSPF area. They are broadcast to all participating OSPF routers within the autonomous system.
- **Network link advertisements**: These provide a list of routers that are connected to the network. They are broadcast to all participating OSPF routers within the autonomous system.
- **Summary link advertisements**: These provide information about routes outside the area. These advertisements are sent by OSPF border routers to participating OSPF area routers.
- **Autonomous System Extended link advertisements**: These contain routes to external autonomous system and are used by OSPF boundary routers.

OSPF is a dynamic and adaptive protocol. It adjusts to problems in the network and provides very short convergence time to stabilize the routing table. It is designed to prevent looping of traffic in mesh networks, or in networks, where multiple bridges are used to connect different local area networks.

OSPF is an alternative to RIP. It overcomes all the limitations of RIP. RIP is a distance vector protocol, whereas OSPF is a link-state protocol. In a link-state protocol each router actively tests the status of its link to each of its neighbors. It sends this link-state information to its neighbor routers. Each router uses the link-state information to build its routing table. This method offers much faster route convergence than is possible with distance-vector protocols, and is well suited for large networks, whose topology changes frequently. Several other features make OSPF superior to RIP, including the following:

- **Type of Service**: OSPF can calculate a separate set of routes for each type of service (TOS).
- **Load-balancing**: When more than one equal-cost route to a destination exist, OSPF can distribute the data evenly between the routes.
- **VLSM**: OSPF supports variable length subnet masks (VLSM).

> **Note**
>
> Unlike RIP, RIP version 2 also understands subnets.

- Each interface is assigned a cost metric based on round trip time, traffic, reliability, and security. Additionally a separate cost can be assigned for the type of service.
- OSPF uses multicasting for route advertisements to reduce the load on systems not participating in OSPF.

OSPF is the answer to managing complex networks with multi-vendor systems. Common routing protocols, such as RIP, are designed for simple networks that have only a few routers and very little redundancy. These protocols are not efficient in large networks where routing messages can take up a significant amount of network bandwidth. OSPF addresses this problem by using multicasting to exchange routing information with participating routers.

A complete elaboration of the OSPF protocol is beyond the scope of this book. To learn about the details of OSPF, you can refer to the following resources:

- RFC-1131, "OSPF specification"
- RFC-1245, "OSPF Protocol Analysis"
- RFC-1246, "Experience with the OSPF Protocol"
- RFC-1364, "BGP OSPF Interaction"
- RFC-1850, "OSPF Version 2 Management Information Base"
- RFC-2154, "OSPF with Digital Signatures"
- RFC-2328, "OSPF Version 2"

- RFC-2329, "OSPF Standardization Report"
- RFC-2370, "The OSPF Opaque LSA Option"
- RFC-2676, "QoS Routing Mechanisms and OSPF Extensions"
- RFC-2740, "OSPF for IPv6"
- *Internetworking with TCP/IP (Vol I)*, by Douglas Comer
- *TCP/IP Illustrated, Volume I, The Protocols*, by W. Richard Stevens

gated

gated is an all-in-one routing daemon that supports RIP, RIP II, Hello, BGP, EGP, and OSPF. Because gated understands all these protocols, it is better suited for complex networks where several routing protocols are used within the same network. gated combines the routing information learned from all these protocols and selects the best routes. The configuration file of gated, however, is more complex than routed, and if your network is simple, you might opt to run routed instead. Running gated with only RIP or RIP II enabled is quite simple and is preferred over running routed.

SAMPLE gated CONFIGURATIONS Configuring gated for a host system is quite simple, requiring only a few configuration statements. When gated is started, it reads its configuration from the file /etc/gated.conf.

The following configuration shown emulates routed. The protocol used is RIP. Updates are sent if more than one network interface is up and IP forwarding is enabled in the kernel:

```
#
rip yes ;
#
```

To enable IP forwarding in the kernel, use the following command:

```
# echo "1" > /proc/sys/net/ipv4/ip_forward
```

> **Tip**
>
> UDP checksums must be enabled in the kernel. Usually, this is enabled by default in Linux. Also, IP Multicast support must be enabled in the kernel. RIP version 2 uses IP Multicast. This is done when configuring the Linux kernel, during a kernel compile. Consult Chapter 11 for a discussion of recompiling the kernel.

The following configuration runs RIP in quiet mode; it only listens to packets, no matter how many interfaces are configured:

```
#
rip yes {
        nobroadcast ;
};
#
```

The next example is for a host system running RIP, which has a single network interface. It also demonstrates how to specify a default route:

```
# Define the only network interface as passive to prevent timing out
# the only network interface.
interfaces {
        interface eth0 passive ;
} ;

# enable RIP version 2 with multicast.
rip yes {
        broadcast ;
        defaultmetric 5 ;
        interface eth0 version 2 multicast ;
} ;

# Define a default static route
static {
        0.0.0.0 mask 0.0.0.0 gateway 10.2.0.254 retain ;
}
```

The keyword `passive` is used in the `interface` command. In this case, by using the keyword `passive`, you are making sure the permanent route through the host's only network interface will not be removed from the routing table by `gated`. Normally, when `gated` thinks a network interface is down, it removes it from the routing table. In this case, the host has a single network interface, and you do not want `gated` to remove that interface from the routing table, even if `gated` thinks the interface is down. Declaring the interface as passive achieves this purpose.

The `static` statement is used to define a static route. In the preceding example, a static route is defined to use a default gateway, which has an IP address of `10.2.0.254`.

The following example illustrates the use of both RIP II and OSPF routing protocols:

```
interfaces {
        interface eth0 passive ;
} ;

rip yes {
        broadcast ;
        defaultmetric 5 ;
        interface eth0 version 2 multicast ;
} ;

ospf yes {
        backbone {
            authtype simple;
            networks {
            10.2.0.0 mask 255.255.0.0;
            10.3.0.0 mask 255.255.0.0;
            };
            interface eth {
            enabled;
```

```
        authkey "secret";
    };
  };
};
static {
  0.0.0.0 mask 0.0.0.0 gateway 10.2.0.254;
};
```

The statement rip yes enables the RIP protocol. If no rip statement is specified, it is enabled by default. If the system is a host with only one interface, the default option is nobroadcast. In the preceding configuration example, you are specifying RIP broadcast. When broadcast is specified, RIP packets are broadcast regardless of the number of interfaces present. This is useful when you want to propagate static routes or routes learned through another protocol into RIP. The defaultmetric directive defines the metric used when advertising routes via RIP that have been learned from other protocols. The interface command controls the attributes of sending RIP over the specified interfaces. Here, you have specified that RIP version 2 be used over IP multicast on the interface eth0.

The statement ospf yes enables the OSPF protocol. The backbone directive specifies the OSPF area to be the backbone network. If more than one area is configured, at least one area must be the backbone. The backbone area is also known as area 0. Either term can be used to specify the backbone area. The authtype directive can have the value none or simple. If none is specified, no authentication is necessary, whereas simple uses a simple password authentication method. OSPF uses one authentication scheme per area. Each area must use the same authentication scheme. The networks directive describes the scope of an area. The entries are specified as network address and network mask pairs. The interface directive followed by eth specifies all Ethernet interfaces. The enabled directive enables all Ethernet interfaces to participate in OSPF routing. The authkey directive is followed by the password string used by OSPF to verify the authentication field in the OSPF header.

> **Tip**
>
> For complete details of all gated options and how to write a gated.conf file, refer to the online manual pages by running man gated. Also refer to the Gated Configuration Guide and GatedOperation Guide, which are available in /usr/doc/gated-3.5/doc directory in a normal gated installation.

STARTING AND STOPPING gated The gated distribution comes with a program called gdc, which is used to start and stop gated and to check the gated.conf file for correctness. For full details of gdc, check the online manual page by running man gdc. Following are a few sample uses of gdc.

To start gated using gdc, use the following command:

```
# /usr/sbin/gdc start
```

To stop gated using gdc, use the following command:

```
# /usr/sbin/gdc stop
```

To restart gated using gdc, use this command:

```
# /usr/sbin/gdc restart
```

To check the status of gated, use the following command:

```
# /usr/sbin/gdc running
```

After you create or modify a gated.conf file, you can test its correctness using gdc as follows:

```
# /usr/sbin/gdc checkconf
```

After modifying the gated.conf file, you can signal gated to reread its configuration file with the following command:

```
# /usr/sbin/gdc reconfig
```

By default gated reads its configuration from the file /etc/gated.conf. The gdc program can also maintain several versions of the configuration file, with special names, such as /etc/gated.conf+, /etc/gated.conf-, and so on. For example, you can create a new configuration file named /etc/gated.conf+ and instruct gdc to install it. When gdc installs the new configuration file /etc/gated.conf+, it renames it to /etc/gated.conf. The previous version of the configuration file is moved to /etc/gated.conf-. If an older configuration file called /etc/gated.conf- already exists, that is renamed to /etc/gated.conf--.

To check the new configuration file /etc/gated.conf+, use the following command:

```
# /usr/sbin/gdc checknew
```

This command is similar to checkconf, except it checks the new configuration file instead of the current one.

To install the /etc/gated.conf+ file as the /etc/gated.conf file, use the following command:

```
# /usr/sbin/gdc newconf
```

To revert back to an older configuration file, use this command:

```
# /usr/sbin/gdc backout
```

This will rotate the older configuration file /etc/gated.conf- to /etc/gated.conf.

TROUBLESHOOTING

This section covers some common problems relating to network connectivity and routing, and then explores possible solutions. In particular, you will consider the following problems:

- Local host cannot access a remote host
- Host connections fail for certain applications
- Poor performance
- Host and router subnet mask mismatch
- OSPF routers not establishing neighbors

LOCAL HOST CANNOT ACCESS REMOTE HOST

Consider the following scenario: Hosts on one network cannot communicate with hosts on a remote network. The networks are separated by one or more routers and might include WAN or other links. One or more routing protocols are running on the routers. In this case, several possible problems might exist:

- The default gateway is not specified or is misconfigured on the local or remote host.
- routed is misconfigured or missing a default route.
- A DNS entry might be missing for a host.
- Improper configuration of a router or routers between the two hosts might have occurred.

DEFAULT GATEWAY IS NOT SPECIFIED OR IS MISCONFIGURED ON LOCAL OR REMOTE HOST

If hosts are not running routed, a default gateway should be configured. Determine whether the local and remote hosts have a default gateway specified. Use the netstat command to determine whether a default gateway is configured as follows:

```
# netstat -rn
```

Check the output of this command for a default gateway specification. If the default gateway specification is incorrect or if it is not present at all, you can change or add a default gateway using the following command on the host:

```
# /sbin/route add default gw <IP address> 1
```

Here, <IP address> is the IP address of the default gateway. The value 1 is the metric and indicates that the specified gateway is one hop away.

routed IS MISCONFIGURED OR MISSING A DEFAULT ROUTE

If the host is running routed, use the netstat -rn command to view the host's routing table. The entry with destination default denotes the default route.

The default route entry should point to the router that has the route to the remote host. If there is no default route entry, use the route command to manually configure the default gateway as described in the previous section. To permanently fix the problem, add a default route entry in the /etc/gateways file and restart routed.

DNS ENTRY MISSING FOR A HOST

Use the nslookup utility to see if you can resolve the host address as follows:

```
$ nslookup <remote hostname>
```

If nslookup cannot resolve the host address but you can reach the remote host by using its IP address, it is a name resolution problem. Make sure a proper DNS entry is added for the host.

IMPROPER CONFIGURATION OF ROUTERS BETWEEN TWO HOSTS

Check routes on the router, or routers, connecting the two networks and fix any misconfigured or missing routes. Narrow down the specific symptoms and troubleshoot the problem using the procedures outlined in Chapter 13. Check the routing tables on the Linux router using the netstat -nr command.

HOST CONNECTIONS FAIL FOR CERTAIN APPLICATIONS

If connection attempts using some applications are successful but others fail, a firewall might be in place between the two hosts that is not allowing particular protocols to pass through it. Check the firewall rules on any firewalls between the hosts in question and modify them if needed.

POOR PERFORMANCE

If the performance of one or more network hosts is slow or connections to servers take a long time to establish, a likely cause is a misconfigured resolv.conf file on a DNS client.

Check the /etc/resolv.conf file on the affected client machines. If the file is misconfigured, the client waits until a query to the first DNS server times out before trying a second server. This causes long delays. Also, DNS might not be set up for reverse lookups, which causes reverse lookup attempts by end systems to time out. This can cause excessive delays for hosts attempting to establish connections. Fix nameserver entries in the /etc/resolv.conf file and other existing DNS problems such as reverse lookups.

HOST AND ROUTER SUBNET MASK MISMATCH

In classful IP networks, every router and host in the same major network must share a common subnet mask. If there are disagreements on the length of the subnet mask, packets are not routed correctly. Make sure the network mask on all hosts and routers is consistent.

OSPF ROUTERS NOT ESTABLISHING NEIGHBORS

If OSPF routers are not establishing neighbor relationships properly, the result is that routing information is not exchanged between routers. Make sure the OSPF routers are in the same area, and share the same authentication type (authtype) and key (authkey). The networks defined within the area and network masks should also be the same throughout an OSPF area.

## CHAPTER 16

LINUX MAIL SERVICES WITH SENDMAIL

In this chapter

EMAIL SYSTEMS

Setting up or maintaining an electronic mail service for an enterprise is not a trivial task. As a system administrator, you may be faced with the task of setting up a whole new email system or maintaining or expanding your current system. The following sections provide an overview of an electronic mail system and briefly touch upon some basic concepts and terminology. We also look at sendmail, the leading email server software for Linux, and its configuration. Finally, we briefly discuss the IMAP and POP3 mail services.

PHYSICAL COMPONENTS OF A MAIL NETWORK

Four basic components comprise an email system. These components can be combined on the same system or can be provided on separate systems. These are as follows:

- Mail clients
- Mail servers
- Mail host
- Mail gateway

Figure 16.1 illustrates a typical corporate email configuration.

Figure 16.1
A typical corporate email environment.

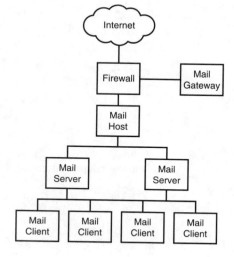

MAIL CLIENTS

A mail client is a machine that reads mail from a mail server. It does not run the mail server application such as the sendmail, smail, or qmail daemons and does not receive mail directly.

Typically, a Linux mail server running `sendmail` receives mail and stores it in user mailboxes in the directory `/var/spool/mail`. A Linux mail client can be configured to mount the mail directory using NFS as discussed in Chapter 14, "Printer and File Sharing with NFS and Samba," and directly access these mailboxes.

In mixed environments, especially those with mixed mail client platforms, mail clients will typically access mailboxes on the mail servers using the POP3 or IMAP protocols. In this case, the mail servers can be Linux-based mail servers or commercial servers such as Microsoft Exchange or Netscape's mail server.

MAIL SERVERS

In the Linux environment, several mail servers are available. By far the most prominent mail server is sendmail.

On a server running sendmail, mail is delivered directly to users' mailboxes. These mailboxes are files stored in the `/var/spool/mail` directory where each file represents a user's inbox and is named with the user's login name. When sendmail is asked to deliver outgoing mail by a mail client, the mail is queued in the directory `/var/spool/mqueue` until the message is successfully delivered.

In a Linux environment, it is common for mail clients to directly access and manipulate these sendmail inboxes, leaving the mail on the mail server at all times. This is commonly done by accessing the inboxes through NFS mounting the `/var/spool/mail` directory to mail clients. This approach provides the advantage of centralizing mailboxes for easy backup, debugging, and management. A notable disadvantage, though, is that if the mail server is down, users cannot access their inboxes.

An alternative approach to mail clients managing centrally maintained inboxes is for mail clients to move messages from these central inboxes to mailboxes in their home directories. Typically, this can be done by direct manipulation of the inbox through NFS mounting or through a mail retrieval protocol such as POP3 or IMAP. While this provides the advantage that mailboxes remain accessible even when a mail server is down, it does suffer from the disadvantage of distributing mail inbox data through many client systems. This can make backup more complex, but not impossible.

MAIL HOST

A mail host is a machine that is designated as the main mail server on the network. It is the system to which other servers at the site forward mail that they cannot deliver. It acts as a central mail hub and routes mail to internal servers or to the external mail gateway. Any mail that needs to go outside your domain will be handed over to the mail host machine.

The sendmail configuration on a mail host is more complex than that of a simple mail server machine.

MAIL GATEWAY

A mail gateway is a machine that handles mail connections between different networks. Typically, a mail gateway is the system defined in a domain's DNS records as the mail exchanger for the domain. DNS records are discussed in Chapter 22, "DNS."

As the mail exchanger, the mail gateway is the primary point of contact from the Internet for incoming mail for a domain. Typically, though, it is not the final destination of an incoming message.

Often, mail gateways have the task of translating between different network and mail protocols. For instance, a mail gateway can connect an external TCP/IP network running Internet-standard SMTP mail to an Internal Windows network running Microsoft Exchange mail.

Note

Because Linux-based networks typically use TCP/IP and SMTP, this is the mail environment on which we will focus.

Typically the sendmail configuration on a gateway machine is quite complex compared to that of simple mail server systems. While a mail server system usually handles mail for a single section of an organization, a mail gateway has the task of receiving all mail from the Internet for an organization and then directing it to the correct internal mail hosts, which then handle further distribution to destination mail servers.

For this reason, a mail gateway has far more decision making to do: It doesn't simply receive messages and place them in the correct user's inbox as is done by a mail server.

SOFTWARE COMPONENTS OF A MAIL SYSTEM

In the previous section, "Physical Components of a Mail System," we discussed the actual physical machines that make up a typical corporate email environment. In addition to this physical division of labor, we need to consider the various software packages that run on these physical systems to provide the actual email functionality.

An email system comprises several software components, including the following:

- Mail user agents
- Mail transport agents
- Mail delivery agents

MAIL USER AGENTS

A mail user agent is a program which users interact with to read, compose, send, and manipulate emails. Numerous mail user agents are available for Linux, including text-based console applications such as Pine and Elm and graphical mail software for X Windows such as Netscape Messenger and Kmail.

These mail user agents communicate with a mail transport agent to handle retrieval and delivery of emails. Mail user agents typically run on mail client systems.

MAIL TRANSPORT AGENTS

A mail transport agent resolves mail addresses and routes mail messages. A mail transport agent generally handles the following tasks:

- Receiving mail from mail user agents
- Resolving mail addresses
- Selecting and delivering mail to the mail delivery agent
- Receiving incoming mail from mail delivery agents

Mail transport agents typically run on mail server systems. By far the most prominent mail transport agent for Linux is sendmail. sendmail is a large, complex, powerful mail server product, which is widely used for large mail installations.

In addition to sendmail, several alternative mail transport agents are available for Linux, including two popular packages:

- Smail (`ftp://ftp.uu.net/networking/mail/smail/`)
- Qmail (`http://www.qmail.org/top.html`)

In this book we focus on the use of sendmail as a mail server for Linux because it represents the accepted standard mail server for Linux.

MAIL DELIVERY AGENTS

A mail delivery agent is a program that implements a particular delivery protocol. In the Linux world, mail delivery agents are typically components of large mail server packages such as sendmail. For example, sendmail includes delivery agents for UUCP, SMTP, and local delivery.

In addition, mail transport agents such as sendmail can also use external mail delivery agents for mail delivery. Newer versions of sendmail, for instance, use `procmail` as the mail delivery agent for local mail delivery.

MAILBOXES

A mailbox is a file, or set of files, on the mail server that is the final destination of an email message. On a Linux mail server using sendmail, the name of the user's mailbox will be the login name of the user. These inbox files are stored in the `/var/spool/mail` directory.

PART

III

CH

16

MAIL ALIASES

A mail alias is an alternative mail name. These aliases associate email addresses with particular inboxes.

For instance, on a mail server, there may be inboxes for user1 and user2. An alias could then be created so that mail addressed to userA would be delivered to the mailbox of user1. No mailbox would exist for userA. Similarly, an alias could allow mail addresses to userB to be delivered to the user2 inbox.

Aliases can also be used to redirect mail to external mailboxes on other mail servers. For instance, on a server, an alias could be created pointing user3 to userC@some.server. This alias would indicate that any mail received by the server for user3 should actually be sent to the mail server some.server for delivery to the mailbox userC. No inbox would actually exist for user3.

Mail aliases can also be used for the creation of simplistic mailing lists: An alias can point to a list of mail recipients so that an email addressed to the alias is actually delivered to all recipients. For instance, if the alias allusers points to the list of users user1, user2, and user5 then all mail addressed to allusers would be delivered to user1, user2, and user5 and no inbox would exist for allusers.

On sendmail systems, mail aliases are normally stored in the file /etc/aliases or /etc/mail/aliases depending on your distribution of Linux and version of sendmail. This is a text file containing one entry per line where each entry takes the form:

```
<alias>: <destination>
```

For instance, all of the aliases discussed above would appear in the aliases file as follows:

```
user1: userA
user2: userB
user3: userC@some.server
allusers: user1, user2, user5
```

> **Note**
>
> When an alias is used to create a simple mailing list, the addresses which are members of the mailing list appear as a comma-separated list of addresses in the destination portion of the entry in the aliases file.

sendmail does not directly read the aliases file. Instead, it is converted into a hash table or dbm database file using the newaliases command. Every time the aliases file is altered, the newaliases program should be executed before sendmail can access the new aliases. The newaliases program does not require any arguments or options:

```
# newaliases
/etc/aliases: 14 aliases, longest 10 bytes, 152 bytes total
```

As an alternative to using the `newaliases` command to rebuild the hash table or dbm file from the `aliases` file, you can use the `sendmail` program itself:

```
# sendmail -bi
/etc/aliases: 14 aliases, longest 10 bytes, 152 bytes total
```

The `newaliases` program will either create a hash table file called `aliases.db` or two files comprising the dbm database called `aliases.dir` and `aliases.pag`.

If you are using NIS on your network to distribute network information as discussed in Chapter 6, "Authenticating User and Network Resources," the aliases databases can actually be maintained as an NIS table on the NIS master server and be replicated on the NIS slave servers.

MAIL ADDRESSES

Internet email addresses typically consist of two sections: a user address and a domain name. For instance, consider the address `user@some.domain`. This address can be broken down into two components separated by the @ sign. To the left of the @ sign is the local address (`user`) and to the right of the @ sign is the domain name (`some.domain`).

Mail delivery agents use the domain portion of the address to determine the hostname and IP address of the appropriate mail exchanger for the domain by querying a DNS server. The mail delivery agent then attempts to connect to that mail exchanger and deliver the message using SMTP.

USING SENDMAIL

Although sendmail is not the only mail transport agent and Smail and Qmail are popular alternatives, sendmail does remain the most widely used mail transport agent for Linux and accordingly is the platform we address in this book.

Unfortunately, sendmail configuration is quite complex. To gain a complete understanding of sendmail configuration and management is beyond the scope of this book. In fact, an entire book is dedicated to the subject: *sendmail* by Bryan Costales and Eric Allman (O'Reilly, 1997). Eric Allman is the original designer and developer of the sendmail package.

Email systems often use a variety of programs and protocols for mail delivery; this is the source of much of the complexity underlying sendmail. For instance, SMTP is used for delivery over TCP/IP networks, UUCP is used for delivery on UUCP networks, and external applications such as `procmail` or `/bin/mail` are used for local delivery. For each delivery mechanism, different delivery agents and addressing schemes are used.

sendmail determines which delivery agent to use through analysis of the email address of a message's recipient. sendmail accepts messages from mail user agents such as Pine or Netscape Messenger, interprets the destination address, reformats the address as required by the appropriate mail delivery agent, and then routes the message to the delivery agent.

Figure 16.2 illustrates the route a message takes from the mail user agent until it is handed to a mail delivery agent for delivery.

Figure 16.2
The role of sendmail in the delivery process.

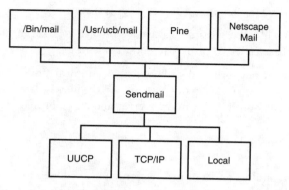

In addition to routing mail, sendmail also receives and delivers SMTP mail and provides for mail aliases.

To receive SMTP mail from the Internet or within the intranet, sendmail is run as a daemon which listens to TCP port 25. sendmail is automatically started at system boot up by the start up scripts in /etc/rc.d/init.d. The following code is typical of the code used in /etc/rc.d/init.d to start sendmail during the boot process:

```
if [ -f /etc/sysconfig/sendmail ] ; then
    . /etc/sysconfig/sendmail
else
    DAEMON=yes
    QUEUE=1h
fi
[ -f /usr/sbin/sendmail ] || exit 0
# See how we were called.
case "$1" in
  start)
    # Start daemons.
    echo -n "Starting sendmail: "
    /usr/bin/newaliases > /dev/null 2>&1
    for i in virtusertable access domaintable mailertable ; do
        if [ -f /etc/mail/$i ] ; then
        makemap hash /etc/mail/$i < /etc/mail/$i
        fi
    done
    /usr/sbin/sendmail $([ "$DAEMON" = yes ] && echo -bd) \
                        $([ -n "$QUEUE" ] && echo -q$QUEUE)
    ;;
```

The script first checks whether the file /etc/sysconfig/sendmail exists. If it does it sources its contents. This file sets the values of two environment variables: DAEMON and QUEUE. If DAEMON is set to yes, it means sendmail should run in daemon mode. The value of the QUEUE variable tells sendmail how often it should process the mail queue. For example if the contents of /etc/sysconfig/sendmail is the following:

```
DAEMON=yes
QUEUE=15m
```

then the sendmail program needs to be invoked with two arguments: -bd to indicate that the program should run in daemon mode and listen to TCP port 25 for incoming SMTP mail and -q15m to indicate a queue processing interval of 15 minutes:

`/usr/sbin/sendmail -bd -q15m`

Prior to starting up the sendmail program, the script runs two other programs, newaliases and makemap.

The program /usr/bin/newaliases is a link to /usr/sbin/sendmail. When sendmail is invoked with the program name newaliases it rebuilds the aliases database.

The makemap program creates a hash or dbm format database files from sendmail configuration files. The above script calls makemap with the argument hash, which tells it to build the databases in a hash table format. The script checks whether the following text files exist and if they do they are converted to hash table files: virtusertable, access, domaintable, and mailertable.

SENDMAIL FILES AND DIRECTORIES

The sendmail package uses numerous files and directories for configuration and processing purposes:

- /usr/sbin/sendmail
- /etc/sendmail.cf
- /usr/bin/newaliases
- /usr/bin/hoststat
- /usr/bin/purgestat
- /var/spool/mqueue
- /usr/bin/mailq
- /var/spool/mqueue/.hoststat
- /etc/aliases
- /usr/lib/sendmail.hf
- /etc/sendmail.st

We will discuss each of these files in turn.

/usr/sbin/sendmail

In Linux the sendmail executable program is located in the /usr/sbin directory. It is setuid root, which means that regardless of who launches the program, it runs as the root user. For security reasons the directories /, /usr, and /usr/sbin should be owned by root, and have the mode 755. This means that only the root user can change the contents of these directories.

PART

III

CH

16

This will prevent the replacement of the sendmail binary by a malicious user who can then take advantage of the fact that sendmail always runs as the root user to compromise system security.

/etc/sendmail.cf

When sendmail starts it reads its configuration from the file /etc/sendmail.cf. The location of the sendmail.cf file is hard coded into the sendmail binary file. For this reason, there are only two ways to change the location of the sendmail configuration file:

- Move the file to a new location and create a link back to /etc using the command:
  ```
  # ln -s <new location of configuration file> /etc/sendmail.cf
  ```
- Recompile the sendmail package after altering the sendmail source code.

/usr/bin/newaliases

The newaliases command is not a distinct file but rather is a link to the sendmail executable. If, for some reason, the newaliases link does not point to your sendmail executable, you can re-create the link as follows:

```
# rm -f /usr/bin/newaliases
# ln -s /usr/sbin/sendmail /usr/bin/newaliases
```

When sendmail is invoked as the newaliases command, it has the effect of starting sendmail with the -bi arguments which causes sendmail to rebuild the aliases hash table or dbm file.

The actual role of newaliases is discussed earlier in this chapter in the section on mail aliases.

/usr/bin/hoststat

The hoststat command is not a distinct file but rather is a link to the sendmail executable in the same way that newaliases is. If, for some reason, the hoststat link does not point to your sendmail executable, you can re-create the link as follows:

```
# rm -f /usr/bin/hoststat
# ln -s /usr/sbin/sendmail /usr/bin/hoststat
```

When sendmail is invoked as the hoststat command, it has the effect of causing sendmail to display a list of the last mail transaction with every remote host that has been communicated with.

For the hoststat command to work, you must perform several preparatory steps:

1. The HostStatusDirectory option must be set in the sendmail.cf file.
2. A .hoststat directory must be created in the /var/spool/mqueue directory with the command:
   ```
   # mkdir /var/spool/mqueue/.hoststat
   ```

/usr/bin/purgestat

The purgestat command is not a distinct file but rather is a link to the sendmail executable in the same way that newaliases is. If, for some reason, the purgestat link does not point to your sendmail executable, you can re-create the link as follows:

```
# rm -f /usr/bin/purgestat
# ln -s /usr/sbin/sendmail /usr/bin/purgestat
```

When sendmail is invoked as the purgestat command, it flushes all information in the HostStatusDirectory directory tree.

/var/spool/mqueue

The /var/spool/mqueue directory is the default mail queue directory for sendmail. This directory should be owned by root and have permissions mode set to 700.

The Q entry in the sendmail.cf file defines the location of the sendmail queue directory. The default value of this entry is /var/spool/mqueue. Normally there is no need to change this, unless you have a very unusual sendmail configuration.

As it operates, sendmail creates mail files in /var/spool/mqueue with prefixes. These prefixes have specific meanings as outlined in Table 16.1.

TABLE 16.1 PREFIXES IN THE /var/spool/mqueue DIRECTORY

Prefix	Description
lf	Lock files
qf	Control files for messages
df	Data files for messages
tf	Temporary versions of control files used during rebuilding of queue files
xf	Transcript files for the current session

/usr/bin/mailq

The mailq command is not a distinct file but rather is a link to the sendmail executable in the same way that newaliases is. If, for some reason, the mailq link does not point to your sendmail executable, you can re-create the link as follows:

```
# rm -f /usr/bin/mailq
# ln -s /usr/sbin/sendmail /usr/bin/mailq
```

When sendmail is invoked as the mailq command, sendmail launches with the -bp argument which causes sendmail to display the current contents of the /var/spool/mqueue directory.

`/var/spool/mqueue/.hoststat`

If you enable the `HostStatusDirectory` option in `sendmail.cf`, the default value of the entry is `/var/spool/mqueue/.hoststat`. This directory contains one file for every host that `sendmail` has communicated with recently which is used by the `hoststat` command to display the last transaction with each host.

`/etc/aliases`

Mail aliases are stored in the file `/etc/aliases`. A sample `aliases` file is usually created when `sendmail` is first installed. The sample file is also provided with the sendmail source distribution. The `aliases` file contains required aliases as well as custom aliases for your site. Required aliases include an alias for the `postmaster` email address.

If you are installing a sendmail system from scratch, you should copy the aliases file from the sendmail source distribution's `lib/aliases` directory to `/etc/aliases` and then edit it to suit the needs of your site.

The `newaliases` program converts the `/etc/aliases` text file to a hash file or dbm database format. sendmail uses the database version of the file instead of the actual `/etc/aliases` text file. The default format for the aliases database is the ndbm format. The path to the `aliases` file is defined by the `AliasFile` entry in `sendmail.cf` file.

`/usr/lib/sendmail.hf`

The `sendmail.hf` is the help file used by the SMTP `HELP` command. The path to this file is set by the `HelpFile` option in `sendmail.cf` file.

`/etc/sendmail.st`

If you create an empty `/etc/sendmail.st` file using the following command:

```
# touch /etc/sendmail.st
```

then sendmail will collect statistics about your mail traffic. The file itself does not change or grow in size but simply indicates to sendmail to start collecting statistics. The path to this file is set by the `S` entry in the `sendmail.cf` file.

THE `sendmail.cf` CONFIGURATION FILE

The sendmail configuration file is `/etc/sendmail.cf`. The location of this file is compiled into the `sendmail` executable. `sendmail` reads it every time it starts.

Tip

If you want to configure sendmail quickly and get it up and running, read the next section "Configuring sendmail with `m4`" first, and later come back to this section to learn the gory details of sendmail's configuration file.

Because the `sendmail.cf` file is designed to be read and parsed quickly and efficiently by sendmail, it uses a format and syntax which is far from easy for humans to read. By way of example, consider the following extracts from a `sendmail.cf`:

```
H?P?Return-Path: <$g>
HReceived: $?sfrom $s $.$?_($?s$¦from $.$_)
        $.by $j ($v/$Z)$?r with $r$. id $i$?u
        for $u; $¦;
        $.$b
H?D?Resent-Date: $a
H?D?Date: $a
H?F?Resent-From: $?x$x <$g>$¦$g$.
H?F?From: $?x$x <$g>$¦$g$.
H?x?Full-Name: $x
# HPosted-Date: $a
# H?l?Received-Date: $b
H?M?Resent-Message-Id: <$t.$i@$j>
H?M?Message-Id: $t.$i@$j
```

PART

III

CH

16

> **Note**
>
> This sample from the `sendmail.cf` file illustrates a more cryptic section of the file. Some parts of the file are easier to read for humans, but generally the file is obscure, as this example illustrates.

Even though the file is hard to read, the contents of the `sendmail.cf` file control the behavior of sendmail. The file provides several key pieces of information to sendmail including the following:

- The location of files and directories sendmail needs to use during regular operation
- The definitions that sendmail uses when rewriting addresses
- The mail header lines sendmail should modify, or pass through when it routes a message
- The sets of rules sendmail should use to select the appropriate delivery agent
- The definitions of mailer delivery agents

GENERAL STRUCTURE OF THE `sendmail.cf` FILE

Luckily, it is not necessary to write a `sendmail.cf` file from scratch. Generally, you can use the default `sendmail.cf` file that comes with your sendmail distribution and then modify it to suit the needs of your site. The structure of the file will remain generally unchanged and you will only need to edit specific entries.

Unfortunately, this is still not a trivial task. The `sendmail.cf` configuration commands use a terse syntax and command set and are difficult to remember or remain fluent in. Each configuration command consists of a single letter starting at the beginning of a line. The single command character is followed by other information pertinent to the command being used. Lines beginning with the hash symbol (#) are comment lines and the commands continue to the end of the line.

Table 16.2 outlines the main `sendmail.cf` configuration command characters.

TABLE 16.2   `sendmail.cf` CONFIGURATION COMMAND CHARACTERS

Command Character	Description	Example/Meaning
#	A comment line	Comment lines are ignored
space	Continue the previous line	
Tab	Continue the previous line	
C	Define a class macro	`CO @ % !` defines class O as the list of characters @, %, and !
D	Define a macro	For example, `DShost.some.domain` defines S as `some.host.domain`
F	Define a class macro from a file or pipe	`Fw/etc/sendmail.cw` indicates that the value of w is read from the file `/etc/sendmail.cw`
H	Define a header	`H?P?Return-Path: <$g>`
K	Create a keyed map entry	`Kaccess hash -o /etc/mail/access` defines the access list database
M	Define a mail delivery agent	`Mprocmail` Defines the program `procmail` as a mail delivery agent
O	Define an option	For example, `O AliasFile=/etc/aliases` defines the location of the aliases file
P	Define delivery priorities	`Pfirst-class=0` indicates that the name `first-class` is given the number 0
R	Define a rule	
S	Declare start of a rule-set	`S0` declares the start of rule-set 0
T	Declare trusted users	`Troot` defines root as a trusted user
V	Version number of the configuration file	`V8/Berkeley` defines the configuration file version as V8/Berkley

DEFINING CLASS COMMANDS

Two commands define classes: `C` and `F`. A class defines an array of values. When multiple values are handled in the same way, a class definition can be used. Classes allow `sendmail` to compare against a list of values instead of a single value.

For example to assign the values bwc and dmz to the class w you can use the following:

```
Cw bwc dmz
```

A class can also be defined specifying list values in multiple lines:

```
Cw bwc
Cw dmz
```

Class values can be loaded from a file by using the F command. For example to read the values for a class w from a file you can use the following:

```
Fw/etc/sendmail.cw
```

The file /etc/sendmail.cw should contain all the strings that you want to assign to class w. For instance, to assign the values bwc and dmz to class w using the /etc/sendmail.cw file, it should contain these values, one per line as follows:

```
bwc
dmz
```

DEFINING MACRO COMMAND

The D command defines a macro and stores a value in it. When the value is defined it can be used by other commands in the sendmail.cf file. This makes it possible to share the same configuration file among different systems. The only changes needed are to define a few system-specific macros.

User-defined macros use uppercase letters. Lowercase macro names are reserved for internal use by sendmail. If a macro called x is defined, its value can be retrieved later using $x. The following are some example macro definitions:

```
Dwphoenix
DDbwc.org
Dj$w.$D
```

Here we have one user-defined macro and two system macros. The lowercase letter w is a system macro reserved for hostname. We have defined w as phoenix in this example. The letter D is a user-defined macro for the domain name. We have defined D as bwc.org. The sendmail system macro definition Dj$w.$D defines the macro j as $w.$D. The lowercase letter j is a system macro reserved for the official domain name of a site. After we expand the values of the macros $w and $D, the final value of j becomes phoenix.bwc.org.

DEFINING HEADER COMMAND

Mail header formats are defined with the H command. Generally the header format definitions that come with the standard sendmail.cf file need no tweaking. The standard headers are listed here:

```
H?P?Return-Path: <$g>
HReceived: $?sfrom $s $.$?_($?s$¦from $.$_)
    $.by $j ($v/$Z)$?r with $r$. id $i$?u
    for $u; $¦;
    $.$b
```

```
H?D?Resent-Date: $a
H?D?Date: $a
H?F?Resent-From: $?x$x <$g>$¦$g$.
H?F?From: $?x$x <$g>$¦$g$.
H?x?Full-Name: $x
H?M?Resent-Message-Id: <$t.$i@$j>
H?M?Message-Id: <$t.$i@$j>
```

The syntax of the header command is the letter H, followed by an optional flag enclosed between two question marks, the name of the header, a colon, and the header template. The header template consists of literals and macros. The macros are expanded before the header is inserted into a message.

The header flags control whether the header is inserted into mail bound for a specific mailer. The flag definitions in the above example are as follows:

- **P:** Use when the mailer requires a Return-Path line.
- **D:** Use when the mailer requires a Date: header line.
- **F:** Use when the mailer requires a From: header line.
- **X:** Use when the mailer requires a Full-Name: header line.
- **M:** Use when the mailer requires a Message-Id: header line.

For a complete list of mailer flags refer to the "Sendmail Installation and Operations Guide." This document is available with the standard Linux distribution as a postscript file /usr/doc/sendmail/op.ps. It can also be downloaded from http://www.sendmail.org.

DEFINING KEYED MAP ENTRIES

The use of external keyed databases was introduced in Version 8 of sendmail. An external keyed database can provide certain information such as a list of UUCP hosts for faster access. Keyed databases come in several forms, such as hash table or dbm formatted files. Pointers to the keyed maps are done with the K command in the sendmail.cf file.

For instance, the following command indicates that the hash table file /etc/mail/uucphosts contains a list of UUCP hosts:

```
Kuucp hash /etc/mail/uucphosts
```

Other typical applications of the K command are using the access database to control spam:

```
Kaccess hash -o /etc/mail/access
```

or to provide virtual user lists:

```
Kvirtuser hash -o /etc/mail/virtusertable
```

DEFINING MAIL DELIVERY PROGRAMS

Mail delivery programs are defined using the M command in the sendmail.cf file. The following is the syntax of this command:

```
M<program>, <field1>=<value1>, <field2>=<value2>, etc.
```

Consider an example:

```
Mprocmail,    P=/usr/bin/procmail, F=DFMSPhnu9, S=11/31, R=21/31,
    T=DNS/RFC822/X-Unix, A=procmail -Y -m $h $f $u
```

Here the `procmail` mailer program is being defined as a delivery agent:

- `Mprocmail` defines the name of the mailer.
- `P=/usr/bin/procmail` specifies the path to the mailer.
- `F=DFMSPhnu9` are the flags used for this mailer.
- The `S` and `R` fields specify rewriting rule sets that need to be applied to the sender and recipient addresses. When two rule sets are specified with a slash in between, it means apply the first rule set to the envelope, and the second rule set to the message header. Therefore S=11/31 says apply ruleset 11 to rewrite the sender envelope address and ruleset 13 to the sender header address. Similarly R=21/23 says apply ruleset 21 to rewrite the recipient envelope address and ruleset 31 to rewrite the recipient header.
- The `T` field sets the type information used in MIME error messages. It is 3 values separated by slashes: the mail transport agent type which describes how hosts are named, the address type which specifies how emails are addressed, and the diagnostic type which provides a description of error diagnostic codes. In the above example these three values are `DNS`, `RFC822`, and `X-Unix`.
- The `A` field specifies the program and all the command-line arguments that are passed to it. The macros are expanded and passed to the program. For example, here the `$h`, `$f` and `$u` macros are internal `sendmail` system macros. `$h` expands to the recipient host, `$f` is the sender's from address, and `$u` is the recipient user.

DEFINING OPTIONS

Options are assigned values with the `O` command. Defining options is straightforward. The following is the syntax:

```
O <option name>=<value>
```

For instance, the `AliasFile` option specifies the location of the aliases file:

```
O AliasFile=/etc/aliases
```

The `MinFreeBlocks` option indicates the minimum number of free blocks that should be maintained on the file system:

```
O MinFreeBlocks=100
```

The `MaxMessageSize` places an upper limit on the size of mail messages, including all attachments:

```
O MaxMessageSize=1000000
```

The `sendmail.cf` includes all the possible options with comments describing the meaning and usage of the options. Usually the default values of these options work well unless your mail site requires some unique settings.

DEFINING MAIL PRIORITY

Each message entering the mail queue is assigned a priority by sendmail. The P command in the sendmail.cf file defines the priority values available to users. By default, messages receive a priority of 0 unless otherwise indicated. Negative priority values lower message priorities, and positive values raise message priorities.

Tip

In addition to being lower on the priority scale, messages with negative priority values do not generate error messages. This means negative priority values can be useful for bulk mailing lists that are likely to generate large numbers of mail messages.

The default sendmail.cf file includes the following priority definitions:

```
Pfirst-class=0
Pspecial-delivery=100
Plist=-30
Pbulk=-60
Pjunk=-100
```

DEFINING RULES AND RULE SETS

In this section we will take a brief look at address rewriting concepts. A detailed discussion of this topic is beyond the scope of this book. For a complete discussion of this topic refer to *sendmail* by Brian Costales and Eric Allman, published by O'Reilly.

Rules and rule sets make more sense when they are looked at together. Address rewriting rules are defined by the R command. Rule sets are defined by the S command. A rule set may contain zero or more individual rules. The following shows the syntax of the R and S commands:

```
S0
R<left side>      <right side>      <comment>
```

The line S0 marks the start of rule set 0. The next line starting with R defines a rule.

The fields in a rule must be separated by one or more tab characters and not by white spaces. White spaces can be used inside a field. The comment field is ignored.

The syntax of rules is extremely cryptic. Therefore if you do not write good comments when you write a rule, it can be very difficult to determine the purpose of the rule at a later date.

We will use the abbreviated terms LHS (left-hand-side), and RHS (right-hand-side) to describe the syntax. The input address is applied to the pattern on the left-hand-side. If the left-hand-side evaluates to true, then the right-hand-side is executed. If LHS evaluates false, then that rule is skipped and it moves on to the next rule in the set.

THE LEFT-HAND-SIDE PATTERN   The left-hand-side pattern consists of normal words and meta-symbols. Normal words are matched directly. Meta-symbols are specified using a dollar sign. Table 16.3 outlines the meta symbols used in the LHS of rules.

TABLE 16.3   LEFT-HAND-SIDE META SYMBOLS

Symbol	Meaning
$*	Match zero or more tokens
$+	Match one or more tokens
$-	Match exactly one token
$=x	Match any phrase in class x
$~x	Match any word not in class x

If any of the symbols match on the left-hand-side, they are assigned to the symbol $n for replacement on the right-hand-side, where n is the index in the lhs. For example, if the LHS is the following:

`$-@$+`

and the following input address

`user@some.domain`

is applied to the LHS rule, it will match. The meta-symbol `$-` matches `user`, the literal `@` matches the `@` in the address, and the meta-symbol `$+` matches `some.domain`.

The $n values passed to the RHS will be $1 (`user`) and $2 (`some.domain`).

THE RIGHT-HAND-SIDE PATTERN   When the left-hand-side of a rewriting rule matches, the input is replaced by the right-hand-side. Tokens are copied directly from the right-hand-side unless they begin with a dollar sign, in which case they are treated as macros or meta-symbols and expanded.

The right-hand-side meta-symbols are outlined in Table 16.4.

TABLE 16.4   RIGHT-HAND-SIDE META-SYMBOLS

Symbols	Meaning
$*x*	Expands macro *x*
$<*n*>	Substitutes indefinite token *n* from LHS; *n* is a digit
$><*n*>	Calls rule set *n*; *n* is a digit
$#<*mailer*>	Resolves to *mailer*
$@<*host*>	Specifies host
$:<*user*>	Specifies *user*
$[host$]	Maps to primary hostname

To illustrate how we test the left-hand-side and assign values to the right-hand-side, consider the following simple rule:

```
R$*<$*>$*      $2        basic RFC822 parsing
```

If you apply the following input address to the rule:

```
Full Name <user@some.domain>
```

on the LHS, the first $* matches the string Full Name and this value is assigned to $1, < matches the literal < in the address, the second $* matches user@some.domain, and is assigned to the variable $2. The literal > matches > in the address. The third $* matches a null value.

The RHS is assigned the value $2 which resolves to user@some.domain.

The third field is a comment.

THE SEMANTICS OF RULE SETS   A rule set is a group of rules that can be referenced as a set, and the set is given a number. The S<*n*> command marks the beginning of a rule set, where n is the number that references the rule set.

Rule sets are like subroutines or functions that process email addresses. They are called from individual rules, mailer definitions, and directly by sendmail itself. Six rule sets have special functions and are called directly by sendmail:

- Rule set 3 is applied first to all addresses. It converts an address to the canonical form: local-part@host.domain. If the address contains no @ sign then the host.domain part may be appended by sendmail. This happens only if the mail is received from a mailer that sets the C flag. SMTP mailers set this flag.

- Rule set 0 is applied after rule set 3 only to the recipient addresses actually used for mail delivery. It resolves the address to the mailer, host, and user triple. The triple is composed of the name of the mailer, the recipient's hostname, and the recipient's username.

- Rule set 1 is applied to all sender addresses in the message. It is usually not used. A standard sendmail.cf file will not have a definition for rule set 1. A custom rule set 1 is written at some sites to make all outgoing mail to appear to come from a central mail server.

- Rule set 2 is applied to all recipient addresses in the message. Like rule set 1, rule set 2 is also generally not used. Rule set 2 is sometimes used for debugging purposes.

- Rule set 4 is applied to all addresses in the message and is used to translate internal address formats to external address formats. Just like rule set 3, which is applied first to all addresses, rule set 4 is applied last to all addresses. Its purpose is to undo any special processing done by rule set 3. It removes trailing dots from fully qualified domain names. If rule set 3 had converted the commas of source route addresses to colons, rule set 4 restores the commas. It removes any angle brackets inserted by rule set 3 to focus on the host part of the address. It converts any UUCP addresses modified by rule set 3 back to the original form.

■ Rule set 5 is applied to all local addresses that do not have aliases. If a local address makes it through aliasing without change, it is given to rule set 5, which may select a new delivery agent. Any special rewriting after aliases have been expanded can be done by rule set 5.

DEFINING TRUSTED USERS

Trusted users are defined with the T command. Trusted users are allowed to override the sender address using the mailer -f flag. Normally the trusted users are defined to be the root, uucp, and daemon users. The default sendmail.cf file contains the following T commands:

```
Troot
Tdaemon
Tuucp
```

There is generally no need to modify this default list of trusted users. The concept of trusted users was eliminated in sendmail Version 8. If your system uses version 8, then you do not need to define or use trusted users.

DEFINING VERSION NUMBER

The configuration file version number is defined using the DZ command. The default version number does not require any modification. However, if you make changes to your sendmail.cf, it is a good idea to keep track of changes you have made by using the version number.

For example, if the version number is initially defined as the following:

```
DZ8.9.3
```

then after making changes to the sendmail.cf file you could change the version number to 8.9.3-1:

```
DZ8.9.3-1
```

CONFIGURING SENDMAIL WITH M4

As seen in the last section, directly configuring sendmail by editing the sendmail.cf file is difficult and attempting to do so from scratch would be nearly impossible. Fortunately, sendmail provides a mechanism for configuration through the m4 macro processor.

Using a collection of macros designed for sendmail, you build your configuration files using more concise and clearer directives than any that you find in the sendmail.cf file. For instance, a basic m4 configuration file for a sendmail server can be less than 10 lines:

```
include('../m4/cf.m4')
OSTYPE('linux')
undefine('UUCP_RELAY')
```

```
undefine('BITNET_RELAY')
FEATURE(redirect)
FEATURE(always_add_domain)
MAILER(local)
MAILER(smtp)
```

This m4 configuration produces a fairly standard sendmail.cf file that provides for delivery of incoming mail to local user mailboxes and delivery of outgoing mail through SMTP.

The directives in this m4 file have the following effect:

- **include('../m4/cf.m4')**: This directive includes generic configuration directives necessary for all sendmail.cf files.

- **OSTYPE('linux')**: This directive indicates that you are building a sendmail.cf file for a Linux-based sendmail system and forces inclusion of the necessary Linux-specific configuration information.

- **undefine('UUCP_RELAY')**: This directive indicates that your sendmail system does not need to support UUCP routing of mail and, accordingly, the relevant sections of sendmail.cf are excluded.

- **undefine('BITNET_RELAY')**: This directive indicates that your sendmail system does not need to support BITNET routing of mail and, accordingly, the relevant sections of sendmail.cf are excluded.

- **FEATURE(redirect)**: This directive indicates that any mail of the form *<address>*.REDIRECT should be rejected with the message indicating the user's new address. When users leave your organization their email addresses can be aliased to *<address>*.REDIRECT so that people who attempt to contact them can be informed of their new address.

- **FEATURE(always_add_domain)**: This directive indicates that the From line of all outgoing messages should contain the domain portion of the address and if a From line doesn't have a domain portion the local domain should be appended.

- **FEATURE(local)**: This directive indicates that sendmail should allow delivery of messages to local Unix mailboxes through the standard sendmail local mailer.

- **FEATURE(smtp)**: This directive indicates that sendmail should allow delivery of messages to remote servers using SMTP.

As this example illustrates, using m4 greatly simplifies the generation of sendmail.cf files. m4 increases the clarity of the configuration process and leads to succinct configuration files. However, m4 also provides a great wealth of configuration directives that allow you to control the finer aspects of your sendmail configuration. The wealth of possibilities presented through m4 configurations is beyond the scope of this book. In fact, several chapters could be devoted to the numerous possibilities afforded by m4 configuration for sendmail.

An excellent discussion of how to configure sendmail with m4 can be found at the sendmail Web site at http://www.sendmail.org/m4/readme.html.

GENERATING A `sendmail.cf` FILE FROM AN `m4` CONFIGURATION FILE

Of course, the `m4` files we have discussed are not directly used by sendmail. Instead, we have to process the `m4` configuration file with the `m4` macro processor to generate the final `sendmail.cf` file.

Typically, `m4` configuration files are created and stored in the directory `/usr/lib/sendmail-cf/cf` and have the file extension `.mc`. For instance, we could create a sample `m4` configuration file `/usr/lib/sendmail-cf/test.mc`.

PART

III

CH

16

Once the file is created, use the following steps to create and install your `sendmail.cf` file from the `m4` configuration file:

1. Change your current directory to `/usr/lib/sendmail-cf/cf/`:

   `# cd /usr/lib/sendmail-cf/cf/`

2. Process your `m4` configuration file with `m4` to generate a `sendmail.cf`-style file:

   `# m4 test.mc > test.cf`

3. Make a backup of your existing `sendmail.cf` file:

   `# cp /etc/sendmail.cf /etc/sendmail.cf.old`

4. Copy the new `sendmail.cf` file you generated to `/etc`:

   `# cp test.cf /etc/sendmail.cf`

5. Force sendmail to reload the new configuration file by sending it the SIGHUP signal:

   `# kill -HUP `cat /var/run/sendmail.pid``

ADDRESSING SECURITY ISSUES WITH SENDMAIL

Using a mail transport agent such as sendmail is a double-edged sword: In today's online world email is an essential communication tool, but mail daemons are among the most susceptible to attacks.

sendmail, in particular, has a long history of security problems and while current versions address most of these problems, it is wise to keep your system up-to-date with the most recently available version of sendmail. It can always be downloaded from the sendmail Web site at `http://www.sendmail.org/`.

The two most well-known security issues with sendmail are the following:

■ **Mail Relay Abuse:** Depending on your version of sendmail it is easy for remote individuals to abuse your sendmail system as a redirector of mass junk mailing. This would make it seem like a large spam mailing originates from your network and uses your server resources to deliver the large number of messages. From version 8.9 of sendmail, the default is to deny this type of mail relaying so that you have to selectively allow mail relaying from outside hosts. By contrast, earlier versions of sendmail allowed mail relaying from external hosts by default. Administrators had to know this in order to disable the feature.

- **Gaining Root Access:** Several bugs have cropped up with various versions of sendmail which if not addressed allow remote or local users to gain root access to your system. For instance, one well-known bug with version 8.8.4 of sendmail allowed a user with shell access to create a root account for their own use. Another similar bug reported up to version 8.8.2 provides a mechanism for a user with shell access to gain root access.

By all accounts, version 8.9.3 fixes most of these known security bugs found in earlier versions of sendmail. Still, it pays to be vigilant:

- Make sure you keep your sendmail up-to-date with the most recent stable version from `http://www.sendmail.org/`.
- Pay heed to security alerts put out by CERT/CC of the Carnegie Mellon University at `http://www.cert.org`. Join their security mailing list to be promptly alerted by email as soon as new vulnerabilities are unearthed. CERT meant Computer Emergency Response Team but now does not stand for anything specific.
- Monitor newsgroups such as `comp.mail.sendmail`.
- Regularly read Web pages which discuss sendmail security and security in general, including the following:
  - The Computer Incident Advisory Capability at `http://ciac.llnl.gov/ciac/`.
  - Rootshell at `http://www.rootshell.com/`.
  - Bugtraq at `http://www.securityfocus.com/`.
- Regularly review your system logs to watch for suspicious activity.

SENDMAIL LOGS

sendmail uses the standard Unix system log facility to write its logs. The `syslogd` daemon provides the system log facility as outlined in Chapter 20, "Log Management and Analysis." All messages from sendmail are logged using the LOG_MAIL facility. The system log can be found at `/var/log/syslog`.

Each line in the system log generated by sendmail consists of a timestamp, the name of the machine that generated it, the word `sendmail:`, and a message. Most messages are a sequence of *<name>=<value>* pairs.

The most common log entries from sendmail are generated when a message is processed. For each message processed, two log entries are created:

- An entry logging receipt of the message.
- An entry logging each delivery attempt for a message. There may be more than one of these entries associated with each message.

The message receipt entry log may contain some or all of the following fields:

- **from**: The sender address.
- **size**: The size of the message in bytes.
- **class**: The class of the message.
- **pri**: The initial message priority.
- **nrcpts**: The number of recipients for this message (after aliasing and forwarding is applied).
- **msgid**: The message id of the message from the message header.
- **proto**: The protocol used to receive this message (such as ESMTP or UUCP).
- **relay**: The host from which the message was received.

For each delivery attempt, the log entry can contain some or all of the following fields:

- **to**: A comma-separated list of the recipients of the message.
- **ctladdr**: The controlling user; that is, the name of the user whose credentials are used for delivery.
- **delay**: The total delay between the time this message was received and the time it was delivered.
- **xdelay**: The amount of time needed in this delivery attempt (normally indicative of the speed of the connection).

LOGGING LEVELS

A large amount of information about sendmail's activities can be logged. The log is arranged in a succession of levels. At the lowest level only extremely strange situations are logged. At the highest level, even the most mundane and uninteresting events are logged.

Log levels are identified numerically. Levels under ten are considered generally useful. Log levels above 64 should only be used for debugging purposes. Levels from 11 to 64 provide verbose information that some sites may want but are not generally needed to monitor the health of your system.

The default logging level set in a standard configuration file is level 9. This means messages at levels 9 and below will be logged. When generating sendmail.cf with m4, you can set the desired logging level by defining the value of the variable confLOG_LEVEL. The default value of this variable is 9 as defined in /usr/lib/sendmail-cf/m4/cfhead.m4. The meanings of the various levels are described in Table 16.5.

PART
III

CH
16

TABLE 16.5 SENDMAIL LOG LEVELS

Level	Description
0	Minimal logging
1	Log Serious system failures and potential security problems
2	Log lost communication connections (network problems) and protocol failures
3	Log other serious failures, malformed addresses, transient forward/include errors, and connection timeouts
4	Log minor failures, out-of-date alias databases, and connection rejections through check rulesets
5	Log message collection statistics
6	Log creation of error messages, VRFY and EXPN commands
7	Log delivery failures (host or user unknown, etc.)
8	Log successful deliveries and alias database rebuilds
9	Log messages being deferred (due to a host being down, etc.)
10	Log database expansion (aliases, forwarding, and user database lookups)
11	Log NIS errors and end of job processing
12	Log all SMTP connections
13	Log bad user shells, files with improper permissions, and other questionable situations
14	Log refused connections
15	Log all incoming and outgoing SMTP commands
20	Log attempts to run locked queue files that can be useful in determining if your queue appears to be clogged
30	Log lost locks (only if using lockf instead of flock)

Additional values above 64 are reserved for extremely verbose debugging output. No normal site would ever use these.

SUMMARIZING STATISTICS GENERATED BY SENDMAIL IN THE SYSTEM LOG

Several free tools are available on the Internet that can summarize sendmail log information written to the system log:

- **syslog_stats:** ftp://ftp.his.com/pub/brad/sendmail/syslog_stats. This script assumes the syslog file is rotated daily and the name of each copy ends with a dot and a digit, as in syslog.0, syslog.1, and so on. It summarizes each file, printing total incoming and outgoing message statistics, and the average for sizes and delays.

- **ssl**: `ftp://ftp.his.com/pub/brad/sendmail/ssl`. This script summarizes incoming and outgoing mail by user. The total message count and message traffic are printed, along with the grand total for all users.

- **smtpstats**: `ftp://ftp.his.com/pub/brad/sendmail/smtpstats`. This script prints statistics about message count, message traffic, and average and maximum delays.

For summarizing POP statistics, a tool called `popstats.pl` is available at `ftp://ftp.his.com/pub/brad/sendmail/popstats`.

IMAP AND POP3 SERVERS

IMAP (Internet Message Access Protocol) provides a method for accessing mail messages stored on a remote mail server. To an IMAP email client, the remote message store appears to be local. In IMAP, messages are stored and manipulated on the mail server. This allows for email clients to access the mail store from a variety of locations. For example, email messages stored on an IMAP server can be accessed from your work computer, your home computer, and your laptop while you are traveling, without the need to transfer messages between these client machines.

POP (Post Office Protocol) version 3 is a much older protocol than IMAP. As opposed to IMAP, in POP3 the client connects to the server and after authenticating, the mail store is transferred to the client. If the user connects from different client machines then mail messages get scattered across these machines. This is one of the biggest disadvantages of POP3 when compared to IMAP. However, POP3 has the advantage of being able to work offline once the mail store is transferred to the client. IMAP generally requires maintaining an open connection to the IMAP server throughout an email session.

Most Linux distributions include IMAP and POP3 servers. The IMAP and POP3 servers are `imapd` and `ipop3d`. By default these daemons are not enabled. To enable the service requires editing the `/etc/inetd.conf` and `/etc/services` files. Follow these steps:

1. Open `/etc/inetd.conf` in a text editor.
2. Find a line similar to the following:

   ```
   #pop-3 stream tcp   nowait root   /usr/sbin/tcpd ipop3d
   ```

3. Remove the hash mark (#) at the start of the line.
4. Find a line similar to the following:

   ```
   #imap  stream tcp   nowait root   /usr/sbin/tcpd imapd
   ```

5. Remove the hash mark (#) at the start of the line.
6. Save the file and close your text editor.
7. Open `/etc/services` in a text editor.

8. Check to see if two lines similar to the following are in the file and if not add them to the file or uncomment them:

```
pop-3       110/tcp
pop-3       110/udp
```

9. Check to see if two lines similar to the following are in the file and if not add them to the file or uncomment them:

```
imap2       143/tcp     imap
imap2       143/udp     imap
```

10. Save the file and close your text editor.

11. Force inetd to re-read its configuration file by sending it a SIGHUP signal:

```
# kill -HUP `cat /var/run/inetd.pid`
```

When you have enabled IMAP and POP3, you need to make sure that the services are responding to requests. You can do this by using Telnet to connect to the appropriate ports for each of the services.

To test POP3 on a host named somehost, Telnet to port 110 on somehost:

```
$ telnet somehost 110
Trying 10.20.30.40 ...
Connected to somehost.
Escape character is '^]'.
+OK POP3 somehost v7.59 server ready
^]telnet> q
```

To test IMAP on a host named somehost, Telnet to port 143 on somehost:

```
$ telnet somehost 143
Trying 10.20.30.40 ...
Connected to somehost.
Escape character is '^]'.
* OK somehost IMAP4rev1 v12.250 server ready
^]
telnet> q
```

If both tests succeed, your IMAP and POP3 servers are working and users with a login account on the server can use either protocol to access their mailboxes.

USING PROCMAIL

As discussed earlier in this chapter, sendmail can use external mailers as mail delivery agents. One such external mailer is procmail, which is designed as a replacement for a local mailer.

Because procmail is generally considered to be roughly 30 percent faster than other local mailers and because it is also known to be extremely secure and stable, procmail is frequently used as the local mailer with sendmail.

procmail's most important feature is that it provides a standard way to create rules ("recipes" in procmail terminology) for processing mail messages before they are added to a mailbox.

These rules can be used to create mail filters. A large percentage of routine mail-related work can be automated by applying such filters.

You can enable procmail as a local mailer for sendmail version 8 in one of two ways:

- As a replacement for the standard local mailer using the m4 configuration directive FEATURE(local_procmail).
- As an additional mailer to the standard local mailer using the m4 configuration directive FEATURE(procmail).

PART
III

CH
16

Note

Users can also install procmail and run it through their .forward files so that mail is processed by procmail when it hits their mailboxes. This is less efficient than running procmail as a sendmail local mailer.

More information about procmail can be found at http://www.procmail.org/ and the latest version can be found at ftp://ftp.procmail.org/pub/procmail/.

Tip

procmail is at the core of a mailing list management package called SmartList. If you are already using procmail, consider SmartList as a possible mailing list system. While SmartList has fewer adherents than Majordomo and Listserv, the most widely used mailing list packages, you may find it preferable and easier to use.

TROUBLESHOOTING

Several problems need to be considered with sendmail systems:

- Problems with .forward files
- Knowing when to manually process the mail queue
- Determining the version of sendmail being used
- SMTP connections taking too long
- Relaying denied errors
- Issues dealing with file and directory permissions
- Using wildcard mail exchangers

PROBLEMS WITH .forward FILES

When troubleshooting mail delivery problems to a particular user, check whether the user affected has a .forward file in their home directory. Often the problem may lie with misconfigured .forward files. For users with accounts on two or more machines, it is possible to create a mail loop by using a .forward on hostA to forward mail to hostB, and another .forward file on hostB to forward mail back to hostA.

MANUALLY PROCESSING THE MAIL QUEUE

Sometimes a host cannot handle a message immediately. For instance, the remote host might be down or too busy, and accordingly is refusing connections. The sending host then saves the message in its mail queue and attempts to deliver it later.

Under normal conditions the mail queue is processed transparently. However, there are times when manual intervention becomes necessary. For example, if a major host is down for a long time the /var/spool/mqueue directory may fill up with hundreds or thousands of messages. In general sendmail will recover gracefully when the remote host comes up, but in the meantime performance can become seriously affected by the large size of the queue because sendmail may spend a large amount of time sorting the queue.

If this happens you can rename the current queue to a name such as mqueue.old, create a new queue for sendmail to use, and process the old queue manually when the remote host is up again using the following steps:

1. List the contents of the current queue.
2. Rename the current queue.
3. Create a new queue.
4. Force delivery of the old queue.

LISTING CONTENTS OF THE CURRENT QUEUE

You can use the mailq command to print the contents of the current queue. You can also use the command sendmail -bp to display a list of the current queue contents.

The listing that is generated will include the queue ID, size, date, sender, and recipients of each message in the queue. Use this information to determine whether the queue is growing too large and you need to manually intervene.

RENAMING THE QUEUE

If you need to manually intervene, use the following steps:

1. Stop sendmail with the following command:
   # /etc/rc.d/init.d/sendmail stop

2. Rename the queue as follows
   # mv /var/spool/mqueue /var/spool/mqueue.old

CREATING A NEW QUEUE

To create a new queue, use the following steps:

1. Create a new directory:
   # mkdir /var/spool/mqueue

2. Change the group ownership of the directory:

```
# chggrp daemon /var/spool/mqueue
```

3. Change file permissions of the directory:

```
# chmod 700 /var/spool/mqueue
```

4. Restart sendmail:

```
# /etc/rc.d/init.d/sendmail start
```

FORCING DELIVERY OF THE OLD QUEUE

You can forcibly process the old mail queue by running sendmail with the following flags:

```
# /usr/sbin/sendmail -oQ/var/spool/mqueue.old -q -v
```

The -oQ flag specifies an alternate queue directory and the -q flag says to just run every job in the queue. The -v flag says to run in verbose mode so that you can monitor the progress of the queue processing. You can drop the -v flag if you want the queue to be processed silently without displaying progress information. After the old queue is emptied, you should remove the old queue directory:

```
# rmdir /var/spool/mqueue.old
```

DETERMINING THE VERSION OF SENDMAIL

There are two ways of determining what version of sendmail you are running.

- Telnet to port 25 of the host running sendmail:

```
$ telnet somehost 25
Trying IP_address 10.20.30.40
Connected to somehost
Escape character is '^]'.
220 somehost ESMTP Sendmail 8.9.3/8.9.3; Mon, 2 Aug 1999 11:39:34 -0700
^]
telnet> q
```

- In this example version 8.9.3 of sendmail is being used.

- Use the debug flag of sendmail, which forces display of the version number along with the domain name and the results of an address test:

```
$ echo \$Z ¦ /usr/sbin/sendmail -bt -d0
Version 8.9.3
 Compiled with: LOG MATCHGECOS MIME7TO8 MIME8TO7 NAMED_BIND NETINET
                NETUNIX NEWDB NIS QUEUE SCANF SMTP USERDB
============ SYSTEM IDENTITY (after readcf) ============
    (short domain name) $w = cstlx001
  (canonical domain name) $j = cstlx001.bwc.org
      (subdomain name) $m = bwc.org
          (node name) $k = cstlx001.bwc.org
========================================================
ADDRESS TEST MODE (ruleset 3 NOT automatically invoked)
Enter <ruleset> <address>
> 8.9.3
```

```
collect: I/O errors on connection
Syslog shows sendmail logging the following errors:
"collect: I/O error on connection"
or
"reply: read error from host.name"
```

Generally, any errors generated using `sendmail` in this way can be ignored. They usually indicate that `sendmail` had problems communicating with a remote host at some time and message delivery will be retried.

CONNECTIONS TO THE SMTP PORT TAKING A LONG TIME

If you upgrade to sendmail version 8 from an earlier version of sendmail, you may find that SMTP connections can take a long time. On some systems, sendmail version 8 attempts a callback to the connecting host to validate the username. Normally, if the connecting host does not support this service, the connection should quickly fail. However, some types of firewalls and TCP/IP implementations wait for a timeout to occur which leads to the delay in establishing an SMTP connection with your sendmail system.

To fix this problem, disable the use of the IDENT protocol by setting the IDENT timeout to zero. Use the following m4 directive when configuring sendmail:

```
define(`confTO_IDENT',`0s')dnl
```

If setting the IDENT timeout to zero fails to solve the problem, it may be related to misconfiguration of name servers. Double check your `/etc/resolv.conf` file and ensure that all name servers listed there are functional. If you control any of the name servers listed in `resolv.conf` on the sendmail system in question, double-check your root cache file to ensure it is up-to-date as outlined in Chapter 22, "DNS."

RELAYING DENIED ERRORS

If you receive relaying denied errors from your sendmail system, you need to add a list of fully qualified hostnames or IP addresses of each client allowed to send mail through the sendmail system to the file `/etc/mail/relay-domains`. Each hostname or IP address should appear on a separate line in the file. After editing the `relay-domains` file, send a SIGHUP signal to the sendmail daemon:

```
# kill -HUP `cat /var/run/sendmail.pid`
```

Note

This problem and the related solution only apply to sendmail version 8.9 and higher.

FILE AND DIRECTORY PERMISSIONS FOR SENDMAIL VERSION 8.9 AND HIGHER

For sendmail to run without complaining, you must ensure that the correct file and directory ownership and permissions are set as outlined in the following commands:

```
# chown root / /etc /etc/mail /usr /var /var/spool /var/spool/mqueue
```

```
# chmod go-w / /etc /etc/mail /usr /var /var/spool /var/spool/mqueue
```

To check whether you have file or directory permission problems, run `sendmail` as follows:

```
# sendmail -v -bi
```

`sendmail` will attempt to initialize the aliases database. If you see errors similar to the following then you have incorrect directory and file permissions set and you need to fix the problem to ensure maximum security of your sendmail system:

```
WARNING: writable directory /etc
WARNING: writable directory /usr/spool/mqueue
```

PART
III

CH
16

USING WILDCARD MAIL EXCHANGERS FOR YOUR DOMAIN

While it is technically possible to define wildcard mail exchangers for your domain in your DNS records, this should be avoided if at all possible. By using wildcards to define the hostnames or IP addresses of mail exchangers, several problems arise. In particular, it is possible for mail to invalid hosts within your domain to be delivered to your mail servers. You may see errors such as `MX list for hostname somehost points back to somehost` or `config error: mail loops back to myself` in bounced messages sent back to senders of incoming emails.

OTHER MAIL RELAYING PROBLEMS

You may see bounce errors such as the following:

```
553 MX list for do.main points back to relay.do.main
554 <user@do.main>... Local configuration error
```

This means you have set up an MX record for mail to `do.main`, which points to the host `relay.do.main`. However, the relaying machine does not have `do.main` specified as a legal domain for which it relays mail. Add `do.main` in `/etc/mail/relay-domains` and restart sendmail to fix this problem.

## CHAPTER 17

FAX SERVERS

In this chapter

WHAT ARE FAX SERVERS?

In the environment of the personal home computer, users generally have their own fax modems, which they can use to send faxes from their computers. However, in an organization which needs to allow users to send faxes from their computers, placing a fax modem on each PC or workstation makes little sense: It is both costly and hard to control.

Not only do you incur the hardware cost of a fax modem on each PC plus the software licenses for your fax software, you have no central control of access to fax services or central management and analysis of usage and billing information.

Fax servers solve this problem: A single fax server can have a bank of fax modems and can send and receive faxes on behalf of users on the network. This can be done with fewer modems and less hardware cost than placing a modem on each desktop. Users can still send faxes from their desktop applications either by printing to the fax server or sending an email to the fax server. The server can be configured to control access to fax services on the basis of the originator of the fax, the destination phone number, and even the time of day. Fax servers can also reduce costs, for instance, by queuing non-priority long-distance faxes to send during off-peak, low-cost time periods.

Fax servers also improve management: Control of the settings of the fax server and software and access to call records is all maintained in a central location. Administrators do not need to support modems and fax software on each desktop and the call log information can easily be integrated into enterprise accounting systems.

FAX SOFTWARE FOR LINUX

Several commercial and free software packages are available for Linux that can be used to configure a Linux system to act as a fax server:

- **Fax2Send (`http://www.fax.2send.com/`):** Fax2Send is a commercial fax server package for Linux. It comes in a free version for four users and a full commercial version for unlimited users. The server can be configured and administered from a Web browser. Users can compose and send messages from a browser or by email. The server provides central logging of all fax transmissions.

- **HylaFAX (`http://www.hylafax.org/`):** HylaFAX is a long-standing fax server platform for Unix systems. It is available freely. HylaFAX has all the features one expects of a robust fax server including sending and receiving faxes, automatic cover page generation, and email to fax gateway capabilities. Full access control is available and outgoing faxes can be scheduled for off-peak hours. Although HylaFAX does not come packaged with a default Linux distribution, it is by far the best free fax server software for Linux and Unix systems in general, and will be covered in detail in this chapter.

- **Efax (`http://metalab.unc.edu/pub/Linux/apps/serialcomm/fax/`):** Efax is the fax software commonly included with most Linux systems. While not as well suited to large-scale fax server installations, it provides faxing-via-printing and can be extended into a fax email server using the Qfax package available from the same site as Efax. Because Efax is included with most Linux distributions, we will briefly cover the installation and configuration of a Linux fax server using Efax.

- **Faximum Messaging Server (`http://www.faximum.com/`):** Faximum is an email-based Fax server product free for personal non-commercial use but which must be purchased for corporate or enterprise use. Faxes are both sent and received by email. The server provides for centralized cost control and management of fax traffic.

- **VSI-FAX (`www.vsifax.com`):** This software offers a well-integrated networked fax solution for Linux. It is very well suited for large corporate environments. VSI-FAX is not free software.

HylaFAX

HylaFAX is a freely available enterprise class fax software. Sam Leffler of Silicon Graphics is the primary developer of this software, although many others have contributed to its development and testing. HylaFAX started out originally under the name FlexFAX, in 1990. It was subsequently renamed to HylaFAX. The name HylaFAX is copyrighted by Silicon Graphics.

HylaFAX is a client server fax solution for UNIX systems. In addition to sending and receiving facsimiles, it can be used to send alphanumeric pages. The fax server can run on a single networked system with one or more fax modems attached. Clients can submit outbound faxes from anywhere on the network. HylaFAX is very robust and reliable and can support heavy traffic loads by sharing jobs between multiple modems. Broadcast faxing, and off-peak-hour scheduling are supported. Access control to restrict use of certain classes of phone numbers is possible.

All modems that provide a standard interface for facsimile operation, such as Class 1, Class 2, and Class 2.0, are supported by HylaFAX. Outgoing faxes are converted from document formats, such as plain text, or postscript to TIFF Class F files and transmitted to remote fax machines. HylaFAX requires a PostScript to facsimile imaging utility. On Linux systems, this is provided by the freely available Ghostscript software.

Obtaining HylaFAX

Binary distributions of HylaFAX for Linux can be downloaded in either RPM, or tar-gzipped format from `ftp://ftp.hylafax.org/pub/hylafax/binary/linux`. The versions available at this location were compiled for Red Hat Linux Versions 4 and 5. To get the latest binary

RPM version for Red Hat Linux 6 go to `ftp://ftp.hylafax.org/pub/hylafax/hylafax-4.1/` `binary/linux/RPMS/i386`. Download either hylafax-4.0pl2-3rh5.i386.rpm, or `hylafax-` `4.1beta1-1rh6.i386.rpm` depending on what version of Linux you are running. The older version will run on Linux 6.x.

In addition to the HylaFAX package you will find additional Ghostscript font packages that may be necessary to install before you can proceed with installation of the HylaFAX RPM package.

INSTALLING HYLAFAX

Before installing the HylaFAX binaries it is recommended that you remove any other fax software you may have on the system. If you have older versions of HylaFAX or FlexFAX installed you must remove them. It is advisable to backup the older version of HylaFAX or FlexFAX before deleting it, so that you can restore any configurations, logs, or setups if you need to refer to them later on.

To install HylaFAX run the following command:

```
# rpm -Uv hylafax-4.1beta1-1rh6.i386.rpm
```

When `rpm` is run with the -U flag it installs a new package, or upgrades a currently installed package to a newer version. This is similar to running rpm with the `-i` (install) flag, except that any other version of the package is first removed from the system.

HylaFAX is a large software package and installs many files on the system. It is good to know where all these files reside after the installation.

The following programs, scripts, and daemons are installed in `/usr/sbin`:

- choptest
- cqtest
- dialtest
- faxabort
- faxaddmodem
- faxanswer
- faxconfig
- faxcron
- faxgetty
- faxinfo
- faxmodem
- faxmsg
- faxq
- faxqclean
- faxquit

- faxsend
- faxstate
- faxwatch
- hfaxd
- lockname
- ondelay
- pagesend
- recvstats
- tag
- test
- textfmt
- tiffcheck
- tsitest
- typetest
- faxsetup
- faxsetup.bsdi
- faxsetup.irix
- faxsetup.linux
- probemodem
- xferfaxstats

HylaFAX also installs the following shared libraries in /usr/lib:

- libfaxserver.so
- libfaxserver.so.4.0.1
- libfaxutil.so
- libfaxutil.so.4.0.1

The following client programs and utilities are installed in /usr/bin:

- faxalter
- faxcover
- faxmail
- faxrm
- faxstat
- sendfax
- sendpage

A system startup script is installed as /etc/rc.d/init.d/hylafax, which starts and stops HylaFAX daemons at system bootup and shutdown.

Two scripts to run from crond are installed as /etc/cron.daily/hylafax and /etc/cron.hourly/hylafax.

Rotation of HylaFAX log files is done by the script /etc/logrotate.d/hylafax.

The following postscript templates and configuration files are installed in /usr/share/fax:

- faxcover.ps
- faxmail.ps
- hfaxd.conf
- pagesizes
- typerules

In addition numerous Adobe Font Metric files are installed in /usr/share/fax/afm.

HylaFAX places the incoming and outgoing fax queues, modem configuration files, and various scripts and binaries in /var/spool/fax and its subdirectories. The subdirectories are as follows:

- archive
- bin
- client
- config
- dev
- docq
- doneq
- etc
- faxrcvd
- info
- log
- pollq
- recvq
- sendq
- status
- tmp

Several programs and scripts that are used while processing the send and receive queues are placed in /var/spool/fax/bin:

- mkcover
- notify
- notify.awk
- pcl2fax
- pollrcvd
- ps2fax
- ps2fax.dps
- ps2fax.gs
- ps2fax.imp
- tiff2fax
- wedged

The etc directory under /var/spool/fax holds more configuration files, templates, and the fax transmission log file. These are as follows:

- cover.templ
- dialrules
- dialrules.europe
- dialrules.sf-ba
- dpsprinter.ps
- hosts
- lutRS18.pcf
- xferfaxlog

Plain text and html documentation are installed in /usr/doc/hylafax-*n.n.n*, where *n.n.n* is the software version number.

CONFIGURING HYLAFAX SERVER

The term HylaFAX server is used to define a machine that has one or more fax modems installed on it and is capable of servicing fax requests both from itself and from networked client machines. Basically the server machine has the complete set of fax client and server software installed.

The faxsetup program must be run to configure HylaFAX before it can be used as a fax server. However it is necessary to have one or more properly functioning fax modems installed on the fax server before you run faxsetup.

If you haven't done that already, now is the time to install and test the fax modems that will be used on the server. After the modem is installed, make sure it is connected to the phone line, and also powered on in case of an external modem. Use cu or minicom to verify the modem is functioning properly. An example using of the cu program to check a modem connected to /dev/ttyS1 is shown here:

```
# cu -l /dev/ttyS1
Connected.
at
OK
at+fclass=?
0,1,2
OK
~[localhost].

Disconnected.
```

After connecting to the modem with cu, try a few modem AT commands to verify the modem is communicating properly. The at+fclass=? command queries the modem to find out what classes it is capable of supporting. The reply 0,1,2 in this example means the modem can support classes 0, 1, and 2. Class 0 is for data use. Classes 1 and 2 are fax capabilities. HylaFAX can use any modems that support classes 1, 2, and 2.0. A modem that supports digital voice will report additional classes. Next exit cu with the tilde (~) followed by the dot (.) command as illustrated above.

Tip

A word on modem classes: Class 2.0 is the best, followed by Class 2, and Class 1. Select the highest class if your modem supports it.

After you have verified the modem is working properly, you are ready to run faxsetup by issuing the following command:

```
# /usr/sbin/faxsetup
```

The faxsetup program will ask many questions and you are required to provide the answers. Except for the telephone number and the Local Identification string, in most cases the default answers will work. You also must provide the serial ports to which the modem or modems are connected. In addition by default there is no limit to the number of pages that can be faxed out. You might want to set a limit. A typical session of running faxsetup is shown in the following code listing. Line numbers have been added to the output to aid the discussion:

```
01: # /usr/sbin/faxsetup

02: Setup program for HylaFAX (tm) 4.1beta1.

03: Created for i686-pc-linux on Thu Jul  1 15:05:50 BST 1999.

04: Checking system for proper client configuration.
05: Checking system for proper server configuration.
```

06: Warning: /sbin/vgetty does not exist or is not an executable program!

07: The file:

08: /sbin/vgetty

09: does not exist or this file is not an executable program. The
10: HylaFAX software optionally uses this program and the fact that
11: it does not exist on the system is not a fatal error. If the
12: program resides in a different location and you do not want to
13: install a symbolic link for /sbin/vgetty that points to your program
14: then you must reconfigure and rebuild HylaFAX from source code.

15: Warning: /bin/egetty does not exist or is not an executable program!

16: The file:

17: /bin/egetty

18: does not exist or this file is not an executable program. The
19: HylaFAX software optionally uses this program and the fact that
20: it does not exist on the system is not a fatal error. If the
21: program resides in a different location and you do not want to
22: install a symbolic link for /bin/egetty that points to your program
23: then you must reconfigure and rebuild HylaFAX from source code.

24: Make /var/spool/fax/bin/ps2fax a link to /var/spool/fax/bin/ps2fax.gs.

25: You do not appear to have a "fax" user in the password file.
26: HylaFAX needs this to work properly, add it [yes]?
27: Added user "fax" to /etc/passwd.

28: Modem support functions written to /var/spool/fax/etc/setup.modem.
29: Configuration parameters written to /var/spool/fax/etc/setup.cache.

30: No scheduler config file exists, creating one from scratch.
31: Country code [1]? 972
32: Area code []? 4
33: Long distance dialing prefix [1]? 0
34: International dialing prefix [011]? 00
35: Dial string rules file (relative to /var/spool/fax) ["etc/dialrules"]?
36: Tracing during normal server operation [1]?
37: Default tracing during send and receive sessions [0xffffffff]?
38: Continuation cover page (relative to /var/spool/fax) []?
39: Timeout when converting PostScript documents (secs) [180]?
40: Maximum number of concurrent jobs to a destination [1]?
41: Define a group of modems []?
42: Time of day restrictions for outbound jobs ["Any"]?
43: Pathname of destination controls file (relative to /var/spool/fax) []?
44: Timeout before purging a stale UUCP lock file (secs) [30]?
45: Max number of pages to permit in an outbound job [0xffffffff]? 25
46: Syslog facility name for ServerTracing messages [daemon]?

47: The non-default scheduler parameters are:

48: CountryCode: 972
49: AreaCode: 4

```
50: LongDistancePrefix:     0
51: InternationalPrefix:      00
52: MaxSendPages:          25

53: Are these ok [yes]?

54: Creating new configuration file /var/spool/fax/etc/config...

55: Restarting HylaFAX server processes.
56: Should I restart the HylaFAX server processes [yes]?

57: /etc/rc.d/init.d/hylafax start
58: HylaFAX: faxq hfaxd (without old protocol or SNPP support).

59: You do not appear to have any modems configured for use.  Modems are
60: configured for use with HylaFAX with the faxaddmodem(1M) command.
61: Do you want to run faxaddmodem to configure a modem [yes]?
62: Serial port that modem is connected to []? ttyS1
63: Hmm, there does not appear to be an fuser command on your machine.
64: This means that I am unable to insure that all processes using the
65: modem have been killed.  I will keep going, but beware that you may
66: have competition for the modem.

67: Ok, time to setup a configuration file for the modem.  The manual
68: page config(4F) may be useful during this process.  Also be aware
69: that at any time you can safely interrupt this procedure.

70: Reading scheduler config file /var/spool/fax/etc/config.

71: No existing configuration, let's do this from scratch.

72: Country code [1]? 972
73: Area code [415]? 4
74: Phone number of fax modem [+1.999.555.1212]? __ _+972.4.8331039
75: Local identification string (for TSI/CIG) ["NothingSetup"]? "MyFaxServer"
76: Long distance dialing prefix [1]? 0
77: International dialing prefix [011]? 00
78: Dial string rules file (relative to /var/spool/fax) [etc/dialrules]?
79: Tracing during normal server operation [1]?
80: Tracing during send and receive sessions [11]?
81: Protection mode for received facsimile [0600]?
82: Protection mode for session logs [0600]?
83: Protection mode for ttyS2 [0600]?
84: Rings to wait before answering [1]?
85: Modem speaker volume [off]?
86: Command line arguments to getty program ["-h %l dx_%s"]?
87: Pathname of TSI access control list file (relative to /var/spool/fax) [""]?
88: Pathname of Caller-ID access control list file (relative to /var/spool/fax)
[""]?
89: Tag line font file (relative to /var/spool/fax) [etc/lutRS18.pcf]?
90: Tag line format string ["From %%l¦%c¦Page %%p of %%t"]?
91: Time before purging a stale UUCP lock file (secs) [30]?
92: Hold UUCP lockfile during inbound data calls [Yes]?
93: Hold UUCP lockfile during inbound voice calls [Yes]?
94: Percent good lines to accept during copy quality checking [95]?
95: Max consecutive bad lines to accept during copy quality checking [5]?
96: Max number of pages to accept in a received facsimile [25]?
```

```
97: Syslog facility name for ServerTracing messages [daemon]?
98: Set UID to 0 to manipulate CLOCAL [""]?

99: Your facsimile phone number (+972.4.8331039) does not agree with your
100: country code (972) or area code (4).  The number
101: should be a fully qualified international dialing number of the form:

102: +972 4 <local phone number>

103: Spaces, hyphens, and periods can be included for legibility.  For example,

104: +972.4.555.1212

105: is a possible phone number (using your country and area codes).

106: The non-default server configuration parameters are:

107: CountryCode:          972
108: AreaCode:             4
109: FAXNumber:            +972.4.8331039
110: LongDistancePrefix:   0
111: InternationalPrefix:   00
112: DialStringRules:      etc/dialrules
113: SessionTracing:        11
114: RingsBeforeAnswer:    1
115: SpeakerVolume:        off
116: GettyArgs:            "-h %l dx_%s"
117: LocalIdentifier:      "MyFaxServer"
118: TagLineFont:          etc/lutRS18.pcf
119: TagLineFormat:         "From %%l¦%c¦Page %%p of %%t"
120: MaxRecvPages:          25

121: Are these ok [yes]?

122: Now we are going to probe the tty port to figure out the type
123: of modem that is attached.  This takes a few seconds, so be patient.
124: Note that if you do not have the modem cabled to the port, or the
125: modem is turned off, this may hang (just go and cable up the modem
126: or turn it on, or whatever).

127: Probing for best speed to talk to modem: 38400 OK.

128: This modem looks to have support for both Class 1 and 2;
129: how should it be configured [2]? 1

130: Hmm, this looks like a Class 1 modem.
131: Product code (ATI0) is "28800".
132: Other information (ATI3) is "V1.302-V34_DP".
133: DTE-DCE flow control scheme [default]?
134: grep: defaults: Is a directory
135: Modem manufacturer is "ROCKWELL".
136: Modem model is "RC288DPi".

137: Using prototype configuration file rc288dpi-1...

138: The modem configuration parameters are:
```

```
139: ModemDialCmd:          ATDT%s
140: ModemFlowControl:      rtscts
141: ModemHardFlowCmd:      AT&K3
142: ModemMfrQueryCmd:      !Rockwell
143: ModemModelQueryCmd:     !RC288DPi
144: ModemNoFlowCmd:         AT&K0
145: ModemRate:         38400
146: ModemRevQueryCmd:      ATI3
147: ModemSetupDCDCmd:      AT&C1
148: ModemSetupDTRCmd:      AT&D2
149: ModemSoftFlowCmd:      AT&K4

150: Are these ok [yes]?

151: Creating new configuration file /var/spool/fax/etc/config.ttyS1...
152: Creating fifo /var/spool/fax/FIFO.ttyS1 for faxgetty... done.
153: Done setting up the modem configuration.

154: Checking /var/spool/fax/etc/config for consistency...
155: ...some parameters are different.

156: The non-default scheduler parameters are:

157: CountryCode:          972
158: AreaCode:          4
159: LongDistancePrefix:     0
160: InternationalPrefix:     00
161: DialStringRules:      etc/dialrules
162: MaxSendPages:          25

163: Are these ok [yes]?

164: Creating new configuration file /var/spool/fax/etc/config...
165: ...saving current file as /var/spool/fax/etc/config.sav.

166: Don't forget to run faxmodem(1M) (if you have a send-only environment)
167: or configure init to run faxgetty on ttyS2.
168: Do you want to run faxaddmodem to configure another modem [yes]? no

169: You do not appear to be using faxgetty to notify the HylaFAX scheduler
170: about new modems and/or their status.  This means that you must use the
171: faxmodem program to inform the new faxq process about the modems you
172: want to have scheduled by HylaFAX.  Beware that if you have modems that
173: require non-default capabilities specified to faxmodem then you should
174: read faxmodem(1M) manual page and do this work yourself (since this
175: script is not intelligent enough to automatically figure out the modem
176: capabilities and supply the appropriate arguments).

177: Should I run faxmodem for each configured modem [yes]?
178: /usr/sbin/faxmodem ttyS1

179: Done verifying system setup.
180: #
```

This session can be analyzed as follows:

- On lines 6-23 the faxsetup program issues warnings about not finding the vgetty, and egetty programs. These warnings can be safely ignored.

- On line 24 faxsetup indicates that a soft link needs to be created from /var/spool/fax/bin/ps2fax pointing to /var/spool/fax/bin/ps2fax.gs. Linux systems use ghostscript as the imaging engine, instead of the other default program. The RPM installation takes care of this and it can be safely ignored, unless you have compiled and installed HylaFAX from source.

- On lines 25-27 the fax user is created. HylaFAX runs its daemons as this user. However when you later check the processes with ps you will discover that HylaFAX daemons are running as the user uucp. This is fine, HylaFAX creates the fax user with the same UID as uucp.

- On lines 28 and 29 faxsetup informs you of the filenames where it has written the modem support functions and configuration parameters. This is useful information if you later need to tweak any of the values in these files.

- On lines 31-34 you provide faxsetup with the country code, area code, and local telephone number for the fax modem.

- On line 45 you get the chance to change the maximum number of pages for an outbound fax job.

- On line 54 faxsetup informs you where it saved the new configuration file.

- On lines 55-58 the HylaFAX daemons, hfaxd and faxq, are started up by running the script /etc/rc.d/init.d/hylafax. You are also informed that the daemons do not support the older fax protocol, or SNPP. If you need to support older fax clients or pagers, you must recompile from source code enabling these options.

- On lines 61 and 62 you are prompted to run the faxaddmodem program. This program queries the serial port where a fax modem is connected and then proceeds to configure it for use by HylaFAX.

- On lines 71-98 the modem connected to the serial port specified on line 62 is configured.

- On lines 99-120 the current configuration is displayed. On line 121 you are prompted to accept the configuration or make changes.

- On lines 122-149 faxsetup runs the probemodem program and tries to learn all its capabilities. The output of this section is modem specific and may not match your faxsetup output.

- On line 150 you are prompted to accept the modem configuration parameters. On acceptance the configuration is written and you are informed of its location.

- On line 151 a FIFO buffer is created for use by HylaFAX.

- On line 164 and 165 the configuration file is saved and any older configuration file from a previous run is backed up.

- On lines 166 and 167 you are reminded to either run `faxmodem` if this is a send only modem, or `faxgetty` to run both send and receive.
- On line 168 you are prompted to configure another fax modem.
- On line 177 in this example `faxsetup` has been told to run the `faxmodem` program, and on line 178 it informs the user it has done so.

CONFIGURING `faxgetty`

It is recommended to run `faxgetty` on a modem port even if the port is not configured to provide inbound service. `faxgetty` informs the HylaFAX scheduler process when a modem is in use, and it identifies the modem's capabilities and passes that information to the scheduler, which uses this information to make better scheduling decisions. In addition, `faxgetty` does an excellent job of resetting difficult modems.

To get `faxgetty` running you must edit the `/etc/inittab` file and add a line similar to the following to the file:

```
t2:2345:respawn:/usr/sbin/faxgetty ttyS1
```

> **Tip**
>
> The above example assumes your modem is connected to `/dev/ttyS1`. If it is connected to `/dev/ttyS2` instead, don't forget to change `t2` in the beginning of the line to `t3`. Serial port 1 or `t1` corresponds to `ttyS0`; serial port 2 or `t2` corresponds to `ttyS1` and so on. Do not use the older serial devices such as `/dev/cua0` or `/dev/cua1`.

Next signal the `init` program to rescan the `/etc/inittab` file as follows:

```
# telinit q
```

You are now ready to test the fax server.

TESTING HYLAFAX

Check that the HylaFAX daemons are running. Remember for security reasons these daemons don't run as the root user. They run as user `fax`, which is the same as user `uucp`. Use the `ps` command as follows to find the fax daemons:

```
# ps -aef|grep uucp
uucp      331     1  0 14:42 ?        00:00:00 /usr/sbin/faxq
uucp      333     1  0 14:42 ?        00:00:00 /usr/sbin/hfaxd -i hylafax
uucp      396     1  0 14:44 ?        00:00:00 /usr/sbin/faxgetty ttyS1
root      424   378  0 14:48 tty1     00:00:00 grep uucp
```

You should see three daemons running: `faxq`, `hfaxd`, and `faxgetty` as shown in the output above.

Now use the `faxstat` command to check the status of the daemons as follows:

```
# faxstat
HylaFAX scheduler on orion.bwc.org: Running
Modem ttyS1 (+972.4.8331039): Running and idle
```

You should see output similar to the above.

SENDING A TEST FAX MESSAGE

On the fax server host create a quick test message as follows:

```
# cat > /tmp/testfax
This is a fax message to test the newly installed HylaFAX server.
FaxMaster
^D
```

Now use the `sendfax` command to send this test message to a remote fax machine or server as follows:

```
# sendfax -n -D -d 8358525 /tmp/testfax
```

It is not necessary to prepare a fax file ahead of time; `sendfax` can input from the standard input also. To use standard input to deliver a message to `sendfax` use the following command:

```
# sendfax -n -D -d 8358525 <
This is a fax message to test the newly installed HylaFAX server.
FaxMaster
^D
```

Remember to use a different destination fax number instead of the one shown in the example. Here's what the various flags used in the example mean:

- **-n**: This tells `sendfax` to not send a cover page.
- **-D**: This tells `sendfax` to email the status after the job is done.
- **-d**: This flag is followed by the destination fax number.

Once you have sent the message, check the status of the fax server with the `faxstat` command as follows:

```
# faxstat
HylaFAX scheduler on orion.bwc.org: Running
Modem ttyS1 (+972.4.8331039): Sending job 1
```

A status report similar to the above should be printed. Run `faxstat` again after a minute or so and you should see something like the following:

```
# faxstat
HylaFAX scheduler on orion.bwc.org: Running
Modem ttyS1 (+972.4.8331039): Running and idle
```

In addition to the status you just checked using `faxstat` to verify the message was sent successfully, you should receive a status report emailed to you by the fax server. Check the root user's mailbox and there should be a message similar to the following:

PART
III

CH
17

```
From fax@orion.bwc.org Mon Mar 20 18:59:12 2000
Date: Mon, 20 Mar 2000 15:00:17 +0200
From: Facsimile Agent <fax@orion.bwc.org>
To: root@orion.bwc.org
Subject: facsimile job 1 to 8358525 completed

Your facsimile job to 8358525 was completed successfully.

        Pages: 1
      Quality: Fine
   Page Width: 215 (mm)
  Page Length: 279 (mm)
  Signal Rate: 9600 bit/s
  Data Format: 1-D MR
Submitted From: orion.bwc.org
        JobID: 1
      GroupID: 1
       CommID: c00000002

Processing time was 0:59.
```

RECEIVING A TEST FAX MESSAGE

Now that you have successfully sent a test fax message, it is time to verify that you can also receive fax messages.

Either from a fax machine or from some other fax server, send a test message to your newly installed HylaFAX server. Immediately after sending the message, start monitoring the fax status with the faxstat command as follows:

```
# faxstat -a
HylaFAX scheduler on orion.bwc.org: Running
Modem ttyS1 (+972.4.8331039): Receiving from ''+972 4 8358591"
```

A status report similar to the above should appear, indicating that a fax message receipt is in progress, and will normally identify the sending fax modem's number, unless it is suppressed by the sending modem for security reasons.

After the fax message is received, the FaxMaster, who is the root user in this case, is notified that a fax message has arrived and is in the /var/spool/fax/recvq directory. The email message in this case is listed below:

```
From fax@orion.bwc.org Mon Mar 20 15:49:48 2000
Date: Mon, 20 Mar 2000 15:47:32 +0200
From: The HylaFAX Receive Agent <fax@orion.bwc.org>
To: FaxMaster@orion.bwc.org
Subject: facsimile received from  +972 4 8358591

recvq/fax00002.tif (ftp://orion.bwc.org:4559/recvq/fax00002.tif):
     Sender: +972 4 8358591
      Pages: 1
    Quality: Normal
       Page: ISO A4
   Received: 2000:03:20 15:47:17
  TimeToRecv: 0:49
  SignalRate: 4800 bit/s
```

```
DataFormat: 1-D MR
ReceivedOn: ttyS2
CommID:    c00000003 (ftp://orion.bwc.org:4559/log/c00000003)
```

We can verify the fax message has really been received by checking the contents of the /var/spool/fax/recvq directory. A directory listing reveals the specified file.

```
# ls /var/spool/fax/recvq
fax00002.tif
```

The FaxMaster can view the file with a suitable TIFF viewer such as xv, viewfax, or kfax. Because the email includes a URL for the fax message, it can be viewed by simply clicking the URL, as long as you are reading email using a mail client that is configured to launch an external TIFF viewer such as xv. The FaxMaster can then forward the received fax to the intended recipient. Since the HylaFAX protocol supports the FTP protocol, you can use any FTP client to retrieve incoming faxes from the server by connecting to port 4559 of the fax server. For this scheme to work, however, the permissions on the files in /var/spool/fax/recvq must be opened up for world reading.

This brings us to the subject of how to automate the handling of received faxes and reduce human intervention as much as possible. This is addressed in the next section.

AUTOMATING DISTRIBUTION OF RECEIVED FAXES

Inbound facsimile is handled by the program /var/spool/fax/bin/faxrcvd. This program is a shell script, and can be easily extended to gain some degree of automation.

There are two possibilities. The first is to send inbound facsimiles to a network printer. In this case receiving inbound facsimile is similar to receiving them on a fax machine. This can be done by slightly modifying the faxrcvd script. A line must be added to first convert the received facsimile to postscript format, and then send that to a postscript printer. For example, adding the following line will send all inbound faxes to the printer called faxprinter:

```
$TIFFBIN/fax2ps $1 ¦ lpr -Pfaxprinter
```

The TIFFBIN variable is defined in the file /var/spool/fax/etc/setup.cache. If required, you can change the default path of TIFFBIN in the setup.cache file.

The second possibility is to direct facsimiles received from well-known senders to designated recipients by using email. This can be done by adding a shell script called FaxDispatch in the /var/spool/fax/etc directory. An example FaxDispatch script is shown below. Line numbers are added to aid in the discussion; they are not part of the actual script.

```
01: #!/bin/sh
02: # File: /var/spool/fax/etc/FaxDispatch
03: # Description: Email inbound faxes to designated recipients based on
04: #              sender's TSI.
05: #
06: case "$SENDER" in
07:     *972*4*8358519) SENDTO="gautam@bwc.org" ;;
08:     *972*4*8358599) SENDTO="armand@juxta.com" ;;
```

```
09:    *)         SENDTO="FaxSec@bwc.org" ;;
10: esac
```

The script is quite simple. It is invoked from within the `/var/spool/fax/bin/faxrcvd` script. It can be analyzed as follows:

- Lines 1-5 are comment lines.
- Lines 6-10 are part of one case statement. The case statement matches each TSI against well-known ones. If a match is found, the SENDTO variable is assigned the designated user's email address. At the end we have a default case that matches everything that did not match earlier. These fax messages are sent to an individual who serves as a fax processor and prints and distributes hard copies to the recipients.

HylaFAX currently does not support the Direct Inward Dial (DID) service, because the DID hardware devices use non-standard programming interfaces. In the future, when updated versions of the ITU facsimile protocols are supported in commercial fax modems HylaFAX will be able to use routing information provided in the protocol to do automatic delivery of inbound facsimile.

HYLAFAX CLIENT SETUP

So far everything you have done was on the Fax Server machine. Now it is time to setup a fax client machine and make sure you can send faxes from it using the HylaFAX server.

HylaFAX uses a client/server architecture. A single server is capable of servicing several network client machines. Client and server machines communicate with each other using a special HylaFAX protocol that runs on top of the TCP/IP protocols. Clients can also use other methods of submitting fax jobs to the server, such as email. Email-fax gateways are discussed in the next section.

A client machine will require the following programs be installed in the `/usr/bin` directory:

- `sendfax`
- `sendpage`
- `faxstat`
- `faxrm`
- `faxalter`
- `fax2ps`

In addition, the following configuration and supporting files are needed in the `/usr/share/fax` directory:

- afm
- faxcover.ps
- faxmail.ps
- hfaxd.conf

- pagesizes
- typerules

`afm` is directory that contains the Adobe Font Metric files used by HylaFAX.

You can use `rdist` to transfer the client programs and the entire `/usr/share/fax` directory from the fax server to the client machines. This assumes all the machines are of compatible x86 architecture. If the architectures are different, you must compile and install just the client software from the source code. After downloading the source code and unpacking it, run `configure` and `make installClient` to install the client programs and supporting files.

Testing a HylaFAX Client

Next you can proceed to test that the client is capable of sending outbound fax messages using the fax server. Before you can use the fax server, however, it must be set up to allow access by clients. The fax server maintains a file called `hosts` in the `/var/spool/fax/etc` directory. Examine the default contents of the file. It should look similar to the following:

```
localhost
127.0.0.1
```

These entries grant access to fax client programs running on the local host, which is the fax server, to use the services of the HylaFAX server. To grant access to the client machine you are about to test, add its fully qualified domain name or IP address to this file. For example, if your fax client is called `client1.bwc.org`, add it to the `hosts` file, which should now look like the following:

```
localhost
127.0.0.1
client1.bwc.org
```

Send a test fax message from `client1` to the fax server using the `sendfax` command. Replace the hostname of the fax server and the recipient fax machine's telephone number, as shown in the following example, with your fax server's hostname and the telephone number of a nearby fax machine to which you have access.

```
$ sendfax -h orion.bwc.org -D -n -d 5551212 test
request id is 14 (group id 14) for host orion.bwc.org (1 file)
```

If all goes well you will see output similar to what's shown above. If you get a password prompt then you have not edited the `hosts` file correctly. Fix any mistakes and try again.

The `hosts` file provides a higher level of access control than we have just discussed. You can provide usernames and passwords to allow only certain users to use the fax server. A sample `hosts` file specifying user and password access control is shown below:

```
localhost
127.0.0.1
^user1@client1\.bwc\.org$:10:xxxxxxxxxxxx:yyyyyyyyyyyy:
^user2@client2\.bwc\.org$:11:xxxxxxxxxxxx::
^user3@client3\.bwc\.org$:12:xxxxxxxxxxxx::
!^client4\.bwc\.org$
```

The format of entries in the hosts file consists of four fields separated by colons. The most general form is of the type:

`<client>:<UID>:<password>:<admin-password>`

Only the first field is necessary. All other fields are optional. The client field can be of user@hostname format, or just hostname format. Regular expressions are supported for this field. To avoid unpleasant side effects, it is advisable to demarcate the beginning and end of a string with the ^ and $ symbols. If the client string does not contain an @ symbol, the string is considered a hostname, and any user from that host is allowed access. A negation (!) in front of the client name denies access to the server from that client.

The UID field is a number within the range from 0-6002. You can assign any numeric ID number in this range to users. Multiple users can be assigned the same UID. hfaxd uses the UID to control access to server resources such as jobs and documents. The value is used to set the group ID of files created by a client. If no UID is specified, hfaxd uses the default value of 6002.

The password field contains a Unix-style encrypted password. This can be copied from the /etc/shadow file. If this field is blank the user is not required to provide a password to use the fax server. The last field holds the encrypted administrator password. A user can gain administrative privileges by providing this password. If this field is empty, the user is not permitted to have administrative privileges.

Try adding an entry to the hosts file with username and password fields specified, and then access the fax server. An example of connecting as user1 is shown below:

```
$ sendfax -h orion.bwc.org -D -d 8523 -n -f user1 test
Password:
request id is 15 (group id 15) for host orion.bwc.org (1 file)
```

The -f flag of sendfax is used to specify a user different from the one you are currently logged in as. In the above example we have used -f user1 to send the fax message as user1. Since we have an entry in the host file that matches user1@client1.bwc.org, and this entry also contains the UID, and password fields, hfaxd prompts for the password. After the correct password for user1 is supplied the fax message is accepted for delivery.

You can use the faxstat command to view the status of the submitted fax messages as follows:

```
$ faxstat -h orion.bwc.org -s
HylaFAX scheduler on localhost: Running
Modem ttyS1 (+972.4.8331039): Waiting for modem to come free

JID Pri S  Owner  Number     Pages Dials     TTS Status
14  127 W gautam 8523        0:0   0:12
15  127 W user1  8523        0:0   0:12
```

> **Tip**
>
> Use the -s flag with the faxstat command to list the contents of the send queue. To list the faxes that have arrived and are waiting in the receive queue, use the -r flag of the faxstat command.

SETTING CLIENT DEFAULTS

Systemwide default settings for HylaFAX clients can be set using a configuration file called hyla.conf. The HylaFAX installation does not create this file. You must create it in the /usr/share/fax directory.

So far we have been specifying the hostname of the fax server when using the sendfax command with the -h flag. This is not necessary if you set a value of the default fax server in the hyla.conf file. Add a line like the following to /usr/share/fax/hyla.conf:

```
Host:   orion.bwc.org
```

Replace orion.bwc.org with the fully qualified domain name of your fax server. Next time you use sendfax it will use this host as the default fax server host.

The same can also be achieved by setting the value of the environment variable FAXSERVER with the name of the fax server. In addition, a per user .hylarc file can be created to set default values for sendfax and other HylaFAX client programs. Check the manual page for sendfax to get a complete list of all the parameters that can be set using the hyla.conf or .hylarc files.

SETTING UP AN EMAIL-FAX GATEWAY

The HylaFAX source distribution comes with several shell scripts and instructions on how to set up an email-fax gateway. Download the HylaFAX source distribution and unpack it in a suitable place such as /usr/local/src. Change your current directory to the HylaFAX source directory and look for a sub-directory called faxmail. Within this sub-directory three scripts are provided to set up email-fax gateways. They are the following:

- **faxmail/mailfax.sh-sendmail**: Suitable for systems using sendmail
- **faxmail/mailfax.sh-smail**: Suitable for systems using smail
- **faxmail/mailfax.sh-qmail**: Suitable for systems using qmail

We will look at the sendmail version of the script. If you are using smail or qmail, the procedure is quite similar. Follow the instructions mentioned in these script files.

Look at the different pieces involved in setting up an email-fax gateway. First, we must define a specification of how to address the message. Second, we must add an address-rewriting rule for sendmail to recognize our special address specification. Third, we must define a custom FAX mailer. And last, we have to write the mailer script.

We will describe the process of editing the sendmail.cf file to add the address-rewriting rule, and the fax mailer definition. However, there is an easier way of doing this. You can generate a sendmail configuration with HylaFAX mailer support using m4 macros. An m4 mailer definition for HylaFAX is included with the sendmail distribution on your Linux system. This process is described further in this chapter in the section "Adding HylaFAX Support to sendmail.cf Using m4."

DEFINING THE ADDRESS SPECIFICATION

Fortunately we don't have to devise a new address specification. One has already been defined and we can just use it. The general format of the email address is *<user>@<number>.<fax>* (*<Full Name of User>*).

For example, to send a fax to user patsmith, whose fax number is 5551212, and full name is Pat Smith, the email address would be patsmith@5551212.fax (Pat Smith). The full name between parentheses is optional. It is used on the fax cover sheet. If you send a fax message suppressing the coversheet, the full name is not used.

ADDING AN ADDRESS-REWRITING RULE

This step requires editing the sendmail.cf file. You must add the following address rewriting rule to rule set 0 in /etc/sendmail.cf:

```
# forward FAX messages to HylaFAX software
R$+<@$+.FAX>              $#fax $@ $2 $: $1              user@host.FAX
```

In addition, it is necessary to ensure that rule set 3 will not attempt a hostname lookup on FAX addresses. This is achieved by creating a pseudo domain called FAX.

Adding the following line in the sendmail.cf file creates the pseudo domain FAX:

```
CPFAX
```

DEFINING A FAX MAILER

Next edit the sendmail configuration file to include the following mailer definition:

```
Mfax, P=/usr/share/fax/mailfax, F=DFMShu, M=100000,
      A=mailfax $u $h $f
```

WRITING THE mailfax MAILER SCRIPT

The last step is to write the mailer script /usr/share/fax/mailfax. This is quite simple. This script uses the faxmail program supplied with the HylaFAX distribtion. A possible mailfax script is listed below:

```
#!/bin/sh
/usr/bin/faxmail -n -d "$1" "$2"
```

The mailfax script is invoked by sendmail and is passed three arguments: $u, $h, and $f. This default mailfax script does not use the last argument passed by sendmail (the full name). This is because `faxmail` is being invoked with the `-n` flag to suppress coversheet generation. The argument `$1` is replaced by `$u`, which is the destination fax number. The argument `$2` is replaced by `$h`, which is the UID of the sender.

ADDING HYLAFAX SUPPORT TO sendmail USING m4

The steps involved in adding HylaFAX support to `sendmail` on a Red Hat Linux system are quite easy. They are the following:

1. Change your current directory to the directory containing m4 definition files with the command `cd /usr/lib/sendmail-cf/cf`.

2. Make a copy of your current Red Hat m4 configuration file with the command `cp redhat.mc redhat+hylafax.mc`.

3. Edit the new m4 definition file and add the following line:
    ```
    MAILER(fax)
    ```

4. Run the make command:
    ```
    # make redhat+hylafax.cf
    rm -f redhat+hylafax.cf
    m4 ../m4/cf.m4 redhat+hylafax.mc > redhat+hylafax.cf ||\
     (rm -f redhat+hylafax.cf && exit 1 )
    chmod 444 redhat+hylafax.cf
    ```

5. Browse the newly created configuration file `redhat+hylafax.cf`, and make sure you see a mailer definition, `Mfax`, address rewriting rules to support the `.FAX` address format, and the pseudo domain definition `CPFAX`. In the `Mfax` mailer section, verify the path to the `faxmail` program is correct. If it is not correct fix it by hand. Now you can install the newly created `sendmail` configuration file. First, stop `sendmail`:
    ```
    # /etc/rc.d/init.d/sendmail stop
    ```

6. Save the current configuration file:
    ```
    # mv /etc/sendmail.cf /etc/sendmail.cf.old
    ```

7. Copy the new configuration file to `sendmail.cf`:
    ```
    # cp redhat+hylafax.cf /etc/sendmail.cf
    ```

8. Restart the sendmail daemon:
    ```
    # /etc/rc.d/init.d/sendmail start
    ```

TESTING THE EMAIL-FAX GATEWAY

You are now ready to test the newly configured E-mail-Fax gateway. This can be done using any mail program. The command line mail utility `/bin/mail` is very handy for quickly sending email from the command line. Run the following command:

```
# mail -v joe@5551212.fax < test
```

Needless to say, you must replace the destination fax number in the above-mentioned command to a valid fax number where you can receive faxes.

Check the send queue on the fax server by running the `faxstat` command as follows:

```
# faxstat -h faxhost.bwc.org -s
```

Again replace the name of the fax host with the correct name of your fax server.

If you see the job either queued, or being processed, you have successfully installed an email-fax gateway.

> **Tip**
>
> For `faxmail` to work, you must ensure users can access the fax server without supplying passwords. This is necessary because the `faxmail` program runs with the UID of the user submitting the job through `sendmail`. The `hosts` file on the fax server must allow access from all users without asking for a password. Because the `faxmail` program runs in the background and is not interactive, it is not possible to collect a password from the user and supply it to the `hfaxd` process on the fax server.

HYLAFAX TRANSFER LOGS

HylaFAX maintains accurate logging of all faxes sent and received in the log file `/var/spool/fax/etc/xferfaxlog`. The default name of the file is `xferlog`, which has been changed in RPM packages to `xferfaxlog`, to distinguish it from the `xferlog` file used by WU-FTPD.

This file contains one line per inbound or outbound call, except for faxes received by polling, when multiple entries may be present for a single call. The records are fixed format, with fields separated by the tab character.

A transmission record has the following format:

```
date  SEND  commid  modem jobid jobtag sender dest-number CSI params #pages job-
time
➥conntime reason
```

A receive record has the following format:

```
date RECV commid modem _<null> _<null> fax local-number TSI params #pages jobtime
➥conntime reason
```

Two typical sample entries in the `xferfaxlog` file are shown below.

```
# more xferfaxlog

03/20/00 14:59    SEND    00000002    ttyS1    1    " "    gautam    "8358525"
➥"972 4 8358525"    33031    1    0:55    0:37    " "

03/20/00 15:46    RECV    00000003    ttyS1    " "    fax    "+972.4.8331039"
➥"+972 4 8358591"    258    1    1:02    1:02    " "
```

As is clearly evident the data contains valuable information such as the call time, user name, local and remote phone numbers, number of pages sent or received, and the connect time. If necessary, this data can be easily processed by a script to generate billing information.

HYLAFAX crond JOBS

HylaFAX comes with two programs that run from crond. One runs once a day, and the other runs every hour. Let us take a brief look at what these programs do.

The /usr/sbin/faxqclean program runs every hour from crond. It processes completed jobs and removes document files that are not referenced. faxqclean scans the /var/spool/fax/doneq directory and processes each file according to the doneop specified in the job description file. Jobs marked for removal are deleted and any references to them are removed.

Jobs marked for archival are moved into the /var/spool/fax/archive directory. After scanning the doneq directory, faxqclean examines the /var/spool/fax/docq directory. Files that are not referenced by any job and files that are older than a specified threshold are deleted.

The /usr/sbin/faxcron script runs once a day from crond. It generates daily and weekly statistics about faxes sent and received. It reports any recent calls that failed suspiciously and returns the associated trace log files. It purges data older than 30 days from the remote machine information directory. It deletes information older than 30 days from session trace log files. It cleans the /var/spool/fax/tmp directory removing files that are older than a day. It cleans the /var/spool/fax/recvd directory by removing received faxes that are older than 7 days. It reports sites that are currently rejecting faxes. It makes sure all session log files are owned by the user fax and have file protection mode 644. A summary report is mailed to the Fax Master.

TROUBLESHOOTING HYLAFAX

We will now discuss some common problems you may face when setting up or running HylaFAX. We will look at the server-side and client-side problems separately. For effective troubleshooting, you must have a good overall understanding of the various components of HylaFAX.

The client-side components are sendfax, faxstat, faxrm, and sendpage.

The server-side components support four distinct job functions. The hfaxd daemon's function is to communicate with the client programs. The faxq daemon schedules outbound jobs. The faxsend and pagesend programs handle delivery of faxes and pages. The faxgetty daemon services the modems and received inbound faxes.

In addition, periodic processes such as faxqclean and faxcron are run from crond.

When you are having a problem it is first necessary to identify whether it is a client-side problem, a server-side problem, or a problem relating to periodic jobs that run from crond.

Generally, HylaFAX is a very stable and robust piece of software and is designed for uninterrupted operation. Once set up correctly, it requires little or no intervention from the system administrator.

AN EXAMPLE OF A CLIENT-SIDE PROBLEM

A client cannot contact the fax server. You run the `faxstat` program and see output similar to the following:

```
$ faxstat
Can not reach server at host "faxhost1.bwc.org", port 4559.
```

Make sure the server name is correct. If not, set the proper name of the server in `/usr/share/hyla.conf`, or `.hylarc`, or the environment variable FAXSERVER. General network connectivity problems cannot be ruled out. Use `ping` and other TCP/IP diagnostics programs to verify the remote fax server can be reached from the client.

After fixing the server name, or any network problems, run `faxstat` again and you should see something like the following:

```
$ faxstat
HylaFAX scheduler on orion.bwc.org: Running
Modem ttyS1 (+972 4 833-1029): Running and idle
```

If the output is as shown below then your client is communicating with the server but there is a problem on the server:

```
HylaFAX scheduler on faxhost.bwc.org: Not running.
```

AN EXAMPLE OF A SERVER-SIDE PROBLEM

If `faxstat` output shows the scheduler is not running such as shown in the `faxstat` output below, then the `faxq` daemon is either dead or has a problem:

```
$ faxstat
HylaFAX scheduler on orion.bwc.org: Not running
Modem ttyS1 (+972.4.8331039): Running and idle
```

To fix this problem, do a process listing and check whether the `faxq` process is running. If it is not running you can start it by running the following command as the root user:

```
# /usr/sbin/faxq
```

The program will put itself in the background and change its UID to fax.

If the `ps` output shows `faxq` is running, but `faxstat` reports the scheduler is not running, you should check the server tracing log for `faxq` to see what the problem is. The `faxstat` communicates with `hfaxd` on the fax server to get the status information. `hfaxd` decides if `faxq` is running based on whether it can open the FIFO special file `/var/spool/fax/FIFO`. Make sure this file is the correct type and has the appropriate permission. The proper ownership and permissions of the FIFO file are as shown by the following ls listing:

```
# ls -l /var/spool/fax/FIFO
prw-------  1 uucp     uucp          0 Mar 22 17:43 FIFO
```

`faxq` creates the FIFO file when it starts up if it does not already exist. If there is a problem, stop `faxq`, stop `hfaxd`, remove the file, and restart `faxq` and `hfaxd` using the following commands:

```
# /usr/sbin/faxquit
# /etc/rc.d/init.d/hylafax stop
# rm -f /var/spool/fax/FIFO
# /etc/rc.d/init.d/hylafax start
```

After running faxquit verify the faxq process has really terminated. Otherwise you may need to use kill -9 to end this process. This is an extreme example and probably will never happen. Before killing faxq in this way make sure no outbound jobs are in progress. Killing faxq while outbound jobs are processing can leave the system in an inconsistent state, and can require a reboot of the server.

DEBUGGING COMMUNICATION PROBLEMS

Modem communication problems can be debugged by looking at session log files. Session log files are stored in the /var/spool/fax/log directory. Session logs are easy to understand. A sample extract of a session log file follows:

```
Mar 20 14:59:22.38: [  492]: SESSION BEGIN 00000002 97248358525
Mar 20 14:59:22.38: [  492]: SEND FAX: JOB 1 DEST 8358525 COMMID 00000002
Mar 20 14:59:22.38: [  492]: DELAY 2600 ms
Mar 20 14:59:24.98: [  492]: <-- [15:ATE0V1Q0S0=0H0\r]
Mar 20 14:59:24.99: [  492]: --> [2:OK]
Mar 20 14:59:24.99: [  492]: <-- [21:ATS8=2S7=60&K3&D2&C1\r]
Mar 20 14:59:25.00: [  492]: --> [2:OK]
Mar 20 14:59:25.00: [  492]: <-- [12:AT+FCLASS=1\r]
Mar 20 14:59:25.01: [  492]: --> [2:OK]
Mar 20 14:59:25.01: [  492]: <-- [5:ATM0\r]
Mar 20 14:59:25.02: [  492]: --> [2:OK]
Mar 20 14:59:25.02: [  492]: <-- [12:AT+FCLASS=1\r]
Mar 20 14:59:25.13: [  492]: --> [2:OK]
Mar 20 14:59:25.15: [  492]: DIAL 8358525
Mar 20 14:59:25.15: [  492]: <-- [12:ATDT8358525\r]
Mar 20 14:59:40.22: [  492]: --> [7:CONNECT]
Mar 20 14:59:41.56: [  492]: --> [2:OK]
Mar 20 14:59:41.56: [  492]: <-- [9:AT+FRH=3\r]
Mar 20 14:59:41.57: [  492]: --> [7:CONNECT]
Mar 20 14:59:42.26: [  492]: --> [2:OK]
Mar 20 14:59:42.26: [  492]: REMOTE CSI "972 4 8358525"
Mar 20 14:59:42.26: [  492]: <-- [9:AT+FRH=3\r]
Mar 20 14:59:42.27: [  492]: --> [7:CONNECT]
Mar 20 14:59:42.52: [  492]: --> [2:OK]
Mar 20 14:59:42.52: [  492]: REMOTE best rate 9600 bit/s
Mar 20 14:59:42.52: [  492]: REMOTE max page width 1728 pixels in 215 mm
Mar 20 14:59:42.52: [  492]: REMOTE max unlimited page length
Mar 20 14:59:42.52: [  492]: REMOTE best vres 7.7 line/mm
Mar 20 14:59:42.52: [  492]: REMOTE best format 1-D MR
Mar 20 14:59:42.52: [  492]: REMOTE best 20 ms, 10 ms/scanline
Mar 20 14:59:42.52: [  492]: USE 9600 bit/s
Mar 20 14:59:42.52: [  492]: USE 20 ms, 10 ms/scanline
Mar 20 14:59:42.52: [  492]: SEND file "docq/doc1.ps;31"
Mar 20 14:59:42.52: [  492]: USE page width 1728 pixels in 215 mm
Mar 20 14:59:42.52: [  492]: USE unlimited page length
Mar 20 14:59:42.52: [  492]: USE 7.7 line/mm
Mar 20 14:59:42.52: [  492]: USE 1-D MR
Mar 20 14:59:42.52: [  492]: SEND training at v.29 9600 bit/s
```

```
Mar 20 14:59:42.52: [   492]: <-- [9:AT+FTH=3\r]
Mar 20 14:59:42.56: [   492]: --> [7:CONNECT]
Mar 20 14:59:42.56: [   492]: <-- data [23]
Mar 20 14:59:42.56: [   492]: <-- data [2]
Mar 20 14:59:44.38: [   492]: --> [7:CONNECT]
Mar 20 14:59:44.38: [   492]: <-- data [6]
Mar 20 14:59:44.38: [   492]: <-- data [2]
Mar 20 14:59:44.79: [   492]: --> [2:OK]
Mar 20 14:59:44.79: [   492]: DELAY 75 ms
Mar 20 14:59:44.87: [   492]: <-- [10:AT+FTM=96\r]
Mar 20 14:59:44.91: [   492]: --> [7:CONNECT]
Mar 20 14:59:44.91: [   492]: <-- data [1024]
Mar 20 14:59:44.91: [   492]: <-- data [776]
Mar 20 14:59:44.91: [   492]: <-- data [2]
Mar 20 14:59:46.86: [   492]: --> [2:OK]
Mar 20 14:59:46.86: [   492]: <-- [9:AT+FRH=3\r]
Mar 20 14:59:47.47: [   492]: --> [7:CONNECT]
Mar 20 14:59:48.35: [   492]: --> [2:OK]
Mar 20 14:59:48.35: [   492]: TRAINING succeeded
Mar 20 14:59:48.35: [   492]: <-- [10:AT+FTM=96\r]
Mar 20 14:59:48.38: [   492]: --> [7:CONNECT]
Mar 20 14:59:48.38: [   492]: SEND begin page
Mar 20 14:59:48.39: [   492]: <-- data [1027]
... ... ...
Mar 20 15:00:06.18: [   492]: <-- data [270]
Mar 20 15:00:06.67: [   492]: SENT 25870 bytes of data
Mar 20 15:00:06.67: [   492]: <-- data [1033]
Mar 20 15:00:07.15: [   492]: <-- data [1029]
Mar 20 15:00:08.12: [   492]: <-- data [124]
Mar 20 15:00:08.12: [   492]: SENT 2172 bytes of data
Mar 20 15:00:08.12: [   492]: SEND 1D RTC
Mar 20 15:00:08.12: [   492]: <-- data [29]
Mar 20 15:00:08.12: [   492]: <-- data [2]
Mar 20 15:00:08.12: [   492]: SEND end page
Mar 20 15:00:12.24: [   492]: --> [2:OK]
Mar 20 15:00:12.24: [   492]: DELAY 95 ms
Mar 20 15:00:12.34: [   492]: SEND send EOP (no more pages or documents)
Mar 20 15:00:12.34: [   492]: <-- [9:AT+FTH=3\r]
Mar 20 15:00:12.38: [   492]: --> [7:CONNECT]
Mar 20 15:00:12.38: [   492]: <-- data [3]
Mar 20 15:00:12.38: [   492]: <-- data [2]
Mar 20 15:00:13.70: [   492]: --> [2:OK]
Mar 20 15:00:13.70: [   492]: <-- [9:AT+FRH=3\r]
Mar 20 15:00:14.20: [   492]: --> [7:CONNECT]
Mar 20 15:00:15.12: [   492]: --> [2:OK]
Mar 20 15:00:15.12: [   492]: SEND recv MCF (message confirmation)
Mar 20 15:00:15.12: [   492]: SEND FAX (00000002): FROM root@orion.bwc.org
 TO 8358525 (page 1 of 1 sent in 0:33)
Mar 20 15:00:15.12: [   492]: SEND FAX (00000002): FROM root@orion.bwc.org
 TO 8358525 (docq/doc1.ps;31 sent in 0:33)
Mar 20 15:00:15.12: [   492]: <-- [9:AT+FTH=3\r]
Mar 20 15:00:15.16: [   492]: --> [7:CONNECT]
Mar 20 15:00:15.16: [   492]: <-- data [3]
Mar 20 15:00:15.16: [   492]: <-- data [2]
Mar 20 15:00:16.47: [   492]: --> [2:OK]
```

```
Mar 20 15:00:16.47: [  492]: <-- [5:ATH0\r]
Mar 20 15:00:17.15: [  492]: --> [2:OK]
Mar 20 15:00:17.15: [  492]: SESSION END
```

Messages sent to the modem are the lines marked with a <-- (left-arrow). Data received from the modem are the lines marked with a --> right-arrow. Timestamps show the date and time. Time stamps are displayed with 10 millisecond precision, which is typical for real time clocks on UNIX systems. Unimportant binary data is generically shown as data.

These log files can pinpoint modem-related problems when talking to different fax machines and fax modems. It is highly recommended that you do not use a generic modem on your fax server. Trying to save money on a modem is a sure way of introducing problems. Buy a good brand name, high-end modem and you will save yourself a lot of aggravation. A list of modems that have been used with HylaFAX can found on the HylaFAX Web site at

http://www.hylafax.org/modems.html

USING EFAX

By using Efax you can easily set up the following:

- A fax server using the Linux print spool to send faxes in the same way you print documents.
- An email-to-fax gateway using the additional Qfax software.
- An automated logging system that can produce logs of user's calls.

Although Efax does not offer the features needed for a large enterprise faxing system and you should be considering a full-scale product such as HylaFAX or Fax2Send for larger installations, Efax is easy to set up and use for small installations. Specifically, Efax is not ideally suited to sites which need to use a fax server with multiple fax modems and is not well-suited to the task of acting as an incoming fax server which can automatically route incoming faxes by email.

To set up a fax server with Efax, it is necessary to first install Efax. After it is installed, a firm understanding of Efax and how it works will assist you in configuring your fax server and managing it in the future. We will cover these fundamentals of Efax and then outline standard configurations for print spool and email-based fax servers.

INSTALLING EFAX

The current version of Efax is 0.9 and is available as the file efax-0.9.tar.gz from http://metalab.unc.edu/pub/Linux/apps/serialcomm/fax/efax-0.9.tar.gz. Download the file and extract it in a convenient location with the command:

```
# tar xzvf efax-0.9.tar.gz
```

Efax will be extracted into the directory efax-0.9. Change to this directory and compile the software with the following command:

```
# make
```

Install the compiled binaries, the Efax scripts and the manual pages with the command:

```
# make install
```

The following Efax files will be installed in /usr/bin:

- **efax**: Sends and receives faxes
- **efix**: Converts between the fax format and text, bitmap and grayscale formats
- **fax**: Main control script for making, sending, viewing, receiving, and printing faxes

CONFIGURING EFAX

To use Efax for sending and receiving faxes from the local system where it is installed with a fax modem requires minimal configuration. You only need to edit the /usr/bin/fax script with your preferred text editor and set the value of the following variables as outlined in the script:

- **DEV**: Your modem device. Typically this will be a serial device such as ttyS0 or ttyS1.

Note

The comments about the DEV variable refer to dial-out devices such as cua0 and cua1. These are references to older versions of Linux that distinguished between outgoing and incoming serial devices. In all current versions of Linux, this distinction no longer exists.

- **FROM**: Your fax number that should be written in standard international form. This format allows for numbers, spaces, and the plus sign (+) which indicates that the international access code needs to be dialed before dialing the number. If you are in North America and your phone number is 416-555-1212, then the value of this variable should be "+1 416 555 1212".

Note

Notice the quotation marks around the value that are necessary because of the spaces in the value.

- **NAME**: Your name as it should appear on the header of outgoing faxes. You should put quotation marks around the name if it contains any spaces.
- **PAGE**: Your preferred page size. Possible values are letter, legal and a4. a4 is the typical letter size sheet outside North America.
- **PRTYPE**: Your printer type. Generally, you should choose ps or pcl depending on whether you have a PostScript or Hewlett-Packard PCL-compatible printer. This setting governs how Efax will print received faxes.

- **PRCMD**: Your printer command. On most Linux systems this will be lpr but if you are using a non-standard print spooler, you can provide the appropriate command here. The command should be able to accept the data to print on the standard input.

- **VIEWCMD**: The command used to view a fax. Typically this will be an X Windows application such as xloadimage or xv which is capable of viewing TIFF images. xloadimage is the default value and you can use this unless you need a viewer with more capabilities.

- **GS**: The name of your Ghostscript executable that Efax will use to send PostScript faxes. Typically this will be gs.

- **DIALPREFIX**: Your dialing string's prefix. This should include T for tone dialing or P for pulse dialing followed by any numbers needed to obtain an outside line.

- **DIALSUFFIX**: Your dialing string's suffix.

Additional variables in the fax file normally do not require changes. You can consult the comments in the file to determine whether you want to change those values.

After you have edited the file, save your changes.

SENDING FAXES WITH EFAX

After Efax is configured, you can test it by attempting to send a fax. Even though Efax consists of three components, the fax script is the one you will use to interact with the majority of Efax's functionality. The fax script brings together efax, efix, and other Linux applications to provide a single point of contact for your faxing software.

The general form of the fax command for sending a fax is:

```
$ fax send <options> <phone number> <file to send>
```

You can use the following options:

- **-l**: Send the fax in low resolution mode at 96 dots per inch.
- **-v**: Display verbose status messages as the fax is sent.
- **-m**: Assume the phone number has already been dialed.

The phone number to dial can be specified in a standard form with or without dashes. For instance, 4165551212 and 416-555-1212 can both be used.

You can easily send text files, PostScript files, and fax-formatted TIFF image files using Efax. For instance, if you have a text file at /tmp/foo.txt, you can send it to 416-555-1212 with the command:

```
$ fax 416-555-1212 /tmp/foo.txt
```

If you have multiple text files you can send them in one fax by listing them all on the command line:

```
$ fax 416-555-1212 /tmp/foo.txt /tmp/foo2.txt
```

PART
III

CH
17

Note You can only send multiple text files by listing them on the command line. If you list multiple PostScript files or combine text and PostScript files in the same command, Efax will not be able to prepare and send the fax.

RECEIVING FAXES WITH EFAX

You can configure Efax to automatically receive faxes using the `wait` option of the `fax` command:

```
$ fax wait
```

Efax will run as a daemon waiting for an incoming phone call, will answer the phone after the second ring, then save the fax, and reset itself to wait for the next call.

Tip While waiting for incoming faxes, your modem will not be locked, so outgoing faxes can be sent while Efax waits for incoming faxes on the same modem.

All incoming faxes are stored in the directory `/var/spool/fax/`. Each fax is named after the date and time it is received as a 10-digit number such as `1201104531`, which is January 12 at 10:45:31. Faxes are split into separate files for each page with extensions starting at `001` and incremented by one. For instance, if you receive a three-page fax on January 12 at 10:45:31 then the pages of the fax will be stored in three files named `1201104531.001`, `1201104531.002`, and `1201104531.003`. All three faxes are saved as fax-formatted TIFF images in the `/var/spool/fax/` directory.

To view the contents of the fax spool directory, use the `fax queue` command:

```
$ fax queue

Fax files in /var/spool/fax:

-rw-r--r--   1 root     root             247 Jan 12 10:45 1201104531.001
-rw-r--r--   1 root     root             247 Jan 12 10:45 1201104531.002
-rw-r--r--   1 root     root             247 Jan 12 10:45 1201104531.003
```

You can view any page of any fax stored in the fax spool directory using the `fax view` command:

```
$ fax view 1201104531.002
```

Depending on the value you set for the `VIEWCMD` variable in the `/usr/bin/fax` file, you might need to be running X Windows to view a fax page.

To print any page of any stored fax in the fax spool directory, use the `fax print` command:

```
$ fax print 1201104531.002
```

While Efax is waiting for incoming faxes, you can check the status of the Efax daemon using the `fax status` command:

```
$ fax status
USER        PID %CPU %MEM  SIZE  RSS TTY STAT START   TIME COMMAND
root        253  0.1  0.6   936  456 p0 S <  13:22   0:00 /usr/bin/efax \d/dev/
ttyS0

from: /var/spool/fax/modem.253

efax: 28:14 opened /dev/ttyS0
efax: 28:16 waiting for activity
```

If Efax is running as a daemon waiting for incoming faxes, you can stop the daemon using the `fax stop` command.

Tip

If you want Efax to enter wait mode every time you boot your system, add the fax `wait` command to the `/etc/rc.d/rc.local` start-up file on your system and the daemon will run each time you boot.

PART
III

CH
17

SETTING UP A FAX PRINT SERVER

Efax can easily integrate with your print spooler to allow users to send faxes by printing. Three steps are involved in configuring a fax print server using Efax:

1. Configure the printer queue.
2. Prepare the `faxlpr` script.
3. Prepare the spool directory.

CONFIGURING THE PRINTER QUEUE

To print to a fax through Efax, edit your `/etc/printcap` file to create an entry for a fax printer queue which uses an input filter to send print jobs to the `faxlpr` script. Typically, this entry would look like the following:

```
fax:\
      :sd=/var/spool/fax:\
      :lp=/dev/null:\
      :if=/usr/bin/faxlpr:
```

This entry creates a printer queue named `fax` which uses the print spool directory `/var/spool/fax`. The `lp=/dev/null` field indicates that any output generated by the input filter is sent to the null device so it doesn't reach a printer. The `if=/usr/bin/faxlpr` field indicates that `lpr` should redirect all files sent to this printer to the `/usr/bin/faxlpr` script.

PREPARING THE `faxlpr` SCRIPT

The fax script has a special property. If it is invoked with the name `faxlpr` it assumes that you are attempting to send a fax through the `lpd` printer daemon instead of on the command line.

This means that you need to create a link to the `fax` script named `faxlpr` so that it can be invoked by this name as the input filter for a printer queue. Create the link with the `ln` command:

```
# ln /usr/bin/fax /usr/bin/faxlpr
```

PREPARING THE SPOOL DIRECTORY

The print queue created in the `/etc/printcap` file uses the spool directory `/var/spool/fax`. You need to check that this directory exists and if it doesn't, create it with the appropriate permissions (world readable and writable):

```
# mkdir /var/spool/fax
# chmod 777 /var/spool/fax
```

The spool directory needs a `lock` file that is readable by all users but only writable by the root user. Create this file as follows:

```
# touch /var/spool/fax/lock ; chmod 644 /var/spool/fax/lock
```

SENDING FAXES THROUGH THE PRINTER QUEUE

Having configured Efax to accept print jobs through the printer queue `fax`, you can send documents by fax by printing them to this queue. To do this, you need to specify the destination phone number using the `-J` option of the `lpr` command:

```
$ lpr -Pfax -J 14165551212 <file to fax>
```

Any application that uses `lpr` to print and generates PostScript output to the printer can print to the `fax` queue in this way.

By using Linux's capability to print to remote print queues you can then use this print server to provide printing services to your network. In order to do this, the following steps are required:

1. Ensure that your fax server system has the necessary security settings to allow printing from each client that needs to use the fax server. This is done using the `hosts.allow`, `hosts.equiv`, and `hosts.lpd` files as outlined in Chapter 18, "General Security Issues."

2. Add the following entry to `/etc/printcap` on each client system that needs to print to the `fax` print queue:
   ```
   fax:\
     :sd=/var/spool/lpd/fax:\
     :mx#0:\
     :sh:\
     :rm=<fax server host name>:\
     :rp=fax:
   ```

3. Create the spool directory /var/spool/lpd/fax on each client system that will be printing to the fax queue.

EXTENDING EFAX WITH QFAX

Although Efax can easily be used to deploy an outgoing fax server for small businesses and workgroups, it lacks some key features necessary for a more robust, large-scale fax server. Some of these missing features are provided for with the Qfax packages:

- Sending outgoing faxes by email
- Automatically generating cover pages
- Spooling outgoing faxes

INSTALLING QFAX

The current version of Qfax is 1.3 and is available as the file qfax1.3.tar.gz from http://metalab.unc.edu/pub/Linux/apps/serialcomm/fax/qfax1.3.tar.gz. Download the file and extract it in a convenient location with the command:

```
# tar xzvf qfax1.3.tar.gz
```

Qfax is extracted into the current directory, so make sure you are in the exact directory where you want to place the source code distribution. Qfax does not extract into a subdirectory of the current directory.

After you have extracted Qfax, installation requires several steps:

1. Create a fax user.
2. Create a FaxMaster mail alias.
3. Create an email to fax gateway.
4. Create a spool directory for faxes.
5. Create a fax configuration directory.
6. Configure Qfax.
7. Specify privileged users.
8. Edit the fax.rc file.
9. Create the fax.db file.
10. Create the .fax file.
11. Compile and install Qfax.
12. Schedule fax queue processing.

These steps presume that you have installed and configured Efax already.

Tip

> If you want to use Qfax in a networked environment, you probably will need to install Efax, Qfax, and your fax modem on the Sendmail server, which will handle all mail messages sent by users on your network.

CREATE A fax USER

When Qfax is installed, it runs Efax as a non-root user, which is atypical on a single-user system. Instead, Efax should be configured to run as the uucp user. The uucp user is common on most Linux systems. However, the name is less than easy to recognize and use in scripts. Instead, it is convenient to create a second user, fax, with the same user ID and group ID as the uucp user on your system. For instance, if your uucp user's entry in /etc/passwd is:

```
uucp:*:10:15:UUCP Agent:/usr/lib/uucp:/bin/false
```

then you need to add the following entry to the /etc/passwd file:

```
fax:*:10:15:Fax Agent:/var/spool/fax:/bin/false
```

Notice that the home directory for the account is your fax spool directory, which comes into play later in the installation process.

To add this entry to the /etc/passwd file, you can edit the file with the vipw command, which safely opens the file in your default text editor.

CREATE A FAXMASTER MAIL ALIAS

Qfax will generate messages to the FaxMaster mail account for administrative purposes. To create this alias on a sendmail system you need to add an entry to the /etc/aliases file. The entry should take the following form:

```
FaxMaster: <user name>
```

The username should be name of the user that should receive all emails addressed to the FaxMaster email alias by Qfax.

When the entry is in the /etc/aliases file and the file is saved, you need to rebuild the sendmail aliases database with the newaliases command.

CREATE AN EMAIL TO FAX GATEWAY

Qfax expects that outgoing faxes generated by email will be addressed using the form <person>@<company>.fax. In order for this to work, sendmail needs to know how to redirect faxes addressed to the .fax domain.

This is a three-step process:

1. Create an address-rewriting rule.
2. Create a mailer definition.
3. Bypass name services.

CREATE AN ADDRESS-REWRITING RULE   The /etc/sendmail.cf file contains a series of rules known as Ruleset 0 as discussed in Chapter 16, "Linux Mail Services with sendmail." In this section you will find a series of messages related to error messages including several $#error entries, such as the following:

```
R<@>                    $@ <@>                         special case error msgs
R$* : $* ; <@>          $#error $@ 5.1.3 $:
    ➥"List:; syntax illegal for recipien$#R@ <@ $* >          < @ $1 >\
                catch "@@host" bogosity
R<@ $+>                 $#error $@ 5.1.3 $: "User address required"
R$*                     $: <> $1
R<> $* < @ [ $+ ] > $*  $1 < @ [ $2 ] > $3
R<> $* <$* : $* > $*    $#error $@ 5.1.3 $: "Colon illegal in host name part"
R<> $*                  $1
R$* < @ . $* > $*       $#error $@ 5.1.2 $: "Invalid host name"
R$* < @ $* .. $* > $*   $#error $@ 5.1.2 $: "Invalid host name"
```

Immediately after this series of entries, add the following address rewriting rule:

```
R$+ < @ $+ .fax >  $#fax $@ $2 $: $1  user@company.fax
```

This entry will forward fax messages to Qfax.

CREATE A MAILER DEFINITION   The /etc/sendmail.cf file contains a series of mailer definitions as discussed in Chapter 16. In this section of the file, you need to add the following mailer definition for fax messages:

```
Mfax,   P=/usr/bin/qfax, F=lsDFheu, S=14, R=24, M=100000,   A=qfax $u
```

BYPASS NAME SERVICES   The /etc/sendmail.cf file contains a series of rules to handle special name cases known as Ruleset 96 as discussed in Chapter 16. In this section you will find the following entry:

```
R$* < @ $* $~P > $*     $: $1 < @ $[ $2 $3 $] > $4
```

Comment this entry out by placing a # at the start of the line.

```
#R$* < @ $* $~P > $*     $: $1 < @ $[ $2 $3 $] > $4
```

This entry normally passes hostnames to a name server to make them canonical. This is generally not needed because names are almost always canonical. By avoiding this, the .fax domain will not cause problems.

CREATE A SPOOL DIRECTORY FOR FAXES

You need to create five directories for spooling purposes:

- **/var/spool/fax/recvq**: A directory for saving incoming faxes.
- **/var/spool/fax/sendq**: A directory for spooling outgoing faxes.
- **/var/spool/fax/docq**: A directory for storing inactive faxes such as those that couldn't be sent properly.
- **/var/spool/fax/log**: A directory where log files will be written.
- **/var/spool/fax/result**: A directory for storing the most recent fax operation.

These directories all need to have their permissions set to being readable by all users:

```
# mkdir /var/spool/fax
# cd /var/spool/fax
# mkdir recvq sendq docq log result
# chmod 755 recvq sendq docq log result
```

CREATE A FAX CONFIGURATION DIRECTORY

Qfax needs a directory to store its configuration files. Possible locations for this directory include `/conf/fax` and `/etc/conf/fax`. We will use the latter.

Create the directory and then copy the `fax.rc`, `fax.db`, and `cover-template.ps` files from the Qfax source directory to the new configuration directory.

CONFIGURE QFAX

Before compiling Qfax, customize the `config.h` file in the Qfax source directory to meet the specific requirements of your system. This file contains a series of entries of the form:

```
#define <variable name> <value>
```

Table 17.1 outlines the variables that need to be set in the `config.h` file.

TABLE 17.1   VARIABLES IN THE QFAX `config.h` FILE

Variable Name	Description
DATABASE	The location of the `fax.db` file. If you copied the file to `/etc/conf/fax`, then the value should be `/etc/conf/fax/fax.db`.
CONFIG	The location of the `fax.rc` file. If you copied the file to `/etc/conf/fax`, then the value should be `/etc/conf/fax/fax.rc`.
TEMPLATE	The location of the `cover-template.ps` file. If you copied the file to `/etc/conf/fax`, then the value should be `/etc/conf/fax/cover-template.ps`.
FAXQUEUE	The directory created for storing outgoing faxes (in this case, `/var/spool/fax/sendq`).
STOREDIR	The directory for storing inactive faxes (in this case, `/var/spool/fax/docq`).
FAXSCRIPT	The location of the Efax `fax` script (usually, `/usr/bin/fax`).
RESULT	The filename which should contain the status of the last attempt to send a fax (in this case, `/var/spool/fax/result/result`).
LS	Your `ls` command (usually this is just `ls`).
MAXFAXES	The maximum number of faxes which should be stored in the outgoing fax queue (the default value is 15).
MAXTRIES	The maximum number of times to attempt sending a failed fax before giving up (the default value is 3).

TABLE 17.1   CONTINUED

Variable Name	Description
LDPERIOD	The time period during which long-distance calls can be placed in the form `<start time>-<end time>` where the times are specified using the 24-hour clock as in `2200-0700`.
FAXGROUP	The name of the user group containing the users who are allowed to send faxes immediately without waiting for the regularly scheduled queue processing. The default group name of `faxnow` is a good choice.
USE_DAEMON	This definition does not take a value. If you want allow Efax to accept incoming faxes, leave the entry as is and if you do not plan to receive faxes, comment the entry out by adding an additional # to the start of the entry.

SPECIFY PRIVILEGED USERS

Normally, Qfax only sends faxes at a scheduled interval when the outgoing spool directory is processed. Users specified in the group indicated by the FAXGROUP variable in the config.h file in the Qfax source directory can override this and send faxes immediately. Typically, this group is called faxnow. You need to create the group faxnow by creating the appropriate entry in the /etc/group file:

```
faxnow::<group ID>:<user1>,<user2>,<user3>,...
```

The group ID should be unique for all groups in the /etc/group file.

EDIT THE fax.rc FILE

The fax.rc file, stored in your Qfax configuration directory created earlier in the installation process, is where you define information which appears on fax headers and the fax cover page and where you indicate the font to use on cover pages.

The comments in the file are self-explanatory. Edit the file to meet your needs.

CREATE THE fax.db FILE

The fax.db file, stored in your Qfax configuration directory created earlier in the installation process, is the global phone book file which contains information needed to map fax email addresses of the form `<person>@<company>.fax` to fax numbers. The entries in this phone book file are accessible to all users.

Each entry is five or more lines in length and is of the following form:

```
<company alias>    <company name>
<voice phone number>
<fax number>
<person alias 1>    <person name 1>
<person alias 2>    <person name 2>
...
+
```

The + on a line by itself delimits the end of the entry. The company and person aliases are then used by users to address faxes by email in the form *<person alias>@<company alias>*.fax. The phone number and fax number can be of any standard format including 1-604-555-1212 and 1 416 555 1212. The leading 1 or 0 on long-distance numbers is essential for Qfax to dial correctly.

CREATE THE .fax FILE

In addition to the global phonebook, fax.db, users can create personal phone books in the .fax file in their home directories. This file takes the same format as just described for the global phonebook file.

COMPILE AND INSTALL QFAX

Compiling and installing Qfax requires one step. Change your current directory to the Qfax source directory and use the following command:

```
# make install
```

Qfax will be compiled and the binary files will be copied to their installation directory (which is /usr/bin). In addition, the Qfax manual pages will be installed.

SCHEDULE FAX QUEUE PROCESSING

When faxes are sent by email through Qfax, Qfax saves them in the outgoing spool directory specified earlier in the installation. The faxes will stay there until Qfax processes the spool. The qrun command processes the spool directory. While you can manually run qrun, you really need to schedule it to run automatically at an interval. For instance, 15-minute intervals work well when you need faxes to be sent quickly. Otherwise, scheduling qrun to run one or twice per day may suffice.

Schedule qrun to run from the fax user's crontab file as outlined in Chapter 7, "Scheduling Tasks." In summary, as the root user, you can open the fax user's crontab file for editing with the command:

```
# crontab -u fax -e
```

If you want to schedule qrun to execute every 15 minutes, add the following entry to the crontab file:

```
0,15,30,45 * * * * /usr/bin/qrun
```

If you want to run qrun every day at 6:00 a.m., add the following entry:

```
0 6 * * * /usr/bin/qrun
```

SENDING FAXES BY EMAIL

Users can send faxes by email simply by addressing a text message to *<person alias>@<company alias>*.fax where the person alias and company alias reflect entries in the global Qfax phonebook or the user's personal Qfax phonebook.

Emails to be sent by fax must be plain text messages. They should not include any attachments. If users want to place a comment on the cover page of their outgoing fax, they need to use the fax comment start and end delimiters defined in the `fax.rc` file.

The `fax.rc` file has two fields, `Fax-Comment-Start` and `Fax-Comment-End`, which indicate the start and end of cover page comments. For instance, if you have defined `Fax-Comment-Start` as `<COMMENT>` and `Fax-Comment-End` as `</COMMENT>`, then you can add cover page comment to your fax as follows:

1. Make the first line of your email message `<COMMENT>`. If it is not the first line, Qfax will treat it as part of the body text of your message.
2. On the lines following `<COMMENT>`, write your cover page comment.
3. On the line following your cover page comment, place `</COMMENT>` on the line by itself.
4. On the lines following `</COMMENT>`, write the body text of your fax.

For instance, a complete message might look like the following:

```
<COMMENT>
Cover page
comment here
</COMMENT>
Body text
goes here
```

MANAGING QFAX

Qfax provides two tools for managing your Qfax-based fax server:

- **qstat**: Users can view a list of faxes they have spooled for delivery with the qstat command. When used by the root user, the qstat command will display a list of all spooled faxes. Each fax is uniquely identified as follows: `fax.<user name>.<timestamp>` such as `fax.user1.10Jan220311`. For each fax listed, the following information is displayed:
  - **Prefix:** A unique identifier for the fax
  - **Sender:** The sender's username
  - **Recipient:** The recipient's dialing string and name
  - **Subject:** The subject of the fax
  - **Queued:** The time the fax entered the queue
  - **Status:** The current status of the fa>
- **qdel**: Users can delete faxes they have queued but which have not yet been sent using the qdel command. To delete all faxes placed in the queue, use the command qdel -a. To delete a particular fax, specify the prefix for the fax on the command line. For example, qdel `<prefix>` should match the one displayed by the qstat command for the fax in question. The root user can delete any or all faxes in the queue with qdel.

PART

III

CH

17

TROUBLESHOOTING EFAX AND QFAX

Several problems can occur when installing and configuring Efax and Qfax, including those outlined in Table 17.2.

TABLE 17.2 COMMON FAX PROBLEMS

Problem	Possible Solution
Efax fails to dial.	Efax might be improperly configured for your modem. Check your modem device in the /usr/bin/fax script.
You are denied permission to send a fax when using Efax.	Efax generally needs to run as the root user; if you are not logged in as root, try logging in as the root user and sending your fax.
When you send a fax through the print queue, it is not sent.	Either your print queue is not specified correctly in the /etc/printcap file or you forgot to specify a phone number with the -J option of 1pr. Check the contents of the fax queue's definition in /etc/printcap and confirm that you specified the phone number.
When you send a fax with qfax, it doesn't send immediately.	Either you forgot to schedule qrun in the fax user's crontab file to run at reasonable intervals or you have sent a long-distance fax but are not in the long-distance time bracket specified in the LDPERIOD variable in the config.h file. Make sure that qrun is scheduled to run with the command crontab -u fax -1 and double-check your long-distance period. If you are not in the long-distance period and have sent a long-distance fax, it will stay in the queue until qrun executes within the long-distance period.
Qfax doesn't generate mail messages to the fax administrator.	Check that you have defined the FaxMaster alias correctly in /etc/aliases and then run newaliases again.

SECURITY AND STABILITY

## CHAPTER 18

GENERAL SECURITY ISSUES

In this chapter

SECURITY IN A NETWORKED WORLD

In the modern computing world, security is of paramount importance. Only if a computer is left turned off in a room with no door or windows and with no data stored on its disks or in static memory can it be considered completely secure.

A culture of challenge exists that renders any computer susceptible to attack. With the propagation of networks and the Internet, security is an acute concern: Organizations not only want to keep their data secure and their systems running smoothly, they also want to prevent unauthorized use, or abuse, of their network's resources.

Security problems emerge for several reasons:

- Many software packages, including operating systems, ship with their security settings in a fairly open mode.
- Many operating systems ship with security tools, which are disabled by default.
- Many software packages contain security bugs.
- Systems are often misconfigured.

Security can be broadly categorized in five levels:

- **Physical Security:** Are your systems physically secure? Can they be accessed by unauthorized personnel? Can they be stolen?
- **Usage and Security Policies:** What are your user access policies? What are your password policies? Have you reviewed your security policies and procedures?
- **System Security:** Does each system on the network implement the necessary security policies? Do unnecessary user accounts exist on systems? Is data secure and, if needed, encrypted? Do systems have modems that allow incoming access? Is sufficient virus protection in place?
- **Network Security:** Are unnecessary services running? Have you used `hosts.allow` and `hosts.deny` to deny access to your system? Are passwords traveling on the network as plain text?
- **Internet Security:** Do you have a suitable firewall in place? Do you need a DMZ? Are you susceptible to denial of service attacks?

Although it may seem that these levels of security are mostly independent, in reality they are layers which build on each other. For instance, it makes no sense to have strong network security if you do not apply a policy of strong passwords or allow completely open physical access to any system on a network. Basically, you must implement each level of security fully as you move through the chain to ensure you have a complete and effective security policy.

PHYSICAL SECURITY

It is simple to say that systems must be physically secure. However, simple as this may seem, it is usually neglected in the focus on software and network security as a result of well-publicized security breaches on the Internet.

Consider this dilemma: If you have the best security software running, effective firewalls, and close monitoring of your system logs for potential breaches, and if you allow uncontrolled access to your server's consoles, you have created a security breach. This breach is at least as large as not implementing any form of system or network security. Not only can a potential attacker walk up to a server and attempt to breach its security, a malicious individual could even walk up to a server, unplug it, and steal it.

Servers are not the only location where sufficient physical security is warranted. You also must consider the security of your desktop systems: While open concept offices make it impossible to individually secure access to each host, you should take care not to place hosts in locations where strangers could, unseen, gain unauthorized physical access to systems on your network.

In addition, consider the need for desktops to have any type of removable media drives. If you run centralized application servers, file servers, and information servers, it is possible that most desktops do not need removable media. By eliminating these drives or physically locking them you prevent attackers from rebooting those systems from boot floppy disks or CD-ROMs and bypassing any security on those systems.

In addition, consider locking access to power switches on all systems in public spaces to prevent them from being turned off and rebooted, perhaps from media other than the intended internal hard drives.

Physical security also must be considered in a campus setting. For instance, if multiple buildings are connected in a large campus-wide LAN, consideration needs to be given to the accessibility of those cables. If they are easy to access (for instance, they run outdoors or in easy-to-access tunnels) then it is possible for an attacker to leverage access to those cables to sniff packets on your network or even gain access to the network.

In addition, if you use wireless communication within a building or between buildings, you must consider how easy it would be for an attacker to position an unauthorized receiver or transmitter that would provide access to your network or network traffic.

USAGE AND SECURITY POLICIES

Before attacking any security system implementation, consider a robust, thorough security and usage policy that should include, but not be limited to, addressing the following questions:

- What criteria will you use to determine who should be provided with user accounts?
- What rules will you use to decide which users should have access to which systems and services?

- Do you need usage guidelines and policies to help your user base be a proactive part of network security?

- How often should you require passwords to be changed?

- What are your password guidelines? Do you require that users adhere to a set of rules when selecting their passwords?

- Do you need additional security measures such as biometric security or smart cards to help prevent unauthorized system access?

- Does your network need to be connected to the Internet? If so, what services and systems actually need access to the Internet?

- Do you need to provide remote dial-up access for mobile users? If so, what resource do they need to access remotely?

USER ACCOUNT POLICIES

It is crucial that you develop a sound user account policy. This policy should take into account the following factors:

- Never have more accounts on your network than necessary. Each additional user account is one more potential doorway through which an attacker can gain access to your systems and network.

- Consider when to delete expired accounts. In some organizations it makes sense to immediately delete user accounts as soon as an individual leaves an organization. In other organizations, accounts need to exist in some limited form after an individual leaves, for instance to provide mail-forwarding or limited access to personal files and data.

- Do not create any form of guest accounts unless it is absolutely necessary to provide guest access to your system. While guest accounts are typically configured with minimal access to system resources, they still provide an easy-to-access initial point of access to your network for an attacker.

- Consider monitoring user activity in user accounts. By monitoring the applications users run and their patterns of disk and CPU usage, you can detect suspicious behavior which could be caused by an attacker gaining access to a user's account or by a user who, himself, is attacking your network.

PASSWORD SECURITY

Implement a sound password policy that can help prevent password-guessing from becoming an easy source of access to your network. Many attacks begin with attackers running software that attempts to guess users' passwords repeatedly until a match is found.

This is a reasonable approach to attacking a system because on many networks no rigorous password policies are applied. This leads to problems such as the following:

- Passwords are too short.
- Passwords are simple dictionary words.
- Passwords are not changed often enough.

To prevent these problems, you must develop a password policy similar to the following:

- Passwords should not include any part of the user's name or relative's names.
- Passwords should not use important dates.
- Passwords should not use dictionary words.
- Passwords should not be strictly numeric.
- Passwords should combine upper and lowercase letters.
- Passwords should combine letters and numbers.
- Passwords should include punctuation symbols.
- Passwords should be long enough (preferably eight characters or longer).
- Passwords should change on a regular basis.

The actual way in which you implement these policies is particular to your network. For instance, the frequency of password changes depends on your environment. It is not uncommon to change sensitive passwords as often as weekly or monthly while allowing regular user accounts to keep their passwords for as long as six months. If you are going to include time limits on the life of passwords in your policies, make sure you have mechanisms in place to enforce the changing of passwords.

You can enforce a password change policy using the shadow password suite that is standard on many modern Linux distributions, including Red Hat Linux 6.2. The shadow password suite separates user account information such as the username, user ID, and group ID, which all exist in the `/etc/passwd` file (readable by all users) from the passwords themselves, which are stored in the `/etc/shadow` file (only readable by the root user).

Entries in the `shadow` file take the following form:

```
testuser:$1$QquzRC5m$dVx4MNDkvD5dmJeiQ1SgV.:10960:-1:99999:-1:-1:-1:135481524
```

Each entry consists of fields separated by colons:

```
<user name>:<encrypted password>:<date of last password change>:<days before
password may be changed>:<days after which password must be changed>:<days
after expiry that account is disabled>:<date that the account is disabled>:
<reserved for system use>
```

The date of the last password change and the date that the account is disabled are expressed as the number of days since January 1, 1970.

Using these fields you can define when a password expires either relative to the previous change or as an absolute date, and you can enforce account disabling if the user fails to change a password in a reasonable amount of time after expiry.

If your system does not have shadow passwords installed and enabled, you can enable the software suite from `ftp://i17linuxb.ists.pwr.wroc.pl/pub/linux/shadow/shadow-current.tar.gz`. The Shadow Password HOWTO is on-line at `http://linux.com/howto/Shadow-Password-HOWTO.html`.

In addition to password expiry, the importance of using a wide range of characters in your passwords cannot be underestimated. For instance, if you use six-character passwords but only use numbers, the possible number of passwords is 10^6 or 1000000. By comparison, a much shorter password of four characters made up of any combination of uppercase letters, lowercase letters, numbers, and punctuation leads to 724 or 26873856 possible passwords (or even more, depending on which punctuation characters are allowed). If you combine this large number of possible characters with longer randomly selected passwords of 8 or more characters, you reach 722204136308736 possible passwords, making the task of guessing a password much more difficult.

Tip

To ensure adherence to this type of policy, consider providing randomly generated passwords to users and not allowing users to change their passwords themselves. However, users who want to select their own passwords generally do not appreciate this type of hard-line approach.

SYSTEM SECURITY

Care must be taken to secure each individual system, whether it is a server or workstation, so that it is fairly secure from attacks. To secure a system, do several things, including the following:

- Ensure that no unneeded user accounts exist on any system.
- Ensure that any sensitive data is secured using an encryption scheme such as PGP public-key encryption.
- Do your systems have modems attached to them? If so, are they necessary? If so, are they in auto-answer mode? If possible, no modems on workstations or random servers should be accepting incoming connections. Instead dial-up access should route through dial-up servers dedicated to that task.
- Does each system on the network include the necessary virus protection?
- Are users required to log in to every workstation or do you have workstations that can be used without login? The latter is a bad idea as it circumvents other security policies such as taking care to only issue accounts to users who should have access and not creating guest accounts.

NETWORK SECURITY

Every system connected to your LAN should be secured against attacks from the network to the highest degree possible. There are several key strategies that you can use to help secure systems:

- Turn off as many services as possible. A default Linux distribution usually has numerous unnecessary services running. If you are not offering content to the network through FTP, turn off `ftpd`. If you don't require Telnet for remote access and management, turn off `telnetd`.

- Remove unnecessary daemons from starting up through `inetd`. For others use TCP wrappers if possible to launch the services from within `inetd`. This provides finer control and greater security.

- Use `/etc/hosts.allow` and `/etc/hosts.deny` to control access to the services that are running on your system as outlined in Chapter 13, "Linux Network Configuration and TCP/IP."

- Try to prevent unencrypted passwords from traveling across the network. For instance, Telnet sends plain text passwords across the network when you log in remotely. You can prevent this by using `ssh` instead of Telnet for remote login. `ssh` is a secure replacement for `Telnet` and `rsh`, and can be downloaded from `http://www.ssh.org/`.

INTERNET SECURITY

If your network will be connected to the Internet, it is essential that you implement sufficient security at the gateway connecting you to the Internet. If not, you expose all systems on your network to potential attack by any user on the Internet and eventually a security hole or misconfiguration will be found and capitalized on by an attacker.

Two key steps must be taken in securing your network against attack from the Internet:

- Create a firewall to prevent unwanted packets from reaching your internal network from the Internet.

- Move services which must be accessed from the Internet to a demilitarized zone and allow limited access to these from the Internet while preventing all access to other systems from the Internet. Services that are candidates for this include email, Web, FTP, and DNS.

The creation of a firewall and a DMZ are discussed in Chapter 19, "Linux and Firewalls."

SECURITY TOOLS

A wide range of tools exists that are useful in implementing and monitoring your security policies. Most of these tools are focused on Internet and network security. These tools include the following:

- **AIDE** (`http://www.cs.tut.fi/~rammer/aide.html`): The Advanced Intrusion Detection Environment, which can be used to monitor the integrity of critical system files and report changes to the files. AIDE is free software.

- **Bastille Linux** (`http://bastille-linux.org/`): Bastille Linux is an effort at a comprehensive, educational tool for hardening the security of a Red Hat Linux 6.0 or 6.2 system. Drawing on well-known sources of information about Linux security, it proposes security measures to system administrators only after educating the system administrator about the finer points related to the particular security issue.

- **Check-PS** (`http://checkps.alcom.co.uk/`): Check-PS attempts to find processes that are hidden from the system administrator because they do not appear in the output generated by ps. Often, attackers will place software onto a system to run without the administrator's knowledge. This software can gather security information such as passwords and send them to the attacker or provide back doors into the system. Check-PS looks for differences between the process list in the /proc file system and the output generated by ps and warns the administrator of hidden processes or even kills them automatically.

- **Check.pl** (`http://opop.nols.com/proggie.html`): Check.pl scans your file system for directories that are not sufficiently secured. The script also looks for suid, sgid, sticky and writeable files.

- **The Deception Toolkit** (`http://all.net/dtk/dtk.html`): The Deception Toolkit is designed to provide an advantage over attackers. It makes it appear as if a system has a wide range of known vulnerabilities, thereby making it harder to attack a system because apparently successful attacks actually are failures the attacker doesn't immediately know about. For instance, if an attacker attempts to steal your password file, he will actually obtain a false file provided by the Deception Toolkit and will waste time and resources cracking the passwords before he realizes the file is false. Also, if an attacker tries multiple attacks it is possible to track his activities.

- **Dsniff** (`http://www.monkey.org/~dugsong/dsniff/`): Dsniff is a suite of tools for penetration testing. These tools allow you to simulate different types of attacks on your systems and see how your systems respond and whether your security system is effective.

- **HostSentry** (`http://www.psionic.com/abacus/hostsentry/`): HostSentry performs login anomaly detection in an attempt to identify strange login behavior. The system learns users' normal login behavior and then attempts to identify activity that falls outside the patterns.

- **John the Ripper** (`http://www.openwall.com/john/`): John the Ripper is a password cracker that you can use to attempt to crack your system's passwords to determine any weak passwords.

- **Linux Intrusion Detect System** (`http://www.lids.org/`): The Linux Intrusion Detect System (LIDS) is a kernel patch which provides for detecting intrusion and allows limiting of many system operations, even for root, on a selective basis.

- **Nessus (`http://www.nessus.org/`):** Nessus is a free remote security scanner which can be used to perform more than 300 security scans of your network to determine your level of exposure to an attack.

- **Osiris (`http://www.shmoo.com/osiris/`):** Osiris catalogs critical system executable files on your system and then monitors those files for changes and warns the administrator when these executable files change.

- **PortSentry (`http://www.psionic.com/abacus/portsentry/`):** PortSentry detects scans against hosts on your network and responds to them by blocking the ports in real-time. This can prevent an attacker from scanning your system for vulnerabilities.

- **Saint (`http://www.wwdsi.com/saint/`):** Saint is a security assessment tool based on the infamous SATAN suite. It can be used to examine network services for security flaws. Saint can scan through a firewall and offers an HTML-based interface.

- **Tripwire (`http://www.tripwiresecurity.com/`):** Tripwire maintains a catalogue of critical system files and monitors those files for changes that it can report to the administrator.

KEEPING SYSTEMS SECURE

Once you have developed a security policy and implemented it, you can take the following steps to ensure the ongoing security of your systems:

- Monitor log entries
- Apply software updates
- React to security breaches
- Monitor sources of security information

MONITOR LOG ENTRIES

The system logging facility, `syslogd`, logs numerous security-related events to the system log files. On most Linux systems, this information is logged to `/var/log/messages`. You can check where your system is logging information by consulting the `/etc/syslog.conf` file.

Scan the log files for the following two main problems:

- Suspicious login activity such as attempts to use the `su` command to become the root user, repeated failed login attempts by one or more users, and strange activity as the root user.

- Signs that your log files have been tampered with, including extended periods of time that cannot be accounted for in the log files.

APPLY SOFTWARE UPDATES

One benefit of the Linux Open Source model of software development is that the developer community is generally fast to respond to security bugs and other alerts which affect Linux and Linux software. For this reason, it is best to keep your system up-to-date with the latest versions of the stable Linux kernel, network software, and any networking services you run. You should also consult your distribution's Web site for their latest security alerts and fixes because these will be easier to install and manage than upgrading software in your distribution from another source.

REACT TO SECURITY BREACHES

As soon as you become aware of a security breach or possible security breach, take action. If you think you have identified an attempt to breach your security while it is occurring, consider some or all of the following:

- If it appears that someone is trying to breach security through an existing user's account, first verify with the user that the activity you see isn't being caused by him.
- If the attempted compromise is coming from the network, disconnect your network from the affected system or systems and disconnect all connections to external networks such as the Internet and dial-up servers.
- Deny access to your systems and network from the host or network the attack appears to be coming from by changing your packet filters on the router or firewall, or changing your /etc/hosts.allow and /etc/hosts.deny settings.
- Log all users off the system.
- Monitor your site after you reconnect it to see if the attacker tries again.

If you become aware that a breach has occurred after the fact, take the following corrective action:

- Determine the hole that was used to create the breach and close the hole.
- Assess the damage. If you were running a product such as TripWire, which can identify changes to critical system files, consult its reports to see what files have changed.
- If the intruder has gained root access, reinstall your systems and restore user data from backups. Do not restore your operating system or applications from backups: You may have backed up software altered by the attacker and you will reintroduce it to your system if you restore from the backups.
- Track down the intruder and prosecute them if necessary.

MONITOR SOURCES OF SECURITY INFORMATION

Numerous sources of security information exist, and you should monitor at least some of them on a regular basis to keep track of new developments and security alerts. Some of the leading security sites include the following:

- **Rootshell.com (http://www.rootshell.com/):** This site offers information about the current exploits of crackers.

- **The BugTRAQ Archives** (`http://www.securityfocus.com/`): This site offers news and security updates.

- **The Computer Emergency Response Team** (`http://www.cert.org/`): CERT is the main response agency to security breaches on the Internet and is an excellent source of advisories and security alerts.

- **The Computer Incident Advisory Capability** (`http://ciac.llnl.gov/cgi-bin/index/bulletins`): This agency of the U.S. Government tracks security vulnerabilities and suggests actions.

## CHAPTER 19

LINUX AND FIREWALLS

In this chapter

FIREWALLS AND THE INTERNET

The Internet is growing at a phenomenal rate. With every passing day new organizations are joining the Internet. Businesses and agencies use the Internet for a variety of purposes, including exchanging email, sharing agency information through FTP and Web servers, and conducting research. Many organizations connect their local area networks to the Internet. Although there are many benefits in connecting to the Internet, security is a major consideration. Many security risks are not immediately obvious to new users. Hackers are at large on the Internet and exploit system vulnerabilities to gain access to private networks. Network administrators are rightfully concerned about exposing their private networks to attacks from Internet hackers.

This chapter focuses on Internet firewalls as one mechanism in the arsenal of security tools available to network administrators to protect sites against attacks from the Internet. It is highly recommended that organizations use firewall technology to filter connections and limit access.

An Internet firewall provides protection to an organization by implementing a security policy that prevents unauthorized access to the computing resources of its private network. The Internet firewall can be a single system or a group of systems that enforce a security policy between an organization's internal network and the Internet. The firewall decides which internal services can be accessed from outside the network and which outside services can be accessed from within the network.

To have an effective firewall, all traffic entering or leaving a site must pass through it. If a private network has multiple connections to the Internet it must ensure that all these network connections pass through the firewall system. If this is not possible, multiple firewall systems must be installed to guard all of the Internet access points. Needless to say, the firewall system itself must be made as immune to penetration as possible. The firewall host is not the only component that guarantees a site's security. Rather, it is one element of a large security system that implements an organization's security policies.

One of the most significant benefits of having a firewall is that all access to the Internet is managed on the firewall machine. Securing one firewall machine and instituting a well-defined security policy guarantees the security of the internal network. If there were no firewall, all the internal hosts would be subject to attacks and any single host with some vulnerability would compromise the security of the entire internal network.

Another advantage of running a firewall is its capability for network address translation, or NAT. Internet network addresses are already a scarce commodity. Acquiring large numbers of new IP addresses for any organization can prove extremely difficult, if not impossible. With a firewall capable of running NAT, an organization can make do with a few legal IP addresses for crucial Internet systems such as DNS, Mail, Web, and FTP servers. All other systems in the private network can use a very large IP address space reserved for private use by IANA. These special reserved addresses are not routed on the Internet and therefore any organization is free to use them internally.

With NAT, as data packets pass through the firewall from systems using these reserved internal IP addresses, the firewall translates the private addresses to registered legal IP addresses, which can reach any system on the Internet. A reverse address translation is performed by the firewall when the reply packets return from systems on the Internet bound for the hosts in the private network. There are many different ways network address translation is implemented on different firewall systems. We will look at the IP masquerade method, which is used to perform NAT in Linux-based firewalls.

TYPES OF FIREWALLS

Many different firewall technologies are in use today. In this chapter we will focus on the following types:

- Packet filtering
- Proxy serving
- IP Masquerading

By combining these three technologies we can build effective firewalls on Linux systems that can match many expensive commercial firewall systems both in performance and in features.

PACKET-FILTERING FIREWALLS

One way a firewall can be implemented is by running it as a packet-filtering router. This is a very powerful capability and is used to implement many firewall functions. Packet-filtering capability is built into the Linux kernel.

Packet filtering is a process in which each datagram, or packet of data, routed through the router is examined against a set of rules. The filtering rules are based on packet header information, which is available to the IP forwarding process of the kernel. The IP packet header provides the following information:

- IP source address
- IP destination address
- The protocol: UDP, TCP, ICMP, or IP Tunnel
- The source port for UDP or TCP
- The destination port for UDP or TCP
- The ICMP message type
- The incoming interface of the packet
- The outgoing interface of the packet

Packet-filtering rules can use any of the fields in the IP header to permit or deny a packet from being forwarded to its destination interface.

Packet-filtering rules are used in firewalls to permit or deny traffic based on service type, source IP addresses, and destination IP address. Most Internet services use well-known ports to provide specific services. For example the FTP service uses TCP ports 20 and 21, while Telnet uses TCP port 23, SMTP uses TCP port 25, and DNS uses UDP port 53. Some services use a default port, but can be configured to use another. For example, the default HTTP port is TCP port 80 but it can easily be configured to use any arbitrary TCP port.

With packet filtering you can, for example, permit incoming SMTP traffic only to a designated mail exchanger host on the internal network and block all incoming Telnet. At the same time, incoming FTP and HTTP connections can be allowed to specific FTP and Web servers. With packet filtering these rules are easy to define and implement.

Packet filtering is also used to protect against IP spoofing attacks. In IP spoofing, the attacker sends packets from the outside that pretend to originate from internal hosts; in other words, the packet header falsely contains the source address of an internal host. This kind of attack can be easily detected and the packets discarded; the router simply checks packets arriving on external network interfaces and if their source address is that of an internal host, the packets are not permitted entry to the network.

Packet filtering is also useful for defending against tiny fragment and source routing attacks. Tiny fragment attacks use the IP fragmentation feature to create very small packets that split the TCP header information into separate packet fragments. The purpose behind this kind of attack is to trick filtering rules, which after permitting the initial fragment, might let subsequent fragments pass through without further examination. Tiny fragment attacks can be avoided by denying all TCP packets that have the IP `FragmentOffset` header set to 1. Similarly, creating rules that discard all packets that contain the source route option can defeat source routing attacks.

Several advantages and disadvantages to packet filtering are outlined in Table 19.1.

TABLE 19.1   PRINCIPAL ADVANTAGES AND DISADVANTAGES OF PACKET-FILTERING FIREWALLS

Advantages	Disadvantages
Low overhead	Does not examine a packet's payload, only the header
Low latency	
Transparent to users and applications	
Efficient	

PROXY SERVER FIREWALLS

Proxy servers are used primarily to monitor and control outbound traffic. For example, you can run the squid proxy server to cache Web and FTP data for all users in your network. This can lower the Internet bandwidth requirement and speed up access by supplying the cached data. Proxies also provide detailed logs of all data transfers. Because proxy servers can examine the payload of packets, they can also be used to filter inappropriate content.

There are two types of proxy servers:

- **Applications proxy servers**—These provide separate proxy services for each protocol that needs to be run through the proxy server. A typical example of an application proxy server is the squid proxy server that provides HTTP and FTP application proxy servers. Squid is available at `http://www.squid-cache.org/`.

- **SOCKS proxy servers**—These provide generalized proxy services for applications which know how to communicate with a SOCKS proxy server. Information about SOCKS proxy servers is available at `http://www.socks.nec.com/`.

IP MASQUERADING PROXY SERVERS

Linux uses IP masquerading to provide the functionality of one-to-many NAT (Network Address Translation). NAT provides two major benefits as a firewall tool:

- Using addresses that are not routed over the Internet for a private network makes the internal network into a black box that cannot be directly examined from the Internet. The topology of the internal network is hidden from external networks, which enhances the security of the internal network significantly.

- The need for a large number of registered valid IP addresses for each host on your network is eliminated and only a small number of valid addresses is required.

IP masquerading allows all internal machines to hide behind the firewall machine and use its IP address to access the Internet. To all machines on the Internet the traffic from the internal hosts appears to originate from the single masquerading firewall machine. This provides a foundation for a very secure internal network. The Internet only sees the well-secured firewall machine and nothing beyond that. Breaking through a properly secured Linux IP masquerading host into the internal network is an extremely difficult task generally considered virtually impossible.

PART
IV

CH
19

Note   The key here is that your IP masquerading firewall must be properly configured and secured. If it is incorrectly configured and secured, your internal network can easily be as accessible as if you had no firewall at all.

FIREWALLS AND NETWORK ARCHITECTURE

There are different ways to structure the network architecture to use a firewall. The simplest architecture is to have two networks, an internal network and external network, with the firewall system sitting between these networks, as illustrated in Figure 19.1.

Figure 19.1
A firewall connecting an internal network to the Internet.

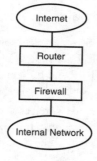

A typical corporate firewall architecture will most likely include several additional networks in addition to the internal and external networks. Commonly a separate network is created to house the public access servers, such as Mail, DNS, FTP, and Web servers, and this network is generally referred to, in firewalling jargon, as the demilitarized zone or DMZ network. The DMZ network is configured to provide limited access from the Internet to specific public information servers. In addition there can be a network to house the remote access servers and modem pools, which we will call the RAS network. If your company subscribes to private financial services such as Bloomberg, you might need additional network legs on the firewall to support them. Figure 19.2 illustrates a typical corporate network firewall architecture.

Figure 19.2
A typical corporate network firewall architecture.

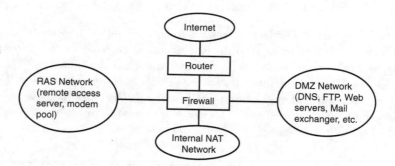

The purpose of creating these different networks is to allow the application of different sets of security rules to these various networks.

For example, one security policy might be as follows:

- The internal network has unrestricted access to all services on DMZ and Internet
- Internet hosts are
  - Denied all access to the Private Internal Network
  - Allowed access to the DMZ Mail exchanger on TCP port 25
  - Allowed access to the DMZ DNS server on UDP port 53
  - Allowed access to the DMZ Web server on TCP port 80
  - Allowed access to the DMZ FTP server on TCP ports 20 and 21
- News feed hosts are allowed access to the DMZ News server on port 119
- DMZ hosts have the following allowances:
  - DMZ mail exchanger is allowed access to internal mail server on TCP port 25
  - DMZ DNS server is allowed access to Internal DNS server on UDP port 53
- The RAS Network consists of RAS servers that use Caller-ID verification and allow authenticated dial-in access from authorized employee home phones. The modem pool in the RAS network only allows dial-in access using callback to authorized employee home phones. Authentication is done on Radius servers. RAS has the following allowances:
  - Remote Access Servers are allowed access to Radius server on the appropriate ports
  - The RAS network is allowed access to internal mail server.
  - The RAS network is allowed Telnet access to specific internal hosts

PART
IV

CH
19

Caution

Many sites permit dial-in access to modems located at various points throughout the site. This is a potential back door and defeats all the protection provided by the firewall. A proper way to provide dial-in access is to place dial-in servers outside the firewall and apply security rules to them just as any other inbound connection. Using caller-ID verification and callback to authorized numbers, in addition to password authentication, is obligatory to provide secure dial-in access.

Note

This security scheme is just a suggested guideline. You must decide what security policy meets your organization's needs and devise your own firewall rules.

SETTING UP A LINUX FIREWALL

In the following sections we will describe how to compile, install, and configure a Linux firewall system that features IP packet filtering using IPCHAINS and IP masquerading to provide for a secure private NAT network.

Note

> The examples in this chapter are based on Linux version 2.2.14. Do not use a kernel source version earlier than 2.2.11. An IPCHAINS fragmentation bug existed in kernels older than 2.2.11.

To configure the kernel for firewalling, which will include IP packet filtering using IPCHAINS and network address translation using IP masquerading, the following options must be enabled:

- **CONFIG_EXPERIMENTAL**—This option allows the kernel to create the masquerading modules and enable the option for port forwarding.
- **CONFIG_MODULES**—This option allows loading of kernel IP masquerading modules.
- **CONFIG_NET**—This option enables the network subsystem.
- **CONFIG_PACKET**—This options allows tcpdump to be used to debug IP masquerading problems.
- **CONFIG_NETLINK**—This option allows logging of firewall hits.
- **CONFIG_FIREWALL**—This option enables the IPCHAINS firewall tool.
- **CONFIG_INET**—This option enables the TCP/IP protocol.
- **CONFIG_IP_ROUTE_VERBOSE**—This option is useful if you want to drop IP spoofed packets at the router.
- **CONFIG_IP_FIREWALL**—This option enables firewalling.
- **CONFIG_IP_FIREWALL_NETLINK**—This option enhances logging of firewall hits.
- **CONFIG_IP_ALWAYS_DEFRAG**—This option is required to enable IP masquerading or transparent proxy features and also optimizes IP masquerading connections.
- **CONFIG_IP_MASQUERADE**—This option enables IP Masquerading to re-address internal TCP/IP packets to external ones.
- **CONFIG_IP_MASQUERADE_ICMP**—This option enables support for ICMP ping packets which is useful for troubleshooting.
- **CONFIG_IP_MASQUERADE_MOD**—This option makes it possible to enable TCP/IP Port forwarding to allow external computers to directly connect to specific internal masqueraded systems.
- **CONFIG_IP_MASQUERADE_IPPORTFW**—This option enables TCP/IP port forwarding to allow external computers to directly connect to specific internal masqueraded systems.

- **CONFIG_IP_ROUTER**—This option optimizes the kernel for the network subsystem although significant performance benefits have yet to be documented.
- **CONFIG_SYN_COOKIES**—This is useful for basic network security.
- **CONFIG_NETDEVICES**—This option enables the Linux network subsystem.
- **CONFIG_DUMMY**—This option helps when debugging problems.
- **CONFIG_PROC_FS**—This option is required to enable the Linux network forwarding system.

The kernel should be compiled with these options enabled as outlined in Chapter 11, "Building the Linux Kernel."

After the kernel is installed and the system is rebooted, the IPCHAINS and IP masquerading features should be available. This can be checked by looking for the files `/proc/net/ip_fwchains` and `/proc/net/ip_masquerade`. If the files exist then the features are enabled.

IP PACKET FILTERING AND IP MASQUERADING USING IPCHAINS

The `ipchains` tool is used to add and remove rules from the kernel's packet filtering section.

> **Tip**
>
> In older kernels (version 2.0.x), `ipfwadm` was used instead of `ipchains`. If you are running the older kernel, it is highly recommended that you upgrade to a 2.2.x version kernel that uses the newer firewall code and `ipchains`.

The kernel has three built-in lists of rules, referred to as chains. These are the `input`, `output`, and `forward` chains. When a packet arrives, for example on the external Ethernet interface of the firewall, the kernel uses the input chain to decide what to do with the packet. If it is permitted to pass according to the rules in this chain, the kernel routes the packet. If the packet is destined for another machine, the kernel consults the forward chain before forwarding. Finally, when the packet is ready to go out, the kernel consults the output chain.

A chain is a list of rules. Each rule is equivalent to an `if-then` statement. The `if` part of the rule tries to match the packet header to a specified criteria. If the `if` part of the rule matches, the `then` part of the rule is applied. If there is no match, the packet is examined by the next rule in the chain. Finally after all the rules of the chain have been applied, the kernel consults the chain policy to decide the fate of the packet. The final fate is usually to permit or deny the packet.

In addition to using the kernel's built-in chains, you can define your own chains. The built-in chains (`input`, `output`, and `forward`) cannot be deleted.

The `ipchains` command takes several flags. A brief description of the `ipchains` flags is provided in Table 19.2. For full details of the `ipchains` command refer to the online manual page by running `man ipchains`.

TABLE 19.2 FLAGS OF THE ipchains COMMAND

Flag	Description
-N	Create a new chain
-X	Delete an empty chain
-L	List the rules in a chain
-F	Flush the rules out of a chain
-Z	Zero the packet and byte counters of all rules in a chain
-A	Append a new rule to a chain
-I	Insert a rule at some position in a chain
-R	Replace a rule at some position in a chain
-D	Delete a rule at some position in a chain
-M -L	List the currently masqueraded connections
-M -S	Set masquerading timeout values
-C	Check packet against the selected chain
-s [!] *<address>/<mask>*	Specify a source IP address/netmask
-d [!]*<address>/<mask>*	Specify a destination IP address/netmask
-p [!] *<protocol>*	Specify a protocol
-j	Specify a target to jump to
-I	Name of the network interface
[!] -f	Rule refers to only second or further fragments of fragmented packets
-b	Bi-directional—Rule matches IP packets in both directions
-v	Verbose output
-n	Print IP addresses and port numbers in numeric format
-l	Turn on kernel logging of matched packets
-o *<maxsize>*	Copy matched packets to user space device
-m *<markvalue>*	Mark matched packets
-t *<mask>*	Mask used to modify TOS field
-x -L	Display exact value of the packet and byte counters
[!] -y	Only match packets with the SYN bit set

Adding a Rule

A rule can be added using the -A (append), -I (insert), and -R (replace) options of the ipchains command. A rule specifies a set of conditions a packet must meet. For example, to deny all ping packets coming from the IP address 10.0.0.1, add the following rule to the input chain:

```
# ipchains -A input -s 10.0.0.1 -p icmp -j DENY
```

Here -A input indicates that the rule should be appended to the input chain, -s 10.10.10.1 specifies the source address to which the rule applies, -p icmp specifies the protocol of packets to which the rule applies, and -j DENY indicates that when packets match this rule, ipchains should jump to a target named DENY.

You can verify that this rule has been added to the input chain by listing rules in the input chain as follows:

```
# ipchains -n -L input
Chain input (policy ACCEPT):
target     prot opt    source          destination        ports
DENY       icmp ------  10.0.0.1        0.0.0.0/0          * ->    *
```

Deleting a Rule

A rule can be deleted in one of two ways: by specifying the exact rule number in the chain or by specifying the exact rule. If we know the rule we want to delete is the first rule in the input chain, we can delete it with the following command:

```
# ipchains -D input 1
```

Alternately, if we know the rule definition we can delete the rule in the same way we appended a rule while replacing the -A flag with -D. For example, the following command deletes the rules we previously appended to the input chain:

```
# ipchains -D input input -s 10.0.0.1 -p icmp -j DENY
```

Specifying Source and Destination IP Addresses

Source or destination IP addresses can be specified in rules in several ways:

- As simple IP addresses as in the case of 10.10.10.1.
- As a combination of an IP address and a network mask as in the case of 10.10.10.1/255.255.255.0.
- As a combination of an IP address and the number of bits which belong to the network portion of the address as in 10.10.10.1/24.

To specify any and all IP addresses, the address and network mask combination should be specified as 0.0.0.0/0 or 0.0.0.0/0.0.0.0.

PART
IV

CH
19

SPECIFYING PROTOCOLS

Protocols are specified with the -p flag as names or numbers. When protocols are specified by name, case does not matter; for instance udp and UDP indicate the same protocol.

SPECIFYING UDP AND TCP PORTS

When UDP or TCP protocols are specified, an extra argument can be passed to specify the UDP or TCP port number, or a range of port numbers. For instance, the following command accepts TCP packets destined for the host 10.10.10.1 on the WWW port (which is port 80):

```
# ipchains -A input -p TCP -d 10.10.10.1/24 www -j ACCEPT
```

The following command uses a range of ports to deny access to packets destined for the host 10.10.10.1 between ports 6000 and 6009:

```
# ipchains -A input -p TCP -d 10.10.10.1/24 6000:6009 -j DENY
```

Open-ended port ranges can also be defined as in the following command, which defines a rule to deny all packets bound for any host below port 1024:

```
# ipchains -A input -p TCP -d 0.0.0.0/0 :1023 -j DENY
```

SPECIFYING INVERSION

Many ipchains flags such as -s, -d, and -p can be preceded with the ! (not) flag, to invert the meaning of the match. For instance, using ! 10.10.10.1 in a rule will mean all other IP addresses except 10.10.10.1.

The following example allows WWW traffic to all destination IP addresses except 10.10.10.1:

```
# ipchains -A input -p TCP -d ! 10.10.10.1 www -j ACCEPT
```

Similarly, the following rule allows all incoming traffic except WWW traffic to all destination hosts:

```
# ipchains -A input -p TCP -d 0.0.0.0/0 ! www -j ACCEPT
```

SPECIFYING ICMP TYPE AND CODE

Several ICMP packet types are used for different purposes such as the ping command and routing. The ipchains -h icmp command will display a list of all ICMP type names. Table 19.3 lists commonly used ICMP packet types and their respective names and codes.

TABLE 19.3   COMMONLY USED ICMP PACKET TYPES AND CODES

Number	Name	Required By
0	echo-reply	ping
3	destination-unreachable	Any TCP/UDP traffic
5	redirect	routing

TABLE 19.3   CONTINUED

Number	Name	Required By
8	echo-request	ping
11	time-exceeded	traceroute

Note

The ! (not) flag cannot be used for ICMP names.

Tip

Do not block ICMP type 3 messages. They are used by TCP and UDP applications. ICMP packets are used to indicate failure for protocols such as TCP and UDP. If you block these packets you will never receive Host unreachable or No route to host errors; connections will just wait for a reply that never comes. While not fatal in most cases, the failure to receive these messages can be irritating and problematic when troubleshooting connectivity problems.

ICMP packets are also used in MTU discovery. The TCP implementations in Linux use MTU discovery to calculate the largest packet size that can be sent to a destination without fragmenting. Fragmenting slows performance, especially when occasional fragments are lost. MTU discovery works by sending packets with the Don't Fragment bit set, and then sending smaller packets if it gets an ICMP packet indicating Fragmentation Needed But DF Set (fragmentation-needed). This is a type of destination-unreachable packet, and if it is never received, the local host will not reduce MTU, and performance will be extremely poor or non-existent.

PART
IV

CH
19

It is common to block all ICMP redirect messages (type 5) because these can be used to manipulate routing. However good IP stacks have safeguards against this type of manipulation, and therefore this is generally not considered a significant risk.

SPECIFYING AN INTERFACE

The interface to match is specified with the -i option. An interface is the physical device on which a packet arrives or through which a packet leaves the firewall system. The input chain controls the interface for incoming packets. The output chain and the forward chain control the interface for outgoing packets.

You can specify an interface that currently does not exist, but is expected to be operational in the future. When the interface comes up, any existing rules will begin applying to that interface. This is very useful for dial-up PPP links where interfaces come into existence and then cease to exist with regularity.

An interface name that ends with a + will match all interfaces which begin with that string. For example, the eth+ option will match all Ethernet interfaces.

The ! (not) flag can precede an interface name, which will match all interfaces other than the specified one.

SPECIFYING TCP SYN PACKETS

There can be times when you want to permit TCP connections in one direction and not the other. For example, you have an external Web server and you want to allow connections to it, but you do not want to allow connections originating from that server.

This can be achieved by blocking only those packets that are used to request a connection. These packets are called SYN packets; they have the SYN flag set, and the FIN and ACK flags cleared. By disallowing only SYN packets, connection attempts can be stopped.

The -y flag is used for this purpose: It only applies to the TCP protocol. For example, to deny TCP connection attempts from 10.10.10.1 you can use this command:

```
# ipchains -A input -p TCP -s 192.168.1.1 -y -j DENY
```

The ! (not) flag can precede the -y option to match all packets excluding the SYN packets.

FRAGMENTED PACKETS

When a packet is too large to fit in a single frame, it is divided into fragments, and sent as multiple packets. The fragments are re-assembled at the receiving end to reconstruct the whole packet.

Filtering fragments poses a difficulty because only the first fragment contains certain header information such as the source port, destinations port, ICMP type, ICMP code, and the TCP SYN flag. The second and further fragments do not have this information. Therefore filtering rules trying to match this kind of information will succeed with the first fragment but will fail to match further fragments. It is generally safe to let later fragments through, because filtering will discard the first fragment, and without it re-assembly of the packet on the target host will fail. However, bugs are known to exist that will crash a system simply by sending it lots of fragments.

If the firewall machine is the only connection to the external network, then the kernel can be compiled with the option IP: always defragment enabled. This option tells the Linux kernel to reassemble all fragments that pass through it. This is a clean solution.

The other option is to disallow all fragmented packets by specifying the -f flag in a rule as in the following example:

```
# ipchains -A output -f -d 10.10.10.1 -j DENY
```

This rule will drop any fragments destined for 10.10.10.1.

THE FILTERING PROCESS

We have looked at all the different ways rules are used to match packets. We now consider what happens when the packet matches a rule:

- The byte counter for that rule is increased by the size of the packet including header.
- The packet counter for the rule is incremented.
- If the rule requested logging, the packet is logged.
- If the rule requested it, the packet's Type Of Service field is changed.
- If the rule requested it, the packet is marked (only in 2.2.x kernels).
- The rule target is examined to decide the fate of the packet.

The target tells the kernel what to do with a packet that matches a rule. The -j flag of the ipchains command is used to specify the name of the target. The target name can be a maximum of eight characters in length, and it is case sensitive.

It is possible to specify a rule with no target. These are sometimes called accounting rules, and are used to count particular types of packets. For example, to count the number of packets from 10.10.10.1 you can create a new rule as follows:

```
# ipchains -N mycntr
# ipchains -A mycntr -s 10.10.10.1
# ipchains -A input -j mycntr
```

Now send some test ping packets to 10.10.10.1 and check the counters by running ipchains with the -L, -v, and -n flags as follows:

```
# ping -c 5  10.10.10.1
# ipchains -L mycntr -v -n
Chain mycntr (1 references):
pkts bytes target prot opt tosa tosx ifname mark outsize source          destination
➥ports
   5   420 -       all --- 0xFF 0x00 *                      10.10.10.1   0.0.0.0/0   n/a
```

This report shows 5 packets and 420 bytes received from source IP 10.10.10.1. The -n flag displays the IP addresses in numeric format.

There are six pre-defined targets. The first three targets are ACCEPT, REJECT, and DENY. ACCEPT allows a packet through. DENY drops a packet as if it had never been received. REJECT drops a packet, and if it is not an ICMP packet, sends a destination-unreachable ICMP reply to the source.

The target MASQ tells the kernel to masquerade the packet. The kernel must be compiled with IP masquerading enabled for this to work. This target is only valid for packets traversing the forward chain.

The target REDIRECT tells the kernel to send a packet to a local port instead of its original destination. This can only be used with rules specifying TCP or UDP as their protocol. Optionally, a port (name or number) can be specified following -j REDIRECT, which will cause the packet to be redirected to that particular port, even if it was addressed to another port. This target is only valid for packets traversing the input chain.

The last pre-defined target is RETURN, which is identical to falling off the end of the chain immediately.

Any other target indicates a user-defined chain. The packet will begin traversing the rules in that chain. If that chain does not decide the fate of the packet, traversal continues with the next rule in the current chain.

To understand how rules are traversed let us look at the following example. Consider two chains: the built-in `input` chain and a user-defined chain called `mycntr`.

The `input` chain consists of three rules:

- `-j mycntr`
- `-p TCP -j ACCEPT`
- `-p UDP -j REJECT`

The `mycntr` chain has one rule. It is an accounting rule specifying a source address `-s 10.10.10.1`.

Consider a `ping` reply packet originating from `10.10.10.1`. It enters the `input` chain and gets tested against rule 1. It matches, and jumps to the user-defined chain `mycntr`. Rule 1 in `mycntr` matches, but no target is specified, so the counters are incremented and it returns to Rule 2 of the `input` chain. It then traverses the second and third rules of the input chain.

LOGGING

The `-l` flag can be specified in a rule to request logging of the matching packet. In general you will not want to log all packets, as that would create very large logs and have a negative impact on performance. However, it is a useful feature to be able to track exceptional packets.

For instance, to log rejected ICMP ping packets from source address `192.115.144.5`, use the following commands:

```
# ipchains -N TEST
# ipchains -A TEST -p ICMP -s 192.115.144.5 -l -j REJECT
# ipchains -A input -j TEST
# ping 192.115.144.5
```

A sample packet log by these rules is shown here:

```
Jan 28 22:54:11 linux kernel: Packet log: TEST REJECT eth0 PROTO= \
1 192.115.144.5 :0 10.2.0.252:0 L=84 S=0x00 I=41553 F=0x4000 T=252 (#1)
```

The log message can be broken down as follows:

- **TEST**—The chain that contained the rule that matched the packet, causing the log message.
- **REJECT**—The target specified by the rule.
- **eth0**—The interface name. Because this was the input chain, it means that the packet arrived on `eth0`.
- **PROTO=1**—This means that the packet was protocol 1.
- **192.115.144.5**—The packet's source IP address. And `:0` means it was an ICMP `echo-reply` packet.

- ■ **10.2.0.252**—The destination IP address and **:0** means an ICMP echo-reply was requested.
- ■ **L=84**—Indicates that the packet was 84 bytes long.
- ■ **S=0x00**—This is the Type of Service field.
- ■ **I=41553**—This is the IP ID.
- ■ **F=0x4000**—This is the 16-bit fragment offset plus flags.
- ■ **T=252**—This is the Time To Live of the packet. One is subtracted from this value for every hop, and it usually starts at 15 or 255.
- ■ **(#1)**—This indicates that rule number 1 in the TEST chain caused the packet log entry.

TYPE OF SERVICE

Four bits called the type of service (TOS) bits are in the IP header. These bits can be manipulated to change the way packets are treated. The four bits are Minimum Delay, Maximum Throughput, Maximum Reliability, and Minimum Cost. Only one of these bits can be set.

The most common use for the TOS bits is to set Telnet and FTP control connections to Minimum Delay and FTP data to Maximum Throughput. This can be done as follows:

```
# ipchains -A output -p tcp -d 0.0.0.0/0 telnet -t 0x01 0x10
# ipchains -A output -p tcp -d 0.0.0.0/0 ftp -t 0x01 0x10
# ipchains -A output -p tcp -s 0.0.0.0/0 ftp-data -t 0x01 0x08
```

The -t flag takes two parameters, both in hexadecimal. These allow alteration of the TOS bits: The first mask is ANDed with the packet's current TOS, and the second mask is XORed with it. Table 19.4 lists the appropriate mask values to use to achieve the desired outcome.

TABLE 19.4   TYPE OF SERVICE BITS

TOS Name	Value	Typical Uses
Minimum Delay	0x01 0x10	ftp, telnet
Maximum Throughput	0x01 0x08	ftp-data
Maximum Reliability	0x01 0x04	snmp
Minimum Cost	0x01 0x02	nntp

PART
IV

CH
19

WORKING WITH CHAINS

User-defined chains can be named in any way given that the maximum length of the name is 8 characters and names are case sensitive.

New chains are created with the -N flag. For instance, to create a chain named mychain, use the following command:

```
# ipchains -N mychain
```

Chains can be deleted with the -X flag as follows:

```
# ipchains -X mychain
```

Chains must be empty before they can be deleted. Also the built-in chains input, output, and forward cannot be deleted.

All rules can be flushed out of a chain using the -F flag as follows:

```
# ipchains -F mychain
```

If a chain is not specified all chains are flushed.

Chains can be listed using the -L flag as follows:

```
# ipchains -L
Chain input (policy ACCEPT):
target     prot opt    source                destination   ports
mycntr     all  ------ anywhere              anywhere      n/a
TEST       all  ------ anywhere              anywhere      n/a
Chain forward (policy ACCEPT):
Chain output (policy ACCEPT):
Chain mycntr (1 references):
target     prot opt    source                destination   ports
-          all  ------ bwc.bwc.org           anywhere      n/a
Chain TEST (1 references):
target     prot opt    source                destination   ports
REJECT     icmp ----1- storm.bwc.org         anywhere      any -> any
```

When the -v option is used with -L more details about the packets and counter are displayed. Using the -n option causes numeric IP addresses to be displayed instead of hostnames.

The counters can be reset to zero using the -Z flag.

SETTING CHAIN POLICY

Each chain can have a policy that acts as a default target for packets. The policies can be any of the first four special targets: ACCEPT, DENY, REJECT, or MASQ. MASQ is only valid for the forward chain.

NETWORK ADDRESS TRANSLATION USING IP MASQUERADE

IP Masquerade is a networking feature in Linux that performs the one-to-many Network Address Translation (NAT) function found in many commercial routers and firewalls. Masquerading enhances network security. It hides many internal hosts behind one IP address on the firewall. This allows for the use of private network addresses for hosts in the internal network. The non-routable private IP addresses are translated to the IP address of the firewall by the IP Masquerading Linux kernel, when they communicate with hosts on the Internet. IP Masquerade is very powerful and flexible. It has filtering and accounting capabilities that can be configured to work with complex network topologies.

Linux IP Masquerade not only does pure NAT, or rewriting of IP packet headers, but also does "impure" NAT, or packet re-writing, in order to cater to services such as FTP, IRC, quake, RealAudio, CUSeeMe, VDO Live, and Microsoft PPTP from behind the firewall.

IP Port Forwarding is a variation of NAT that has been implemented in Linux under the name Port Forwarding. This is a patch against the masquerading code in recent Linux kernels that allows IP traffic to certain ports on the masquerading firewall to be forwarded to internal hosts. As in masquerading, the IP addresses are re-written so that incoming IP (TCP and UDP) packets are forwarded, and the reply packets are rewritten to appear to be coming from the firewall. See the "IP Port Forwarding" section later in the chapter for more details.

SETTING MASQUERADING PARAMETERS   The IP Masquerading flag is -M. It can be combined with -L to list currently masqueraded connections, or -S to set the masquerading parameters.

The -L command can be accompanied by -n to show numbers instead of hostnames and port names or -v to show deltas in sequence numbers for masqueraded connection.

The -S command should be followed by three timeout values, each in seconds: for TCP sessions, for TCP sessions after a FIN packet, and for UDP packets. If you don't want to change one of these values, simply give a value of 0. The default values are currently 15 minutes, 2 minutes, and 5 minutes respectively.

To change the default timeout values to

- 2 hours (=7200 seconds) timeout for TCP sessions
- 10 seconds timeout after a TCP FIN packet is received
- 160 seconds timeout for UDP traffic

the following ipchains command can be used:

```
# /sbin/ipchains -M -S 7200 10 160
```

SAVING AND RESTORING DEFINED CHAINS WITH ipchains-save **AND** ipchains-restore

After you have defined your firewall chains using the ipchains commands, they are installed in memory and will be lost after you reboot the system. Two scripts are available to save the defined ipchains to a file and later restore them at boot time.

ipchains-save is a script that saves the currently defined chains to a file. ipchains-save can save a single chain or all chains. If no chain names are specified, all chains are saved. If the -v flag is specified with ipchains-save, it prints the rules to STDERR as the chains are being saved. The policies for input, output and forward chains are also saved:

```
# ipchains-save > firewall-rules
Saving `input'.
Saving `output'.
Saving `forward'.
Saving `mychain'.
```

ipchains-restore restores chains that have been saved with ipchains-save. ipchains-restore has two flags: -v and -f. The -v flag causes the script to describe each rule as it is being added. If a user-defined chain is found in the input chain, ipchains-restore checks if that chain already exists. If it does, ipchains-restore will prompt if the chains should be flushed or if restoring the chain should be skipped. Specifying the `-f` flag to `ipchains-restore` causes the user-defined chains to be quietly flushed and no prompting occurs. To use the command, provide the contents of a file containing saved chains on the standard input:

```
# ipchains-restore < firewall-rules
Restoring `input'.
Restoring `output'.
Restoring `forward'.
Restoring `mychain1'.
Chain `mychain1' already exists. Skip or flush? [S/f]? s
Skipping `mychain1'.
Restoring `mychain2'.
Chain `mychain2' already exists. Skip or flush? [S/f]? f
Flushing `mychain2'.
```

PUTTING IT ALL TOGETHER

We will now consider a complete example of a firewall implementing IP packet filtering and IP masquerading. There are many ways to setup firewall rules, and we will cover one such method.

Note

This is just an example offered to illustrate typical firewall rules; you must adapt it to suit the requirements of your site.

Our example firewalled network is shown in Figure 19.3.

This example network comprises an internal masqueraded network, a demilitarized zone, and an external network that connects to the Internet. The firewall machine has three Ethernet interfaces connecting these three networks. The name of the firewall machine is FW.

The external network connects the firewall to a router that connects to the Internet through the ISP's router. The name of the external network is EXT. This network uses four IP addresses in the range from 192.115.144.16 through 192.115.144.19. The network mask for this network is 255.255.255.252. The IP address of the external Ethernet interface of the firewall (`eth0`) is 192.115.144.17/255.255.255.252.

The name of the masqueraded internal network is PRIV, indicating it is a network using private IP addresses. This is a Class A private network using the 10.0.0.0/255.0.0.0 address range. The IP address of the Ethernet interface (`eth1`) on the firewall serving this network is 10.0.0.1/255.0.0.0. If you want to use a Class B or Class C private network instead, you can adjust the network mask appropriately.

The public servers will sit in the demilitarized zone. The name of this network is DMZ. This network uses registered Internet IP addresses. This network is sub-netted to use 16 IP addresses ranging from 192.115.144.0 through 192.115.144.15. The network mask for this network is 255.255.255.240. There are four servers in the DMZ network:

Figure 19.3
A firewalled
network.

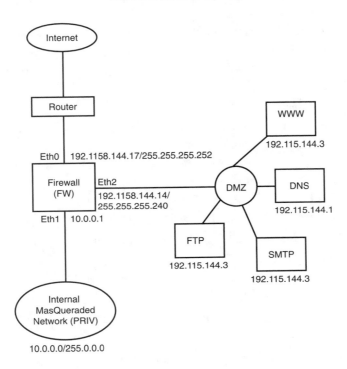

External Network (EXT)

- A DNS server with IP address 192.115.144.1/255.255.255.240
- A SMTP mail server with IP address 192.115.144.2/255.255.255.240
- An FTP server with IP address 192.115.144.3/255.255.255.240
- A WWW server with IP address 192.115.144.4/255.255.255.240

> **Note**
>
> The Internet IP addresses used here are registered with the Baha' World Centre in Haifa, Israel. Make sure you do not try using any of them in your own scripts because they will not work. Replace the IP addresses on the DMZ and EXT networks with IP addresses appropriate for your network.

The first order of business is to record the security policy that we want to enforce on this firewalled network. The security goals of the various components of the firewalled network are stated here:

- **Firewall Machine (FW):**
  - Secure the firewall machine.
  - Protect the network interfaces of the firewall machine from IP spoofing.

- The firewall machine must be able to ping any network. This is useful to test network connectivity.
- The firewall machine must be able to trace-route any network. Again this is useful for diagnosis.
- The firewall machine must have access to a DNS server for name lookup.

- **The DMZ Network:**
  - Name Server:
    - Must service DNS queries from internal network, external network, and the firewall machine.
    - Must allow zone transfers to secondary DNS servers residing in the external network.
  - SMTP Mail server:
    - Must allow SMTP to external mail servers.
    - Must accept SMTP from internal and external mail servers and clients.
  - FTP server
    - Must allow FTP from internal and external hosts.
    - Web server
    - Must accept HTTP from internal and external hosts.

- **Internal Network:**
  - Must allow everything to internal machines.

SECURING THE FIREWALL MACHINE

It is extremely important to make sure the firewall machine itself is not left open to attacks. All unnecessary services must be turned off. Rename or delete the current /etc/inetd.conf file and create a new one with only one line in it as follows:

```
telnet stream tcp   nowait root /usr/sbin/in.telnetd in.telnetd
```

This allows only the Telnet service for remote management of the firewall system. Send the SIGHUP signal to inetd after creating the new inetd.conf file as outlined in Chapter 8, "Linux Process Management and Daemons."

The firewall system's /etc/passwd file and corresponding /etc/shadow file should contain the minimum necessary accounts such as root, bin, daemon, sync, shutdown, halt, and operator as well as local accounts for the firewall administrators. The system should not be used for any purposes other than firewall administration and operation. The system should not be part of an NIS domain.

Direct root login to the firewall system through Telnet should be prohibited. Passwords should be secure (for instance, you could enforce a policy including minimum password lengths, non-use of dictionary words, and combinations of upper- and lowercase letters with numbers and punctuation) and should change frequently (even as often as every three months).

X Windows as well as unneeded daemons including `nfsd`, `named`, `dhcpd`, `atd`, and other non-essential services should not run on the firewall system.

> **Tip**
>
> To disable particular daemons from starting at run level 3, change your current directory to `/etc/rc.d/rc3.d` and rename the links starting with uppercase s to lowercase s for each service you want to disable. For instance, to disable NFS, rename `S60nfs` to `s60nfs`.

To enhance security, consider disabling Telnet and `inetd` and installing the SSH package on the firewall system and connecting through SSH only from designated secure hosts.

SSH (secure shell) is a secure login program that should be safe to use even across the Internet. It uses strong cryptography to protect all transmitted data including passwords, binary files, and administrative commands.

The SSH package can be downloaded from `ftp://ftp.cs.hut.fi/pub/ssh`. The latest stable version at the time of this writing is 2.0.13. Download `ssh-2.0.13.tar.gz`, configure, compile, and install it. Read the file `SSH2.QUICKSTART` that comes with the package. It provides instructions about how to build and install the package, generate the public and private keys, install keys on local and remote systems, and edit the `/etc/ssh2/sshd2-config` file to allow only designated hosts to connect to a machine. Finally, remember to create a `bootup` script to start `/usr/local/sbin/sshd` at boot time.

> **Note**
>
> SSH is not open source software. It is for non-commercial and educational use but is not freely available for any other use or redistribution.

Part

IV

Ch

19

Protect Against IP Spoofing

To protect the firewall machine and subsequently the networks attached to it from IP spoofing, anti-spoofing can be turned on for all interfaces using the kernel's built-in anti-spoofing feature. To do this, run the following command:

```
# for f in /proc/sys/net/ipv4/conf/*/rp_filter; do echo 1 > $f; done
```

Set Up Filtering Rules

When setting up the filtering rules, the safest approach is to deny all traffic until the firewall rules are in place. Then you can allow permitted traffic to come into your various networks only after you have defined all your chains and rules.

To deny all traffic except loopback traffic on the firewall system, use the following commands:

```
# ipchains -A input -i ! lo -j DENY
# ipchains -A output -i ! lo -j DENY
# ipchains -A forward -j DENY
```

If specific protocol masquerading modules need to be loaded, they should be loaded next. The per-protocol modules can be loaded using the depmod and modprobe commands as follows:

```
# /sbin/depmod -a
# /sbin/modprobe ip_masq_ftp
# /sbin/modprobe ip_masq_raudio
# /sbin/modprobe ip_masq_irc
# /sbin/modprobe ip_masq_quake ports=26000,27000,27910,27960
# /sbin/modprobe ip_masq_cuseeme
# /sbin/modprobe ip_masq_vdolive
```

> **Note**
>
> You only need to load the modules for protocols that you want to support at your site.

At this point you must enable IP forwarding, which is disabled by default.

For Red Hat Linux, this can be done by changing the variable FORWARD_IPV4=false to FORWARD_IPV4=true in /etc/sysconfig/network.

For other Linux systems this is achieved by setting the value of the kernel parameter ip_forward to 1 by executing the following command:

```
# echo "1" > /proc/sys/net/ipv4/ip_forward
```

Because we are using IP masquerading it is best to filter using the forward chain. We will split the forward chain into various user-defined chains based on the three networks attached to the firewall machine.

The user-defined chains are created using ipchains -N. The names of the chains are chosen based on their source and destination networks as follows:

```
# ipchains -N priv-dmz
# ipchains -N dmz-priv
# ipchains -N ext-dmz
# ipchains -N dmz-ext
# ipchains -N priv-ext
# ipchains -N ext-priv
```

After the chains have been created, the forward chain must be configured to call these user-defined chains. The forward chain is only known to the outgoing interface; therefore, the source address of packets must be examined to determine where the packet originated. Because the system is protected against IP spoofing, there is no risk in using the source address instead of the incoming interface to determine the origin of packets. The following rules direct all outgoing packets to the appropriate chain based on their point of origin and outgoing interface:

```
# ipchains -A forward -s 10.0.0.0/255.0.0.0 -i eth2 -j priv-dmz
# ipchains -A forward -s 10.0.0.0/255.0.0.0 -i eth0 -j priv-ext
# ipchains -A forward -s 192.115.144.0/255.255.255.240 -i eth1 -j dmz-priv
# ipchains -A forward -s 192.115.144.0/255.255.255.240 -i eth0 -j dmz-ext
# ipchains -A forward -i eth2 -j ext-dmz
# ipchains -A forward -i eth1 -j ext-priv
```

Although it is unlikely that packets that don't match one of these six rules should be encountered, the following rule should be implemented to log all packets that fail to match one of the rules:

```
# ipchains -A forward -j DENY -l
```

In addition, a chain should be created to accept ICMP errors as follows:

```
# ipchains -N icmp-err
```

Packets that are one of the error ICMPs are accepted; otherwise, control passes back to the calling chain. This is achieved using the following rules:

```
# ipchains -A icmp-acc -p icmp --icmp-type destination-unreachable -j ACCEPT
# ipchains -A icmp-acc -p icmp --icmp-type source-quench -j ACCEPT
# ipchains -A icmp-acc -p icmp --icmp-type time-exceeded -j ACCEPT
# ipchains -A icmp-acc -p icmp --icmp-type parameter-problem -j ACCEPT
```

DEFINE THE priv-dmz CHAIN The priv-dmz chain is setup as follows:

```
# ipchains -A priv-dmz -p udp -d 192.115.144.1 domain -j ACCEPT
# ipchains -A priv-dmz -p tcp -d 192.115.144.1 domain -j ACCEPT
# ipchains -A priv-dmz -p tcp -d 192.115.144.2 smtp -j ACCEPT
# ipchains -A priv-dmz -p tcp -d 192.115.144.3 ftp -j ACCEPT
# ipchains -A priv-dmz -p tcp -d 192.115.144.3 ftp-data -j ACCEPT
# ipchains -A priv-dmz -p tcp -d 192.115.144.4 www -j ACCEPT
# ipchains -A priv-dmz -p icmp -j icmp-err
# ipchains -A priv-dmz -j DENY -l
```

These rules allow DNS connections to the DNS server, SMTP connections to the mail server, FTP connections to the FTP server, HTTP connections to the Web server, and ping connections to any host.

DEFINE THE ext-dmz CHAIN The ext-dmz chain is set up as follows:

```
# ipchains -A ext-dmz -p udp -d 192.115.144.1 domain -j ACCEPT
# ipchains -A ext-dmz -p tcp -d 192.115.144.1 domain -j ACCEPT
# ipchains -A ext-dmz -p tcp -d 192.115.144.2 smtp -j ACCEPT
# ipchains -A ext-dmz -p tcp -d 192.115.144.3 ftp -j ACCEPT
# ipchains -A ext-dmz -p tcp -d 192.115.144.3 ftp-data -j ACCEPT
# ipchains -A ext-dmz -p tcp -d 192.115.144.4 www -j ACCEPT
# ipchains -A ext-dmz -p icmp -j icmp-err
# ipchains -A ext-dmz -j DENY
```

These rules allow DNS connections to the DNS server, SMTP connections to the mail server, FTP connections to the FTP server, HTTP connections to the Web server, and ping connections to any host.

PART IV

CH 19

DEFINE THE priv-ext **CHAIN** The priv-ext chain is set up as follows:

```
# ipchains -A priv-ext -j MASQ
```

This rule allows all connections from the internal network to the Internet using IP masquerading.

DEFINE THE dmz-priv **CHAIN** The dmz-priv chain is set up as follows:

```
# ipchains -A dmz-priv -p udp -s 192.115.144.1 domain -j ACCEPT
# ipchains -A dmz-priv -p tcp ! -y -s 192.115.144.1 domain -j ACCEPT
# ipchains -A dmz-priv -p tcp ! -y -s 192.115.144.2 smtp -j ACCEPT
# ipchains -A dmz-priv -p tcp ! -y -s 192.115.144.3 ftp -j ACCEPT
# ipchains -A dmz-priv -p tcp ! -y -s 192.115.144.3 ftp-data -j ACCEPT
# ipchains -A dmz-priv -p tcp ! -y -s 192.115.144.4 www -j ACCEPT
# ipchains -A dmz-priv -p icmp -j icmp-acc
# ipchains -A dmz-ext -j DENY -l
```

These rules allow DNS, MAIL, FTP, Web, and ping traffic from the DMZ to the internal machines.

DEFINE THE dmz-ext **CHAIN** The dmz-ext chain is set up as follows:

```
# ipchains -A dmz-ext -p udp -s 192.115.144.1 domain -j ACCEPT
# ipchains -A dmz-ext -p tcp -s 192.115.144.1 domain -j ACCEPT
# ipchains -A dmz-ext -p tcp -s 192.115.144.2 smtp -j ACCEPT
# ipchains -A dmz-ext -p tcp -s 192.115.144.3 ftp -j ACCEPT
# ipchains -A dmz-ext -p tcp -s 192.115.144.3 ftp-data -j ACCEPT
# ipchains -A dmz-ext -p tcp ! -y -s 192.115.144.4 www -j ACCEPT
# ipchains -A dmz-ext -p icmp -j icmp-err
# ipchains -A dmz-ext -j DENY -l
```

These rules allow DNS, MAIL, FTP, Web, and ping traffic from the DMZ to external network.

DEFINE THE ext-priv **CHAIN** The ext-priv chain is set up as follows:

```
# ipchains -A ext-priv -j REJECT
```

This rule allows nothing to go from the external network (Internet) into the private internal network. The internal network uses private IP addresses and there is no way to send packets from the external network to the internal network. If you need to provide access from the Internet to a particular host in the private internal network this can be done using IP Port Forwarding (IPPORTFW).

CREATE CHAINS FOR THE FIREWALL

To filter packets coming into the firewall host itself you must filter on the input chain. This requires a chain for each destination interface as follows:

```
# ipchains -N ext-if
# ipchains -N dmz-if
# ipchains -N priv-if
```

The input chain must be configured to use the user-defined chains as follows:

```
# ipchains -A input -d 192.115.144.17 -j ext-if
# ipchains -A input -d 192.115.144.14 -j dmz-if
# ipchains -A input -d 10.0.0.1 -j priv-if
```

DEFINE THE ext-if CHAIN   The ext-if chain is set up as follows:

```
# ipchains -A ext-if -i ! eth0 -j DENY -l
# ipchains -A ext-if -p TCP --dport 61000:65096 -j ACCEPT
# ipchains -A ext-if -p UDP --dport 61000:65096 -j ACCEPT
# ipchains -A ext-if -p ICMP --icmp-type pong -j ACCEPT
# ipchains -A ext-if -j icmp-err
# ipchains -A ext-if -j DENY
```

These rules allow DNS, traceroute, and ping connections from any external network to the firewall machine. Linux IP masquerading code uses destination ports 61000 and above. By default 4096 ports are reserved for this purpose, thus we get the range 61000-65096. Therefore we have the rules to accept all UDP and TCP packets marked with these destination ports.

DEFINE THE dmz-if CHAIN   The dmz-if chain is set up as follows:

```
# ipchains -A dmz-if -i ! eth2 -j DENY
# ipchains -A dmz-if -p TCP ! -y -s 192.115.144.1 domain -j ACCEPT
# ipchains -A dmz-if -p UDP -s 192.115.144.1 domain -j ACCEPT
# ipchains -A dmz-if -p ICMP --icmp-type pong -j ACCEPT
# ipchains -A dmz-if -j icmp-err
# ipchains -A dmz-if -j DENY -l
```

These rules allow DNS replies, ping replies, and ICMP errors to the firewall from the DMZ.

DEFINE THE priv-if CHAIN   The priv-if chain is set up as follows:

```
# ipchains -A priv-if -i ! eth1 -j DENY
# ipchains -A priv-if -p ICMP --icmp-type ping -j ACCEPT
# ipchains -A priv-if -p ICMP --icmp-type pong -j ACCEPT
# ipchains -A priv-if -j icmp-err
# ipchains -A priv-if -j DENY -l
```

These rules allow the internal interface of the firewall to receive ping replies and traceroute packets.

UNBLOCK THE input, output, AND forward CHAINS

After all the rules are defined, the blocking rules from the input, forward, and output chains can be removed as follows:

```
# ipchains -D input 1
# ipchains -D forward 1
# ipchains -D output 1
```

PART

IV

CH

19

CREATE A FIREWALL SCRIPT

After all these rules have been defined, a startup script, /etc/rc.d/init.d/firewall, must be created so that the chains and rules are re-created each time you boot your firewall system. You must add a link to this script in rc.3d directory as follows:

```
# cd /etc/rc.d/rc3.d
# ln -s /etc/rc.d/init.d/firewall S90firewall
```

Note

The name S90firewall is an example. Refer to Chapter 4, "Booting Up and Shutting Down," which explains how to add startup scripts.

The complete script should look like the following, based on the examples used in this chapter:

```
#!/bin/bash
PATH=/sbin:/usr/sbin:/bin:/usr/bin
export PATH
# Setup anti-spoofing
for f in /proc/sys/net/ipv4/conf/*/rp_filter; do echo 1 > $f; done
# Block input, output, and forward chains while firewall \
rules are being # installed
ipchains -A input -i ! lo -j DENY
ipchains -A output -i ! lo -j DENY
ipchains -A forward -j DENY
# Load protocol specific special masquerade modules
/sbin/depmod -a
/sbin/modprobe ip_masq_ftp
/sbin/modprobe ip_masq_raudio
/sbin/modprobe ip_masq_irc
/sbin/modprobe ip_masq_quake ports=26000,27000,27910,27960
/sbin/modprobe ip_masq_cuseeme
/sbin/modprobe ip_masq_vdolive
# Make sure IP forwarding is turned on
echo "1" > /proc/sys/net/ipv4/ip_forward
# Create user-defined chains
ipchains -N priv-dmz
ipchains -N dmz-priv
ipchains -N ext-dmz
ipchains -N dmz-ext
ipchains -N priv-ext
ipchains -N ext-priv
# Set up the user-defined chains to be called from the forward chain
ipchains -A forward -s 10.0.0.0/255.0.0.0 -i eth2 -j priv-dmz
ipchains -A forward -s 10.0.0.0/255.0.0.0 -i eth0 -j priv-ext
ipchains -A forward -s 192.115.144.0/255.255.255.240 -i eth1 -j dmz-priv
ipchains -A forward -s 192.115.144.0/255.255.255.240 -i eth0 -j dmz-ext
ipchains -A forward -i eth2 -j ext-dmz
ipchains -A forward -i eth1 -j ext-priv
# Log anything that doesn't match any of these
# This should never happen
ipchains -A forward -j DENY -l
```

```
# Create a chain to ACCEPT ICMP errors
ipchains -N icmp-err
ipchains -A icmp-acc -p icmp --icmp-type destination-unreachable -j ACCEPT
ipchains -A icmp-acc -p icmp --icmp-type source-quench -j ACCEPT
ipchains -A icmp-acc -p icmp --icmp-type time-exceeded -j ACCEPT
ipchains -A icmp-acc -p icmp --icmp-type parameter-problem -j ACCEPT
# priv-dmz chain
# Allow DNS to DNS server, SMTP to mail server, FTP to FTP server, HTTP #
   to Web server, and ping to any host.
ipchains -A priv-dmz -p udp -d 192.115.144.1 domain -j ACCEPT
ipchains -A priv-dmz -p tcp -d 192.115.144.1 domain -j ACCEPT
ipchains -A priv-dmz -p tcp -d 192.115.144.2 smtp -j ACCEPT
ipchains -A priv-dmz -p tcp -d 192.115.144.3 ftp -j ACCEPT
ipchains -A priv-dmz -p tcp -d 192.115.144.3 ftp-data -j ACCEPT
ipchains -A priv-dmz -p tcp -d 192.115.144.4 www -j ACCEPT
ipchains -A priv-dmz -p icmp -j icmp-err
ipchains -A priv-dmz -j DENY -l
# ext-dmz chain
# Allow DNS to DNS server, SMTP to mail server, FTP to FTP server, HTTP #
   to Web server and ping to any host.
ipchains -A ext-dmz -p udp -d 192.115.144.1 domain -j ACCEPT
ipchains -A ext-dmz -p tcp -d 192.115.144.1 domain -j ACCEPT
ipchains -A ext-dmz -p tcp -d 192.115.144.2 smtp -j ACCEPT
ipchains -A ext-dmz -p tcp -d 192.115.144.3 ftp -j ACCEPT
ipchains -A ext-dmz -p tcp -d 192.115.144.3 ftp-data -j ACCEPT
ipchains -A ext-dmz -p tcp -d 192.115.144.4 www -j ACCEPT
ipchains -A ext-dmz -p icmp -j icmp-err
ipchains -A ext-dmz -j DENY
# priv-ext chain
# Allow everything from the internal network to the Internet using IP
# masquerading.
ipchains -A priv-ext -j MASQ
# dmz-priv chain
# Allow DNS, MAIL, FTP, Web, and ping traffic from the DMZ to the
# internal machines.
ipchains -A dmz-priv -p udp -s 192.115.144.1 domain -j ACCEPT
ipchains -A dmz-priv -p tcp ! -y -s 192.115.144.1 domain -j ACCEPT
ipchains -A dmz-priv -p tcp ! -y -s 192.115.144.2 smtp -j ACCEPT
ipchains -A dmz-priv -p tcp ! -y -s 192.115.144.3 ftp -j ACCEPT
ipchains -A dmz-priv -p tcp ! -y -s 192.115.144.3 ftp-data -j ACCEPT
ipchains -A dmz-priv -p tcp ! -y -s 192.115.144.4 www -j ACCEPT
ipchains -A dmz-priv -p icmp -j icmp-acc
ipchains -A dmz-ext -j DENY -l
# dmz-ext chain
# Allow DNS, MAIL, FTP, Web, and ping traffic from DMZ to external
# network.
ipchains -A dmz-ext -p udp -s 192.115.144.1 domain -j ACCEPT
ipchains -A dmz-ext -p tcp -s 192.115.144.1 domain -j ACCEPT
ipchains -A dmz-ext -p tcp -s 192.115.144.2 smtp -j ACCEPT
ipchains -A dmz-ext -p tcp -s 192.115.144.3 ftp -j ACCEPT
ipchains -A dmz-ext -p tcp -s 192.115.144.3 ftp-data -j ACCEPT
ipchains -A dmz-ext -p tcp ! -y -s 192.115.144.4 www -j ACCEPT
ipchains -A dmz-ext -p icmp -j icmp-err
ipchains -A dmz-ext -j DENY -l
# ext-priv chain
# Reject everything from external to private internal network
ipchains -A ext-priv -j REJECT
```

```
# Create firewall interface chains
ipchains -N ext-if
ipchains -N dmz-if
ipchains -N priv-if
# Setup input chain to use the user-defined chains
ipchains -A input -d 192.115.144.17 -j ext-if
ipchains -A input -d 192.115.144.14 -j dmz-if
ipchains -A input -d 10.0.0.1 -j priv-if
# ext-if chain
# allow DNS, traceroute, and ping from any external network to the
# firewall machine.
ipchains -A ext-if -i ! eth0 -j DENY -l
ipchains -A ext-if -p TCP --dport 61000:65096 -j ACCEPT
ipchains -A ext-if -p UDP --dport 61000:65096 -j ACCEPT
ipchains -A ext-if -p ICMP --icmp-type pong -j ACCEPT
ipchains -A ext-if -j icmp-err
ipchains -A ext-if -j DENY
# dmz-if chain
# Allow DNS replies, ping replies and ICMP errors to the firewall from
# the DMZ.
ipchains -A dmz-if -i ! eth2 -j DENY
ipchains -A dmz-if -p TCP ! -y -s 192.115.144.1 domain -j ACCEPT
ipchains -A dmz-if -p UDP -s 192.115.144.1 domain -j ACCEPT
ipchains -A dmz-if -p ICMP --icmp-type pong -j ACCEPT
ipchains -A dmz-if -j icmp-err
ipchains -A dmz-if -j DENY -l
# priv-if chain
# Allow the internal interface of the firewall to receive ping replies
# and traceroute packets.
ipchains -A priv-if -i ! eth1 -j DENY
ipchains -A priv-if -p ICMP --icmp-type ping -j ACCEPT
ipchains -A priv-if -p ICMP --icmp-type pong -j ACCEPT
ipchains -A priv-if -j icmp-err
ipchains -A priv-if -j DENY -l
# Unblock input, output, and forward chains
ipchains -D input 1
ipchains -D forward 1
ipchains -D output 1
```

IP PORT FORWARDING

IP port forwarding is needed if you must provide access to an internal masqueraded host from the Internet. As a general rule, it is preferable to locate the servers that need access from the Internet in your DMZ network. However, this might not always be possible and you might have to devise a way to access one of your internal masqueraded servers from the external network.

This is best done on Linux kernel 2.2.x, using a tool called ipmasqadm. You must also select the IPPORTFW option when compling the Linux kernel for the IP port-forwarding feature to be available. You can download the package ipmasqadm-0.4.2.tar.gz from http://juanjox.kernelnotes.org.

Next, unpack the source in /usr/src and compile and install the ipmasqadm tool as follows:

```
# cd /usr/src
# tar xvzf  ipmasqadm-0.4.2.tar.gz
# cd ipmasqadm-0.4.2
# make
# make install
```

This will install the ipmasqadm tool in /usr/sbin, and the modules autofw.so, mfw.so, portfw.so, and user.so in /usr/lib/ipmasqadm. A manual page for ipmasqadm is also installed in /usr/man/man8.

IP port forwarding is best illustrated by an example. Consider an HTTP server in your internal masqueraded network that you want to provide direct access to from the Internet. Assume the IP address of this server is 10.0.0.10 and the IP address of the external interface firewall machine is 192.115.144.17. To enable the desired port forwarding, you must add the following commands to your firewall startup script.

```
# /usr/sbin/ipmasqadm portfw -f
# /usr/sbin/ipmasqadm portfw -a -P tcp -L 192.115.144.17 80 -R 10.0.0.10 80
```

The first command clears the port-forwarding table. The second command adds a port-forwarding entry to forward all traffic coming to port 80 of the firewall's external interface 192.115.144.17 to port 80 of the internal host 10.0.0.10.

TROUBLESHOOTING

Several common problems can occur when implementing a Linux-based firewall:

- ipchains -L freezes.
- DNS lookups fail part of the time.
- IP masquerading does not work.
- 4096 masqueraded TCP and UDP connections are insufficient.

ipchains -L FREEZES

The command ipchains -L might freeze if DNS traffic is blocked because the command will attempt to convert IP addresses to domain names through DNS. By adding the -n flag to the command, name lookups will be suppressed.

Alternately, you can enable traffic for UDP port 53 and TCP port 53 so that DNS traffic will be allowed.

DNS LOOKUPS FAIL PART OF THE TIME

If you allow only UDP port 53 for DNS queries, some DNS queries might fail. This is because some replies from DNS servers will be more than 512 bytes, which causes the client to use a TCP connection on port 53 to retrieve the data. Both UDP and TCP ports 53 should allow packets through the firewall if you want to allow DNS lookups.

IP MASQUERADING DOES NOT WORK

For IP masquerading to work you must have packet forwarding enabled. This is done by tweaking a kernel variable through the /proc file system as follows:

```
# echo 1 > /proc/sys/net/ipv4/ip_forward
```

Masquerading uses the forward chain; without ip_forwarding enabled the packets never reach this chain.

> **Tip**
>
> In Red Hat Linux 6.2, you can enable packet forwarding by editing the /etc/sysconfig/network file and setting IP_FORWARDING = Yes.

4096 MASQUERADED TCP AND UDP CONNECTIONS ARE INSUFFICIENT

The Linux kernel limits the number of masqueraded connections to 4096 TCP and UDP ports. This number can be changed by adjusting the value of the PORT_MASQ_BEGIN and PORT_MASQ_END constants in /usr/src/linux/include/net/ip_masq.h. The default values of these constants are 61000 and 65096 respectively. You can choose an appropriate range of destination port numbers starting above 32768 and ending below 65536. After changing these values you must recompile the kernel. If you adjust these values, do not forget to change any firewall rules that you have defined using the destination port range of 61000-65096. Note that the kernel will use more memory when you increase kernel limits.

CHAPTER **20**

LOG MANAGEMENT AND ANALYSIS

In this chapter

LOGGING ACTIVITY IN LINUX

Linux and other UNIX systems provide a standardized mechanism for logging system activity from daemons and programs running on the system. These logs can be used not only to analyze and debug system problems, but also to track system usage and security. The logs can sometimes provide advance warning about failing hardware, which if heeded in a timely manner will guarantee better system uptime. All user access to the system is logged, including failed attempts to log in.

Of paramount importance are logs of successful super user logins and failed attempts to gain root access. Such security logs can alert system administrators about possible attempts by malicious users or hackers to breach the system security, and provide an opportunity to take precautionary measures to thwart such attempts before any real harm is done. In the unfortunate event of a security breach, detected after the fact, system logs can still provide valuable clues as to what the hacker was after, and help ascertain the level of damage the system has suffered. However, after a system is compromised, it is very probable that the logs have been tampered with and cannot be trusted.

On Linux systems, all logs are generally written to files and directories under the `/var/log` directory. When a Linux system is booted, several log files are created or log entries are appended to existing log files. These files are `/var/log/dmesg`, `/var/log/boot.log`, and `/var/log/messages` among others. The `/var/log/messages` file records all messages produced during system bootup and startup of system daemons. The system continues to write various other log messages to this file. During system bootup, specific bootup messages are duplicated into the `dmesg` file. These messages relate to probing of system hardware, initialization of the Linux kernel, and drivers. The `boot.log` file contains logs of system daemon startup messages and output of the file system checker. The following directory listing of the `/var/log/` directory illustrates Linux log files and directories for a typical Linux server:

```
boot.log          lastlog       messages.2    savacct       spooler.2    xferlog.1
cron              lastlog.1     messages.3    secure        spooler.3    xferlog.2
cron.1            maillog       messages.4    secure.1      spooler.4    xferlog.3
cron.2            maillog.1     netconf.log   secure.2      squid/       xferlog.4
cron.3            maillog.2     netconf.log.1 secure.3      usracct
cron.4            maillog.3     netconf.log.2 secure.4      uucp/
dmesg             maillog.4     news/         sendmail.st   wtmp
htmlaccess.log    messages      pacct         spooler       wtmp.1
httpd/            messages.1    samba/        spooler.1     xferlog
```

This listing shows various logs generated by the system. Some of these files are system specific, while others are application specific log files and directories. For instance, `boot.log`, `dmesg`, `lastlog`, `messages*`, `netconf.log*`, `secure*`, and `wtmp*` are system-specific log files, while `cron`, `maillog`, `httpd/*`, `news/*`, `squid/*`, `uucp/*`, and `xferlog` files are generated by the `cron`, `sendmail`, `httpd`, `news`, `squid`, `uucp`, and `ftp` daemons respectively. The system provides a special logging daemon called `syslogd`, which allows centralized configuration of logging levels and the location of log files.

THE syslog DAEMON

System logs are generated by the syslog daemon, which is called syslogd. syslogd is started when the system boots. At startup it reads the configuration file /etc/syslog.conf, which controls the behavior of syslogd. Although most programs use the syslog facility to log messages, the messages need not all be logged to the same file. The syslog.conf file controls how log messages are disposed of.

The default pathname of the syslog configuration file is /etc/syslog.conf. An alternate path can be specified by invoking syslogd with the -f flag followed by the pathname of the syslog.conf file. This file contains routing commands for use by the syslog daemon. The syntax of the file is slightly complicated because it is designed to log messages for many programs. Entries in the syslog.conf file have the following format:

```
<facility>.<level>   <target>
```

The facility represents the type of program that is producing the log message. For example, the Linux kernel uses the facility type kern to log kernel messages.

The syslog manual page describes the facilities and severity levels. A complete list of all the facility types is shown in Table 20.1.

TABLE 20.1   LOG FACILITY TYPES IN THE syslog.conf FILE

Facility	Used By
auth	The authorization subsystem
authpriv	The authorization subsystem (private)
cron	The crond and atd daemons
daemon	System daemons
ftp	The FTP daemon
kern	The kernel
lpr	The printing subsystem
mail	The mail subsystem
mark	Timestamps generated internally by syslogd
news	The network news subsystem
security	The authorization subsystem (Use auth instead)
syslog	Messages internally generated by syslogd
user	User processes
uucp	The UUCP subsystem
local0-7	Facilities reserved for local use
*	All of the above

PART

IV

CH

20

The logging level indicates the minimum severity at which log messages should be handled. The complete list of logging levels is shown in Table 20.2.

TABLE 20.2 LOGGING LEVELS IN syslog.conf FILE

Log Level	Meaning
emerg	Panic situation, system is unusable
alert	Condition requires immediate corrective action
crit	Critical condition
err	Other errors
warning	Warning messages
notice	Non-error condition that might require special handling
info	Informational messages
debug	Debugging level messages
none	Do not log messages at this level

The target has several possibilities, including sending the logs to a remote host where the syslogd daemon is running. The possible targets are listed in Table 20.3.

TABLE 20.3 TARGETS IN THE syslog.conf FILE

Target	Description
@host	Forward messages to the specified host
Filename	Append messages to the specified file
user,user,...	Write messages to user's screens, if logged in
*	Write to all logged-in users' screens

The following syslog.conf file illustrates how entries are built from these elements:

Note

Comments in the syslog.conf file start with a hash mark (#) and continue to the end of the line.

Note

Line numbers have been added to the following file for reference purposes and are not part of the file.

```
01: # Log all kernel messages to the console.
02: kern.*                         /dev/console
03:
04: # Messages of the priority alert will be directed to the operators
05: *.alert                        root,gautam,armand
06:
07: # Log everything of level info or higher, except mail, news, or
08: # private authentication messages in /var/log/messages
09: *.info;mail.none;news.none;authpriv.none      /var/log/messages
10:
11: # Log private authentication messages to /var/log/secure file.
12: # This file has restricted access.
13: authpriv.*                     /var/log/secure
14:
15: # Sitewide sendmail logs are stored in a central loghost machine
16: mail.*                         @loghost
17:
18: # Emergency messages are broadcast to all logged in users
19: *.emerg                              *
20:
21: # Save uucp errors in /var/log/spooler file.
22: uucp                           /var/log/spooler
23:
24: # Save boot messages also to boot.log
25: local7.*                       /var/log/boot.log
26:
27: # Separate news log messages of varying severity in different log files
28: news.=crit                     /var/log/news/news.crit
29: news.=err                      /var/log/news/news.err
30: news.notice                    /var/log/news/news.notice
```

The first point to note is that log messages are separated and directed to different files. This provides flexibility and control over these files on an individual basis and allows the application of different aging rules. For instance, it is necessary to keep some log files for extended periods of time while others can be deleted on a daily basis. In addition, the sizes of log files can be managed better by not amalgamating all log messages into one monolithic log file.

The compartmentalizing of log files by category also provides easier browsing and identifying of specific messages when needed. If all messages were in a single file, this browsing and searching task would be unmanageable in the midst of a large volume of log messages.

The sample configuration file above breaks down as follows:

- Line 2 instructs syslogd to send all kernel messages to the system console.
- Line 5 specifies that all system alert messages should be sent to the root user and other system operators.
- Line 9 specifies that all log messages of level info or higher, with the exception of mail, news or private authentication messages should be logged in the file /var/log/messages.
- Line 13 instructs syslogd to store user login authentication messages in the file /var/log/secure.

PART

IV

CH

20

- Line 16 specifies that all mail log messages should be sent to a remote host called `loghost`. The `syslog.conf` file on `loghost` will determine where on that host the mail logs are stored. It is useful, for example, to store `sendmail` log messages for all machines in a site on a central log machine.

- Lines 28-30 specify special log handling for the news program. The syntax `.=level` has different meaning from the more general `.level` specification. The general syntax `.level` indicates that log messages of the specified level and higher should be sent to the designated target. When the equal sign (=) is used it restricts the logging to only the specified level. Thus, line 28 instructs `syslogd` to log only critical messages generated by the news program to `/var/log/news/news.crit` file.

MAKING CHANGES TO THE `syslog.conf` FILE

The sample `syslog.conf` file that comes with the standard Linux distribution might be adequate for your needs, or you might want to customize it to suit the specific needs of your site. To make changes to the logging strategy, edit the `syslog.conf` file and then signal syslogd to re-read its configuration file. Sending it a SIGHUP signal to `syslogd`, as illustrated by the following command, does this:

```
# kill -HUP `cat /var/run/syslogd.pid`
```

LOG ROTATION

For logs to remain useful, and to prevent file systems from filling up with log files, they must be rotated on a regular basis. Log file rotation trims the log file sizes down to manageable levels, and old and useless information is purged from the system, allowing valuable disk space to be regained.

Log files can be managed in one of two ways:

- On Red Hat Linux and other distributions, a program called `logrotate` is available that can be used for rotation.

- You can write your own simple scripts to delete old log files and restart `syslogd`. These scripts can then be scheduled to run from `crond`.

The following sample script illustrates how to write your own log rotation utility for managing the `/var/log/messages` log file:

```
#!/bin/sh
# File: /usr/local/sbin/rotate-messages
# Example script to manage /var/log/messages
# To run from cron once a day
# Keep a week worth of old logs online
cd /var/log
[ -f messages.5 ] && mv messages.5 messages.6
[ -f messages.4 ] && mv messages.4 messages.5
[ -f messages.3 ] && mv messages.3 messages.4
[ -f messages.2 ] && mv messages.2 messages.3
```

```
[ -f messages.1 ] && mv messages.1 messages.2
[ -f messages.0 ] && mv messages.0 messages.1
[ -f messages ] && mv messages messages.0
touch messages
chmod 600 messages
kill -HUP `/var/run/syslogd.pid`
```

Save the above script to a file, for example /usr/local/sbin/rotate-messages, and make it executable using the chmod command as follows:

```
# chmod +x /usr/local/sbin/rotate-messages
```

Next add an entry such as the following to the root user's crontab to make it run once every night:

```
15 3 * * * /usr/local/sbin/rotate-messages
```

> **Tip**
>
> You can extend this idea to manage all the log files on your system, create monthly, weekly, or daily crontab entries to control the aging of the log files, and maintain the requisite level of log history that suits the needs of your site.

THE logrotate UTILITY

The logrotate utility is packaged with several Linux distributions including Red Hat Linux. If your Linux system does not have this utility you can download and install it from one of the Linux distribution sites. Pre-built RPM packages are available for logrotate. The current version at the time of writing this book is logrotate-3.3-1.

The logrotate utility is a very elegant way of managing rotation for a large number of log files by writing specifications in a single configuration file. The logrotate utility is designed to simplify the administration of log files on a system that generates numerous log files. logrotate allows for the automatic rotation, compression, removal, and mailing of log files. logrotate can be instructed to manage log files on a daily, weekly, or monthly basis or when files cross a size threshold. Normally, logrotate is run from the root user's crontab file as a daily job.

Consider the following sample logrotate.conf file. When logrotate runs it reads the /etc/logrotate.conf file, which will be similar to the following:

```
01: # File: /etc/logrotate.conf
02: # Description: sample logrotate configuration file
03: # Global options can be overridden by local options
04: weekly
05: rotate 4
06: errors root@some.host
07: compress
08: create
09: # Also read configuration directives in logrotate.d directory,
10: # where rotation instructions for individual applications
11: # are specified
```

PART
IV

CH
20

```
12: include /etc/logrotate.d
13: /var/log/messages {
14: rotate 5
15: weekly
16: nocompress
17: postrotate
18:           /sbin/killall -HUP syslogd
19: endscript
20: }
21: /var/log/httpd/access.log {
22: rotate 5
23: mail webmaster@some.host
24: errors webmaster@some.host
25: size=100k
26: postrotate
27:           /sbin/killall -HUP httpd
28: endscript
29: }
30: /var/log/wtmp {
31: monthly
32: create 0664 root utmp
33: rotate 1
34: }
35: /var/log/lastlog {
36: monthly
37: rotate 1
38: }
```

Note

The lines starting with the hash symbol (#) are comment lines, and are ignored by the logrotate program.

Note

Line numbers have been added to the following file for reference purposes and are not part of the file.

Lines 4–8 set global options. The weekly directive sets the default log rotation interval to once a week. The rotate 4 directive specifies maintaining 4 history files. The errors directive specifies to whom errors generated during log processing are mailed. In this example root@some.host gets all error output, unless overridden by local options. The compress directive specifies that history logs should be compressed after they are rotated.

The include directive on line 12 specifies that additional log rotation configuration files might need to be read from the /etc/logrotate.d directory. The contents of this directory on a particular Linux system show the following:

```
# ls /etc/logrotate.d
apache  ftpd       mars-nwe.log  samba    slrnpull  syslog
cron    linuxconf  mgetty        sendfax  squid     uucp
```

These files contain instructions for log rotation for specific daemons. Packages installed using Red Hat's RPM package manager place log rotation scripts in this directory.

Lines 13-20 define how to process the log file /var/log/messages. This log will go through five weekly rotations before it is removed. Notice the local rotation directive on line 14 overrides the global rotation directive on line 5. The nocompress local directive overrides the global compress directive. This means the messages history files (messages.0, messages.1 and so forth) are not compressed. The postrotate section specifies commands that must run after the logs are rotated. In this case the syslogd daemon is sent the SIGHUP signal. This section ends with the endscript directive.

Lines 21-29 define the parameters for /var/log/httpd/access.log. It is rotated whenever the size of the log file exceeds 100KB. The file is mailed to the webmaster@some.host and five history versions are kept in compressed format. If any errors occur while processing the log file, the error messages are mailed to webmaster@some.host and not to root@some.host as specified in the global options. This is a local override of the global errors directive.

Lines 30-38 set options for rotating the wtmp and lastlog files. These are rotated on a monthly schedule instead of a weekly schedule as globally specified. Also the create mode for the new /var/log/wtmp file is specified to be 0644. When the file is created, its owner and group will be adjusted so that it is owned by root and belongs to the utmp group. Only one history file will be maintained for these log files.

The status of logrotate is written to the file /var/lib/logrotate.status.

The logrotate configuration file can contain many directives, all of which are not covered in the above example. A complete set of all logrotate directives is listed in Table 20.3.

TABLE 20.3 logrotate DIRECTIVES

Directive	Description
compress	Compress the older versions of log files using GNU gzip.
copytruncate	Truncate the original log file in place after creating a copy, instead of moving the old log file and optionally creating a new one. It can be used when some program cannot be told to close its log file and thus might continue appending to the previous log file. Note that there is a very small time slice between copying the file and truncating it, so some logging of data can be lost. When this option is used, the create option has no effect, as the old log file stays in place.
create <mode> <owner> <group>	Immediately after rotation, before running the postrotate script, the log file is created with the same name as the log file just rotated. mode specifies the mode for the log file as used in chmod, owner specifies the owner of the log file, and group specifies the group to which the log file will belong. If any of the log file attributes are omitted, the attributes for the new file are kept the same as the original log file. The nocreate option overrides this directive.

PART **IV**

CH **20**

TABLE 20.3   CONTINUED

Directive	Description
`daily`	Rotate log files every day.
`delaycompress`	Do not compress the previous log file until the next rotation cycle. This is effective only when used in combination with `compress`. This is used when a particular program cannot be told to close its log file and thus might continue writing to the previous log file for some time.
`errors address`	Any errors that occur during log file processing are mailed to the given address.
`ifempty`	Rotate the log file even if it is empty, overriding any global `notifempty` option. `ifempty` is enabled by default.
`include file¦ directory`	Include other configuration files inline. If a directory is given, the files in that directory are read. The only files that are ignored are files that are not regular files, such as directories and named pipes, and files with names ending in one of the taboo extensions, as specified by the `tabooext` directive. The `include` directive cannot appear inside of a log file definition.
`mail address`	When a log is rotated and removed, it is mailed to the specified address. The `nomail` directive overrides this directive.
`missingok`	If the log file is missing, go on to the next one without issuing an error message.
`nocopytruncate`	Do not truncate the original log file in place after creating a copy. This overrides the `copytruncate` option.
`nocreate`	New log files are not created. This overrides the `create` option.
`nodelaycompress`	Do not postpone compression of the previous log file until the next rotation cycle. This overrides the `delaycompress` option.
`nomissingok`	If a log file does not exist, issue an error. This is the default.
`noolddir`	Logs are rotated in the same directory that they normally reside in. This overrides the `olddir` option.
`notifempty`	Do not rotate the log if it is empty. This overrides the `ifempty` option.
`olddir <directory>`	Logs are moved into the specified directory for rotation. The directory must be on the same physical device as the log file being rotated. When this option is used all old versions of the log end up in the specified directory. This option can be overriden by the `noolddir` option.
`postrotate/ endscript`	The `postrotate` and `endscript` directives must appear on lines by themselves. The commands in between are executed after the log file is rotated. These definitions must appear inside a log file definition.

TABLE 20.3   CONTINUED

Directive	Description
prerotate/endscript	The prerotate and endscript directives must appear on lines by themselves. The commands in between are executed before the log file is rotated. These directives must appear inside a log file definition.
rotate <number>	Log files are rotated the specified number of times before being removed or mailed to the address specified by a mail directive. If the number is zero, old versions are removed instead of being rotated.
size <size>	Log files are rotated when they grow bigger than the specified size in bytes. The size is specified in kilobytes or megabytes, by appending a K or M to the number, such as 100K or 10M.
tabooext [+] <list>	The tabooext directive works in conjunction with the include directive. Filename extensions specified with the tabooext directive are ignored by logrotate when scanning an include directory for logrotate specification files. If a + precedes the list of extensions, the current taboo extension list is augmented, otherwise it is replaced. At startup, the taboo extension list contains .rpmorig, .rpmsave, v, and ~.
weekly	Log files are rotated if the current weekday is less than the weekday of the last rotation or if more then a week has passed since the last rotation. This is normally the same as rotating logs on the first day of the week, but it works better if logrotate is not run every night.

CASE STUDY: USEFUL SCRIPTS

Two scripts can help you monitor your system logs for security information:

- su-report examines the /var/log/messages file and creates a report of all successful super-user logins during the past two days, and mails the report to root.
- failed-su finds all unsuccessful attempts to gain super-user access during the past two days, and creates a report and mails it to root.

You should create these scripts in a convenient location such as /usr/local/bin/ and then make them executable with the commands:

```
# chmod +x /usr/local/bin/su-report
# chmod +x /usr/local/bin/failed-su
```

Ideally, you should schedule these scripts to run on a regular basis such as daily by adding the relevant entries to the root user's crontab file as outlined in Chapter 7, "Scheduling Tasks." To schedule the scripts to run daily at 1 a.m., use the following entries:

```
0 1 * * * /usr/local/bin/su-report
0 1 * * * /usr/local/bin/failed-su
```

PART
IV

CH
20

SOURCE CODE FOR su-report

```
#!/bin/sh
# File: su-report
# Description: Report all successful super user
➥logins during past 2 days to root.
# Runs from cron once every 24 hours
#
# Create an entry in root's crontab as follows:
# 0 12 * * * /usr/local/sbin/su-report
PATH=/bin:/usr/bin:/sbin:/usr/sbin:/usr/ucb:/usr/local/bin:.
export PATH
MAILTO=root
progname=`#180;basename $0`
thishost=`hostname`
sureport=/tmp/sureport.$$
# write the header for our logfile
#
cat <<EOF > $sureport
`hostname`: SU report`date`
EOF
#
# Check super user logins over the past 2 days
#
# Print a header line
cat <<EOF >> $sureport
Super user logins reported in /var/log/messages
EOF
today=`date| awk '{printf "%s %s\n", $2, $3}`
yesterday=`#180;date | awk '{printf "%s %s\n", $2, $3-1}'`
grep "$yesterday" /var/log/messages | grep '(su)' >> $sureport
grep "$today" /var/log/messages | grep '(su)' >> $sureport

Mail -n -s "SU Report: `date`" $MAILTO < $sureport

rm -f $sureport
```

SOURCE CODE FOR failed-su

```
#!/bin/sh
#
# File: failed-su
# Description: Report all failed attempts to gain super user access
# during past 2 days to root.
# Runs from cron once every 24 hours
#
# Create an entry in root's crontab as follows:
# 0 12 * * * /usr/local/sbin/failed-su

PATH=/bin:/usr/bin:/sbin:/usr/sbin:/usr/ucb:/usr/local/bin:.
export PATH
MAILTO=root
progname=`basename $0`
thishost=`hostname`
report=/tmp/failed-su-report.$$
# write the header for our logfile
#
```

```
cat <<EOF > $report
`hostname`: Failed SU report:`date`
EOF
#
# Check failed attempts to gain super user access over the past 2 days
#
# Print a header line
cat <<EOF >> $report
Failed Super user login attempts reported in /var/log/messages
EOF
today=`date¦ awk '{printf "%s %s\n", $2, $3}`
yesterday=`date ¦ awk '{printf "%s %s\n", $2, $3-1}'`
grep "$yesterday" /var/log/messages ¦ grep 'authentication failure' \
     ¦ grep 'su service' >> $report
grep "$today" /var/log/messages ¦ grep 'authentication failure' \
     ¦ grep 'su service' >> $report

Mail -n -s "Failed SU Report: `date`" $MAILTO < $report

rm -f $report
```

PART V

THE INTERNET AND THE INTRANET

## CHAPTER 21

USING LINUX AS AN INTRANET SERVER

In this chapter

UNDERSTANDING INTRANETS

The server market has primarily fueled Linux's quick rise to prominence as an operating system. Linux has quickly emerged as a platform of choice next to Windows NT for deploying corporate intranets.

In the simplest sense, an intranet is a network which uses Internet technologies and protocols such as HTTP, FTP, and SMTP for distributing and sharing information within a closed corporate network.

Typically, an intranet will use Web browsers and servers for sharing documents and information within the network, and will use Internet-standard mail servers and clients running SMTP for email communication within the intranet. An intranet may also include discussion facilities through a platform such as Lotus Notes or Microsoft Exchange or through standard Internet newsgroup technologies.

In addition, corporate databases are often made accessible across departments and divisions through the integration of Web technology and back-end databases. This allows access to information to be simplified and made more efficient throughout the organization.

Linux provides a platform on which all of these technologies can be deployed quickly, efficiently, and cheaply. This platform includes the following:

- **HTTP:** Linux provides an ideal platform for implementing a Web server.
- **Database Access:** Numerous free and commercial database servers are available for Linux. Even if you choose to run your corporate database on another platform, a Linux-based Web server can still provide a Web browser front-end to these databases for your intranet.
- **NNTP:** Linux provides a complete newsgroup system through the use of the Internet-standard NNTP protocol. Numerous clients can access NTTP servers, including Microsoft Outlook and Netscape Communicator.
- **SMTP:** Linux provides a powerful, scalable platform for delivering Simple Mail Transfer Protocol (SMTP) services. SMTP is the Internet standard for mail delivery and almost all mail clients, including Microsoft Outlook and Netscape Communicator, can communicate with SMTP servers.

LINUX AS A WEB SERVER

Linux is a popular platform for Web servers. Web servers use the Hypertext Transfer Protocol (HTTP) to make documents available transparently to any HTTP-capable client. All Web browsers are HTTP-capable clients. Web servers aasdre discussed in detail in Chapter 23, "Apache and the World Wide Web." HTTP is a stateless protocol for document delivery. A typical HTTP transaction works like this:

1. The client requests a document using a URL.

2. The appropriate Web server receives the request and interprets the URL, mapping it to a physical file on the system.

3. The Web server checks that the client has permission to retrieve the file.

4. If the client has permission to receive the file, the server returns it to the client and terminates the connection.

In addition to simple retrieval of static files, Web servers can also be used to provide a limited degree of interactivity between the client and server. You can see this interactivity every day on the World Wide Web in the use of forms for submitting information, e-commerce sites with "shopping carts," and Internet search engines.

This interactivity is provided through one of two types of extensions to the basic Web server concept: The Common Gateway Interface and Server Application Program Interfaces.

THE COMMON GATEWAY INTERFACE

The Common Gateway Interface (CGI) is the longest standing mechanism for deploying interactive content on the World Wide Web. CGI is a simple mechanism:

1. The client requests a CGI program using a URL.

2. The appropriate Web server receives the request and interprets the URL, mapping it to a CGI script on the system.

3. The Web server checks that the client has permission to access the script.

4. If the client has permission to access the script, the server passes the user's data from any forms to the CGI script and waits for the program to run and return data.

5. The CGI program runs and returns data, usually in HTML form, to the Web server.

6. The Web server returns the data from the CGI program to the client.

While CGI has worked quite well, problems have emerged with this approach to delivering interactive applications on the World Wide Web, including the following:

- **Significant security holes:** If an application is poorly written it can expose the Web server to significant security breaches. CGI scripts run as individual programs on the server and enjoy all the privileges and security risks this entails. A poorly written script can allow an attacker to run an arbitrary command on the server.

- **Inefficiency:** Each time the client requests a CGI program, the Web server launches that program as a separate process. If a site is busy, this entails a large number of new CGI processes being started in short periods of time. This is a highly inefficient way to handle multiple requests for CGI applications.

SERVER APPLICATION PROGRAM INTERFACES

Application Program Interfaces (APIs) provide a powerful alternative to traditional CGI Web application programming. Using APIs, developers write applications that integrate closely

PART

V

CH

21

with the Web server. Normally, API-based applications load as part of the Web server and don't require separate processes for each request being handled.

Generally, API-based applications perform the same tasks as CGI programs, including processing data submitted from forms, generating dynamic HTML pages from data stored in databases, and verifying credit card numbers. The key difference is that API-based programming is generally more efficient and scalable, allowing a Web server to handle more simultaneous requests than with CGI applications. In addition, server API-based development environments often cache requests for dynamic pages, significantly improving performance, which is not done with traditional CGI programs.

A key drawback of API programming is that each Web server has its own API. Moving an API-based application to a new server often requires significant reprogramming. Generally, applications written for API-based development environments are limited to the platforms on which the API is implemented and cannot be truly multi-platform in the way a Perl CGI-BIN script or C CGI-BIN program can be.

Server APIs generally address the primary security risk of CGI scripts: Applications written for server API environments do not run as individual processes on the server. This means that their capability to compromise system security when written poorly is restricted to the privileges and security holes in the server API itself. A well-designed server API environment can prevent poorly written scripts from opening up unnecessary security holes on your server. Equally a poorly designed API could, in theory, create a larger security risk than with traditional CGI applications.

While Web developer's can use a high-level language such as C or C++ to directly write applications on top of a Web-server's API, it is much more common to develop Web applications using a development environment which has been implemented on top of an API. Typically, these development environments implement a custom programming language designed specifically for Web application development. Common API-based development environments include the following:

- Microsoft's Active Server Pages
- Allaire's ColdFusion
- TalentSoft's Web+
- PHP
- Zope

PHP is a freely available development environment that uses the Apache Web server's API for Web server integration. PHP is discussed in more detail in Chapter 25, "Dynamic, Data-Driven Web Sites."

USEFUL REFERENCES

A wealth of useful information regarding the use of Linux as a Web server on the Internet is available. The following are some good starting points:

- The Linux WWW HOWTO (http://www.linuxdoc.org/HOWTO/WWW-HOWTO.html)
- The Apache Web Site (http://www.apache.org/)
- The Linux.com Web Server List (http://www.linux.com/links/Software/Web_servers/)
- The World Wide Web Consortium (http://www.w3c.org/)

LINUX AS A DATABASE SERVER

Until recently, one area that Linux had failed to gain widespread acceptance in was database serving. Linux has long had a full range of free relational database packages including the well-known PostgreSQL (or *Postgres* for short), mSQL, and MySQL.

Since 1998, however, this situation has gradually changed. Most major commercial database vendors now offer Linux versions of their products including Oracle, Sybase, and Informix. This extends Linux into the realm of scalable, fully supported database platforms and makes it a viable option for organizations looking at moving some or all of their back-end processing to Linux-based systems.

The following are some of the leading commercial and free database platforms for Linux:

- **IBM:** IBM's DB2 database server is available for Linux. It offers Java support and reportedly high levels of scalability. A free development and testing version of the software is available at http://www.software.ibm.com/data/db2/linux.

- **Informix:** Informix ranks in the top five commercial database platforms for Linux. The company offers two Linux servers: Informix SE, a freely available, small-scale database system and Informix Dynamic Server Linux Edition Suite, a more powerful database environment. Full details are available at http://www.informix.com/.

- **Mini SQL:** Mini SQL, or mSQL, is one of the best known and most widely used relational databases for Linux. mSQL started as shareware which was available for free non-commercial and educational use and has now matured into a modestly priced, efficient, commercial product which is freely available for non-commercial and educational use from http://www.hughes.com.au/.

- **MySQL:** MySQL is a relational database server from Sweden that is available at no charge for use on non-Microsoft systems. As long as the server is not sold, no charges are made for installation, and the software is not included in a commercial distribution. Well-known for superb performance, MySQL can be downloaded from http://www.mysql.com/.

- **PostgreSQL:** PostgreSQL is considered the most robust server for Linux available under an open source license. PostgreSQL can be downloaded from http://looking-glass.usask.ca/.

PART
V

CH
21

- **Oracle:** Oracle is a top database player and by some counts is the market leader for enterprise databases. Traditionally available only on commercial Unix and Windows NT systems, Oracle now offers a Linux version of its flagship Oracle 8 database system. A free 30-day trial can be obtained from `http://platforms.oracle.com/linux/index_lin.htm`.

- **Sybase:** One of the top-five database vendors, Sybase offers its Adaptive Server Enterprise (ASE) product for free on Linux. With few limitations, ASE can be run for any use on a Linux system. More information is available from `http://www.sybase.com/`.

The process of deploying Linux as a database server is discussed in depth in Chapter 24, "Linux Database Servers."

LINUX AS A NEWS SERVER

A common feature of many corporate intranets is some form of discussion forum such as that offered by Microsoft Exchange or Lotus Notes. The Internet-standard NNTP protocol is the underpinning of the well-known Usenet newsgroup network on the Internet.

Newsgroups provide for non-real-time discussions. That is, users can post at any time and then read other posts at their leisure because the posts remain in the group for future reading and reference. This is in contrast to chat systems, which require real-time interaction among the participants.

On Linux systems, NNTP services are provided using the INN package. Installation and management of an INN news server is discussed in Chapter 26, "News Services."

LINUX AS A MAIL SERVER

Mail services are typically divided into two components:

- **Mail User Agents (MUAs):** MUAs are normally the mail client software that users see such as Eudora, Pegasus, pine, Netscape Messenger, or Outlook Express.

- **Mail Transport Agents (MTAs):** MTAs are the back-end server systems that provide mail delivery and storage facilities to the MUAs.

In Internet terms, MTAs use the Simple Mail Transport Protocol (SMTP) to route and deliver email messages. The majority of the Internet email system is routed through SMTP-based MTAs.

In the UNIX world, Linux included, the leading MTA is sendmail. As the dominant MTA, sendmail has not only come to be widely deployed but has also grown in complexity and capabilities in order to address the diverse needs of this large user base. This degree of complexity is reflected in the fact that most mail administrators never attempt to master sendmail and rely on printed references. In fact, entire books are devoted to the installation, configuration, and maintenance of sendmail systems.

Many Linux distributions come with the sendmail system. The installation and implementation of sendmail-based mail servers is covered in more depth in Chapter 16, "Linux Mail Services with sendmail." In addition to sendmail, several other MTAs are available for Linux which offer better security or performance or simplified configuration and management. These include the following:

- **smail:** smail is widely used as an MTA in the Linux world. It offers simpler configuration than sendmail for most installations.

- **qmail:** qmail focuses on security in an attempt to address the well-known security lapses in sendmail. qmail attempts to avoid hidden holes and tries to provide superior delivery reliability with a minimum change of inbox corruption.

HARDWARE REQUIREMENTS

There are no simple ways to assess the hardware needs of your intranet. Much of this depends on the number of intranet services you plan to provide, the number of users, and the level of their use.

Nonetheless, a few guidelines do apply:

- Unless you are running an extremely small intranet, you will not want to run multiple intranet services on the same Linux system. That is, it is wise to provide separate hardware for your Web, database, news, and mail servers. Not only does this provide for better performance and room to scale, but you also eliminate having a single point of failure. If you run all these services on a single system without redundant systems and the system's hardware fails, all services fail instead of just one.

- If your hardware budget allows it, provide for redundancy by running at least two Web, database, news, and mail servers. In the case of database and news servers, automatic data mirroring can take place for all services. The multiple servers can share the load and when one server fails, the other can take over while you repair or replace the problematic server. This can help you achieve near 100% uptime.

- News servers tend to have heavy hardware requirements. If you plan to have local news groups plus partial feeds of Internet news groups, then a single-processor Pentium 300, with 256MB of memory and 16GB of hard disk space on Ultra Wide SCSI-2 disks should meet your needs. If you want to provide complete Internet news feeds to your Intranet users, you may need to go as high as 4 CPUs, 2GB of RAM and one terabyte (1 TB) of disk space. It is never wise to share your news server with other intranet services. News servers are discussed in detail in Chapter 26.

- The performance of Web servers is determined mainly by available RAM, especially if any interactive or data-driven applications are being deployed on the Web server. The goal is to prevent swapping at any time on your Web server because this incurs a noticeable performance hit for the end user. Fast CPUs and network cards are important but should not be used if the cost of them means less than sufficient RAM is available. Web servers are discussed in detail in Chapter 23.

PART

V

CH

21

- Always use the fastest disks available in your intranet servers. The best choice is usually Ultra-Wide SCSI 2 disks.

- If your mail server has a large number of users, disk space can easily be at a premium. Make sure you have enough space to store your mail queues plus any inboxes stored on your mail server. Mail servers were discussed in detail in Chapter 16.

Specific hardware requirements for the different types of intranet services are discussed in more detail in the relevant chapters.

CHAPTER 22

DNS

THE DOMAIN NAME SYSTEM

Paul Mockapetris wrote the original version of DNS in 1984-85. This system was called JEEVES. Kevin Dunlap wrote a later version for Berkeley's 4.3BSD UNIX system. It was called *BIND*, which stands for *Berkeley Internet Name Domain*. BIND software has gone through many revisions since then.

The version of BIND discussed in this chapter is Version 8 and is written and maintained by the Internet Software Consortium (www.isc.org). BIND provides Domain Name System services.

The Domain Name System is one of the Internet's basic building blocks. It is a distributed hosts database, used to translate hostnames to IP addresses. It is a hierarchical, tree-structured system; a vast network that connects numerous networks across the world.

Organizations join the Internet by applying for membership. They can join an organizational domain or a geographic domain. The root of the domain tree is .(dot). Under . there are many *top-level domains* (*TLD*s), such as .com, .org, .net, .gov, .edu, .mil, .int, with two-letter country codes such as .au (Australia), .in (India), .uk (United Kingdom), .il (Israel), and .us (United States) and so on.

Table 22.1 outlines the Internet organizational domains.

TABLE 22.1   INTERNET ORGANIZATIONAL DOMAINS

Domain	Purpose
.com	Commercial Organizations
.org	Not-for-Profit Organizations
.edu	Educational Institutions
.gov	Governmental Institutions
.net	Major Network Support Center
.mil	Military Groups
.int	International Organizations

The geographic hierarchy assigns each country in the world two or three letter identifiers. You can find a complete list of country codes at ftp://rs.internic.net/netinfo/iso3166-countrycodes.

The *second-level domains* are below these TLDs in the hierarchy. These include domains such as sun.com, linux.org, and nasa.gov, which are normally controlled by organizations, and other second-level domains, which must be further subdivided for individual organizational use such as ac.il (educational institutions in Israel).

Below these second-level domains you will find two types of names:

- Individual hostnames, such as `metalab.unc.edu` or `www.cnn.com`.

- Further sub-divided domains such as `ca.bahai.org`, which can be divided into hostnames such as `www.ca.bahai.org` and further sub-domains.

DNS was designed with decentralized administration in mind. Domains are delegated to organizations. The organization so delegated becomes responsible for maintaining host and subdomain data for their domain. The organization can change their domain data without worrying about the parent domain. The parent domain only keeps pointers to the subdomain's name servers, to which it can direct queries. The domain `bahai.org`, for example, is delegated to the Bah' World Centre. The Bah' World Centre can delegate a sub-domain such as `us.bahai.org`. The subdomain can maintain its own data, without bothering the domain administrators of `bahai.org`. All `bahai.org` must do is keep a pointer to the name servers of `us.bahai.org`. This is the power and convenience of decentralized DNS administration.

DNS NAME RESOLUTION

DNS provides the mechanism to translate hostnames to IP addresses and reverse translations of IP addresses to hostnames.

A name lookup is done starting at the root of the tree at `.` and traversing the various branches until the process arrives at a leaf node (which contains a hostname). Each `.` in the name is a branching point. Branching points will become clear as we consider examples using the `nslookup` utility.

The process of translating names to IP addresses is called *name resolution*. DNS stores all names and IP Addresses of hosts in a domain in a set of maps, which are called *zone files*.

You can also look up names for IP addresses. This process is called *reverse name resolution*. DNS uses a special domain called `in-addr.arpa` for this purpose. We will discuss reverse lookups in detail later in this chapter.

DNS zones are made up of a set of resource records that define hostnames, administrative information, and other information which can be stored in a DNS database. Some of the most commonly used record types are outlined in Table 22.2.

TABLE 22.2   COMMON DNS RECORD TYPES

Record Identifier	Record Name	Description
SOA	Start of Authority	Marks the start of a zone of authority. Each zone must contain one, and only one, SOA record.
A	Address	Defines an IP address for a hostname in the domain.

TABLE 22.2 CONTINUED

Record Identifier	Record Name	Description
NS	Name Server	Specifies a name server for the domain.
MX	Mail Exchanger	Specifies a mail exchanger, which handles incoming email for the domain.
CNAME	Canonical Name	Specifies an alias for a hostname.
NULL	Null	A null record containing no format or data information.
RP	Responsible Person	Specifies a person responsible for the domain.
PTR	Pointer	Specifies a pointer (typically used for reverse name lookup).
HINFO	Host Information	Specifies information about a host such as the CPU and operating system type.
TXT	Text Information	Specifies a text description of a host.

SETTING UP NAME SERVERS

To set up a name server in the best way possible you must first identify the purpose of the server. In particular you need to determine whether the server will be an authoritative name server for a domain name registered on the Internet or will provide private name services for your internal domain from behind a firewall.

For any domain, a registered domain or a private internal domain, two types of name servers can be created: primary master servers and secondary master servers. A domain will always have one primary master and can have any number of secondary master servers. While the primary master server is required, the secondary servers are optional.

The primary master server obtains its data from zone files stored on the system running the primary master while the secondary servers obtain their data from the primary master. Every time a secondary server starts it contacts the master to obtain a copy of the zone data in a process known as a *zone transfer*. This arrangement allows a DNS administrator to only edit files on the primary master and allows the changes to propagate automatically to other DNS servers for the domain.

Note

Because of the simplicity of maintaining secondary master name servers, it is recommended that you maintain at least one. This provides redundancy should the primary name server be down and can be used for load balancing should the primary name server be under heavy use for a period of time.

PRIMARY NAME SERVER CONFIGURATION (AUTHORITATIVE FOR REGISTERED DOMAIN)

Three steps are involved in setting up a primary name server for a registered Internet domain:

1. Create a `named.conf` file.
2. Create the zone files.
3. Start `named`.

For the purposes of the examples in this section, we will create a primary name server for the fictitious `foo.edu` domain.

> **Tip**
>
> In addition, to make the name resolver work you must create an `/etc/resolv.conf` file. On some systems such as Linux or Solaris you might also need to modify the name server switch file (`/etc/nsswitch.conf`).

> **Note**
>
> Since BIND Version 8 the format of the `named` configuration file has changed completely. Earlier versions of `bind` used a file called `named.boot` and its format was different from the current `named.conf` file. A shell script is available to convert Bind version 4 `named.boot` files to the new `named.conf` format. It is called `named-bootconf` and how to obtain it is mentioned at the end of this chapter.

CREATING A `named.conf` FILE

> **Note**
>
> In these examples we create a name server for the fictitious `foo.edu` domain. You must substitute your domain name for this domain. In addition, these examples use private IP addresses even when providing examples for external servers. This prevents problems if you attempt to use these files on your server without changing the IP addresses.

The `named.conf` file for the primary server for the `foo.edu` domain is as follows:

```
// File: /etc/named.conf
// Primary Name Server for foo.edu
//
options {
        directory "/var/named";
};
zone "." {
        type hint;
        file "root.hints";
};
```

```
zone "foo.edu" {
        type master;
        file "zone.foo.edu";
};
zone "1.168.192.in-addr.arpa" {
    type master;
    file "one.192.168.1";
};
zone "0.0.127.in-addr.arpa" {
        type master;
        file "zone.127.0.0";
};
```

Note The lines that start with // are comments.

This file contains an options section and then several zone sections. The options section contains a single directive which defines the directory where named will find all other configuration files referred to in the named.conf file:

```
directory   "/var/named";
```

Each zone section defines a zone being served by the server, the type of zone it is, and where to find the relevant files. This file contains information about three zones:

■   .: This is a hint type zone. It indicates where the server should look for the initial set of name servers used to begin resolving names that are not part of zones for which the server is the primary server. In this case, the file root.hints is in the directory /var/named. The contents of this file are provided from the FTP server rs.internic.net and are updated regularly. A typical root.hints file is shown below:

```
; root.hints
;
.               6D IN NS    G.ROOT-SERVERS.NET.
.               6D IN NS    J.ROOT-SERVERS.NET.
.               6D IN NS    K.ROOT-SERVERS.NET.
.               6D IN NS    L.ROOT-SERVERS.NET.
.               6D IN NS    M.ROOT-SERVERS.NET.
.               6D IN NS    A.ROOT-SERVERS.NET.
.               6D IN NS    H.ROOT-SERVERS.NET.
.               6D IN NS    B.ROOT-SERVERS.NET.
.               6D IN NS    C.ROOT-SERVERS.NET.
.               6D IN NS    D.ROOT-SERVERS.NET.
.               6D IN NS    E.ROOT-SERVERS.NET.
.               6D IN NS    I.ROOT-SERVERS.NET.
.               6D IN NS    F.ROOT-SERVERS.NET.
G.ROOT-SERVERS.NET.    5w6d16h IN A   192.112.36.4
J.ROOT-SERVERS.NET.    5w6d16h IN A   198.41.0.10
K.ROOT-SERVERS.NET.    5w6d16h IN A   193.0.14.129
L.ROOT-SERVERS.NET.    5w6d16h IN A   198.32.64.12
M.ROOT-SERVERS.NET.    5w6d16h IN A   202.12.27.33
A.ROOT-SERVERS.NET.    5w6d16h IN A   198.41.0.4
K.ROOT-SERVERS.NET.    5w6d16h IN A   193.0.14.129
```

```
L.ROOT-SERVERS.NET.    5w6d16h IN A    198.32.64.12
M.ROOT-SERVERS.NET.    5w6d16h IN A    202.12.27.33
A.ROOT-SERVERS.NET.    5w6d16h IN A    198.41.0.4
H.ROOT-SERVERS.NET.    5w6d16h IN A    128.63.2.53
B.ROOT-SERVERS.NET.    5w6d16h IN A    128.9.0.107
C.ROOT-SERVERS.NET.    5w6d16h IN A    192.33.4.12
D.ROOT-SERVERS.NET.    5w6d16h IN A    128.8.10.90
E.ROOT-SERVERS.NET.    5w6d16h IN A    192.203.230.10
I.ROOT-SERVERS.NET.    5w6d16h IN A    192.36.148.17
F.ROOT-SERVERS.NET.    5w6d16h IN A    192.5.5.241
```

- **foo.edu**: This the master zone for the `foo.edu` domain. This indicates that this name server is the primary master for the `foo.edu` domain and that it can find the zone definition in the file `/var/named/zone.foo.edu`.

- **1.168.192.in-addr.arpa**: This is the master zone for reverse name lookups for the `foo.edu` domain. The zone information is contained in the file `/var/named/zone.192.168.1` and specifies the hostnames corresponding to specific IP addresses.

- **0.0.127.in-addr.arpa**: This indicates that the server is the primary master server for reverse name lookups for the local loopback network 127.0.0.0. This information is not relevant to the Internet but it allows reverse name lookups for the local system. The zone information is stored in the file `/var/named/zone.127.0.0`.

CREATING ZONE FILES   After `named.conf` is configured, you must create the zone files indicated in the configuration. In particular, the three files `zone.foo.edu`, `zone.192.168.1`, and `zone.127.0.0` must be created in the directory `/var/named`.

The zone file for the `foo.edu` (`zone.foo.edu`) domain illustrates a typical zone file on a primary master server for an Internet-registered domain name:

```
; zone.foo.edu   file
;
@       IN      SOA     fake.foo.edu.   hostmaster.foo.edu. (
                                1999042800      ;Serial
                                8H              ;Refresh
                                2H              ;Retry
                                1W              ;Expire
                                1D)             ;Minimum
;
; Name-servers
;

        IN      NS      fake.foo.edu.
;
; Addresses for canonical names
;
fake        IN      A    192.168.1.1
pinky       IN      A    192.168.1.2
brain       IN      A    192.168.1.3
www         IN      CNAME   brain.foo.edu.

; Mail exchangers
;
foo.edu.    IN      MX   10 mail.foo.edu.
```

```
foo.edu.    IN    MX    20 mail2.foo.edu.
mail        IN    A     192.168.1.4
mail2       IN    A     192.168.1.5
```

Tip

In DNS zone files, comments run from a semicolon (;) to the end of the line and are ignored by `named`.

The first entry in the zone file covers multiple lines:

```
@       IN    SOA    fake.foo.edu.    hostmaster.foo.edu. (
                            1999042800      ;Serial
                            8H              ;Refresh
                            2H              ;Retry
                            1W              ;Expire
                            1D)             ;Minimum
```

The entry breaks down as follows:

- `@`: A special symbol which maps to the domain name, which in this case is `foo.edu`.
- `IN`: A special symbol, which stands for `Internet`.
- `SOA`: Indicates this is a Start of Authority record, which is required in every zone and should be the first record in the zone file.
- **`fake.foo.edu.`: Indicates the server on which the SOA record is defined. Generally, this is the name of the primary master DNS server for the domain and is the host on which the zone file exists.**

Note

Notice that the hostname `fake.foo.edu.` includes a dot at the end. All fully qualified hostnames in zone files include the trailing dot, which indicates that the name is written relative to the global root . domain. If you don't include the dot then the name is presumed to be relative to the domain defined by the zone file. For instance, if the dot were omitted from `fake.foo.edu.` this would actually indicate the hostname `fake.foo.edu.foo.edu.`.

- **`hostmaster.foo.edu.`:** Indicates the email address of the DNS server's administrator, which in this case is `hostmaster@foo.edu.`. The @ symbol cannot be used in the email address in a zone file because it has a special meaning as outlined previously. Therefore, a dot is used in its place.
- **Inside the parentheses is a series of values separated by commas:** The values are as follows:
    - **The serial number:** Indicates the current revision of the zone file. It must be incremented by at least one each time you make changes to the zone file because secondary name servers for the domain rely on this number to decide to update their zone information from the primary name server. A common

practice is to use the date as the serial number in the format YYYYMMDDNN where YYYY is the year, MM is the month, DD is the day of the month, and NN is a specific revision on the given day. This means that up to 100 changes (from 00-99) can be made on any given day to the zone file.

- **The refresh value**: Indicates how often secondary name servers should consult the primary to see whether changes need to be downloaded. Typically, this value is in seconds but can be specified in other units such as 8H, which indicates 8 hours.

- **The retry value**: Indicates how long a secondary name server should wait after a failed attempt at a zone transfer from the primary before trying again. Typically, this value is in seconds but can be specified in other units such as 2H, which indicates 2 hours.

- **The expiry value**: Indicates the maximum amount of time a secondary name server can use the zone information before it must refresh its zone information from the primary. Typically, this value is in seconds but can be specified in other units such as 1W, which indicates 1 week.

- **The minimum value:** Indicates the time to live (TTL) value. A name server must retain an answer from the primary master in its cache for at least this amount of time before it can query the server again for the same information. Typically this value is in seconds but can be specified in other units such as 1D, which indicates one day.

The remainder of this zone file contains four types of records:

- NS records
- A records
- CNAME records
- MX records

The NS record indicates a server acting as a name server for the zone. Zone files can contain more than one record indicating the primary and secondary servers for the domain. In this case, a single record exists of the form:

```
IN   NS   <host name>
```

Note

You should have A records for any name server which is part of the domain being defined by the zone file. If you use a backup name server which is part of another domain, no A record is needed in the zone file and instead will appear in the zone file for the primary name server of the other domain.

The A records associate default hostnames in the domain with IP addresses. For instance, the record

```
fake   IN   A   192.168.1.1
```

indicates that the host `fake` in the domain `foo.edu` (which is the host `fake.foo.edu.`) has the IP address `192.168.1.1`. A records take the form:

```
<host name>   IN   A   <IP address>
```

The CNAME record indicates an alias for a hostname. In this case, `www` is an alias for the host `brain.foo.edu.`:

```
www      IN   CNAME   brain.foo.edu.
```

This means that any requests to resolve `www.foo.edu` will actually be resolved as if they were requests for `brain.foo.edu.`.

The MX records indicate the hostnames of mail exchangers for the domain. When a mail message is addressed to the `foo.edu` domain, the mail server delivering the message uses this information to determine to which mail exchanger to deliver the message. MX entries take the following form:

```
<domain>   IN   MX   <preference> <host name>
```

The preference number indicates the order in which mail delivery attempts should be made: The lower the preference number the higher the priority to go to the server. In this example, `mail.foo.edu` has a preference of `10` and `mail2.foo.edu` has a preference of `20`. This means `mail.foo.edu` is the primary mail exchanger and `mail2.foo.edu` is the backup. If, for some reason, mail cannot be delivered to `mail.foo.edu`, delivery will be attempted to `mail2.foo.edu`.

Note

You should have A records for any mail exchanger which is part of the domain being defined by the zone file. If you use a backup mail exchanger which is part of another domain, no A record is needed in the zone file and instead will appear in the zone file for the primary name server of the other domain.

The zone file for reverse name lookups for `foo.edu`, `/var/named/zone.192.168.1`, is similar to the zone file for `foo.edu` but contains some different records:

```
; File: zone.192.168.1
;
1.168.192.in-addr.arpa.   IN      SOA     fake.foo.edu.  hostmaster.foo.edu. (
                                  1998021700       ;Serial
                                  8H               ;Refresh
                                  2H               ;Retry
                                  1W               ;Expire
                                  1D)              ;Minimum
             IN     NS     fake.foo.edu.
       1     IN     PTR    fake.foo.edu.
       2     IN     PTR    pinky.foo.edu.
       3     IN     PTR    brain.foo.edu.
       4     IN     PTR    mail.foo.edu.
       5     IN     PTR    mail2.foo.edu.
```

Like the `foo.edu` zone file, this file contains an `SOA` record and at least one `NS` record.

In addition, it contains a series of PTR records, which define the IP addresses that can be used as pointers for reverse name lookup. The form of the PTR records is as follows:

```
<IP address>   IN   PTR   <host name>
```

Notice that the IP addresses are specified without the trailing dots. This makes them relative to the network for which the zone file provides reverse name lookup data. Therefore, the following entry:

```
3   IN   PTR   brain.foo.edu.
```

indicates that the IP address 192.168.1.3 points to the host `brain.foo.edu`.

The reverse name lookup file for the local loopback network, `/var/named/127.0.0`, is similar to the reverse lookup zone for `foo.edu`:

```
;
; File: zone.127.0.0
@       IN      SOA             fake.foo.edu.           hostmaster.foo.edu. (
                        19960101401     ;Serial
                        8H              ;Refresh
                        2H              ;Retry
                        1W              ;Expire
                        1D)             ;Minimum
        IN      NS              fake.foo.edu.
1       IN      PTR             localhost.
```

This file contains an `SOA` record, one or more `NS` records and one or more `PTR` records.

STARTING named   We are now ready to start `named`. In version 8 a new program called `ndc` has been introduced for managing and controlling `named` but you can still invoke `named` directly if you prefer. However, `ndc` provides a clean way of starting, stopping, and checking the status of `named`.

With the configuration file `/etc/named.conf`, and the zone files defined in `/var/named`, we can start `named` using `ndc` as `follows`:

```
# ndc start
```

Check `/var/log/messages` after you start `named` and make sure no errors are reported. If there are errors the log entries will give you an idea of what's wrong. You will need to fix any errors you might have made in the configuration or zone files and restart `named`.

After it is started you can check the status of `named` with the command:

```
# ndc status
```

You can also stop named using the `ndc` command:

```
# ndc stop
```

PRIMARY NAME SERVER FOR PRIVATE NETWORK BEHIND A FIREWALL

The following is a typical `named.conf` file for a primary name server for a private network behind a corporate firewall:

```
// File: /etc/named.conf
// Primary Name Server for foo.dom
//           Internal Network
options {
    directory "/var/named";
    // Uncommenting this might help if you have to go through a
    // firewall and things are not working out:
    fake-iquery yes;
    query-source address * port 53;
    forward first;
    forwarders {
        192.168.1.1
    }
};
zone "." {
    type hint;
    file "root.hints";
};
zone "foo.dom" {
    type master;
    file "zone.foo.dom";
};
zone "10.in-addr.arpa" {
    type master;
    file "zone.10";
};
zone "0.0.127.in-addr.arpa" {
    type master;
    file "zone.127.0.0";
};
```

Note several differences between this `named.conf` file and the one previously used to illustrate a primary name server for a registered domain:

- In the `options` section, several new directives have been added:
  ```
  fake-iquery yes;
  query-source address * port 53;
  forward first;
  forwarders {
     192.168.1.1
  }
  ```

  The `fake-iquery` and `query-source` directives are necessary with some firewalls to allow the internal DNS server to query external DNS servers. The forward and forwarders directives indicate that queries for any domains not handled by this server as the primary master should be forwarded to 192.168.1.1 for resolution instead of attempting to resolve the queries directly. The server the request has been forwarded to will return any response to the queries.

■ A `foo.dom` domain has been defined with the associated reverse lookup zone. This domain is for internal use on the private network for the purpose of using DNS to resolve internal hostnames. The `foo.dom` domain is not part of the standard domain name hierarchy, does not affect the Internet, and does not require registration. Names in the `foo.dom` domain only work locally and cannot be used as hostnames on the Internet.

The zone files can be created using the same techniques for zones and reverse lookup zones described in the section "Creating Zone Files" earlier in this chapter.

After this is done, start `named` as outlined previously in the "Starting `named`" section.

SECONDARY NAME SERVERS

After understanding how to set up a primary name server, creating a secondary name server for a domain is quite simple. For the secondary server, only a `named.conf` file is needed. All zone file information will be transferred from the primary name server when the secondary server starts.

A secondary name server for the `foo.edu` domain would have a `named.conf` file similar to the following:

```
// Secondary Name Server for foo.edu
options {
        directory "/var/named";
};
zone "." {
        type hint;
        file "root.hints";
};
zone "0.0.127.in-addr.arpa" {
        type master;
        file "zone.127.0.0";
};
zone "foo.edu" {
        type slave;
        file "zone.foo.edu";
        masters {
                192.168.1.1;
        };
};
zone "1.168.192.in-addr.arpa" {
        type slave;
        file "zone.192.168.1";
        masters {
                192.168.1.1;
        };
};
```

This file is quite similar to the named.conf file for a primary master, except some zones are defined as slave zones. For each slave zone, you still must specify a zone file so that the downloaded information can be saved in this file. In addition, you need to specify the IP address of the primary name server (master) for the domain from which the secondary server can obtain zone information.

You must define a zone file for the loopback network as described earlier in the section about creating a primary name server for a registered Internet domain.

After the named.conf file is in place as well as the zone file for the loopback network and the root.hints file, start named as outlined earlier in the "Starting named" section.

RESOLVING NAMES

Resolvers are library routines that perform name lookup of the DNS name space on systems that need to resolve names. These are configured with the /etc/resolv.conf. In addition, the order in which different name spaces such as DNS and NIS are searched when resolving names is specified in the /etc/nsswitch.conf file.

Consider the following resolv.conf file for a host behind a corporate firewall in a private network:

```
; File: /etc/resolv.conf
domain foo.dom        ; internal private domain
search foo.dom foo.edu  ; foo.edu is the internet domain
nameserver    10.0.0.1 ; primary for foo.dom
nameserver    10.0.0.2 ; secondary for foo.dom
```

This file works in the following way:

- Comments start with semicolons (;) and continue to the end of the line.
- The domain directive specifies the domain to which the host belongs.
- The search directive specifies one or more domains that should be searched when an attempt is made to resolve incomplete hostnames that are not fully qualified with a domain name.
- The nameserver directives specify the IP addresses of your name servers in the order in which you should query them. When resolving names your system will query the first server listed and if that server is unavailable or fails to respond, your system will move on to the next server specified and so on down the list. You can have as many nameserver directives as you have name servers.

Depending on your system's configuration, you might need to add DNS resolution to the /etc/nsswitch.conf file. For example, say the file contains an entry similar to the following:

```
hosts: files nis
```

You would add dns to the line as follows:

```
hosts: files nis dns
```

This tells the host's name resolution libraries to perform name resolution by first consulting the /etc/hosts file, then checking your network's NIS server, and finally consulting your DNS servers. If you don't run NIS, you can remove it from the list in the /etc/nsswitch.conf file as follows:

```
hosts: files dns
```

RESOLVING NAMES WITH nslookup

You can check whether you have name resolution configured correctly on a host using the nslookup tool. This utility queries the DNS servers you have specified in resolv.conf for names. To look up a specific hostname, provide the hostname as an argument to nslookup:

```
$ nslookup www.yahoo.com
Server:  fake.foo.edu
Address:  192.168.1.1

Non-authoritative answer:
Name:    www.yahoo.com
Addresses:  204.71.200.67, 204.71.200.74, 204.71.200.75, 204.71.200.68
            204.71.202.160
```

You can also use nslookup interactively:

```
$ nslookup
Default Server:  fake.foo.edu
Address:  192.168.1.1

> www.cnn.com
Default Server:  fake.foo.edu
Address:  192.168.1.1

Name:    www.cnn.com
Address:  207.25.71.20

> www.bahai.org
Default Server:  fake.foo.edu
Address:  192.168.1.1

Name:    www.bahai.org
Address:  207.217.239.32

> cfcomm.juxta.com
Default Server:  fake.foo.edu
Address:  192.168.1.1

Name:    cfcomm.juxta.com
Address:  204.50.107.156

> exit
```

You can query a host in your local domain without specifying the complete domain name as follows:

```
> pinky
Default Server:  fake.foo.edu
Address: 192.168.1.1

Name:    pinky.foo.edu
Address:  192.168.1.2
```

To perform a reverse name lookup, provide the IP address to nslookup and it should respond with the hostname:

```
> 192.168.1.2
Default Server:  fake.foo.edu
Address:  192.168.1.2

Name:    pinky.foo.edu
Address:  192.168.1.2
```

When you query a name that is an alias defined with a CNAME record, it returns the actual name of the host as well as its aliases along with the IP address:

```
> www
Server:  fake.foo.edu
Address:  192.168.1.1

Name:    brain.foo.edu
Address:  192.168.1.3
Aliases:  www.foo.edu
```

If you want to obtain a specific type of record from a domain such as a nameserver record, use the set type command:

```
> set type=ns
> foo.edu.
Default Server:  fake.foo.edu
Address:  192.168.1.1

foo.edu nameserver = fake.foo.edu
fake.foo.edu    internet address = 192.168.1.1
```

Here the set type=ns command indicates you are looking for NS records and the result of the query for the foo.edu. domain returns the name server name and address for the domain.

Similarly, you can check the MX records for a domain using set type=mx:

```
> set type=mx
> foo.edu.
Default Server:  fake.foo.edu.
Address:  192.168.1.1

foo.edu preference = 10, mail exchanger = mail.foo.edu
foo.edu preference = 20, mail exchanger = mail2.foo.edu
foo.edu nameserver = fake.foo.edu
```

```
mail.foo.edu      internet address = 192.168.1.4
mail2.foo.edu     internet address = 192.168.1.5
fake.foo.edu      internet address = 192.168.1.1
```

A start of authority record for a domain can also be obtained using the set type command:

```
> set type=soa
> foo.org.
Default Server:  fake.foo.edu.
Address:  192.168.1.1
foo.edu
    origin = fake.foo.edu
    mail addr = hostmaster.foo.edu
    serial = 1999042800
    refresh = 28800 (8H)
    retry   = 7200 (2H)q
    expire  = 604800 (1W)
    minimum ttl = 86400 (1D)
foo.edu nameserver = fake.foo.edu
fake.foo.edu      internet address = 192.168.1.1
```

Note	In some of the examples in this section, you will notice that the responses to queries include the Non-authoritative answer indicator. This indicates that the name server had the data in its cache and is returning this data instead of querying the name server for the domain or host being queried.

You can obtain extra debugging information about a query by using the debug or d2 option:

```
> set d2
> cnn.com.
Server:  bwc.bwc.org
Address:  192.115.144.1

;; res_nmkquery(QUERY, cnn.com, IN, A)
------------
Got answer:
    HEADER:
        opcode = QUERY, id = 59442, rcode = NOERROR
        header flags:  response, want recursion, recursion avail.
        questions = 1,  answers = 18,  authority records = 0,  additional = 0
QUESTIONS:
        cnn.com, type = A, class = IN
    ANSWERS:
    ->  cnn.com
        internet address = 207.25.71.199
        ttl = 280 (4m40s)
    ->  cnn.com
        internet address = 207.25.71.5
        ttl = 280 (4m40s)
    ->  cnn.com
        internet address = 207.25.71.6
        ttl = 280 (4m40s)
```

```
     ->  cnn.com
         internet address = 207.25.71.7
         ttl = 280 (4m40s)
..............
     ->  cnn.com
         internet address = 207.25.71.82
         ttl = 280 (4m40s)
............
Non-authoritative answer:
Name:    cnn.com
Addresses:  207.25.71.199, 207.25.71.5, 207.25.71.6, 207.25.71.7
            207.25.71.8, 207.25.71.9, 207.25.71.12, 207.25.71.20, 207.25.71.22
            207.25.71.23, 207.25.71.24, 207.25.71.25, 207.25.71.26, 207.25.71.27
            207.25.71.28, 207.25.71.29, 207.25.71.30, 207.25.71.82
```

You can disable the extra debugging information with the nodebug option:

```
> set nodebug
```

To quit nslookup, use the exit command:

```
> exit
```

To learn more about the details of nslookup and other options, consult the nslookup manual page with the command man nslookup.

> **Tip**
>
> Another useful DNS tool is dig (the Domain Information Groper), which can be used for gathering information from DNS servers. Consult the dig manual page with the command man dig for details about dig and techniques for using the tool.

DNS MAINTENANCE

All updates and management of DNS zone data should be done on the primary master server. The key to remember is that after adding, removing, or changing any resource records in a zone file it is essential to increase the serial number in the SOA record in that file. Failure to do so causes the secondary servers for the domain to ignore the changes and not obtain the new data when they should. The amount by which you increment the serial number is not significant as long as it increases; follow your own numbering scheme consistently when increasing the serial numbers and you shouldn't have a problem.

After changing the contents of a zone file you must signal named on the primary master to read its configuration files. You do this by sending a SIGHUP signal to the named process:

```
# kill -HUP `cat /var/run/named.pid`
```

Alternately, use the ndc command to restart named:

```
# ndc restart
```

Tip

Whenever you restart `named` it is a good idea to use `nslookup` to verify operation of the name server. Alternately you can check the system log file `/var/log/messages` to ensure named restarted properly.

LOAD BALANCING WITH DNS

As some of the examples in the "Resolving Names with `nslookup`" section showed, it is possible for a single hostname to resolve to multiple IP addresses. Where this is possible, the DNS server rotates through these IP addresses in a round-robin fashion when resolving names for client applications.

This round-robin approach with multiple IP addresses provides a simple mechanism for distributing load across a number of parallel servers.

Consider an example in our sample `foo.edu` domain used in this chapter: You have a heavily used Web site at www.foo.edu which is aliased to `brain.foo.edu`. To handle the heavy load, you need to distribute this traffic across three servers but want to make www.foo.edu the hostname that is consistently used to access the site, regardless of which physical server answers an HTTP query.

To do this, first create three `A` records for `brain` in the `zone.foo.edu` file:

```
; zone.foo.edu  file
;
@       IN      SOA     fake.foo.edu.    hostmaster.foo.edu. (
                                1999042800      ;Serial
                                8H              ;Refresh
                                2H              ;Retry
                                1W              ;Expire
                                1D)             ;Minimum
;
; Name-servers
;
                IN      NS      fake.foo.edu.
;
; Addresses for canonical names
;
fake            IN      A       192.168.1.1
pinky           IN      A       192.168.1.2
brain           IN      A       192.168.1.3
                IN      A       192.168.1.4
                IN      A       192.168.1.5
www             IN      CNAME   brain.foo.edu.
;
; Mail exchangers
;
foo.edu.        IN      MX      10 mail.foo.edu.
                IN      MX      20 mail2.foo.edu.
mail            IN      A       192.168.1.4
mail2           IN      A       192.168.1.5
```

Note the three A records for host brain. After restarting named, a query for www or www.foo.edu using nslookup reports the list of three IP addresses but rotates them for each query:

```
> www
Default Server:  fake.foo.edu
Address:  192.168.1.1

Name:     brain.foo.edu
Addresses:  192.168.1.3, 192.168.1.5, 192.168.1.4
Aliases:  www.foo.edu

> www
Default Server:  fake.foo.edu
Address:  192.168.1.1

Name:     brain.foo.edu
Addresses:  192.168.1.4, 192.168.1.3, 192.168.1.5
Aliases:  www.foo.edu

> www
Default Server:  fake.foo.edu
Address:  192.168.1.1

Name:     brain.foo.edu
Addresses:  192.168.1.5, 192.168.1.4, 192.168.1.3
Aliases:  www.foo.edu
```

SECURING DNS

As a domain administrator you must be vigilant about security.

> **Tip**
>
> Consider joining the CERT mailing list by sending an email to cert-advisory-request@cert.org. This list includes announcements of new vulnerabilities and suggested fixes. Although the security issues are not specific to DNS, it is an excellent source of security information for all your servers and your network.

BIND Version 8 offers some added security features over older versions, including:

- Restricts zone transfers to designated slave servers only
- Restricts zone transfers from secondary servers
- Restricts queries to your name server

RESTRICTING ZONE TRANSFERS TO DESIGNATED SLAVE SERVERS ONLY

You can restrict zone transfers to designated slave servers using the allow-transfer directive in the options section of the named.conf file:

```
allow-transfer {
```

```
        <IP address of secondary 1>;
        <IP address of secondary 2>;
        ...
};
```

This restricts zone transfers for all domains for which the server acts as the primary master. Alternately, you can restrict zone transfers on a zone-by-zone basis in the zone sections of the `named.conf` file:

```
zone "foo.edu" {
    type master;
    file "zone.foo.edu";
    allow-transfer {
        <IP address of secondary 1>;
        <IP address of secondary 2>;
        ...
    };
};
```

It is a good security measure to restrict zone transfers to designated slave servers only. This prevents hackers from listing the contents of your zones and obtaining host demographic information about your network. The less you can let the hacker know about your network the safer you are.

RESTRICTING ZONE TRANSFERS FROM SECONDARY SERVERS

In addition to restricting zone transfers from the primary master to the secondary name servers, you should also restrict zone transfers from secondary servers.

If you are using dynamic updates, restrict dynamic updates for the domain using the `allow-update` directive in the zone sections of the `named.conf` file on the primary server:

```
zone "foo.edu" {
    type master;
    file "zone.foo.edu";
    allow-update {
        <IP address of updater 1>;
        <IP address of updater 2>;
        ...
    };
};
```

In addition, you can prevent spoofing by denying recursion with the recursion directive in the options section of your name servers:

```
recursion no;
```

RESTRICTING QUERIES TO YOUR NAME SERVER

You can restrict queries for records outside the authoritative zone for which your server is the primary master or secondary name server to a restricted list of hosts (usually only hosts on the internal network or in the domains in the authoritative zones). To implement this type of restriction, use access control lists (ACLs) by adding an `acl` section to your `named.conf` file and then adding an `allow-query` directive to the `options` section of the files:

```
acl internal {
    <network or host address>;
    <network or host address>;
};
options {
    ...
    allow-query {
        internal;
    };
};
```

You can specify a network of hosts using standard `<network address>/<bits>` notation such as `10.10.10.0/24` for the 10.10.10.0 Class C network.

USEFUL SCRIPTS

A useful script `named-bootconf` is provided with BIND version 8 source distribution to convert version 4 `named.boot` files to version 8 `named.conf` files. To obtain this script, download and unpack the BIND source distribution from `http://www.isc.org`.

In addition, other available utilities help ease administration of zone files for DNS, including the following:

- **h2n**: A Perl script that converts host tables such as `/etc/hosts` into zone data files. This script is useful in moving from an existing host table-based name resolution environment on your network to a DNS-based solution. You can obtain h2n with anonymous FTP from `ftp://ftp.uu.net/published/oreilly/nutshell/dnsbind/dns.tar.Z`.

- **makezones**: A Perl script that generates zone files from special files with syntax for special cases. The script is included with the current version of Bind and can be obtained with FTP from `ftp://ftp.cus.cam.ac.uk:/pub/software/programs/DNS/makezones`.

TROUBLESHOOTING

DNS problems are often caused by subtle mistakes in `named` configuration and zone files. Other DNS errors are caused by lack of communication between parent and child domain administrators. This section lists some of the common DNS errors and discusses how you can avoid them.

DOMAIN NAMES MISSING THE TRAILING DOT

This subtle mistake can have potentially disastrous consequences. In BIND when a domain name does not end with a dot, it is considered to be a relative name to the domain currently being defined.

For instance an entry like the following:

```
foo.edu.    IN  NS  fake.foo.edu
```

will produce the following result:

```
foo.edu.    IN  NS  fake.foo.edu.foo.edu
```

Clearly this is far from what was intended. Notice the hostname `fake.foo.edu` is missing a dot at the end. Without the trailing dot the hostname is considered a relative name and the current domain name is appended to it. The resultant hostname therefore becomes `fake.foo.edu.foo.edu`.

Pay special attention to trailing dots when defining hostnames and domain names in zone files. Always test the entries you add to a zone file with `nslookup` to ensure the name resolution is what you expect it to be.

FORGETTING TO INCREMENT THE SOA SERIAL NUMBER

This is a very common cause of DNS errors. After making changes to zone data you must remember to increment the serial number in the Start of Authority record. Without the serial number increment, the secondary name servers will not recognize that a change has been made to the zone data on the primary name server, and the changes will not be downloaded by the secondary.

Any changes made on the primary name server's zone data must be accompanied by a change in the SOA record's serial number. The serial number must be incremented by at least one every time you make changes to the zone file. The secondary name servers for the domain check this number to decide whether an update to the zone information has been made on the primary name server. When it detects the serial number has been incremented, it downloads the updated zone files from the primary name server. Whenever you make changes to zone data, remember to test a secondary name server to ensure it recognized the change. How often the secondary name servers consult the primary to see whether changes need to be downloaded depends on the refresh value in the SOA record or the secondary name server.

If you need to force an immediate update of zone data on a secondary name server, restart `named` on that name server. When `named` starts on a secondary name server, it checks the serial numbers of the primary name server's zone files, and downloads fresh copies of all updated zones.

FORGETTING TO SIGNAL named AFTER MAKING CHANGES TO ZONE DATA

Sometimes you can forget to signal the primary name server after making changes to the `named.conf` file or the zone data files. The name server will not know that it needs to load the new data. As a result changes you have made will not take effect.

It is very important to check system logs to make sure the name server properly reinitialized, after you have made changes to zone data, and signaled `named` to restart. Syntax errors in the configuration or zone files may prevent `named` from starting up. It is also recommended to run nslookup or dig to verify the changes you have made are as you expect them to be. If there are subtle mistakes, like missing a trailing dot for instance, the output of nslookup will reveal that, and you can fix the error promptly.

FORGETTING REVERSE DNS RECORDS

When you add new hosts to the zone files remember to add the reverse DNS or PTR entries. Many network applications do reverse DNS lookups for IP addresses. A common symptom of missing reverse DNS records is very slow startup of client applications that do reverse DNS lookups. The traceroute program, for example, runs very slow when tracing hosts with missing reverse DNS entries.

INVALID GLUE RECORD

A common symptom of invalid glue record is when you can access a host in another domain using its IP address, but you cannot access it using its domain name.

This problem commonly happens with delegated sub-domains. Delegated sub-domains must inform parent domains to change their glue records whenever the IP address or alias of its primary or secondary name server changes. If a delegated sub-domain does not inform its parent about the change, the associated glue records maintained by the parent domain become invalid.

LACK OF COORDINATION AMONG DNS ADMINISTRATORS

The distributed administration of DNS is its strength. However it can also become its weakness, if the parent and child zone administrators fail to communicate with each other about zone changes.

Two common errors that result from this are lame delegations and missing delegations. A *lame delegation* occurs when a parent domain lists a name server for a delegated sub-domain in its zone files, but that name server is completely unaware of its assigned role. A *missing delegation*, on the other hand, is the opposite scenario. In this case, the parent domain does not list a name server for a delegated sub-domain. Missing delegations happen when the IP address of an organization's primary server is changed without informing the parent domain to incorporate the change into its zone data. A common symptom of missing delegation is when hosts in your domain can reach other hosts on the Internet but no host outside your domain can reach your hosts.

MISCONFIGURED resolv.conf FILE

There are several possibilities for errors creeping into the resolv.conf file. The resolv.conf file contains the domain name of the organization. This domain name is automatically appended to any hostname that is not fully qualified. If the resolv.conf file contains an incorrect domain name entry, erroneous domain names are appended to hostnames, which result in non-existent hosts and name lookup failures.

The `resolv.conf` file lists IP addresses of name servers. The name server that appears first in the file is queried first. It is important to ensure all name servers listed in the `resolv.conf` file are functional. A non-functioning name server entry followed by a functioning name server entry will cause name lookups to work; however, it will introduce long delays in name lookups.

Check the contents of the `resolv.conf` file and make sure all information in it is up to date and accurate.

OUTDATED `root.hints` FILE

The `root.hints` file contains the domain names and IP addresses of the root servers for each domain. Changes to the `root.hints` file are not automatically propagated to your name server. You must update this file manually. Check for updated root servers information at `rs.internic.net`. You can get the latest root server information from `rs.internic.net` by running the following command:

```
# dig @rs.internic.net . ns > root.hints.new
```

The output of the `dig` command is saved to the file `root.hints.new`. Compare the contents of this file with your current `root.hints` file and if it differs use the new `root.hints` file. It is possible to set up a `cron` job to automatically retrieve information about the root servers once a month, install the updated information, restart named, and notify the administrator of the update via email. A ready script that performs this function is listed in the Linux DNS HOWTO file, which is available on-line in the `/usr/doc/HOWTO directory`.

CHAPTER 23

APACHE AND THE WORLD WIDE WEB

In this chapter

LINUX AS A WEB SERVER PLATFORM

As Linux has emerged from obscurity and been accepted as a general purpose server and network operating system, it has evolved through many stages to gain acceptance, and even prominence, as an operating system for a specific task.

One of the first domains where Linux gained this prominence was as a Web server. As a free operating system with powerful HTTP (HyperText Transfer Protocol) daemons, Linux was ideally suited as a low-cost Web server in an era when Windows was ill suited to the task and lacked the necessary tools and robustness to do so.

This allowed Linux to emerge as the platform of choice for Web servers in many organizations, including Internet providers and universities.

APACHE'S ROLE AS A LINUX HTTP SERVER

Many different HTTP daemons are available to allow Linux to act as a Web server. These include numerous freely available daemons and commercial servers such as the Netscape FastTrack Web server.

Of all these, the Apache Web server is clearly the de facto standard Web server for Linux. Almost every Linux distribution ships with the Apache Web server and Apache development occurs at a fast pace.

Apache is a freely available Web server that emerged in 1995 as an alternative to the then standard NCSA HTTP daemon, which grew out of collective efforts to patch the NCSA daemon. Within a year, Apache was ranked the top Web server on the Internet and today it is more widely used than all other available Web servers combined.

Apache exists as a commercial-grade reference implementation that provides numerous leading-edge features, including:

- HTTP 1.1 compliance
- Configurable with third-party plug-in module support
- Runs on most versions of UNIX without alteration
- Supports DBM databases for authentication
- Provides customized error messages
- Allows an unlimited number of aliases and redirections
- Supports content negotiation
- Supports virtual hosting

CONFIGURING APACHE

Apache is configured through three files:

- **httpd.conf**: This file is Apache's main configuration file and controls how Apache will run.
- **srm.conf**: This file is used to configure the resources made available with Apache.
- **access.conf**: This file is used to define access permissions for resources served by Apache.

> **Tip**
>
> The httpd.conf file is the only required configuration file for Apache. All the configuration directives normally placed in srm.conf and access.conf can also be placed in httpd.conf, allowing you to maintain your Apache configuration in one place. Although the current Apache documentation recommends placing all directives in the httpd.conf file and not using the srm.conf and access.conf files, many sites still maintain the three-file approach and the version of Apache 1.3.9 which ships with Red Hat 6.2 still uses the three-file structure for Apache configuration directives. Many administrators find that the separation of configuration into three files simplifies the organization of the configuration files and limits the size of any single configuration file.

These files are stored in a configuration directory that can be located in different places depending on your Linux distribution. If you download and install Apache from the Apache source code at http://www.apache.org/ the default configuration directory is /usr/local/apache/conf/. Red Hat Linux's bundled Apache distribution places its configuration files in /etc/httpd/conf/.

> **Note**
>
> Apache's configuration files can be stored in any location. They do not need to be stored in the default location. As outlined in the section "Starting and Stopping Apache" later in this chapter, you can specify an alternate location for your configuration files when launching Apache.

All Apache configuration files are text files and can be edited using any standard text editor such as Emacs.

THE httpd.conf FILE

The httpd.conf is the primary configuration file used by Apache. It is normally located in the default Apache configuration directory (/usr/local/apache/conf/httpd.conf if Apache is installed from the source code distribution using default settings).

As normally used, this configuration file defines the core parameters that define the operation of the Apache server. This file consists of a series of directives of the general form:

`<Directive Name> <Directive Value>`

A typical `httpd.conf` file will likely contain the directives outlined in Table 23.1.

TABLE 23.1 TYPICAL `httpd.conf` DIRECTIVES

Directive Name	Description
AddModule	Specifies a pre-compiled module to be enabled when Apache starts. The module must be loaded with a LoadModule directive to be enabled with an AddModule directive. The httpd.conf normally will have multiple AddModule directives and the default httpd.conf contains numerous AddModule directives enabling a set of standard modules that are part of the Apache distribution. Apache modules are discussed in more detail later in this chapter in the "Apache Modules" section.
ClearModuleList	Specifies that Apache's default list of enabled modules should be cleared. This allows the AddModule directive to specify modules to enable instead of using the default pre-loaded list.
CustomLog	Specifies the location of the log file for logging successful access attempts. It also identifies the type of log entries to write. The format of the value is <Complete path of log file> <Entry type>. The file must be writable by the user the Apache daemon will run as; the user and group of the Apache daemon are specified with the User and Group directives. The entry type should be the alias name of a log format specified with a LogFormat directive.
ErrorLog	Specifies the location of the file used for logging error messages. This file should be writable by the user the Apache daemon will run as; the user and group of the Apache daemon are specified using the User and Group directives.
Group	Specifies the group the Apache daemon will run as. This should be a valid Linux user group as specified in the /etc/group file. Take care to restrict the access privileges of the Apache daemon by using a group with limited access. Typically, Apache daemons run in the nobody group.
HostNameLookups	Specifies whether Apache should attempt to look up the hostnames of clients using DNS when they connect. This allows Apache to log the hostname instead of the IP address of the client but incurs substantial overhead because DNS lookups can be time consuming. In addition, if enabled and the connection fails, the client connection can time out. Possible values are on or off.

TABLE 23.1 CONTINUED

Directive Name	Description
KeepAlive	Specifies whether Apache's KeepAlive feature should be enabled when running the server in standalone mode as specified with the ServerType directive. When enabled, Apache establishes persistent connections with clients that allow for improved performance because a new connection does not need to be created for each page request. Possible values are on or off. The default value, which conforms to the HTTP 1.1 specification is on, which enables the feature.
KeepAliveTimeout	Specifies the period of inactivity after which persistent connections are closed when the server is running in standalone mode as specified with the ServerType directive. The time is specified in seconds and the default value of 100 seconds is normally suitable.
LoadModule	Specifies what compiled modules to load when Apache starts. Values take the form <External module name> <Compiled module object file>. Typically, Apache httpd.conf files contain a number of pre-specified modules to load at start time. You do not need to change this list unless you are adding third-party modules that do not have an automated installation process.
LogFormat	Specifies the format of log file entry types. Normally more than one LogFormat directive will appear in the httpd.conf file. The value of a LogFormat directive takes the form <Entry definition> <Entry alias>. The entry alias name is used in other directives, such as the CustomLog directive, to indicate the type of log entries to write to log files. The default httpd.conf file normally contains four LogFormat entries for the following alias names: combined, common, referrer, and agent. The referrer and agent formats specify log formats that are then used in the combined and common log formats. The common log format defines the Common Log Format, a standard Web server log entry format that is the default format used in the CustomLog directive. The combined format is an alternative to the common format that adds the referrer and user agent information specified in the referrer and agent formats to the Common Log Format.
LogLevel	Specifies the level of error logging Apache should perform. The possible levels are: emerg (log all emergency errors), alert (log alert conditions), critical (log critical errors), warn (log all warnings), and debug (logs almost all messages from the server). The debug error level is useful for determining problems with your server configuration but generates excessive disk activity for logging that can impact the performance of your server. The default level warn is usually best for normal server use.

TABLE 23.1 CONTINUED	
Directive Name	**Description**
MaxClients	Specifies the maximum number of simultaneous requests that are supported when the server is running in standalone mode as specified by the ServerType directive. The maximum value is 256. The value of this setting needs to be carefully considered especially if persistent connections are enabled with the KeepAlive directive. If persistent connections are enabled and you have set the maximum number of clients to too small a value, you will have contention for connection resources as new clients connect. At the same time, as you increase the number of open connections, you incur a performance hit that on a smaller Web server might be significant.
MaxKeepAliveRequest	Specifies the maximum number of requests that can be serviced with each persistent connection before the connection must be closed when the server is running in standalone mode as specified by the ServerType directive. This helps prevent a client from maintaining a permanent persistent connection by making repeated requests for documents. The default value of 100 will work well for most servers. Keep in mind that the value of 0 effectively disables persistent connections even when KeepAlive is set to on.
MaxRequestsPerChild	Specifies the maximum number of requests processed by each child server process when the server is running in standalone mode as specified by the ServerType directive. When running in standalone mode, the Apache daemon will launch a number of child processes to listen for connections and try to keep a minimum number of child processes available waiting for new incoming connections. After a child has serviced the specified number of requests, it will die and be replaced by a new child process. The default value of 30 will work well for most servers.
MaxSpareServers	Specifies the maximum number of child servers waiting for incoming connections at any one time when the server is running in standalone mode as specified by the ServerType directive. When running in standalone mode, the Apache daemon will launch a number of child processes to listen for connections and try to keep a minimum number of child processes available waiting for new incoming connections. After a child has serviced the specified number of requests, it will die and be replaced by a new child process. On a busy server, this value can have significant effect on server performance. As you increase the number of spare servers, you can quickly answer a larger number of incoming connections. However, this means that resources are allocated to the waiting server processes and you effectively allow a larger number of simultaneous connections to occur within the limit specified by the MaxClients directive.

TABLE 23.1   CONTINUED

Directive Name	Description
MinSpareServers	Specifies the minimum number of child servers waiting for incoming connections at any one time when the server is running in standalone mode as specified by the ServerType directive. When running in standalone mode, the Apache daemon will launch a number of child processes to listen for connections and try to keep a minimum number of child processes available waiting for new incoming connections. After a child has serviced the specified number of requests, it will die and be replaced by a new child process. On a busy server, this value can have a significant effect on server performance. As you increase the number of spare servers, you can quickly answer a larger number of incoming connections. This means that resources are allocated to the waiting server processes and you are effectively allowing a larger number of simultaneous connections to occur within the limit specified by the MaxClients directive. You should not set this value too high because it will unnecessarily waste resources. Apache will adjust the number of spare servers in the range between the minimum and maximum specified with the MinSpareServers and MaxSpareServers based on current system load. If you set this value too high, Apache does not have the option to reduce the number of spare servers as needed by load demands.
PidFile	Specifies the filename used to store the main parent Apache server daemon's process ID when the server is running in standalone mode as specified by the ServerType directive.
Port	Specifies the port on which the Apache server will listen for incoming connections when the server is running in standalone mode as specified by the ServerType directive. The default HTTP port for incoming connections is port 80. Do not change this unless you want to run a server on a non-standard port.
ServerAdmin	Specifies the email address of the server administrator that is displayed in Apache's default error messages displayed for users.
ServerName	Specifies your Web server's default hostname. This name should have a valid DNS entry that points to the server running Apache.
ServerRoot	Specifies the top-level directory where your Apache configuration, error, and log files are kept. If you installed Apache from the source code archives, this is likely /usr/local/apache/.
ServerType	Specifies whether you want to run Apache as a standalone process or invoke Apache through the standard inetd mechanism. Possible values are standalone and inetd. The issues surrounding the choice of standalone or inetd operation are discussed later in the section "Choosing Between Standalone and inetd Apache Operation."

TABLE 23.1 CONTINUED

Directive Name	Description
StartServers	Specifies the initial number of child servers Apache will launch to wait for incoming connections when the server is running in standalone mode as specified by the ServerType directive. When running in standalone mode, the Apache daemon launches a number of child processes to listen for connections and tries to keep a minimum number of child processes available waiting for new incoming connections. You can keep this at the default value because Apache will adjust the number of spare servers in the range between the minimum and maximum specified with the MinSpareServers and MaxSpareServers based on current system load.
Timeout	Specifies the amount of time in seconds that the Apache server waits for a client to respond before it gives up. The default value of 300 works well for most servers.
UseCanonicalNames	Specifies whether Apache should build URLs for self-referencing links using the server and port specified in the ServerName and Port directives or using the server name and port specified by the client in the document request. Self-referencing links are of the type specified relative to the current document. When set to on, the feature is enabled and the server and port specified in the directives are used. When set to off, the feature is disabled and the values specified in the client request are used.
User	Specifies the user the Apache daemon will run as. This should be a valid Linux user group as specified in the /etc/passwd file. You need to take care to restrict the access privileges of the Apache daemon by using a user with limited access. Typically, Apache daemons run as nobody. Do not allow Apache to run as the root user because this may provide users of interactive Web server features such as CGI-BIN scripts access to your system as the root user, especially if CGI-BIN scripts are poorly written.

CHOOSING BETWEEN STANDALONE AND inetd APACHE OPERATION

The Apache daemon can run in standalone mode or through the inetd daemon:

- In standalone mode, Apache keeps a number of child Apache processes running at all times to handle incoming requests. These processes persist for a period before they die and are replaced by new child processes.

- When running through inetd, no Apache processes are run. Instead, inetd listens for incoming Web connections and when one is made, it launches a new Apache process.

The choice of mode is defined by the ServerType directive of the httpd.conf file. (Refer to Table 23.1.)

Which mode to run in is primarily governed by the performance demands on your Web server. Without any doubt, the standalone mode offers better system performance than is possible with `inetd` operation. This is because when running through `inetd`, a new Apache process must be launched to handle each incoming connection where standalone mode keeps child processes running ready to receive connections. On a heavily used Web server, there is no choice but to run Apache in standalone mode. If you are running a low-usage Web server, you have the option to choose either mode and if you configure all your incoming network connections through `inetd`, you may want to configure Apache in this way as well.

CONFIGURING APACHE TO RUN WITH `inetd`

If you opt to run Apache through `inetd` as discussed previously in "Choosing Between Standalone and `inetd` Apache Operation," you must create an appropriate entry in the `/etc/inetd.conf` file for Apache. The use of `inetd` is discussed in detail in Chapter 13, "Linux Network Configuration and TCP/IP."

For Apache, add the following entry to the `inetd.conf` file:

```
httpd stream tcp nowait httpd /usr/sbin/httpd -f /usr/local/apache/conf/httpd.conf
```

The path to the `httpd` binary file and the `httpd.conf` configuration file in this example assumes you have installed Apache from source code using the default settings. This entry indicates that `httpd` should be launched using the specified `httpd.conf` file each time `inetd` receives an HTTPD connection.

In addition, you must specify the port on which incoming HTTPD connections will be made. This is specified in the `/etc/services` file. This file must have the following entry to support HTTPD on the standard port 80:

```
httpd 80/tcp httpd
```

Once these entries have been created, `inetd` should be restarted with the following commands:

```
# /etc/rc.d/init.d/inet stop
# /etc/rc.d/init.d/inet start
```

Alternately, you can force `inetd` to reload its configuration file by sending it the SIGHUP signal:

```
# kill -1 `cat /var/run/inetd.pid`
```

Tip

If you run Apache through `inetd`, you don't want it to be included in the `rc` scripts for launching at startup. Check your startup scripts to be sure you are not launching `httpd` at startup time. Consult Chapter 4, "Booting Up and Shutting Down," for details of the `rc` startup scripts.

A TYPICAL httpd.conf FILE

A typical httpd.conf for an Apache Web server might look like the following:

```
ServerType standalone
Port 80
HostnameLookups off
User nobody
Group nobody
ServerAdmin reqeusts@juxta.com
ServerRoot /usr/local/apache
ServerName www.juxta.com
ErrorLog /usr/local/apache/logs/error_log
LogLevel warn
LoadModule env_module          modules/mod_env.so
LoadModule config_log_module   modules/mod_log_config.so
LoadModule agent_log_module    modules/mod_log_agent.so
LoadModule referer_log_module  modules/mod_log_referer.so
LoadModule mime_module         modules/mod_mime.so
LoadModule negotiation_module  modules/mod_negotiation.so
LoadModule status_module       modules/mod_status.so
LoadModule info_module         modules/mod_info.so
LoadModule includes_module     modules/mod_include.so
LoadModule autoindex_module    modules/mod_autoindex.so
LoadModule dir_module          modules/mod_dir.so
LoadModule cgi_module          modules/mod_cgi.so
LoadModule asis_module         modules/mod_asis.so
LoadModule imap_module         modules/mod_imap.so
LoadModule action_module       modules/mod_actions.so
LoadModule userdir_module      modules/mod_userdir.so
LoadModule proxy_module        modules/libproxy.so
LoadModule alias_module        modules/mod_alias.so
LoadModule rewrite_module      modules/mod_rewrite.so
LoadModule access_module       modules/mod_access.so
LoadModule auth_module         modules/mod_auth.so
LoadModule anon_auth_module    modules/mod_auth_anon.so
LoadModule db_auth_module      modules/mod_auth_db.so
LoadModule digest_module       modules/mod_digest.so
LoadModule expires_module      modules/mod_expires.so
LoadModule headers_module      modules/mod_headers.so
LoadModule usertrack_module    modules/mod_usertrack.so
LoadModule setenvif_module     modules/mod_setenvif.so
ClearModuleList
AddModule mod_env.c
AddModule mod_log_config.c
AddModule mod_log_agent.c
AddModule mod_log_referer.c
AddModule mod_mime.c
AddModule mod_negotiation.c
AddModule mod_status.c
AddModule mod_info.c
AddModule mod_include.c
AddModule mod_autoindex.c
AddModule mod_dir.c
AddModule mod_cgi.c
AddModule mod_asis.c
AddModule mod_imap.c
```

```
AddModule mod_actions.c
AddModule mod_userdir.c
AddModule mod_proxy.c
AddModule mod_alias.c
AddModule mod_rewrite.c
AddModule mod_access.c
AddModule mod_auth.c
AddModule mod_auth_anon.c
AddModule mod_auth_db.c
AddModule mod_digest.c
AddModule mod_expires.c
AddModule mod_headers.c
AddModule mod_usertrack.c
AddModule mod_so.c
AddModule mod_setenvif.c
LogFormat "%h %l %u %t \"%r\" %>s %b \"%{Referer}i\" \"%{User-Agent}i\"" combined
LogFormat "%h %l %u %t \"%r\" %>s %b" common
LogFormat "%{Referer}i -> %U" referer
LogFormat "%{User-agent}i" agent
CustomLog /usr/local/apache/logs/access_log common
PidFile /var/run/httpd.pid
UseCanonicalName on
Timeout 300
KeepAlive On
MaxKeepAliveRequests 100
KeepAliveTimeout 15
MinSpareServers 8
MaxSpareServers 20
StartServers 10
MaxClients 150
MaxRequestsPerChild 100
```

Note

The httpd.conf file normally contains substantial comments that describe entries and their purposes. These have been removed for brevity and clarity of presentation in this book. Comments start with the hash mark (#) and continue to the end of the line, as is typical of most Linux configuration files.

Note

Where the complete absolute path of a file is not specified (such as in the LoadModule directives), the specified path of the file is relative to the directory specified with the ServerRoot directive. Therefore, the file modules/mod_env.so is actually /usr/local/apache/modules/mod_env.so in this example.

THE srm.conf FILE

The srm.conf file is typically used to specify configuration information related to resources being served by the Apache Web server. For instance, the document root directory for your Web server, supported languages, and directory aliases is defined in this file. The srm.conf file is normally located in the default Apache configuration directory (/usr/local/apache/conf/srm.conf if Apache is installed from the source code distribution using default settings).

> **Note**
>
> As mentioned earlier, the configuration directives listed here can also be placed in the httpd.conf file. Apache recommends placing the directives in httpd.conf but both approaches can be used.

As normally used, this configuration file defines the core parameters that define the operation of the Apache server. This file consists of a series of directives of the general form:

<Directive Name> <Directive Value>

A typical srm.conf file will likely contain the directives outlined in Table 23.2.

TABLE 23.2 TYPICAL srm.conf DIRECTIVES

Directive Name	Description
AccessFileName	Specifies the name of the access control file. An access control file of the specified name can be placed in a directory in your server's document tree to specify server-specific access control settings overriding general settings defined in the access.conf file. Normally this file is called .htaccess and this is the default value of the AccessFileName directive. Because this is a commonly known filename, you can enhance the security of your system by changing the filename for your Web server. The filename should always start with a dot so that it is hidden from directory listings; otherwise, the purposes of changing the filename (to make it harder for attackers to guess the name and download the file for viewing and analyis) are defeated.
AddEncoding	Specifies a MIME encoding for files with a particular filename extension. Multiple AddEncoding directives normally appear in the srm.conf file and the default file contains a pre-defined set of encoding to which you can add your own entries.
AddHandler	Specifies an application handler for files with a given filename extension. The value of this directive takes the form *<Handler name> <File name extension>*.
AddIcon	Specifies the icon to display in directory listings for files with a specific filename extension when FancyIndexing is enabled. The value of this directive takes the form *<Icon file name> <File name extension>*. The icon filename should be a path from the root of your Web site. That is, if you access the file as http://my.host/icons/file.gif then you want to specify /icons/file.gif as the filename. The filename extension should contain the leading dot as in .txt. The default srm.conf contains a set of icon definitions to which you can add your own AddIcon directives as needed.

TABLE 23.2 CONTINUED	
Directive Name	**Description**
AddIconBy Encoding	Specifies the icon to display in directory listings for files of a specific MIME encoding when FancyIndexing is enabled. The MIME encoding must be defined with an AddEncoding directive. The value of this directive takes the form (*<Text name>,<Icon file name>*) *<MIME Encoding>*. The icon filename should be a path from the root of your Web site. That is, if you would access the file as http://my.host/icons/file.gif then specify /icons/file.gif as the filename. The text name is the text to display in place of an icon in text-only browsers. The MIME encoding should be specified with a name specified in an AddEncoding directive. The default srm.conf contains a set of icon definitions to which you can add your own AddIconByEncoding directives as needed.
AddIconByType	Specifies the icon to display in directory listings for files of a specific MIME type when FancyIndexing is enabled. The MIME encoding must have been defined with an AddEncoding directive. The value of this directive takes the form (*<Text name>,<Icon file name>*) *<MIME Type>*. The icon filename should be a path from the root of your Web site. That is, if you would access the file as http://my.host/icons/file.gif then specify /icons/file.gif as the filename. The text name is the text to display in place of an icon in text-only browsers. The MIME type should be a standard MIME type such as text/html or a broad grouping of MIME types specified with a wildcard such as image/*. The default srm.conf contains a set of icon definitions to which you can add your own AddIconByType directives as needed.
AddLanguage	Specifies language-specific MIME encodings to be associated with specific filename extensions. The value of this directive takes the form *<MIME language> <Filename extension>*. The MIME language is a two-letter MIME language code such as en for English or de for German. The filename extension specifies the extension of files in the given language; the extension should include the leading dot as in .en. The default srm.conf file contains a default list of language encodings to which you can add your own AddLanguage directives as needed.
Alias	Specifies an alias for a physical directory. The value of this directive takes the form *<Alias directory> <Physical directory>*. For instance if you want the physical directory /some/directory to be accessible as /foo on your Web site using the URL http://my.domain/foo, you need the following directive: Alias /foo /some/directory.
BrowserMatch	Specifies environment variables based on the user agent HTTP header provided by the browser. Each browser provides a user agent header that identifies the maker and version of the browser. With the BrowserMatch directive you can define environment variables based on the value of this header. The value of the directive takes the form *<Regular expression> <Variable name>=<Variable value> <Variable name>=<Variable value>* .... The regular expression should be a standard POSIX.2 regular expression such as ^Mozilla or ^Mozilla/[3-4]. The variable name-value pairs take one of three forms: to set a variable to 1 simply use its name as in foo which sets the environment variable foo to 1; to remove a variable if it is already set use the ! Symbol as in !foo which deletes the variable foo from the environment; and to assign an actual value to a variable, use = symbol as in foo="Some value" which sets foo to the string Some value.

TABLE 23.2   CONTINUED

Directive Name	Description
DefaultIcon	Specifies the default icon to display in directory listings for files with no other icon specified when `FancyIndexing` is enabled. The icon filename should be a path from the root of your Web site. That is, if you access the file as `http://my.host/icons/file.gif` then specify `/icons/file.gif` as the filename.
DefaultType	Specifies the default MIME type for files that have no other MIME type associated with them. The default value of `text/plain` is a good choice as is `text/html`.
DirectoryIndex	Specifies the default filename to serve from a directory when the browser requests a directory with no filename specified. For instance, if a browser requests `http://my.domain/` from your system, Apache must know which file in your root document directory to send to the browser. This directive takes a list of filenames, separated by spaces, as its value. Apache will search through the list until finds a matching file in the requested directory and then will send this file to the client. Specifying more than one filename on this list is useful when you might be serving HTML files from some directories but special application files such as PHP applications or ColdFusion applications from another. However, you should take care to keep the list of directory index files to a minimum for two reasons. The server must search through the list each time a directory is requested and with a longer list this is inefficient.If you have two files in the directory that match files on the list, the file you want sent to the browser may not be the one that Apache will select to send.
DocumentRoot	Specifies the physical directory to use as the root document directory for your Web server. For instance, if you want the root URL for your site (such as `http://my.domain/`) to point to the physical directory `/usr/local/apache/htdocs/`, use the following directive: `DocumentRoot /usr/local/apache/htdocs`.
FancyIndexing	Specifies whether fancy indexing should be used when displaying a listing of files in a directory on the Web site. With fancy indexing, enabled icons you specify in the `srm.conf` file will be used to display the files in the directory listing. To enable fancy indexing, set the directive to `on`; to disable the feature, set the directive to `off`.
HeaderName	Specifies the name of a file that will be displayed before a directory listing. The value of this directive specifies a file name that must exist in the directory being listed. This allows you to specify a filename and have different versions of the file in different directories.
IndexIgnore	Specifies the name of files that will be ignored and not displayed in directory listings displayed to the user. The value of this directive is one or more filenames or POSIX.2 regular expressions separated by spaces.
Language Priority	Sets the preferred order of languages to server to the browser where the browser indicates a list of acceptable languages. The value of this directive is a space-separated list of MIME language encodings such as `en de`. The value specified in the default `srm.conf` file is ideal for an English-only site.

TABLE 23.2   CONTINUED

Directive Name	Description
ReadmeName	Specifies the name of a file that will be displayed at the end of a directory listing. The value of this directive specifies a filename that must exist in the directory being listed. This allows you to specify a filename and have different versions of the file in different directories.
TypesConfig	Specifies the name and location of the MIME types configuration file for your server. Keep the default value of this directive unless you create a custom file in a different location.
UserDir	Specifies the directory name of a subdirectory in a user's home directory which can server as the document root for the user's personal Web files. This allows a user to place files in this directory and have them accessed through the Web as http://my.domain/~<username>/.

PART
V

CH
23

PERMISSIONS AND SECURITY FOR YOUR ROOT DOCUMENT DIRECTORY

The purpose behind using a root document directory as specified by the DocumentRoot directive is to prevent a Web browser from gaining access to your entire system through the Web server. This effectively limits access to the document tree specified in the DocumentRoot directive unless you use a directive such as Alias to enable access to other directories. Care should be taken in selecting your root document directory and any other directories such as aliases to ensure that only files which you want to be available on the Web are being served by Apache.

However, taking care to choose an appropriate document root and aliases is not sufficient to protect your file systems. For instance, if you have symbolic links somewhere in the root document directory tree to directories or files outside this hierarchy, you are enabling access to data located outside the document tree, negating any security you gain by limiting Apache to a particular root document directory tree.

> **Note**
>
> As we will learn later in the "The access.conf File" section, if FollowSymLinks is disabled for a directory, this is not a problem because disabling this feature prevents this security hole.

A TYPICAL srm.conf FILE

A typical srm.conf file for an Apache Web server might look like the following:

```
DocumentRoot /home/httpd/html
UserDir public_html
DirectoryIndex index.html index.shtml index.cgi
FancyIndexing on
AddIconByEncoding (CMP,/icons/compressed.gif) x-compress x-gzip
AddIconByType (TXT,/icons/text.gif) text/*
```

```
AddIconByType (IMG,/icons/image2.gif) image/*
AddIconByType (SND,/icons/sound2.gif) audio/*
AddIconByType (VID,/icons/movie.gif) video/*
AddIcon /icons/binary.gif .bin .exe
AddIcon /icons/binhex.gif .hqx
AddIcon /icons/tar.gif .tar
AddIcon /icons/world2.gif .wrl .wrl.gz .vrml .vrm .iv
AddIcon /icons/compressed.gif .Z .z .tgz .gz .zip
AddIcon /icons/a.gif .ps .ai .eps
AddIcon /icons/layout.gif .html .shtml .htm .pdf
AddIcon /icons/text.gif .txt
AddIcon /icons/c.gif .c
AddIcon /icons/p.gif .pl .py
AddIcon /icons/f.gif .for
AddIcon /icons/dvi.gif .dvi
AddIcon /icons/uuencoded.gif .uu
AddIcon /icons/script.gif .conf .sh .shar .csh .ksh .tcl
AddIcon /icons/tex.gif .tex
AddIcon /icons/bomb.gif core
AddIcon /icons/back.gif ..
AddIcon /icons/hand.right.gif README
AddIcon /icons/folder.gif ^^DIRECTORY^^
AddIcon /icons/blank.gif ^^BLANKICON^^
DefaultIcon /icons/unknown.gif
ReadmeName README
HeaderName HEADER
IndexIgnore .??* *~ *# HEADER* README* RCS
AccessFileName .htaccess
TypesConfig /etc/mime.types
DefaultType text/plain
AddEncoding x-compress Z
AddEncoding x-gzip gz
AddLanguage en .en
AddLanguage fr .fr
AddLanguage de .de
AddLanguage da .da
AddLanguage el .el
AddLanguage it .it
LanguagePriority en fr de
Alias /icons/ /home/httpd/icons/
ScriptAlias /cgi-bin/ /home/httpd/cgi-bin/
AddType text/html .shtml
AddHandler server-parsed .shtml
AddHandler imap-file map
BrowserMatch "Mozilla/2" nokeepalive
BrowserMatch "MSIE 4\.0b2;" nokeepalive downgrade-1.0 force-response-1.0
BrowserMatch "RealPlayer 4\.0" force-response-1.0
BrowserMatch "Java/1\.0" force-response-1.0
BrowserMatch "JDK/1\.0" force-response-1.0
```

Note

The srm.conf file normally contains substantial comments that describe entries and their purposes. These have been removed for brevity and clarity of presentation in this book. Comments start with the hash mark (#) and continue to the end of the line as is typical of most Linux configuration files.

THE access.conf FILE

The access.conf file is typically used to specify access control information for resources being served by the Apache Web server. The access.conf file is normally located in the default Apache configuration directory (/usr/local/apache/conf/access.conf if Apache is installed from the source code distribution using default settings).

> **Note**
>
> As mentioned earlier, the configuration directives listed here can also be placed in the httpd.conf file. Apache recommends placing the directives in httpd.conf but both approaches can be used.

The format of this file differs from that of the httpd.conf and srm.conf file in that it consists of directive blocks which span multiple lines and run from an opening marker or tag such as <Directory ...> to a closing tag such as </Directory>.

Inside these directive blocks, one or more directives are used to specify access control for a particular directory. The opening <Directory ...> tag takes the form:

<Directory <Directory name>>

This indicates to which directory the directives in the block apply. Within <Directory ...> block you will find directives of the general form:

<Directive Name> <Directive Value>

A typical access.conf file will likely contain the directives outlined in Table 23.3 in its <Directory ...> blocks.

TABLE 23.3 TYPICAL access.conf DIRECTIVES

Directive Name	Description
allow from	Specifies the hostnames or IP addresses that are allowed to access this directory and its subdirectories. Spaces separate hosts using the following rules: The special keyword all allows access from all clients; the tail end of a hostname can be used to match all hosts ending in that tail (such as cnn.com); and the front part of an IP address can be used to match all IP addresses starting with that front end (such as 192.168.147), or a <network address>/<network mask> pair.
AllowOverride	Specifies what features can be overridden by a local access file (usually .htaccess) stored in a particular directory. Possible values are AuthConfig (allow overriding of directives related to authentication and authorization); FileInfo (allow overriding of directives related to document types and languages); Indexes (allow overriding of directives related to directory indexing); Limit (allow overriding of directives related to the control of host access); and Options (allow overriding of the Options and XbitHack directives). Multiple values can be listed separated by spaces.

TABLE 23.3   CONTINUED

Directive Name	Description
deny from	Specifies the hostnames or IP addresses that are not allowed to access this directory and its subdirectories. Hosts are listed separated by spaces using the following rules: The special keyword all allows access from all clients; the tail end of a hostname can be used to match all hosts ending in that tail (such as cnn.com); and the front part of an IP address can be used to match all IP addresses starting with that front end (such as 192.168.147), or a *<network address>*/*<network mask>* pair.
Options	Specifies the server options enabled in the directory and its subdirectories. Possible values are None (no options are enabled), All (all options are enabled), ExecCGI (CGI scripts can be executed), FollowSymLinks (symbolic links can be followed), Includes (server-side includes are allowed), Includes NOEXEC (server-side includes are allowed with the exception of #exec and #include), Indexes (directory listings are allowed), SymLinksIfOwnerMatch (symbolic links can be followed only if the target file or directory has the same owner as the link itself), and MultiViews (content negotiation should be performed on the basis of a document's language). A list of multiple options separated by spaces can be included in the value of this directive.
order	Specifies the order in which allow and deny directives are processed. Possible values are: deny,allow (evaluate the deny directives before the allow directives), allow,deny (evaluate the allow directives before the deny directives), and mutual-failure (only allow hosts which appear in the allow list and do not appear in the deny list).

These directives can also be used in local access control files such as .htaccess to override settings from access.conf where the AllowOverride directive in access.conf allows this.

Note

Remember that access configurations in a subdirectory override those in parent directories. For this reason, you must take care when you use multiple <Directory ...> blocks that the necessary access control settings are in place for all directories in your system.

A TYPICAL access.conf FILE

A typical access.conf file for an Apache Web server might look like the following:

```
<Directory />
Options None
AllowOverride None
</Directory>

<Directory /home/httpd/html>
Options Indexes Includes FollowSymLinks
```

```
AllowOverride None
order allow,deny
allow from all
</Directory>

<Directory /home/httpd/cgi-bin>
AllowOverride None
Options ExecCGI
</Directory>

<Directory /usr/doc>
order deny,allow
deny from all
allow from localhost
Options Indexes FollowSymLinks
</Directory>
```

PART
V

CH
23

Note

The `access.conf` file normally contains substantial comments that describe entries and their purposes. These have been removed for brevity and clarity of presentation in this book. Comments start with the hash mark (#) and continue to the end of the line as is typical of most Linux configuration files.

APACHE MODULES

Apache provides the capability to dynamically load pre-compiled modules at start time without requiring that the module be compiled into the `httpd` binary itself. Apache ships with a large number of these pre-compiled binaries, which provide the bulk of the capabilities of Apache, including access control, directory aliasing, and authorization. Table 23.4. outlines these modules.

TABLE 23.4   APACHE PRE-COMPILED MODULES

Module Name	Functionality
mod_access	Provides access control on the basis of the client's host name or IP address.
mod_actions	Provides CGI-BIN script support through file MIME type of HTTP request headers.
mod_alias	Provides the capability to create directory aliases.
mod_asis	Provides the capability to send a document to the browser without the standard HTTP headers.
mod_auth	Provides basic HTTP authentication against standard Apache htpasswd text files containing user accounts.
mod_auth_anon	Provides for anonymous access to authenticated areas in a manner similar to FTP anonymous access.

TABLE 23.4 CONTINUED	
Module Name	**Functionality**
mod_auth_db	Provides basic HTTP authentication against user accounts stored in Berkeley DB files.
mod_auth_dbm	Provides basic HTTP authentication against user accounts stored in DBM files.
mod_auth_external	Provides basic HTTP authentication using an external program to perform the actual authorization.
mod_autoindex	Provides control over the way in which Apache generates automatic directory indexes.
mod_cern_meta	Provides support for additional meta information such as additional HTTP headers.
mod_cgi	Provides CGI-BIN script support.
mod_digest	Provides user authentication using the MD5 digest authentication scheme.
mod_dir	Provides the capability to redirect any request for a directory that does not include the trailing slash.
mod_env	Provides the capability to pass environment variables to CGI-BIN scripts or server-side include files.
mod_expires	Provides control over Apache's handling of the Expires HTTP header.
mod_headers	Provides the capability to manipulate HTTP headers.
mod_imap	Provides image map support.
mod_include	Provides server-side include support.
mod_info	Provides an overview of server operation and status.
mod_log_agent	Provides the capability to store user agent information in log files.
mod_log_config	Provides the capability to control the format of log entries.
mod_log_referer	Provides the capability to store incoming Referer headers in log files.
mod_mime	Provides clients with meta-information about files.
mod_mime_magic	Provides the capability to determine the MIME type of files from a magic file.
mod_negotiation	Provides support for content negotiation.
mod_proxy	Provides HTTP proxy capabilities.
mod_rewrite	Provides URL rewriting capabilities.
mod_setnenvif	Provides the capability to create custom environment variables for later decision making.
mod_spelling	Provides the capability to handle mis-spelling and mis-capitalization of URLs requested by clients.

TABLE 23.4   CONTINUED

Module Name	Functionality
mod_status	Provides the capability to monitor the status of the Apache server through the Web.
mod_unique_id	Provides a unique ID for each request.
mod_usertrack	Provides support for HTTP Cookies.

Each of these modules when enabled in the httpd.conf file provides configuration directives that can be used to configure the features of the module. Complete details of these directives and the use of these modules are found in the Apache documentation at http://www.apache.org/.

Note

Numerous third-party modules are available for Apache. The Apache Modules Registry at http://modules.apache.org/ is a good source of these modules.

MANAGING APACHE

Several management tasks are routinely performed with an Apache Web server, including:

- Starting the Server
- Stopping the Server
- Restarting the Server
- Checking the Server's Status
- Testing the Server's Configuration Files

STARTING THE SERVER

The Apache server can be started by simply starting the httpd daemon, which is normally located in the /usr/sbin/ directory:

```
# /usr/sbin/httpd
```

Launch Apache as the root user. Apache will proceed to launch daemons to listen for connections using the user and group specified in the httpd.conf file.

If your Apache configuration files are not in the default location for your Apache installation or if you want to insure that Apache uses the correct files, specify the path to your httpd.conf file using the -f flag:

```
# /usr/sbin/httpd -f /usr/local/apache/conf/httpd.conf
```

Apache will look in the same directory as httpd.conf for the other configuration files or will follow any directives in httpd.conf, pointing to the location of alternate access.conf and srm.conf files.

STOPPING THE SERVER

You can stop the server using the kill command. Apache stores its process ID in the file /var/run/httpd.pid so you can kill Apache with the command:

```
# kill `cat /var/run/httpd.pid`
```

RESTARTING THE SERVER

You can force a running Apache daemon to reload its configuration files by sending it the SIGHUP signal using the kill command:

```
# kill -HUP `cat /var/run/httpd.pid`
```

If you really need to stop Apache and restart it you can use the following commands:

```
# kill `cat /var/run/httpd.pid`
# /usr/sbin/httpd
```

TESTING THE SERVER'S STATUS AND CONFIGURATION FILES

You can check the accuracy of your Apache configuration files using the -t and -S flags of the httpd command:

```
# /usr/sbin/httpd -t -S
```

The -t flag tests your configuration syntax and the -S flag displays the parsing of your virtual host configuration, if any. If you need to specify the exact location of your configuration files, indicate the location of your httpd.conf file using the -f flag:

```
# /usr/sbin/httpd -t -S -f /usr/local/apache/conf/httpd.conf
```

VIRTUAL HOSTING WITH APACHE

Although many Web servers serve a single Web site, it is not uncommon for intranet and Internet Web servers to host multiple sites, each with their own unique document trees and domain names. For instance, Internet Service Providers may offer Web hosting to their customers or each department in an organization may have a separate, and distinct, Web site on the Intranet.

To support hosting of multiple sites from a single Web server requires the use of virtual hosting. Virtual hosting can be implemented in two ways:

- IP address-based virtual hosting (or hardware virtual hosting) in which the Web server has multiple IP addresses and a different IP address is associated with each site.

- Hostname-based virtual hosting (or software virtual hosting) in which the Web server responds to a single IP address but multiple hostnames are associated with that address and each hostname is associated with a different Web site on the server.

IP address-based hosting provides the advantage that the client does not need to provide any special information to the server in order for the server to select and serve the correct site. However, because IP addresses are increasingly in short supply, this option is unattractive for servers offering Web sites on the public Internet.

Name-based virtual hosting requires that the client provide a host header field in which the hostname of the desired site is indicated. This is an HTTP 1.1 feature supported by all newer browsers, but some older browsers do not support this. With these browsers, the server will receive a request on its IP address but have no information to determine which site to serve. Nonetheless, software virtual hosting of this type is increasingly the norm because it does not strain the availability of IP addresses unnecessarily. In this chapter we will consider implementation of hostname-based virtual hosting.

Implementing name-based virtual hosting requires three steps:

- Creating DNS entries for each site
- Creating a directory hierarchy for the sites
- Configuring Apache to serve each site

CREATING DNS ENTRIES FOR EACH SITE

A Web server on the Internet needs a primary A record for itself, which indicates the primary domain name for the server. If your Web server's primary domain name is `www.my.domain` and its IP address is `1.2.3.4`, the DNS A record for the server would be:

`www.my.domain.  IN  A  1.2.3.4`

For each additional site you want to host on the system using name-based virtual hosting, you must create a *canonical name* (CNAME) record which serves as an alias for the server. For instance, to associate a second domain name, `fun.my.domain`, with the same server you would use the following CNAME record:

`fun.my.domain.  IN  CNAME  www.my.domain.`

Even if you want to create virtual hosts in domains other than the domain of the primary hostname, you can still use CNAME records. For instance, you can alias `www.another.domain` to `www.my.domain` using the following CNAME entries in the DNS records for `another.domain`:

`www.another.domain.  IN  CNAME  www.my.domain.`

Complete details of DNS management and the creation and editing of DNS zone files is discussed in Chapter 22, "DNS."

CREATING A DIRECTORY HIERARCHY FOR THE SITES

Each site being served by your Apache system requires a separate and distinct document root directory from which to serve files. Typically, it is advisable to consolidate these document roots in a single location for ease of management. For instance, if your single-site Web server normally uses `/usr/local/apache/htdocs/` as its document root directory, when you move to virtual hosting you may want create subdirectories in this location where each subdirectory is a document root for a different site. Consider the three hostnames defined previously for a server: `www.my.domain`, `fun.my.domain`, and `www.another.domain`.

In this situation, you could create three directories for the sites:

- `/usr/local/apache/htdocs/www.my.domain`
- `/usr/local/apache/htdocs/fun.my.domain`
- `/usr/local/apache/htdocs/www.another.domain`

You can use any organizational scheme for your Web site's root document directories. Using a consistent scheme such as the one created here can help ensure ease of management as your sites develop and grow.

CONFIGURING APACHE TO SERVE EACH SITE

You can configure Apache in two ways to serve multiple virtual sites:

- By running a separate Apache daemon for each site
- By running a shared Apache daemon for all sites

Unless you plan to have significantly different configurations for each site including a different `ServerRoot` value, different users and groups, or different `ServerType` values, consider the latter option. Running a single Apache daemon makes management easier: You need to only maintain one set of configuration files and you need to only monitor one daemon to keep track of the health of your sites.

The first step in configuring name-based virtual hosting using a single Apache daemon is to add the `NameVirtualHost` directive to your `httpd.conf` file. This indicates which IP address Apache should listen on for virtual host connections and takes the following form:

```
NameVirtualHost 1.2.3.4
```

1.2.3.4 is the IP address of the server.

Next, you need to add special `<VirtualHost ...> ... </VirtualHost>` sections to your `httpd.conf` file. The `VirtualHost` sections allow you to specify settings specific to a given virtual server including a unique document root and server name. Each `VirtualHost` section takes the general form:

```
<VirtualHost <IP Address>>
   <Directives>
</VirtualHost>
```

In the case of name-based virtual hosting, each `VirtualHost` section is associated with the same IP address but the `ServerName` directive inside the section identifies the name with which a server is associated. For instance, in the previous example of three virtual Web servers for `www.my.domain`, `fun.my.domain` and `www.another.domain`, you would need three `VirtualHost` sections each with at least a `ServerName` and `DocumentRoot` directive:

```
<VirtualHost 1.2.3.4>
    ServerName www.my.domain
    DocumentRoot /usr/local/apache/htdocs/www.my.domain
</VirtualHost>

<VirtualHost 1.2.3.4>
    ServerName fun.my.domain
    DocumentRoot /usr/local/apache/htdocs/fun.my.domain
</VirtualHost>

<VirtualHost 1.2.3.4>
    ServerName www.another.domain
    DocumentRoot /usr/local/apache/htdocs/www.another.domain
</VirtualHost>
```

Inside each `VirtualHost` section you can also place additional directives to create settings specific to each site.

After you configure Apache for your virtual sites, restart the Apache daemon to reload its configuration files as outlined earlier in this chapter in the section "Restarting the Server."

PROVIDING BACKWARD COMPATIBILITY

Name-based virtual hosting provides a simple, elegant solution to the need to run multiple Web sites on a single server without excessive use of scarce IP addresses. However, it suffers from incompatibility with older Web browsers that do not use the HTTP 1.1 Host header field to indicate the name of the site they are requesting. With these browsers, you must set up a logical default Web site from which users can link to the virtual sites.

The basic model is this:

- Define each virtual site using a `VirtualHost` section as outlined above but add a `ServerPath` directive to the section.

- Add a default `VirtualHost` section that catches any connection to an unspecified or non-existent site. This site should have links to all the virtual sites.

The end result is the following directives to define your virtual hosts for the example server used in this chapter:

```
<VirtualHost 1.2.3.4?
    DocumentRoot /usr/local/apache/htdocs/
</VirtualHost>
```

```
<VirtualHost 1.2.3.4>
   ServerName www.my.domain
   DocumentRoot /usr/local/apache/htdocs/www.my.domain
    ServerPath /www.my.domain/
</VirtualHost>

<VirtualHost 1.2.3.4>
   ServerName fun.my.domain
   DocumentRoot /usr/local/apache/htdocs/fun.my.domain
   ServerPath /fun.my.domain/
</VirtualHost>

<VirtualHost 1.2.3.4>
   ServerName www.another.domain
   DocumentRoot /usr/local/apache/htdocs/www.another.domain
   ServerPath /www.another.domain/
</VirtualHost>
```

The first VirtualHost section does not contain a ServerName directive. This means that when Apache can't match a connection to one of the other VirtualHost sections it will use this one. This will default to the parent directory of the root directory for all other sites (/usr/local/apache/htdocs) and provide the default index file from that directory. This file can then contain links to the relative directory www.my.domain/, fun.my.domain/, and www.another.domain/ without the need to specify the host header name.

The ServerPath directives have the effect of ensuring that connections to http://www.my.domain/ and http://www.my.domain/www.my.domain/ end up at the same place and similarly for each site.

All this means the following:

■ Connections to http://www.my.domain/, http://fun.my.domain/, or http://www.another.domain/ from hosts that support HTTP 1.1's Host header field will access the directories /usr/local/apache/htdocs/www.my.domain/, /usr/local/apache/htdocs/fun.my.domain/, and /usr/local/apache/htdocs/www.another.domain/ respectively.

■ Connections to http://www.my.domain/, http://fun.my.domain/, or http://www.another.domain/ from hosts that do not support HTTP 1.1's Host header field will access the directory /usr/local/apache/htdocs/.

■ Connections to http://www.my.domain/www.my.domain/, http://fun.my.domain/fun.my.domain/, or http://www.another.domain/www.another.domain/ from any host will access the directories /usr/local/apache/htdocs/www.my.domain/, /usr/local/apache/htdocs/fun.my.domain/, and /usr/local/apache/htdocs/www.another.domain/ respectively.

> **Tip**
>
> For this backward compatibility solution to work it is crucial that all links in your sites be relative links or include the leader `ServerPath` directory in their URLs. For instance, in the `www.my.domain` site, the file `/usr/local/apache/htdocs/www.my.domain/index.html` can link to the file `/usr/local/apache/htdocs/www.my.domain/test.html` with the relative URL `test.html` or the absolute URL `/www.my.domain/test.html`.

> **Note**
>
> One major limitation to virtual-hosting is when the number of sites being served becomes too large. Each process is only able to use a limited number of file handles, typically 64. Apache uses a file handle for each log file it opens plus between 10-20 for internal use. If you create separate log files for each virtual server instead of allowing them to share the main Apache log files, you may find that you quickly run out of file handles. To remedy the situation, consider reducing the number of unique log files you are using.

MONITORING YOUR WEB SITE THROUGH THE LOGS

Apache can be configured to write its logs to any number of files as well as to write some messages to the `syslogd` logging daemon. By default, most Apache sites are configured to write log messages to two files:

- **`logs/access_log` (relative to the `ServerRoot` directory):** This files contains log entries for each access to the system.

- **`logs/error_log` (relative to the `ServerRoot` directory):** This file contains errors, warning messages, and notices.

THE ACCESS LOG FILE

The access log file (typically `access_log`) contains one entry for each access connection it receives. This means there is one entry for each individual document, graphic, or other file requested from the Web server.

Normally, log entries are written in the Common Log Format (CLF) as outlined earlier in this chapter in the section on the `httpd.conf` file. CLF makes the Apache logs readable by any standard log analysis tool for the purpose of generating comprehensive traffic reports. Although the format of entries can be extended using the `LogFormat` directive, CLF entries normally contain enough information for most reporting purposes.

CLF entries take the following format:

<host name> <client identity> <user name> <date> <request> <status> <bytes>

These fields represent the following information:

- **Host name**: This is the hostname or IP address of the client requesting a document.
- **Client identity**: If the client is running `identd` and the `IdentityCheck` directive is enabled, the identity information provided by the client is placed in this field.
- **Username**: If the requested URL required basic HTTP authentication, the username used to authenticate appears in this field.
- **Date**: The date and time of the request in the form `[dd/mmm/yyyy:hh:mm:ss zzzzz]`. For instance, a typical date might be `[30/Jan/2000:04:23:35 -0800]`. The `zzzzz` portion of the field (in this case `-0800`) is the time zone's offset from GMT.
- **Request**: This field contains the exact text of the client's `Request` header surrounded by double quotes. This field makes it possible to determine which document was requested. A typical entry is similar to `"GET /manual/mod/core.html HTTP/1.1"`.
- **Status**: This field contains a three-digit code specifying the HTTP status code returned by Apache. HTTP status codes are outlined in Table 23.5.
- **Bytes**: This field contains the number of bytes transferred.

Where a field does not contain any information (as can be the case with the client identity and username fields), the field will simply contain a dash (-). The status field will contain one of the status codes outlined in Table 23.5.

TABLE 23.5 HTTP 1.1 STATUS CODES

Status Code	Name	Description
100	Continue	The server is ready to receive the rest of the request from the client.
101	Switching Protocols	The server is willing to switch to an application protocol specified by the client in an `Upgrade` header.
200	OK	The server has processed a request successfully and is returning it to the client.
201	Created	The server has created a new URL based on a `Location` header.
202	Accepted	The server has accepted a request and will process it.
203	Non-Authoritative Information	The information in the response header was copied from another server.
204	No Content	The server has successfully processed a request but no new information need be displayed by the client.
205	Reset Content	The client should reset the currently displayed document.
206	Partial Content	The server has successfully processed a partial `GET` request.

TABLE 23.5   CONTINUED

Status Code	Name	Description
300	Multiple Choices	A requested resource is associated with a set of documents rather than a single document.
301	Moved Permanently	A requested resource no longer exists on the server and a Location header is being provided by the server, indicating the new location of the resource.
302	Moved Temporarily	A requested resource temporarily does not exist on the server and a Location header is being provided by the server, indicating the new location of the resource.
303	See Other	A requested resource is located in a different location and a Location header is being provided by the server, indicating the correct location of the resource.
304	No modified	A requested document has not been modified since the date specified by the client.
305	Use Proxy	Indicates that the client should use the proxy server specified in the Location header provided by the server.
307	Temporary Redirect	A requested resource is temporarily being redirected to the Location specified in the Location header provided by the server.
400	Bad Request	A syntax error was found in the client request.
401	Unauthorized	The resource requested by the client required authentication as indicated in the Authenticate header being returned by the server.
402	Payment Required	Reserved for future use.
403	Forbidden	Access to the requested resource is forbidden.
404	Not Found	The requested resource does not exist on the server.
405	Method No Allowed	The client has used an unacceptable method to request a resource and the client should use a method specified in the Allow header returned by the server.
406	Not Acceptable	The requested resource cannot be provided in a format the client can use based on information indicated in the client's accept headers.
407	Proxy Authentication Required	The client must first authenticate with the proxy server before it will be provided access.
408	Request Time-Out	The request failed to complete within the timeout period the server used.
409	Conflict	The request conflicts with another request.
410	Gone	The requested resources have been permanently removed from the server.
411	Length Required	The client must provide a ContentLength header.

TABLE 23.5   CONTINUED

Status Code	Name	Description
412	Precondition Failed	The request failed to pass the If headers provided by the client.
413	Request Entity Too Large	The message body of the request is too large and the server will not process the request.
414	Request URL Too Long	The URL specified by the client is too long and the server will not process the request.
415	Unsupported Media Type	The request's body is in an unsupported format and the server will not process the request.
417	Expectation Failed	The server does not meet the requirements specified by the client in the Expect header of its request.
500	Internal Server Error	The server's configuration is invalid if an external program invoked by the server generated an error.
501	Not Implemented	The server does not support the features needed to fulfill a request.
502	Bad Gateway	The server received an invalid response from another server or a proxy upstream from itself.
503	Service Unavailable	The requested service is temporarily unavailable.
504	Gateway Time-Out	A gateway or proxy exceeded the time out limit.
505	HTTP Version Not Supported	The client used a version of HTTP not supported by the server.

Put together, a typical access log file would contain entries similar to the following:

```
10.10.10.10 - - [30/Jan/2000:04:24:35 -0800] "GET /manual/mod/core.html \
HTTP/1.0" 200 118574
10.10.10.10 - - [30/Jan/2000:04:44:02 -0800] "GET /manual/mod/mod_access.html \
HTTP/1.0'" 200 8819
10.10.10.10 - - [30/Jan/2000:14:15:17 -0800] "GET /manual/mod/index.html \
HTTP/1.0'" 200 5296
10.10.10.10 - - [30/Jan/2000:14:27:20 -0800] "GET /manual HTTP/1.0" 301 235
10.10.10.10 - - [30/Jan/2000:14:27:21 -0800] "GET /manual/ HTTP/1.0" 200 2277
10.10.10.10 - - [30/Jan/2000:14:27:25 -0800] "GET /manual/invoking.html \
HTTP/1.0" 200 8759
10.10.10.10 - - [30/Jan/2000:14:27:39 -0800] "GET /manual/stopping.html \
HTTP/1.0'" 200 8466
10.10.10.10 - - [02/Feb/2000:15:34:00 -0800] "GET / HTTP/1.0" 200 1945
```

THE ERROR LOG FILE

The error log file (typically error_log) contains error notices up to the level specified in the LogLevel directive in the httpd.conf file as outlined in the section of this chapter discussing the httpd.conf file.

The following is the format of entries in the error log file:

`[<date>] [<error level>] [<error message>]`

The fields have the following meanings:

- **Date**: This indicates the date and time of the error. The date and time are specified in the format `ddd mmm dd hh:mm:ss yyyy`. For instance, a typical date is Sun Jan 30 04:02:02 2000.

- **Error Level**: This field indicates the type of error message and is one of the following:
  - **emerg**: Emergency messages
  - **alert**: Alert messages
  - **crit**: Critical messages
  - **error**: Error messages
  - **warn**: Warning messages
  - **notice**: Notification messages
  - **info**: Information messages
  - **debug**: Messages logged for debugging purposes

- **Error Message**: This field contains the text of the error message.

Typical error log entries look like the following:

```
[Sun Jan 30 04:02:02 2000] [notice] Apache/1.3.9 (Unix) \
(Red Hat/Linux) configured -- resuming normal operations
[Sun Jan 30 04:02:02 2000] [notice] suEXEC mechanism enabled \
(wrapper: /usr/sbin/suexec)
[Sun Jan 30 21:12:46 2000] [notice] caught SIGTERM, shutting down
[Mon Jan 31 05:14:31 2000] [notice] Apache/1.3.9 (Unix) \
(Red Hat/Linux) configured -- resuming normal operations
[Mon Jan 31 05:14:31 2000] [notice] suEXEC mechanism enabled \
(wrapper: /usr/sbin/suexec)
[Sun Jan 30 21:42:03 2000] [notice] caught SIGTERM, shutting down
[Mon Jan 31 11:17:18 2000] [notice] Apache/1.3.9 (Unix) \
(Red Hat/Linux) configured -- resuming normal operations
[Mon Jan 31 11:17:18 2000] [notice] suEXEC mechanism enabled \
(wrapper: /usr/sbin/suexec)
[Mon Jan 31 13:46:08 2000] [notice] caught SIGTERM, shutting down
[Tue Feb  1 16:53:17 2000] [notice] Apache/1.3.9 (Unix) \
(Red Hat/Linux) configured -- resuming normal operations
[Tue Feb  1 16:53:18 2000] [notice] suEXEC mechanism enabled \
(wrapper: /usr/sbin/suexec)
[Wed Feb  2 08:34:25 2000] [notice] caught SIGTERM, shutting down
[Wed Feb  2 11:43:27 2000] [notice] Apache/1.3.9 (Unix) \
(Red Hat/Linux) configured -- resuming normal operations
```

MANAGING LOGS

Do not allow your log files to grow excessively large. Not only can they consume large amounts of disk space on an average server, but they also become less useful as they grow too large because they do not provide self-contained pictures of activity over logical time periods.

For this reason, rotate your log files on a regular basis: daily, weekly, or monthly depending on the amount of traffic on your Web server. Apache includes the `rotatelogs` tool for this purpose. Typically, this tool is located at `/usr/sbin/rotatelogs`.

To use `rotatelogs` to manage your log rotation, add or replace the `CustomLog` directive that normally defines your `access_log` file with a `TransferLog` directive. This directive sends all logging messages in Common Log Format (CLF) to the `rotatelogs` program:

```
TransferLog "¦ <path to rotatelogs> <path to log gile> <rotation time in seconds>"
```

The `rotatelogs` program will write log messages to the specified file but will rotate the log file at the interval specified by the rotation time, creating backups of the current log file using the name `<log file name>.<arbitrary long number>`.

For instance, to rotate the log file at `/usr/local/apache/logs/access_log` every week (604,800 seconds), use the following entry in `httpd.conf`:

```
TransferLog "/usr/sbin/rotatelogs /usr/local/apache/logs/access_log 604800"
```

> **Note**
>
> Apache's logs can also be rotated using the standard `logrotate` utility as outlined in Chapter 20, "Log Management and Analysis."

BASIC WEB SITE SECURITY

Web server security is a large topic that easily deserves a book of its own or at least several chapters in a Web administration and management text. Nonetheless, several basic principles should still be applied to all Web sites to ensure a minimum of security. These principles include the following:

- Set your file and directory permissions correctly.
- Consider your use of server-side includes carefully.
- Consider allowing users access to CGI-BIN scripts carefully.
- Examine your CGI-BIN scripts.
- Do not allow users to override global settings.
- Deny default access.

SET YOUR FILE AND DIRECTORY PERMISSIONS CORRECTLY

Apache is typically started by the root user and then run as a non-privileged user as specified in `httpd.conf`. However, ensure that all files in your server root except the document trees (which can be editable by other users) are only modifiable by the root user. For instance, if you install Apache in the default `/usr/local/apache`, ensure that the installation directory and the `bin`, `conf`, and `logs` directories are only modifiable by the root user:

```
# cd /usr/local
# chown root apache
# chgrp root apache
# chmod 755 apache
# cd apache
# chown -R root bin conf logs
# chgrp -R root bin conf logs
# chmod -R 755 bin conf logs
```

In addition, ensure that the `httpd` binary is only executable by the root user. If your Apache binary is located at `/usr/local/apache/bin/httpd`, then use the following commands to restrict access appropriately:

```
# chown root /usr/local/apache/bin/httpd
# chgrp root /usr/local/apache/bin/httpd
# chmod 511 /usr/local/apache/bin/httpd
```

CONSIDER YOUR USE OF SERVER-SIDE INCLUDES CAREFULLY

Server-side includes are a powerful extension to your HTML files. They make it possible to include other files in your HTML files as well as to execute arbitrary programs from your HTML files and include the output as part of the document sent to the user.

However, this is a serious security risk that should only be allowed in the rarest of exceptional circumstances. Ideally, you want to disable server-side includes altogether by not including the `Includes` option of the `Options` directive as outlined in the section discussing the `access.conf` file earlier in this chapter.

If you need to include limited server-side include capabilities but want to disable the capability to execute arbitrary programs on the server, change the `Includes` option of the `Options` directive to `IncludesNOEXEC`.

CONSIDER ALLOWING USERS ACCESS TO CGI-BIN SCRIPTS CAREFULLY

To allow users who develop their own Web content on your server access to CGI-BIN scripts, you are creating a potential security hole:

- If you allow non-script aliased CGI-BIN scripts then users can place executable content anywhere in their personal Web document root directories. In this case, you need to implicitly trust users not to use scripts that accidentally or deliberately attack your system or create security holes on the network.

- If you allow script-aliased GI-BIN scripts then you maintain control over where scripts are placed but any users with write access to those locations must still be implicitly trusted.

- Any form of CGI-BIN scripting has the potential to create security holes and risks if mistakes exist in the code of the script.

If you can avoid allowing users to directly create their own CGI-BIN scripts you prevent a large security risk. However, this means either denying all CGI-BIN access to users with personal Web content or limiting them to the use of centrally stored and maintained scripts which are all vetted by an administrator. This creates a potentially significant management task.

EXAMINE YOUR CGI-BIN SCRIPTS

Any CGI-BIN scripts you do run must be examined carefully. All CGI-BIN scripts run as the same user, which means they can interfere accidentally or deliberately with data used by other scripts. In addition, a CGI-BIN script can execute an arbitrary application on the server, which means it can be used as a staging ground for some attacks when the script contains security holes.

The entire topic of writing secure CGI-Bin applications is complex, but the following basic principles apply:

- Validate all input provided by the user to the script before processing the data.

- Scan input data for illegal characters to prevent embedded system calls from being passed to your script. In particular, look for forward slashes, semi-colons, brackets, redirection symbols, and the vertical pipe.

- When invoking external programs, do so carefully. In particular, do not rely on the PATH variable and specify the exact path to each executable. Also, avoid passing unparsed and checked, user-provided data directly to an external application.

- If you write your CGI-BIN scripts in Perl, use Perl's taint checking to avoid passing unchecked user variables to the shell. To invoke taint-checking, add the -T flag to the Perl invocation on the first line of your CGI-BIN scripts:

  ```
  #!/usr/bin/perl -T
  ```

DO NOT ALLOW USERS TO OVERRIDE GLOBAL SETTINGS

If you use the AllowOverride directive in your access.conf file to allow overriding of security settings for a directory through the .htaccess file and then you allow non-administrators who develop Web content to write to content directories, they can override your well-conceived security policies.

It is best to deny overriding on all directories by adding the following to the start of your access.conf file:

```
<Directory />
   AllowOverride None
   Options None
   allow from all
</Directory>
```

This will prevent overriding of any directory's security policies (as well as prevent server-side includes) unless you explicitly allow this in another Directory block in the access.conf file.

DENY DEFAULT ACCESS

By default, if a user creates a symbolic link from a content directory to the top-level Linux directory (/) then the entire file system of the Web server can be browsed through the Web. To prevent this, you must deny access to all directories with the following Directory block at the start of your access.conf file and then explicitly allow access to individual directories with subsequent Directory blocks:

```
<Directory />
    Order deny, allow
    Deny from all
</Directory>
```

You can combine this with appropriate Options and AllowOverride directives to further limit default behavior:

```
<Directory />
    AllowOverride None
    Options None
    Order deny, allow
    Deny from all
</Directory>
```

TROUBLESHOOTING

There are several problems that can occur when launching the Apache daemon:

- **Starting httpd causes a "setgid: Invalid argument" error**: This problem is caused when the group directive in the httpd.conf file specifies a non-existent group. Make sure this directive specifies the name of a group which exists in the /etc/group file.

- **Starting httpd causes an "httpd: could not set socket option TCP_NODELAY" error in the error log**: This indicates that a client disconnected before Apache created a socket for the connection. It is not a sign of a serious problem and should only occur in 1% or less of requests.

- **Starting httpd causes a "shmget: function not found" error**: This error indicates that your Linux kernel does not have SysV IPC support compiled into it. You will need to rebuild your kernel to include this support as outlined in Chapter 11, "Building the Linux Kernel."

Discussion of other problems can be found in the Apache documentation at http://www.apache.org/docs/.

Linux Database Servers

LINUX AS A DATABASE SERVER

Linux has come late to the database server market. Early Linux successes came in the Web server and mail server arenas and only recently has Linux gained acceptance as a corporate enterprise database server.

The problems Linux faced originally in this market are twofold:

- Technical limitations in earlier versions of Linux restricted its scalability for mission-critical database applications.

- A dearth of commercial database servers for Linux was apparent.

In many ways, the first problem fueled the latter: As long as there were perceived technical limitations for Linux in this capacity, there was no demand for corporate database vendors to port their products to Linux. As Linux's technology has matured, it has gained a foothold in corporate information technology architectures and now every major database vendor offers versions of their products for Linux, including:

- Oracle (http://www.oracle.com/)
- Sybase (http://www.sybase.com/)
- Informix (http://www.informix.com/)
- IBM (http://www.ibm.com/)

Even before these commercial products emerged, numerous database platforms were available for Linux, many offering the capabilities and performance promised by their commercial counterparts. The following are the most notable among these database servers:

- **PostgreSQL:** (http://www.postgresql.org/): Widely regarded as the most full-featured and powerful database server for Linux outside the commercial products, PostgreSQL is still one of the most widely used database platforms on Linux servers.

- **MySQL:** (http://www.mysql.org/): This is a lightweight database server known for its stability and speed. Although it doesn't have as many features as PostgreSQL, it is far more lightweight and is easier to learn and use.

- **mSQL:** (http://www.hughes.com.au/): This is another lightweight database server platform similar in features and functionality to MySQL. This is a commercial product except for very limited use but is widely regarded as an excellent database platform for servers requiring efficient performance with large tables.

In this book we consider deploying a Linux system using MySQL as a database platform because this is a product that is easy-to-install and manage. It is freely available for Linux and does not require access to costly commercial products.

CREATING A LINUX DATABASE SERVER

In this chapter we will consider installation and configuration of a Linux database system by using MySQL, a widely used, freely available database environment for Linux available from `http://www.mysql.org/`.

> **Note**
>
> Each database server environment has its own installation, configuration, and usage techniques that can differ considerably. Consult the documentation for your chosen server for guidance in this regard if you do not use MySQL.

Getting your database server up and running involves several steps:

1. Determining your database server's hardware requirements.
2. Obtaining and installing MySQL.
3. Configuring and testing MySQL.

DETERMINING YOUR DATABASE SERVER'S HARDWARE REQUIREMENTS

The question of what hardware you need to run a successful database server is largely dependent on the types of database applications you will run on the server, the size and number of tables in your databases, and the number of simultaneous users.

A few general rules of thumb can be applied to this assessment:

- Place your MySQL databases on partitions with plenty of excess room to spare. It is easier to provide your databases with plenty of room to grow rather than being forced into moving them to a new partition. For instance, if you expect your databases to amount to 10GB in size over the next year, consider using a 15-20GB partition for those databases.

- Use the fastest disks possible. Disk seeks are considered the largest performance bottleneck with MySQL. If disk performance becomes a severe bottleneck for your databases, consider using disk striping in which data is spread over multiple disks that appear to the operating system like one large disk. Or, consider some form of RAID, which offers redundant disks for extra reliability (consult Chapter 9, "Installing and Using RAID," for a discussion of RAID with Linux).

- With larger tables and larger queries, memory can provide additional performance benefits because it enables you to avoid swapping to disk. Always use substantial memory on your database servers, especially if they will be heavily used.

OBTAINING AND INSTALLING MySQL

At the time of writing, the latest stable release of MySQL is 3.22, available in source code form for Linux from `http://www.mysql.org/download_3.22.html`. The download source code archive file is named `mysql-3.22.30.tar.gz`. Download this file and then extract the archive using the command:

```
# tar xzvf mysql-3.22.30.tar.gz
```

The source code will be extracted into the `mysql-3.22.30` subdirectory. Change your current directory to that directory:

```
# cd mysql-3.22.30
```

Next, configure the release for compiling with the configure command:

```
# ./configure
```

By default, MySQL will be configured to be installed in the `/usr/local/` directory. This chapter assumes you have installed MySQL in the default location. If you prefer to install in an alternate directory, use the `--prefix` argument of the `configure` command:

```
# ./configure -prefix=<directory>
```

Next, compile and install the MySQL software with the commands:

```
# make
# make install
```

MySQL will be installed under the `/usr/local/` directory. Files will be installed as outlined in Table 24.1.

TABLE 24.1 LOCATIONS OF MySQL FILES

Directory	Directory Contents
/usr/local/bin/	Subdirectory containing client programs and scripts
/usr/local/include/mysql/	Header files
/usr/local/info/	Documentation
/usr/local/lib/mysql/	Libraries
/usr/local/libexec/	The mysqld binary file
/usr/local/share/mysql/	Error message files
/usr/local/sql-bench/	Benchmark tests
/usr/local/var/	Databases and log files

There are several useful Internet resources providing information and support about MySQL:

- MySQL Documentation (`http://web.mysql.com/doc.html`)
- Developer Shed (`http://www.devshed.com/Server_Side/MySQL/`)
- Setting up a MySQL Based Web Site (`http://www.linuxplanet.com/linuxplanet/tutorials/1046/1/`)

CONFIGURATION OPTIONS

The configure command used to configure the release for compilation can take a number of options. The most useful options are outlined in Table 24.2.

TABLE 24.2   USEFUL CONFIGURATION OPTIONS

Option	Description
`--prefix=<directory>`	Sets the installation directory to an alternate location (the default is `/usr/local/`).
`--without-server`	Only builds and installs the client software. Does not install the server software.
`--localstatedir=<directory>`	Installs log files and databases in an alternate location (the default is `/usr/local/var/`).
`--with-mysqld-ldflags=all-static`	Statically links the `mysqld` daemon. This can improve performance or solve some problems encountered when building MySQL on some distributions.
`--with-client-ldflags=all-static`	Statically links the client software. This can improve performance or solve some problems encountered when building MySQL on some distributions.
`--with-charset=<character set>`	Changes the default character set from ISO-8859-1 (Latin 1) to one of the following: big5, cp1251, cp1257, czech, danish, dec8, dos, euc_kr, gb2312, gbk, german1, hebrew, hp8, hungarian, koi8_ru, koi8_ukr, latin1, latin2, sjis, swe7, tis620, ujis, usa7, win1251 or win1251ukr.
`--with-debug`	Configures MySQL to compile with debugging options enabled.

PART

V

CH

24

CONFIGURING AND TESTING MySQL

After it is compiled and installed, some configuration steps need to be performed before you can use MySQL to create databases and applications:

1. Install the grants table.
2. Start `mysqld`.

3. Verify that the server is running.

4. Edit the configuration files.

INSTALL THE GRANTS TABLE

Before MySQL can be used you need to install the grants table. The grants table is a database which contains user information and permissions. You can install the initial grants table using the `mysql_install_db` script, which is located in the `/usr/local/bin/` directory:

```
# /usr/local/bin/mysql_install_db
Creating db table
Creating host table
Creating user table
Creating func table
Creating tables_priv table
Creating columns_priv table

To start mysqld at boot time you have to copy support-files/mysql.server
to the right place for your system

PLEASE REMEMBER TO SET A PASSWORD FOR THE MySQL root USER !
This is done with:
/usr/local/mysql//bin/mysqladmin -u root password 'new-password'
See the manual for more instructions.

Please report any problems with the /usr/local/mysql//bin/mysqlbug script!

The latest information about MySQL is available on the web at http://www.mysql.c
om
Support MySQL by buying support/licenses at http://www.tcx.se/license.htmy.
```

The initial grants table contains the following settings:

- A MySQL root user is created with super-user privileges. The root user can only be used for connections from the local server host.

- An anonymous user is created which can perform any operation on databases named test or databases with names starting with test_. The anonymous user can only be used for connections from the local server host.

- Other privileges are denied.

START mysqld

To start the `mysqld` daemon, do not directly invoke the `/usr/local/libexec/mysqld` program but instead use the `/usr/local/bin/safe_mysqld` script, which sets up the necessary environment and then starts `mysqld`:

```
# cd /usr/local
# bin/safe_mysqld &
Starting mysqld daemon with databases from /usr/local/var
```

VERIFY THAT THE SERVER IS RUNNING

You can verify that your MySQL installation is functioning properly using the `mysqladmin` command. First, display current version information:

```
# /usr/local/bin/mysqladmin version
/usr/local/bin/mysqladmin  Ver 7.15 Distrib 3.22.30, for pc-linux-gnu on i686
TCX Datakonsult AB, by Monty

Server version          3.22.30
Protocol version        10
Connection              Localhost via UNIX socket
UNIX socket             /tmp/mysql.sock
Uptime:                 3 min 10 sec

Threads: 1  Questions: 1  Slow queries: 0  Opens:
➥6  Flush tables: 1  Open tables: 2
```

Next, you can display the current value of MySQL's variables:

```
# /usr/local/bin/mysqladmin variables
+------------------------------+----------------------------------------+
| Variable_name                | Value                                  |
+------------------------------+----------------------------------------+
| back_log                     | 5                                      |
| connect_timeout              | 5                                      |
| basedir                      | /usr/local/                            |
| datadir                      | /usr/local/var/                        |
| delayed_insert_limit         | 100                                    |
| delayed_insert_timeout       | 300                                    |
| delayed_queue_size           | 1000                                   |
| join_buffer                  | 131072                                 |
| flush_time                   | 0                                      |
| key_buffer                   | 8388600                                |
| language                     | /usr/local/share/mysql/english/        |
| log                          | OFF                                    |
| log_update                   | OFF                                    |
| long_query_time              | 10                                     |
| low_priority_updates         | OFF                                    |
| max_allowed_packet           | 1048576                                |
| max_connections              | 100                                    |
| max_connect_errors           | 10                                     |
| max_delayed_insert_threads   | 20                                     |
| max_join_size                | 4294967295                             |
| max_sort_length              | 1024                                   |
| max_write_lock_count         | 4294967295                             |
| net_buffer_length            | 16384                                  |
| pid_file                     | /usr/local/var/micron.pid              |
| port                         | 3306                                   |
| protocol_version             | 10                                     |
| record_buffer                | 131072                                 |
| skip_locking                 | ON                                     |
| skip_networking              | OFF                                    |
| socket                       | /tmp/mysql.sock                        |
```

```
¦ sort_buffer              ¦ 2097144                              ¦
¦ table_cache              ¦ 64                                   ¦
¦ thread_stack             ¦ 65536                                ¦
¦ tmp_table_size           ¦ 1048576                              ¦
¦ tmpdir                   ¦ /tmp/                                ¦
¦ version                  ¦ 3.22.30                              ¦
¦ wait_timeout             ¦ 28800                                ¦
+-------------------------+-------------------------------------+
```

Finally, you can conduct further tests using the `mysqlshow` command to show existing databases, tables, and records. For instance, to display a list of existing tables, use the command without any parameters:

```
# /usr/local/bin/mysqlshow
+-----------+
¦ Databases ¦
+-----------+
¦ mysql     ¦
¦ test      ¦
+-----------+
```

SET THE root PASSWORD

When the initial grants table is installed, the `root` user has no password. This is a gaping security hole because it enables any user with shell access to use the MySQL server as the `root` database user. After you have verified correct operation of the server, your first order of business should be to set a root password.

To do this, use the `mysqladmin` command:

```
# /usr/local/bin/mysqladmin -u root password <new password>
```

After you have set a password, it is necessary to specify the username and password for most actions. For instance, the mysqladmin version command used above now needs to be issued as follows:

```
# /usr/local/bin/mysqladmin -u root --password=<password> version
```

EDIT THE CONFIGURATION FILES

You can specify default start-up options for all MySQL applications such as `mysqladmin`, `mysql`, or `mysqld` using options files. You can create three possible options files:

- `/etc/my.conf`
- `/usr/local/var/my.conf`
- `~/.my.conf`

MySQL applications will read the files in this order and settings from later options file will always take precedence over earlier files.

An options file consists of a series of sections of the general form:

```
[<section name>]
<option entry>
<option entry>
<option entry>
etc.
```

The section name generally is the name of the application for which the option entries will apply so that a typical options file might take the following form:

```
[mysqld]
<option entry>
<option entry>
<option entry>
etc.

[mysqladmin]
<option entry>
<option entry>
<option entry>
etc.

[mysql]
<option entry>
<option entry>
<option entry>
etc.
```

The options entries reflect the possible long options that can be issued at the command line. For any command, you can get a list of possible options with the --help option for the command:

```
# /usr/local/bin/mysqladmin --help
/usr/local/bin/mysqladmin  Ver 7.15 Distrib 3.22.30, for pc-linux-gnu on i686
TCX Datakonsult AB, by Monty
This software comes with NO WARRANTY: see the file PUBLIC for details.

Administer program for the mysqld demon
Usage: bin/mysqladmin [OPTIONS] command command....

  -#, --debug=...       Output debug log. Often this is 'd:t:o,filename`
  -f, --force           Don't ask for confirmation on drop database; with
                        multiple commands, continue even if an error occurs
  -?, --help            Display this help and exit
  -C, --compress        Use compression in server/client protocol
  -h, --host=#          Connect to host
  -p, --password[=...]  Password to use when connecting to server
                        If password is not given it's asked from the tty
  -P  --port=...        Port number to use for connection
  -i, --sleep=sec       Execute commands again and again with a sleep between
  -r, --relative        Show difference between current and previous values
                        when used with -i. Currently works only with
                        extended-status
  -s, --silent          Silently exit if one can't connect to server
  -S, --socket=...      Socket file to use for connection
  -t, --timeout=...     Timeout for connection to the mysqld server
  -u, --user=#          User for login if not current user
  -V, --version         Output version information and exit
  -w, --wait[=retries]  Wait and retry if connection is down
```

```
Where command is a one or more of: (Commands may be shortened)
  create databasename   Create a new database
  drop databasename     Delete a database and all its tables
  extended-status       Gives an extended status message from the server
  flush-hosts           Flush all cached hosts
  flush-logs            Flush all logs
  flush-status          Clear status variables
  flush-tables          Flush all tables
  flush-privileges      Reload grant tables (same as reload)
  kill id,id,...        Kill mysql threads
  password new-password Change old password to new-password
  ping                  Check if mysqld is alive
  processlist           Show list of active threads in server
  reload                Reload grant tables
  refresh               Flush all tables and close and open logfiles
  shutdown              Take server down
  status                Gives a short status message from the server
  variables             Prints variables available
  version               Get version info from server

Default options are read from the following files in the given order:
/etc/my.cnf ~/.my.cnf
The following groups are read: mysqladmin client
The following options may be given as the first argument:
--print-defaults      Print the program argument list and exit
--no-defaults         Don't read default options from any options file
--defaults-file=#       Only read default options from the given file #
```

The long options are those which start with two dashes such as --compress or --port=<port>.

These options take a slightly different form in the options files as outlined in Table 24.3.

TABLE 24.3   OPTIONS IN OPTIONS FILES

Command-Line Format	Options File Format
--<option>	<option>
--<option>=<value>	<option>=<value>
--set-variable <variable>=<value>	set-variable = <variable>=<value>

For instance, a typical global options file in /etc/my.conf or in /usr/local/var/my.conf might look like the following:

```
[client]
port=3306
socket=/tmp/mysql.sock


[mysqld]
port=3306
socket=/tmp/mysql.sock
set-variable = max_allowed_packet=1M

[mysqldump]
quick
```

> **Note**
>
> The client section applies to several applications including `mysql`, `mysqladmin`, and `mysqldump`.

Notice the use of all three types of options: those without values, those with values, and variable set options.

Common options for the `mysql` client, `mysqld`, and `mysqladmin` are outlined in Table 24.4.

TABLE 24.4 COMMON OPTIONS FOR `mysql`, `mysqld`, AND `mysqladmin`

Option	Applications	Description
`--basedir= <directory>`	`mysqld`	Use the specified path as the installation directory.
`--bind- address= <IP address>`	`mysqld`	Bind to the specified address on a system with multiple IP addresses.
`--compress`	`mysql, mysqladmin`	Use compression in client/server protocol.
`--database= <database>`	`mysql`	Connect to the specified database on the server.
`--datadir= <directory>`	`mysqld`	Use the specified path as the database and log file directory.
`--execute= <command>`	`mysql`	Execute the specified command and then exit.
`--force`	`mysql, mysqladmin`	Don't ask for confirmation for database drops.
`--host=<host>`	`mysql, mysqladmin`	Connect to the specified host.
`--html`	`mysql`	Generate HTML output.
`--log=<file>`	`mysqld`	Log errors to the specified file.
`--password`	`mysql, mysqladmin`	Prompt for a password.
`--password= <password>`	`mysql, mysqladmin,`	Use the specified password.
`--port=<port>`	`mysqld, mysql, mysqladmin`	Connect to the server using the specified port.
`--skip-name- resolve`	`mysqld`	Don't resolve host names.
`--skip- networking`	`mysqld`	Don't enable connections through TCP/IP.

TABLE 24.4	CONTINUED	
Option	**Applications**	**Description**
--socket= <socket file>	mysqld, mysql, mysqladmin	Socket file to use for the connection.
--table	mysql	Generate output in table format.
--timeout= <seconds>	mysqladmin	Timeout for the connection to the server specified in seconds.
--user=<user>	mysql, mysqladmin	User to use in connecting (the default is the current logged in user).
--user=<user>	mysqld	Run the daemon as the specified user.
--vertical	mysql	Generate output of rows vertically.

DATABASE MANAGEMENT

Managing your MySQL database consists of several tasks:

- Starting and stopping the server
- Connecting to the server
- Creating and deleting databases and tables
- Interacting with databases using SQL
- Backing up your databases
- Managing users and permissions

STARTING AND STOPPING THE SERVER

The mysqld daemon is started using the safe_mysqld script. This script checks the state of your system and sets numerous environment variables before invoking the mysqld daemon.

To start the server, simply use this command with no arguments:

```
# /usr/local/bin/safe_mysqld &
```

The trailing ampersand runs the program in the background so that the MySQL daemon starts but you retain use of your shell.

To stop mysqld, use the mysqladmin command:

```
# /usr/local/mysqladmin -u root -password=<password> shutdown
```

CONNECTING TO THE SERVER

The most direct way of interacting with a running MySQL server is to use the mysql client which is included as part of the MySQL package. To connect to your server, use the command:

```
# /usr/local/bin/mysql -u <user name> --password=<password>
Welcome to the MySQL monitor.  Commands end with ; or \g.
Your MySQL connection id is 1 to server version: 3.22.30

Type 'help' for help.

mysql>
```

At the command prompt, all commands for the SQL server must end with a semicolon or the \g combination. Any commands processed by the client which do not get sent to the server do not need to end in the semicolon or \g, such as the help command which simply displays the client's local help information:

```
mysql> help

MySQL commands:
help     (\h)    Display this text
?        (\h)    Synonym for `help'
clear    (\c)    Clear command
connect  (\r)    Reconnect to the server. Optional arguments are db and host
edit     (\e)    Edit command with $EDITOR
exit     (\q)    Exit mysql. Same as quit
go       (\g)    Send command to mysql server
ego      (\G)    Send command to mysql server; Display result vertically
print    (\p)    Print current command
quit     (\q)    Quit mysql
rehash   (\#)    Rebuild completion hash
status   (\s)    Get status information from the server
use      (\u)    Use another database. Takes database name as argument

Connection id: 1   (Can be used with mysqladmin kill)

mysql>
```

To disconnect from the server, use the \q command:

```
mysql> \q
Bye
```

Alternately, you can use Ctrl+D to close the client and disconnect from the server.

CREATING AND DELETING DATABASES AND TABLES

The creation of databases with MySQL is done with the `mysqladmin` tool:

```
# /usr/local/bin/mysqladmin -u <user> --password=<password> create <database name>
```

For instance, to create a database named mydbase, use the following command:

```
# /usr/local/bin/mysqladmin -u root --password=<password> create mydbase
Database "mydbase" created.
```

To delete a database you have created, you also use the `mysqladmin` command:

```
# /usr/local/bin/mysqladmin -u <user> --password=<password> drop <database name>
```

Caution

When you drop a database, `mysqladmin` prompts you to make sure you want to delete the database. Take care at this point. If you indicate you want to delete the database, all tables in the database and the data they contain will be deleted and can only be retrieved from backups. Do not delete a database without first backing up its contents unless you are entirely sure you do not need the data it contains.

After you have created a database, you must connect to the server with the `mysql` client first:

```
# mysql -u <username> --password=<password>
```

Next select the database you want to work with using the `USE` command:

```
mysql> USE <database name>;
Database changed
```

For instance, to work with the `mydbase` database, use the command:

```
mysql> USE mydbase;
```

If you are not sure of the name of the database you want to work with, use the `SHOW DATABASES` command:

```
mysql> SHOW DATABASES;
+-----------+
| Database  |
+-----------+
| mydbase   |
| mysql     |
| test      |
+-----------+
3 rows in set (0.00 sec)
```

After you have connected to a database, you can create tables using the `CREATE TABLE` command, which takes the general form:

```
mysql> CREATE TABLE <table name> (<field name> <field type>, <field name> <field type>,
<field name> <field type> ...);
```

Because `mysql` doesn't send a command to the server until it receives the semicolon, you can actually split a long command over multiple lines:

```
mysql> CREATE TABLE <table name> (
    -> <field name> <field type>,
    -> <field name> <field type>,
    -> <field name> <field type> ...);
```

The fields in a record can be one of the types outlined in Table 24.5.

TABLE 24.5 MYSQL DATA TYPES

Data Type	Description
TINYINT	Integer in the range -128-127
TINYINT UNSIGNED	Integer in the range 0-255

TABLE 24.5 CONTINUED

Data Type	Description
SMALLINT	Integer in the range -32768-32767
SMALLINT UNSIGNED	Integer in the range 0-65535
MEDIUMINT	Integer in the range -8388608-8388607
MEDIUMINT UNSIGNED	Integer in the range 0-16777215
INT	Integer in the range -2147483648-2147483647
INT UNSIGNED	Integer in the range 0-4294967295
INTEGER	Integer in the range -2147483648-2147483647
INTEGER UNSIGNED	Integer in the range 0-4294967295
BIGINT	Integer in the range -9223372036854775808-9223372036854775807
BIGINT UNSIGNED	Integer in the range 0-18446744073709551615
FLOAT	Floating point number in the range $-3.402823466E+38$--$1.175494351E-38$ and $1.175494351E-38$ to $3.402823466E+38$ as well as 0
DOUBLE	Floating point number in the range $-1.7976931348623157E+308$--$2.2250738585072014E-308$ and $2.2250738585072014E-308$-$1.7976931348623157E+308$ as well as 0
DOUBLE PRECISION	Floating point number in the range $-1.7976931348623157E+308$--$2.2250738585072014E-308$ and $2.2250738585072014E-308$-$1.7976931348623157E+308$ as well as 0
REAL	Floating point number in the range $-1.7976931348623157E+308$--$2.2250738585072014E-308$ and $2.2250738585072014E-308$-$1.7976931348623157E+308$ as well as 0
DECIMAL	Floating point number in the range $-1.7976931348623157E+308$--$2.2250738585072014E-308$ and $2.2250738585072014E-308$-$1.7976931348623157E+308$;the number is stored as a string of characters rather than a numeric value
NUMERIC	Floating point number in the range $-1.7976931348623157E+308$--$2.2250738585072014E-308$ and $2.2250738585072014E-308$-$1.7976931348623157E+308$ as well as a number is stored as a string of characters rather than a numeric value
DATE	A date in the range 1000-01-01-9999--12-31
DATETIME	A date and time in the range 1000-01-01 00:00:00-9999-12-31 23:59:59

TABLE 24.5 CONTINUED

Data Type	Description
TIMESTAMP	A timestamp in the range 1970-01-01 00:00:00 to the year 2037
TIME	A time in the range of -838:59:59-838:59:59
YEAR	A year in the range 1901 to 2155 as well as 0000
CHAR(<length>)	A string of the specified number of characters up to 255 characters
VARCHAR(<maximum length>)	A variable-length string of at most the specified number of characters with a maximum of 255 characters
TINYBLOB	A binary large object of at most 255 characters
TINYTEXT	A string of at most 255 characters
BLOB	A binary large object of at most 65535 characters
TINYBLOB	A string of at most 65535 characters
MEDIUMBLOB	A binary large object of at most 16777215 characters
MEDIUMTEXT	A string of at most 16777215 characters
LONGBLOB	A binary large object of at most 4294967295 characters
LONGTEXT	A string of at most 4294967295 characters
ENUM(`<value 1>','<value 2>',...)	A string taking as its value one of the values in the enumerated list
SET(`<value 1>','<value 2>',...)	A string taking as its value zero or more values in the enumerated list

For instance, the following table definition creates a table named mytable with four fields: an ID number as an integer, a last name field as a 255-character string, a first name field as a 255-character string, and a birth date field as a date field:

```
mysql> CREATE TABLE mytable (
    -> ID INTEGER,
    -> last_name TINYTEXT,
    -> first_name TINYTEXT,
    -> birth_date DATE);
```

To delete a table you have created, you can use the following command:

```
mysql> drop table <table name>
```

Caution

When you drop a table, all data in the table will be deleted and can only be retrieved from backups. Do not delete a table without first backing up its contents unless you are entirely sure you do not need the data it contains.

INTERACTING WITH DATABASES USING SQL

With MySQL, you interact with your databases and their contents using the Structured Query Language, or SQL. Many modern databases use SQL as the basis for querying the database as well as inserting new records in tables and updating existing records.

SQL is a rich language with wide possible actions. The three basic commands, however, are as follows:

- SELECT
- INSERT
- UPDATE

All these commands can be entered from the `mysql` client's prompt after connecting to the `mydbase` database:

```
$ /usr/local/bin/mysql
Welcome to the MySQL monitor.  Commands end with ; or \g.
Your MySQL connection id is 1 to server version: 3.22.30

Type 'help' for help.

mysql> USE mydbase;
Database changed
```

> **Tip**
>
> Several good sources of SQL support and information are on the Internet, including an SQL tutorial at `http://w3.one.net/~jhoffman/sqltut.htm` and SQL for Web Nerds at `http://photo.net/sql/`.

For the purpose of discussing these commands, we will consider the `mydbase` database we created earlier in this chapter with the `mytable` table with four fields: an ID number, the last name, the first name, and the birth date.

Suppose the database initially contains three records as outlined in Table 24.6.

TABLE 24.6 RECORDS IN THE `mytable` TABLE

ID	Last Name	First Name	Birth Date
1	Smith	Joe	14-Jun-1965
2	Sawyer	Jane	22-Oct-1973
3	Walters	Bob	01-Jan-1969

QUERYING THE DATABASE WITH THE SELECT STATEMENT

The SELECT statement can be used to extract some or all the records from a database table. In its simplest form you can use it to select all fields of all records from mytable:

```
mysql> SELECT * FROM mytable;
+------+-----------+------------+------------+
| ID   | last_name | first_name | birth_date |
+------+-----------+------------+------------+
|    2 | Sawyer    | Jane       | 1973-10-22 |
|    1 | Smith     | Joe        | 1969-06-14 |
|    3 | Walters   | Bob        | 1969-01-01 |
+------+-----------+------------+------------+
3 rows in set (0.00 sec)
```

The * in the SELECT statement indicates that you want to select all fields in the table.

You can indicate specific records by using the WHERE clause. For instance, to select the record with ID number 2, use the following:

```
mysql> SELECT * FROM mytable WHERE ID = 2;
+------+-----------+------------+------------+
| ID   | last_name | first_name | birth_date |
+------+-----------+------------+------------+
|    2 | Sawyer    | Jane       | 1973-10-22 |
+------+-----------+------------+------------+
1 row in set (0.01 sec)
```

You can specify multiple criteria in the WHERE clause by using the Boolean AND or OR operators:

```
mysql> SELECT * FROM mytable WHERE last_name = 'Smith' OR first_name = 'Jane';
+------+-----------+------------+------------+
| ID   | last_name | first_name | birth_date |
+------+-----------+------------+------------+
|    2 | Sawyer    | Jane       | 1973-10-22 |
|    1 | Smith     | Joe        | 1969-06-14 |
+------+-----------+------------+------------+
2 rows in set (0.00 sec)
```

Notice the use of the single quotes around both names. In SQL, strings are surrounded by single quote marks.

At times you might not want to display every field in each record. For instance, if you just want a list of names, you might only want to display the last name and first name. In this case, you need to replace the * with a comma-separated list of field names that you want to extract from the table:

```
mysql> SELECT last_name, first_name FROM mytable;
+-----------+------------+
| last_name | first_name |
+-----------+------------+
| Sawyer    | Jane       |
| Smith     | Joe        |
| Walters   | Bob        |
+-----------+------------+
3 rows in set (0.00 sec)
```

You can specify the order of results using the ORDER BY clause. For instance, to sort the results by the ID number, use the following:

```
mysql> SELECT * FROM mytable ORDER BY ID;
+------+-----------+------------+------------+
| ID   | last_name | first_name | birth_date |
+------+-----------+------------+------------+
|    1 | Smith     | Joe        | 1969-06-14 |
|    2 | Sawyer    | Jane       | 1973-10-22 |
|    3 | Walters   | Bob        | 1969-01-01 |
+------+-----------+------------+------------+
3 rows in set (0.00 sec)
```

If you want to sort by multiple fields, you can specify them all in a comma-separated list. The results will be first sorted on the first field specified, then the second, and so on. For instance, to sort by the first name and then the last name, use the following command:

```
mysql> SELECT * FROM mytable ORDER BY first_name, last_name;
+------+-----------+------------+------------+
| ID   | last_name | first_name | birth_date |
+------+-----------+------------+------------+
|    3 | Walters   | Bob        | 1969-01-01 |
|    2 | Sawyer    | Jane       | 1973-10-22 |
|    1 | Smith     | Joe        | 1969-06-14 |
+------+-----------+------------+------------+
3 rows in set (0.00 sec)
```

To sort on a field in descending order, add the DESC keyword to the field name:

```
mysql> SELECT * FROM mytable ORDER BY last_name DESC;
+------+-----------+------------+------------+
| ID   | last_name | first_name | birth_date |
+------+-----------+------------+------------+
|    3 | Walters   | Bob        | 1969-01-01 |
|    1 | Smith     | Joe        | 1969-06-14 |
|    2 | Sawyer    | Jane       | 1973-10-22 |
+------+-----------+------------+------------+
3 rows in set (0.00 sec)
```

When you use both the WHERE clause and the ORDER BY clause, the WHERE clause should come first:

```
mysql> SELECT * FROM mytable WHERE last_name = 'Smith' or first_name = 'Jane'
ORDER BY last_name DESC;
+------+-----------+------------+------------+
| ID   | last_name | first_name | birth_date |
+------+-----------+------------+------------+
|    1 | Smith     | Joe        | 1969-06-14 |
|    2 | Sawyer    | Jane       | 1973-10-22 |
+------+-----------+------------+------------+
2 rows in set (0.00 sec)
```

PART

V

CH

24

ADDING NEW RECORDS WITH THE INSERT STATEMENT

The INSERT command enables you to add records to a table. In its most simple form, you specify a list of values corresponding to the number and order of fields in the table. For instance, to add a fourth record to the mytable table, use the following command:

```
mysql> INSERT INTO mytable VALUES (4,'Roberts','Susan','1982-11-15');
Query OK, 1 row affected (0.00 sec)
```

Now, if you display all the records in the table, there will be four records in the table:

```
mysql> SELECT * FROM mytable;
+------+-----------+------------+------------+
| ID   | last_name | first_name | birth_date |
+------+-----------+------------+------------+
|    2 | Sawyer    | Jane       | 1973-10-22 |
|    1 | Smith     | Joe        | 1969-06-14 |
|    3 | Walters   | Bob        | 1969-01-01 |
|    4 | Roberts   | Susan      | 1982-11-15 |
+------+-----------+------------+------------+
4 rows in set (0.00 sec)
```

If you want to insert a record but only want to specify data for some of the fields, you need to indicate a list of field names and then only list values for those fields. For instance, to insert a record with no birth date specified, use the following:

```
mysql> INSERT INTO mytable (ID, last_name, first_name)
➥VALUES (5,'Philips','Peter');
Query OK, 1 row affected (0.00 sec)
```

If you display the contents of the table, you will note that the birth date has a null value because it wasn't specified in the INSERT command:

```
mysql> SELECT * FROM mytable;
+------+-----------+------------+------------+
| ID   | last_name | first_name | birth_date |
+------+-----------+------------+------------+
|    2 | Sawyer    | Jane       | 1973-10-22 |
|    1 | Smith     | Joe        | 1969-06-14 |
|    3 | Walters   | Bob        | 1969-01-01 |
|    4 | Roberts   | Susan      | 1982-11-15 |
|    5 | Philips   | Peter      | NULL       |
+------+-----------+------------+------------+
5 rows in set (0.00 sec)
```

CHANGING EXISTING RECORDS WITH THE UPDATE STATEMENT

The UPDATE command enables you to change the values of one or more fields in an existing record. For instance, to set the birth date field in the last record we added, you would use the following command:

```
mysql> UPDATE mytable SET birth_date = '1999-02-01' WHERE ID = 5;
Query OK, 1 row affected (0.00 sec)
Rows matched: 1  Changed: 1  Warnings: 0
```

This command indicates a new value to assign to the birth date field. The WHERE clause is used to specify the records which should be affected in the same way the WHERE clause indicates which records to display in the SELECT command. The result is a birth date in the correct field:

```
mysql> SELECT * FROM mytable;
+------+-----------+------------+------------+
| ID   | last_name | first_name | birth_date |
+------+-----------+------------+------------+
|    2 | Sawyer    | Jane       | 1973-10-22 |
|    1 | Smith     | Joe        | 1969-06-14 |
|    3 | Walters   | Bob        | 1969-01-01 |
|    4 | Roberts   | Susan      | 1982-11-15 |
|    5 | Philips   | Peter      | 1999-02-01 |
+------+-----------+------------+------------+
5 rows in set (0.00 sec)
```

Take care to specify the WHERE clause and to specify it correctly. For instance, if you fail to specify a WHERE clause, all records will be updated:

```
mysql> UPDATE mytable SET birth_date = '2000-02-02';
Query OK, 5 rows affected (0.00 sec)
Rows matched: 5  Changed: 5  Warnings: 0

mysql> SELECT * FROM mytable;
+------+-----------+------------+------------+
| ID   | last_name | first_name | birth_date |
+------+-----------+------------+------------+
|    2 | Sawyer    | Jane       | 2000-02-02 |
|    1 | Smith     | Joe        | 2000-02-02 |
|    3 | Walters   | Bob        | 2000-02-02 |
|    4 | Roberts   | Susan      | 2000-02-02 |
|    5 | Philips   | Peter      | 2000-02-02 |
+------+-----------+------------+------------+
5 rows in set (0.00 sec)
```

You can specify multiple fields to update by listing all the fields separated by commas:

```
mysql> UPDATE mytable SET last_name = 'Kent', first_name = 'Clark' WHERE ID = 5;
Query OK, 1 row affected (0.00 sec)
Rows matched: 1  Changed: 1  Warnings: 0

mysql> SELECT * FROM mytable;
+------+-----------+------------+------------+
| ID   | last_name | first_name | birth_date |
+------+-----------+------------+------------+
|    2 | Sawyer    | Jane       | 2000-02-02 |
|    1 | Smith     | Joe        | 2000-02-02 |
|    3 | Walters   | Bob        | 2000-02-02 |
|    4 | Roberts   | Susan      | 2000-02-02 |
|    5 | Kent      | Clark      | 2000-02-02 |
+------+-----------+------------+------------+
5 rows in set (0.00 sec)
```

PART
V
CH
24

You can also specify multiple criteria to define the record you want to update:

```
mysql> UPDATE mytable SET ID = 10 WHERE last_name = 'Kent' and first_name = 'Clark';
Query OK, 1 row affected (0.00 sec)
Rows matched: 1  Changed: 1  Warnings: 0

mysql> SELECT * FROM mytable;
+-------+-----------+------------+------------+
| ID    | last_name | first_name | birth_date |
+-------+-----------+------------+------------+
|     2 | Sawyer    | Jane       | 2000-02-02 |
|     1 | Smith     | Joe        | 2000-02-02 |
|     3 | Walters   | Bob        | 2000-02-02 |
|     4 | Roberts   | Susan      | 2000-02-02 |
|    10 | Kent      | Clark      | 2000-02-02 |
+-------+-----------+------------+------------+
5 rows in set (0.00 sec)
```

BACKING UP YOUR DATABASES

To back up your databases, lock your tables so that they cannot be changed and then back up the files in the /usr/local/var/ directory which contains your database files. In the /usr/local/var/ directory you will find a subdirectory for each database you have created. The directory contains all the files needed to make your database function correctly. You should back up your databases one at a time as follows:

1. Run mysql and connect to the database you want to back up. For instance, to back up the mydbase database used as an example in this book, use the following commands:

   ```
   # /usr/local/bin/mysql -u <user name> --password=<password>
   Welcome to the MySQL monitor.  Commands end with ; or \g.
   Your MySQL connection id is 12 to server version: 3.22.30

   Type 'help' for help.

   mysql> use mydbase;
   Reading table information for completion of table and column names
   Database changed
   mysql>
   ```

2. Lock all tables to enable only reading. This will enable users to continue to query the database while ensuring that no new data is written to the tables while they are being backed up. To lock tables for reading, use the LOCK TABLES command:

   ```
   mysql> LOCK TABLES <table name> READ, <table name> READ, ...;
   ```

   Lock all tables in the database you plan to back up. In the case of the mydbase database, we have a single table:

   ```
   mysql> LOCK TABLES mytable READ;
   Query OK, 0 rows affected (0.00 sec)
   ```

3. Back up all files in the directory /usr/local/var/mydbase/. Ideally you should quickly copy them to another location which can then be backed up to tape or other backup media with your regular system backups. By doing this you can quickly unlock the tables so that the database can resume normal operation.

4. Unlock the tables with the UNLOCK TABLES command:

```
mysql> UNLOCK TABLES;
Query OK, 0 rows affected (0.00 sec)
```

You can automate this process so that your databases are backed up automatically. For instance, you can schedule copying of the databases files to the /backups directory and then include the /backups directory in your regular system backups.

The following script will lock tables in the mydbase database, copy the relevant files, and then unlock the tables:

```
#!/bin/sh

/usr/local/bin/mysql --user=<user name> --password=<password>
➥--database=mydbase --execute='LOCK TABLES mytable READ'
cp /usr/local/var/mydbase/* /backups
/usr/local/bin/mysql --user=<user name> –password=<password>
➥--database=mydbase --execute='UNLOCK TABLES'
```

Create this script in a logical location such as /usr/local/bin/ and give it a descriptive name such as backupmysql. Make the script executable:

```
# chmod 755 /usr/local/bin/backupmysql
```

You can then schedule the script to run regularly using crond as outlined in Chapter 7, "Scheduling Tasks." For instance, to run this script once a day at 11:00 p.m., add the following entry to the root user's crontab file:

```
* 23 * * * /usr/local/bin/backupmysql
```

MANAGING USERS AND PERMISSIONS

MySQL permits control of access to databases and tables with user accounts that you create in the MySQL grant tables.

You can create user accounts and assign system access permissions at four levels:

- **Global**: Privileges that apply to all databases
- **Database**: Privileges that apply to all tables in a particular database
- **Table**: Privileges that apply to all columns in a particular table
- **Column**: Privileges that apply to a single column in a given table

The GRANT statement enables you to grant access privileges and takes the general form:

```
mysql> GRANT <privilege>, <privilege>, ... ON <object to which privileges apply>
➥ TO <user name> IDENTIFIED BY <password>, <user name> IDENTIFIED BY <password>,
...
```

Possible privileges are outlined in Table 24.7.

PART
V
CH
24

TABLE 24.7 MYSQL ACCESS PRIVILEGES

Privilege	Description
ALL PRIVILEGES	Grants superuser access to all operations.
ALTER	Grants the ability to use the ALTER command.
CREATE	Grants the ability to use the CREATE command.
DELETE	Grants the ability to use the DELETE command.
DROP	Grants the ability to use the DROP command.
FILE	Grants the ability to perform file access.
INDEX	Grants the ability to index tables.
INSERT	Grants the ability to use the INSERT command.
PROCESS	Grants the ability to view a list of active threads in the server.
RELOAD	Grants the ability to issue reload, refresh, and flush commands.
SELECT	Grants the ability to use the SELECT command.
SHUTDOWN	Grants the ability to shut down the server.
UPDATE	Grants the ability to use the UPDATE command.
USAGE	Grants no privileges.

The scope of privileges being granted is determined by the ON clause as follows:

- To grant global privileges, use the following ON clause: ON *.*.
- To grant database privileges, use the following ON clause: ON <database name>.*. Alternatively, connect to the desired database with USE <database name> and then use the following ON clause: ON *.
- To grant table privileges, use the following ON clause: ON <database name>.<table name>. Alternatively, connect to the database in question using USE <database name> and then use the following ON clause: ON <table name>.
- To grant column privileges, specify the table name in the ON clause and then specify a list of columns and permissions in the privilege list: GRANT <privilege> <column name>, <privilege> <column name>, ... ON <database name>.<table name>.

The TO clause specifies the user to whom permissions are being granted. The username can be specified in several ways:

- *<user name>*: Corresponds to the user connecting from any host.
- *<user name>*@%: Corresponds to the user connecting from any host.
- *<user name>*@*<host name>*: Corresponds to the user connecting from a specific host.
- *<user name>*@*localhost*: Corresponds to the user connecting from the server machine itself.

For any given GRANT statement, the privileges only apply to the specified hosts.

Note

If the specified username does not exist in MySQL's user database then that user will be created.

Tip

Always specify specific permissions for a user on the local host system using **@localhost because otherwise the user will receive the anonymous user permissions when connecting from the local host instead of any permissions specified with a *<user name>*@% or *<user name>* entry.

The IDENTIFIED BY clause enables you to specify the password for the user in question. Table 24.8 provides some examples of the granting of permissions.

TABLE 24.8 EXAMPLES OF GRANTING PRIVILEGES IN MySQL

GRANT Command	Result
GRANT ALL PRIVILEGES ON *.* TO someuser@localhost IDENTIFIED BY somepassword	Enables the user someuser to have global super-user privileges when connecting from the local system.
GRANT SELECT, INSERT, UPDATE ON somedatabase.* TO someuser IDENTIFIED BY somepassword	Enables the user someuser to select, insert, and update on any table in the somedatabase database.
GRANT ALTER, SELECT, INSERT, UPDATE ON somedatabase.sometable TO someuser @somehost IDENITIFED BY somepassword	Enables the user someuser to use the ALTER, SELECT, INSERT, and UPDATE statements on the sometable table in the somedatabase database when connecting from the host somehost.
GRANT USAGE ON *.* TO someuser@% IDENTIFIED BY somepassword	Denies the user someuser connecting from any host any privileges on any object.

To revoke a privilege that has been granted to the user, use the REVOKE command. The REVOKE command looks like the GRANT command except for two changes:

- You use a FROM clause instead of a TO clause to specify the users the REVOKE command applies to.
- You do not use an IDENTIFIED BY clause.

For instance, consider the GRANT command:

```
mysql> GRANT SELECT, INSERT, UPDATE ON somedatabase.*
➥TO someuser IDENTIFIED BY somepassword
```

You would revoke the permissions this command grants with the following REVOKE command:

```
mysql> REVOKE SELECT, INSERT, UPDATE ON somedatabase.* FROM someuser
```

TROUBLESHOOTING

Numerous problems can occur when you are setting up and learning to use MySQL. The following are some of the more commonly reported problems:

- Receiving the MySQL server has gone away error.
- Receiving the Host <host name> is blocked error.
- Receiving the Too many connections error.
- Receiving the Out of memory error when executing a SQL command.
- Receiving the Access Denied error.

In addition to these problems, numerous other problems are discussed in the MySQL reference manual. The relevant chapter is online at http://www.mysql.org/Manual_chapter/manual_Problems.html.

RECEIVING THE MySQL server has gone away ERROR

This error occurs when you have an open connection (such as an open instance of the mysql client) and you leave it idle for an extended period of time. The mysqld daemon will close a connection after eight hours if no activity has occurred on the connection. If you close your connection and reconnect, the server should be running fine.

If you typically need to leave connections open, but idle, for longer than eight hours, you can set the wait_timeout variable when you start mysqld by adding the following line to the mysqld section of your MySQL options file with an appropriate time value:

```
set-variable = wait_timeout = <time>
```

Alternately, pass the variable definition on the command line to safe_mysqld:

```
# /usr/local/bin/safe_mysqld -set-variable wait_timeout=<time>
```

RECEIVING THE Host <host name> is blocked ERROR

If too many connections are received from a host that is subsequently interrupted before they are closed, mysqld will stop accepting connections from the host. The number of connections of this sort that are allowed before a host is blocked is determined by the max_connect_errors variable and the default value is 10. You can change the number of connections before blocking by adding the line

```
set-variable = max_connect_errors = <number of connections>
```

to the mysqld section of your MySQL options file with an appropriate time value. Alternately, pass the variable definition on the command line to safe_mysqld:

```
# /usr/local/bin/safe_mysqld -set-variable
➥max_connect_errors=<number of connections>
```

If the number of interrupted connections has been exceeded, you can reset the counter with the mysqladmin program:

```
# /usr/local/bin/mysqladmin -u root –password=<password> flush-hosts
```

RECEIVING THE Too many connections ERROR

If you receive the Too many connections error, it means too many open connections to the server exist. By default mysqld allows up to 100 simultaneous connections to the server. The maximum number of connections allowed is determined by the max_connections variable. You can change the maximum number of connections by adding the line

```
set-variable = max_connections = <number of connections>
```

to the mysqld section of your MySQL options file with an appropriate time value. Alternately, pass the variable definition on the command line to safe_mysqld:

```
# /usr/local/bin/safe_mysqld -set-variable max_connections=<number of connections>
```

RECEIVING THE Out of memory ERROR WHEN EXECUTING A SQL COMMAND

When you receive an Out of memory error, it is indicative of a problem caused by the mysql client and not the mysqld daemon. The error indicates that the system running mysql does not have enough memory available to store the entire result of a query to the server.

Sometimes this is caused by an incorrectly formed query that generates an excessive number of rows in the result. If this is not the problem and you cannot add more memory to the server, try running mysql with the --client argument:

```
# /usr/local/bin/mysql -u <user name> --password=<password> --client
```

This places more load on the server but frees the client, which can eliminate the memory error.

RECEIVING THE Access Denied ERROR

A number of reasons why you might receive Access Denied errors when connecting to mysqld exist. These include the following:

- The mysql_install_db script was not run after installing MySQL as outlined earlier in this chapter. This means that the necessary grant tables do not exist. Try running the script as outlined in the installation section of this chapter.

- If you change the grant tables directly with SQL INSERT and UPDATE commands, you must issue a FLUSH PRIVILEGES command or execute mysqladmin flush-privileges in order for mysqld to re-read the tables and establish the new privileges.

- The user table might be corrupt. Try connecting to the mysql database and using the command SELECT * FROM user to display the contents of the table.

A detailed discussion of Access Denied errors and their causes and solutions can be found at http://www.mysql.org/Manual_chapter/manual_Privilege_system.html#Access_denied.

DYNAMIC, DATA-DRIVEN WEB SITES

In this chapter

UNDERSTANDING DYNAMIC, INTERACTIVE WEB SITES

Although it used to be the case that Web sites consisted of collections of static HTML documents and image files, this is no longer true except for the smallest, simplest sites.

Even a moderately complex site can benefit from being stored in a back-end database and any site requiring interactivity almost definitely needs to be generated programmatically from a store of data on the server.

Several reasons exist for a Web site to be driven from a database:

- The need to provide simple, distributed management tools for site content.
- The need for frequent, regular changes to site contents.
- The need to provide dynamic data such as catalog information through the Web.
- The need to create interactive applications such as search engines and shopping carts.

To create Web sites driven from dynamic data sources, use a mechanism for dynamic content generation. In this model, when a user requests a document, the document does not exist as a static document but, instead, the request causes some form of a script or program to execute. This obtains data from some dynamic data source and then builds an HTML document on-the-fly to return to the user's browser.

Two main models exist for generating this type of dynamically generated Web site:

- Traditional CGI-BIN programming
- Server API programming

CGI-BIN PROGRAMMING

The Common Gateway Interface is the original model for dynamic programming for the Web. Under CGI-BIN, scripts or binary programs are executed by the Web server as separate processes every time the user requests execution of the script or program. Any data provided by the user is directed to the application that performs the required processing and then returns HTML to the Web server for sending to the browser (see Figure 25.1).

CGI-BIN scripts or programs can be developed in any language which supports reading data from the standard input and outputting results to the standard output. This includes Perl, TCL, shell languages such as Bash and C Shell, and compiled languages such as C, C++, and Java.

The advantage of CGI-BIN programming is that it is Web server-independent. All modern Web servers support CGI-BIN so a CGI-BIN program can easily be moved between Web server platforms, especially if it is written in an interpreted language such as Perl, which is available for any operating system.

Figure 25.1
A typical CGI-BIN interaction.

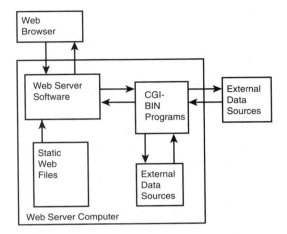

However, CGI-BIN programming has disadvantages. In particular, for each request for a CGI-BIN script or program a separate instance of the application must be launched as a separate process. Overhead is incurred for each process started by the Web server and in the case of interpreted languages this overhead is even larger because a separate instance of the language's interpreter is started as well.

For any site with a high volume of requests, especially simultaneous requests, this presents a serious efficiency and performance problem and for this reason, many sites opt for API-based solutions instead of CGI-BIN programming.

In addition, CGI-BIN generally uses general-purpose programming languages instead of the programming languages of many API-based development environments. Such environments have languages optimized specifically for the task of creating applications to obtain data from back-end data sources and then generate HTML from the data.

Of course, this does not mean that CGI-BIN has no benefits. CGI-BIN programming's reliance on general-purpose programming languages provides some advantages, including the following:

- Easy integration with other applications
- Access to features of full-fledged programming languages such as custom data types and linked lists
- The option to use full-fledged object-oriented programming for application development
- Access to system at a low-level including, if needed, access to stacks and registers

SERVER API PROGRAMMING

Modern Web servers such as Apache include application program interfaces (APIs) which allow applications to directly interact with the server. This allows the creation of application development environments that are integrated parts of the Web server and run either as part of the Web server process itself or as a single external process.

When requests are made for applications run through that application development environment, the Web server can simply direct the request to the application engine through the API without starting a new process or launching a command interpreter as required for CGI-BIN. The application can produce dynamic HTML and return it to the browser directly through the Web server's API rather than sending the data to the standard output and then letting the Web server read it back in from there. The relationship of API-based application development environments with Web servers is illustrated in Figure 25.2.

Figure 25.2
API Web application environments.

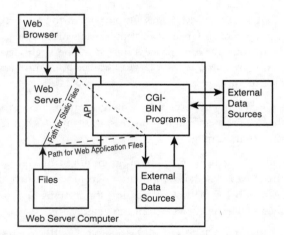

This direct interaction between the Web server and the application engine allows for more efficient dynamic and interactive Web applications that can generally handle more requests and larger numbers of simultaneous requests than CGI-BIN solutions on the same system. For this reason, API-based solutions are commonly used on interactive and dynamic Web sites today.

In addition to efficiency advantages as compared to CGI-BIN programming, API-based solutions provide the following potential advantages:

- Easy access to features of the Web server through the API
- Integration with the Web server's security and authentication mechanisms

However, Web application environments have disadvantages. Most notably, the programming languages of most of these environments are focused on a particular task: obtaining dynamic data and using it to generate HTML for the browser. This focus means the languages lack many features found in the general-purpose programming languages commonly used for CGI-BIN programming.

In addition, API-based solutions often lock you into a particular Web server and, at times, a particular operating system platform which means your applications are harder to move between systems.

Software for Connecting Web Sites to Databases

Linux benefits from a wide range of free and commercial server-based API Web application development environments for the Apache server. These include the following:

- PHP
- Zope
- Web+
- ColdFusion

PHP

PHP is one of the most popular Web-application development environments for Apache and Linux. As a freely available Web application framework, it adheres to the open-source ideals of Linux and Apache, which makes it an attractive choice for many Linux Web servers.

It uses a Perl-like syntax and provides many features of Perl and other general-purpose programming languages. PHP includes wide-ranging support for external data sources including all available databases for Linux such as Oracle, Sybase, Informix, MySQL, mSQL, PostreSQL, and Adabas D as well as support for IMAP and LDAP data sources and FTP servers.

In addition, PHP can be integrated with several Linux libraries including the GD library, which allows PHP to generate dynamic graphics on-the-fly, FreeType, which provides support for TrueType fonts in PHP, and PDFLib for working with PDF files within PHP.

PHP can be downloaded as source code for more platforms including Linux from `http://www.php.net/`. We will consider PHP in more detail as an example Web application environment for database integration in this chapter because it is widely used and because it is freely available and included with many Linux distributions including Red Hat Linux 6.2.

Zope

Zope is a newer API-based Web application environment for Linux under the open-source model. Although it is new, it has gained a lot of attention for its unique approach to Web application development.

Zope was developed in Python and can be extended using Python and C. However, application developers do not need to know or use the Python programming language for most development work.

Instead, Zope provides a unique solution in the Web application development problem domain. Unlike most application development environments that provide a language with which to develop scripts which generate HTML pages, Zope provides a complete content management and development environment, which allows developers to keep a clear separation of data, logic, and design. Zope handles all issues of data persistence and access control, tasks that often require manual programming in other application environments and in CGI-BIN.

Zope provides a complete Web-based environment for management and development. The system allows complete access control, delegation of responsibility for development of different sections of a site, data sharing, and search tools. Zope is well suited to creating complex, distributed sites that require delegation of responsibility to a wide group of people.

Zope can be downloaded from `http://www.zope.org/`.

Web+

Web+ is a commercial application development environment that was among the earliest available application development environments for Linux and Apache. Web+ is produced by TalentSoft.

Web+ uses a simple tag-based language for application development, which makes it an attractive choice for developers without a strong programming background coming from a strong HTML background. Using this tag-based language, developers can build applications that interact with most Linux databases, the file system, Web servers, and TCP/IP applications through direct socket communication.

Web+ can also be extended with Web+Shop, which provides a complete e-commerce solution built on Web+. Web+Shop allows the building of complete online shopping applications as well as providing inventory management, customer management, and online transaction processing. Web+Shop provides full integration with CyberCash Register for online payment processing. A trial version of Web+ can be downloaded from `http://www.webplus.com/`.

ColdFusion

ColdFusion is the well-regarded commercial Web application development environment from Allaire. Originally available only for Windows and Solaris, the beta of the Linux version is now available and the Linux version should be shipping by the time you read this book.

ColdFusion, like Web+, provides a tag-based language that is easy to learn for experienced HTML developers with no programming background. ColdFusion provides easy integration with most back-end data sources including leading relational databases for Linux, the Linux file system, FTP and HTTP servers, IMAP and POP3 servers, and LDAP servers.

ColdFusion can be extended through the creation of custom tags written in the ColdFusion markup language or as compiled executables written in C++ or Java. This allows for adherence to the principle of writing code once and then reusing it as widely as possible.

ColdFusion provides an integrated development environment in the form of ColdFusion Studio and allows for remote development. ColdFusion also includes a complete security model for building secured applications and can integrate with applications written in other languages through the XML-based WDDX protocol.

A trial version of ColdFusion can be downloaded from `http://www.allaire.com/`.

INSTALLING PHP

The latest version of PHP is available for download from `http://www.php.net/` in source code form. The version available at time of publication was PHP 3.0.14 and was available for download in a compressed tape archive file named `php-3.0.14.tar.gz`.

Download the archive and extract it using the command:

```
# tar xzvf php-3.0.14.tar.gz
```

Next, change the directory to the subdirectory containing the extract source code:

```
# cd php-3.0.14
```

You can build PHP from the source code in one of two ways:

- **As a Dynamic Shared Object (DSO) for Apache:** Using this option, you do not need to recompile Apache. Apache will load the PHP module from an external file. This is the preferred method for compiling and installing PHP. If you are using Apache 1.3.6 or higher you can use this option. In this chapter we will address building PHP as a DSO for Apache.

- **As a Static Object for Apache:** Using this option, you need to recompile Apache with PHP support. Use this method for earlier versions of Apache or if you have opted not to use Dynamic Apache modules.

PART
V

CH
25

Note   The installation instructions in this chapter assume that Apache has been installed as outlined in Chapter 23, "Apache and the World Wide Web."

Compilation and installation require four steps:

1. Configure the source code for installation using the `configure` command. The following is the most basic `configure` command:

   ```
   # ./configure --with-apxs=/usr/local/apache/bin/apxs
   ```

   The value of the `--with-apxs` parameter should be the complete path to the `apxs` script which comes with the Apache distribution. If you installed Apache from the Apache source code using the default settings, this path will be `/usr/local/apache/bin/apxs`.

On Red Hat 6.2, this script is normally installed at /usr/sbin/apxs. In addition to the --with-apxs option, PHP's configure script supports a large number of parameters which allow you to customize the features supported by PHP. These parameters are discussed later in this chapter under "PHP Installation Configuration Parameters."

2. Compile the source code with the following command:

   ```
   # make
   ```

3. Install the compiled software with this command:

   ```
   # make install
   ```

4. Restart Apache with this command:

   ```
   # /usr/local/apache/bin/apachectl restart
   ```

   On Red Hat Linux, you can restart Apache with the following command:

   ```
   # /etc/rc.d/init.d/httpd restart
   ```

Once you have PHP installed and running it is a good idea to test the installation. To do this, create a test PHP document. The simplest PHP document will contain a single command:

```
<? phpinfo(); ?>
```

Create a file in your Web server's document root directory containing this single command. The file should have a name with the extension .php3 such as test.php3.

Note

PHP documents normally have the extension .php3. You can alter this with the AddType directive in the srm.conf Apache configuration file. To define an extension for PHP, use a directive of the form AddType application/x-httpd-php3 <extension>.

If you request this document with your browser, PHP will generate a page of PHP information like the one shown in Figure 25.3 as long as PHP is installed correctly and Apache is running.

PHP INSTALLATION CONFIGURATION PARAMETERS

The configuration steps of the PHP installation outlined above allow you great flexibility over the features compiled into your PHP module and the configuration of the module and the installation process. These configuration directives can be generally classified into the following groups:

- General Parameters
- Directory and File Parameters
- Feature and Package Parameters

Figure 25.3
The PHP information page.

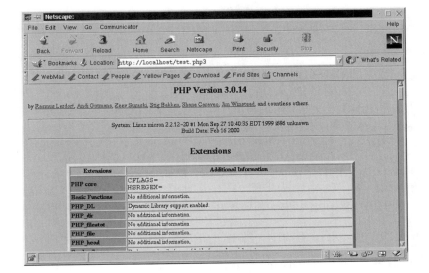

GENERAL PARAMETERS

The general parameters outlined in Table 25.1 allow you to specify basic aspects of the operation of the `configure` script.

TABLE 25.1 APACHE GENERAL INSTALLATION CONFIGURATION PARAMETERS

Parameter	Description
`--cache-file=` `<file name>`	Cache results of tests run during execution in the specified file for later reference.
`--help`	Display a complete list of configuration parameters instead of configuring the source code.
`--no-create`	Run the configuration but do not create the resulting configuration files in order to test the configuration process.
`--quiet, --silent`	Do not print test messages during configuration.
`--version`	Display the version of `autoconf` that was used to create the configuration instead of configuring the source code.

DIRECTORY AND FILENAME PARAMETERS

The directory and filename installation configuration parameters outlined in Table 25.2 specify the locations where files should be placed during installation and where the configuration and installation process can find the files it needs.

PART **V**

CH **25**

TABLE 25.2   DIRECTORY AND FILENAME INSTALLATION/CONFIGURATION PARAMETERS

Parameter	Description	Default Value
--prefix= *<directory>*	Install architecture-independent files in the specified directory (this value is referred to as PREFIX in the remainder of this table)	/usr/local
--exec-prefix= *<directory>*	Install architecture-dependent files in the specified directory (this value is referred to as EPREFIX in the remainder of this table)	The value of the - prefix parameter.
--bindir= *<directory>*	Install user executable binary in the specified directory	EPREFIX/bin
--sbindir= *<directory>*	Install system administration executable files in the specified directory	EPREFIX/sbin
--libexecdir= *<directory>*	Install program executable files in the specified directory	EPREFIX/libexec
--datadir= *<directory>*	Install read-only, architecture-independent data files in the specified directory	PREFIX/share
--sysconfdir= *<directory>*	Install read-only single-machine data in the specified directory	PREFIX/etc
--sharedstatedir= *<directory>*	Install modifiable architecture-independent data in the specified directory	PREFIX/com
--localstatedir= *<directory>*	Install modifiable single-machine data in the specified directory	PREFIX/var
--libdir= *<directory>*	Install object code libraries in the specified directory	EPREFIX/lib
-includedir= *<directory>*	Install C header files in the specified directory	PREFIX/include
--oldincludedir= *<directory>*	Install C header files for non-gcc compilers in the specified directory	/usr/include
--infodir= *<directory>*	Install info style documentation in the specified directory	PREFIX/info
--mandir= *<directory>*	Install man style documentation in the specified directory	PREFIX/man
--srcdir=*<directory>*	The directory containing the source code	The directory containing the configure script
--x-includes= *<directory>*	X include files are in the specified directory	
--x-libraries= *<directory>*	X library files are in the specified directory	
--program- prefix=*<directory>*	Directory prefix for installed program names	
--program-suffix= *<directory>*	Suffix to append to installed program names	

TABLE 25.2   CONTINUED

Parameter	Description	Default Value
`--program-transform-name=<program name>`	Run sed `<program name>` on installed program names	

FEATURE AND PACKAGE PARAMETERS

The feature and package installation configuration parameters outlined in Table 25.3 enable you to specify which features of PHP beyond the core functionality to build when compiling PHP. These features include support for different databases and support for special libraries (such as the `gd` graphics generation libraries).

TABLE 25.3   FEATURE AND PACKAGE INSTALLATION CONFIGURATION PARAMETERS

Parameter	Description
`--with-apxs=<file name>`	Indicates that PHP should be built as a dynamic shared object for Apache and optionally specifies the path to the `apxs` script.
`--enable-versioning`	Indicates that PHP should take advantage of versioning and scoping in Solaris 2.x and Linux.
`--with-apache=<directory>`	Indicates that PHP should be built as a static object for Apache and optionally specifies the path to the top-level Apache directory. If no path is specified, the default is `/usr/local/etc/httpd`.
`--with-system-regex`	Build PHP using the system's regular expression library instead of PHP's regular expression library.
`--with-mod_charset`	Enable support for transfer tables for the Apache `mod_charset` module in Russian Apache.
`--with-fhttpd=<directory>`	Indicates that PHP should be built as an `fhttpd` module and optionally specifies the path to the `fhttpd` source code directory. If no path is specified, the default is `/usr/local/src/fhttpd`.
`--with-imap=<directory>`	Indicates that PHP should be built with IMAP support and optionally specifies the IMAP include directory.
`--with-imsp=<directory>`	Indicates that PHP should be built with IMSP support and optionally specifies the IMSP include directory containing `libimsp.a`.
`--with-aspell=<directory>`	Indicates that PHP should be built with ASPELL support and optionally specifies the path to the ASPELL files.
`--with-mcal=<directory>`	Indicates that PHP should be built with MCAL support and optionally specifies the path to the MCAL files.
`--with-ftp`	Build PHP with FTP support.

PART
V
CH
25

TABLE 25.3 CONTINUED

Parameter	Description
`--without-gd`	Build PHP without support for the GD graphics library.
`--with-gd=<directory>`	Indicates that PHP should be built with support for the GD graphics library and optionally specifies that path to the GD installation directory.
`--with-ttf=<directory>`	Indicates that PHP should be built with support for the FreeType font library and optionally specifies the path to the FreeType files.
`--enable-freetype-4bit-antialias-hack`	Build PHP with patches needed to support the FreeType 2 font library.
`--enable-t1lib`	Build GD support for PHP with `t1lib` support.
`--with-get-text=<directory>`	Indicates that PHP should be built with support for GNU `gettext` and optionally specifies the path to the GNU `gettext` files. If no path is specified, the default is `/usr/local`.
`--with-ima-gick=<directory>`	Indicates that PHP should be built with support for ImageMagick and optionally specifies the path to ImageMagick. If no path is specified, PHP will attempt to determine the location.
`--with-x`	Build PHP with support for X Windows.
`--with-oracle=<directory>`	Indicates that PHP should be built with support for Oracle databases and optionally specifies the path to the Oracle home directory. If no path is specified, the default is the value of the `ORACLE_HOME` environment variable.
`--with-iodbc=<directory>`	Indicates that PHP should be built with support for the iODBC ODBC driver package and optionally specifies the location of the iODBC base installation directory. If no path is specified, the default value is `/usr/local`.
`--with-openlink=<directory>`	Indicates that PHP should be built with support for the OpenLink ODBC driver package and optionally specifies the location of the OpenLink base installation directory. If no path is specified, the default value is `/usr/local/openlink`.
`--with-adabas=<directory>`	Indicates that PHP should be built with support for the Adabas D database and optionally specifies the location of the Adabas D base installation directory. If no path is specified, the default value is `/usr/local`.
`--with-sybase=<directory>`	Indicates that PHP should be built with support for the Sybase database and optionally specifies the location of the Sybase home directory. If no path is specified, the default value is `/home/sybase`.

TABLE 25.3 CONTINUED	
Parameter	**Description**
--with-sybase-ct= <directory>	Indicates that PHP should be built with support for Sybase-CT and optionally specifies the location of the Sybase home directory. If no path is specified, the default value is /home/sybase.
--with-mysql=<directory>	Indicates that PHP should be built with support for the MySQL database and optionally specifies the location of the MySQL installation directory. If no path is specified, PHP attempts to determine the location of the installation directory.
--with-msql=<directory>	Indicates that PHP should be built with support for the mSQL database and optionally specifies the location of the mSQL installation directory. If no path is specified, the default value is /usr/local/Hughes.
--with-pgsql=<directory>	Indicates that PHP should be built with support for the PostgreSQL database and optionally specifies the location of the PostgreSQL base installation directory. If no path is specified, the default value is /usr/local/pgsql.
--with-ibm-db2= <directory>	Indicates that PHP should be built with support for the IBM DB2 database and optionally specifies the location of the DB2 base installation directory. If no path is specified, the default value is /home/db2inst1/sqllib.
--with-solid=<directory>	Indicates that PHP should be built with support for the Solid database and optionally specifies the location of the Solid base installation directory. If no path is specified, the default value is /usr/local/solid.
--with-empress= <directory>	Indicates that PHP should be built with support for the Empress database and optionally specifies the location of the Empress base installation directory. If no path is specified, the default value is the value of the EMPRESSPATH environment variable.
--with-ldap=<directory>	Indicates that PHP should be built with support for LDAP and optionally specifies the location of the LDAP base installation directory. If no path is specified, the default value is /usr and /usr/local.
--with-mck=<directory>	Indicates that PHP should be built with support for Cybercash MCK and optionally specifies the location of the Cybercash MCK build directory. If no path is specified, the default value is /usr/src/mck-3.2.0.3-linux.
--with-snmp=<directory>	Indicates that PHP should be built with support for SNMP and optionally specifies the location of the SNMP base installation directory. If no path is specified, PHP attempts to locate the SNMP installation directory.

PART

V

CH

25

TABLE 25.3 CONTINUED

Parameter	Description
--with-velocis=<directory>	Indicates that PHP should be built with support for Velocis and optionally specifies the location of the Velocis base installation directory. If no path is specified, the default value is /usr/local/velocis.
--with-informix=<directory>	Indicates that PHP should be built with support for the Informix database and optionally specifies the location of the Informix base installation directory.
--with-inter-base=<directory>	Indicates that PHP should be built with support for the Interbase database and optionally specifies the location of the Interbase base installation directory. If no path is specified, the default value is /usr/interbase.
--with-custom-odbc=<directory>	Indicates that PHP should be built with support for user-defined ODBC drivers and optionally specifies the location of the ODBC drivers. If no path is specified, the default value is /usr/local.
--with-hyperwave	Build PHP with Hyperwave support.
--with-xml	Build PHP with XML support.
--with-yp	Build PHP with support for YP (NIS).
--with-zlib=<directory>	Indicates that PHP should be built with support for zlib and optionally specifies the location of the zlib installation directory. If no path is specified, the default value is /usr.
--with-pdflib=<directory>	Indicates that PHP should be built with support for pdflib and optionally specifies the location of the pdflib installation directory. If no path is specified, the default value is /usr/local.
--with-zlib-dir=<directory>	Indicates the zlib directory for pdflib 2.0 or indicates that zlib support should be included if pdflib is not being included.
--with-jpeg-dir=<directory>	Indicates the JPEG directory for pdflib 2.0.
--with-tiff-dir=<directory>	Indicates the TIFF directory for pdflib 2.0.
--with-cpdflib=<directory>	Indicates that PHP should be built with support for ClibPDF and optionally specifies the location of the CLibPDF installation directory. If no path is specified, the default value is /usr/local.
--with-fdftk=<directory>	Indicates that PHP should be built with support for fdftk and optionally specifies the location of the fdftk installation directory. If no path is specified, the default value is /usr/local.
--with-dbase	Indicates that PHP should be built with the bundled support for Dbase databases.

TABLE 25.3 CONTINUED

Parameter	Description
`--with-filepro`	Indicates that PHP should be built with the bundled read-only support for FilePro databases.
`--with-mod-dav=<directory>`	Indicates that Apache should be built with DAV support through Apache's `mod_dav` module and indicates the location of the `mod_dav` installation directory.
`--disable-unified-odbc`	Indicates that unified ODBC support should be disabled if iODBC, Adabas, Solid, Velocis or custom ODBC is enabled.
`--with-config-file-path=<directory>`	Specifies the path where PHP should look for the `php3.ini` file. By default, PHP will look in `/usr/local/lib`.
`--enable-debug`	Build PHP with debugging symbols enabled.
`--enable-safe-mode`	Build PHP with safe mode enabled by default.
`--with-exec-dir=<directory>`	Indicates that PHP should only allow executable scripts in the specified directory when running in safe mode. By default, PHP only allows executables in `/usr/local/php/bin` when running in safe mode.
`--enable-track-vars`	Indicates that support for GET, POST and Cookies tracking variables should be enabled by default.
`--enable-magic-quotes`	Indicates that magic quotes should be enabled by default.
`--enable-debugger`	Build PHP with support for remote debugging.
`--disable-bcmath`	Build PHP without `bc`-style precision math support.
`--enable-force-cgi-redirect`	Indicates that the security check for the internal server should be enabled.
`--enable-discard-path`	Allows the PHP CGI binary to be placed outside the Web document tree for security reasons when using PHP through CGI.
`--enable-memory-limit`	Build PHP with memory limit support.
`--disable-short-tags`	Disable support for the short-form `<?` Start tag by default.
`--disable-url-fopen-wrapper`	Disable the URL-aware `fopen` wrapper which allows PHP to access files through HTTP or FTP.
`--enable-sysvsem`	Build PHP with System V semaphore support.
`--enable-sysvshm`	Build PHP with System V shared memory support.
`--disable-display-source`	Build PHP without support for displaying source code.

PART

V

CH

25

TABLE 25.3 CONTINUED

Parameter	Description
`--with-gdbm=<directory>`	Indicates that PHP should be built with support for GDBM and specifies the location of the GDBM files.
`--with-ndbm=<directory>`	Indicates that PHP should be built with support for NDBM and specifies the location of the NDBM files.
`--with-db2=<directory>`	Indicates that PHP should be built with support for Berkeley DB2 and specifies the location of the DB2 files.
`--with-dbm=<directory>`	Indicates that PHP should be built with support for DBM and specifies the location of the DBM files.
`--with-cdb=<directory>`	Indicates that PHP should be built with support for CDB and specifies the location of the CDB files.
`--with-mcrypt=<directory>`	Indicates that PHP should be built with support for mcrypt and specifies the location of the mcrypt installation directory.
`--with-mhash=<directory>`	Indicates that PHP should be built with support for mhash and specifies the location of the mhash installation directory.
`--enable-ucd-snmp-hack`	Build PHP with support for the UCD SNMP hack.
`--without-pcre-regex`	Build PHP without support for Perl-compatible regular expressions.
`--without-posix`	Build PHP without POSIX functions.
`--with-recode=<directory>`	Build PHP with GNU recode support.
`--enable-dmalloc`	Build PHP with dmalloc support.

AN OVERVIEW OF PHP SCRIPTING

A complete tutorial on PHP development is beyond the scope of a book focusing on Linux system administration. Still, if you plan to administer a Web site running PHP, a basic understanding of PHP development can help when you need to interact with developers to analyze and debug apparent system problems with the Web and PHP server.

PHP files seamlessly integrate HTML and PHP code. In order for the PHP engine to know which portions of a file to process as PHP code and which to leave untouched as HTML code, PHP code is marked in one of four ways:

- Using the <? and ?> opening and closing tags:

```
<?
PHP code goes here
?>
```

- Using the `<?php` and `?>` opening and closing tags:

```
<?php
PHP code goes here
?>
```

- Using the `<SCRIPT LANGUAGE="php">` and `</SCRIPT>` opening and closing tags:

```
<SCRIPT LANGUAGE="php">
</SCRIPT>
```

- Using the `<%` and `%>` opening and closing tags:

```
<%
PHP code goes here
%>
```

By far the most common format for PHP code is the `<? PHP code goes here ?>` format.

PHP code normally consists of a series of statements. A statement can be one of the following:

- A single statement ending with a semi-colon:

```
phpinfo();
```

- A series of statements enclosed in parentheses:

```
{
  $a = 1;
  $b = 2;
  $c = a + b;
}
```

- A flow control command followed by a statement (either of the following):

```
if ($x > 1)
  phpinfo();

if ($x > 1) {
  $a = 1;
  $b = 2;
  $c = a + b;
}
```

PHP supports a variety of basic data types:

- Integers
- Floating point numbers
- Strings

Complex data types are also available:

- Arrays
- Objects

PART

V

CH

25

Variable names are identified by a leading $ as in Perl: $<variable name>. For instance, $x, $myvar, and $some_var are all variable names. Variables in PHP do not need to be initialized and can be used at any point a script. They are also easily converted between types; for instance, assigning an integer to a string converts it to a string.

Several operators are available for building expressions:

- Arithmetic operators such as +, -, *, /, and %.
- Assignment operators such as =, +=, and .=.
- Bitwise operators such as &, |, ^, ~, <<, and >>.
- Comparison operators such as ==, ===, !=, <, >, <=, and >=.
- Incrementing and decrementing operators such as ++ and -.
- Logical operators such as and, or, xor, !, &&, and ||.

Complete discussion of PHP operators is in the online PHP manual at http://www.php.net/manual/language.operators.string.php3.

PHP provides a large set of built-in functions that provide the functionality of PHP including support for all external data sources and integrated libraries. Programmers can also create their own functions in PHP. A complete discussion of functions and a complete reference of all built-in functions is in the PHP online manual at http://www.php.net/manual/.

CREATING A SIMPLE DYNAMIC WEB SITE WITH PHP

To illustrate the use of PHP for dynamic Web site creation, consider the following simple case: You have a MySQL database named mydbase with a table named mytable containing four fields in each record: ID number, last name, first name, and birth date (this database and table were created in Chapter 24, "Linux Database Servers"). You want to create a simple Web application to allow users to enter an ID number or last name and view all matching records.

This requires two files:

- A file to present a form that the user can use to specify the ID number or last name of the records to display. Let's call this file form.html.
- A file to process the contents of the data submitted from the form and display any matching records from the database. Let's call this file query.php3.

The form.html file is a simple HTML form:

```
<HTML>
    <HEAD>
        <TITLE>form.html PHP example</TITLE>
    </HEAD>
    <BODY>
        <FORM METHOD=POST ACTION="query.php3">
            ID Number: <INPUT TYPE=TEXT NAME="ID"><BR>
            Last Name: <INPUT TYPE=TEXT NAME="Name"><BR>
```

```
          <INPUT TYPE=SUBMIT>
      </FORM>
   </BODY>

</HTML>
```

This produces a form like the one in Figure 25.4.

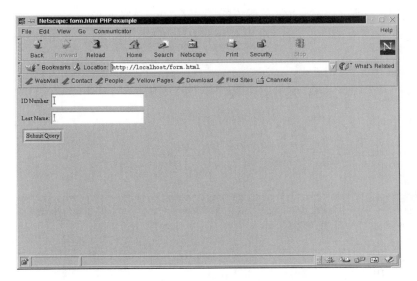

Figure 25.4
A query form for retrieving database records.

The form will be submitted to the query.php3 file:

```
01: <?
02:     $link = mysql_connect("localhost","root","");
03:     $dbase = mysql_select_db("mydbase","$link");
04:     if ($ID <> "") {
05:         $result = mysql_query("SELECT * FROM mytable WHERE ID = $ID",$dbase);
06:     } else {
07:         $result = mysql_query("SELECT * FROM mytable WHERE last_name =
➥'$Name'",$$
08:     }
09:     $numresults = mysql_num_rows($result);
10: ?>
11: <HTML>
12:     <HEAD>
13:         <TITLE>query.php3 Results</TITLE>
14:     </HEAD>
15:     <BODY>
16:         <H1>Search Results</H1>
17:         <?
18:             if ($numresults > 0) {
19:                 echo "
20:                 <TABLE BORDER=0 CELLPADDING=3>
21:                     <TR VALIGN=TOP>
22:                         <TD ALIGN=LEFT><STRONG>ID</STRONG></TD>
23:                         <TD ALIGN=LEFT><STRONG>Last Name</STRONG></TD>
24:                         <TD ALIGN=LEFT><STRONG>First Name</STRONG></TD>
```

```
25:                         <TD ALIGN=LEFT><STRONG>Birth Date</STRONG></TD>
26:                     </TR>
27:
28:                     ";
29:                 for ($i = 1; $i <= $numresults; $i ++) {
30:                     $row = mysql_fetch_array($result);
31:                     echo "
32:                         <TR VALIGN=TOP>
33:                             <TD ALIGN=LEFT>$row[0]</TD>
34:                             <TD ALIGN=LEFT>$row[1]</TD>
35:                             <TD ALIGN=LEFT>$row[2]</TD>
36:                             <TD ALIGN=LEFT>$row[3]</TD>
37:                         </TR>
38:                     ";
39:                 }
40:                 echo "</TABLE>";
41:             } else {
42:                 echo "No matches.";
43:             }
44:         ?>
45:     </BODY>
46: </HTML>
```

Note The line numbers in the previous file have been added for reference and are not part of the script.

This PHP file produces results similar to those shown in Figure 25.5.

Figure 25.5
Search results
with PHP.

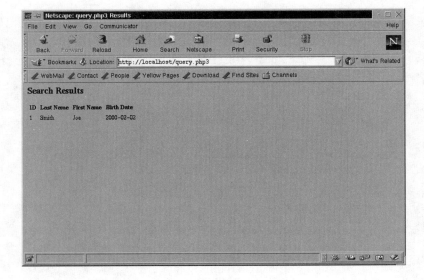

The resulting HTML code generated by this script and sent to the browser looks something like the following:

```
<HTML>
    <HEAD>
        <TITLE>query.php3 Results</TITLE>
    </HEAD>
    <BODY>
        <H1>Search Results</H1>

                <TABLE BORDER=0 CELLPADDING=3>
                    <TR VALIGN=TOP>
                        <TD ALIGN=LEFT><STRONG>ID</STRONG></TD>
                        <TD ALIGN=LEFT><STRONG>Last Name</STRONG></TD>
                        <TD ALIGN=LEFT><STRONG>First Name</STRONG></TD>
                        <TD ALIGN=LEFT><STRONG>Birth Date</STRONG></TD>
                    </TR>

                    <TR VALIGN=TOP>
                        <TD ALIGN=LEFT>1</TD>
                        <TD ALIGN=LEFT>Smith</TD>
                        <TD ALIGN=LEFT>Joe</TD>
                        <TD ALIGN=LEFT>2000-02-02</TD>
                    </TR>
                </TABLE>    </BODY>
</HTML>
```

The query.php3 script can be broken down as follows:

- Lines 1-10: These commands connect to the MySQL server, open the mydbase database, and then perform the appropriate query based on whether the user has submitted an ID number or a last name.

- Lines 17-40: One table row is displayed for each record in the returned results. For each record, the record is fetched from the results and stored in an array and then the contents of the array are displayed in the appropriate table cell.

- Line 42: If no results were obtained from the database, this information is displayed.

TROUBLESHOOTING

Numerous possible problems can exist when installing and using PHP, including those specific to interaction with particular databases and data sources. Some broad general problems do arise, however, including the following:

- PHP stops working after installing FrontPage extensions for Apache.
- PHP files are displayed as source code by Apache.
- PHP fails to compile because of a missing library.
- PHP fails to connect to my database.

PART

V

CH

25

PHP STOPS WORKING AFTER INSTALLING FRONTPAGE EXTENSIONS FOR APACHE

When you install the FrontPage extensions, they alter some Apache structures. PHP will need to be recompiled after this change. In your PHP source code directory, use the following commands to recompile and install PHP:

```
# make clean
# make
# make install
```

After this, restart Apache.

PHP FILES ARE DISPLAYED AS SOURCE CODE BY APACHE

If you request a PHP file from your Apache server and it returns the source code of the file instead of the processed result, you are missing an appropriate `AddType` directive in your `srm.conf` Apache configuration file. Add an entry similar to the following to `srm.conf` and restart Apache:

```
AddType application/x-hhtpd-php3 .php3
```

PHP FAILS TO COMPILE BECAUSE OF A MISSING LIBRARY

If you try to build PHP with external features such as GD support, FreeType, or LDAP, you must have the appropriate development libraries installed and available for PHP to compile successfully. A partial list of libraries and their locations can be found in the PHP FAQ at `http://www.php.net/FAQ.php3#1`, and include the following:

- LDAP: `ftp://ftp.openldap.org/pub/openldap/openldap-stable.tgz`
- Berkeley DB2: `http://www.sleepycat.com/`
- GD: `http://www.boutell.com/gd/#buildgd`
- mSQL: `http://www.hughes.com.au/`
- MySQL: `http://www.mysql.com/`
- IMAP: `ftp://ftp.cac.washington.edu/imap/old/`
- FreeType: `http://www.freetype.org/`
- ZLib: `http://www.cdrom.com/pub/infozip/zlib/`
- expat XML parser: `http://www.jclark.com/xml/expat.html`
- PDFLib: `http://www.pdflib.com`
- mcrypt: `ftp://argeas.cs-net.gr/pub/unix/mcrypt/`
- mhash: `http://sasweb.de/mhash/`
- t1lib: `http://www.neuroinformatik.ruhr-uni-bochum.de/ini/PEOPLE/rmz/t1lib/t1lib.html`
- dmalloc: `http://www.dmalloc.com/`
- aspell: `http://metalab.unc.edu/kevina/aspell/`
- Readline: `ftp://prep.ai.mit.edu/pub/gnu/readline/`

PHP FAILS TO CONNECT TO MY DATABASE SERVER

Assuming you are using the correct username and password for your server, this problem is most likely to occur when the PHP server and the database server are on different machines on the network. If your database server restricts based on the host of origin of the connection, be sure to add the PHP server to the list of valid clients on the database server. Otherwise, connections will be refused.

Also, ensure that the host table (/etc/hosts) on the PHP server has an entry for the database server and that the host table on the database server has an entry for the PHP server.

Another problem when accessing a database with PHP is that your PHP installation may not have the appropriate library compiled into for the database server you are trying to access. In this case, you should recompile PHP as outlined earlier in the "Installing PHP" section.

PART

V

CH

25

NEWS SERVICES

In this chapter

A Brief History of Usenet

In late 1979, soon after the release of V7 UNIX with UUCP, Steve Bellowin, a grad student of the University of North Carolina, released the first version of news software. It was installed on two computers, one at UNC and the other at Duke University. The first version was written with shell scripts and was later rewritten in C. This enabled shared discussions to take place at the two universities.

Since then many versions of news software have been written; the major ones are A News, B News, C News, NNTP, and INN. In addition there are some commercial implementations of news-type software such as DNews and Netscape Collabra.

In 1986 a news software was released that used the NNTP protocol over TCP/IP for news transport instead of UUCP. This was called NNTP. It was developed at UC San Diego. Soon after, in 1987, a very popular version of news called C News was developed at the University of Toronto. C News was widely used across the Internet.

The current news software used almost exclusively on the Internet is called INN. It was originally developed by Rich Salz of UUNET and released in 1992. It provides for both NNTP and UUCP-based news delivery.

Since version 1.4 of INN, the Internet Software Consortium handles development of the software. Now at version 2.2.1, INN can be obtained from `ftp://ftp.isc.org/isc/inn`. We will look at INN version 2.2.1 in this chapter.

News Group Hierarchies

The current structure of news groups on the Internet is known as Usenet. Usenet is a decentralized collection of sites exchanging news articles. Users on member sites read and write articles and post new articles to their local servers, which in turn feed them, server-by-server, to the rest of the Usenet community.

Newsgroups are structured hierarchically to varying levels of detail. The name of the group indicates the group's position within the hierarchy. For instance, a group by the name of `comp.languages` is within the `comp` category and might discuss computer languages in general but the group `comp.languages.pascal` is more finely focused, being part of the `languages` subcategory of the `comp` category and discusses the Pascal language.

The most well-known and widely used top-level categories are the following:

- **`alt`**: Alternative topics
- **`comp`**: Computer topics
- **`rec`**: Recreational topics
- **`soc`**: Social and societal topics

In addition, numerous targeted top-level categories exist including national top-level categories such as can for Canadian discussions and topic-related categories such as k12 for Kindergarten through grade 12 discussions.

In addition to these public Usenet categories, Usenet sites can create their own local categories which they can either keep private or make available for sharing by those sites which wish to receive feeds of the groups within those categories.

HARDWARE REQUIREMENTS

The hardware required to operate a viable INN news server is dependent on two factors:

- The size of a news feed you plan to receive: Do you plan to receive a complete Usenet news feed or a partial feed of select groups?
- The number of concurrent news readers that you expect to use the server.

For a partial feed site, a system could be as small as a single Pentium II 300 system with 256MB of RAM and 16GB of disk space on ultra-wide SCSI-2 hard disks connected to your news provider through a T1 connection. Typically a partial feed of this sort will not take the alt.* hierarchy and any *binaries groups.

At the high end, a full-feed site with a large number of users could easily require 4 Pentium III 500 CPUs with 2GB of RAM and more than 1KB of hard disk capacity. These could be on ultra-wide SCSI-2 hard disks connected through multiple ultra-wide SCSI controllers such as an Adaptec 2940 UW controller. With a full-feed site, it is recommended to connect to the Internet through a T3 connection, or at the very least you must have 4 or 5 T1 connections to your news provider.

PART
V

CH
26

INSTALLING INN 2.2.1

> **Tip**
>
> To install INN, you must first have Perl 5.004 or later installed. Perl is part of all major Linux distributions; you can obtain the latest version of Perl from http://www.perl.com/.

Precompiled INN software is packaged with many standard Linux distributions such as Red Hat 6.2. You can use RPM package add commands to install it on your server. However if you want to build INN binaries from source code, you can do so by following these steps:

1. Download the INN archive from ftp://ftp.isc.org/isc/inn/inn-2.2.1.tar.gz to a convenient location on your system such as /usr/local/src.

2. Change your current directory to the directory where you downloaded INN:
   ```
   # cd /usr/local/src
   ```

3. Unpack the INN distribution archive:
   ```
   # tar xzvf inn-2.2.1.tar.gz
   ```

4. Change your current directory to the directory created during extraction of the archive:
   ```
   # cd inn-2.2.1
   ```

5. Create the group news:
   ```
   # groupadd news
   ```

6. Create the user news and set the account's home directory to /usr/local/news/:
   ```
   # useradd -g news -d /usr/local/news/ news
   ```

7. Configure the INN source code for compiling with the command:
   ```
   # ./configure –with-perl
   ```

8. The configure script will build a Makefile suited to your system to be used during compilation.

9. Compile the INN software:
   ```
   # make
   ```

10. The INN source code will be compiled into binary files.

11. Install the compiled INN software:
    ```
    # make install
    ```

12. The compiled binary files along with the INN man pages and other documentation will be installed in its default locations.

GENERAL OVERVIEW OF INN

The operations performed by INN can be divided into five main areas:

- Receiving incoming news feeds
- Processing outgoing news feeds
- Servicing news readers and facilitating the reading and posting of articles
- Expiring old articles
- Logging all activity

When a system which runs INN boots, it starts the script /etc/rc.d/rc.news. This script runs as the root user and launches innd, the INN daemon, which runs as the news user for security reasons. rc.news actually starts innd using the inndstart script which opens the NNTP port, sets the port's user ID and group ID to the news user and group, and then launches innd with the -p flag.

The purpose of this multi-level launching of innd and the change in user is to prevent security problems. If a service such as INN runs as the root user then the software has root privileges and if someone compromises the service they may be able to gain root privileges. The ps command executed shortly after running rc.news shows innd running as the news user:

```
# ps auxw|grep news
news      13735  0.3  4.6  6212 2932 ?      S    16:33   0:01 /usr/local/news/
➥bin/innd -p4
root      13737  0.0  1.5  1836  988 pts/0  S    16:33   0:00 sh /usr/local/news/
➥bin/rc.news
news      13741  0.0  0.9  1516  616 ?      SN   16:33   0:00 /usr/local/news/
➥bin/overchan
news      13742  0.0  1.2  1760  804 ?      SN   16:33   0:00 /usr/local/news/
➥bin/innfeed
root      13761  0.0  1.5  1852 1008 pts/0  S    16:34   0:00 sh /usr/local/news/
➥bin/innwatch
news      13981  0.0  1.2  1756  772 pts/0  S    16:40   0:00 /usr/local/news/
➥bin/actived
```

innd is the master daemon and performs certain tasks, while it invokes other programs to do other tasks. The daemon takes care of all incoming article feeds and writes them to disk. To send articles out, it uses external programs such as nntpsend or innfeed.

When it starts, innd reads three configuration files:

- ~news/etc/active
- ~news/etc/newsfeeds
- ~news/etc/incoming.conf

Note

The tilde (~) character before news is a special shell variable, which causes the term ~news to be replaced by the home directory of user news as specified in /etc/passwd map. In other words, if the home directory of user news is /usr/local/news, the shell (csh, ksh, or bash) replaces ~news by this path.

After loading the configuration, innd listens on port 119 for incoming NNTP connection requests.

Note

If you are using the version of INN included with Red Hat Linux 6.2, the INN configuration files are stored in /etc/news/ instead of ~news/etc.

RECEIVING INCOMING NEWS FEEDS

When a connection is received from an authorized feeder site listed in the incoming.conf file, the article feeds are accepted.

PROCESSING OUTGOING NEWS FEEDS

For outgoing news feeds, innd uses nntpsend or innfeed to send posted articles out to feeder sites. These processes run on a scheduled basis from cron (as outlined in Chapter 7, "Scheduling Tasks") to regularly scan for and send outgoing articles.

SERVICING NEWS READERS AND FACILITATING THE READING AND POSTING OF ARTICLES

If the request comes from an authorized news reader as identified in the file ~news/etc/nnrp.access, innd starts an nnrpd process to handle the reader connection. This leaves innd free to handle incoming news feed connections.

EXPIRING ARTICLES

In the INN model, articles do not remain in newsgroups permanently. Instead, they are expired on a schedule to ensure that newsgroups do not grow to unmanageable sizes. Expiring of articles is handled by the script news.daily, which is scheduled with cron (as outlined in Chapter 7); normally news.daily is scheduled to run once a day. The news.daily script reads the ~news/etc/expire.ctl configuration file which defines policies for expiring articles.

LOGGING ALL ACTIVITY

Most INN log messages are written to log files in /usr/local/news/log directory. In addition some log messages are written to /var/log/messages. Of course this depends on how logging of news messages is set up in the system's /etc/syslog.conf file.

CONFIGURING INN

INN normally stores its configuration files in ~news/etc/. The version of INN which ships with Red Hat Linux 6.2 stores the files in /etc/news/.

These files are used to achieve several configuration tasks. We will consider the following tasks:

- Selecting a storage method for news articles
- Editing inn.conf
- Editing the newsfeeds file
- Editing incoming.conf
- Using the cycbuff.conf file for CNFS
- Editing storage.conf for CNFS and timehash
- Using the overview.ctl file with CNFS and timehash storage
- Controlling client access with the nnrp.access file
- Controlling article expiration with expire.ctl

- Creating an article spool for CNFS storage
- Specifying sites to feed to with the `nntpsend.ctl` file
- Controlling daily maintenance with the `news.daily` utility
- Starting INN at boot time with `rc.news`

SELECTING A STORAGE METHOD FOR NEWS ARTICLES

Three methods are available for storing news articles with INN:

- **Traditional:** This method is used by older versions of INN. Articles are stored in individual files named after the article numbers. These files are stored in a directory hierarchy based on news group names. For instance, article 12345 in `comp.os.linux.networking` is stored in the spool directory; typically this would be at `/usr/local/news/spool/comp/os/linux/networking/12345`. The traditional method is based on time-tested code and has wide compatibility with third-party INN applications. This method also provides fine-grained control over article expiration times. This comes at the expense of storing large numbers of files in single directories, which generates performance bottlenecks. This method requires extremely fast computers, disks, and disk controllers for large news feed sites.

- **Timehash:** This method is a variation of the traditional method. Articles are still stored as individual files but in a directory hierarchy based on their arrival time. This avoids bottlenecks associated with directories containing large numbers of files, which can easily happen. Directories are structured according to group names. This method also allows fine control over article expiration time but at the expense of still requiring very fast computers, disks, and disk controllers to handle the performance requirements of file-based storage of articles.

- **CNFS:** This method stores articles sequentially in pre-configured, cyclic buffer files. When the end of the buffer is reached, new articles are stored from the beginning of the buffer, overwriting the oldest articles in the buffer. This method provides extremely fast performance: No files need to be created or deleted during operation and no expiration processes need to run because articles are automatically overwritten as buffers fill. In addition, the disk space used by INN remains constant and assigning them to different buffers of fixed sizes can control the sizes of individual groups. These benefits come at the expense of less control over expiration of articles. However CNFS storage method can cause problems if you want greater retention time for a group that suddenly starts receiving a very high volume of traffic.

Generally, experienced news administrators select CNFS over other storage methods because the CNFS method's advantages far outweigh its sole disadvantage. The fact that I/O performance is blazingly fast and that you never have to worry about full file systems are sufficient reasons to consider using this method.

PART

V

CH

26

EDITING `inn.conf`

The first and most important file you should configure is `inn.conf`. Most settings in the sample `inn.conf` file included with INN can be left unchanged with the defaults provided. We will only look at the ones that are essential to change. Table 26.1 outlines these key settings.

TABLE 26.1   KEY SETTINGS IN `inn.conf`

Settings	Description
`organization`	Set this to the name of your organization.
`pathhost`	Set this to the fully qualified domain name of your news server. If you leave it blank INN will try to use the FQDN of the server.
`domain`	Set this to the domain name of your server.
`complaints`	You may want to set this to `postmaster@your.domain`. If not specified it will try to use the `newmaster@your.domain` address.
`storageapi`	Set to `true` if articles should be stored using CNFS or timehash methods.
`overviewmap`	If set to `true`, overview data will be memory mapped and reading overviews will be faster.
`allownewnews`	If set to `yes`, INN will support NEWNEWS command for news readers. This adversely affects server performance and the recommended setting is `no`.
`nnrpdoverstats`	If set to `yes` nnrpd will log statistics about how much time was spent during various stages of reading article overview information. The recommended setting is `no`.
`hiscachesize`	This sets the size of the cache in kilobytes for recently used history file entries. To disable history caching set the value to 0. However, for better server performance, it is highly recommended that you set a cache size of 16MB if you have the memory to spare.

EDITING THE `newsfeeds` FILE

The `newsfeeds` file specifies how incoming articles should be distributed to other sites and to other INN processes. Where articles are sent and how that is done is determined by the contents of this file. We will cover the basics of the `newsfeeds` file in this chapter. To learn about all the options, you need to consult the man page with the command `man newsfeeds`.

The `newsfeeds` file consists of a series of `newsfeed` entries. A `newsfeed` entry consists of four colon-separated fields:

```
sitename:pattern:flag:param
```

The first field is the name of the feed. It must be unique. It is best to use the fully qualified domain name of the remote server for the name of the feed because this keeps things simple. A slash and an exclude list can follow the name of the feed. If the feed name or any of the names in the exclude list appear in the Path line of an article, then that article will not be forwarded to the feed, as it is assumed to have passed once through that site already. The exclude list is useful when the server's name is not the same as the name it puts in the path header of its articles or when you don't want to receive articles from a certain source.

The second field specifies a set of desired newsgroups and distribution lists. The pattern is a wildcard-matching pattern with one addition. Patterns that start with @ will cause any articles posted to groups matching that pattern to be dropped, even if they match patterns for groups that are wanted. Otherwise articles that match both want and don't want patterns are sent.

The third field is a comma-separated list of flags that determine the type of feed and set some parameters for the entry. Possible flags are summarized in Table 26.2.

TABLE 26.2   FLAGS FOR newsfeeds ENTRIES

Flag	Description
`<size>`	Articles must be smaller than the specified size in bytes.
`<size>`	Articles must be larger than the specified size in bytes.
`A<items>`	A list of one or more article checks: d (articles must have a distribution header), p (INN should not check for the site in the path header), c (control messages are not allowed), C (only control messages are allowed), e (all groups that an article is destined for must exist).
`B<high or low>`	Internal buffer size before writing an article to output.
`F<name>`	Indicates the name of the spool file for the feed.
`G<count>`	Limits cross postings to count groups.
`H<count>`	Articles must have less than the specified number of hops. If no value is specified, the default number of hops is 1.
`I<size>`	Internal buffer size if using a file feed.
`Nm`	Only allows moderated groups that match the entry's patterns.
`Nu`	Only allows unmoderated groups that match the entry's patterns.
`P<priority>`	Sets the priority of the channel or feed.
`O<originator>`	The first field of an article's X-Trace must match the specified originator.
`S<size>`	Starts spooling the feed if more than the specified number of bytes are queued.
`T<type>`	Indicates the type of feed being specified by the entry. Possible field types are: f (file), m (funnel), p (pipe to program), c (send the feed to the standard input of the parameter's sub-process), x (log entry only).

PART
V

CH
26

TABLE 26.2 CONTINUED

Flag	Description
W<items>	A list of one or more items to write: b (article size in bytes), f (the full path of an article), g (the first newsgroup of an article posting), h (the message ID hash of an article), m (the message ID), n (the relative path of an article), p (the posted time of an article), s (the site that fed the article), t (the time an article was received), * (the names of funnel feed-in's or all sites that receive the article), N (the newsgroups header of an article), D (the distribution header of an article), H (all headers of an article), O (the overview data of an article), P (the path header of an article), R (an article's replication information).

The fourth field is a multi-purpose parameter. Its usage depends on the type of flags used in the third field.

SAMPLE newsfeeds ENTRIES

The newsfeeds file controls how articles posted on the local site are fed out to other NNTP servers. Because of the inherent complexity of entries in the newsfeeds file, the easiest way to grasp how to use entries is to analyze some sample entries.

First, consider the following entry:

```
ME:*,!junk,!control*,!local*\
/world,usa,na,gnu,bionet,pubnet,u3b,eunet,vmsnet,inet,ddn,k12::
```

Every newsfeeds file requires a single ME site entry. This entry lists a set of defaults that affect all other entries in the newsfeeds file. The subscription list from the ME entry is automatically added to the start of the subscription list for all other entries. In this example, the subscription list is *,!junk,!control,!local*/world,usa,na,gnu,bionet,pubnet,u3b, eunet,vmsnet,inet,ddn,k12. This subscription list has two parts: the part before the forward slash and the exceptions list after the forward slash.

The part before the forward slash is *,!junk,!control,!local*. This indicates that local postings, control postings, and junk postings are not propagated unless a group is explicitly indicated in an entry's subscription list.

If a distribution field appears in a ME entry, only articles which match the distribution list are accepted and all other articles are rejected.

In addition to the required ME entry, several special entries provide the program feeds for the overchan, innfeed, controlchan, and crosspost utilities. These entries are provided with the default newsfeeds file and can simply be uncommented if you need to use them.

For the traditional storage method, uncomment the following entries:

```
overview!:*:Tc,WO:/usr/local/news/bin/overchan
crosspost:*:Tc,Ap,WR:/usr/local/news/bin/crosspost
innfeed!:!*:Tc,Wnm*,S16384:/usr/local/news/bin/startinnfeed -y
```

For the CNFS or timehash storage methods, uncomment the following entries:

```
overview!:*:Tc,Ao,WhR:/usr/local/news/bin/overchan
innfeed!:!*:Tc,Wnm*,S16384:/usr/local/news/bin/startinnfeed -y
```

To enable controlchan to remove the task of handling control messages from innd, uncomment the following entries:

```
controlchan!:!*,control,control.*,!control.cancel\
:Tc,Wnsm:/usr/local/news/bin/controlchan
```

Use of controlchan is recommended as it reduces the load of processing control messages, especially when several of them arrive within a short span of time.

In addition to the required ME entry and special entries, you need to create entries for each site to which you will be feeding news.

```
news-feed.netvision.net.il\
:*,!junk,!control,!bwc.*,!general.*/!bwc:Tf,Wnm\
:news-feed.netvision.net.il
```

The first field (news-feed.netvision.net.il) is the fully qualified domain name of the site we feed news articles to.

The second field specifies which articles should be sent to this site. This field indicates that all posted articles except local groups bwc.*, general.*, junk, and control messages should be sent. The /!bwc portion of the field indicates that articles with the local distribution header bwc should not be sent to news-feed.netvision.net.il.

In the third field flags are specified. The flags used here indicate the type of feed (Tf indicates a file feed) and the data to write to the file (Wmn indicates that the relative path name and message ID of articles should be written).

The last field is optional, and its interpretation depends on the type of feed indicated in the third field. For file feeds, the fourth field specifies the relative pathname of the feed file as it appears in the ~news/spool/outgoing directory. In this example, the fourth field indicates that an output file should be created in the ~news/spool/outgoing directory and the file should be called news-feed.netvision.net.il; every article destined for this site will have its filename and message ID written to this file.

EDITING incoming.conf

The incoming.conf file controls incoming newsfeeds and is quite straightforward. This file specifies what machines are allowed to connect to your news host and feed articles. In earlier versions of INN this file was named hosts.nntp and the format has changed since then. A simple incoming.conf file might look like the following:

```
streaming:              true
max-connections:        8

peer ME {
  hostname:             "localhost, 127.0.0.1"
}
```

```
peer netvision {
  hostname:            news-feed.netvision.net.il
}
```

This file can be broken down as follows:

- The streaming entry indicates that streaming of newsfeeds is allowed by default.
- The max-connections entry indicates the maximum number of connections allowed per feed.
- Each peer section indicates the host from which incoming newsfeeds are accepted. Typically, the localhost and any other external systems that act as sources of incoming newsfeeds are listed as peers.

USING THE cycbuff.conf FILE FOR CNFS

CNFS stores articles in logical objects called *metacycbuffs* . Each metacycbuff is composed of one or more physical buffers called *cycbuffs*. Each cycbuff can be spread across multiple physical disks for load balancing.

These cycbuffs are defined in the cycbuff.conf file. Consider the following cycbuff.conf file:

```
cycbuff:ONE:/disk1/cycbuffs/one:20480000
cycbuff:TWO:/disk1/cycbuffs/two:20480000
cycbuff:THREE:/disk2/cycbuffs/three:20480000
cycbuff:FOUR:/disk2/cycbuffs/four:20480000
cycbuff:FIVE:/disk3/cycbuffs/five:20480000
cycbuff:SIX:/disk3/cycbuffs/six:20480000
metacycbuff:SMALLAREA:ONE,TWO

metacycbuff:BIGAREA:THREE,FOUR,FIVE,SIX
```

This file specifies two metacycbuffs named SMALLAREA and BIGAREA. SMALLAREA is composed of two cycbuffs named ONE and TWO while BIGAREA is composed of four cycbuffs named THREE, FOUR, FIVE, and SIX.

The actual creation of these cycbuffs is discussed later in this chapter in the section "Creating an Article Spool for CNFS Storage."

EDITING storage.conf FOR CNFS AND TIMEHASH

The storage.conf file maps newsgroups into storage classes. This determines where and how articles are stored. Each line defines a storage class for articles. The first matching storage class is used to store any given article; if no storage class matches an article then INN will reject that article.

In a general sense, a storage class is defined as follows:

```
method <methodname> {
        newsgroups: <wildcard expression>
        class: <storage class>
```

```
    size: <minsize>,<maxsize>
    expires: <mintime>,<maxtime>
    options: <options>
}
```

The method name is either cnfs or timehash indicating the storage method to which the class is applied. A special method called trash can also be used to define a storage class for which all messages are thrown away.

Inside each class are five parameters:

- **newsgroups:** A wildcard expression indicating which newsgroups are accepted by the storage class.

- **class:** A unique number identifying the storage class. The number should be between 0 and 255 and should be unique among all the storage classes in storage.conf.

- **size:** The minimum size in bytes of articles accepted by the class and, optionally, the maximum size of articles accepted by the class. A maximum size of zero indicates that there is no upper limit on article size and a minimum size of zero indicates that there is no lower limit on article size.

- **expires:** The minimum expire time for articles accepted by the class and, optionally, the maximum time for articles accepted by the class. A maximum time or zero indicates that there is no maximum on the expire time for articles accepted in the class.

- **options:** The name of the metacycbuff used to store articles accepted by this storage class. This parameter is only used for CNFS storage classes.

The following is a sample storage.conf file:

```
method cnfs {
    newsgroups: alt.binaries.*
    class: 0
    size: 0,1000000
    expires: 0,4d
    options: SMALLAREA
}
method cnfs {
    newsgroups: *
    class: 2
    size: 0,0
    expires: 0,0
    options: BIGAREA
}
```

The first storage class indicates that articles destined for groups whose names start with alt.binaries that are between 0 and 1MB in size and expire within 4 days should be stored in the SMALLAREA metacycbuff. The second storage class accepts any articles that are rejected by the first storage class and stores them in the BIGAREA metacycbuff.

If your system uses timehash storage, you might use the following storage.conf file to achieve a similar result:

```
method timehash {
    newsgroups: alt.binaries.*
    class: 0
    size: 0,1000000
}
method timehash {
    newsgroups: *
    class: 2
}
```

For timehash methods, storage class IDs (indicated in the `class` parameter) are used to store articles in separate directory trees so that different expiration policies can be applied to each storage class. The newsgroups must be divided based on retention time of articles in those groups, and a storage class created for each collection. The storage class IDs that are assigned are used in the `expire.ctl` file to control expiration of articles.

USING THE `overview.ctl` FILE WITH CNFS AND `timehash` STORAGE

The `overview.ctl` file determines where article overview information will be stored for each newsgroup. Overview information is stored in one or more storage files identified by unique numbers between 0 and 254. Each line consists of the storage file number followed by a single colon and a wildcard pattern list of which newsgroups are to be stored in that file. As with `storage.conf`, the first matching line is used to determine where to store overview information for a given article.

The goal is to spread the overview files across a number of smaller files rather than one large file. One suggested method is to create 27 storage areas; the first 26 will be for newsgroups a* through z*, and the 27th will be for * to catch all articles which fail to match the alphabetic wildcard patterns in the first 26 entries. The layout can be modified later by editing the `overview.ctl` file and running `expire`. The overview data will be rearranged during the expiration process.

CONTROLLING CLIENT ACCESS WITH THE `nnrp.access`

The `nnrp.access` file controls who can access the news server as a reader using a news client. Consider the following `nnrp.access` file:

```
stdin:RP:::*
localhost:RP:::*
127.0.0.1:RP:::*
*.bwc.org:RP:::*
192.115.144.*:RP:::*
```

Each line in the file takes the following format:

<host>:*<access privileges>*:*<username>*:*<password>*:*<newsgroups>*

These five fields are used as follows:

- The `host` field can be a hostname (as in line 2 in the example), an IP address (as in line 3 in the example), an IP address range or a wildcard pattern (as in the last line in the example). The field specifies to which host or hosts the rule applies.

- The access privileges field is a set of letters chosen from the following list: R (the client can read articles), P (the client can post new articles), N (the client can override global settings), and L (the client can post articles to groups which normally prohibit local posting). Using these letters, this field indicates the permissions granted to users connecting from the specified client. In all cases in the example, clients can both read existing articles and post new articles.

- The username field indicates the username that a client must use to authenticate to the news server. If left blank, no username is required.

- The password field indicates the password that a client must use to authenticate to the news server. If left blank, no password is required.

- The newsgroups field is a set of wildcard patterns indicating which newsgroups the client has permission to access. In the set, commas separate each individual wildcard pattern from others. For instance, *,!alt.binaries.* allows access to all groups except the alt.binaries hierarchy.

CONTROLLING ARTICLE EXPIRATION WITH expire.ctl

Expiration of old articles is a very important process because it allows for control over the size of the news store on a news server. Without article expiration, the amount of disk space consumed by newsgroups would grow endlessly and newsgroups would become unreadable and unmanageable.

Control over expiration policies is managed through the expire.ctl configuration file. Consider the following extracts from an expire.ctl file:

```
/remember/:14
*:A:1:10:21
*.answers:M:1:35:90
news.announce.*:M:1:35:90
```

The /remember/:14 entry tells the expire program to keep history entries for 14 days after the articles are expired. The reason for retaining records of expired articles for a period of time is to handle the situation where a feeder offers old articles that have been previously accepted and expired. In this case the server would be able to reject the old articles. If no record were kept, the server would accept old articles again.

All other entries in the example take the following basic format:

<pattern>:*<modification flag>*:*<keep>*:*<default>*:*<purge>*

Each entry contains five colon-separated fields:

- The pattern field is a wildcard pattern indicating to which newsgroups the rule applies.

- The modification flag field indicates to which types of newsgroups matching the pattern field the rule applies. Possible values for the modification flag field are: A (all news groups), M (only moderated newsgroups), U (only unmoderated newsgroups).

PART

V

CH

26

A fourth special value is possible (X), which indicates that articles that are cross-posted should be removed even if they are still listed in groups which have not expired the article yet.

- The keep field indicates the minimum length of time in days an article should remain the group.

- The default field indicates the default time in days an article should remain in the group when the article does not provide an Expires header with an alternate expire time.

- The purge field indicates the maximum time in days an article should remain in the group regardless of any alternate expire time specified with an Expires header.

Keep in mind that if you are using the CNFS storage method, the expire time is effectively automatic because the size of groups is limited by the size of pre-existing buffer files. In this case, only the /remember/ entry is used from the expires.ctl file. Instead, the entries in the storage.conf file control the expire time of articles in the CNFS storage method as outlined earlier in the section, "Editing storage.conf for CNFS and timehash."

CREATING AN ARTICLE SPOOL FOR CNFS STORAGE

If you are using the CNFS storage method, you can create the article spool as follows:

1. For each cycbuff you need to create a buffer file. This can be done using the dd command. For example to create the cycbuffs we have mentioned in our example cycbuff.conf file we need to do the following:

```
% dd if=/dev/zero of=/disk1/cycbuffs/one bs=1k count=2048000
% dd if=/dev/zero of=/disk1/cycbuffs/two bs=1k count=2048000
% dd if=/dev/zero of=/disk2/cycbuffs/three bs=1k count=2048000
% dd if=/dev/zero of=/disk2/cycbuffs/four bs=1k count=2048000
% dd if=/dev/zero of=/disk3/cycbuffs/five bs=1k count=2048000
% dd if=/dev/zero of=/disk3/cycbuffs/six bs=1k count=2048000
% chmod 0644 /disk1/cycbuffs/one
% chmod 0644 /disk1/cycbuffs/two
% chmod 0644 /disk2/cycbuffs/three
% chmod 0644 /disk2/cycbuffs/four
% chmod 0644 /disk3/cycbuffs/five
% chmod 0644 /disk3/cycbuffs/six
```

2. Each dd command creates a file of the size specified in the count argument filled with zeros. The chmod commands ensure the cycbuffs have the necessary permissions.

CREATING NEWS HISTORY DATABASE FILES

To build the news history database, you need two files—the newsgroups file, and the active file. The makehistory command uses these files to create the initial history database. The various steps involved to create the history database are described here:

1. Obtain the newsgroup and active files. If you don't have them with your distribution of INN, download them from ftp.isc.org:/pub/usenet/CONFIG and save them in the db subdirectory of the news user's home directory (~news/db).

2. Become the news user using the command su news.

3. Change to the db subdirectory:

   ```
   $ cd ~/news
   ```

4. Create new history files for your news spool with the following command:

   ```
   $ makehistory -I
   ```

5. This command creates two files: history.n.dir and history.n.pag.

6. Rename history.n.dir to history.dir:

   ```
   $ mv history.n.dir history.dir
   ```

7. Rename history.n.pag to history.pag:

   ```
   $ mv history.n.pag history.pag
   ```

8. Set the permissions on all files in the db directory:

   ```
   $ chmod 644 *
   ```

SPECIFYING SITES TO FEED TO WITH THE nntpsend.ctl FILE

The nntpsend.ctl file specifies the site that feeds from your server. The file is read by the nntpsend process and consists of a series of entries, one per line. Each entry consists of four colon-separated fields:

<site>:<domain name>:<maximum size>:<arguments>

The fields are used as follows:

- The site field indicates the name used in the newsfeeds file for this site. The name is used to create a batch file for the feed.
- The domain name field is the fully qualified domain name of the site receiving the feed and the name is passed as an argument to the innxmit process.
- The maximum size indicates the size limit for a batch file. The file will be truncated at this size.
- The arguments are other optional arguments to be passed to the innxmit process.

For example, consider the following entry from an nntpsend.ctl file:

```
news-feed.netvision.net.il:news.netvision.net.il:4m:-T1800 -t300
```

This entry indicates that articles should be sent to the host news-feed.netvision.net.il and that the batch file should be named news-feed.netvision.net.il. The fully qualified domain name of the site is specified in the next field (news.netvision.net.il). The maximum size field indicates that the maximum batch file size is four megabytes. The final field indicates the arguments to pass to innxmit.

To ensure orderly, regular sending of articles to feed recipients, you must invoke nntpsend from the cron daemon. To do this, create a cron entry similar to the following in the news user's crontab file as outlined in Chapter 7.

```
0,10,20,30,40,50 * * * * /usr/local/news/bin/nntpsend
```

This `crontab` entry causes `nntpsend` to run every 10 minutes and send out posted articles which have been queued for transmission.

CONTROLLING DAILY MAINTENANCE WITH THE `news.daily` SCRIPT

INN needs to perform daily server maintenance tasks such as expiring old articles and rotating log files. For this to happen you need to create a cron entry for `news.daily` as follows:

```
0 3 * * * /usr/local/news/bin/news.daily expireover lowmark
```

Create this entry in the `news` user's `crontab` file. The entry will cause `news.daily` to run every day at 3 a.m. to perform daily maintenance tasks such as the expire time of articles. Article expire time can be an intensive process and, accordingly, should be run at low usage, off-peak hours.

The `news.daily` script creates a summary report when it runs which is mailed to the news administrator. The report includes disk usage information, log file sizes, the number of entries in the log, incoming article and newsgroups statistics, article expire data, and post-expire data.

STARTING INN AT BOOT TIME WITH `rc.news`

Generally, you will want to start INN at boot time. Some Linux distributions that include INN will already be configured to do this. If not, you can configure your system to do so by adding the following command to the end of your `/etc/rc.d/rc.local` file:

```
su news -c /usr/local/news/bin/rc.news
```

UNDERSTANDING INN LOG FILES

INN records its activities in the `/usr/local/news/log/news` file. Entry in the file takes the following format:

```
<date> <time> + <feed> <message ID> <site>
```

Optionally, two fields may appear after the message ID field depending on the configuration in the `inn.conf` file:

```
<date> <time> <status> <feed> <message ID> <host name> <size> <site>
```

The feed field indicates the site that sent the article. The message ID field is the article's ID.

The critical field is the status field. This field can take several possible values as outlined in Table 26.3.

TABLE 26.3   STATUS IN THE INN LOG FILE

Value	Description
+	Article was accepted.
j	Article was accepted but filed in the junk newsgroup.
c	A cancel message was accepted before the original article arrived; the article is accepted.
-	Article was rejected.

If the article is accepted then the site field contains a site-separated list of sites where the article will be sent.

OTHER LOG FILES

INN generates several other log files, including the following:

- **expire.log**: Logs article expiration activities.
- **innfeed.log**: Generated if you use innfeed instead of nntpsend.
- **innfeed.status**: Logs innfeed connections.
- **nntpsend.log**: Logs start and stop times of outgoing connections with nntpsend.
- **unwanted.log**: Logs unwanted newsgroups that have been offered.

INN also generates entries logged through the system log facility, syslog. To configure where syslog will store news-related logfiles, edit /etc/syslog.conf file.

ADMINISTERING INN

INN comes with a tool called ctlinnd for managing the innd daemon. ctlinnd sends messages to the control channel of innd requesting action. innd performs the requested action and sends a message back to ctlinnd.

Common ctlinnd commands include those outlined in Table 26.4.

TABLE 26.4   COMMON ctlinnd COMMANDS

Command	Description
ctlinnd mode	Checks the current mode of the server.
ctlinnd shutdown reason	Shuts down the server and records the reason in the news log file.
ctlinnd pause reason	Pauses the server and records the reason in the news log file.
ctlinnd reload all reason	Forces the server to reload all its configuration files.

PART

V

CH

26

TABLE 26.4 CONTINUED	
Command	**Description**
`ctlinnd newgroup` `<group name>`	Creates a new newsgroup with the specified group name.
`ctlinnd rmgroup` `<group name>`	Removes the specified news group.
`ctlinnd checkfile`	Checks the accuracy of the INN configuration.

TROUBLESHOOTING

Several common troubleshooting situations arise with INN:

- Dealing with server throttling
- Handling a history file which is too large
- Managing multiple `innwatch` processes
- Editing the active file
- Dealing with `history.n.*` files
- Dealing with a corrupt or deleted active file

WHEN A SERVER IS THROTTLED

If the system runs out of space or inodes while `innd` is writing the active file, an article file, or the history database, `innd` will send itself a throttle command. In a throttled state, `innd` will continue to accept reader connections, but will stop receiving feeds and article posts from `nnrpd` or `rnews` processes.

To bring a server out of the throttled condition when the problem is insufficient disk space, you must free up some disk space. The best approach to freeing up space is to run `expire`. First, edit `expire.ctl` to reduce the retention time of articles as outlined earlier in this chapter in the section "Controlling Article Expiration with `expire.ctl`" and then run `expire`.

Before running `expire`, check that the partition containing the history database has sufficient space to write a copy of the database because `expire` will attempt to build a new copy of this file while the old one is in use. The old database is deleted when the new one is built.

If you run out of inodes, the problem is more severe than running out of disk space. To solve the problem you will need to re-create the file system that holds the article spool directory with a larger number of inodes than when it was originally created.

If you frequently encounter throttling of the server, consider switching to CNFS storage, which can ensure that you never run out of disk space or inodes.

WHEN THE HISTORY FILE IS TOO LARGE

The history file is supposed to be large and you need not take any action if you find it getting larger. At first, it might seem prudent to change the value of the `remember` entry in the `expire.ctl` file to fewer days than the typical 14 days. While this will reduce the size of your history file, it may lead to re-accepting expired articles that are re-offered by a server more than seven days after they were expired.

WHEN MULTIPLE innwatch PROCESSES RUN

When you shut down the news server for maintenance by running `ctlinnd shutdown`, it terminates `innd` but `innwatch` is not affected. Later when you restart `innd` by running `rc.news` it also starts `innwatch`.

> **Tip**
>
> Always remember to kill `innwatch` after you manually shut down `innd`.

EDITING THE active FILE

It is far better to add or remove entries from the `active` file using the `ctlinnd newgroup` and `ctlinnd rmgroup` commands than to do this manually. However, if you must create or delete a large number of entries, it will be more efficient to do so by directly editing the `active` file using the following steps:

1. Pause the server:
   ```
   $ ctlinnd pause "edit active"
   ```

2. Edit the active file.

3. Run `inncheck` to check that the `active` file is accurate.

4. Force `innd` to reread the active file:
   ```
   $ ctlinnd reload active "edit active"
   ```

5. Restart the paused server:
   ```
   $ ctlinnd go "edit active"
   ```

> **Tip**
>
> Never edit the `active` file manually without pausing or shutting down the `innd` process using `ctlinnd`.

HANDLING THE history.n.* FILES

When `expire` runs, it recreates the history database files. It does this by creating the `history.n`, `history.n.pag` and `history.n.dir` files and then renames them to `history`, `history.pag`, and `history.dir` once the files are created.

At times, however, you may find these `history.n.*` files left behind after running `expire`. This can be caused by one of two reasons:

- Insufficient disk space on the partition containing the history database files.
- Incorrect lines in the history file.

In either case, expire will abort and leave the `history.n.*` files behind.

If `expire` is aborting because of insufficient disk space, move the history files to another partition, create a soft link to the files in their original location, and run `expire` to completion.

> **Tip**
>
> It is best to try and avoid a file system full situation on a news server. Closely watch disk space usage on the news server and rearrange files to free up space before a disk full state occurs. Automatically monitor disk space usage running a script such as `fschecker` from `cron` as outlined in Chapter 7.

WHEN THE `active` FILE IS CORRUPTED OR DELETED

The best way to recover from a corrupted `active` file is to use an older one. Old copies of active files are compressed and saved in the `~news/log/OLD` directory by expire. To recover in this manner, use the following steps:

1. Shut down `innd`.
2. Copy and uncompress an older `active` file.
3. Restart `innd`.

If you need to force a renumber of the `active` file after copying an older version, use the command `ctlinnd renumber "active"`.

CHAPTER 27

FTP SERVERS

UNDERSTANDING FTP

FTP is the File Transfer Protocol. With Web servers and Mail servers, FTP servers are among the most common types of Internet information servers. FTP client software is available on all Internet hosts, either as standalone client software or through any Web browser.

In fact, FTP is so widely deployed that the September 1999 traffic statistics at NSFNET show 34 percent of its backbone traffic was FTP traffic. NSFNET is a backbone network of the National Science Foundation that connects several supercomputer centers in the United States. The reason for this high figure is that most Internet users today access FTP servers in the same way they access Web sites: through their Web browser. From the user's perspective, use of FTP servers is transparent and doesn't require the separate command-line client software it once did. Web browsers have hidden the complexities of using FTP servers behind simple point and click interfaces.

As a protocol, FTP can be used to transfer any type of data including text files, PostScript files, images, and compressed file archives such as ZIP files, audio files, and video files. The protocol supports anonymous guest access without a password as well as authenticated user access. The protocol provides commands for directory and file manipulation and upload and download of files. Restrictions can be placed on the actions that particular users can take.

> **Note**
>
> It is a misnomer to say that anonymous access happens without a password. In reality, anonymous access occurs when a user logs in as one of two different users, `ftp` or `anonymous`, and then provides an email address as a password. The email address is, however, only used for logging purposes, and not for authentication.

When an anonymous user logs in, the ftp daemon executes a `chroot` system call. This system call makes the user's FTP home directory the root directory. By doing this, anonymous users have restricted system access: Users will not be able to change to a directory above the home directory in the directory tree. For instance, if the FTP user's home directory is `/home/ftp/` then an anonymous user will see `/home/ftp/` as `/` and cannot change to a directory above `/home/ftp/`. Only files and directories below `/home/ftp/` will be accessible to anonymous users.

Accordingly, anonymous FTP access can provide a secure way to offer public access to files without inadvertently providing unauthenticated users widespread access to a system. This has made FTP ideal for deployment of large-scale file archives on the Internet.

WASHINGTON UNIVERSITY FTP SERVER—WU-FTPD

All major Linux distributions include FTP server software. While many different FTP server software packages are available, most Linux distributions include the WU Archive FTP Server (WU-FTPD) from Washington University in St. Louis, Missouri. WU-FTPD is commonly used in Linux distributions because it offers many features not included in standard FTP daemons that are the norm on many Unix systems. The most recent version of WU-FTPD is available at `ftp://ftp.wu-ftpd.org/`.

One of the advantages of WU-FTPD is that it is well suited to handling FTP sites with large collections of files. There are several reasons why WU-FTPD is well adapted to this task:

- The server can automatically tar, compress, and uncompress files and directories as it transfers them.

- The server can limit the maximum number of simultaneous ftp connections based on classes of users. These limits can be varied based on time of day and day of week. Classes of users can be defined and managed by the administrator. As an example, a class of users who are archive maintainers can be given access at all times without any connection limits. At the same time, anonymous users can have a maximum number of connections enforced with fewer connections allowed during peak hours. Access can also be limited based on hostname, domain name, or IP address from which a client connects.

- The server can log all file transfers as well as all commands issued by FTP clients. Accesses also can be tracked by user class.

- The server simplifies shutdown and maintenance by providing a graceful shutdown method. You can first disallow new users from connecting and then inform current users of an impending shutdown and log them off, if they are still connected, through a simple procedure.

WU-FTPD CONFIGURATION FILES

To provide a wide range of features, WU-FTPD has several configuration files, listed in Table 27.1.

PART
V

CH
27

TABLE 27.1   WU-FTPD CONFIGURATION FILES

Filename	Description
ftphosts	You can deny access from particular hosts, and allow access to certain accounts from specified hosts only. The ftphosts file allows you to specify the IP addresses and hostnames of hosts to which you plan to deny or allow access.
ftpconversions	Using the ftpconversions file, you can specify the tools to use for on-the-fly compression and decompression of files and archives.

TABLE 27.1   CONTINUED

Filename	Description
ftpaccess	The ftpaccess file is used to define user classes, based on the account accessed and the host from which the user connects. You can also deny access to a certain class of users or limit their number of connections during specific times of the week in this file, as well as specify who has permission to perform particular actions such as directory creation and file uploading.
ftpusers	Usernames listed in the ftpusers file are not allowed access to the FTP server.
ftpservers	The ftpservers file allows you to implement support for FTP Virtual domains. Through this file, you can specify different sets of configuration files for different virtual servers that can be distinguished by their IP addresses or their virtual domain names.
ftpgroups	The ftpgroups file provides support for FTP site groups and FTP site passwords.

The use of these files is discussed within the context of various tasks throughout this chapter.

BUILDING WU-FTPD FROM SOURCE

Generally, WU-FTPD comes with most Linux distributions as pre-built binary packages. Accordingly, building WU-FTPD from source code is not necessary. However, if you want to upgrade to a newer version of WU-FTPD before a binary package becomes available for your distribution or if your distribution includes a different FTP server and you want to use WU-FTPD, then you might need to build WU-FTPD from source code.

The source code for WU-FTPD is available online at `ftp://ftp.wu-ftpd.org/`. The current version of the software is 2.6 and is available at `ftp://ftp.wu-ftpd.org/pub/wu-ftpd/ wu-ftpd-2.6.tar.gz`.

Tip

The latest stable release might have changed by the time you download the software, but you should always use the latest stable version to be sure that you have the latest security and bug fixes.

You can unpack and build WU-FTPD as follows:

1. Download the archive to a convenient location such as `/tmp/`.
2. Unpack the source in a suitable place, where you keep all software source code, for example, `/usr/local/src/` or `/opt/src/`. To unpack the archive in `/usr/local/src/`, use the following commands:

```
# cd /usr/local/src/
# tar xzvf /tmp/wu-ftpd-2.6.tar.gz
```

3. This will create a directory called `/usr/local/src/wu-ftpd-2.6`. Change your current directory to this new directory with the following command:

    `# cd wu-ftpd-2.6`

4. Read the file `INSTALL` to verify the steps needed for installation. The steps outlined here should work for version 2.6 but might have been changed for newer versions. You can read this file with the following command:

    `# less INSTALL`

5. Configure the source code for compilation using the `configure` utility:

    `# ./configure`

    If `configure` runs without any errors it will produce a file named `Makefile` tailored for your system.

6. Compile the software with the following command:

    `# make >& make.out&`

    The `>& make.out` section of the command redirects all output to the file `make.out`. You can monitor new data in this file as it is added with the command `tail -f make.out` and the file will be retained after compilation completes. This way you can refer to it later, should compilation fail.

7. If compilation succeeds, install the compiled software with the command:

    `# make install`

8. This command will install the following binaries as well as the man pages for WU-FTPD in the directory `/usr/man/`:

    - `/usr/sbin/in.ftpd`
    - `/usr/sbin/ftpshut`
    - `/usr/bin/ftpcount`
    - `/usr/bin/ftpwho`
    - `/usr/sbin/ckconfig`
    - `/usr/sbin/ftprestart`

9. If this is your first installation of WU-FTPD, default `/etc/ftpaccess` and `/etc/ftpconversions` files will also be created.

10. Customize the `/etc/ftpaccess` file as outlined later in this chapter, in the section "Using the `ftpaccess` file."

11. The default `/etc/ftpconversions` file can be used as is with any customization. For a complete understanding of this file see the section "Using the `ftpconversions` File" later in the chapter.

12. Check `/etc/inetd.conf` for a line similar to this:

    `ftp    stream tcp   nowait root   /usr/sbin/tcpd in.ftpd -l -a`

PART

V

CH

27

13. If this line is missing from inetd.conf, add the line, save the file, and restart inetd by sending it a SIGHUP signal as outlined in Chapter 8, "Linux Process Management and Daemons."

When installed using these steps, you will have a standard password-protected FTP server.

TESTING YOUR NEW WU-FTPD INSTALLATION

After you have installed WU-FTPD, you should double-check that it is running properly. To do this, use the FTP client included with your Linux distribution to connect to the new FTP server and log in as an existing user to whom you have allowed access to your FTP server in /etc/ftpaccess:

```
# ftp localhost
Connected to localhost.
220 linux.juxta.com FTP server (Version wu-2.6.0 (1) \
        Mon Apr 19 09:21:53 EDT 1999) ready.
Name (localhost:root): username
331 Password required for username.
Password:
230 User username logged in.
Remote system type is UNIX.
Using binary mode to transfer files.
ftp> pwd
257 "/home/username" is the current directory.
ftp> bye
```

If you can successfully connect to the server, log in and display the current directory as shown in this example. You have successfully installed WU-FTPD.

ANONYMOUS FTP SETUP

When you have a functioning FTP server either installed with your distribution or compiled from the source code, you can configure it to accept anonymous access using the following steps:

> **Note**
>
> Many Linux distributions that install WU-FTPD as a binary package will pre-configure the software to accept anonymous connections. You can check this by connecting to your FTP server as an anonymous user.

1. Create a user to be used for anonymous access. Usually, this user is called ftp. The account you create should have a unique home directory. On most Linux systems this home directory will be /home/ftp/. You can create this user and home directory using the procedures described in Chapter 3, "User and Group Administration."

2. Set the default shell for the user you created to `/bin/false`. You can do this by editing the `/etc/passwd` file using the command `/usr/sbin/vipw` and changing the final field in the entry for the ftp account to `/bin/false` as shown in the following sample entry from an `/etc/passwd` file:

```
ftp:x:14:50:Anonymous FTP User:/home/ftp:/bin/false
```

3. When someone logs in as user `anonymous` or `ftp` the server does a `chroot()` (change root) system call and the home directory of user ftp becomes the server's root directory. As a result, everything outside of the ftp user's home directory becomes invisible to the server and the anonymous user.

4. To allow anonymous users to do useful things, create a restricted environment within the `/home/ftp/` directory which contains the minimum tools to allow for a useful FTP environment. To do this, first create the following directories:

   - `/home/ftp/bin/`
   - `/home/ftp/etc/`
   - `/home/ftp/lib/`
   - `/home/ftp/pub/`

5. You can create these directories with the following commands:

```
# mkdir /home/ftp/bin/
# mkdir /home/ftp/etc/
# mkdir /home/ftp/lib/
# mkdir /home/ftp/pub/
```

Note

You are free to create additional directories. For instance, many FTP servers have an incoming directory where anonymous users can upload files. For this, you could create the directory `/home/ftp/incoming/`.

Caution

Only create an `incoming` directory if it is absolutely necessary. An `incoming` directory can quickly become the staging ground for unethical transfer of questionable material by third parties on the Internet.

6. Any commands which you want to allow anonymous users to use, such as `ls` or `cp`, need to be copied to `/home/ftp/bin/`. To create a highly restricted environment, copy the `ls` program to this directory. If you want to support on-the-fly compression and decompression, copy the necessary programs such as `tar`, `compress`, or `gzip` to `/home/ftp/bin/` as well.

PART
V

CH
27

> **Caution**
>
> Remember that anonymous users need to have a restricted environment because they amount to unauthenticated users with access to part of your system. Only put essential tools in /home/ftp/bin/.

7. The /home/ftp/etc/ directory needs to contain a passwd file and a group file. Do not add any real users to these files. The passwd file should contain minimal entries such as the following:

    ```
    root:*:0:0::/:
    bin:*:1:1:::
    ftp:*:14:50:::
    ```

8. Similarly, a minimal group file should contain entries such as the following:

    ```
    root::0:
    bin::1:
    daemon::2:
    wheel::10:
    ftp::50:
    ```

9. In the /home/ftp/lib/ directory place any dynamic libraries needed by the programs placed in the /home/ftp/bin/ directory. Generally this will include the ld and libc libraries and possibly the libnsl and libnss libraries.

10. In the /home/ftp/pub/ directory place any files you want to make accessible for download by anonymous FTP users.

OWNERSHIPS AND PERMISSIONS FOR ANONYMOUS FTP

Because anonymous FTP users are effectively unauthenticated users with access to part of your system, it is essential that you use file and directory permissions properly to prevent abuse of your system through anonymous FTP access. There are several key principles you should follow:

■   The anonymous FTP user's home directory (that is, /home/ftp/ in all the examples in this chapter) should be owned by the root user and the group root or wheel.

■   The anonymous FTP user's home directory's permissions should be 555: Read and execute for all users.

■   The bin directory (that is, /home/ftp/bin/ in all the examples in this chapter) should be owned by the root user and the group root or wheel.

■   The bin directory's permissions should be 111: Execute for all users. This exceptionally tight restriction means that anonymous users can execute commands stored in this directory but they cannot view the list of commands stored in the directory. This helps ensure that they only use the limited repertoire of commands you want to make available to them.

- The applications in the bin directory should have permission set to 111: Execute for all users.

- The etc directory (that is, /home/ftp/etc/ in all the examples in this chapter) should be owned by the root user and the group root or wheel.

- The etc directory's permissions should be 111: Execute for all users.

- The passwd and group files in the etc directory must have 444 as their permission: Readable by all users.

- The lib directory (that is, /home/ftp/lib/ in all the examples in this chapter) should be owned by the root user and the group root or wheel.

- All files in the lib directory should have 555 as their permission: Readable and executable by all users.

- The pub directory (that is, /home/ftp/pub/ in all the examples in this chapter) should be owned by the root user or the user who is assigned to maintain the archive.

- The pub directory's permission should be 555: Readable and executable by all users.

The following directory listings show file and directory permissions from the anonymous FTP user's directory on a sample FTP site:

```
# cd /home/ftp
# ls -l
 d--x--x--x   2 root      root            1024 Nov 11 21:14 bin
 d--x--x--x   2 root      root            1024 Nov 11 21:14 etc
 d--x--x--x   2 root      root            1024 Nov 11 21:14 lib
 dr-xr-xr-x   2 root      root         1024 Nov 11 21:14 pub
# ls -l etc
 -r--r--r--   1 root      root              29 Nov 10 20:26 group
 -r--r--r--   1 root      root              91 Nov 10 20:25 passwd
# ls -l bin
 ---x--x--x   1 root      wheel          50148 Nov 10 20:20 ls
# ls -l lib
 -r-xr-xr-x   1 root      root          342206 Nov 10 22:29 ld-2.1.1.so
 lrwxrwxrwx   1 root      root              11 Nov 10 22:29 ld-linux.so.2 -> \
ld-2.1.1.so
 -r-xr-xr-x   1 root      root         4016683 Nov 10 22:30 libc-2.1.1.so
 lrwxrwxrwx   1 root      root              13 Nov 10 22:30 libc.so.6 -> \
libc-2.1.1.so
 -r-xr-xr-x   1 root      root          364235 Nov 10 22:38 libnsl-2.1.1.so
 lrwxrwxrwx   1 root      root              15 Nov 10 22:40 libnsl.so.1 -> \
libnsl-2.1.1.so
 -r-xr-xr-x   1 root      root          243964 Nov 10 22:39 libnss_files-2.1.1.so
 lrwxrwxrwx   1 root      root              21 Nov 10 22:39 libnss_files.so.2 ->\
libnss_files-2.1.1.so
```

TESTING YOUR ANONYMOUS FTP SERVER

When you have configured WU-FTPD for anonymous access, double-check that it is running properly. To do this, use the FTP client included with your Linux distribution to connect to the new FTP server and log in as the anonymous user. Once connected, you need to test several things:

PART

V

CH

27

- Confirm that you can log in as the anonymous user.
- Check that the commands in the bin directory can be used by trying the ls command.
- Check that the pub directory is accessible by changing to that directory and listing the files there.

The following is an example FTP client session illustrating these tests:

```
# ftp localhost
Connected to localhost.
220 linux.juxta.com FTP server (Version wu-2.6.0 (1) \
      Mon Apr 19 09:21:53 EDT 1999) ready.
Name (localhost:root):ftp
331 Guest login ok, send your complete e-mail address as password.
Password:
230 Guest login ok, access restrictions apply.
Remote system type is UNIX.
Using binary mode to transfer files.
ftp> ls
200 PORT command successful.
150 Opening ASCII mode data connection for /bin/ls.
total 4
d--x--x--x   2 root     root         1024 Nov 11 19:42 bin
d--x--x--x   2 root     root         1024 Nov 11 20:23 etc
d--x--x--x   2 root     root         1024 Nov 11 19:14 lib
dr-xr-xr-x   2 root     root         1024 Nov 11 19:14 pub
226 Transfer complete.
ftp> cd pub
250-Please read the file README
250-  it was last modified on Wed Nov 10 20:37:24 1999 - 2 days ago
250 CWD command successful.
ftp> ls
200 PORT command successful.
150 Opening ASCII mode data connection for /bin/ls.
total 1
-r--r--r--   1 ftp      ftp            27 Nov 10 18:37 README \
226 Transfer complete.
ftp> bye
```

USING THE ftpaccess FILE

The ftpaccess file is used to define user classes, based on the account accessed and the host from which the user connects. You can deny access to a certain class of users or limit their number of connections during specific times of the week in this file. You can also specify who has permission to perform particular actions such as directory creation and file uploading.

SPECIFYING CLASSES OF USERS

Three classes of users are available with WU-FTPD as outlined in Table 27.2.

TABLE 27.2   CLASSES OF USERS WITH WU-FTPD

Class	Description
real	This class is for users who can access using regular accounts on the FTP server. When these users connect, the server does not execute a chroot system call to the FTP user's home directory (which is /home/ftp/ in all the examples in this book).
anonymous	This class is for users accessing the account anonymous or ftp. When these users connect, the server executes a chroot system call to the anonymous FTP user's home directory.
guest	This class is for users accessing with unique user IDs and passwords and having special access rights that are greater than anonymous users but less than real users. When these users connect, the server executes a chroot but to a specified location. Guest users are discussed later in this chapter in the section "Guest Users."

ftpaccess DIRECTIVES

The ftpaccess file consists of a series of directives, one per line. More than 60 different directives can be used in the ftpaccess file. These directives are all defined in the ftpaccess man page, which can be viewed with the command man ftpaccess.

Normally, however, only a small subset of these directives is used in an ftpaccess file. Most FTP server configurations are straightforward. The following ftpaccess is representative of typical files for servers that use anonymous access. We will analyze it to learn how basic directives are used:

```
01: class   all    real,guest,anonymous   *
02: email root@localhost
03: deny    *.denied.com     /etc/ftpmsgs/deny-msg
04: limit        anonymouses 100    SaSu    /etc/msg.full.capacity
05: limit        anonymouses 50     Any     /etc/msg.full.capacity
06: message /welcome.msg          login
07: message .message     cwd=*
08: compress        yes            all
09: tar             yes            all
10: chmod           no             guest,anonymous
11: delete          no             guest,anonymous
12: overwrite       no             guest,anonymous
13: rename          no             guest,anonymous
14: readme  README*    login
15: readme  README*    cwd=*
16: log transfers anonymous,real inbound,outbound
17: shutdown /etc/shutmsg
```

PART
V

CH
27

Note   The line numbers have been added for reference purposes only and are not part of the ftpaccess file.

Let's consider this file on a line-by-line basis.

LINE 1   The class directive allows you to define composite classes. The directive takes the following form:

```
class <class name> <class members> <address expression>
```

The class name is the name of the class you are defining. Class members are one or more of the base user classes (anonymous, guest or real) separated by commas. The address expression specifies one or more hostnames; an asterisk can be used as a wildcard and hosts can be specified by name or IP address. The specified class will only apply to connections from the specified host or hosts.

In our example, one class is defined, named all, which encompasses all real, guest, and anonymous users connecting from any host. This class name can then be used throughout the ftpaccess file where a class needs to be specified.

Multiple classes can be specified in an ftpaccess file.

LINE 2   The email directive specifies the email address of the FTP server administrator. In our example, this email address is root@localhost.

LINE 3   The deny directive is used to specify particular hosts which should be denied access. The directive takes the following form:

```
deny <address expression> <message file>
```

The address expression specifies one or more hostnames; an asterisk can be used as a wildcard and hosts can be specified by name or IP address. The specified message file will be displayed to the user when denying access to the specified host or hosts.

In this example, anyone connecting from any host in the denied.com domain will be denied access and the message contained in the file /etc/ftpmsgs/deny-msg will be presented to users when access is denied.

LINES 4 AND 5   The limit directive is used to specify limitations on the number of users allowed to connect to the server at a particular time. This directive takes the following form:

```
limit <user class> <maximum users> <time> <message file>
```

The user class indicates what group or groups of users the limit applies to (such as anonymous, real, or guest). The maximum users field is a numeric value specifying the maximum number of users from the specific class allowed to connect. The time field specifies the times when the limit is in effect. The message file is the message to display when users attempt to connect when the maximum number of connections is already in use.

Times are specified in the format used in the UUCP L.sys file. This is a flexible format that allows you to specify times by the day of the week and time. First, consider limiting a connection between 12:00 and 2:00 p.m. every day. To do this, the time would be specified as Any1200-1400. The Any indicates the limit applies to any day of the week and 1200-1400 specifies the time range every day. By contrast, if you want a limit to apply all day every day, simply omit the time range: Any. If you want to specify a limit that applies only on Saturday and Sunday, set the time to SaSu.

You can also specify multiple times when a filter applies by separating multiple time definitions with a vertical pipe. For instance, SaSu¦Any1200-1400 indicates that a filter applies all weekend and between 12:00 and 2:00 p.m. every day.

The ftpaccess file can contain multiple limit directives. In this case, the first directive that matches a connection will be applied. Therefore, in our example, the first directive indicates that on the weekend anonymous connections will be limited to 100 users but on weekdays, only 50 users will be allowed. In each case, the message in the file /etc/msg.full.capacity is displayed if a user attempts to connect when the maximum number of connections is already in use.

LINES 6 AND 7 The message directive is used to specify a text file to display either upon login or when a change directory command is issued. The directive takes the form:

```
message <message file> <time> <class>
```

The message file specified will be displayed at the time the directive indicates. Two possible times can be used: LOGIN or CWD=*directory* where the directory is the directory which triggers the display of the message; you can specify all directories with an asterisk. In the case of the LOGIN time, the message file indicates the file path to the file to display. However in the case of the CWD time, the file specified is relative to the directory to which it is being changed. The class field is optional and is used to specify the class of users (such as anonymous, real, or group) for which the message should be displayed.

In our example, line 6 indicates that the file welcome.msg in the root FTP directory should be displayed when a user logs in and line 7 indicates that the file .message in each directory should be displayed when a user changes the current directory.

LINES 8-13 These directives indicate the permissions for specific capabilities including on-the-fly compression (compress and tar), changing file permissions (chmod), deleting files (delete), overwriting files (overwrite) and renaming files (rename).

The second field in each line can be yes or no indicating whether the directive is being used to show who is or is not allowed to perform a particular action. The third field indicates the class of users (such as guest, anonymous, or real) to which the directive applies.

In our example, lines 8 and 9 indicate that all users can use compress and tar for on-the-fly compression. Lines 10-13 indicate that guest and anonymous users cannot change file permissions, delete files, overwrite files, or rename files.

LINES 14 AND 15 The readme directive is used to specify a text file considered the readme file for a particular directory. When a user changes to a given directory they will be informed that the file is available and the modification date of the file. The directive takes the following form:

```
readme <message file> <time> <class>
```

The message file specified will be displayed at the time the directive indicates. Two possible times can be used: LOGIN or CWD=*directory* where the directory is the directory which triggers the display of the message; you can specify all directories with an asterisk. In the case of the LOGIN time, the message file indicates the file path to the file to display but in the case of the CWD time, the file specified is relative to the directory being changed to. The class field is optional and is used to specify the class of users (such as anonymous, real, or group) for which the message should be displayed.

In our example, any file with a name beginning with README in a directory will be considered the readme file for the directory.

LINE 16 The log transfers directive is used to indicate which types of transfer should be logged to the log file (usually /var/log/xferlog). The directive takes the following form:

```
log transfers <class> <direction>
```

The class indicates which classes of users should have their transfers logged and the direction indicates which type of transfers to log. Possible transfer directions are inbound or outbound. You can specify both directions by separating them with a comma: inbound,outbound.

In our example, inbound and outbound transfers by anonymous and real users will be logged.

LINE 17 The shutdown directive points to a file that indicates when a shutdown will occur as well as a warning message to display to users prior to the shutdown. Generally, this file will be created with the ftpshut program which is discussed later this chapter in the section "Other WU-FTPD Programs."

USING THE ftpconversions FILE

The ftpconversions file is used to tell WU-FTPD to perform on-the-fly compression and archiving using tar, compress, or gzip during file transfer.

The file consists of multiple entries. Each entry appears on a separate line and takes the form:

```
<strip prefix>:<strip postfix>:<addon prefix>:<addon postfix>:
➥ <external command>:<types>:<options>:<description>
```

The strip prefix and addon prefix are currently not used by WU-FTPD and are in place for future use.

The strip postfix indicates that files with the indicated ending should be passed through the specified external command and the extension removed. By contrast, the addon postfix indicates the extension to add a file when compressed with a particular external command.

The external command indicates how to perform the specific compression or decompression. In the command, %s is a symbol used to indicate the place where WU-FTPD should insert the filename in the command.

The types field indicates which types of files are affected by the entry. For instance, T_ASCII indicates that the entry applies to ASCII files. Multiple types are separated by vertical bars as in `T_REG¦T_ASCII`. The options field indicates whether the entry is for compression (`O_COMPRESS`) or decompression (`O_DECOMPRESSION`).

The `description` field is used to provide a meaningful description of the entry's purpose for future reference.

The following file is a sample `ftpconversions` file:

```
01:    :.Z:  :  :/bin/compress -d -c %s:T_REG¦T_ASCII:O_UNCOMPRESS:UNCOMPRESS
02:    :   :  :.Z:/bin/compress -c %s:T_REG:O_COMPRESS:COMPRESS
03:    :.gz:  :  :/bin/gzip -cd %s:T_REG¦T_ASCII:O_UNCOMPRESS:GUNZIP  :  :
04:    :.gz:/bin/gzip -9 -c %s:T_REG:O_COMPRESS:GZIP  :  :
05:    :.tar:/bin/tar -c -f - %s:T_REG¦T_DIR:O_TAR:TAR  :  :
06:    :.tar.Z:/bin/tar -c -Z -f - %s:T_REG¦T_DIR:O_COMPRESS¦\
➥O_TAR:TAR+COMPRESS  :  :
07:    :.tar.gz:/bin/tar -c -z -f - %s:T_REG¦T_DIR:O_COMPRESS¦O_TAR:TAR+GZIP
```

> **Note**
>
> The line numbers have been added for reference purposes only and are not part of the `ftpconversions` file.

In this example, the first two lines allow for on-the-fly compression and decompression of .Z files using the `compress` utility. Similarly, lines 3 and 4 allow for on-the-fly compression and decompression of `.gz` files using the `gzip` utility. Lines 5-7 provide for tarring, and compress tarring with `gzip` or `compress` on-the-fly.

ALLOWING UPLOADS INTO THE INCOMING DIRECTORY

By default, the WU-FTPD server does not allow uploads by anonymous FTP users. However, some distributions of Linux can preconfigure WU-FTPD in a different way and allow anonymous uploads. You can double-check this by looking for a line similar to the following in the `ftpaccess` file:

```
upload /home/ftp * no
```

The key is that the `upload` directive exists, that the appropriate directory (`/home/ftp/` here) and users (all users in this case) are specified, and that `no` is present to indicate that permission is denied.

If you want to allow uploads by anonymous users you need to take care to properly restrict their access. Generally, you will want the following restrictions in place:

- Anonymous users should not be able to create directories under incoming.
- Anonymous users should not be able to see the contents of incoming.

To implement these restrictions and enable anonymous uploads, use the following steps:

1. Create a special user to own the incoming directory. Typically, this user is called `ftpadmin`. Create the user as outlined in Chapter 3, "User and Group Administration." The user's home directory should be `/home/ftp/`.

2. Create a group in the /etc/group file called ftpadmin and make ftpadmin a member of the group in the /etc/passwd file. These procedures are outlined in Chapter 3.

3. Make the ftpadmin owner and group the owner of the incoming directory with the following command:

```
# chown ftpadmin.ftpadmin /home/ftp/incoming/
```

4. Apply permissions to the incoming directory so that the directory is only writable by non-owners with the following command:

```
# chmod 3773 /home/ftp/incoming/
```

5. Here, the permissions for world (in other words, users who are not the owner or member of the group owner) are only allowed write permissions (3 in the last position).

6. Enable upload access by adding the following line to /etc/ftpaccess:

```
upload /home/ftp /incoming yes ftpadmin ftpadmin 0440 nodirs
```

7. This line allows upload to /home/ftp/incoming and makes uploaded files owned by ftpadmin and group ftpadmin. The mode 0440 makes the files readable only for ftpadmin, ensuring that they cannot be downloaded by anonymous FTP users. Finally, permission to create directories under incoming is not granted (with nodirs).

With the scenario implemented here, users must email the FTP administrator after uploading files so that these files can be moved to a directory visible to FTP users if it is appropriate to do so.

You should also consider implementation of controls on the filenames of upload files. For instance, it is a good idea to disallow creation of files whose names start with a dot or a dash. You can implement these restrictions with a path-filter directive in the /etc/ftpaccess file.

It is advisable to use a path-filter to control the filenames users can create to upload files. For example you might not want to allow anonymous users to upload files with names starting with a dot (.) or dash (-). To do this you need to add a path-filter directive to the ftpaccess file. A good one is provided with the WU-FTP distribution:

```
path-filter anonymous,guest /etc/pathmsg ^[-A-Za-z0-9_\.]*$ ^\. ^-
```

There are several fields in this directive:

- **anonymous,guest**: This field indicates the user classes to which the directive applies. In this case all anonymous and guest users are affected by the path-filter directive.

- **/etc/pathmsg**: This field indicates the file containing a message to display when a user attempts to violate the restrictions of the path-filter directive.

- **^[-A-Za-z0-9 \.]*$**: This field is a regular expression indicating that valid uploaded filenames can only start with an alphanumeric character or a dot, an underscore, or a dash.

- `^\.`: This field is a regular expression indicating that filenames starting with a dot are prohibited.
- `^\-`: This field is a regular expression indicating that filenames starting with a dash are prohibited.

USING HIDDEN DIRECTORIES

An alternative approach to allowing file uploads is to allow only authorized users to upload files. This can be achieved by providing each of these users with a hidden directory under the incoming directory where they can upload files and the name of which is only known to the appropriate user.

To upload a file, users must know the exact name of the hidden directory where they will upload the file. Because the directories are hidden, the directory names effectively act as passwords that only allow authorized users to read or write to them.

Consider an example: A hidden directory called `secret` under `incoming` will be created and the name will only be made known to authorized users. This is achieved with the following steps after setting up the incoming directory as outlined in the previous section of this chapter:

1. Change your current working directory to the `incoming` directory:

   `# cd /home/ftp/incoming/`

2. Create a subdirectory called `secret`:

   `# mkdir secret/`

3. Make the `ftpadmin` user and group the owner of the `secret` directory:

   `# chown ftpadmin.ftpadmin secret/`

4. Make the directory readable and writable by all users:

   `# chmod 777 secret/`

5. Add an upload directive to the `/etc/ftpaccess` file allowing uploads to the `secret` directory:

   `upload /home/ftp /incoming/secret   yes  ftpadmin ftpadmin 0440 nodirs`

At this point, users who know about the existence of the secret directory can change their working directory to this directory and be able to upload files to the directory as well as view and read the files in the directory. You can test this by connecting to the FTP server as an anonymous user:

```
# ftp localhost
Connected to localhost.
220 linux.juxta.com FTP server (Version wu-2.6.0 (1) \
     Mon Apr 19 09:21:53 EDT 1999) ready.
Name (localhost:root):ftp
331 Guest login ok, send your complete e-mail address as password.
Password:
230 Guest login ok, access restrictions apply.
```

PART

V

CH

27

```
Remote system type is UNIX.
Using binary mode to transfer files.
ftp> ls
200 PORT command successful.
150 Opening ASCII mode data connection for /bin/ls.
total 5
---------    1 root     root            0 Nov 12 15:52 .notar
d--x--x--x   2 root     root         1024 Nov 11 19:42 bin
d--x--x--x   2 root     root         1024 Nov 12 16:02 etc
drwxrws-wt   3 ftpadmin ftpadmin     1024 Nov 12 16:09 incoming
d--x--x--x   2 root     root         1024 Nov 11 19:14 lib
dr-xr-xr-x   2 root     root         1024 Nov 11 19:14 pub
226 Transfer complete.
ftp> cd incoming
250 CWD command successful.
ftp> ls
200 PORT command successful.
150 Opening ASCII mode data connection for /bin/ls.
226 Transfer complete.
ftp> cd secret
250 CWD command successful.
ftp> put test
local: test remote: test
200 PORT command successful.
150 Opening BINARY mode data connection for test.
226 Transfer complete.
50 bytes sent in 0.000167 secs (2.9e+02 Kbytes/sec)
ftp> ls
200 PORT command successful.
150 Opening ASCII mode data connection for /bin/ls.
total 1
-r--r-----   1 ftpadmin ftpadmin       50 Nov 12 19:02 test
226 Transfer complete.
ftp> bye
```

Executing ls inside the incoming directory does not reveal the existence of the secret directory, but if you know the name of the directory, you can use cd to change to that directory.

OTHER WU-FTPD UTILITIES

WU-FTPD includes several utilities that are useful for administering your FTP server:

- **ftpwho**: This utility displays current process information for any users connected to your server at any given time.

- **ftpcount**: This utility displays the number of users of each class connected to your server at any given time.

- **ftpshut**: This utility initiates a shutdown of the FTP server and prevents new connections until the shutdown is complete.

- **ftprestart**: This utility removes the /etc/shutmsg file and allows users to connect and use the server.

SAMPLE `ftpwho` OUTPUT

The following illustrates typical output of the `ftpwho` utility:

```
# ftpwho
Service class all:
    1 ?        S       0:05
ftpd: localhost: anonymous/user@some.host: IDLE    -   1 users (50 maximum)
```

SAMPLE `ftpcount` OUTPUT

The following illustrates typical output of the `ftpcount` utility:

```
# ftpcount
Service class all                    -   1 users (50 maximum)
```

USING `ftpshut`

The `ftpshut` utility allows you to schedule a shutdown of the FTP server. In its most basic form, the `ftpshut` command needs to be provided with a time for the shutdown:

```
# ftpshut time
```

The `time` can be specified as a specific time in the form `HHMM` (in other words `1430` for 2:30 p.m.), as an offset of minutes in the form `+minutes` (in other words, to shutdown the server in 30 minutes, use `+30`), or immediately using `now`.

Ten minutes prior to the scheduled shutdown, the FTP server will stop accepting new connections. If the scheduled shutdown time is fewer than 10 minutes away then new logins will immediately be prevented. This 10-minute threshold can be altered with the `-l` argument to the `ftpshut` command. For instance, to shut down WU-FTPD in 30 minutes and start preventing logins 20 minutes prior to the shutdown, use the following command:

```
# ftpshut -l 20 +30
```

Five minutes prior to the scheduled shutdown, the FTP server will terminate all existing connections. If the scheduled shutdown time is fewer than 5 minutes away then all connections will immediately be terminated. This 5-minute threshold can be altered with the `-d` argument to the `ftpshut` command. For instance, to shut down WU-FTPD at 2:30 p.m. and disconnect existing logins 10 minutes prior to the shutdown, use the following command:

```
# ftpshut -d 10 1430
```

Optionally, you can warn users of the imminent shutdown of the server by providing a warning message as the last argument to the `ftpshut` command. The message should be a string of text enclosed in double quotation marks. Several special symbols can be used in your message text to force the inclusion of dynamic information. These symbols are outlined in Table 27.3.

PART

V

CH

27

TABLE 27.3 SPECIAL SYMBOLS FOR ftpshut MESSAGES

Symbol	Description
%s	Time at which the FTP server will shut down
%r	Time at which new connections will be refused by the FTP server
%d	Time at which the FTP server will terminate existing connections
%C	Current working directory
%E	Email address of the FTP administrator as defined in /etc/ftpaccess
%F	Free space in kilobytes available in the current working directory
%L	Local hostname
%M	Maximum number of users allowed in the user's class
%N	Current number of users logged in the user's class
%R	Remote hostname
%T	Local time
%U	Username given at login time

THE FTP xferlog FILE

The WU-FTPD daemon logs transfer information to the xferlog file. Typically, this log file is created in /var/log/. The xferlog file consists of a series of entries, one per line, each taking the following form:

```
<current time> <transfer time> <remote host> <file size> <filename>
➥<transfer type> <special action flag> <direction> <access mode>
➥<username> <service name> <authentication method>
➥<authenticated user ID> <completion status>
```

These fields have the following meaning:

- current time: The date and time of the transfer
- transfer time: The total transfer time in seconds
- remote host: The remote hostname
- file size: The size of the transferred file in bytes
- filename: The name of the transferred file
- transfer type: The transfer type (a for ASCII or b for binary)
- special action flag: A flag indicating if special action (such as compressing, decompressing, tarring, or no action) was taken
- direction: The direction of the transfer (o for outgoing or i for incoming)
- access mode: The access class of the user (a for anonymous, g for guest, or r for real)
- username: The email address provided by an anonymous user

- `service name`: The service being used (this will always be `ftp`)

- `authentication method`: Indicates the authentication method used (typically, this is either no authentication or RFC931 authentication)

- `authenticated user ID`: The username of an authenticated user or `*` to indicate that the user was not authenticated (for instance, an anonymous user)

- `completion status`: Indicates the status of the transfer (`c` for complete or `i` for incomplete)

The following are examples of typical entries for an anonymous FTP user:

```
Fri Nov 12 21:23:20 1999 1 localhost 27 /home/ftp/pub/README \
      b _ o a user@some.host ftp 0 * c
Fri Nov 12 21:23:25 1999 1 localhost 33 /home/ftp/pub/README \
      b C o a user@some.host ftp 0 * i
Fri Nov 12 21:24:29 1999 1 localhost 50 /home/ftp/incoming/test \
      b _ i a user@some.host ftp 0 * c
```

THE PROFESSIONAL FTP DAEMON—PROFTPD

ProFTPD is a new development that is gaining popularity, especially in the Linux community for better security and excellent support for virtual FTP servers.

The developers of ProFTPD were inspired by the Apache Web Server design. The ProFTPD server has many more features than are available with WU-FTPD. Instead of trying to extend the WU-FTPD code, they decided to write the server from scratch. One of the design goals was better security. Although WU-FTPD is likely the most widely used FTP daemon, and it performs very well, it has suffered several security vulnerabilities over the past few years. As a result, the developers of ProFTPD decided to write a completely new FTP daemon from ground up with tighter security and many more features.

ProFTPD compiles and runs on many versions of Unix, and Linux is one of them. In fact, Linux is one of the core platforms on which ProFTPD is heavily tested.

ProFTPD offers the following features:

- It uses a single main configuration file akin to the Apache web server. The configuration directives are designed to be intuitive, and especially easy for administrators who already manage the Apache web server.

- It offers a per directory access control by use of a `.ftpaccess` file similar to Apache's `.htaccess` file.

- It has excellent support for virtual FTP servers.

- It is very easy to configure for anonymous access.

- It can run as a standalone daemon or can be started up from the `inetd` daemon.

- It does not require any special binaries in its `bin` or `lib` directories to support anonymous FTP.

PART
V

CH
27

- Unlike most FTP servers, for better security, it does not support any SITE EXEC commands. In addition it does not use any external programs, which are also a major source of security problems in most FTP daemons.

- It runs as a configurable, non-privileged user, and thereby offers a higher level of security.

- It supports hidden directories and files.

- It provides logs that are compatible with the WU-FTPD logs. More extended logging is possible.

- It supports shadow passwords.

INSTALLING A PRECOMPILED BINARY

Precompiled binary distributions of ProFTPD for Linux are available from ftp:// ftp.proftpd.net/pub/proftpd. The latest version at the time of this writing is proftpd-1.2.0pre10. Note these are development releases; a stable version is yet to be released.

To install the standalone version on an Intel architecture machine with support for Red Hat package files, download proftpd-core-1.2.0pre10-1.686.rpm and proftpd-standalone-1.2.0pre10-1.i686.rpm, and run the following commands:

```
# rpm -i proftpd-core-1.2.0pre10-1.i686.rpm
# rpm -i proftpd-standalone-1.2.0pre10-1.i686.rpm
```

To install the inetd version instead, download proftpd-core-1.2.0pre10-1.686.rpm and proftpd-inetd-1.2.0pre10-1.i686.rpm, and run the following commands:

```
# rpm -i proftpd-core-1.2.0pre10-1.i686.rpm
# rpm --install proftpd-inetd-1.2.0pre10-1.i686.rpm
```

The ProFTPD RPM packages install the following files:

- /usr/sbin/proftpd
- /usr/sbin/ftpshut
- /usr/bin/ftpwho
- /usr/bin/ftpcount
- A symbolic link /usr/sbin/in.proftpd pointing to /usr/sbin/proftpd

In addition a default configuration file proftpd.conf is placed in /etc directory.

The RPM installation for the inetd version of ProFTPD edits the /etc/inetd.conf file, and signals inetd with a SIGHUP signal. It adds an entry to start proftpd when a connection attempt to port 21 is detected.

The RPM installation for the standalone version of ProFTPD also edits the /etc/inetd.conf file to remove any invocation of the FTP daemon, and sends a SIGHUP signal to inetd. In addition, it places a startup script called proftpd in the /etc/rc.d/init.d directory. After the installation of the standalone version is complete you can start ProFTPD by executing the following command:

```
# /etc/rc.d/init.d/proftpd start
```

BUILDING FROM SOURCE

Building ProFTPD from source code is quite straightforward. Download the ProFTPD source archive, `proftpd-1.2.0pre10.tar.gz`, in a suitable directory such as `/usr/local/src`. Unpack it as follows:

```
# cd /usr/local/src
# tar xzf proftpd-1.2.0pre10.tar.gz
```

This will create a directory called `proftpd-1.2.0pre10`. Change your current directory to this directory and run `configure` as follows:

```
# cd proftpd-1.2.0pre10
# ./configure -prefix=/usr
```

After the configure script executes, it will create a top level `makefile` and a `makefile` in the modules sub-directory. Now run `make` to build the executables:

```
# make
```

This will create the `proftpd` daemon, and three utility programs: `ftpwho`, `ftpcount`, and `ftpshut`.

Now install the binaries:

```
# make install
```

This will install `proftpd` and `ftpshut` in `/usr/sbin`, and the utilities `ftpwho` and `ftpcount` in `/usr/bin`. If you want to install the executables in a different path then specify the value of prefix accordingly when you run `configure`. After that you must run `make` and `make install`.

> **Tip**
>
> Before you install ProFTPD you might want to remove any other FTP daemon that might be installed on the system. This is not absolutely necessary, as long as you are aware of it and know how to make sure the correct FTP server answers when an FTP sessions is initiated.

PART
V

CH
27

CONFIGURING PROFTPD

After installing ProFTPD the next step is to configure it. You must decide at this point if you want to run ProFTPD from `inetd` or as a standalone program. If you have installed pre-built binaries you have already made that choice by installing either the `inetd` version or the standalone version.

RUNNING PROFTPD FROM `inetd`

If you built ProFTPD from the source code distribution, you need to edit `/etc/inetd.conf` to run ProFTPD from `inetd`. In the `inetd.conf` file, find a line similar to the following:

```
ftp stream tcp nowait root  /usr/sbin/in.ftpd in.ftpd -l -a
```

Replace it with the following line:

```
ftp stream tcp nowait root  /usr/sbin/proftpd proftpd
```

If you decide to run `proftpd` with TCP wrappers, then use the following line instead:

```
ftp stream tcp nowait root  /usr/sbin/tcpd   proftpd
```

After editing `inetd.conf`, the `inetd` daemon must be sent a SIGHUP signal to reload its configuration file using the following command:

```
# kill -HUP `cat /var/run/inetd.pid`
```

RUNNING PROFTPD IN STANDALONE MODE

If you decide to run ProFTPD in standalone mode, make sure `inetd.conf` file is not configured to start an FTP daemon. If it is then remove the relevant line from `/etc/inetd.conf` and send a SIGHUP signal to `inetd`.

You can start the ProFTP daemon in standalone with the following command:

```
# /usr/sbin/proftpd
```

To automatically start `proftpd` in standalone mode when the system reboots, add a startup script in `/etc/rc.d/init.d`. For details on how to add startup scripts refer to Chapter 4, "Booting Up and Shutting Down."

THE `proftpd.conf` FILE

At startup `proftpd` reads its configuration from `/etc/proftpd.conf`, or `/usr/etc/proftpd.conf`, or `/usr/local/etc/proftpd.conf` depending on how the package was compiled. If you have installed the pre-built RPM binary the configuration file `/etc/proftpd.conf` is consulted.

A sample configuration file is shown here. This is followed by a line-by-line explanation of the file. Line numbers have been added to aid discussion. They are not part of the real configuration file:

```
01: # This is a basic ProFTPD configuration file
02: # It establishes a single server and a single anonymous
03: # login.  It assumes that you have a user/group
04: # "nobody" and "ftp" for normal and anonymous operation.
05: ServerName            "ProFTPD Default Installation"
06: ServerType            standalone
07: User                   nobody
08: Group                  nobody
09: Port                  21
10: Umask                 022
```

```
11: MaxInstances            30
12: <Directory /*>
13: AllowOverwrite          on
14: </Directory>
15: # A basic anonymous configuration, no upload directories.
16: <Anonymous ~ftp>
17: User                    ftp
18: Group                   ftp
19: UserAlias               anonymous ftp
20: MaxClients              10
21: DisplayLogin            welcome.msg
22: DisplayFirstChdir       .message
23: <Limit WRITE>
24: DenyAll
25: </Limit>
26: </Anonymous>
```

It is clearly evident from the structure of this configuration file that it closely resembles the Apache Web server configuration file. Lines beginning with the hash symbol (#) are comment lines and are ignored by the daemon. The file can be analyzed as follows:

■ On line 5 the server is given a name. Change the default name to whatever name you want your server to have. This name is printed as part of the login banner when users connect to the server with an FTP client.

■ The operating mode of the server is set on line 6. Decide between standalone or inetd modes.

■ On lines 7 and 8 the user and group that the server runs as is set. The default value of nobody is a good security measure.

■ On line 9 the standard FTP port 21 is specified for use.

■ On line 10 the umask is specified. A umask of 022 is good choice. It prevents new directories and files from being created as group and world writable.

■ On line 11 the MaxInstances directive sets the maximum number of child processes that can be spawned by a parent proftpd process in standalonemode. This directive has no effect when a server is running in inetdmode. This is a good security measure against DOS attacks.

■ Lines 12, 13, and 14 specify the AllowOverwrite directive. This directive permits newly transferred files to overwrite existing files. By default, FTP clients cannot overwrite existing files.

■ Lines 15-26 specify a typical anonymous FTP configuration. The Anonymous configuration block is used to create an anonymous FTP login. This block is terminated by a matching </Anonymous> directive on line 27. The ~ftp after Anonymous on line 17 specifies that the daemon will execute a chdir to the user ftp's home directory, and then execute a chroot system call, for an anonymous login. After the chroot operation completes, higher level directories are not accessible to the child process and consequently to the logged in user.

PART

V

CH

27

- Lines 18 and 19 specify the anonymous ftp session will run as the user ftp and group ftp.
- Line 20 allows the anonymous user to login with the user ID of either anonymous or ftp.
- Line 21 sets a limit to the maximum number of simultaneous anonymous ftp connections.
- Lines 23 and 24 specify that the file welcome.msg be displayed at login, and the file .message be displayed when the user changes to any directory that contains a .message file.
- Lines 24-26 deny write access to all anonymous users.
- Line 27 ends the Anonymous section.

Virtual FTP Servers

Originally it was only possible to host a single FTP server on a machine. As the Internet grew in leaps and bounds it soon became necessary to devise a mechanism whereby multiple sites could be hosted on the same server. This capability of many sites hosted on one server is called *virtual hosting*.

ProFTPD provides an elegant mechanism for handling virtual hosts, which is very similar to with the method used by the Apache Web server. Serving multiple hosts is accomplished by assigning more than one IP address to a machine and then having ProFTPD bind differently to those different IP addresses. For example a host can be assigned two IP addresses 192.115.144.3 and 192.115.144.4 which are associated with the virtual servers named ftp.site1.org and ftp.site2.org respectively. When a connection to 192.115.144.3 is initiated it is directed to the virtual server ftp.site1.org, while a connection to 192.115.144.4 is directed to ftp.site2.org. ProFTPD allows completely separate environments for its virtual servers.

Virtual hosts are configured by using a <VirtualHost ...> configuration block in proftpd.conf. The block is terminated by the </VirtualHost> directive. This is best illustrated by examining a sample configuration file. A relevant section of a proftpd.conf file showing virtual host configurations for two fictitious hosts ftp.site1.org and ftp.site2.org is displayed here. Line numbers have been added to aid the discussion. They are not part of an actual configuration file:

```
01: # Anonymous access, and no incoming

02: <VirtualHost ftp.site1.org>
03: ServerAdmin            ftpmaster@site1.org
04: ServerName             "Site1 FTP Server"
05: TransferLog            /var/spool/syslog/xfer/ftp.site1.org
06: MaxLoginAttempts       3
07: RequireValidShell      no
08: DefaultRoot            /home/ftp/ftp.site1.org
09: User                   site1
10: Group                  site1
```

```
11: AllowOverwrite          yes

12: # Auth files....

13: AuthUserFile     /var/conf/ftp/authfiles/passwd.ftp.site1.org
14: AuthGroupFile    /var/conf/ftp/authfiles/group.ftp.site1.org

15: <Anonymous /home/ftp/ftp.site1.org>
16:    User                 ftp
17:    Group                ftp
18:    UserAlias            anonymous ftp
19:    RequireValidShell    no
20:    MaxClients           10

21:    <Limit WRITE>
22:        DenyAll
23:    </Limit>
24: </Anonymous>
25: </VirtualHost>


26: # ftp.site2.org
27: # Anonymous ftp, and no incoming

28: <VirtualHost ftp.site2.org>
29: ServerAdmin          ftpmaster@site2.org
30: ServerName           "Site 2 FTP Server"
31: TransferLog          /var/spool/syslog/xfer/ftp.site2.org
32: MaxLoginAttempts     3
33: RequireValidShell    no
34: DefaultRoot          /home/ftp/ftp.site2.org
35: User                 site2
36: Group                site2
37: AllowOverwrite       yes

38: # Auth files....

39: AuthUserFile     /var/conf/ftp/authfiles/passwd.ftp.site2.org
40: AuthGroupFile    /var/conf/ftp/authfiles/group.ftp.site2.org

41: <Anonymous /home/ftp/ftp.site2.org>
42:    User                 ftp
43:    Group                ftp
44:    UserAlias            anonymous ftp
45:    RequireValidShell    no
46:    MaxClients           10

47:    <Limit WRITE>
48:        DenyAll
49:    </Limit>

50: </Anonymous>
51: </VirtualHost>
```

PART

V

CH

27

Lines starting with the hash symbol (#) are comment lines and are ignored by the ProFTPD daemon. The file can be analyzed as follows:

- Lines 2-25 define a virtual host named ftp.site1.org.
- Lines 26-51 define a second virtual host named ftp.site2.org.
- Line 3 specifies the email address of the first site's administrator. Line 3 also specifies the name of the server that the banner page displays when you connect to this server.
- Line 5 specifies the location of the transfer log file for the first site virtual host.
- Line 8 specifies the root directory of the first site.

> **Note**
>
> Each virtual host has its private root directory and separate transfer log files.

- Lines 9 and 10 specify that the ProFTPD daemon servicing this virtual host will run as user site1 and group site1. Needless to say, the specified user and group must be defined when setting up the virtual sites.
- Lines 13 and 14 specify the AuthUserFile and AuthGroupFile locations. AuthUserFile specifies an alternate password file, that has the same format as the system /etc/passwd file. When it is specified, it is used for authentication and directory access control.

> **Note**
>
> The alternate password file need not reside inside a chroot'ed directory structure for anonymous or normal logins.

- Lines 15-24 define an anomymous FTP access using directives we have already discussed in the previous section.
- Lines 25-51 define the second virtual host named ftp.site2.org, and use similar directives as in defining ftp.site1.org.

For more details on the configuration options of ProFTPD, use the online documentation in the /usr/local/src/proftpd-1.2.0pre10/doc directory or visit the ProFTPD Web site at http://www.proftpd.net.

USEFUL SCRIPTS

The data often saved in the xferlog file is valuable but hard to use. Because each individual file transferred is logged in the file in chronological order, it is difficult to get a grasp on the usage of your server simply by reading the log file.

WU-FTPD includes a utility called xferstats that is useful for analyzing and summarizing the log information stored in the xferlog file. The output of xferstats includes the following information:

- Total and average daily bytes transferred
- Daily statistics
- Breakdown of files and bytes sent by each server directory
- Hourly traffic statistics

The xferstats program takes several arguments, including `-f filename` to indicate the full path and filename of the xferlog file; `-r` to include real users in the statistics; `-a` to include anonymous users in the statistics; `-h` to generate hourly traffic reports; `-d` to generate domain-specific traffic reports; and `-t` to generate total traffic reports by section.

The following is sample output from xferstats:

```
# xferstats -f /var/log/xferlog -r -a -h -t
TOTALS FOR SUMMARY PERIOD Sun Nov  7 1999 TO Sat Nov 13 1999
Files Transmitted During Summary Period          107
Bytes Transmitted During Summary Period      8217300
Systems Using Archives                            43

Average Files Transmitted Daily                   15
Average Bytes Transmitted Daily              1173900


Daily Transmission Statistics

                  Number Of    Number of    Average     Percent Of  Percent Of
        Date      Files Sent   Bytes  Sent  Xmit  Rate  Files Sent  Bytes Sent
 ----------------  ----------  ----------   ----------   ----------  ----------
Sun Nov  7 1999           29     2756399    2.2 KB/s        27.10       33.54
Mon Nov  8 1999           11      161781    3.2 KB/s        10.28        1.97
Tue Nov  9 1999           12      506230    2.9 KB/s        11.21        6.16
Wed Nov 10 1999           10      602695    0.9 KB/s         9.35        7.33
Thu Nov 11 1999            9      498994    1.2 KB/s         8.41        6.07
Fri Nov 12 1999           19     1904576    0.6 KB/s        17.76       23.18
Sat Nov 13 1999           17     1786625    1.7 KB/s        15.89       21.74


Total Transfers from each Archive Section (By bytes)

                                                 ---- Percent  Of ----
        Archive Section    Files Sent Bytes Sent  Files Sent  Bytes Sent
 ----------------------    ---------- ----------   ----------  ----------
/bahai/authors/bahaullah          38    3072276       35.51       37.39
/bahai/authors/other              14    2269853       13.08       27.62
/bahai/authors/abdulbaha           9    1463654        8.41       17.81
/bahai/authors/shoghi_eff          9     897391        8.41       10.92
/bahai/authors/bab                 2     211318        1.87        2.57
/bahai                            32     159146       29.91        1.94
/bahai/compilations/bahai          1      55624        0.93        0.68
```

```
/bahai/compilations/peace       1      51099    0.93      0.62
/bahai/compilations/schol       1      36939    0.93      0.45
```

Hourly Transmission Statistics

Time	Number Of Files Sent	Number of Bytes Sent	Average Xmit Rate	Percent Of Files Sent	Percent Of Bytes Sent
00	4	344770	3.2 KB/s	3.74	4.20
01	30	2607905	2.1 KB/s	28.04	31.74
02	5	422711	3.7 KB/s	4.67	5.14
03	2	37908	0.7 KB/s	1.87	0.46
04	1	3127	3.1 KB/s	0.93	0.04
05	1	1826	1.8 KB/s	0.93	0.02
06	13	721616	0.8 KB/s	12.15	8.78
07	6	1121640	0.9 KB/s	5.61	13.65
09	4	40445	0.5 KB/s	3.74	0.49
10	1	4992	2.5 KB/s	0.93	0.06
12	1	1826	1.8 KB/s	0.93	0.02
13	3	89864	0.7 KB/s	2.80	1.09
15	8	1353225	1.9 KB/s	7.48	16.47
16	1	92	0.1 KB/s	0.93	0.00
17	2	28298	4.0 KB/s	1.87	0.34
18	5	116513	2.9 KB/s	4.67	1.42
19	4	153783	4.0 KB/s	3.74	1.87
20	4	399828	4.3 KB/s	3.74	4.87
21	4	203706	0.1 KB/s	3.74	2.48
22	2	226956	2.1 KB/s	1.87	2.76
23	6	336269	2.3 KB/s	5.61	4.09

In addition to xferstats, there are several freely available third-party tools for summarizing the contents of xferlog files:

- dumpxfer processes xferlog files and gives more humanly readable output (available through anonymous ftp at ftp://tnt.microimages.com/tools/; requires Perl).

- Koos van den Hout has written a Perl script to process the xferlog file, mail daily statistics and upload files, and create a top-most downloaded files list (available at ftp://ftp.cetis.hvu.nl/pub/koos/ftplogcheck).

- iistat generates nice transfer graphs from xferlog files and from many other sources (available from ftp://ftp.support.lotus.com/pub/utils/InternetServices/iisstat/iisstat.html).

- Webalizer is available from ftp.mrunix.net/pub/webalizer. It analyzes WU-FTPD format log files and creates reports in HTML pages that can be viewed with a Web browser.

TROUBLESHOOTING

Two problems commonly occur when configuring a WU-FTPD server:

- `ls` works for real users, but produces no output for anonymous users. To resolve this problem, you need the dynamic libraries used by `ls` in the lib directory in the FTP user's home directory (`/home/ftp/lib/` in the examples in this chapter). You can test if `ls` will work for FTP users with the following command:

```
# chroot ~ftp /bin/ls
```

If `ls` doesn't work you can use the `ldd` command to determine which libraries are needed by the `ls` command and copy these files to `/home/ftp/lib/`:

```
# ldd /bin/ls
    libc.so.6 => /lib/libc.so.6 (0x40000000)
    /lib/ld-linux.so.2 => /lib/ls-linux.so.2 (0x40000000)
```

The same principles hold true for other programs in the `/bin` directory such as `compress` and `gzip`. If FTP users cannot use them then check that the libraries needed are present using `ldd`.

- `ls` works fine but the file and directory owner and group names are not shown; UID and GID numbers are displayed instead of names. There are two possible causes of this problem. One is that the user and group names for the UIDs and GIDs have not been added to `/home/ftp/etc/passwd` and `/home/ftp/etc/group`. A second possible cause for the problem is related to missing dynamic libraries in `/home/ftp/lib/`. WU-FTPDS needs the `libnsl.*` and `libnss_files.*` libraries on Linux in order to display this information.

Two common problems can occur when starting the ProFTPD server:

- After installing ProFTPD for the first time, when you try to start it up either from inetd or as standalone you might see the error "Group nogroup not found." This is because the default `proftpd.conf` file calls for the user `nobody` and group `nogroup` to run the daemon. Commonly, Linux systems don't have the group `nogroup` defined in `/etc/group`. To fix it you can either define the group `nogroup` in `/etc/group` or change the `proftpd.conf` file to use the group `nobody` instead.

- When starting ProFTPD in standalone mode you might see the error "Unable to bind to port/Address already in use." This problem happens when a line for the FTP service exists in the `/etc/inetd.conf` file. To solve the problem, comment out the line starting with "ftp" in `/etc/inetd.conf` and send inetd a hang-up signal. Alternatively, make sure another copy of ProFTPD or another FTP daemon is not already running in standalone mode.

PART
V

CH
27

APPENDIXES

A

LINUX COMMAND REFERENCE

The following are reproductions of selected manual pages as shipped with Red Hat Linux 6.2. They are copyrighted by their respective authors or copyright holders and are freely redistributable, as is Linux.

AT

NAME

at, batch, atq, and atrm queue, examine, or delete jobs for later execution.

SYNOPSIS

at [-V] [-q queue] [-f file] [-mldbv] TIME

at -c job [job...]

atq [-V] [-q queue] [-v]

atrm [-V] job [job...]

batch [-V] [-q queue] [-f file] [-mv] [TIME]

DESCRIPTION

at and batch, which are to be executed at a later time, read commands from standard input or from a specified file using /bin/sh.

- at—Executes commands at a specified time.
- atq—Lists the user's pending jobs, unless the user is the super-user; in that case, everybody's jobs are listed.
- atrm—Deletes jobs.
- batch—Executes commands when system load levels permit; in other words, when the load average drops below 0.8, or the value specified in the invocation of atrun.

at allows fairly complex time specifications, extending the POSIX.2 standard. It accepts times of the form HH:MM to run a job at a specific time of day. (If that time is already past, the next day is assumed.) You can also specify midnight, noon, or teatime (4 p.m.) and you can have a time-of-day suffixed with AM or PM for running in the morning or the evening. You can also say what day the job will be run by giving a date in the form month-name day with an optional year, or giving a date in the form of MMDDYY, MM/DD/YY, or DD.MM.YY. The specification of a date *must* follow the specification of the time of day. You can also give times such as now + *count time-units*, where the time-units can be minutes, hours, days, or weeks and you can tell at to run the job today by suffixing the time with today or to run the job tomorrow by suffixing the time with tomorrow.

For example, to run a job at 4:00 p.m. three days from now, you would enter at 4pm + 3 days; to run a job at 10:00 a.m. on July 31; you would enter at 10am Jul 31; and to run a job at 1:00 a.m. tomorrow, you would enter at 1am tomorrow.

The exact definition of the time specification can be found in /usr/doc/at-3.1.7/timespec.

For both at and batch, commands are read from standard input or the file specified with the -f option and executed. The working directory, the environment (except for the variables TERM, DISPLAY, and _), and the umask are retained from the time of invocation. An at - or batch - command invoked from a su(1) shell will retain the current user ID. The user will be mailed standard error and standard output from his commands, if any. Mail will be sent using the command /usr/sbin/sendmail. If at is executed from a su(1) shell, the owner of the login shell will receive the mail.

The super-user can use these commands in any case. For other users, permission to use at is determined by the files /etc/at.allow and /etc/at.deny.

If the file /etc/at.allow exists, only usernames mentioned in it are allowed to use at.

If /etc/at.allow does not exist, /etc/at.deny is checked, and every username not mentioned in it is then allowed to use at.

If neither exists, only the super-user is allowed use of at.

An empty /etc/at.deny means that every user is allowed to use these commands; this is the default configuration.

OPTIONS

- ■   -V—Prints the version number to standard error.
- ■   -q queue—Uses the specified queue.

A queue designation consists of a single letter; valid queue designations range from a to z and A to Z. The a queue is the default for at and the b queue is the default for batch. Queues with higher letters run with increased niceness. The special queue = is reserved for jobs which are currently running. If a job is submitted to a queue designated with an uppercase letter, it is treated as if it had been submitted to batch at that time. If atq is given a specific queue, it will only show jobs pending in that queue.

- ■   -m—Sends mail to the user when the job has completed even if there was no output.
- ■   -f file—Reads the job from file rather than standard input.
- ■   -l—Is an alias for atq.

- ■   -d—Is an alias for atrm.

- ■   -v—For atq, shows completed but not yet deleted jobs in the queue; otherwise shows the time the job will be executed. Times displayed will be in the format "1997-02-20 14:50' unless the environment variable POSIXLY_CORRECT is set; then, it will be "Thu Feb 20 14:50:00 1996'.

- ■   -c—Cats the jobs listed on the command line to standard output.

FILES

/var/spool/at

/var/spool/at/spool

/proc/loadavg

/var/run/utmp

/etc/at.allow

/etc/at.deny

SEE ALSO

cron(1), nice(1), sh(1), umask(2), atd(8)

BUGS

The correct operation of batch for Linux depends on the presence of a proc type directory mounted on /proc.

If the file /var/run/utmp is not available or corrupted, or if the user is not logged on at the time at is invoked, the mail is sent to the userid found in the environment variable LOGNAME. If that is undefined or empty, the current userid is assumed.

at and batch as presently implemented are not suitable when users are competing for resources. If this is the case for your site, you might want to consider another batch system, such as nqs.

AUTHOR

at was written mostly by Thomas Koenig, ig25@rz.uni-karlsruhe.de.

CAT

NAME

cat—Concatenate files and print on the standard output.

SYNOPSIS

cat [OPTION] [FILE]...

DESCRIPTION

Concatenate FILE(s), or standard input, to standard output.

- `-A, --show-all`—Equivalent to `-vET`
- `-b, --number-nonblank`—Numbers nonblank output lines
- `-e`—Equivalent to `-vE`
- `-E, --show-ends`—Displays $ at end of each line
- `-n, --number`—Numbers all output lines
- `-s, --squeeze-blank`—Never more than one single blank line
- `-t`—Equivalent to `-vT`
- `-T, --show-tabs`—Displays TAB characters as ^I
- `-u`—(ignored)
- `-v, --show-nonprinting`—Uses ^ and M- notation, except for LFD and TAB
- `--help`—Displays this help and exits
- `--version`—Outputs version information and exits

With no FILE, or when FILE is -, read standard input.

REPORTING BUGS

Report bugs to <bug-textutils@gnu.org>.

SEE ALSO

The full documentation for `cat` is maintained as a Texinfo manual. If the `info` and `cat` programs are properly installed at your site, the command

`info cat`

should give you access to the complete manual.

COPYRIGHT

Copyright © 1999 Free Software Foundation, Inc. This is free software; see the source for copying conditions. There is NO warranty; not even for MERCHANTABILITY or FITNESS FOR A PARTICULAR PURPOSE.

CHGRP

NAME

`chgrp`—Change group ownership.

SYNOPSIS

```
chgrp [OPTION]... GROUP FILE...
chgrp [OPTION]... --reference=RFILE FILE...
```

DESCRIPTION

Change the group membership of each FILE to GROUP.

- `-c, --changes`—Like verbose but report only when a change is made
- `-h, --no-dereference`—Affects symbolic links instead of any referenced file (available only on systems with lchown system call)
- `-f, --silent, --quiet`—Suppresses most error messages
- `--reference=RFILE`—Uses RFILE's group instead of using a GROUP value
- `-R, --recursive`—Changes files and directories recursively
- `-v, --verbose`—Outputs a diagnostic for every file processed
- `--help`—Displays this help and exits
- `--version`—Outputs version information and exits

REPORTING BUGS

Report bugs to <bug-fileutils@gnu.org>.

SEE ALSO

The full documentation for `chgrp` is maintained as a Texinfo manual. If the `info` and `chgrp` programs are properly installed at your site, the command

```
info chgrp
```

should give you access to the complete manual.

CHMOD

NAME

chmod—Change file access permissions.

SYNOPSIS

```
chmod [OPTION]... MODE[,MODE]... FILE...
chmod [OPTION]... OCTAL_MODE FILE...
chmod [OPTION]... --reference=RFILE FILE...
```

PART
VI

APP
A

DESCRIPTION

This manual page documents the GNU version of chmod. chmod changes the permissions of each given file according to *mode*, which can be either a symbolic representation of changes to make or an octal number representing the bit pattern for the new permissions.

The format of a symbolic mode is:

`'[ugoa...][[+-=][rwxXstugo...]...][,...]'`

Multiple symbolic operations can be given, separated by commas.

A combination of the letters ugoa controls which user's access to the file will be changed: the user who owns it (u), other users in the file's group (g), other users not in the file's group (o), or all users . If none of these are given, the effect is as if a were given, but bits that are set in the umask are not affected.

The operator + causes the permissions selected to be added to the existing permissions of each file; - causes them to be removed; and = causes them to be the only permissions that the file has.

The letters rwxXstugo select the new permissions for the affected users: read (r), write (w), execute (or access for directories) (x), execute only if the file is a directory or already has execute permission for some user (X), set user or group ID on execution (s), save program text on swap device (t), the permissions that the user who owns the file currently has for it (u), the permissions that other users in the file's group have for it (g), and the permissions that other users not in the file's group have for it (o).

A numeric mode is from one to four octal digits (0-7), derived by adding the bits with values 4, 2, and 1. Any omitted digits are assumed to be leading zeros. The first digit selects the set user ID (4) and set group ID (2) and saves text image (1) attributes. The second digit selects permissions for the user who owns the file: read (4), write (2), and execute (1); the third selects permissions for other users in the file's group, with the same values; and the fourth for other users not in the file's group, with the same values.

chmod never changes the permissions of symbolic links; the chmod system call cannot change their permissions. This is not a problem because the permissions of symbolic links are never used. However, for each symbolic link listed on the command line, chmod changes the permissions of the pointed-to file. In contrast, chmod ignores symbolic links encountered during recursive directory traversals.

OPTIONS

- -c, --changes—Like verbose but reports only when a change is made
- -f, --silent, --quiet—Suppresses most error messages
- -v, --verbose—Outputs a diagnostic for every file processed
- --reference=RFILE—Uses RFILE's mode instead of MODE values

- -R, --recursive—Changes files and directories recursively
- --help—Displays this help and exits
- --version—Outputs version information and exits

Each MODE is one or more of the letters ugoa, one of the symbols + - = and one or more of the letters rwxXstugo.

REPORTING BUGS

Report bugs to <bug-fileutils@gnu.org>.

SEE ALSO

The full documentation for chmod is maintained as a Texinfo manual. If the info and chmod programs are properly installed at your site, the command

info chmod

should give you access to the complete manual.

CHOWN

NAME

chown—Change file owner and group.

SYNOPSIS

chown [OPTION]... OWNER[.[GROUP]] FILE...

chown [OPTION]... .GROUP FILE...

chown [OPTION]... –reference=RFILE FILE...

DESCRIPTION

This manual page documents the GNU version of chown. chown changes the user or group ownership of each given file, according to its first non-option argument, which is interpreted as follows. If only a username (or numeric user ID) is given, that user is made the owner of each given file, and the file's group is not changed. If the username is followed by a colon or dot and a group name (or numeric group ID), with no spaces between, the group ownership of the files is changed as well. If a colon or dot but no group name follows the username, that user is made the owner of the files and the group of the files is changed to that user's login group. If the colon or dot and group are given, but the username is omitted, only the group of the files is changed; in this case, chown performs the same function as chgrp.

PART

VI

APP

A

OPTIONS

Change the owner and/or group of each FILE to OWNER and/or GROUP.

- `-c, --changes`—Is verbose whenever change occurs
- `--dereference`—Affects the referent of each symbolic link, rather than the symbolic link itself
- `-h, --no-dereference`—Affects symbolic links instead of any referenced file (available only on systems that can change the ownership of a symlink)
- `-f, --silent, --quiet`—Suppresses most error messages
- `--reference=RFILE`—Uses the owner and group of RFILE instead of using explicit OWNER.GROUP values
- `-R, --recursive`—Operates on files and directories recursively
- `-v, --verbose`—Explains what is being done
- `--help`—Displays this help and exits
- `--version`—Outputs version information and exits

Owner is unchanged if missing. Group is unchanged if missing, but changed to login group if implied by a period. A colon can replace the period.

REPORTING BUGS

Report bugs to <bug-fileutils@gnu.org>.

SEE ALSO

The full documentation for chown is maintained as a Texinfo manual. If the info and chown programs are properly installed at your site, the command

`info chown`

should give you access to the complete manual.

CP

NAME

cp—Copy files and directories.

SYNOPSIS

```
cp [OPTION]... SOURCE DEST
cp [OPTION]... SOURCE... DIRECTORY
```

DESCRIPTION

- ■ Copy SOURCE to DEST, or multiple SOURCE(s) to DIRECTORY.
- ■ `-a, --archive`—Same as `-dpR`
- ■ `-b, --backup`—Makes backup before removal
- ■ `-d, --no-dereference`—Preserves links
- ■ `-f, --force`—Removes existing destinations, never prompt
- ■ `-i, --interactive`—Prompts before overwrite
- ■ `-l, --link`—Links files instead of copying
- ■ `-p, --preserve`—Preserves file attributes if possible
- ■ `-P, --parents`—Appends source path to DIRECTORY
- ■ `-r`—Copies recursively, non-directories as files
- ■ `--sparse=WHEN`—Controls creation of sparse files
- ■ `-R, --recursive`—Copies directories recursively
- ■ `-s, --symbolic-link`—Makes symbolic links instead of copying
- ■ `-S, --suffix=SUFFIX`—Overrides the usual backup suffix
- ■ `-u, --update`—Copies only when the SOURCE file is newer than the destination file or when the destination file is missing
- ■ `-v, --verbose`—Explains what is being done
- ■ `-V, --version-control=WORD`—Overrides the usual version control
- ■ `-x, --one-file-system`—Stays on this file system
- ■ `--help`—Displays this help and exits
- ■ `--version`—Outputs version information and exits

By default, sparse SOURCE files are detected by a crude heuristic method and the corresponding DEST file is made sparse as well. That is the behavior selected by `--sparse=auto`. Specify `--sparse=always` to create a sparse DEST file whenever the SOURCE file contains a long enough sequence of zero bytes. Use `--sparse=never` to inhibit creation of sparse files.

The backup suffix is ~, unless set with SIMPLE_BACKUP_SUFFIX. The version control can be set with VERSION_CONTROL. Values are:

`t, numbered`

`make numbered backups`

`nil, existing`

`numbered if numbered backups exist, simple otherwise`

`never, simple`

`always make simple backups`

As a special case, cp makes a backup of SOURCE when the force and backup options are given and SOURCE and DEST are the same name for an existing, regular file.

REPORTING BUGS

Report bugs to <bug-fileutils@gnu.org>.

SEE ALSO

The full documentation for cp is maintained as a Texinfo manual. If the info and cp programs are properly installed at your site, the command

```
info cp
```

should give you access to the complete manual.

CRONTAB

NAME

crontab—Maintain crontab files for individual users (V3).

SYNOPSIS

```
crontab [ -u user ] file
crontab [ -u user ] { -l ¦ -r ¦ -e }
```

DESCRIPTION

crontab is the program used to install, uninstall or list the tables used to drive the cron(8) daemon in Vixie Cron. Each user can have their own crontab, and though these are files in /var, they are not intended to be edited directly.

If the *allow* file exists, you must be listed therein to be allowed to use this command. If the *allow* file does not exist but the *deny* file does exist, you must not be listed in the deny file in order to use this command. If neither of these files exists then depending on site-dependent configuration parameters, only the super-user will be allowed to use this command, or all users will be able to use this command.

If the *-u* option is given, it specifies the name of the user whose crontab is to be tweaked. If this option is not given, crontab examines your crontab, that is, the crontab of the person executing the command. Note that *su*(8) can confuse crontab and that if you are running inside of *su*(8) you should always use the *-u* option for safety's sake.

The first form of this command is used to install a new crontab from some named file or standard input if the pseudo-filename '-' is given.

The *-l* option causes the current crontab to be displayed on standard output.

The *-r* option causes the current crontab to be removed.

The -e option is used to edit the current crontab using the editor specified by the VISUAL or EDITOR environment variables. After you exit from the editor, the modified crontab will be installed automatically.

SEE ALSO

crontab(5), cron(8)

FILES

/etc/cron.allow

/etc/cron.deny

STANDARDS

The crontab command conforms to IEEE Std1003.2-1992 ('POSIX'). This new command syntax differs from previous versions of Vixie Cron, as well as from the classic SVR3 syntax.

DIAGNOSTICS

A fairly informative usage message appears if you run it with a bad command line.

AUTHOR

Paul Vixie paul@vix.com

DF

NAME

df—Report file system disk space usage.

SYNOPSIS

df [OPTION]... [FILE]...

DESCRIPTION

This manual page documents the GNU version of df. df displays the amount of disk space available on the file system containing each filename argument. If no filename is given, the space available on all currently mounted file systems is shown. Disk space is shown in 1K blocks by default unless the environment variable POSIXLY_CORRECT is set, in which case 512-byte blocks are used.

If an argument is the absolute filename of a disk device node containing a mounted file system, df shows the space available on that file system rather than on the file system containing the device node (which is always the root file system). This version of df cannot show the space available on unmounted file systems because on most kinds of systems, doing so requires very nonportable intimate knowledge of file system structures.

PART

VI

APP

A

OPTIONS

Show information about the file system on which each FILE resides, or all file systems by default.

- -a, --all—Includes file systems having 0 blocks
- --block-size=SIZE—Uses SIZE-byte blocks
- -h, --human-readable—Prints sizes in human readable format (for example, 1K 234M 2G)
- -H, --si—Likewise, but uses powers of 1000 not 1024
- -i, --inodes—Lists inode information instead of block usage
- -k, --kilobytes—Like --block-size=1024
- -l, --local—Limits listing to local file systems
- -m, --megabytes—Like --block-size=1048576
- --no-sync—Does not invoke sync before getting usage info (default)
- -P, --portability—Uses the POSIX output format
- --sync—Invokes sync before getting usage info
- -t, --type=TYPE—Limits listing to file systems of type TYPE
- -T, --print-type—Prints file system type
- -x, --exclude-type=TYPE—Limits listing to file systems not of type TYPE
- -v—(ignored)
- --help—Displays this help and exits
- --version—Outputs version information and exits

REPORTING BUGS

Report bugs to <bug-fileutils@gnu.org>.

SEE ALSO

The full documentation for df is maintained as a Texinfo manual. If the info and df programs are properly installed at your site, the command

info df

should give you access to the complete manual.

DU

NAME

du—Estimate file space usage

Synopsis

```
du [OPTION]... [FILE]...
```

Description

Summarize disk usage of each FILE, recursively for directories.

- `-a, --all`—Writes counts for all files, not just directories
- `--block-size=SIZE`—Uses SIZE-byte blocks
- `-b, --bytes`—Produces a grand total
- `-c, --total`—Produces a grand total
- `-D, --dereference-args`—Dereferences PATHs when symbolic link
- `-h, --human-readable`—Prints sizes in human readable format (for example, 1K 234M 2G)
- `-H, --si`—Likewise, but uses powers of 1000 not 1024
- `-k, --kilobytes`—Like –block-size=1024
- `-l, --count-links`—Dereferences all symbolic links
- `-L, --dereference`—Dereferences all symbolic links
- `-m, --megabytes`—Like `--block-size=1048576`
- `-S, --separate-dirs`—Does not include size of subdirectories
- `-s, --summarize`—Displays only a total for each argument
- `-x, -one-file-system`—Skips directories on different file systems
- `-X FILE, --exclude-from=FILE`—Excludes files that match any pattern in FILE
- `--exclude=PAT`—Excludes files that match PAT
- `--max-depth=N`—Prints the total for a directory (or file, with `--all`) only if it is N or fewer levels below the command line argument; `--max-depth=0` is the same as `--summarize`
- `--help`—Displays this help and exits
- `--version`—Outputs version information and exits

Reporting Bugs

Report bugs to <bug-fileutils@gnu.org>.

See Also

The full documentation for du is maintained as a Texinfo manual. If the info and du programs are properly installed at your site, the command

```
info du
```

should give you access to the complete manual.

FDISK

NAME

fdisk—Partition table manipulator for Linux.

SYNOPSIS

fdisk [-u] device

fdisk -l [-u] *device* ...

fdisk -s *partition* ...

fdisk -v

DESCRIPTION

Hard disks can be divided into one or more logical disks called partitions. This division is described in the partition table found in sector 0 of the disk.

In the BSD world, one talks about *disk slices* and a *disk label*.

Linux requires at least one partition, namely for its root file system. It can use swap files or swap partitions, but the latter are more efficient. Usually one will want a second Linux partition dedicated as swap partition. On Intel-compatible hardware, the BIOS that boots the system can often only access the first 1024 cylinders of the disk. For this reason people with large disks often create a third partition, just a few MB in size, typically mounted on /boot, to store the kernel image and a few auxiliary files needed at boot time, to make sure that this is accessible to the BIOS. There can be reasons of security, ease of administration and backup, or testing, to use more than the minimum number of partitions.

fdisk (in the first form of invocation) is a menu-driven program for creation and manipulation of partition tables. It understands DOS-type partition tables and BSD or SUN-type disk labels.

The *device* is usually one of the following:

/dev/hda

/dev/hdb

/dev/sda

/dev/sdb

(/dev/hd[a-h] for IDE disks, /dev/sd[a-p] for SCSI disks, /dev/ed[a-d] for ESDI disks, /dev/xd[ab] for XT disks). A device name refers to the entire disk.

The *partition* is a device name followed by a partition number. For example, /dev/hda1 is the first partition on the first IDE hard disk in the system. IDE disks can have up to 63 partitions, SCSI disks up to 15. See also /usr/src/linux/Documentation/devices.txt.

A BSD/SUN type disk label can describe 8 partitions, the third of which should be a whole disk partition. Do not start a partition that actually uses its first sector (such as a swap partition) at cylinder 0 because that will destroy the disk label.

An IRIX/SGI-type disk label can describe 16 partitions, the eleventh of which should be an entire volume partition, while the ninth should be labeled volume header. The volume header will also cover the partition table, that is, it starts at block zero and extends by default over five cylinders. The remaining space in the volume header can be used by header directory entries. No partitions can overlap with the volume header. Also do not change its type and create some file system on it, because you will lose the partition table. Use this type of label only when working with Linux on IRIX/SGI machines or IRIX/SGI disks under Linux.

A DOS-type partition table can describe an unlimited number of partitions. In sector 0 there is room for the description of four partitions (called primary). One of these can be an extended partition; this is a box holding logical partitions, with descriptors found in a linked list of sectors, each preceding the corresponding logical partitions. The four primary partitions, present or not, get numbers 1-4. Logical partitions start numbering from 5.

In a DOS-type partition table, the starting offset and the size of each partition are stored in two ways: as an absolute number of sectors (given in 32 bits) and as a Cylinders/Heads/ Sectors triple (given in 10+8+6 bits). The former is okay—with 512-byte sectors this will work up to 2TB. The latter has two different problems. First, these C/H/S fields can be filled only when the number of heads and the number of sectors per track are known. Second, even if we know what these numbers should be, the 24 bits that are available do not suffice. DOS uses C/H/S only, Windows uses both, and Linux never uses C/H/S.

If possible, fdisk will obtain the disk geometry automatically. It is not necessarily the physical disk geometry (indeed, modern disks do not really have anything like a physical geometry, certainly not something that can be described in simplistic Cylinders/Heads/ Sectors form), but is the disk geometry that MS-DOS uses for the partition table.

Usually all goes well by default, and there are no problems if Linux is the only system on the disk. However, if the disk must be shared with other operating systems, it is often a good idea to let an fdisk from another operating system make at least one partition. When Linux boots, it looks at the partition table and tries to deduce what (fake) geometry is required for good cooperation with other systems.

Whenever a partition table is printed, a consistency check is performed on the partition table entries. This check verifies that the physical and logical start and end points are identical, and that the partition starts and ends on a cylinder boundary (except for the first partition).

Some versions of MS-DOS create a first partition that does not begin on a cylinder boundary, but on sector two of the first cylinder. Partitions beginning in cylinder one cannot begin on a cylinder boundary, but this is unlikely to cause difficulty unless you have OS/2 on your machine.

PART
VI
APP
A

A sync() and a `BLKRRPART` ioctl() (reread partition table from disk) are performed before exiting when the partition table has been updated. Long ago it was necessary to reboot after the use of `fdisk`. I do not think this is the case anymore—indeed, rebooting too quickly might cause loss of not-yet-written data. Note that both the kernel and the disk hardware can buffer data.

DOS 6.x Warning

The DOS 6.x FORMAT command looks for some information in the first sector of the data area of the partition, and treats this information as more reliable than the information in the partition table. DOS FORMAT expects DOS FDISK to clear the first 512 bytes of the data area of a partition whenever a size change occurs. DOS FORMAT will look at this extra information even if the /U flag is given—we consider this a bug in DOS FORMAT and DOS FDISK.

The bottom line is that if you use `cfdisk` or `fdisk` to change the size of a DOS partition table entry then you must also use `dd` to zero the first 512 bytes of that partition before using DOS FORMAT to format the partition. For example, if you were using `cfdisk` to make a DOS partition table entry for /dev/hda1, (after exiting `fdisk` or `cfdisk` and rebooting Linux so that the partition table information is valid) you would use the command `dd if=/dev/zero of=/dev/hda1 bs=512 count=1` to zero the first 512 bytes of the partition.

Be extremely careful if you use the `dd` command because a small typo can make all the data on your disk useless.

For best results, always use an OS-specific partition table program. For example, create DOS partitions with the DOS FDISK program and Linux partitions with the Linux `fdisk` or Linux `cfdisk` program.

Options

- -v—Prints version number of `fdisk` program and exits.
- -l—Lists the partition tables for /dev/hd[a-d], /dev/sd[a-h], /dev/ed[a-d], and then exits.
- -u—When listing partition tables, gives sizes in sectors instead of cylinders.
- -s partition—The size of the partition (in blocks) is printed on the standard output.

Bugs

Several `fdisk` programs exist and each has its problems and strengths. Try them in the order `cfdisk`, `fdisk`, and `sfdisk`. (Indeed, `cfdisk` is a beautiful program that has strict requirements on the partition tables it accepts, and it produces high-quality partition tables. Use it if you can. `fdisk` is a buggy program that does fuzzy things—usually it produces reasonable results. Its single advantage is that it has some support for BSD disk labels and other non-DOS partition tables. Avoid it if you can. `sfdisk` is for hackers only—the user interface is terrible, but it is more correct than `fdisk` and more powerful than both `fdisk` and `cfdisk`. Moreover, it can be used noninteractively.)

The IRIX/SGI type `disklabel` is currently not supported by the kernel. Moreover, IRIX/SGI header directories are not fully supported yet.

The option `dump partition table to file` is missing.

FIND

NAME

find—Search for files in a directory hierarchy.

SYNOPSIS

find [path...] [expression]

DESCRIPTION

This manual page documents the GNU version of `find`. `find` searches the directory tree rooted at each given filename by evaluating the given expression from left to right, according to the rules of precedence (see section OPERATORS), until the outcome is known (the left-hand side is false for `and` operations, true for `or`), at which point `find` moves on to the next filename.

The first argument that begins with -, (,), , , or ! is taken as the beginning of the expression; any arguments before it are paths to search, and any arguments after it are the rest of the expression. If no paths are given, the current directory is used. If no expression is given, the expression -print is used.

`find` exits with status 0 if all files are processed successfully, greater than 0 if errors occur.

EXPRESSIONS

The expression is made up of options (which affect overall operation rather than the processing of a specific file, and always return true), tests (which return a true or false value), and actions (which have side effects and return a true or false value), all separated by operators. -and is assumed where the operator is omitted. If the expression contains no actions other than -prune, -print is performed on all files for which the expression is true.

OPTIONS

All options always return `true`. They always take effect, rather than being processed only when their place in the expression is reached. Therefore, for clarity, it is best to place them at the beginning of the expression.

- ■ -daystart—Measures times (for -amin, -atime, -cmin, -ctime, -mmin, and -mtime) from the beginning of today rather than from 24 hours ago.

- **-depth**—Processes each directory's contents before the directory itself.

- **-follow**—Dereferences symbolic links. Implies **-noleaf**.

- **-help, --help**—Prints a summary of the command-line usage of **find** and exits.

- **-maxdepth levels**—Descends at most levels (a non-negative integer) of directories below the command-line arguments. **-maxdepth 0** means only apply the tests and actions to the command-line arguments.

- **-mindepth levels**—Does not apply any tests or actions at levels less than **levels** (a non-negative integer). **-mindepth 1** means process all files except the command-line arguments.

- **-mount**—Does not descend directories on other file systems. An alternate name for **-xdev**, for compatibility with some other versions of **find**.

- **-noleaf**—Does not optimize by assuming that directories contain two fewer subdirectories than their hard link count. This option is needed when searching file systems that do not follow the UNIX directory link convention, such as CD-ROM or MS-DOS file systems or AFS volume mount points. Each directory on a normal UNIX file system has at least two hard links: its name and its entry. Additionally, its subdirectories (if any) each have a .. entry linked to that directory. When **find** is examining a directory, after it has statted two fewer subdirectories than the directory's link count, it knows that the rest of the entries in the directory are non-directories (**leaf** files in the directory tree). If only the files' names need to be examined, there is no need to stat them; this results in a significant increase in search speed.

- **-version, --version**—Do not descend directories on other file systems. Print the **find** version number and exit.

- **-xdev**—Does not descend directories on other file systems.

TESTS

Numeric arguments can be specified as

- **+n**—For greater than n.

- **-n**—For less than n.

- **n**—For exactly n.

- **-amin n**—File was last accessed n minutes ago.

- **-anewer file**—File was last accessed more recently than **file** was modified. **-anewer** is affected by **-follow** only if **-follow** comes before **-anewer** on the command line.

- **-atime n**—File was last accessed n*24 hours ago.

- **-cmin n**—File's status was last changed n minutes ago.

- **-cnewer file**—File's status was last changed more recently than **file** was modified. **-cnewer** is affected by **-follow** only if **-follow** comes before **-cnewer** on the command line.

- **-ctime n**—File's status was last changed n*24 hours ago.

- -empty—File is empty and is either a regular file or a directory.

- -false—Always false.

- -fstype type—File is on a file system of type type. The valid file system types vary among different versions of UNIX; an incomplete list of file system types that are accepted on one version of UNIX or another is: ufs, 4.2, 4.3, nfs, tmp, mfs, S51K, S52K. You can use -printf with the %F directive to see the types of your file systems.

- -gid n—File's numeric group ID is n.

- -group gname—File belongs to group gname (numeric group ID allowed).

- -ilname pattern—Like -lname, but the match is not case sensitive.

- -iname pattern—Like -name, but the match is not case sensitive. For example, the patterns 'fo*' and 'F??' match the filenames 'Foo', 'FOO', 'foo', 'fOo', and so forth.

- -inum n—File has inode number n.

- -ipath pattern—Like -path, but the match is not case sensitive.

- -iregex pattern—Like -regex, but the match is not case sensitive.

- -links n—File has n links.

- -lname pattern—File is a symbolic link whose contents match shell pattern pattern. The metacharacters do not treat '/' or '.' in a special way.

- -mmin n—File's data was last modified n minutes ago.

- -mtime n—File's data was last modified n*24 hours ago.

- -name pattern—Base of filename (the path with the leading directories removed) matches shell pattern pattern. The metacharacters ('*', '?', and '[]') do not match a '.' at the start of the base name. To ignore a directory and the files under it, use -prune; see an example in the description of -path.

- -newer file—File was modified more recently than file. -newer is affected by -follow only if -follow comes before -newer on the command line.

- -nouser—No user corresponds to file's numeric user ID.

- -nogroup—No group corresponds to file's numeric group ID.

- -path pattern—Filename matches shell pattern pattern. The metacharacters do not treat '/' or '.' in a special way; so, for example,

  ```
  find . -path './sr*sc'
  ```

  will print an entry for a directory called './src/misc' (if one exists). To ignore a whole directory tree, use -prune rather than checking every file in the tree. For example, to skip the directory 'src/emacs' and all files and directories under it, and print the names of the other files found, do something like this:

  ```
  find . -path './src/emacs' -prune -o -print
  ```

- -perm mode—File's permission bits are exactly mode (octal or symbolic). Symbolic modes use mode 0 as a point of departure.

- -perm -mode—All the permission bits mode are set for the file.

PART

VI

APP

A

- ■ -perm +mode—Any of the permission bits mode are set for the file.

- ■ -regex pattern—Filename matches regular expression pattern. This is a match on the whole path, not a search. For example, to match a file named ./fubar3, use the regular expression .*bar. or .*b.*3, but not b.*r3.

- ■ -size n[bckw]—File uses n units of space. The units are 512-byte blocks by default or if b follows n, bytes if c follows n, kilobytes if k follows n, or 2-byte words if w follows n. The size does not count indirect blocks, but does count blocks in sparse files that are not actually allocated.

- ■ -true—Always true.

- ■ -type c—File is of type c:.

- ■ b—Block (buffered) special.

- ■ c—Character (unbuffered) special.

- ■ d—Directory.

- ■ p—Named pipe (FIFO).

- ■ f—Regular file.

- ■ l—Symbolic link.

- ■ s—Socket.

- ■ -uid n—File's numeric user ID is n.

- ■ -used n—File was last accessed n days after its status was last changed.

- ■ -user uname—File is owned by user uname (numeric user ID allowed).

- ■ -xtype c—The same as -type unless the file is a symbolic link. For symbolic links: if -follow has not been given, true if the file is a link to a file of type c; if -follow has been given, true if c is l. In other words, for symbolic links, -xtype checks the type of the file that -type does not check.

ACTIONS

- ■ -exec command ;—Execute command; true if 0 status is returned. All following arguments to find are taken to be arguments to the command until an argument consisting of ; is encountered. The string {} is replaced by the current filename being processed everywhere it occurs in the arguments to the command, not just in arguments where it is alone, as in some versions of find. Both these constructions might need to be escaped (with a \) or quoted to protect them from expansion by the shell. The command is executed in the starting directory.

- ■ -fls file—True; like -ls but write to file like -fprint.

- ■ -fprint file—True; print the full filename into file file. If file does not exist when find is run, it is created; if it does exist, it is truncated. The filenames /dev/stdout and /dev/stderr are handled specially; they refer to the standard output and standard error output, respectively.

- ■ -fprint0 file—True; like -print0 but write to file like -fprint.

- -fprintf file format—True; like -printf but write to file like -fprint.
- -ok command ;—Like -exec but ask the user first (on the standard input); if the response does not start with 'y' or 'Y', do not run the command, and return false.
- -print—True; print the full filename on the standard output, followed by a new line.
- -print0—True; print the full filename on the standard output, followed by a null character. This allows filenames that contain new lines to be correctly interpreted by programs that process the find output.
- -printf format—True; print format on the standard output, interpreting '\' escapes and '%' directives. Field widths and precisions can be specified as with the 'printf' C function. Unlike -print, -printf does not add a new line at the end of the string. The escapes and directives are:
  - \a—Alarm bell
  - \b—Backspace
  - \c—Stop printing from this format immediately and flush the output
  - \f—Form feed
  - \n—Newline
  - \r—Carriage return
  - \t—Horizontal tab
  - \v—Vertical tab
  - \\—A literal backslash (\)

A \ character followed by any other character is treated as an ordinary character, so they both are printed.

- %%—A literal percent sign.
- %a—File's last access time in the format returned by the C ctime function.
- %Ak—File's last access time in the format specified by k, which is either @ or a directive for the C strftime function. The possible values for k are listed in the following text; some of them might not be available on all systems, due to differences in strftime between systems.
  - @
  - Seconds since Jan. 1, 1970, 00:00 GMT—Time fields:
  - H—Hour (00..23)
  - I—Hour (01..12)
  - k—Hour (0..23)
  - l—Hour (1..12)
  - M—Minute (00..59)
  - p—locale's AM or PM
  - r—time, 12-hour (hh:mm:ss [AP]M)

- s—Second (00..61)
- t—Time, 24-hour (hh:mm:ss)
- x—Locale's time representation (H:M:S)
- z—Time zone (for example, EDT), or nothing if no time zone is determinable

Date fields:

- a—Locale's abbreviated weekday name (Sun..Sat)
- A—Locale's full weekday name, variable length (Sunday..Saturday)
- b—Locale's abbreviated month name (Jan..Dec)
- B—Locale's full month name, variable length (January..December)
- c—Locale's date and time (Sat Nov 04 12:02:33 EST 1989)
- d—Day of month (01..31)
- D—Date (mm/dd/yy)
- h—Same as b
- j—Day of year (001..366)
- m—Month (01..12)
- U—Week number of year with Sunday as first day of week (00..53)
- w—Day of week (0..6)
- W—Week number of year with Monday as first day of week (00..53)
- x—Locale's date representation (mm/dd/yy)
- y—Last two digits of year (00..99)
- Y—Year (1970...)
- %b—File's size in 512-byte blocks (rounded up).
- %c—File's last status change time in the format returned by the C ctime function.
- %Ck—File's last status change time in the format specified by k, which is the same as for %A.
- %d—File's depth in the directory tree; 0 means the file is a command line argument.
- %f—File's name with any leading directories removed (only the last element).
- %F—Type of the file system the file is on; this value can be used for -fstype.
- %g—File's group name, or numeric group ID if the group has no name.
- %G—File's numeric group ID.
- %h—Leading directories of file's name (all but the last element).
- %H—Command-line argument under which file was found.
- %i—File's inode number (in decimal).
- %k—File's size in 1K blocks (rounded up).

- %l—Object of symbolic link (empty string if file is not a symbolic link).
- %m—File's permission bits (in octal).
- %n—Number of hard links to file.
- %p—File's name.
- %P—File's name with the name of the command-line argument under which it was found removed.
- %s—File's size in bytes.
- %t—File's last modification time in the format returned by the C 'ctime' function.
- %Tk—File's last modification time in the format specified by k, which is the same as for %A.
- %u—File's username, or numeric user ID if the user has no name.
- %U—File's numeric user ID.

A % character followed by any other character is discarded (but the other character is printed).

- -prune—If -depth is not given, true; does not descend the current directory. If -depth is given, false; no effect.
- -ls—True; list current file in ls -dils format on standard output. The block counts are of 1K blocks unless the environment variable POSIXLY_CORRECT is set, in which case 512-byte blocks are used.

OPERATORS

Listed in order of decreasing precedence:

- (expr)—Force precedence
- ! expr—True if expr is false
- -not expr—Same as ! expr
- expr1 expr2—And (implied); expr2 is not evaluated if expr1 is false
- expr1 -a expr2—Same as expr1 expr2
- expr1 -and expr2—Same as expr1 expr2
- expr1 -o expr2—Or; expr2 is not evaluated if expr1 is true
- expr1 -or expr2—Same as expr1 -o expr2
- expr1 , expr2—List; both expr1 and expr2 are always evaluated. The value of expr1 is discarded; the value of the list is the value of expr2.

SEE ALSO

locate(1L), locatedb(5L), updatedb(1L), xargs(1L) Finding Files (online in Info, or printed)

PART VI

APP A

GREP

NAME

`grep, egrep, fgrep`—Print lines matching a pattern.

SYNOPSIS

```
grep [-[AB] NUM] [-CEFGVabchiLlnqrsvwxyUu] [-e PATTERN ¦ -f FILE] [-d ACTION]
[--directories=ACTION] [--extended-regexp] [--fixed-strings] [--basic-regexp]
[--regexp=PATTERN] [--file=FILE] [--ignore-case] [--word-regexp] [--line-regexp]
[--line-regexp] [--no-messages] [--revert-match] [--version] [--help] [--byte-offset]
[--line-number] [--with-filename] [--no-filename] [--quiet] [--silent] [--text]
[--files-without-match] [--files-with-matcces] [--count] [--before-context=NUM]
[--after-context=NUM] [--context] [-binary] [--unix-byte-offsets] [--recursive]
files...
```

DESCRIPTION

grep searches the named input *files* (or standard input if no files are named, or the filename - is given) for lines containing a match to the given *pattern*. By default, grep prints the matching lines.

Three major variants of grep are controlled by the following options:

- -G, --basic-regexp—Interpret pattern as a basic regular expression (see the following). This is the default.
- -E, --extended-regexp—Interpret pattern as an extended regular expression (see the following).
- -F, --fixed-strings—Interpret pattern as a list of fixed strings, separated by newlines, any of which are to be matched.

In addition, two variant programs, egrep and fgrep, are available. egrep is similar (but not identical) to grep-E, and is compatible with the historical UNIX egrep. Fgrep is the same as grep-F.

All variants of grep understand the following options:

- -A NUM, --after-context=NUM—Print NUM lines of trailing context after matching lines.
- -B NUM, --before-context=NUM—Print NUM lines of leading context before matching lines.
- -C, --context[=NUM]—Print NUM lines (default 2) of output context.
- -NUM—Same as --context=NUM lines of leading and trailing context. However, grep will never print any given line more than once.

- -V, --version—Print the version number of grep to standard error. This version number should be included in all bug reports (see below).

- -b, --byte-offset—Print the byte offset within the input file before each line of output.

- -c, --count—Suppress normal output; instead print a count of matching lines for each input file. With the -v, --revert-match option (see below), count non-matching lines.

- -d ACTION, --directories=ACTION—If an input file is a directory, use ACTION to process it. By default, ACTION is read, which means that directories are read just as if they were ordinary files. If ACTION is skip, directories are silently skipped. If ACTION is recurse, grep reads all files under each directory, recursively; this is equivalent to the -r option.

- -e PATTERN, --regexp=PATTERN—Use PATTERN as the pattern; useful to protect patterns beginning with -.

- -f FILE, --file=FILE—Obtain patterns from FILE, one per line. The empty file contains zero patterns, and therefore matches nothing.

- -h, --no-filename—Suppress the prefixing of filenames on output when multiple files are searched.

- -i, --ignore-case—Ignore case distinctions in both the pattern and the input files.

- -L, --files-without-match—Suppress normal output; instead print the name of each input file from which no output would normally have been printed. The scanning will stop on the first match.

- -l, --files-with-matches—Suppress normal output; instead print the name of each input file from which output would normally have been printed. The scanning will stop on the first match.

- -n, --line-number—Prefix each line of output with the line number within its input file.

- -q, --quiet, --silent—Quiet; suppress normal output. The scanning will stop on the first match. Also see the -s or --no-messages option below.

- -r, --recursive—Read all files under each directory, recursively; this is equivalent to the -d recurse option.

- -s, --no-messages—Suppress error messages about nonexistent or unreadable files. Portability note: unlike GNU grep, BSD grep does not comply with POSIX.2, because BSD grep lacks a -q option and its -s option behaves like GNU grep's -q option. Shell scripts intended to be portable to BSD grep should avoid both -q and -s and should redirect output to /dev/null instead.

- -a, --text—Do not suppress output lines that contain binary data. Normally, if the first few bytes of a file indicate that the file contains binary data, grep outputs only a message saying that the file matches the pattern. This option causes grep to act as if the file is a text file, even if it would otherwise be treated as binary.

- -v, --revert-match—Invert the sense of matching, to select non-matching lines.

- `-w`, `--word-regexp`—Select only those lines containing matches that form whole words. The test is that the matching substring must either be at the beginning of the line, or preceded by a non-word constituent character. Similarly, it must be either at the end of the line or followed by a non-word constituent character. Word-constituent characters are letters, digits, and the underscore.

- `-x`, `--line-regexp`—Select only those matches that exactly match the whole line.

- `-y`—Obsolete synonym for `-i`.

- `-U`, `--binary`—Treat the file(s) as binary. By default, under MS-DOS and MS-Windows, `grep` guesses the file type by looking at the contents of the first 32KB read from the file. If `grep` decides the file is a text file, it strips the CR characters from the original file contents (to make regular expressions with `^` and `$` work correctly). Specifying `-U` overrules this guesswork, causing all files to be read and passed to the matching mechanism verbatim; if the file is a text file with CR/LF pairs at the end of each line, this will cause some regular expressions to fail. This option is only supported on MS-DOS and MS-Windows.

- `-u`, `--unix-byte-offsets`—Report UNIX-style byte offsets. This switch causes `grep` to report byte offsets as if the file were a UNIX-style text file, that is, with CR characters stripped off. This will produce results identical to running `grep` on a UNIX machine. This option has no effect unless the `-b` option is also used; it is only supported on MS-DOS and MS-Windows.

REGULAR EXPRESSIONS

A regular expression is a pattern that describes a set of strings. Regular expressions are constructed analogously to arithmetic expressions by using various operators to combine smaller expressions.

Grep understands two different versions of regular expression syntax: basic and extended. In GNUgrep, there is no difference in available functionality using either syntax. In other implementations, basic regular expressions are less powerful. The following description applies to extended regular expressions; differences for basic regular expressions are summarized afterward.

The fundamental building blocks are the regular expressions that match a single character. Most characters, including all letters and digits, are regular expressions that match themselves. Any metacharacter with special meaning can be quoted by preceding it with a backslash.

A list of characters enclosed by `[` and `]` matches any single character in that list; if the first character of the list is the caret `^` then it matches any character *not* in the list. For example, the regular expression `[0123456789]` matches any single digit. A range of ASCII characters can be specified by giving the first and last characters, separated by a hyphen. Finally, certain named classes of characters are predefined. Their names are self-explanatory, and they are `[:alnum:]`, `[:alpha:]`, `[:cntrl:]`, `[:digit:]`, `[:graph:]`, `[:lower:]`, `[:print:]`, `[:punct:]`,

[:space:], [:upper:], and [:xdigit:]. For example, [[:alnum:]] means [0-9A-Za-z], except the latter form is dependent upon the ASCII character encoding, whereas the former is portable. (Note that the brackets in these class names are part of the symbolic names, and must be included in addition to the brackets delimiting the bracket list.) Most metacharacters lose their special meaning inside lists. To include a literal] place it first in the list. Similarly, to include a literal ^ place it anywhere but first. Finally, to include a literal - place it last.

The period . matches any single character. The symbol \w is a synonym for [[:alnum:]] and \W is a synonym for [^[:alnum]].

The caret ^ and the dollar sign $ are metacharacters that respectively match the empty string at the beginning and end of a line. The symbols \< and \> respectively match the empty string at the beginning and end of a word. The symbol \b matches the empty string at the edge of a word, and \B matches the empty string provided it's *not* at the edge of a word.

A regular expression can be followed by one of several repetition operators:

- ?—The preceding item will be matched zero or more times. The preceding item is optional and matched at most once.
- *—The preceding item will be matched zero or more times.
- +—The preceding item will be matched one or more times.
- {n}—The preceding item is matched exactly n times.
- {n,}—The preceding item is matched n or more times.
- {,m}—The preceding item is optional and is matched at most m times.
- {n,m}—The preceding item is matched at least n times, but not more than m times.

Two regular expressions can be concatenated; the resulting regular expression matches any string formed by concatenating two substrings that respectively match the concatenated subexpressions.

Two regular expressions can be joined by the infix operator ¦; the resulting regular expression matches any string matching either subexpression.

Repetition takes precedence over concatenation, which in turn takes precedence over alternation. A whole subexpression can be enclosed in parentheses to override these precedence rules.

The back reference \n, where n is a single digit, matches the substring previously matched by the nth parenthesized subexpression of the regular expression.

In basic regular expressions the metacharacters ?, +, {, ¦, (, and) lose their special meaning; instead use the backslashed versions \?, \+, \{, \¦, \(, and \).

In egrep the metacharacter { loses its special meaning; instead use \{.

DIAGNOSTICS

Normally, exit status is 0 if matches were found, and 1 if no matches were found. (The -v option inverts the sense of the exit status.) Exit status is 2 if there were syntax errors in the pattern, inaccessible input files, or other system errors.

BUGS

Email bug reports to bug-gnu-utils@gnu.org. Be sure to include the word grep somewhere in the Subject: field.

Large repetition counts in the {m,n} construct can cause grep to use lots of memory. In addition, certain other obscure regular expressions require exponential time and space, and can cause grep to run out of memory.

Back references are very slow, and can require exponential time.

GZIP

NAME

gzip, gunzip, zcat—Compress or expand files.

SYNOPSIS

gzip [-acdfhlLnNrtvV19] [-Ssuffix] [name ...]

gunzip [-acfhlLnNrtvV] [-Ssuffix] [name ...]

zcat [-fhLV] [name ...]

DESCRIPTION

gzip reduces the size of the named files using Lempel-Ziv coding (LZ77). Whenever possible, each file is replaced by one with the extension .gz, while keeping the same ownership modes, access, and modification times. (The default extension is -gz for VMS, z for MSDOS, OS/2 FAT, Windows NT FAT, and Atari.) If no files are specified, or if a filename is -, the standard input is compressed to the standard output. gzip will only attempt to compress regular files. In particular, it will ignore symbolic links.

If the compressed filename is too long for its file system, gzip truncates it. gzip attempts to truncate only the parts of the filename longer than 3 characters. (A part is delimited by dots.) If the name consists of small parts only, the longest parts are truncated. For example, if filenames are limited to 14 characters, gzip.msdos.exe is compressed to gzi.msd.exe.gz. Names are not truncated on systems that do not have a limit on filename length.

By default, gzip keeps the original filename and time stamp in the compressed file. These are used when decompressing the file with the -N option. This is useful when the compressed filename was truncated or when the time stamp was not preserved after a file transfer.

Compressed files can be restored to their original form using gzip -d or gunzip or zcat. If the original name saved in the compressed file is not suitable for its file system, a new name is constructed from the original one to make it legal.

gunzip takes a list of files on its command line and replaces each file with a name ending in .gz, -gz, .z, -z, _z or .Z and which begins with the correct magic number with an uncompressed file without the original extension. gunzip also recognizes the special extensions .tgz and .taz as shorthands for .tar.gz and .tar.Z respectively. When compressing, gzip uses the .tgz extension if necessary instead of truncating a file with a .tar extension.

gunzip can currently decompress files created by gzip, zip, compress, compress -H or pack. The detection of the input format is automatic. When using the first two formats, gunzip checks a 32 bit CRC. For pack, gunzip checks the uncompressed length. The standard compress format was not designed to allow consistency checks. However gunzip is sometimes able to detect a bad .Z file. If you get an error when uncompressing a .Z file, do not assume that the .Z file is correct simply because the standard uncompress does not complain. This generally means that the standard uncompress does not check its input, and happily generates garbage output. The SCO compress -H format (lzh compression method) does not include a CRC but also allows some consistency checks.

Files created by zip can be uncompressed by gzip only if they have a single member compressed with the *deflation* method. This feature is only intended to help conversion of tar.zip files to the tar.gz format. To extract zip files with several members, use unzip instead of gunzip.

zcat is identical to gunzip -c. (On some systems, zcat can be installed as gzcat to preserve the original link to *compress*.) zcat uncompresses either a list of files on the command line or its standard input and writes the uncompressed data on standard output. zcat will uncompress files that have the correct magic number whether they have a .gz suffix or not.

gzip uses the Lempel-Ziv algorithm used in zip and PKZIP. The amount of compression obtained depends on the size of the input and the distribution of common substrings. Typically, text such as source code or English is reduced by 60-70%. Compression is generally much better than that achieved by LZW (as used in compress), Huffman coding (as used in pack), or adaptive Huffman coding (compact).

Compression is always performed, even if the compressed file is slightly larger than the original. The worst case expansion is a few bytes for the gzip file header, plus 5 bytes every 32K block, or an expansion ratio of 0.015% for large files. Note that the actual number of used disk blocks almost never increases. gzip preserves the mode, ownership, and time stamps of files when compressing or decompressing.

PART

VI

APP

A

OPTIONS

- `-a --ascii`—ASCII text mode: convert end-of-lines using local conventions. This option is supported only on some non-UNIX systems. For MSDOS, CR LF is converted to LF when compressing, and LF is converted to CR LF when decompressing.

- `-c --stdout --to-stdout`—Write output on standard output; keep original files unchanged. If there are several input files, the output consists of a sequence of independently compressed members. To obtain better compression, concatenate all input files before compressing them.

- `-d --decompress --uncompress`—Decompress.

- `-f --force`—Force compression or decompression even if the file has multiple links or the corresponding file already exists, or if the compressed data is read from or written to a terminal. If the input data is not in a format recognized by `gzip`, and if the option `--stdout` is also given, copy the input data without change to the standard output: Let zcat behave as cat. If `-f` is not given, and when not running in the background, `gzip` prompts to verify whether an existing file should be overwritten.

- `-h --help`—Display a help screen and quit.

- `-l --list`—For each compressed file, list the following fields:

  `compressedsize:sizeofthecompressedfile`

  `uncompressedsize:sizeoftheuncompressedfile`

  `ratio:compressionratio(0.0%ifunknown)`

  `uncompressed_name:nameoftheuncompressedfile`

The uncompressed size is given as `-1` for files not in `gzip` format, such as compressed `.z` files. To get the uncompressed size for such a file, use:

`zcatfile.Z¦wc-c`

In combination with the `--verbose` option, the following fields are also displayed:

`method:compressionmethod`

`crc:the32-bitCRCoftheuncompresseddata`

`date&time:timestampfortheuncompressedfile`

The compression methods currently supported are deflate, compress, lzh (SCO compress -H) and pack. The crc is given as ffffffff for a file not in `gzip` format.

With `--name`, the uncompressed name, date, and time are those stored within the compress file if present.

With `--verbose`, the size totals and compression ratio for all files are also displayed, unless some sizes are unknown. With `-quiet`, the title and totals lines are not displayed.

- -L --license—Display the gzip license and quit.

- -n --no-name—When compressing, do not save the original filename and time stamp by default. (The original name is always saved if the name had to be truncated.) When decompressing, do not restore the original filename if present (remove only the gzip suffix from the compressed filename) and do not restore the original time stamp if present (copy it from the compressed file). This option is the default when decompressing.

- -N --name—When compressing, always save the original filename and time stamp; this is the default. When decompressing, restore the original filename and time stamp if present. This option is useful on systems which have a limit on filename length or when the time stamp has been lost after a file transfer.

- -q --quiet—Suppress all warnings.

- -r --recursive—Travel the directory structure recursively. If any of the filenames specified on the command line are directories, gzip will descend into the directory and compress all the files it finds there (or decompress them in the case of gunzip).

- -S .suf --suffix .suf—Use suffix .suf instead of .gz. Any suffix can be given, but suffixes other than .z and .gz should not be used to avoid confusion when files are transferred to other systems. A null suffix forces gunzip to try decompression on all given files regardless of suffix, as in:

- gunzip -S '' * (*.* for MSDOS)—Previous versions of gzip used the .z suffix. This was changed to avoid a conflict with pack(1).

- -t --test—Test. Check the compressed file integrity.

- -v --verbose—Verbose. Display the name and percentage reduction for each file compressed or decompressed.

- -V --version—Version. Display the version number and compilation options then quit.

- -# --fast --best—Regulate the speed of compression using the specified digit #, where -1 or --fast indicates the fastest compression method (less compression) and -9 or --best indicates the slowest compression method (best compression). The default compression level is -6 (that is, biased towards high compression at expense of speed).

ADVANCED USE

Multiple compressed files can be concatenated. In this case, gunzip will extract all members at once. For example:

```
gzip -c file1 > foo.gz
gzip -c file2 >> foo.gz
```

PART

VI

APP

A

Then

```
gunzip -c foo
```

is equivalent to

```
cat file1 file2
```

In case of damage to one member of a .gz file, other members can still be recovered (if the damaged member is removed). However, you can get better compression by compressing all members at once:

```
cat file1 file2 ¦ gzip > foo.gz
```

compresses better than

```
gzip -c file1 file2 > foo.gz
```

If you want to recompress concatenated files to get better compression, do:

```
gzip -cd old.gz ¦ gzip > new.gz
```

If a compressed file consists of several members, the uncompressed size and CRC reported by the --list option applies to the last member only. If you need the uncompressed size for all members, use:

```
gzip -cd file.gz ¦ wc -c
```

To create a single archive file with multiple members so members can later be extracted independently, use an archiver such as tar or zip. GNU tar supports the -z option to invoke gzip transparently. gzip is designed as a complement to tar, not as a replacement.

ENVIRONMENT

The environment variable GZIP can hold a set of default options for gzip. These options are interpreted first and can be overwritten by explicit command-line parameters. For example:

```
for sh: GZIP='-8v --name'; export GZIP
```

```
for csh: setenv GZIP '-8v --name'
```

```
for MSDOS: set GZIP=-8v --name
```

On Vax/VMS, the name of the environment variable is GZIP_OPT, to avoid a conflict with the symbol set for invocation of the program.

SEE ALSO

```
znew(1), zcmp(1), zmore(1), zforce(1), gzexe(1), zip(1),
```

```
unzip(1), compress(1), pack(1), compact(1)
```

DIAGNOSTICS

Exit status is normally 0; if an error occurs, exit status is 1. If a warning occurs, exit status is 2.

The following is possible usage:

- `gzip [-cdfhlLnNrtvV19] [-S suffix] [file ...]`

  Invalid options were specified on the command line.

- `file: not in gzip format`

  The file specified to `gunzip` has not been compressed.

- `file: corrupt input`

  Use `zcat` to recover some data. The compressed file has been damaged. The data up to the point of failure can be recovered using `zcat file > recover`.

- `file: compressed with xx bits, can only handle yy bits`

  `file` was compressed (using LZW) by a program that could deal with more bits than the decompress code on this machine. Recompress the file with `gzip`, which compresses better and uses less memory.

- `file: already has .gz suffix – no change`

  The file is assumed to be already compressed. Rename the file and try again.

- `file already exists; do you wish to overwrite (y or n)?`

  Respond y if you want the output file to be replaced; n if not.

- `gunzip: corrupt input`

  A `SIGSEGV` violation was detected, which usually means that the input file has been corrupted.

- `xx.x% percentage of the input saved by compression. (Relevant`
  `➥only for -v and -l.) -- not a regular file or directory: ignored`

  When the input file is not a regular file or directory, (for example, a symbolic link, socket, FIFO, or device file), it is left unaltered.

- `--has xx other links: unchanged`

  The input file has links; it is left unchanged. See `ln(1)` for more information. Use the `-f` flag to force compression of multiple-linked files.

CAVEATS

When writing compressed data to a tape, it is generally necessary to pad the output with zeroes up to a block boundary. When the data is read and the whole block is passed to `gunzip` for decompression, `gunzip` detects that there is extra trailing garbage after the compressed data and emits a warning by default. You must use the `--quiet` option to suppress the warning. This option can be set in the `GZIP` environment variable as in:

```
for sh: GZIP='-q' tar -xfz --block-compress /dev/rst0
```

```
for csh: (setenv GZIP -q; tar -xfz --block-compr /dev/rst0
```

In the previous example, `gzip` is invoked implicitly by the `-z` option of GNU `tar`. Make sure that the same block size (`-b` option of `tar`) is used for reading and writing compressed data on tapes. (This example assumes you are using the GNU version of `tar`.)

BUGS

The `--list` option reports incorrect sizes if they exceed 2 gigabytes. The `--list` option reports sizes as -1 and crc as ffffffff if the compressed file is on a non-seekable media.

In some rare cases, the `--best` option gives worse compression than the default compression level (-6). On some highly redundant files, `compress` compresses better than `gzip`.

HALT

NAME

`halt, reboot, poweroff`—Stop the system.

SYNOPSIS

`/sbin/halt [-n] [-w] [-d] [-f] [-i] [-p]`

`/sbin/reboot [-n] [-w] [-d] [-f] [-i]`

`/sbin/poweroff [-n] [-w] [-d] [-f] [-i]`

DESCRIPTION

`halt` notes that the system is being brought down in the file `/var/log/wtmp`, and then either tells the kernel to halt, reboot, or power off the system. If `halt` or `reboot` is called when the system is not in runlevel `0` or `6`, shutdown(8) will be invoked instead (with the flag `-h` or `-r`).

OPTIONS

- `-n`—Don't sync before reboot or halt.
- `-w`—Don't actually reboot or halt but only write the wtmp record (in the `/var/log/wtmp` file).
- `-d`—Don't write the wtmp record. The `-n` flag implies `-d`.
- `-f`—Force halt or reboot, don't call shutdown(8).
- `-i`—Shut down all network interfaces just before halt or reboot.
- `-p`—When halting the system, do a poweroff. This is the default when halt is called as `poweroff`.

DIAGNOSTICS

If you're not the super-user, you will get the message must be superuser.

NOTES

Under previous `sysvinit` releases, `reboot` and `halt` should never be called directly. From this release on `halt` and `reboot`, invoke shutdown(8) if the system is not in runlevel 0 or 6.

AUTHOR

Miquel van Smoorenburg, miquels@cistron.nl

SEE ALSO

shutdown(8), init(1)

KILL

NAME

kill—Terminate a process.

SYNOPSIS

kill [-s signal ¦ -p] [-a] pid ...

kill -l [signal]

DESCRIPTION

kill sends the specified signal to the specified process. If no signal is specified, the TERM signal is sent. The TERM signal will kill processes that do not catch this signal. For other processes, it can be necessary to use the KILL (9) signal, because this signal cannot be caught.

Most modern shells have a built-in kill function.

OPTIONS

- pid ...—Specify the list of processes that kill should signal. Each pid can be one of four things: a process name, where processes called will be signaled; n, where n is larger than 0 (the process with pid n will be signaled); -1, where all processes from MAX_INT to 2 will be signaled, as allowed by the issuing user; or -n where n is larger than 1, in which case processes in process group n are signaled. If a negative argument is given, the signal must be specified first; otherwise it will be taken as the signal to send.

- -s—Specify the signal to send. The signal can be given as a signal name or number.

- -p—Specify that kill should only print the process id (pid) of the named process, and should not send it a signal.

- -l—Print a list of signal names. These are found in /usr/include/linux/signal.h.

SEE ALSO

bash(1), tcsh(1), kill(2), sigvec(2)

PART

VI

APP

A

AUTHOR

Taken from BSD 4.4. The capability to translate process names to process ids was added by Salvatore Valente <svalente@mit.edu>.

LN

NAME

ln—Make links between files.

SYNOPSIS

```
ln [OPTION]... TARGET [LINK_NAME]
ln [OPTION]... TARGET... DIRECTORY
```

DESCRIPTION

Create a link to the specified TARGET with optional LINK_NAME. If there is more than one TARGET, the last argument must be a directory; create links in DIRECTORY to each TARGET. Create hard links by default, symbolic links with --symbolic. When creating hard links, each TARGET must exist.

- -b, --backup—Make a backup of each existing destination file
- -d, -F, --directory—Hard link directories (super-user only)
- -f, --force—Remove existing destination files
- -n, --no-dereference—Treat destination that is a symlink to a directory as if it were a normal file
- -i, --interactive—Prompt whether to remove destinations
- -s, --symbolic—Make symbolic links instead of hard links
- -S, --suffix=SUFFIX—Override the usual backup suffix
- -v, --verbose—Print name of each file before linking
- -V, --version-control=WORD—Override the usual version control
- --help—Display this help and exit
- --version—Output version information and exit

The backup suffix is ~, unless set with SIMPLE_BACKUP_SUFFIX. The version control can be set with VERSION_CONTROL, values are:

t, numbered

make numbered backups

nil, existing

numbered if numbered backups exist, simple otherwise

never, simple

always make simple backups

REPORTING BUGS

Report bugs to <bug-fileutils@gnu.org>.

SEE ALSO

The full documentation for ln is maintained as a Texinfo manual. If the info and ln programs are properly installed at your site, the command

info ln

should give you access to the complete manual.

LS

NAME

ls—List directory contents.

SYNOPSIS

ls [OPTION]... [FILE]...

DESCRIPTION

List information about the FILEs (the current directory by default). Sort entries alphabetically if none of -cftuSUX or --sort.

- -a, --all—Do not hide entries starting with .
- -A, --almost-all—Do not list implied . and ..
- -b, --escape—Print octal escapes for non-graphic characters
- --block-size=SIZE—Use SIZE-byte blocks
- -B, --ignore-backups—Do not list implied entries ending with ~
- -c—Sort by change time; with -l: show ctime
- -C—List entries by columns
- --color[=WHEN]—Control whether color is used to distinguish file types. WHEN can be 'never', 'always', or 'auto'
- -d, --directory—List directory entries instead of contents
- -D, –dired—Generate output designed for Emacs' dired mode
- -f—Do not sort, enable -aU, disable -lst
- -F, --classify—Append indicator (one of */=@¦) to entries

PART

VI

APP

A

- --format=WORD—Across -x, commas -m, horizontal -x, long -l, single-column -1, verbose -l, vertical -C
- --full-time—List both full date and full time
- -g—(ignored)
- -G, --no-group—Inhibit display of group information
- -h, --human-readable—Print sizes in human readable format (for example, 1K 234M 2G)
- -H, --si—Likewise, but use powers of 1000 not 1024
- --indicator-style=WORD—Append indicator with style WORD to entry names: none (default), classify (-F), file-type (-p)
- -i, --inode—Print index number of each file
- -I, --ignore=PATTERN—Does not list implied entries matching shell PATTERN
- -k, --kilobytes—Like --block-size=1024
- -l—Use a long listing format
- -L, --dereference—List entries pointed to by symbolic links
- -m—Fill width with a comma separated list of entries
- -n, --numeric-uid-gid—List numeric UIDs and GIDs instead of names
- -N, --literal—Print raw entry names (don't treat, for example, control characters in a special way)
- -o—Use long listing format without group info
- -p, --file-type—Append indicator (one of /=@¦) to entries
- -q, --hide-control-chars—Print ? rather than non-graphic characters
- --show-control-chars—Show non-graphic characters as-is (default)
- -Q, --quote-name—Enclose entry names in double quotes
- --quoting-style=WORD—Use quoting style WORD for entry names: literal, shell, shell-always, c, escape
- -r, --reverse—Reverse order while sorting
- -R, --recursive—List subdirectories recursively
- -s, --size—Print size of each file, in blocks
- -S—Sort by file size
- --sort=WORD—Extension -X, none -U, size -S, time -t, version -v, status -c, time -t, atime -u, access -u, use -u
- --time=WORD—Show time as WORD instead of modification time: atime, access, use, ctime or status; use specified time as sort key if --sort=time
- -t—Sort by modification time
- -T, --tabsize=COLS—Assume tab stops at each COLS instead of 8

- ■ -u—Sort by last access time; with -l: show atime
- ■ -U—Do not sort; list entries in directory order
- ■ -v—Sort by version
- ■ -w, --width=COLS—Assume screen width instead of current value
- ■ -x—List entries by lines instead of by columns
- ■ -X—Sort alphabetically by entry extension
- ■ -1—List one file per line
- ■ --help—Display this help and exit
- ■ --version—Output version information and exit

By default, color is not used to distinguish types of files. This is equivalent to using --color=*none*. Using the --color option without the optional WHEN argument is equivalent to using --color==*always*. With --color==*auto*, color codes are output only if standard output is connected to a terminal (tty).

REPORTING BUGS

Report bugs to <bug-fileutils@gnu.org>.

SEE ALSO

The full documentation for ls is maintained as a Texinfo manual. If the info and ls programs are properly installed at your site, the command

```
info ls
```

should give you access to the complete manual.

MAIL

NAME

mail—Send and receive mail.

SYNOPSIS

```
mail [ -iInv ] [ -s subject ] [ -c cc-addr ] [ -b bcc-addr ] to-addr...
mail [ -iInNv -f ] [ name ]
mail [ -iInNv [ -u user ] ]
```

INTRODUCTION

mail is an intelligent mail processing system that has a command syntax reminiscent of ed1 with lines replaced by messages.

- ■ -v—Verbose mode—The details of delivery are displayed on the user's terminal.
- ■ -i—Ignore tty interrupt signals. This is particularly useful when using mail on noisy phone lines.
- ■ -I—Forces mail to run in interactive mode even when input isn't a terminal. In particular, the ~ special character when sending mail is only active in interactive mode.
- ■ -n—Inhibits reading /etc/mail.rc upon startup.
- ■ -N—Inhibits the initial display of message headers when reading mail or editing a mail folder.
- ■ -s—Specifies subject on command line (only the first argument after the -s flag is used as a subject; be careful to quote subjects containing spaces).
- ■ -c—Sends carbon copies to list of users.
- ■ -b—Sends blind carbon copies to list. List should be a comma-separated list of names.
- ■ -f—Reads in the contents of your mbox (or the specified file) for processing; when you quit mail writes undeleted messages back to this file.

-u

is equivalent to:

```
mail -f /var/spool/mail/user
```

SENDING MAIL

To send a message to one or more people, mail can be invoked with arguments, which are the names of people to whom the mail will be sent. You are then expected to type in your message, followed by Ctrl and D at the beginning of a line. The following section "Replying to or Originating Mail," describes some features of mail available to help you compose your letter.

READING MAIL

In normal usage, mail is given no arguments and checks your mail out of the post office. It then prints out a one-line header of each message found. The current message is initially the first message (numbered 1) and can be printed using the print command, (which can be abbreviated p). You can move among the messages much as you move between lines in ed1, with the commands + and - moving backward and forward, and simple numbers.

DISPOSING OF MAIL

After examining a message you can delete (d) it or reply (r) to it. Deletion causes the mail program to forget about the message. This is not irreversible; the message can be undeleted (u) by giving its number, or the mail session can be aborted by giving the exit (x) command. Deleted messages will, however, usually disappear, never to be seen again.

SPECIFYING MESSAGES

Commands such as print and delete can be given a list of message numbers as arguments to apply to a number of messages at once. Thus delete 1 2 deletes messages 1 and 2, while delete 1-5 deletes messages 1-5. The special name * addresses all messages, and $ addresses the last message; thus the command top which prints the first few lines of a message could be used in top * to print the first few lines of all messages.

REPLYING TO OR ORIGINATING MAIL

Use the reply command to set up a response to a message, sending it back to the person it was from. Text you then type in, up to an end-of-file, defines the contents of the message. While you are composing a message, mail treats lines beginning with the character ~ in a special way. For instance, typing ~m (alone on a line) will place a copy of the current message into the response, right-shifting it by a tab stop (see indentprefix variable, in the following section). Other escapes will set up subject fields, add and delete recipients to the message, and allow you to escape to an editor to revise the message or to a shell to run some commands. (These options are given in the summary below.)

ENDING A MAIL PROCESSING SESSION

You can end a mail session with the quit (q) command. Messages that have been examined go to your mbox file unless they have been deleted, in which case they are discarded. Unexamined messages go back to the post office. (See the -f option above).

PERSONAL AND SYSTEMWIDE DISTRIBUTION LISTS

It is also possible to create a personal distribution list so that, for instance, you can send mail to cohorts and have it go to a group of people. Such lists can be defined by placing a line such as

alias cohorts bill ozalp jkf mark kridle@ucbcory

in the file .mailrc in your home directory. The current list of such aliases can be displayed with the alias command in mail.Systemwide distribution lists can be created by editing /etc/aliases (see aliases(5) and sendmail(8)); these are kept in a different syntax. In mail you send, personal aliases will be expanded in mail sent to others so that they will be able to reply to the recipients. Systemwide aliases are not expanded when the mail is sent, but any reply returned to the machine will have the systemwide alias expanded as all mail goes through sendmail.

NETWORK MAIL (ARPA, UUCP, BERKNET)

See mailaddr(7) for a description of network addresses.

Mail has a number of options that can be set in the .mailrc file to alter its behavior; thus set askcc enables the askcc feature. (These options are summarized below.)

SUMMARY

(Adapted from the *Mail Reference Manual*)

Each command is typed on a line by itself, and can take arguments following the command word. The command need not be typed in its entirety—the first command, which matches the typed prefix, is used. For commands that take message lists as arguments, if no message list is given then the next message forward that satisfies the command's requirements is used. If there are no messages forward of the current message, the search proceeds backward, and if there are no good messages at all, mail types applicable messages and aborts the command.

- ·—Prints the preceding message. If given a numeric argument n goes to the n 'th previous message and prints it.
- ?—Prints a brief summary of commands.
- !—Executes the shell (see sh(1) and csh(1)) command which follows.
- Print—(P) Like print but also prints out ignored header fields. See also print, ignore, and retain.
- Reply—(R) Replies to originator. Does not reply to other recipients of the original message.
- Type—(T) Identical to the Print command.
- alias—(a) With no arguments, prints out all currently defined aliases. With one argument, prints out that alias. With more than one argument, creates a new alias or changes an old one.
- alternates—(alt) The alternates command is useful if you have accounts on several machines. It can be used to inform mail that the listed addresses are really you. When you reply to messages, mail will not send a copy of the message to any of the addresses listed on the alternates list. If the alternates command is given with no argument, the current set of alternate names is displayed.
- chdir—Changes the user's working directory to that specified, if given. If no directory is given then changes to the user's login directory.
- copy—(co) The copy command does the same thing that save does, except that it does not mark the messages it is used on for deletion when you quit.
- delete—(d) Takes a list of messages as argument and marks them all as deleted. Deleted messages will not be saved in mbox nor will they be available for most other commands.
- dp—(also dt) Deletes the current message and prints the next message. If there is no next message, mail says "at EOF ".
- edit—(e) Takes a list of messages and points the text editor at each one in turn. On return from the editor, the message is read back in.
- exit—(ex or x) Effects an immediate return to the Shell without modifying the user's system mailbox, his mbox file, or his edit file in -f.
- file

- (fi) The same as folder.
- folders—Lists the names of the folders in your folder directory.
- folder—(fo) The folder command switches to a new mail file or folder. With no arguments, it tells you which file you are currently reading. If you give it an argument, it will write out changes (such as deletions) you have made in the current file and read in the new file. Some special conventions are recognized for the name. # means the previous file, % means your system mailbox, %user means user's system mailbox, & means your mbox file, and +folder means a file in your folder directory.
- from—(f) Takes a list of messages and prints their message headers.
- headers—(h) Lists the current range of headers, which is an 18-message group. If a '+' argument is given, then the next 18-message group is printed, and if a '-' argument is given, the previous 18-message group is printed.
- help—A synonym for ?.
- hold—(ho also preserve) Takes a message list and marks each message therein to be saved in the user's system mailbox instead of in mbox. Does not override the delete command.
- ignore—Adds the list of header fields named to the ignored list. Header fields in the ignore list are not printed on your terminal when you print a message. This command is very handy for suppression of certain machine-generated header fields. The Type and Print commands can be used to print a message in its entirety, including ignored fields. If ignore is executed with no arguments, it lists the current set of ignored fields.
- mail—(m) Takes as argument login names and distribution group names and sends mail to those people.
- mbox—Indicates that a list of messages be sent to mbox in your home directory when you quit. This is the default action for messages if you do not have the hold option set.
- next—(n) Like + or CR. Goes to the next message in sequence and types it. With an argument list, types the next matching message.
- preserve—(pre) A synonym for hold.
- print—(p) Takes a message list and types out each message on the user's terminal.
- quit—(q) Terminates the session, saving all undeleted, unsaved messages in the user's mbox file in his login directory, preserving all messages marked with hold or preserve or never referenced in his system mailbox, and removing all other messages from his system mailbox. If new mail has arrived during the session, the message "You have new mail" is given. If given while editing a mailbox file with the -f flag, then the edit file is rewritten. A return to the Shell is effected, unless the rewrite of edit file fails, in which case the user can escape with the exit command.
- reply—(r) Takes a message list and sends mail to the sender and all recipients of the specified message. The default message must not be deleted.
- respond—A synonym for reply.

- retain—Adds the list of header fields named to the retained list. Only the header fields in the retain list are shown on your terminal when you print a message. All other header fields are suppressed. The Type and Print commands can be used to print a message in its entirety. If retain is executed with no arguments, it lists the current set of retained fields.

- save—(s) Takes a message list and a filename and appends each message in turn to the end of the file. The filename in quotes, followed by the line count and character count is echoed on the user's terminal.

- set—(se) With no arguments, prints all variable values. Otherwise, sets option. Arguments are of the form option=value (no space before or after =) or option. Quotation marks can be placed around any part of the assignment statement to quote blanks or tabs, for example, "set indentprefix=->".

- saveignore—Saveignore is to save what ignore is to print and type. Header fields thus marked are filtered out when saving a message by save or when automatically saving to mbox.

- saveretain—Saveretain is to save what retain is to print and type. Header fields thus marked are the only ones saved with a message when saving by save or when automatically saving to mbox. Saveretain overrides saveignore.

- shell—(sh) Invokes an interactive version of the shell.

- size—Takes a message list and prints out the size in characters of each message.

- source—The source command reads commands from a file.

- top—Takes a message list and prints the top few lines of each. The number of lines printed is controlled by the variable toplines and defaults to five.

- type—(t) A synonym for print.

- unalias—Takes a list of names defined by alias commands and discards the remembered groups of users. The group names no longer have any significance.

- undelete—(u) Takes a message list and marks each message as not being deleted.

- unread—(U) Takes a message list and marks each message as not having been read.

- unset—Takes a list of option names and discards their remembered values; the inverse of set.

- Visual—(v) Takes a message list and invokes the display editor on each message.

- write—(w) Similar to save except that only the message body (without the header) is saved. Extremely useful for such tasks as sending and receiving source program text over the message system.

- xit—(x) A synonym for exit.

- z—mail presents message headers in windows as described under the headers command. You can move mail's attention forward to the next window with the z command. Also, you can move to the previous window by using z.

TILDE/ESCAPES

A summary of the tilde escapes follows. These are used when composing messages to perform special functions. Tilde escapes are only recognized at the beginning of lines. The name *tilde escape* is somewhat of a misnomer because the actual escape character can be set by the option `escape`.

- `~! Command`—Execute the indicated shell command, and then return to the message.
- `~b name ...`—Add the given names to the list of carbon copy recipients but do not make the names visible in the Cc: line ("blind" carbon copy).
- `~c name ...`—Add the given names to the list of carbon copy recipients.
- `~d`—Read the file `dead.letter` from your home directory into the message.
- `~e`—Invoke the text editor on the message collected so far. After the editing session is finished, you can continue appending text to the message.
- `~f messages`—Read the named messages into the message being sent. If no messages are specified, read in the current message. Message headers currently being ignored (by the `ignore` or `retain` command) are not included.
- `~F messages`—Identical to `~f` except all message headers are included.
- `~h`—Edit the message header fields by typing each one in turn and allowing the user to append text to the end or modify the field by using the current terminal erase and kill characters.
- `~m messages`—Read the named messages into the message being sent, indented by a tab or by the value of `indentprefix`. If no messages are specified, read the current message. Message headers currently being ignored (by the `ignore` or `retain` command) are not included.
- `~M messages`—Identical to `~m` except all message headers are included.
- `~p`—Print out the message collected so far, prefaced by the message header fields.
- `~q`—Abort the message being sent, copying the message to `dead.letter` in your home directory if `save` is set.
- `~r filename`—Read the named file into the message.
- `~s string`—Cause the named string to become the current subject field.
- `~t name ...`—Add the given names to the direct recipient list.
- `~v`—Invoke an alternate editor (defined by the VISUAL option) on the message collected so far. Usually, the alternate editor will be a screen editor. After you quit the editor, you can resume appending text to the end of your message.
- `~w filename`—Write the message onto the named file.
- `~¦ command`—Pipe the message through the command as a filter. If the command gives no output or terminates abnormally, retain the original text of the message. The command `fmt`(1) is often used as `command` to re-justify the message.

PART
VI
APP
A

- ~: mail-command—Execute the given mail command. Not all commands, however, are allowed.

- ~~ string—Insert the string of text in the message prefaced by a single ~. If you have changed the escape character then you should double that character in order to send it.

MAIL OPTIONS

Options are controlled through set and unset commands. Options can be either binary, in which case it is only significant to see whether they are set; or string, in which case the actual value is of interest. Binary options include the following:

- append—Causes messages saved in mbox to be appended to the end rather than prepended. This should always be set (perhaps in /etc/mail.rc).

- ask, asksub—Causes mail to prompt you for the subject of each message you send. If you respond with simply a newline, no subject field will be sent.

- askcc—Causes you to be prompted for additional carbon copy recipients at the end of each message. Responding with a newline indicates your satisfaction with the current list.

- askbcc—Causes you to be prompted for additional blind carbon copy recipients at the end of each message. Responding with a newline indicates your satisfaction with the current list.

- autoprint—Causes the delete command to behave like dp, thus, after deleting a message, the next one will be typed automatically.

- debug—Setting the binary option debug is the same as specifying -d on the command line and causes mail to output all sorts of information useful for debugging mail.

- dot—The binary option dot causes mail to interpret a period alone on a line as the terminator of a message you are sending.

- hold—This option is used to hold messages in the system mailbox by default.

- ignore—Causes interrupt signals from your terminal to be ignored and echoed as @'s.

- ignoreeof—An option related to dot is ignoreeof, which makes mail refuse to accept a control-d as the end of a message. Ignoreeof also applies to mail command mode.

- metoo—Usually, when a group is expanded that contains the sender, the sender is removed from the expansion. Setting this option causes the sender to be included in the group.

- noheader—Setting the option noheader is the same as giving the -N flag on the command line.

- nosave—Normally, when you abort a message with two RUBOUT (erase or delete) mail copies the partial letter to the file dead.letter in your home directory. Setting the binary option nosave prevents this.

- Replyall—Reverses the sense of reply and Reply commands.

- quiet—Suppresses the printing of the version when first invoked.

- searchheaders—If this option is set, a message-list specifier in the form /x:y will expand to all messages containing the substring y in the header field x. The string search is case insensitive.

- verbose—Setting the option verbose is the same as using the -v flag on the command line. When mail runs in verbose mode, the actual delivery of messages is displayed on the user's terminal.

OPTION STRING VALUES

- EDITOR—Pathname of the text editor to use in the edit command and ~e escape. If not defined, a default editor is used.

- LISTER—Pathname of the directory lister to use in the folders command. Default is /bin/ls.

- PAGER—Pathname of the program to use in the more command or when crt variable is set. The default paginator more(1) is used if this option is not defined.

- SHELL—Pathname of the shell to use in the ! command and the ~! escape. A default shell is used if this option is not defined.

- VISUAL—Pathname of the text editor to use in the visual command and ~v escape.

- crt—The valued option crt is used as a threshold to determine how long a message must be before PAGER is used to read it. If crt is set without a value, the height of the terminal screen stored in the system is used to compute the threshold (see stty(1)).

- escape—If defined, the first character of this option gives the character to use in the place of ~ to denote escapes.

- folder—The name of the directory to use for storing folders of messages. If this name begins with a /, mail considers it to be an absolute pathname; otherwise, the folder directory is found relative to your home directory.

- MBOX—The name of the mbox file. It can be the name of a folder. The default is mbox in the user's home directory.

- record—If defined, gives the pathname of the file used to record all outgoing mail. If not defined, outgoing mail is not so saved.

- indentprefix—String used by the ~m tilde escape for indenting messages, in place of the normal tab character (^I). Be sure to quote the value if it contains spaces or tabs.

- toplines—If defined, gives the number of lines of a message to be printed out with the top command; normally, the first five lines are printed.

ENVIRONMENT

mail utilizes the HOME and USER environment variables.

FILES

- /var/spool/mail/*—Post office
- ~/mbox—User's old mail

PART

VI

APP

A

- ~/.mailrc—File giving initial mail commands
- /tmp/R*—Temporary files
- /usr/lib/mail.*help—Help files
- /etc/mail.rc—System initialization file

SEE ALSO

fmt(1), newaliases(1), vacation(1), aliases(5), mailaddr(7), sendmail(8) and 'The Mail Reference Manual'.

HISTORY

A mail command appeared in AT&T System v6. This man page is derived from 'The Mail Reference Manual' originally written by Kurt Shoens.

BUGS

Some flags are not documented here. Most are not useful to the general user.

MAN

NAME

man—Format and display the online manual pages.

manpath—Determine user's search path for man pages.

SYNOPSIS

man [-acdfFhkKtwW] [-m system] [-p string] [-C config_file] [-M path] [-P pager]
➥[-S section_list] [section] name ...

DESCRIPTION

man formats and displays the online manual pages. This version knows about the MANPATH and (MAN)PAGER environment variables, so you can have your own set(s) of personal man pages and choose whatever program you want to display the formatted pages. If section is specified, man only looks in that section of the manual. You can also specify the order to search the sections for entries and which preprocessors to run on the source files using command-line options or environment variables. If name contains a / then it is first tried as a filename, so that you can do man ./foo.5 or even man /cd/foo/bar.1.gz.

OPTIONS

- -C config_file—Specify the man.conf file to use; the default is /etc/man.config. (See man.conf(5).)

- -M path—Specify the list of directories to search for man pages. If no such option is given, the environment variable MANPATH is used. If no such environment variable is found, the default list is found by consulting /etc/man.config. An empty substring of MANPATH denotes the default list.

- -P pager—Specify which pager to use. This option overrides the MANPAGER environment variable, which in turn overrides the PAGER variable. By default, man uses /usr/bin/less-is.

- -S section_list—List is a colon-separated list of manual sections to search. This option overrides the MANSECT environment variable.

- -a—By default, man will exit after displaying the first manual page it finds. Using this option forces man to display all the manual pages that match name, not just the first.

- -c—Re-format the source man page, even when an up-to-date cat page exists. This can be meaningful if the cat page was formatted for a screen with a different number of columns, or if the preformatted page is corrupted.

- -d—Don't actually display the man pages, but do print gobs of debugging information.

- -D—Don't actually display the man pages, but do print gobs of debugging information. Both display and print debugging info.

- -f—Equivalent to whatis.

- -F or --preformat—Format only—do not display.

- -h—Print a one-line help message and exit.

- -k—Equivalent to apropos.

- -K—Search for the specified string in *all* man pages. Warning: This is probably very slow! It helps to specify a section. (Just to give a rough idea, on my machine this takes about a minute per 500 man pages.)

- -m system—Specify an alternate set of man pages to search based on the system name given.

- -p string—Specify the sequence of preprocessors to run before nroff or troff. Not all installations will have a full set of preprocessors. Some of the preprocessors and the letters used to designate them are: eqn , grap (g), pic (p), tbl (t), vgrind (v), refer (r). This option overrides the MANROFFSEQ environment variable.

- -t—Use /usr/bin/groff -Tps -mandoc to format the manual page, passing the output to stdout. The output from /usr/bin/groff -Tps -mandoc might need to be passed through some filter or another before being printed.

- -w or –path—Don't actually display the man pages, but do print the location(s) of the files that would be formatted or displayed. If no argument is given, display (on stdout) the list of directories that is searched by man for man pages. If manpath is a link to man, manpath is equivalent to man –path.

- -W—Like -w, but print filenames one per line, without additional information. This is useful in shell commands like man -aW man ¦ xargs ls -l.

PART

VI

APP

A

CAT PAGES

man will try to save the formatted man pages to save formatting time the next time these pages are needed. Traditionally, formatted versions of pages in DIR/manX are saved in DIR/catX, but other mappings from man dir to cat dir can be specified in /etc/man.config. No cat pages are saved when the required cat directory does not exist.

It is possible to make man suid to a user man. Then, if a cat directory has owner man and mode 0755 (only writable by man), and the cat files have owner man and mode 0644 or 0444 (only writable by man, or not writable at all), no ordinary user can change the cat pages or put other files in the cat directory. If man is not made suid, a cat directory should have mode 0777 if all users should be able to leave cat pages there.

The option -c forces reformatting a page, even if a recent cat page exists.

ENVIRONMENT

- MANPATH—If MANPATH is set, its value is used as the path to search for manual pages.

- MANROFFSEQ—If MANROFFSEQ is set, its value is used to determine the set of preprocessors run before running nroff or troff. By default, pages are passed through the table preprocessor before nroff.

- MANSECT—If MANSECT is set, its value is used to determine which manual sections to search.

- MANWIDTH—If MANWIDTH is set, its value is used as the width manpages should be displayed. Otherwise the pages can be displayed over the whole width of your screen.

- MANPAGER—If MANPAGER is set, its value is used as the name of the program to use to display the man page. If not, then PAGER is used. If that has no value either, /usr/bin/ less -is is used.

- LANG—If LANG is set, its value defines the name of the subdirectory where man first looks for man pages. Thus, the command LANG=dk man 1 foo will cause man to look for the foo man page in .../dk/man1/foo.1, and if it cannot find such a file, then in ... /man1/foo.1, where ... is a directory on the search path.

- NLSPATH, LC_MESSAGES, LANG—The environment variables NLSPATH and LC_MESSAGES (or LANG when the latter does not exist) play a role in locating the message catalog. (But the English messages are compiled in, and for English no catalog is required.) Note that programs like col(1) called by man also use, for example, LC_CTYPE.

- PATH—PATH is used in the construction of the default search path for man pages.

- SYSTEM—SYSTEM is used to get the default alternate system name (for use with the -m option).

SEE ALSO

apropos(1), whatis(1), less(1), groff(1).

BUGS

The -t option only works if a troff-like program is installed. If you see blinking \255 or <AD> instead of hyphens, put LESSCHARSET=latin1 in your environment.

TIPS

If you add the line

```
(global-set-key[(f1)](lambda()(interactive)(manual-entry(current-word))))
```

to your .emacs file, pressing F1 will give you the man page for the library call at the current cursor position.

MORE

NAME

more—File perusal filter for crt viewing.

SYNOPSIS

```
more [-dlfpcsu ] [-num ] [+/ pattern] [+ linenum] [file ... ]
```

DESCRIPTION

more is a filter for paging through text one screen at a time. This version is especially primitive. Users should realize that less(1) provides more(1) emulation and extensive enhancements.

OPTIONS

Command-line options are described in the following list. Options are also taken from the environment variable MORE (make sure to precede them with a dash (-)) but command-line options will override them.

- -num—This option specifies an integer which is the screen size (in lines).

- -d—more will prompt the user with the message "[Press space to continue, 'q' to quit.]" and will display "[Press 'h' for instructions.]" instead of ringing the bell when an illegal key is pressed.

- -1—more usually treats ^L (form feed) as a special character, and will pause after any line that contains a form feed. The -1 option will prevent this behavior.

- -f—Causes more to count logical, rather than screen lines (for example, long lines are not folded).

- -p—Do not scroll. Instead, clear the whole screen and then display the text.

- -c—Do not scroll. Instead, paint each screen from the top, clearing the remainder of each line as it is displayed.

PART

VI

APP

A

- ■ -s—Squeeze multiple blank lines into one.
- ■ -u—Suppress underlining.
- ■ +/—The +/ option specifies a string that will be searched for before each file is displayed.
- ■ +num—Start at line number num.

COMMANDS

Interactive commands for more are based on vi(1). Some commands can be preceded by a decimal number, which is called k in the descriptions that follow. In the following descriptions, ^X means Control-X.

- ■ h or ?—Help: display a summary of these commands. If you forget all the other commands, remember this one.
- ■ SPACE—Display next k lines of text. Defaults to current screen size.
- ■ z—Display next k lines of text. Defaults to current screen size. Argument becomes new default.
- ■ RETURN—Display next k lines of text. Defaults to 1. Argument becomes new default.
- ■ d or ^D—Scroll k lines. Default is current scroll size, initially 11. Argument becomes new default.
- ■ q or Q or INTERRUPT—Exit.
- ■ s—Skip forward k lines of text. Defaults to 1.
- ■ f—Skip forward k screens of text. Defaults to 1.
- ■ b or ^B—Skip backward k screens of text. Defaults to 1. Go to place where previous search started.
- ■ =—Display current line number.
- ■ / pattern—Search for kth occurrence of regular expression. Defaults to 1.
- ■ n—Search for kth occurrence of last r.e. Defaults to 1.
- ■ !<cmd> or :!<cmd>—Execute <cmd> in a subshell.
- ■ v—Start up /usr/bin/vi at current line.
- ■ ^L—Redraw screen.
- ■ :n Go to kth next file. Defaults to 1.
- ■ :p—Go to kth previous file. Defaults to 1.
- ■ :f—Display current filename and line number.
- ■ .—Repeat previous command.

ENVIRONMENT

more utilizes the following environment variables, if they exist:

- MORE—This variable can be set with favored options to more.
- SHELL—Current shell in use (normally set by the shell at login time).
- TERM—Specifies terminal type, used by more to get the terminal characteristics necessary to manipulate the screen.

SEE ALSO

vi(1) less(1)

AUTHORS

Eric Shienbrood, UC Berkeley

Modified by Geoff Peck, UCB to add underlining, single spacing

Modified by John Foderaro, UCB to add -c and MORE environment variable

HISTORY

The more command appeared in BSD 3.0 This man page documents more version 5.19 (Berkeley 6/29/88), which is currently in use in the Linux community. Documentation was produced using several other versions of the man page and extensive inspection of the source code.

MOUNT

NAME

mount—Mount a file system.

SYNOPSIS

mount [-hV]

mount -a [-fFnrsvw] [-t vfstype]

mount [-fnrsvw] [-o options [,...]] device ¦ dir

mount [-fnrsvw] [-t vfstype] [-o options] device dir

DESCRIPTION

All files accessible in a UNIX system are arranged in one tree, the file hierarchy, rooted at /. These files can be spread out over several devices. The mount command serves to attach the file system found on some device to the file tree. Conversely, the umount(8) command will detach it again.

PART
VI
APP
A

The standard form of the `mount` command is

`mount -t type device dir`

This tells the kernel to attach the file system found on `device` (which is of type `type`) at the directory `dir`. The previous contents (if any) and owner and mode of `dir` become invisible, and as long as this file system remains mounted, the pathname `dir` refers to the root of the file system on `device`.

Three forms of invocation do not actually mount anything:

- `mount -h`—Prints a help message.
- `mount -V`—Prints a version string.
- `mount [-t type]`—Lists all mounted file systems (of type `type`)—see below.

The `proc` file system is not associated with a special device, and when mounting it, an arbitrary keyword, such as `proc` can be used instead of a device specification. (The customary choice *none* is less fortunate: the error message `none busy` from `umount` can be confusing.)

Most devices are indicated by a filename (of a block special device), like `/dev/sda1`, but there are other possibilities. For example, in the case of an NFS mount, *device* can look like `knuth.cwi.nl:/dir`. It is possible to indicate a block special device using its volume label or UUID (see the `-L` and `-U` options below).

The file `/etc/fstab` (see `fstab(5)`), can contain lines describing what devices are usually mounted where, using which options. This file is used in three ways:

- The command

  `mount -a [-t type]`

  (usually given in a bootscript) causes all file systems mentioned in `fstab` (of the proper type) to be mounted as indicated, except for those whose line contains the `noauto` keyword. Adding the `-F` option will make mount fork, so that the file systems are mounted simultaneously.
- When mounting a file system mentioned in `fstab`, it suffices to give only the device, or only the mount point.
- Normally, only the superuser can mount file systems. However, when `fstab` contains the `user` option on a line, then anybody can mount the corresponding system.

Thus, given a line

`/dev/cdrom /cd iso9660 ro,user,noauto,unhide`

any user can mount the `iso9660` file system found on his CDROM using the command

`mount /dev/cdrom`

or

`mount /cd`

For more details, see fstab(5). Only the user that mounted a file system can unmount it again. If any user should be able to unmount, use users instead of user in the fstab line.

The programs mount and umount maintain a list of currently mounted file systems in the file /etc/mtab. If no arguments are given to mount, this list is printed. When the *proc* file system is mounted (say at /proc), the files /etc/mtab and /proc/mounts have very similar contents. The former has somewhat more information, such as the mount options used, but is not necessarily up-to-date (cf. the -n option below). It is possible to replace /etc/mtab by a symbolic link to /proc/mounts, but some information is lost, and in particular working with the loop device will be less convenient.

OPTIONS

The full set of options used by an invocation of mount is determined by first extracting the options for the file system from the fstab table, applying any options specified by the -o argument, and finally applying a -r or -w option, when present.

Options available for the mount command:

- -V—Output version.
- -h—Print a help message.
- -v—Verbose mode.
- -a—Mount all file systems (of the given types) mentioned in fstab.
- -F—(Used in conjunction with -a.) Fork off a new incarnation of mount for each device. This will do the mounts on different devices or different NFS servers in parallel. This has the advantage that it is faster; also NFS timeouts go in parallel. A disadvantage is that the mounts are done in undefined order. Thus, you cannot use this option if you want to mount both /usr and /usr/spool.
- -f—Causes everything to be done except for the actual system call; if it's not obvious, this fakes mounting the file system. This option is useful in conjunction with the -v flag to determine what the mount command is trying to do. It can also be used to add entries for devices that were mounted earlier with the -n option.
- -n—Mount without writing in /etc/mtab. This is necessary, for example, when /etc is on a read-only file system.
- -s—Tolerate sloppy mount options rather than failing. This will ignore mount options not supported by a file system type. Not all file systems support this option. This option exists for support of the Linux autofs-based automounter.
- -r—Mount the file system read-only. A synonym is -o ro.
- -w—Mount the file system read/write. This is the default. A synonym is -o rw.
- -L label—Mount the partition that has the specified label.

- ■ -U uuid—Mount the partition that has the specified uuid. These two options require the file /proc/partitions (present since Linux 2.1.116) to exist.

- ■ -t vfstype—The argument following the -t is used to indicate the file system type. The file system types which are currently supported are listed in linux/fs/filesystems.c: minix, xiafs, ext, ext2, msdos, umsdos, vfat, proc, autofs, devpts, nfs, iso9660, smbfs, ncpfs, adfs, affs, coda, hfs, hpfs, ntfs, qnx4, romfs, ufs, sysv, xenix, coherent. Note that the last three are equivalent and that xenix and coherent will be removed at some point in the future—use sysv instead. Since kernel version 2.1.21 the types ext and xiafs do not exist anymore.

For most types all the mount program must do is issue a simple mount(2) system call, and no detailed knowledge of the file system type is required. For a few types however (such as nfs, smbfs, and ncpfs) ad hoc code is necessary. The nfs ad hoc code is built in, but smbfs and ncpfs have a separate mount program. To treat all types in a uniform way, mount will execute the program /sbin/mount.TYPE (if that exists) when called with type smb or ncp. Because various versions of the smbmount program have different calling conventions, /sbin/mount.smb can need to be a shell script that sets up the desired call.

The type iso9660 is the default. If no -t option is given, or if the auto type is specified, the superblock is probed for the file system type (minix, ext, ext2, xiafs, iso9660, and romfs are supported). If this probe fails, mount will try to read the file /etc/filesystems, or, if that does not exist, /proc/filesystems. All the file system types listed there will be tried, except for those that are labeled nodev (for examplel, proc and nfs).

The auto type can be useful for user-mounted floppies. Creating a file /etc/filesystems is useful to change the probe order (for example, to try vfat before msdos) or if you use a kernel module autoloader. Warning: The probing uses a heuristic method (the presence of appropriate 'magic'), and could recognize the wrong file system type.

More than one type can be specified in a comma-separated list. The list of file system types can be prefixed with no to specify the file system types on which no action should be taken. (This can be meaningful with the -a option.)

For example, the command:

```
mount -a -t nomsdos,ext
```

mounts all file systems except those of type msdos and ext.

- ■ -o—Options are specified with a -o flag followed by a comma-separated string of options. Some of these options are only useful when they appear in the /etc/fstab file. The following options apply to any file system that is being mounted:

- ■ async—All I/O to the file system should be done asynchronously.

- ■ atime—Update inode access time for each access. This is the default.

- ■ auto—Can be mounted with the -a option.

- ■ defaults—Use default options: rw, suid, dev, exec, auto, nouser, and async.

- ■ dev—Interpret character or block special devices on the file system.

- exec—Permit execution of binaries.

- noatime—Do not update inode access times on this file system (for example, for faster access on the news spool to speed up news servers).

- noauto—Can only be mounted explicitly (for example, the -a option will not cause the file system to be mounted).

- nodev—Do not interpret character or block special devices on the file system.

- noexec—Do not allow execution of any binaries on the mounted file system. This option might be useful for a server that has file systems containing binaries for architectures other than its own.

- nosuid—Do not allow set-user-identifier or set-group-identifier bits to take effect. (This seems safe, but is in fact rather unsafe if you have suidperl(1) installed.)

- nouser—Forbid an ordinary (for example, non-root) user to mount the file system. This is the default.

- remount—Attempt to remount an already mounted file system. This is commonly used to change the mount flags for a file system, especially to make a read-only file system writeable.

- ro—Mount the file system read-only.

- rw—Mount the file system read-write.

- suid—Allow set-user-identifier or set-group-identifier bits to take effect.

- sync—All I/O to the file system should be done synchronously.

- user—Allow an ordinary user to mount the file system. This option implies the options noexec, nosuid, and nodev (unless overridden by subsequent options, as in the option line user, exec, dev, suid).

FILE SYSTEM-SPECIFIC MOUNT OPTIONS

The following options apply only to certain file systems. We sort them by file system. They all follow the -o flag.

MOUNT OPTIONS FOR affs

- uid=value and gid=value—Set the owner and group of the root of the file system (default: uid=gid=0, but with option uid or gid without specified value, the uid and gid of the current process are taken).

- setuid=value and setgid=value—Set the owner and group of all files.

- mode=value—Set the mode of all files to value & 0777 disregarding the original permissions. Add search permission to directories that have read permission. The value is given in octal.

- protect—Do not allow any changes to the protection bits on the file system.

- usemp—Set uid and gid of the root of the file system to the uid and gid of the mount point upon the first sync or umount, and then clear this option. Strange...

PART
VI
APP
A

- verbose—Print an informational message for each successful mount.
- prefix=string—Prefix used before volume name, when following a link.
- volume=string—Prefix (of length at most 30) used before / when following a symbolic link.
- reserved=value—(Default: 2.) Number of unused blocks at the start of the device.
- root=value—Give explicitly the location of the root block.
- bs=value—Give blocksize. Allowed values are 512, 1024, 2048, 4096.
- grpquota / noquota / quota / usrquota—These options are accepted but ignored.

MOUNT OPTIONS FOR coherent

None.

MOUNT OPTIONS FOR ext

None. Note that the ext file system is obsolete. Don't use it. Since Linux version 2.1.21, extfs is no longer part of the kernel source.

MOUNT OPTIONS FOR ext2

The ext2 file system is the standard Linux file system. Due to a kernel bug, it can be mounted with random mount options (fixed in Linux 2.0.4).

bsddf / minixdf

Set the behavior for the statfs system call. The minixdf behavior is to return in the f_blocks field the total number of blocks of the file system, while the bsddf behavior (which is the default) is to subtract the overhead blocks used by the ext2 file system and not available for file storage. Thus

```
% mount /k -o minixdf; df /k; umount /k
Filesystem 1024-blocks Used Available Capacity Mounted on
/dev/sda6 2630655 86954 2412169 3% /k
% mount /k -o bsddf; df /k; umount /k
Filesystem 1024-blocks Used Available Capacity Mounted on
/dev/sda6 2543714 13 2412169 0% /k
```

(Note that this example shows that one can add command line options to the options given in /etc/fstab.)

- check / check=normal / check=strict—Set checking level. When at least one of these options is set (and check=normal is set by default) the inodes and blocks bitmaps are checked upon mount (which can take half a minute or so on a big disk). With strict checking, block deallocation checks that the block to free is in the data zone.
- check=none / nocheck—No checking is done.
- debug—Print debugging info upon each (re)mount.

- errors=continue / errors=remount-ro / errors=panic—Define the behavior when an error is encountered. (Ignore the errors and mark the file system erroneous and continue, or remount the file system read-only, or panic and halt the system.) The default is set in the file system superblock, and can be changed using tune2fs(8).

- grpid or bsdgroups / nogrpid or sysvgroups—These options define what group id a newly created file gets. When grpid is set, it takes the group id of the directory in which it is created. Otherwise (the default) it takes the fsgid of the current process, unless the directory has the setgid bit set, in which case it takes the gid from the parent directory. It also gets the setgid bit set if it is a directory itself.

- resgid=n and resuid=n—The ext2 file system reserves a certain percentage of the available space (by default 5%, see mke2fs(8) and tune2fs(8)). These options determine who can use the reserved blocks. (Roughly, whoever has the specified uid, or belongs to the specified group.)

- sb=n—Instead of block 1, use block n as superblock. This could be useful when the file system has been damaged. Usually, copies of the superblock are found every 8192 blocks: in block 1, 8193, 16385, ... (Thus, one gets hundreds or even thousands of copies of the superblock on a big file system. I do not know of options to mke2fs that would cause fewer copies to be written.)

- grpquota / noquota / quota / usrquota—These options are accepted but ignored.

MOUNT OPTIONS FOR fat

(Note: fat is not a separate file system, but a common part of the msdos, umsdos, and vfat file systems.)

- blocksize=512 / blocksize=1024—Set blocksize (default 512).

- uid=value and gid=value—Set the owner and group of all files. (Default: the uid and gid of the current process.)

- umask=value—Set the umask (the bitmask of the permissions that are not present). The default is the umask of the current process. The value is given in octal.

- check=value—Three different levels of strictness can be chosen:

- r[elaxed]—Upper and lowercase are accepted and equivalent, long name parts are truncated (for example, verylongname.foobar becomes verylong.foo), leading and embedded spaces are accepted in each name part (name and extension).

- n[ormal]—Like 'relaxed', but many special characters (*, ?, <, spaces, and so forth) are rejected. This is the default.

- s[trict]—Like 'normal', but names cannot contain long parts and special characters that are sometimes used on Linux, but are not accepted by MS-DOS are rejected (+, =, spaces, and so forth).

- conv=b[inary] / conv=t[ext] / conv=a[uto]—The fat file system can perform CRLF<->NL (MS-DOS text format to UNIX text format) conversion in the kernel. The following conversion modes are available:

PART

VI

APP

A

- binary—No translation is performed. This is the default.
- text—CRLF<-->NL translation is performed on all files.
- auto—CRLF<-->NL translation is performed on all files that don't have a well-known binary extension. The list of known extensions is at the beginning of fs/fat/misc.c. (As of 2.0, the list is: exe, com, bin, app, sys, drv, ovl, ovr, obj, lib, dll, pif, arc, zip, lha, lzh, zoo, tar, z, arj, tz, taz, tzp, tpz, gz, tgz, deb, gif, bmp, tif, gl, jpg, pcx, tfm, vf, gf, pk, pxl, dvi).

Programs that do computed lseeks won't like in-kernel text conversion. Several people have had their data ruined by this translation. Beware!

For file systems mounted in binary mode, a conversion tool (fromdos/todos) is available.

- debug—Turn on the debug flag. A version string and a list of file system parameters will be printed (these data are also printed if the parameters appear to be inconsistent).
- fat=12 / fat=16—Specify either a 12-bit fat or a 16-bit fat. This overrides the automatic FAT-type detection routine. Use with caution!
- quiet—Turn on the quiet flag. Attempts to chown or chmod files do not return errors, although they fail. Use with caution!
- sys_immutable, showexec, dots, nodots, dotsOK=[yes¦no]— Various misguided attempts to force UNIX or DOS conventions onto a FAT file system.

MOUNT OPTIONS FOR hpfs

- uid=value and gid=value—Set the owner and group of all files. (Default: the uid and gid of the current process.)
- umask=value—Set the umask (the bitmask of the permissions that are not present). The default is the umask of the current process. The value is given in octal.
- case=lower / case=asis—Convert all filenames to lowercase, or leave them. (Default: case=lower.)
- conv=binary / conv=text / conv=auto—For conv=text, delete some random CRs (in particular, all followed by NL) when reading a file. For conv=auto, choose more or less at random between conv=binary and conv=text. For conv=binary, just read what is in the file. This is the default.
- For conv=text, delete some random CRs (in particular, all followed by NL) when reading a file. For conv=auto, choose more or less at random between conv=binary and conv=text. For conv=binary, just read what is in the file. This is the default.
- nocheck—Do not abort mounting when certain consistency checks fail.

MOUNT OPTIONS FOR ISO 9660

Normal ISO 9660 filenames appear in an 8.3 format (that is, DOS-like restrictions on filename length), and in addition all characters are in uppercase. Also there is no field for file ownership, protection, number of links, provision for block/character devices, and so forth.

Rock Ridge is an extension to ISO 9660 that provides all of these UNIX-like features. Basically there are extensions to each directory record that supply all the additional information, and when Rock Ridge is in use, the file system is indistinguishable from a normal UNIX file system (except that it is read-only, of course).

- _—Disable the use of Rock Ridge extensions, even if available. (Compare to map.)

- check=r[elaxed] / check=s[trict]—With check=relaxed, a filename is first converted to lowercase before doing the lookup. This is probably only meaningful together with norock and map=normal. (Default: check=strict.)

- uid=value and gid=value—Give all files in the file system the indicated user or group id, possibly overriding the information found in the Rock Ridge extensions. (Default: uid=0,gid=0.)

- map=n[ormal] / map=o[ff]—For non-Rock Ridge volumes, normal name translation maps upper to lowercase ASCII, drops a trailing ;1, and converts ; to .. With map=off no name translation is done. See norock. (Default: map=normal.)

- mode=value—For non-Rock Ridge volumes, give all files the indicated mode. (Default: read permission for everybody.) Since Linux 2.1.37, one no longer needs to specify the mode in decimal. (Octal is indicated by a leading 0.)

- unhide—Also show hidden and associated files.

- block=[512¦1024¦2048]—Set the block size to the indicated value. (Default: block=1024.)

- conv=a[uto] / conv=b[inary] / conv=m[text] / conv=t[ext]—(Default: conv=binary.) Since Linux 1.3.54, this option has no effect anymore. (And non-binary settings used to be very dangerous, often leading to silent data corruption.)

- cruft—If the high byte of the file length contains other garbage, set this mount option to ignore the high order bits of the file length. This implies that a file cannot be larger than 16MB. The cruft option is set automatically if the entire CD-ROM has a weird size (negative, or more than 800MB). It is also set when volume sequence numbers other than 0 or 1 are seen.

MOUNT OPTIONS FOR minix

None.

MOUNT OPTIONS FOR msdos

See mount options for fat. If the msdos file system detects an inconsistency, it reports an error and sets the file system read-only. The file system can be made writeable again by remounting it.

PART

VI

APP

A

MOUNT OPTIONS FOR ncp

Just like nfs, the ncp implementation expects a binary argument (a struct ncp_mount_data) to the mount system call. This argument is constructed by ncpmount(8) and the current version of mount (2.6h) does not know anything about ncp.

MOUNT OPTIONS FOR nfs

Instead of a textual option string, parsed by the kernel, the nfs file system expects a binary argument of type struct nfs_mount_data. The program mount parses the following options of the form tag=value and puts them in the structure mentioned: rsize=n, wsize=n, timeo=n, retrans=n, acregmin=n, acregmax=n, acdirmin=n, acdirmax=n, actimeo=n, retry=n, port=n, mountport=n, mounthost=name, mountprog=n, mountvers=n, nfsprog=n, nfsvers=n, and namlen=n. The option addr=n is accepted but ignored. Also the following Boolean options, possibly preceded by no are recognized: bg, fg, soft, hard, intr, posix, cto, ac, tcp, udp, and lock. For details, see nfs(5).

Especially useful options include the following:

- rsize=8192,wsize=8192—This will make your nfs connection much faster than with the default buffer size of 1024.
- hard—The program accessing a file on a NFS mounted file system will hang when the server crashes. The process cannot be interrupted or killed unless you also specify intr. When the NFS server is back online the program will continue undisturbed from where it was. This is probably what you want.
- soft—This option allows the kernel to time out if the nfs server is not responding for some time. The time can be specified with timeo=time. This option might be useful if your nfs server sometimes doesn't respond or will be rebooted while some process tries to get a file from the server. Usually it just causes lots of trouble.
- nolock—Do not use locking. Do not start lockd.

MOUNT OPTIONS FOR proc

- uid=value and gid=value—These options are recognized, but have no effect as far as I can see.

MOUNT OPTIONS FOR romfs

None.

MOUNT OPTIONS FOR smbfs

Just like nfs, the smb implementation expects a binary argument (a struct smb_mount_data) to the mount system call. This argument is constructed by smbmount(8) and the current version of mount (2.6c) does not know anything about smb.

MOUNT OPTIONS FOR `sysv`

None.

MOUNT OPTIONS FOR `ufs`

None.

MOUNT OPTIONS FOR `umsdos`

See mount options for `msdos`. The `dotsOK` option is explicitly killed by `umsdos`.

MOUNT OPTIONS FOR `vfat`

First, the mount options for `fat` are recognized. The `dotsOK` option is explicitly killed by `vfat`. Furthermore, there is

`uni_xlate`

Translate unhandled Unicode characters to special escaped sequences. This enables you to back up and restore filenames that are created with any Unicode characters. Without this option, a ? is used when no translation is possible. The escape character is : because it is otherwise illegal on the `vfat` file system. The escape sequence that is used where u is the unicode character, is: :, (u & 0x3f), ((u>>6) & 0x3f), (u>>12).

`posix`

Allow two files with names that only differ in case.

`nonumtail`

First try to make a short name without sequence number, before trying `name~num.ext`.

MOUNT OPTIONS FOR `xenix`

None.

MOUNT OPTIONS FOR `xiafs`

None. Although nothing is wrong with `xiafs`, it is not used much and is not maintained. Probably one shouldn't use it. Since Linux version 2.1.21, `xiafs` is no longer part of the kernel source.

THE LOOP DEVICE

One further possible type is a mount using the loop device. For example, the command

```
mount /tmp/fdimage /mnt -t msdos -o loop=/dev/loop3,blocksize=1024
```

sets up the loop device `/dev/loop3` to correspond to the file `/tmp/fdimage`, and then mount this device on `/mnt`. This type of mount knows about three options, namely `loop`, `offset` and `encryption`, that are really options to `losetup(8)`. If no explicit loop device is mentioned (but just an option `-o loop` is given), then `mount` will try to find some unused loop device and use that. If you are not so unwise as to make /etc/mtab a symbolic link to /proc/mounts then any loop device allocated by mount will be freed by umount. You can also free a loop device by hand, using losetup -d (see losetup(8)).

FILES

/etc/fstab file system table

/etc/mtab table of mounted file systems

/etc/mtab~ lock file

/etc/mtab.tmp temporary file

SEE ALSO

mount(2), umount(2), fstab(5), umount(8), swapon(8), nfs(5), mountd(8), nfsd(8), mke2fs(8), tune2fs(8), losetup(8)

BUGS

A corrupted file system can cause a crash.

Some Linux file systems don't support -o sync (the ext2fs *does* support synchronous updates (à la BSD) when mounted with the sync option).

The -o remount might not be able to change mount parameters (all *ext2fs*-specific parameters, except sb, are changeable with a remount, for example, but you can't change gid or umask for the *fatfs*).

HISTORY

A mount command existed in Version 5 AT&T UNIX.

MV

NAME

mv—Move (rename) files.

SYNOPSIS

mv [OPTION]... SOURCE DEST

mv [OPTION]... SOURCE... DIRECTORY

DESCRIPTION

Rename SOURCE to DEST, or move SOURCE(s) to DIRECTORY.

- -b, --backup—Make backup before removal
- -f, --force—Remove existing destinations, never prompt
- -i, --interactive—Prompt before overwrite

- -S, --suffix=SUFFIX—Override the usual backup suffix
- -u, --update—Move only older or brand new non-directories
- -v, --verbose—Explain what is being done
- -V, --version-control=WORD—Override the usual version control
- --help—Display this help and exit
- --version—Output version information and exit

The backup suffix is ~, unless set with SIMPLE_BACKUP_SUFFIX. The version control can be set with VERSION_CONTROL>. Values are

> t, numbered
>
> make numbered backups
>
> nil, existing
>
> numbered if numbered backups exist, simple otherwise
>
> never, simple
>
> always make simple backups

REPORTING BUGS

Report bugs to <bug-fileutils@gnu.org>.

SEE ALSO

The full documentation for mv is maintained as a Texinfo manual. If the info and mv programs are properly installed at your site, the command

```
info mv
```

should give you access to the complete manual.

PASSWD

NAME

passwd—Update a user's authentication token(s).

SYNOPSIS

```
passwd [-k] [-l] [-u [-f]] [-d] [-S] [username]
```

DESCRIPTION

passwd is used to update a user's authentication token(s).

passwd is configured to work through the Linux-PAM API. Essentially, it initializes itself as a passwd service with Linux-PAM and utilizes configured password modules to authenticate and then update a user's password.

PART
VI

APP
A

A simple entry in the Linux-PAM configuration file for this service would be:

```
#
#passwdserviceentrythatdoesstrengthcheckingof
#aproposedpasswordbeforeupdatingit.
#
passwdpasswordrequisite\
 /usr/lib/security/pam_cracklib.soretry=3
passwdpasswordrequired\
 /usr/lib/security/pam_pwdb.souse_authtok
#
```

Note that other module-types are not required for this application to function correctly.

OPTIONS

- -k—The option, -k, is used to indicate that the update should only be for expired authentication tokens (passwords); the user wishes to keep their non-expired tokens as before.

- -l—This option is used to lock the specified account and is available to root only. The locking is performed by rendering the encrypted password into an invalid string (by prefixing the encrypted string with an !).

- -u—This is the reverse of the previous—it will unlock the account password by removing the ! prefix. This option is available to root only. By default passwd will refuse to create a passwordless account (it will not unlock an account that has only ! as a password). The force option -f will override this protection.

- -d—This is a quick way to disable a password for an account. It will set the named account passwordless. Available to root only.

- -s—This will output a small amount of information about the status of the password for a given account. Available to root user only.

REMEMBER THE FOLLOWING TWO PRINCIPLES

PROTECT YOUR PASSWORD

Don't write down your password—memorize it. In particular, don't write it down and leave it anywhere, and don't place it in an unencrypted file! Use unrelated passwords for systems controlled by different organizations. Don't give or share your password, in particular to someone claiming to be from computer support or a vendor. Don't let anyone watch you enter your password. Don't enter your password into a computer you don't trust. Use the password for a limited time and change it periodically.

CHOOSE A HARD-TO-GUESS PASSWORD

passwd will try to prevent you from choosing a really bad password, but it isn't foolproof; create your password wisely. Don't use something you'd find in a dictionary (in any language or jargon). Don't use a name (including that of a spouse, parent, child, pet, fantasy character, famous person, or location) or any variation of your personal or account name. Don't use accessible personal information (such as your phone number, license plate, or social security number) or your environment. Don't use a birthday or a simple pattern (such as backward, followed by a digit, or preceded by a digit. Instead, use a mixture of upper and lowercase letters, as well as digits or punctuation. When choosing a new password, make sure it is unrelated to any previous password. Use long passwords (say 8 characters long). You might use a word pair with punctuation inserted, a passphrase (an understandable sequence of words), or the first letter of each word in a passphrase.

These principles are partially enforced by the system. Vigilance on your part will make the system much more secure.

EXIT CODE

On successful completion of its task, passwd will complete with exit code 0. An exit code of 1 indicates an error occurred. Textual errors are written to the standard error stream.

CONFORMING TO

Linux-PAM (Pluggable Authentication modules for Linux). If your distribution of Linux-PAM conforms to the Linux File System Standard, you can find the modules in /lib/security/ instead of /usr/lib/security/, as indicated in the example.

FILES

/etc/pam.d/passwd - the Linux-PAM configuration file

BUGS

None known.

SEE ALSO

pam(8), and pam_chauthok(2).

For more complete information on how to configure this application with Linux-PAM, see the Linux-PAM System Administrators' Guide at

<http://parc.power.net/morgan/Linux-PAM/index.html>.

PART

VI

APP

A

AUTHOR

Cristian Gafton <gafton@redhat.com>

PS

NAME

ps—Report process status.

SYNOPSIS

ps [options]

DESCRIPTION

ps gives a snapshot of the current processes. If you want a repetitive update of this status, use top. This man page documents the /proc-based version of ps, or tries to.

COMMAND-LINE OPTIONS

This version of ps accepts several kinds of options.

UNIX98 options can be grouped and must be preceded by a dash. BSD options can be grouped and must not be used with a dash. GNU long options are preceded by two dashes.

Options of different types can be freely mixed.

Set the I_WANT_A_BROKEN_PS environment variable to force BSD syntax even when options are preceded by a dash. The PS_PERSONALITY environment variable (described below) provides more detailed control of ps behavior.

SIMPLE PROCESS DESCRIPTION

Switch	Description
-A	Select all processes
-N	Negate selection
-a	Select all with a tty except session leaders
-d	Select all, but omit session leaders
-e	Selects all processes
T	Select all processes on this terminal
a	Select all processes on a terminal, including those of other users
g	Really all, even group leaders (does nothing without SunOS settings)
r	Restrict output to running processes
x	Select processes without controlling ttys
--deselect	Negate selection

PROCESS SELECTION BY LIST

Switch	Description
-C	Select by command name
-G	Select by RGID (supports names)
-U	Select by RUID (supports names)
-g	Select by session leader OR by group name
-p	Select by PID
-s	Select processes belonging to the sessions given
-t	Select by tty
-u	Select by effective user ID (supports names)
U	Select processes for specified users
p	Select by process ID
t	Select by tty
--Group	Select by real group name or ID
--User	Select by real user name or ID
--group	Select by effective group name or ID
--pid	Select by process ID
--sid	Select by session ID
--tty	Select by terminal
--user	Select by effective user name or ID
-123	Implied --sid
123	Implied --pid

OUTPUT FORMAT CONTROL

Switch	Description
-O	Is preloaded '-o'
-c	Different scheduler info for -l option
-f	Does full listing
-j	Jobs format
-l	Long format
-o	User-defined format
-y	Do not show flags; show rss in place of addr
O	Is preloaded 'o' (overloaded)
X	Old Linux i386 register format
j	Job control format
l	Display long format
o	Specify user-defined format
s	Display signal format
u	Display user-oriented format
v	Display virtual memory format
--format	User-defined format

PART

VI

APP

A

OUTPUT MODIFIERS

Switch	Description
-H	Show process hierarchy (forest)
-m	Show threads
-n	Set namelist file
-w	Wide output
C	Use raw CPU time for %CPU instead of decaying average
N	Specify namelist file
O	Indicate sorting order (overloaded)
S	Include some dead child process data (as a sum with the parent)
c	True command name
e	Show environment after the command
f	ASCII-art process hierarchy (forest)
h	Do not print header lines (repeat header lines in BSD personality)
m	All threads
n	Numeric output for WCHAN and USER
w	Wide output
--cols	Set screen width
--columns	Set screen width
--cumulative	Include some dead child process data (as a sum with the parent)
--forest	ASCII art process tree
--html	HTML escaped output
--headers	Repeat header lines
--no-headers	Print no header line at all
--lines	Set screen height
--nul	Unjustified output with NULs
--null	Unjustified output with NULs
--rows	Set screen height
--sort	Specify sorting order
--width	Set screen width
--zero	Unjustified output with NULLs

INFORMATION

Switch	Description
-V	Print version
L	List all format specifiers
V	Show version information
--help	Print help message

--info	Print debugging info
--version	Print version

OBSOLETE

Switch	Description
A	Increase the argument space (DecUnix)
M	Use alternate core (try -n or N instead)
W	Get swap info from ... not /dev/drum (try -n or N instead)
k	Use /vmcore as c-dumpfile (try -n or N instead)

NOTES

The -g option can select by session leader or by group name. Selection by session leader is specified by many standards, but selection by group name is the logical behavior that several other operating systems use. This ps will select by session leader when the list is completely numeric (as sessions are). Group ID numbers will work only when some group names are also specified.

The m option should not be used. Use -m or -o with a list. (m displays memory info, shows threads, or sorts by memory use.)

The h option is problematic. Standard BSD ps uses the option to print a header on each page of output, but older Linux ps uses the option to totally disable the header. This version of ps follows the Linux usage of not printing the header unless the BSD personality has been selected, in which case it prints a header on each page of output. Regardless of the current personality, you can use the long options --headers and --no-headers to enable the printing of headers on each page and disable headers entirely, respectively.

Terminals (ttys, or screens of text output) can be specified in several forms: /dev/ttyS1, ttyS1,or S1. Obsolete 'ps t' (your own terminal) and 'ps t?' (processes without a terminal) syntax is supported, but modern options ('T', 't' with list, 'x', 't' with list) should be used instead.

The BSD O option can act like -O (user-defined output format with some common fields predefined) or can be used to specify sort order. Heuristics are used to determine the behavior of this option. To ensure that the desired behavior is obtained, specify the other option (sorting or formatting) in some other way.

For sorting, BSD O option syntax is O[+¦-]k1[,[+¦-]k2[,...]] Order the process listing according to the multilevel sort specified by the sequence of short keys from SORT KEYS, k1, k2, ... The + is quite optional, merely re-iterating the default direction on a key. - reverses direction only on the key it precedes. The O option must be the last option in a single command argument, but specifications in successive arguments are catenated.

PART

VI

APP

A

GNU sorting syntax is `--sortX[+¦-]key[,[+¦-]key[,...]]`. Choose a multi-letter key from the SORT KEYS section. X can be any convenient separator character. To be GNU-ish use '='. The '+' is really optional since default direction is increasing numerical or lexicographic order; for example, `ps jax --sort=uid,-ppid,+pid`.

This ps works by reading the virtual files in `/proc`. This ps does not need to be suid kmem or have any privileges to run. Do not give this ps any special permissions.

This ps needs access to a namelist file for proper WCHAN display. The namelist file must match the current Linux kernel exactly for correct output.

To produce the WCHAN field, ps needs to read the System.map file created when the kernel is compiled. The search path is:

```
$PS_SYSTEM_MAP
/boot/System.map-'uname -r'
/boot/System.map
/lib/modules/'uname -r'/System.map
/usr/src/linux/System.map
```

The member used_math of task_struct is not shown, since crt0.s checks to see if math is present. This causes the math flag to be set for all processes, and so it is worthless. (Somebody fix libc or the kernel please.)

Programs swapped out to disk will be shown without command-line arguments, and unless the c option is given, in brackets.

%CPU shows the cputime/realtime percentage. It will not add up to 100% unless you are lucky. It is time used divided by the time the process has been running.

The SIZE and RSS fields don't count the page tables and the task_struct of a proc; this is at least 12KB of memory that is always resident. SIZE is the virtual size of the proc (code+data+stack).

Processes marked `<defunct>` are dead processes (so-called 'zombies') that remain because their parent has not destroyed them properly. These processes will be destroyed by init(8) if the parent process exits.

PROCESS FLAGS

ALIGNWARN	001	Print alignment warning msgs
STARTING	002	Being created
EXITING	004	Getting shut down
PTRACED	010	Set if ptrace (0) has been called
TRACESYS	020	Tracing system calls
FORKNOEXEC	040	Forked but didn't exec
SUPERPRIV	100	Used super-user privileges
DUMPCORE	200	Dumped core
SIGNALED	400	Killed by a signal

PROCESS STATE CODES

D	Uninterruptible sleep (usually IO)
R	Runnable (on run queue)
S	Sleeping
T	Traced or stopped
Z	A defunct ('zombie') process

For BSD formats and when the `stat` keyword is used, additional letters can be displayed:

W	Has no resident pages
<	High-priority process
N	Low-priority task
L	Has pages locked into memory (for real-time and custom IO)

SORT KEYS

The values used in sorting are the internal values `ps` uses and not the cooked values used in some of the output format fields. Pipe `ps` output into the `sort(1)` command if you want to sort the cooked values.

KEY	LONG	DESCRIPTION
c	cmd	Simple name of executable
C	cmdline	Full command line
f	flags	Flags as in long format F field
g	pgrp	Process group ID
G	tpgid	Controlling tty process group ID
j	cutime	Cumulative user time
J	cstime	Cumulative system time
k	utime	User time
K	stime	System time
m	min_flt	Number of minor page faults
M	maj_flt	Number of major page faults
n	cmin_flt	Cumulative minor page faults
N	cmaj_flt	Cumulative major page faults
o	session	Session ID
p	pid	Process ID
P	ppid	Parent process ID
r	rss	Resident set size
R	resident	Resident pages
s	size	Memory size in kilobytes
S	share	Amount of shared pages
t	tty	The minor device number of tty
T	start_time	Time process was started

PART

VI

APP

A

U	uid	User ID number
u	user	Username
v	vsize	Total VM size in bytes
y	priority	Kernel scheduling priority

AIX FORMAT DESCRIPTORS

This ps supports AIX format descriptors, which work somewhat like the formatting codes of printf(1) and printf(3). For example, the normal default output can be produced with this: ps -eo '%p %y %x %c'

CODE	NORMAL	HEADER
%C	pcpu	%CPU
%G	group	GROUP
%P	ppid	PPID
%U	user	USER
%a	args	COMMAND
%c	comm	COMMAND
%g	rgroup	RGROUP
%n	nice	NI
%p	pid	PID
%r	pgid	PGID
%t	etime	ELAPSED
%u	ruser	RUSER
%x	time	TIME
%y	tty	TTY
%z	vsz	VSZ

STANDARD FORMAT SPECIFIERS

These can be used to control both output format and sorting; for example: ps -eo pid,user,args --sort user

CODE	HEADER
%cpu	%CPU
%mem	%MEM
alarm	ALARM
args	COMMAND
blocked	BLOCKED
bsdstart	START
bsdtime	TIME
c	C
caught	CAUGHT
cmd	CMD
comm	COMMAND

command	COMMAND
cputime	TIME
drs	DRS
dsiz	DSIZ
egid	EGID
egroup	EGROUP
eip	EIP
esp	ESP
etime	ELAPSED
euid	EUID
euser	EUSER
f	F
fgid	FGID
fgroup	FGROUP
flag	F
flags	F
fname	COMMAND
fsgid	FSGID
fsgroup	FSGROUP
fsuid	FSUID
fsuser	FSUSER
fuid	FUID
fuser	FUSER
gid	GID
group	GROUP
ignored	IGNORED
intpri	PRI
lim	LIM
longtname	TTY
lstart	STARTED
m_drs	DRS
m_trs	TRS
maj_flt	MAJFL
majflt	MAJFLT
min_flt	MINFL
minflt	MINFLT
ni	NI
nice	NI
nwchan	WCHAN
opri	PRI
pagein	PAGEIN
pcpu	%CPU
pending	PENDING

pgid	PGID
pgrp	PGRP
pid	PID
pmem	%MEM
ppid	PPID
pri	PRI
rgid	RGID
rgroup	RGROUP
rss	RSS
rssize	RSS
rsz	RSZ
ruid	RUID
ruser	RUSER
s	S
sess	SESS
session	SESS
sgi_p	P
sgi_rss	RSS
sgid	SGID
sgroup	SGROUP
sid	SID
sig	PENDING
sig_block	BLOCKED
sig_catch	CATCHED
sig_ignore	IGNORED
sig_pend	SIGNAL
sigcatch	CAUGHT
sigignore	IGNORED
sigmask	BLOCKED
stackp	STACKP
start	STARTED
start_stack	STACKP
start_time	START
stat	STAT
state	S
stime	STIME
suid	SUID
suser	SUSER
svgid	SVGID
svgroup	SVGROUP
svuid	SVUID
svuser	SVUSER
sz	SZ

time	TIME
timeout	TMOUT
tmout	TMOUT
tname	TTY
tpgid	TPGID
trs	TRS
trss	TRSS
tsiz	TSIZ
tt	TT
tty	TT
tty4	TTY
tty8	TTY
ucomm	COMMAND
uid	UID
uid_hack	UID
uname	USER
user	USER
vsize	VSZ
vsz	VSZ
wchan	WCHAN

ENVIRONMENT VARIABLES

The following environment variables could affect ps:

COLUMNS	Override default display width
LINES	Override default display height
PS_PERSONALITY	Set to one of posix, old, linux, bsd, sun, digital
CMD_ENV	Set to one of posix, old, linux, bsd, sun, digital
I_WANT_A_BROKEN_PS	Force obsolete command-line interpretation
LC_TIME	Date format
PS_FORMAT	Default output format override
PS_SYSMAP	Default namelist (System.map) location
PS_SYSTEM_MAP	Default namelist (System.map) location
POSIXLY_CORRECT	Don't find excuses to ignore bad features
UNIX95	Don't find excuses to ignore bad features
_XPG	Cancel CMD_ENV=irix non-standard behavior

In general, it is a bad idea to set these variables. The two exceptions are CMD_ENV (or PS_PERSONALITY), to set the desired default personality, and POSIXLY_CORRECT (or UNIX95), which should be set for UNIX98 standard compliance.

PS_PERSONALITY	**Description**
none	"Do the right thing"
aix	Like AIX ps

bsd	Like FreeBSD ps
compaq	Like Digital UNIX ps
debian	Like the old Debian ps
digital	Like Digital UNIX ps
gnu	Like the old Debian ps
hp	Like HP-UX ps
hpux	Like HP-UX ps
irix	Like Irix ps
linux	Deviate from UNIX98 for convenience only
old	Like the original Linux ps
posix	Standard
sco	Like SCO ps
sgi	Like Irix ps
sun	Like SunOS 4 ps
sunos	Like SunOS 4 ps
sysv	Standard
unix	Standard
unix95	Standard
unix98	Standard

EXAMPLES

To see every process on the system using standard syntax:

- ps -e—To see every process on the system using BSD syntax
- ps ax—To see every process except those running as root (real & effective ID)
- ps -U root -u root -N—To see every process with a user-defined format
- ps -eo pid,tt,user,fname,tmout,f,wchan—Odd display with AIX field descriptors
- ps -o '%u : %U : %p : %a'—Print only the process IDs of syslogd: ps -C syslogd -o pid=

SEE ALSO

top(1) pstree(1) proc(5)

STANDARDS

This ps can be set to conform to version 2 of the Single UNIX Specification.

AUTHOR

ps was originally written by Branko Lankester <lankeste@fwi.uva.nl>.

Michael K. Johnson <johnsonm@redhat.com> rewrote it significantly to use the proc file system, changing a few things in the process.

Michael Shields <shields@msrl.com> added the pid-list feature.

Charles Blake <cblake@bbn.com> added multilevel sorting, the dirent-style library, the device name-to-number mapped database, the approximate binary search directly on System.map, and many code and documentation cleanups.

David Mosberger-Tang wrote the generic BFD support for psupdate.

Albert Cahalan <acahalan@cs.uml.edu> rewrote ps for full UNIX98 and BSD support, along with some ugly hacks for obsolete and foreign syntax.

Michael K. Johnson <johnsonm@redhat.com> is the current maintainer.

Please send bug reports to <procps-bugs@redhat.com>.

PWD

NAME

pwd—Print name of current/working directory.

SYNOPSIS

pwd [OPTION]

DESCRIPTION

Print the full filename of the current working directory.

--help

Display this help and exit.

--version

Output version information and exit.

REPORTING BUGS

Report bugs to <bug-sh-utils@gnu.org>.

SEE ALSO

The full documentation for pwd is maintained as a Texinfo manual. If the info and pwd programs are properly installed at your site, the command

info pwd

should give you access to the complete manual.

COPYRIGHT

Copyright © 1999 Free Software Foundation, Inc. This is free software; see the source for copying conditions. There is NO warranty; not even for MERCHANTABILITY or FITNESS FOR A PARTICULAR PURPOSE.

PART
VI

APP
A

RM

NAME

rm—Remove files or directories.

SYNOPSIS

rm [OPTION]... FILE...

DESCRIPTION

This manual page documents the GNU version of rm. rm removes each specified file. By default, it does not remove directories. If a file is unwritable, the standard input is a tty, and the -f or –force option is not given, rm prompts the user for whether to remove the file. If the response does not begin with 'y' or 'Y', the file is skipped.

GNU rm, like every program that uses the getopt function to parse its arguments, enables you to use the -- option to indicate that all following arguments are non-options. To remove a file called -f in the current directory, you could type either

rm -- -f

or

rm ./-f

The UNIX rm program's use of a single - for this purpose predates the development of the getopt standard syntax.

OPTIONS

Remove (unlink) the FILE(s).

- -d, --directory—Unlink directory, even if non-empty (super-user only)
- -f, --force—Ignore nonexistent files, never prompt
- -i, --interactive—Prompt before any removal
- -r, -R, --recursive—Remove the contents of directories recursively
- -v, --verbose—Explain what is being done
- --help—Display this help and exit
- --version—Output version information and exit

REPORTING BUGS

Report bugs to <bug-fileutils@gnu.org>.

SEE ALSO

The full documentation for rm is maintained as a Texinfo manual. If the info and rm programs are properly installed at your site, the command

`info rm`

should give you access to the complete manual.

SHUTDOWN

NAME

shutdown—Bring the system down.

SYNOPSIS

`/sbin/shutdown [-t sec] [-arkhncfF] time [warning-message]`

DESCRIPTION

shutdown brings the system down in a secure way. All logged-in users are notified that the system is going down, and login(1) is blocked. It is possible to shut the system down immediately or after a specified delay. All processes are first notified that the system is going down by the signal SIGTERM. This gives programs like vi(1) the time to save the file being edited, mail and news processing programs a chance to exit cleanly, etc. shutdown does its job by signaling the init process, asking it to change the runlevel. Runlevel 0 is used to halt the system, runlevel 6 is used to reboot the system, and runlevel 1 is used to put the system into a state where administrative tasks can be performed; this is the default if neither the -h nor -r flag is given to shutdown. To see which actions are taken on halt or reboot see the appropriate entries for these runlevels in the file /etc/inittab.

OPTIONS

- ■ -a—Use /etc/shutdown.allow.
- ■ -t sec—Tell init(8) to wait sec seconds between sending processes the warning and the kill signal, before changing to another runlevel.
- ■ -k—Don't really shut down; only send the warning messages to everybody.
- ■ -r—Reboot after shutdown.
- ■ -h—Halt after shutdown.
- ■ -n—[DEPRECATED] Don't call init(8) to do the shutdown but do it ourselves. The use of this option is discouraged, and its results are not always what you'd expect.
- ■ -f—Skip fsck on reboot.
- ■ -F—Force fsck on reboot.

PART

VI

APP

A

- -c—Cancel an already running shutdown. With this option it is of course not possible to give the time argument, but you can enter an explanatory message on the command line that will be sent to all users.
- time—When to shutdown.
- warning-message—Message to send to all users.

The time argument can have different formats. It can be an absolute time in the format hh:mm, in which hh is the hour (1 or 2 digits) and mm is the minute of the hour (in two digits). It can also be in the format +m, in which m is the number of minutes to wait. The word now is an alias for +0.

If shutdown is called with a delay, it creates the advisory file /etc/nologin which causes programs such as login(1) to not allow new user logins. shutdown only removes this file if it is stopped before it can signal init (that is, it is cancelled or something goes wrong). Otherwise it is the responsibility of the system shutdown or startup scripts to remove this file so that users can login.

The -f flag means 'reboot fast'. This only creates an advisory file /fastboot which can be tested by the system when it comes up again. The boot rc file can test if this file is present, and decide not to run fsck(1) if the system has been shut down in the proper way. After that, the boot process should remove /fastboot.

The -F flag means 'force fsck'. This only creates an advisory file /forcefsck, which can be tested by the system when it comes up again. The boot rc file can test whether this file is present, and decide to run fsck(1) with a special 'force' flag so that even properly unmounted file systems get checked. After that, the boot process should remove /forcefsck.

The -n flag causes shutdown not to call init, but to kill all running processes itself. shutdown will then turn off quota, accounting, and swapping and unmount all file systems.

ACCESS CONTROL

shutdown can be called from init(8) when the Ctrl-Alt-Del keys are pressed, by creating an appropriate entry in /etc/inittab. Everyone who has physical access to the console keyboard can shut the system down. To prevent this, shutdown can check to see if an authorized user is logged in on one of the virtual consoles. If shutdown is called with the -a argument (add this to the invocation of shutdown in /etc/inittab), it checks to see if the file /etc/shutdown.allow is present. It then compares the login names in that file with the list of people that are logged in on a virtual console (from /var/run/utmp). Only if one of those authorized users or root is logged in, it will proceed. Otherwise it will write the message

shutdown: no authorized users logged in

to the (physical) system console. The format of /etc/shutdown.allow is one user name per line. Empty lines and comment lines (prefixed by a #) are allowed. Currently there is a limit of 32 users in this file.

FILES

```
/fastboot
/etc/inittab
/etc/init.d/halt
/etc/init.d/reboot
/etc/shutdown.allow
```

BUGS

Not really a bug, but most users forget to give the time argument and are then puzzled by the error message shutdown produces. The time argument is mandatory; in 90 percent of all cases this argument will be the word 'now'.

AUTHOR

Miquel van Smoorenburg, miquels@cistron.nl

SEE ALSO

fsck(8), init(1), halt(8), reboot(8)

SU

NAME

su—Run a shell with substitute user and group IDs

SYNOPSIS

su [OPTION]... [-] [USER [ARG]...]

DESCRIPTION

Change the effective user id and group id to that of USER.

- -, -l, --login—Make the shell a login shell
- -c, --commmand=COMMAND—Pass a single COMMAND to the shell with -c
- -f, --fast—Pass -f to the shell (for csh or tcsh)
- -m, --preserve-environment—Do not reset environment variables
- -p—Same as -m
- -s, --shell=SHELL—Run SHELL if /etc/shells allows it
- --help—Display this help and exit
- --version—Output version information and exit

A mere - implies -l. If USER not given, assume root.

PART

VI

APP

A

REPORTING BUGS

Report bugs to <bug-sh-utils@gnu.org>.

SEE ALSO

The full documentation for su is maintained as a Texinfo manual. If the info and su programs are properly installed at your site, the command

```
info su
```

should give you access to the complete manual.

COPYRIGHT

Copyright © 1999 Free Software Foundation, Inc. This is free software; see the source for copying conditions. There is NO warranty; not even for MERCHANTABILITY or FITNESS FOR A PARTICULAR PURPOSE.

SYNC

NAME

sync—Flush file system buffers

SYNOPSIS

```
sync [OPTION]
```

DESCRIPTION

Force changed blocks to disk, update the super block.

- --help—Display this help and exit
- --version—Output version information and exit

REPORTING BUGS

Report bugs to <bug-fileutils@gnu.org>.

SEE ALSO

The full documentation for sync is maintained as a Texinfo manual. If the info and sync programs are properly installed at your site, the command

```
info sync
```

should give you access to the complete manual.

TAR

NAME

tar—The GNU version of the tar archiving utility.

SYNOPSIS

```
tar [ - ] A --catenate --concatenate ¦ c --create ¦ d --diff --compare ¦
r --append ¦ t --list ¦ u --update ¦ x -extract --get [ --atime-preserve ]
[ -b, --block-size N ] [ -B, --read-full-blocks ] [ -C, --directory DIR ] [ --checkpoint ]
[ -f, --file [HOSTNAME:]F ] [ --force-local ] [ -F, --info-script F --new-volume-script F ]
➥[ -G, --incremental ]
[ -g, --listed-incremental F ] [ -h, --dereference ] [ -i, --ignore-zeros ]
[ --ignore-failed-read ] [ -k, --keep-old-files ] [ -K, --starting-file F ]
[ -l, --one-file-system ] [ -L, --tape-length N ] [ -m, --modification-time ]
[ -M, --multi-volume ] [ -N, --after-date DATE, --newer DATE ]
[ -o, --old-archive, --portability ] [ -O, --to-stdout ]
[ -p, --same-permissions, --preserve-permissions ] [ -P, --absolute-paths ] [ --preserve ]
[ -R, --record-number ] [ --remove-files ] [ -s, --same-order, --preserve-order ]
[ --same-owner ] [ -S, --sparse ] [ -T, --files-from F ] [ --null ]
[ --totals ] [ -v, --verbose ] [ -V, --label NAME ] [ --version ]
[ -w, --interactive, --confirmation ] [ -W, --verify ]
[ --exclude FILE ] [ -X, --exclude-from FILE ] [ -Z, --compress, --uncompress ]
[ -z, --gzip, --ungzip ] [ --use-compress-program PROG ] [ --block-compress ]
[ -[0-7][lmh] ] filename1 [ filename2, ... filenameN ] directory1
➥ [ directory2, ...directoryN ]
```

DESCRIPTION

This manual page documents the GNU version of tar , an archiving program designed to store and extract files from an archive file known as a *tarfile*. A tarfile can be made on a tape drive; however, it is also common to write a tarfile to a normal file. The first argument to tar must be one of the options: Acdrtux, followed by any optional functions. The final arguments to tar are the names of the files or directories that should be archived. The use of a directory name always implies that the subdirectories below should be included in the archive.

FUNCTION LETTERS

One of the following options must be used:

- -A, --catenate, --concatenate—Append tar files to an archive
- -c, --create—Create a new archive

- -d, --diff, --compare—Find differences between archive and file system
- --delete—Delete from the archive (not for use on mag tapes!)
- -r, --append—Append files to the end of an archive
- -t, --list—List the contents of an archive
- -u, --update—Only append files that are newer than copy in archive
- -x, --extract, --get—Extract files from an archive

OTHER OPTIONS

- --atime-preserve—Don't change access times on dumped files
- -b, --block-size N—Block size of Nx512 bytes (default N=20)
- -B, --read-full-blocks—Reblock as we read (for reading 4.2BSD pipes)
- -C, --directory DIR—Change to directory DIR
- --checkpoint—Print directory names while reading the archive
- -f, --file [HOSTNAME:]F—Use archive file or device F (default /dev/rmt0)
- --force-local—Archive file is local even if has a colon
- -F, --info-script F --new-volume-script F—Run script at end of each tape (implies -M)
- -G, --incremental—Create/list/extract old GNU-format incremental backup
- -g, --listed-incremental F—Create/list/extract new GNU-format incremental backup
- -h, --dereference—Don't dump symlinks; dump the files they point to
- -i, --ignore-zeros—Ignore blocks of zeros in archive (normally mean EOF)
- --ignore-failed-read—Don't exit with non-zero status on unreadable files
- -k, --keep-old-files—Keep existing files; don't overwrite them from archive
- -K, --starting-file F—Begin at file F in the archive
- -l, --one-file-system—Stay in local file system when creating an archive
- -L, --tape-length N—Change tapes after writing N*1024 bytes
- -m, --modification-time—Don't extract file modified time
- -M, --multi-volume—Create/list/extract multi-volume archive
- -N, --after-date DATE, --newer DATE—Only store files newer than DATE
- -o, --old-archive, --portability—write a V7 format archive, rather than ANSI format
- -O, --to-stdout—Extract files to standard output
- -p, --same-permissions, --preserve-permissions—Extract all protection information
- -P, --absolute-paths—Don't strip leading '/'s from filenames

- --preserve—Like -p -s
- -R, --record-number—Show record number within archive with each message
- --remove-files—Remove files after adding them to the archive
- -s, --same-order, --preserve-order—List of names to extract is sorted to match archive
- --same-owner—Create extracted files with the same ownership
- -S, --sparse—Handle sparse files efficiently
- -T, --files-from F—Get names to extract or create from file F
- --null—-T reads null-terminated names, disables -C
- --totals—Print total bytes written with -'-create
- -v, --verbose—Verbosely list files processed
- -V, --label NAME—Create archive with volume name NAME
- --version—Print tar program version number
- -w, --interactive, --confirmation—Ask for confirmation for every action
- -W, --verify—Attempt to verify the archive after writing it
- --exclude FILE—Exclude file FILE
- -X, --exclude-from FILE—Exclude files listed in FILE
- -Z, --compress, --uncompress—Filter the archive through compress
- -z, --gzip, –ungzip—Filter the archive through gzip
- --use-compress-program PROG—Filter the archive through PROG (which must accept -d)
- --block-compress—Block the output of compression program for tapes
- -[0-7][lmh]—Specify drive and density

TOUCH

NAME

touch—Change file time stamps.

SYNOPSIS

touch [OPTION]... FILE...

DESCRIPTION

- or
- ../src/touch [-acm] MMDDhhmm[YY] FILE... (obsolescent)—Update the access and modification times of each FILE to the current time

- -a—Change only the access time
- -c—Do not create any files
- -d, --date=STRING—Parse STRING and use it instead of current time
- -f—(ignored)
- -m—Change only the modification time
- -r, --reference=FILE—Use this file's times instead of current time
- -t—STAMP use [[CC]YY]MMDDhhmm[.ss] instead of current time
- --time=WORD—Access -a, atime -a, mtime -m, modify -m, use -a
- --help—Display this help and exit
- --version—Output version information and exit

STAMP can be used without -t if none of -drt, nor -, are used. Note that the three time-date formats recognized for the -d and -t options and for the obsolescent argument are all different.

REPORTING BUGS

Report bugs to <bug-fileutils@gnu.org>.

SEE ALSO

The full documentation for touch is maintained as a Texinfo manual. If the info and touch programs are properly installed at your site, the command

info touch

should give you access to the complete manual.

UMOUNT

NAME

umount—Unmount file systems.

SYNOPSIS

umount [-hV]

umount -a [-nrv] [-t vfstype]

umount [-nrv] device ¦ dir [...]

DESCRIPTION

The umount command detaches the file system(s) mentioned from the file hierarchy. A file system is specified either by giving the directory where it has been mounted, or by giving the special device on which it lives.

Note that a file system cannot be unmounted when it is busy; for example, when there are open files on it, when some process has its working directory there, or when a swap file on it is in use. The offending process could even be umount—it opens libc, and libc in its turn can open, for example, locale files.

Options for the umount command:

- -V—Print help message and exit.
Print version and exit.

- -h—Print help message and exit.
- -v—Verbose mode.
- -n—Unmount without writing in /etc/mtab.
- -r—In case unmounting fails, try to remount read-only.
- -a—All file systems described in /etc/mtab are unmounted. (With umount version 2.7 and later, the proc file system is not unmounted.)
- -t vfstype—Indicate that the actions should only be taken on file systems of the specified type. More than one type can be specified in a comma-separated list. The list of file system types can be prefixed with no to specify the file system types on which no action should be taken.
- -f—Force unmount (in case of an unreachable NFS system). (Requires kernel 2.1.116 or later.)

THE LOOP DEVICE

The umount command will free the loop device (if any) associated with the mount, in case it finds the option loop=... in /etc/mtab. Any pending loop devices can be freed using losetup -d, see losetup(8).

FILES

/etc/mtab—Table of mounted file systems

SEE ALSO

umount(2), mount(8), losetup(8).

HISTORY

A umount command appeared in Version 6 AT&T UNIX.

UPTIME

NAME

uptime—Tell how long the system has been running.

PART
VI

APP
A

SYNOPSIS

```
uptime
uptime [-V]
```

DESCRIPTION

uptime gives a one-line display of the following information: the current time, how long the system has been running, how many users are currently logged on, and the system load averages for the past 1, 5, and 15 minutes.

This is the same information contained in the header line displayed by w(1).

FILES

/var/run/utmp—Information about who is currently logged on /proc process information

AUTHORS

uptime was written by Larry Greenfield <greenfie@gauss.rutgers.edu> and Michael K. Johnson <johnsonm@sunsite.unc.edu>.

Please send bug reports to <procps-bugs@redhat.com>.

SEE ALSO

ps(1), top(1), utmp(5), w(1)

WHICH

NAME

which—Show full path of commands.

SYNOPSIS

```
which [options] [-] programname [...]
```

DESCRIPTION

which takes one or more arguments. For each of its arguments it prints to stdout the full path of the executables that would have been executed when this argument had been entered at the shell prompt. It does this by searching for an executable or script in the directories listed in the environment variable PATH using the same algorithm as bash(1).

Options

- `--all`, `-a`—Print all matching executables in PATH, not just the first.
- `--read-alias`, `-I`—Read aliases from stdin, reporting matching ones on stdout. This is useful in combination with using an alias for which itself. For example `alias which='alias | which -i'`.
- `--skip-alias`—Ignore option `--read-alias`, if any. This is useful to explicate search for normal binaries, while using the `--read-alias` option in an alias for which.
- `--skip-dot`—Skip directories in PATH that start with a dot.
- `--skip-tilde`—Skip directories in PATH that start with a tilde and executables which reside in the HOME directory.
- `--show-dot`—If a directory in PATH starts with a dot and a matching executable was found for that path, then print '/programname' rather than the full path.
- `--show-tilde`—Output a tilde when a directory matches the HOME directory. This option is ignored when which is invoked as root.
- `--tty-only`—Stop processing options on the right if not on tty.
- `--version`, `-v`, `-V`—Print version information on standard output then exit successfully.

Return Value

which returns the number of failed arguments, or -1 when no program name was given.

Example

A useful way to use this utility is by adding an alias to which like the following:

```
alias which='which --tty-only --show-tilde --show-dot'
```

This will print the readable ~/ and ./ when starting which from your prompt while still printing the full path when used from a script:

```
> which q2 ~/bin/q2 > echo 'which q2' /home/carlo/bin/q2
```

Aliases are also supported, through the use of an alias for which. An example alias for which that is using this feature is as follows:

```
alias which='alias | which --tty-only --read-alias --show-tilde --show-dot'
```

This will print the output of alias for each alias that matches one of the given arguments; for example, using this alias on itself in a tcsh:

```
$ alias which alias \| /usr/bin/which -i !\* $ which which which
➥(alias | ./which -i !*) /usr/bin/which
```

Bugs

The HOME directory is determined by looking for the HOME environment variable, which aborts when this variable doesn't exist. This will consider two equivalent directories to be different when one of them contains a path with a symbolic link.

PART

VI

APP

A

AUTHOR

Carlo Wood <carlo@gnu.org>

SEE ALSO

bash(1)

LINUX HARDWARE SUPPORT

In this appendix

THE LINUX HARDWARE COMPATIBILITY HOWTO

This appendix is the complete text of the Linux Hardware Compatibility HOWTO by Patrick Reijnen. It is a useful reference for installing, upgrading, and troubleshooting hardware problems with Linux systems. This document is based on the HTML version of the HOWTO at `http://www.linuxdoc.org/HOWTO/Hardware-HOWTO.html`. The version used for this appendix is 99.3, dated 28 September 1999.

INTRODUCTION

> **Note**
>
> USB is not yet supported by Linux.

WELCOME

Welcome to the Linux Hardware Compatibility HOWTO. This document lists most of the hardware components (not computers with components built in) supported by Linux, so by reading through this document you can choose the components for your own Linux computer. As the list of components supported by Linux is growing rapidly, this document will never be complete. If components are not mentioned in this HOWTO, it is because I am unaware that they are supported. Either I have not found support for the component or no one has told me about support.

Subsections titled "Alpha, Beta Drivers" list hardware with alpha or beta drivers in varying degrees of usability. Note that some drivers only exist in alpha kernels, so if you see something listed as supported but it isn't in your version of the Linux kernel, upgrade.

Some devices are supported by binary-only modules; avoid these when you can. Binary-only modules are modules that are compiled for ONE kernel version. The source code for these modules has NOT been released. This may prevent you from upgrading or maintaining your system. Linus Torvalds said, "I allow binary-only modules, but I want people to know that they are *only* ever expected to work on the one version of the kernel that they were compiled for." See `http://www.kt.opensrc.org/kt19990211_5.html#10` for information on source code availability of components.

The latest version of this document can be found on `http://users.bart.nl/~patrickr/hardware-howto/Hardware-HOWTO.html`, SunSite, and all the usual mirror sites. Translations of this and other Linux HOWTOs can be found at `http://metalab.unc.edu/pub/Linux/docs/HOWTO/translations` and `ftp://metalab.unc.edu/pub/Linux/docs/HOWTO/translations`.

If you know of any Linux hardware incompatibilities not listed here please let me know; just send mail.

Still need some help selecting components after reading this document? Check the "Build Your Own PC" site at http://www.verinet.com/pc/.

Want to have a preconfigured Linux system? Have a look at http://www.linuxresources.com/web/.

Copyright

Copyright 1997, 1998, 1999 Patrick Reijnen

This HOWTO is free documentation; you can redistribute it or modify it under the terms of the GNU General Public License as published by the Free Software Foundation; either version 2 of the license, or (at your option) any later version.

This document is distributed in the hope that it will be useful, but without any warranty, without even the implied warranty of merchantability or fitness for a particular purpose. See the GNU General Public License for more details. You can obtain a copy of the GNU General Public License by writing to the Free Software Foundation, Inc., 675 Mass. Ave, Cambridge, MA 02139, USA.

If you use this or any other Linux HOWTO's in a commercial distribution, it would be nice to send the authors a complimentary copy of your product.

System Architectures

This document only deals with Linux for Intel platforms. For other platforms check the following:

- ARM Linux
  http://www.arm.uk.linux.org/

- Linux/68k
  http://www.clark.net/pub/lawrencc/linux/index.html

- Linux/8086 (The Embeddable Linux Kernel Subset)
  http://www.linux.org.uk/ELKS-Home/index.html

- Linux/Alpha
  http://www.azstarnet.com/~axplinux/

- Linux/MIPS
  http://www.linux.sgi.com

- Linux/PowerPC
  http://www.linuxppc.org/

- Linux for Acorn
  http://www.ph.kcl.ac.uk/~amb/linux.html

- Linux for PowerMac
  http://ftp.sunet.se/pub/os/Linux/mklinux/
  mkarchive/info/index.html

COMPUTERS/MOTHERBOARDS/BIOS

ISA, VLB, EISA, and PCI buses are all supported.

SPECIFIC SYSTEM/MOTHERBOARD/BIOS

- IBM PS/2 MCA systems have been supported since kernel version 2.0.7, but only for the stable kernel releases. For information you can look at the Micro Channel Linux Home Page (http://www.dgmicro.com/default.htm). Software for MCA systems can be found at ftp://ftp.dgmicro.com/pub/linuxmca. Information on the MCA SCSI subsystem can be found at http//www.uni-mainz.de/~langm000/linux.html.

- EFA E5TX-AT motherboard has a solvable problem with Red Hat Linux 5.0 and possibly other versions of Linux. It spontaneously reboots while probing hardware. To solve, update BIOS to version 1.01. Get the BIOS update at http://www.efacorp.com/download/bios/e5tx103.exe.

- The Edom MP080 motherboard needs a BIOS flash for Linux to work. Without the BIOS flash Linux will reboot during the hardware scan. For the BIOS flash check http://www.edom.com/tech/tech.htm and http://www.edom.com/download.

- The Zida 6MLX motherboard with PII Intel LX chipset is mentioned only to work with Linux when the PII cache is disabled in BIOS. BIOS upgrade does not solve the problem. Symptom is random reboots during or shortly after system boot.

Many new PCI boards are causing a couple of failure messages during boot time when "Probing PCI Hardware." The procedure presents the following message

```
Warning : Unknown PCI device (8086:7100). Please read include/linux/pci.h
```

It tells you to read the pci.h file. From this file is the following quote:

```
PROCEDURE TO REPORT NEW PCI DEVICES
    We are trying to collect information on new PCI devices, using
    the standard PCI identification procedure. If some warning is
    displayed at boot time, please report
        - /proc/pci
        - your exact hardware description. Try to find out
          which device is unknown. It may be your mainboard chipset.
          PCI-CPU bridge or PCI-ISA bridge.
        - If you can't find the actual information in your hardware
          booklet, try to read the references of the chip on the board.
        - Send all that to linux-pcisupport@cao-vlsi.ibp.fr,
          and I'll add your device to the list as soon as possible
```

```
BEFORE you send mail, please check the latest linux releases
to be sure it has not been recently added.

    Thanks
        Frederic Potter.
```

Normally your motherboard and the unknown PCI devices will function correctly.

UNSUPPORTED

- Supermicro P5MMA with BIOS versions 1.36, 1.37, and 1.4. Linux will not boot on this motherboard. A new (beta) release of the BIOS which makes Linux boot is available at `ftp.supermicro.com/mma9051.zip`.

- Supermicro P5MMA98. Linux will not boot on this motherboard. A new (beta) release of the BIOS which makes Linux boot is available at `ftp.supermicro.com/a98905.zip`.

- DataExpert Corp. ExpertColor TX531 V1.0 motherboard with chipset ACER M1531 (Date: 9729, TS6) and ACER M1543 (Date: 9732 TS6) seems to present not reproducible segmentations faults, kernel oops, and kernel hangs under heavy load and tape access. The problem seems to be the PCI-bus, respectively the ACER chipset.

LAPTOPS

For more information about Linux and laptops, the following site is a good starting point:

- Linux Laptop Homepage
  `http://www.cs.utexas.edu/users/kharker/linux-laptop/`

Other information related to laptops can be found at the following sites:

- Advanced Power Management
  `ftp://ftp.cs.unc.edu/pub/users/faith/linux/`

- Notebook battery status
  `ftp://metalab.unc.edu/pub/Linux/system/power/`

- Non-blinking cursor
  `ftp://metalab.unc.edu/pub/Linux/kernel/patches/console/noblink-1.7.tar.gz`

- Other general information
  `ftp://tsx-11.mit.edu/pub/linux/packages/laptops/`

SPECIFIC LAPTOPS

- Compaq Concerto (pen driver)
  `http://www.cs.nmsu.edu/~pfeiffer/`

- Compaq Contura Aero
  `http://domen.uninett.no/~hta/linux/aero-faq.html`

- IBM ThinkPad

  http://peipa.essex.ac.uk/tp-linux/tp-linux.html

- IBM ThinkPad 770 series

  http://resources.inw.com/linux/thinkpad770

- NEC Versa M and P

  http://www.santafe.edu:80/~nelson/versa-linux/

- Tadpole P1000

  http://www.tadpole.com/support-trdi/plans/linux.html

- Tadpole P1000 (another one)

- TI TravelMate 4000M

  ftp://ftp.biomath.jussieu.fr/pub/linux/TM4000M-mini-HOWTO.txt.Z

- TI TravelMate 5100

- Toshiba Satellite Pro 400CDT

  http://terra.mpikg-teltow.mpg.de/~burger/T400CDT-Linux.html

PCMCIA

- PCMCIA

  http://hyper.stanford.edu/HyperNews/get/pcmcia/
  home.html

PCMCIA drivers currently support all common PCMCIA controllers, including Databook TCIC/2, Intel i82365SL, Cirrus PD67xx, and Vadem VG-468 chipsets. Motorola 6AHC05GA controller used in some Hyundai laptops is not supported. See "Supported PCMCIA Cards" for a list of supported PCMCIA cards.

CPU/FPU

Intel/AMD/Cyrix 386SX/DX/SL/DXL/SLC, 486SX/DX/SL/SX2/DX2/DX4 are supported. Intel Pentium, Pentium Pro and Pentium II, Pentium III (regular and Xeon versions), and Celeron also work. AMD K5 and K6 work well, although older versions of K6 should be avoided as they are buggy. Setting "internal cache" disabled in bios setup can be a workaround. AMD K6-2 and K6-3 also work. Some early K6-2 300Mhz have problems with the system chips. Cyrix 6x86 works out of the box.

IDT Winchip C6-PSME2006A processors are also supported under Linux (http://www.winchip.com).

Linux has built-in FPU emulation if you don't have a math coprocessor.

Experimental SMP (multiple CPU) support is included in kernel 1.3.31 and newer. Check the Linux/SMP Project page for details and updates.

- Linux/SMP Project

  `http://www.linux.org.uk/SMP/title.html`

Advanced multimedia effects built in to the Cyrix MediaGX are not supported.

A few very early AMD 486DXs may hang in some special situations. All current chips should be okay, and getting a chip swap for old CPUs should not be a problem.

ULSI Math*Co series has a bug in the FSAVE and FRSTOR instructions that causes problems with all protected mode operating systems. Some older IIT and Cyrix chips may also have this problem.

Problems exist with TLB flushing in UMC U5S chips in very old kernels (1.1.x).

- Enable cache on Cyrix processors

  `ftp://metalab.unc.edu/pub/Linux/kernel/patches/`
  `CxPatch030.tar.z`

- Cyrix software cache control

  `ftp://metalab.unc.edu/pub/Linux/kernel/patches/`
  `linux.cxpatch`

- Cyrix 5x86 CPU register settings

  `ftp://metalab.unc.edu/pub/Linux/kernel/patches/`
  `cx5x86mod_1.0c.tgz`

MEMORY

All memory such as DRAM, EDO, and SDRAM can be used with Linux. One thing you must consider is that normally the kernel is not supporting more than 64MB of memory. When you add more than 64MB of memory you must add the following line to your LILO configuration file:

`append="mem=[[number of Mb]]M"`

So, when you have 96MB of memory, this should become like this:

`append="mem=96M"`

Don't type a number higher than the number MB you really have. This can present unpredictable crashes.

VIDEO CARDS

Linux will work with all video cards in text mode. VGA cards not listed in the following text probably will still work with mono VGA or standard VGA drivers.

If you're looking into buying a cheap video card to run X, keep in mind that accelerated cards (ATI Mach, ET4000/W32p, S3) are much faster than unaccelerated or partially accelerated (Cirrus, WD) cards.

32 bpp is actually 24-bit color aligned on 32-bit boundaries. It does NOT mean the cards are capable of 32-bit color; they still display 24-bit color (16,777,216 colors). 24-bit packed pixels modes are not supported in XFree86, so cards that can do 24 bit modes to get higher resolutions in other OSes are not able to do this in X using XFree86. These cards include Mach32, Cirrus 542x, S3 801/805/868/968, ET4000, and others.

AGP (Accelerated Graphics Port) support is growing fast. Most of the X servers (both freely available and commercial versions) have more or less support for AGP.

DIAMOND VIDEO CARDS

Most currently available Diamond cards are supported by the current release of XFree86. Early Diamond cards may not be officially supported by XFree86, but there are ways of getting them to work. Diamond is now actively supporting the XFree86 Project.

SVGALIB (GRAPHICS FOR CONSOLE)

- VGA
- EGA
- ARK Logic ARK1000PV/2000PV
- ATI VGA Wonder
- ATI Mach32
- Cirrus 542x, 543x
- OAK OTI-037/67/77/87
- S3 (limited support)
- Trident TVGA8900/9000
- Tseng ET3000/ET4000/W32

XFREE86 3.3.2

ACCELERATED

- ARK Logic ARK1000PV/VL, ARK2000PV/MT
- ATI Mach8
- ATI Mach32 (16 bpp supported for cards with RAMDAC ATI68875, AT&T20C49x, BT481 and 2MB video ram)
- ATI Mach64 (16/32 bpp supported for cards with RAMDAC ATI68860, ATI68875, CH8398, STG1702, STG1703, AT&T20C408, 3D Rage II, internal, IBM RGB514)
- Chips & Technologies 64200, 64300, 65520, 65525, 65530, 65535, 65540, 65545, 65546, 65548, 65550, 65554
- Cirrus Logic 5420, 542x/5430 (16 bpp), 5434 (16/32 bpp), 5436, 544x, 546x, 5480, 62x5, 754x

- Diamond Viper 330
- Gemini P1 (ET6000 chip)
- IBM 8514/A
- IBM XGA-I, XGA-II
- IIT AGX-010/014/015/016 (16 bpp)
- Matrox MGA2064W (Millennium)
- Matrox MGA1064SG (Mystique)
- Number Nine Imagine I128
- Oak OTI-087
- S3 732 (Trio32), 764 (Trio64), Trio64V+, 801, 805, 864, 866, 868, 86C325 (ViRGE), 86C375 (ViRGE/DX), 86C385 (ViRGE/GX), 86C988 (ViRGE/VX), 911, 924, 928, 964, 968
- See "S3 cards supported by XFree86 3.3.x" for a list of supported S3 cards
- SiS 86c201, 86c202, 86c205
- Trident 9440, 96xx, Cyber938x
- Tseng ET4000/W32/W32i/W32p, ET6000
- Weitek P9000 (16/32 bpp)
- Diamond Viper VLB/PCI
- Orchid P9000
- Western Digital WD90C24/24A/24A2/31/33

UNACCELERATED

- Alliance AP6422, AT24
- ATI VGA Wonder series
- Avance Logic AL2101/2228/2301/2302/2308/2401
- Cirrus Logic 6420/6440, 7555
- Compaq AVGA
- DEC 21030
- Genoa GVGA
- MCGA (320x200)
- MX MX68000/MX68010
- NCR 77C22, 77C22E, 77C22E+
- NVidia NV1
- Oak OTI-037C, OTI-067, OTI-077
- RealTek RTG3106
- SGS-Thomson STG2000

- Trident 8800CS, 8200LX, 8900x, 9000, 9000i, 9100B, 9200CXr, 9320LCD, 9400CXi, 9420, 9420DGi, 9430DGi
- Tseng ET3000, ET4000AX
- VGA (standard VGA, 4 bit, slow)
- Video 7/Headland Technologies HT216-32
- Western Digital/Paradise PVGA1, WD90C00/10/11/30

MONOCHROME

- Hercules mono
- Hyundai HGC-1280
- Sigma LaserView PLUS
- VGA mono

ALPHA, BETA DRIVERS

- EGA (ancient, from c. 1992)
  `ftp://ftp.funet.fi/pub/Linux/BETA/Xega/`

SuSE X-Server

SuSE is building a series of X-servers based on the XFree86 code. These X-servers support new video cards and are bug fix releases for XFree86 X-servers. SuSE is building these X-servers together with The XFree86 Project, Inc. These X-Servers will be in the next XFree86 version and can be found at `http://www.suse.de/index.html`. At this moment SuSE X-Servers are available for the following video cards:

- XSuSE Elsa GLoria X-Server
  - ELSA GLoria L, GLoria L/MX, Gloria S
- Video cards with the Alliance Semiconductor AT3D (also AT25) Chip
  - Hercules Stingray 128 3D
- XSuSE NVidia X-Server (PCI and AGP support, NV1 chipset and Riva128)
  - ASUS 3Dexplorer
  - Diamond Viper 330
  - ELSA VICTORY Erazor
  - STB Velocity 128
- XSuSE Matrox. Support for Mystique, Millennium, Millennium II, and Millennium II AGP
- XSuSE Trident. Support for the 9685 (including ClearTV) and the latest Cyber chipset
- XSuSE Tseng. W32, W32i ET6100 and ET6300 support.

COMMERCIAL X SERVERS

Commercial X servers provide support for cards not supported by XFree86, and might give better performances for cards that are supported by XFree86. In general they support many more cards than XFree86, so I'll only list cards that aren't supported by XFree86 here. Contact the vendors directly or check the Commercial HOWTO for more info.

XI GRAPHICS, INC

Xi Graphics, Inc, formerly known as X Inside, Inc, (`http://www.xig.com`) sells three X server products. (Cards supported are sorted by manufacturer.):

ACCELERATED-X DISPLAY SERVER

- 3Dlabs
  - 300SX
  - 500TX Glint
  - 500MX Glint
  - Permedia 4MB/8MB
  - Permedia II 4MB/8MB
- Actix
  - GE32plus 1MB/2MB
  - GE32ultra 2MB
  - GraphicsENGINE 64 1MB/2MB
  - ProSTAR 64 1MB/2MB
- Alliance
  - ProMotion-3210 1MB/2MB
  - ProMotion-6410 1MB/2MB
  - ProMotion-6422 1MB/2MB
- ARK Logic
  - ARK1000PV 1MB/2MB
  - ARK1000VL 1MB/2MB
  - ARK2000PV 1MB/2MB
- AST
  - Manhattan 5090P (GD5424) 512KB
- ATI
  - 3D Xpression 1MB/2MB
  - 3D Pro Turbo PC2TV 4MB/8MB
  - 3D Pro Turbo PC2TV 6144

- 3D Xpression+ PC2TV 2MB/4MB
- 3D Xpression+ 2MB/4MB
- ALL-IN-WONDER 4MB/8MB
- ALL-IN-WONDER PRO 4MB/8MB
- Graphics Ultra (Mach8) 1MB
- Graphics Pro Turbo (Mach64/VRAM) 2MB/4MB
- Graphics Pro Turbo 1600 (Mach64/VRAM) 2MB/4MB
- Graphics Ultra Plus (Mach32) 2MB
- 8514/Ultra (Mach8) 1MB
- Graphics Ultra Pro (Mach32) 1MB2MB
- Graphics Vantage (Mach8) 1MB
- VGA Wonder Plus 512KB
- VGA Wonder XL 1MB
- Video Xpression 1MB
- XPERT@Play 4MB/6MB/8MB
- XPERT@Work 4MB/6Mb/8MB
- Video Xpression 2MB
- WinBoost (Mach64/DRAM) 2MB
- WinTurbo (Mach64/VRAM) 2MB
- Graphics Wonder (Mach32) 1MB
- Graphics Xpression 1MB/2MB
- Rage II (SGRAM) 2MB/4MB/8MB
- Rage II+ (SGRAM) 2MB/4MB/8MB
- Rage Pro 2MB/4MB/8MB

- Avance Logic
  - ALG2101 1MB
  - ALG2228 1MB/2MB
  - ALG2301 1MB/2MB
- Boca
  - Voyager 1MB/2MB
  - Vortek-VL 1MB/2MB
- Colorgraphic
  - Dual Lightning 2MB
  - Pro Lightning Accelerator 2MB

- Quad Pro Lightning Accelerator 2MB
- Twin Turbo Accelerator 1MB/2MB
■ Chips & Technology
    - 64300 1MB/2MB
    - 64310 1MB/2MB
    - 65510 512KB
    - 65520 1MB
    - 65530 1MB
    - 65535 1MB
    - 65540 1MB
    - 65545 1MB
    - 65550 2MB
    - 82C450 512KB
    - 82C451 256KB
    - 82C452 512KB
    - 82C453 1MB
    - 82C480 1MB/2MB
    - 82C481 1MB/2MB
■ Cirrus Logic
    - GD5402 512KB
    - GD5420 1MB
    - GD5422 1MB
    - GD5424 1MB
    - GD5426 1MB/2MB
    - GD5428 1MB/2MB
    - GD5429 1MB/2MB
    - GD5430 1MB/2MB
    - GD5434 1MB/2MB
    - GD5436 1MB/2MB
    - GD5440 1MB/2MB
    - GD5446 1MB/2MB
    - GD5462 2MB/4MB PCI and AGP
    - GD5464 2MB/4MB PCI and AGP
    - GD5465 2MB/4MB PCI and AGP

- GD54M30 1MB/2MB
- GD54M40 1MB/2MB

■ Compaq
  - ProLiant Series 512KB
  - ProSignia Series 512KB
  - QVision 1024 1MB
  - QVision 1280 1MB/2MB
  - QVision 2000+ 2MB
  - QVision 2000 2MB

■ DEC
  - DECpc XL 590 (GD5428) 512KB

■ Dell
  - 466/M & 466/ME (S3 805) 1MB
  - OnBoard ET4000 1MB
  - DGX (JAWS) 2MB
  - OptiPlex XMT 590 (Vision864) 2MB

■ Diamond
  - Fire GL 1000 Pro 4MB/8MB
  - Fire GL 1000 4MB/8Mb
  - Stealth 3D 2000 2MB/4MB
  - Stealth 3D 3000XL 2MB/4MB
  - Stealth 64 Graphics 2001 1MB/2MB
  - Stealth 64 Graphics 2121XL 1MB/2MB
  - Stealth 64 Graphics 2201XL 2MB
  - SpeedStar 1MB
  - SpeedStar 64 Graphics 2000 1MB/2MB
  - SpeedStar 24 1MB
  - SpeedStar 24X 1MB
  - SpeedStar 64 1MB/2MB
  - SpeedStar Hicolor 1MB
  - SpeedStar PCI 1MB
  - SpeedStar Pro 1MB
  - SpeedStar Pro SE 1MB/2MB
  - Stealth 1MB
  - Stealth 24 1MB

- Stealth 32 1MB/2MB
- Stealth 64 VRAM 2MB/4MB
- Stealth 64 DRAM 1MB/2MB
- Stealth 64 Video VRAM (175MHz) 2MB/4MB
- Stealth 64 Video DRAM 1MB/2MB
- Stealth 64 Video VRAM (220MHz) 2MB/4MB
- Stealth Hicolor 1MB
- Stealth Pro 1MB/2MB
- Stealth SE 1MB/2MB
- Stealth 64 Video 2001TV 2MB
- Stealth 64 Video 2121 1MB/2MB
- Stealth 64 Video 2121TV 1MB/2MB
- Stealth 64 Video 2201 2MB
- Stealth 64 Video 2201TV 2MB
- Stealth 64 Video 3200 2MB
- Stealth 64 Video 3240 2MB/4MB
- Stealth 64 Video 3400 4MB
- Viper 1MB/2MB
- Viper Pro 2MB
- Viper Pro Video 2MB/4MB
- Viper SE 2MB/4MB

- ELSA
- VICTORY 3D 2MB/4MB
- WINNER 1000 1MB/2MB
- WINNER 1000AVI 1MB/2MB
  - WINNER 1000ISA 1MB/2MB
  - WINNER 1000PRO 1MB/2MB
  - WINNER 1000TRIO 1MB/2MB
  - WINNER 1000TRIO/V 1MB/2MB
  - WINNER 100VL 1MB
  - WINNER 2000 2MB/4MB
  - WINNER 2000AVI 2MB/4MB
  - WINNER 2000AVI/3D 2MB/4MB
  - WINNER 2000PRO 2MB/4MB
  - WINNER 2000PRO/X 2MB/4MB/8MB

- WINNER 3000-L 4MB
- WINNER 3000-M 2MB
- WINNER 3000-S 2MB
- WINNER 1024 1MB
- WINNER 1280, TLC34075 Palette 2MB
- WINNER 1280, TLC34076 Palette 2MB
- Gloria-XL
- Gloria-MX
- Gloria-L
- Synergy

■ Everex
  - ViewPoint 64P 1MB/2MB
  - VGA Trio 64P 1MB/2MB

■ Gateway
  - Mach64 Accelerator (Mach64/VRAM) 2MB

■ Genoa
  - 5400 512KB
  - 8500/8500VL 1MB
  - Phantom 32i 8900 2MB
  - Phantom 64 2MB

■ Hercules
  - Dynamite 1MB
  - Dynamite Pro 1MB/2MB
  - Dynamite Power 2MB
  - Dynamite 3D / GL
  - Graphite 1MB
  - Stingray 64 1MB/2MB
  - Stingray Pro 1MB/2MB
  - Stringray 1MB
  - Terminator 3D 2MB/4MB
  - Terminator 64/Video 2MB
  - Graphite Terminator Pro 2MB/4MB

■ HP
  - NetServer LF/LC/LE (TVGA9000i) 512KB
  - Vectra VL2 (GD5428) 1MB

- Vectra XM2i (Vision864) 1MB/2MB
- Vectra XU (Vision864) 1MB/2MB

■ IBM

- 8514/A 1MB
- PC 300 Series (GD5430) 1MB
- PC 300 Series (Vision864) 1MB/2MB
- PC 700 Series (Vision864) 1MB/2MB
- PS/ValuePoint Performance Series (Vision864) 1MB/2MB
- VC550 1MB
- VGA 256KB
- XGA-NI 1MB
- XGA 1MB

■ IIT

- AGX014 1MB
- AGX015 1MB/2MB

■ Integral

- FlashPoint 1MB/2MB

■ Leadtek

- WinFast L2300 4MB/8MB

■ Matrox

- Comet 2MB
- Marvel II 2MB
- Impression (MGA-IMP/3/A/H, MGA-IMP/3/V/H, MGA-IMP/3/M/H) 3MB
- Impression Lite (MGA-IMP+/LTE/P) 2MB
- Impression Plus Lite (MGA-IMP+/LTE/V) 2MB
- Millennium (MGA-MIL) 2MB/4MB/8MB
- Millennium 220 (MGA-MIL) 2MB/4Mb/8MB
- Millennium PowerDoc (WRAM) 2MB/4MB/8MB
- Millennium II (WRAM) 2MB/4MB/8MB PCI and AGP
- Mystique (MGA-MYS) 2MB/4MB
- Mystique 220
- Impression Plus (MGA-IMP+/P, MGA-IMP+/A) 2MB/4MB
- Impression Plus 220 (MGA-IMP+/P/H, MGA-IMP+/A/H) 2MB/4MB

- Impression Pro (MGA-PRO/4.5/V) 4.5MB
- Ultima Plus (MGA-PCI/2+, MGA-VLB/2+) 2MB/4MB
- Ultima (MGA-ULT/2/A, MGA-PCI/2, MGA-VLB/2) 2MB
- Ultima (MGA-ULT/2/A/H, MGA-ULT_2/M/H) 2MB
- Ultima Plus 200 (MGA-PCI/4/200, MGA-VLB/4/200) 4MB

- MaxVision
  - VideoMax 2000 2MB/4MB
- Metheus
  - Premier 801 1MB
  - Premier 928-1M 1MB
  - Premier 928-2M 2MB
  - Premier 928-4M 4MB
- Micronics
  - Mpower 4 Plus (Mach64) 1MB
- MIRO
  - miroCRYSTAL 10AD 1MB
  - miroCRYSTAL 12SD 1MB
  - miroCRYSTAL 12SD 2MB
  - miroCRYSTAL 20PV 2MB
  - miroCRYSTAL 20SD 2MB
  - miroCRYSTAL 20SV 2MB
  - miroCRYSTAL 22SD 2MB
  - miroCRYSTAL 40SV 4MB
  - miroCRYSTAL VR2000 2MB/4MB
  - miroMAGIC 40PV 4MB
  - miroMAGIC plus 2MB
  - miroVIDEO 12PD 1MB/2MB
  - miroVIDEO 20SD 2MB
  - miroVIDEO 20SV 2MB
  - miroVIDEO 20TD 2MB
  - miroVIDEO 22SD 2MB
  - miroVIDEO 40SV 4MB
- NEC
  - Versa P Series 1MB

- Nth Graphics
  - Engine/150 2MB
  - Engine/250 2MB
- Number Nine
  - GXE Level 10, AT&T 20C491 Palette 1MB
  - GXE Level 10, Bt485 or AT&T20C505 Palette 1MB
  - GXE Level 11 2MB
  - GXE Level 12 3MB
  - GXE Level 14 4MB
  - GXE Level 16 4MB
  - GXE64 1MB/2MB
  - GXE64pro 2MB/4Mb
  - GXE64pro (-1600) 2MB/4MB
  - Imagine 128 2MB
  - Image 128 (-1280) 4MB
  - Image 128 Series 2 (DRAM) 2MB/4Mb
  - Image 128 Pro (-1600) 4MB/8MB
  - Image 128 Series 2 (VRAM) 2MB/4MB/8MB
  - Image 128 Series III (Revolution 3D) (WRAM) 8MB/16MB PCI and AGP
  - Revolution 3D "Ticket to Ride" (WRAM) 8MB/16MB PCI and AGP
  - 9FX Motion331 1MB/2MB
  - 9FX Motion531 1MB/2MB
  - 9FX Motion771 2MB/4MB
  - 9FX Reality332 2MB
  - 9FX Reality772 2MB/4MB
  - 9FX Reality 334 PCI and AGP
  - 9FX Vision330 1MB/2MB
- Oak Technology
  - OTI-067 512KB
  - OTI-077 1MB
  - OTI-087 1MB
  - OTI-107 1MB/2MB
  - OTI-111 1MB/2MB

- Orchid
  - Fahrenheit 1280 Plus, ATT20C491 Palette 1MB
  - Fahrenheit 1280 1MB
  - Fahrenheit 1280 Plus, SC15025 Palette 1MB
  - Fahrenheit ProVideo 64 2MB/4MB
  - Fahrenheit Video 3D 2MB
  - Kelvin 64 1MB/2MB
  - Kelvin Video64 1MB/2MB
  - P9000 2MB
- Packard Bell
  - Series 5000 Motherboard 1MB
- Paradise
  - 8514/A 1MB
  - Accelerator 24 1MB
  - Accelerator Value card 1MB
  - Bahamas 64 1MB/2MB
  - Bali 32 1MB/2MB
  - VGA 1024 512KB
  - VGA Professional 512KB
- Pixelworks
  - WhrilWIN WL1280 (110MHz) 2MB
  - WhrilWIN WL1280 (135MHz) 2MB
  - WhirlWIN WW1280 (110MHz) 2MB
  - WhirlWIN WW1280 (135MHz) 2MB
  - WhrilWIN WW1600 1MB
  - Radius
  - XGA-2 1MB
- Reveal
  - VC200 1MB
  - VC300 1MB
  - VC700 1MB
- S3
  - ViRGE 2MB/4MB
  - ViRGE/DX 2MB/4MB
  - ViRGE/GX 2MB/4MB

- ViRGE/GX /2 2MB/4MB
- ViRGE/VX 2MB/4MB
- Trio32 1MB/2MB
- Trio64 1MB/2MB
- Trio64V+ 1MB/2MB
- Trio64V2/DX 1MB/2MB
- Trio64V2/GX 1MB/2MB
- 801 1MB/2MB
- 805 1MB/2MB
- Vision864 1MB/2MB
- Vision866 1MB/2MB
- Vision868 1MB/2MB
- 911 1MB
- 924 1MB
- 928 1MB
- 928 2MB/4MB

- Sierra
  - Falcon/64 1MB/2MB
- Sigma
  - Legend 1MB
  - SPEA/V7
  - Mercury P64 2MB
  - Storm Pro 4MB
  - ShowTime Plus 2MB
  - STB
  - Evolution VGA 1MB
  - Horizon Plus 1MB
  - Horizon VGA 1MB
  - Horizon 64 1MB/2MB
  - Horizon 64 Video 1MB/2MB
  - Horizon Video 1MB
  - LightSpeed 2MB
  - LightSpeed 128 2MB
  - Nitro 3D 2MB/4MB
  - Nitro 64 1MB/2MB

- Nitro 64 Video 1MB/2MB
- PowerGraph VL-24 1MB
- PowerGraph X-24 1MB
- PowerGraph 64 3D 2MB
- PowerGraph 64 1MB/2MB
- PowerGraph 64 Video 1MB/2MB
- PowerGraph Pro 2MB
- Velocity 3D 4MB
- Velocity 64V 2MB/4MB

■ Toshiba
- T4900CT 1MB

■ Trident
- TGUI9400CXi 1MB/2MB
- TGUI9420DGi 1MB/2MB
- TGUI9440 1MB/2MB
- TGUI9660 1MB/2MB
- TGUI9680 1MB/2MB
- TVGA8900B 1MB
- TVGA8900C 1MB
- TVGA8900CL 1MB
- TVGA8900D 1MB
- TVGA9000 512KB
- TVGA9000i 512KB
- TVGA9200CXr 1MB/2MB

■ Tseng Labs
- ET3000 512KB
- ET4000 1MB
- ET6000 2MB/4MB
- VGA/16 (ISA) 1MB
- VGA/16 (VLB) 1MB/2MB
- VGA/32 1MB/2MB
- ET4000/W32 1MB
- ET4000/W32i 1MB/2MB
- ET4000/W32p 1MB/2MB

- VLSI
  - VL82C975 (AT&T RAMDAC) 2MB
  - VL82C975 (BrookTree RAMDAC) 2MB
  - VL82C976 (Internal RAMDAC) 2MB
- Western Digital
  - WD90C00 512KB
  - WD90C11 512KB
  - WD90C24 1MB
  - WD90C26 512KB
  - WD90C30 1MB
  - WD90C31 1MB
  - WD90C33 1MB
  - WD9510-AT 1MB
- Weitek
  - P9100 2MB
  - P9000 2MB
  - W5186 1MB
  - W5286 1MB

LAPTOP ACCELERATED-X DISPLAY SERVER

- Broadax
  - NP8700 (Cyber 9385)
- Chips & Technology
  - 65510 512KB
  - 65520 1MB
  - 65530 1MB
  - 65535 1MB
  - 65540 1MB
  - 65545 1MB
  - 65554 2MB/4MB
  - 65555 2MB
- Cirrus Logic
  - GD7541 1MB/2MB
  - GD7543 1MB/2MB
  - GD7548 2MB

- Compaq
    - LTE 5400 (Cirrus Logic CL5478)
    - Presario 1090ES (NM 2093)
- Dell
    - Latitude XPi 896 (NeoMagic 2070)
    - Latitude XPi (NM 2070)
    - Latitude XPi CD 1MB (NM 2090)
    - Latitude LM (NM 2160)
    - Latitude CP (NM 2160)
    - Inspiron 3000 (NM 2160)
- Digital (DEC)
    - HiNote VP (NeoMagic 2090)
- Fujitsu
    - Lifebook 435DX (NeoMagic 2093)
- Gateway 2000
    - Solo 2300 (NeoMagic 2160)
    - Solo 2300 SE (NM 2160)
    - Solo 9100 (C&T 65554)
    - Solo 9100XL (C&T 65555)
- Hewlett Packard
    - OmniBook 800 (NM 2093)
- Hitachi
    - Notebook E133T (NeoMagic 2070)
- IBM
    - VGA 256KB
    - Thinkpad 380D (NeoMagic 2090)*
    - Thinkpad 385ED (NeoMagic 2090)*
    - Thinkpad 560E (Cyber 9382)
    - Thinkpad 760XD (Cyber 9385)
    - Thinkpad 770 (Cyber 9397)
- Micron
    - TransPort XKE (NeoMagic 2160)
    - Millenia Transport (Cirrus Logic GD7548)

- NEC
  - Versa P Series 1MB
  - Versa 6230 2MB (NeoMagic 2160)
- NeoMagic
  - MagicGraph128 / NM2070 896
  - MagicGraph128 / NM2070
  - MagicGraph128V / NM2090
  - MagicGraph128V+ / NM2097
  - MagicGraph128ZV / NM2093
  - MagicGraph128XD / NM2160
- Sony
  - VAIO PCG-505 (NeoMagic 2097)
- Toshiba
  - T4900CT 1MB
  - Tecra 740CDT (C&T 65554)
- Trident
  - Cyber 9397
  - Cyber 9385
  - Cyber 9382
- Twinhead
  - Slimnote 9166TH (Cyber 9385)

* Numerous XiG customers have confirmed support.

MULTI-HEAD ACCELERATED-X DISPLAY SERVER

METRO-X 4.3.0   Metro Link sales@metrolink.com

TABLE B.1   SUPPORTED CARDS

Graphics	Card Chipset
ATI 3D RAGE	3D RAGE
ATI 3D RAGE II	3D RAGE II
ATI ALL-IN-WONDER PRO AGP	3D RAGE PRO
ATI ALL-IN-WONDER PRO PCI	3D RAGE PRO
ATI Graphics Pro Turbo	Mach64
ATI Graphics Ultra	Mach8
ATI Graphics Xpression	Mach64

TABLE B.1   CONTINUED

Graphics	Card Chipset
ATI Mach32	Mach32
ATI Mach64	Mach64
ATI VGA STEREO-F/X	ATI 28800
ATI Winturbo PCI	Mach64
ATI XPERT@Play	3D RAGE PRO
ATI XPERT@Play AGP	3D RAGE PRO
ATI XPERT@Work	3D RAGE PRO
ATI XPERT@Work AGP	3D RAGE PRO
Diamond Fire GL 1000Pro	PERMEDIA 2
Diamond SpeedStar 24X	Western Digital 90C31
Diamond SpeedStar Pro SE	Cirrus 5430
Diamond Stealth 24	S3 801
Diamond Stealth 32	ET4000/W32p
Diamond Stealth 3D 2000	S3 ViRGE
Diamond Stealth 64	S3 964, Bt485KPJ135
Diamond Stealth 64 DRAM	S3 Trio64
Diamond Stealth 64 DRAM (SDAC)	S3 864, S3 SDAC
Diamond Stealth 64 Graphics 2000 Series	S3 864, S3 SDAC
Diamond Stealth 64 Graphics 2200	S3 Trio64
Diamond Stealth 64 VRAM	S3 968, IBM RGB526CF22
Diamond Stealth 64 Video 3000 Series	S3 968, TI 3026-175
Diamond Stealth 64 Video VRAM	S3 968, TI 3026-175
Diamond Stealth Video (SDAC)	S3 868, S3 SDAC
Diamond Stealth Video 2000 Series	S3 868, S3 SDAC
Diamond Viper (110 MHz RAMDAC)	P9000
Diamond Viper (135 MHz RAMDAC)	P9000
ELSA GLoria Synergy	PERMEDIA 2
ELSA Victory 3D	S3 ViRGE
ELSA WINNER 2000 Office AGP	PERMEDIA 2
ELSA Winner 1000 TRIO/V	S3 Trio64V+
ELSA Winner 2000 AVI	S3 968, TI 3026-175
ELSA Winner 2000 PRO/X-2, -4	S3 968, TI 3026-220

TABLE B.1 CONTINUED	
Graphics	**Card Chipset**
ELSA Winner 2000 PRO/X-8	S3 968, IBM RGB528CF25
EPS Apex L-200	C&T 65550
Generic	ATI 28800
Generic	Alliance ProMotion
Generic	Ark 2000
Generic	Avance Logic 22xx/23xx/24xx
Generic	Chips & Technologies
Generic	Cirrus 5420
Generic	Cirrus 5422/5424
Generic	Cirrus 5426/5428
Generic	Cirrus 5429
Generic	Cirrus 5430
Generic	Cirrus 5434
Generic	Cirrus 5436
Generic	Cirrus 5446
Generic	Cirrus 5462
Generic	Cirrus 5462/5465
Generic	Cirrus 5480
Generic	Cirrus 62x5
Generic	Cirrus 6410/6412/6420/6440
Generic	Cirrus 754x
Generic	ET3000
Generic	ET4000/W32P
Generic	ET4000AX
Generic	ET6000
Generic	Mach32
Generic	Mach64
Generic	Mach8
Generic	P9000
Generic	PERMEDIA 2
Generic	S3 864/868/924/928/964
Generic	S3 968

TABLE B.1 CONTINUED	
Graphics	**Card Chipset**
Generic	S3 Trio64
Generic	S3 Trio64V+
Generic	S3 ViRGE
Generic	S3 ViRGE/GX/DX
Generic	SiS 86c201/86c202/86c205
Generic Trident	TGUI9440
Generic Trident	TGUI96xx
Generic	Trident8900
Generic	VGA
Generic	Western Digital SVGA
Genoa Phantom 64	S3 Trio64V+
Genoa WindowsVGA 8500VL	Cirrus 5426
Hercules Dynamite 128/Video	ET6000
Hercules Dynamite 3D/GL	PERMEDIA 2
Hercules Dynamite 3D/GL AGP	PERMEDIA 2
Hercules Stingray	Avance Logic 2301
Hercules Stingray 128/3D	Alliance ProMotion AT3D
Hercules Stingray 64	Ark 2000
Hercules Terminator 3D	S3 ViRGE/DX
IBM VGA	
Matrox Marvel	ET4000
Matrox Marvel II	ET4000
Matrox Millennium	MGA Storm
Matrox Millennium II AGP	MGA 2164, TI 3026-250
Matrox Millennium II PCI (220 MHz)	MGA 2164, TI 3026-220
Matrox Millennium II PCI (250 MHz)	MGA 2164, TI 3026-250
Matrox Mystique	MGA 1064
Matrox Mystique 220	MGA 1164
Number Nine GXE64	S3 864
Number Nine Imagine 128	Imagine 128
Number Nine Imagine 128 Series 2	Imagine 128 Series 2
Number Nine Motion 531	S3 868

TABLE B.1 CONTINUED	
Graphics	**Card Chipset**
Number Nine Motion 771	S3 968
Number Nine Revolution 3D	Ticket to Ride
Number Nine Vision 330	S3 Trio64
Orchid Kelvin 64	Cirrus 5434
SPEA Mirage Video	S3 Trio64V+
STB NITRO 3D	S3 ViRGE/GX
STB/Symmetric GLyder MAX-2	PERMEDIA 2
Sigma Designs VGA Legend	ET4000
Tech Source Raptor	Imagine 128 Series 2
Trident 64-Bit Providia 9685	
Trident 8900	Trident 8900
Trident 9440	TGUI9440-2
V PCI-53	Cirrus 5434

CONTROLLERS (HARD DRIVE)

Linux will work with standard IDE, MFM, and RLL controllers. When using MFM/RLL controllers it is important to use ext2fs and the bad block checking options when formatting the disk.

Enhanced IDE (EIDE) interfaces are supported with up to two IDE interfaces and up to four hard drives or CD-ROM drives. Linux will detect the following EIDE interfaces:

- CMD-640 (Support for buggy interfaces in kernel 2.2)
- DTC 2278D
- FGI/Holtek HT-6560B VLB (Support for secondary interface in kernel 2.2)
- RZ1000 (Support for buggy interfaces in kernel 2.2)
- Triton I (82371FB) (with busmaster DMA)
- Triton II (82371SB) (with busmaster DMA)

ESDI controllers that emulate the ST-506 (MFM/RLL/IDE) interface will also work. The bad block checking comment also applies to these controllers.

Generic 8 bit XT controllers also work.

Starting with pre-patch-2.0.31-3 IDE/ATAPI is provided.

ALPHA, BETA DRIVERS

- UMC 8672 interfaces (experimental support in kernel 2.2)
- Promise DC4030VL caching interface card (experimental support in kernel 2.2)

CONTROLLERS (HARD DRIVE RAID)

- Tekram D690CD IDE PCI Cache Controller (with RAID level 1 Mirroring and caching)
- ARCO Inc. DupliDisk IDE disk mirroring controller
  - Support for ATA, IDE, E-IDE, and UDMA drive. Controllers available can be plugged into ISA and PCI slots, and directly into the IDE controller. Furthermore, 3.5-inch and 5.25-inch Bay Mount units that fit into the respective drive bays are available. More information is available at http://www.arcoide.com. Make sure you have at least rev 3.00 of the firmware.
- Mylex RAID controllers
  - More information can be found at http://www.dandelion.com/Linux/DAC960.html

CONTROLLERS (SCSI)

It is important to pick a SCSI controller carefully. Many cheap ISA SCSI controllers are designed to drive CD-ROMs rather than anything else. Such low-end SCSI controllers are no better than IDE. See the SCSI HOWTO and look at performance figures before buying a SCSI card.

SUPPORTED

- AMI Fast Disk (**VLB/EISA**) (BusLogic compatible)
- Adaptec AVA-1502E (**ISA/VLB**) (AIC-6360) (AHA1520)
- Adaptec AVA-1505/1515 (**ISA**) (Adaptec AHA-152x compatible)
- Adaptec AVA-1825 (**VLB**) (Adaptec AHA-152x compatible)
- This card has a SCSI, EIDE and floppy port which all work nicely.
- Adaptec AHA-1510/152x (**ISA/VLB**) (AIC-6260/6360)
- Adaptec AHA-154x (**ISA**) (all models)
- Adaptec AHA-174x (**EISA**) (in enhanced mode)
- Adaptec AHA-274x/274xT (**EISA**) (AIC-7771). The 274xT is supported since kernel series 2.1.x (AHA2740)
- Adaptec AHA-284x (**VLB**) (AIC-7770) (AHA2740)
- Adaptec AHA-2910B (**PCI**) (since kernel series 2.1.x)

- Adaptec AHA-2920 (**PCI**). Use the Future Domain driver. LILO parameters are needed when used for hard disks.

- Adaptec AHA-2920C (**PCI**)

- Adaptec AHA-2930/U/U2 (**PCI**)

- Adaptec AHA-2940/U/W/AU/UW/U2W/U2/U2B/U2BOEM (**PCI**) (AIC-7861, AIC-7871, AIC-7844, AIC-7881, AIC-7884). Some of these are only supported since kernel series 2.1.x (AHA2740).

- Adaptec AHA-2944D/WD/UD/UWD (**PCI**). Some of these are only supported since kernel series 2.1.x (AHA2740).

- Adaptec AHA-2950U2/U2B/U2W

- Adaptec AHA-3940/U/W/UW/AUW/U2W (**PCI**) (AIC-7872, AIC-7882) (since 1.3.6). Some of these are only supported since kernel series 2.1.x.

- Adaptec AHA-3950U2B/U2D

- Adaptec AHA-3985U/W/UW (**PCI**) (AIC-7873, AIC-7883). Some of these are only supported since kernel series 2.1.x.

- Adaptec **PCI** controllers with AIC-7850, AIC-7855, AIC-7860

- Adaptec on board controllers with AIC-777x (**EISA**), AIC-785x, AIC-786x, AIC-787x (**PCI**), AIC-788x (**PCI**), AIC-789x, AIC-3860, AIC-786x, and AIC-789x are supported since kernel series 2.1.x.

- AdvanSys ABP510/5150 Bus-Master (**ISA**)
  http://advansys.com/support/software/os/linux.htm

- AdvanSys ABP5140 Bus-Master (**ISA**) PnP
  http://advansys.com/support/software/os/linux.htm

- AdvanSys ABP5142 Bus-Master (**ISA**) PnP with floppy
  http://advansys.com/support/software/os/linux.htm

- AdvanSys ABP920 Bus-Master (**PCI**)
  http://advansys.com/support/software/os/linux.htm

- AdvanSys ABP930/U Bus-Master (**PCI/Ultra**)
  http://advansys.com/support/software/os/linux.htm

- AdvanSys ABP960/U Bus-Master (**PCI/Ultra**) MAC/PC
  http://advansys.com/support/software/os/linux.htm

- AdvanSys ABP542 Bus-Master (**ISA**) with floppy (single channel)
  http://advansys.com/support/software/os/linux.htm

- AdvanSys ABP742 Bus-Master (**EISA**) (single channel)
  http://advansys.com/support/software/os/linux.htm

- AdvanSys ABP842 Bus-Master (**VL**) (single channel)
  http://advansys.com/support/software/os/linux.htm

- AdvanSys ABP940/U Bus-Master (**PCI/Ultra**) (single channel)
  http://advansys.com/support/software/os/linux.htm

- AdvanSys ABP970/U Bus-Master (**PCI/Ultra**) MAC/PC (single channel)
  http://advansys.com/support/software/os/linux.htm

- AdvanSys ABP752 Dual Channel Bus-Master (**EISA**) (dual channel)
  http://advansys.com/support/software/os/linux.htm

- AdvanSys ABP852 Dual Channel Bus-Master (**VL**) (dual channel)
  http://advansys.com/support/software/os/linux.htm

- AdvanSys ABP950 Dual Channel Bus-Master (**PCI**) (dual channel)
  http://advansys.com/support/software/os/linux.htm

- Always IN2000

- AMD AM53C974

- BusLogic FlashPoint LT/DL/LW/DW (BT-930(R), BT-920, BT-932(R), BT-950(R), BT-952(R))
  http://www.dandelion.com/Linux/

- Compaq Smart Array 2

- DPT PM2001, PM2012A (EATA-PIO)

- DPT Smartcache/SmartRAID Plus,III,IV families (**ISA/EISA/PCI**)
  - Take a look at http://www.uni-mainz.de/~neuffer/scsi/dpt/ (EATA-DMA)
  - Cards in these families are PM2011, PM2021, PM2041, PM3021, PM2012B, PM2022, PM2122, PM2322, PM2042, PM3122, PM3222, PM3332, PM2024, PM2124, PM2044, PM2144, PM3224, and PM3334.

- DTC 3180/3280

- DTC 329x (**EISA**) (Adaptec 154x compatible)

- Future Domain TMC-16x0, TMC-3260 (**PCI**)

- Future Domain TMC-8xx, TMC-950

- Future Domain chips TMC-1800, TMC-18C50, TMC-18C30, TMC-36C70

- ICP-Vortex PCI-SCSI Disk Array Controllers (many RAID levels supported)
  - Patches for Linux 1.2.13 and 2.0.29 are available at ftp://icp-vortex.com/download/linux/. The controllers GDT6111RP, GDT6121RP, GDT6117RP, GDT6127RP, GDT6511RP, GDT6521RP, GDT6517RP, GDT6527RP, GDT6537RP, and GDT6557RP are supported. You can also use pre-patch-2.0.31-4 to pre-patch-2.0.31-9.

- ICP-Vortex EISA-SCSI Controllers (many RAID levels supported)
  - Patches for Linux 1.2.13 and 2.0.29 are available at `ftp://icp-vortex.com/download/linux/`. The controllers GDT3000B, GDT3000A, GDT3010A, GDT3020A, and GDT3050A are supported. You can also use pre-patch-2.0.31-4 to pre-patch-2.0.31-9.
- Iomega PPA3 parallel port SCSI Host Bus Adapter embedded in ZIP drive
- Initio Corp. INI-9090U INI-9100, INI-9100W/A/UW, INI-9200U/UW, INI-9400U/UW, INI-9520U/UW, INI-A100U2W
- Initio Corp. INIC-950
- Media Vision Pro Audio Spectrum 16 SCSI (**ISA**)
- Mylex (formerly BusLogic) W Series (**PCI**) (BT-948, BT-958, BT-958D)
- Mylex (formerly BusLogic) C Series (**ISA/EISA/VLB/PCI**) (BT-946C, BT-956C, BT-956CD, BT-445, BT-747C, BT-757C, BT-757CD, BT-545C, BT-540CF)
- Mylex (formerly BusLogic) S Series (**ISA/EISA/VLB**) (BT-445S, BT-747S, BT-747D, BT-757S, BT-757D, BT-545S, BT-542D, BT-742A, BT-542B)
- Mylex (formerly BusLogic) A Series (**ISA/EISA**) (BT-742A, BT-542B)
- NCR 5380 generic cards
- NCR 53C400 (Trantor T130B) (use generic NCR 5380 SCSI support)
- NCR 53C406a (Acculogic ISApport/Media Vision Premium 3D SCSI)
- NCR chips 53C7x0 (the 53C710 is only supported in PCI variant)
- NCR chips 53C810, 53C815, 53C820, 53C825, 53C860, 53C875, 53C895 (53C895 supported "on paper"
- Qlogic/Control Concepts SCSI/IDE (FAS408) (**ISA/VLB**)
- Qlogic FASXXX/FASXX family of chips (**ISA/VLB**)
- QLogic IQ-PCI, IQ-PCI-10, IQ-PCI-D (**PCI**) (ISP1020 chip)
- Quantum ISA-200S, ISA-250MG
- Seagate ST-01/ST-02 (**ISA**)
- SIIG Ultrawide SCSI Pro (Initio chipset). Drivers and kernel patch can be found at `http://www.initio.com/suse.htm`.
- SoundBlaster 16 SCSI-2 (Adaptec 152x compatible) (**ISA**)
- Tekram DC-390, DC-390W/U/F
- Trantor T128/T128F/T228 (**ISA**)
- UltraStor 14F (**ISA**), 24F (**EISA**), 34F (**VLB**)
- Western Digital WD7000 SCSI

ALPHA, BETA DRIVERS

- AMD AM79C974 (**PCI**) (Compaq, HP, Zeos onboard SCSI)

  `ftp://metalab.unc.edu/pub/Linux/kernel/patches/scsi/AM53C974-0.3.tgz`

- Adaptec ACB-40xx SCSI-MFM/RLL bridgeboard

  `ftp://metalab.unc.edu/pub/Linux/kernel/patches/scsi/adaptec-40XX.tar.gz`

- Always Technologies AL-500

  `ftp://metalab.unc.edu/pub/Linux/kernel/patches/scsi/al500-0.2.tar.gz`

- Iomega PC2/2B

  `ftp://metalab.unc.edu/pub/Linux/kernel/patches/scsi/iomega_pc2-1.1.x.tar.gz`

- Ricoh GSI-8

  `ftp://tsx-11.mit.edu/pub/linux/ALPHA/scsi/gsi8.tar.gz`

UNSUPPORTED

- Adaptec AHA 2940UW Pro
- Adaptec AAA-13x RAID Adapters
- Adaptec AAA-113x Raid Port Cards
- Adaptec AIC-7810
- NCR chip 53C710 (**ISA**) (old obsolete chip, but still used in some Compaq models)
- Non Adaptec compatible DTC boards (327x, 328x)

CONTROLLERS (I/O)

Any standard serial/parallel/joystick/combo cards. Linux supports 8250, 16450, 16550, and 16550A UARTs. Cards that support nonstandard IRQs (IRQ 9) can be used.

See National Semiconductor's "Application Note AN-493" by Martin S. Michael. Section 5.0 describes in detail the differences between the NS16550 and NS16550A. Briefly, the NS16550 had bugs in the FIFO circuits, but the NS16550A (and later) chips fixed those. However, there were very few NS16550's produced by National, long ago, so these should be very rare. And many of the "16550" parts in actual modern boards are from the many manufacturers of compatible parts, which may not use the National "A" suffix. Also, some multiport boards will use 16552 or 16554 or various other multiport or multifunction chips from National or other suppliers (generally in a dense package soldered to the board, not a 40-pin DIP). Don't worry about it unless you encounter a very old 40-pin DIP National "NS16550" (no A) chip loose or in an old board, in which case treat it as a 16450 (no FIFO) rather than a 16550A —Zhahai Stewart at `zstewart@hisys.com`.

CONTROLLERS (MULTIPORT)

NONINTELLIGENT CARDS

SUPPORTED

- AST FourPort and clones (4 port)
- Accent Async-4 (4 port)
- Arnet Multiport-8 (8 port)
- Bell Technologies HUB6 (6 port)
- Boca BB-1004, 1008 (4, 8 port) - no DTR, DSR, and CD
- Boca BB-2016 (16 port)
- Boca IO/AT66 (6 port)
- Boca IO 2by4 (4 serial/2 parallel, uses 5 IRQ's)
- Computone ValuePort (4, 6, 8 port) (AST FourPort compatible)
- DigiBoard PC/X, PC/Xem, PCI/Xem, EISA/Xem, PCI/Xr (4, 8, 16 port)
- Comtrol Hostess 550 (4, 8 port)
- PC-COMM 4-port (4 port)
- SIIG I/O Expander 4S (4 port, uses 4 IRQ's)
- STB 4-COM (4 port)
- Twincom ACI/550
- Usenet Serial Board II (4 port)

Nonintelligent cards usually come in two varieties, one using standard com port addresses and 4 IRQs, and another that is AST FourPort-compatible and uses a selectable block of addresses and a single IRQ. (Addresses and IRQs are set using setserial.) If you're getting one of these cards, be sure to check which standard it conforms to; prices are no indication.

INTELLIGENT CARDS

SUPPORTED

- Computone IntelliPort II (4/8/16 port)
  ftp://ftp.computone.com/pub/bbs/beta/ip2linux-1.0.2.tar.gz
- Cyclades Cyclom-Y (RISC-based, 8-32 ports) (**ISA/PCI**)
  http://www.cyclades.com/
- Cyclades-Z (high-end, 16-64 ports) (**PCI**)
  http://www.cyclades.com/
- DigiBoard PC/Xe (**ISA**), PC/Xi (**EISA**) and PC/Xeve
  ftp://ftp.digibd.com/drivers/linux/

- Equinox SST Intelligent serial I/O cards
  `http://www.equinox.com`

- Hayes ESP 1, 2, and 8 port versions

- Included in kernel since 2.1.15. The driver for kernel versions 2.0.x can be found at `http://www.nyx.net/~arobinso`.

- Stallion EasyIO (**ISA**)/EasyConnection 8/32 (**ISA/MCA**)/EasyConnection 8/64 (**PCI**)

- For DIP switch settings and configuration files check `http://www.stallion.com`.

- Stallion EasyConnection 8/64 (**ISA/EISA**)/ONboard (**ISA/EISA/MCA**)/Brumby (**ISA**)
  - The latest driver can be found at `ftp://ftp.stallion.com/drivers/ata5/Linux/v544.tar.gz`.

ALPHA, BETA DRIVERS

- Comtrol RocketPort (8/16/32 port)
  `ftp://metalab.unc.edu/pub/Linux/kernel/patches/`

- `serial/comtrol-1.04.tar.gz` (kernels 1.2.x). A driver for kernels 2.x can be found at `http://ftp.leidenuniv.nl/linux/tsx-11/packages/comtrol/`.

- DigiBoard COM/Xi

- Moxa C102, C104, C168, C218 (8 port), C320 (8/16/24/32 expandable) and C320T
  `ftp://ftp.moxa.com.tw/drivers/linux/`

- RISCom/8

- Specialix SIO/XIO (modular, 4 to 32 ports)
  `ftp://metalab.unc.edu/pub/Linux/kernel/patches/serial/sidrv.taz`

- Specialix IO8+
  - Contact `devices@BitWizard.nl`.

NETWORK ADAPTERS

Ethernet adapters vary greatly in performance. In general the newer the design the better. Some very old cards such as the 3Com 3c501 are only useful because they can be found in junk heaps for $5 apiece. Be careful with clones—not all are good clones, and bad clones often cause erratic lockups under Linux. Read the Ethernet HOWTO, `http://metalab.unc.edu/LDP/HOWTO/`, for detailed descriptions of various cards.

SUPPORTED

ETHERNET

For ethernet cards with the DECchip DC21x4x family the "Tulip" driver is available. More information on this driver can be found at `http://cesdis.gsfc.nasa.gov/linux/drivers/tulip.html`.

- 3Com 3c501— avoid like the plague (3c501 driver)
- 3Com 3c503 (3c503 driver), 3c505 (3c505 driver), 3c507 (3c507 driver), 3c509/3c509B (**ISA**)/3c579 (**EISA**)
- 3Com Etherlink III Vortex Ethercards (3c590, 3c592, 3c595, 3c597) (**PCI**), 3Com Etherlink XL Boomerang (3c900, 3c905) (**PCI**) and Cyclone (3c905B, 3c980) Ethercards (3c59x driver) and 3Com Fast EtherLink Ethercard (3c515) (**ISA**) (3c515 driver)
    - Newer versions of these drivers are available at `http://cesdis.gsfc.nasa.gov/linux/drivers/vortex.html`.
    - Avoid the 3c900 card when possible because the driver is not functioning well for this card.
- 3Com 3ccfe575 Cyclone Cardbus (3c59x driver)
- 3Com 3c575 series Cardbus (3c59x driver) (ALL PCMCIA ??)
- AMD LANCE (79C960) / PCnet-ISA/PCI (AT1500, HP J2405A, NE1500/NE2100)
- AT&T GIS WaveLAN
- Allied Telesis AT1700
- Allied Telesis LA100PCI-T
- Allied Telesyn AT2400T/BT ("ne" module)
- Ansel Communications AC3200 (**EISA**)
- Apricot Xen-II / 82596
- Cabletron E21xx
- Cogent EM110
- Crystal Lan CS8920, Cs8900
    - `http://www.cirrus.com/private/drivers/ethernet/edrivers.html`
- Danpex EN-9400
- DEC DE425 (**EISA**)/DE434/DE435 (**PCI**)/DE450/DE500 (DE4x5 driver)
- DEC DE450/DE500-XA (dc21x4x) (Tulip driver)
- DEC DEPCA and EtherWORKS
- DEC EtherWORKS 3 (DE203, DE204, DE205)
- DEC QSilver's (Tulip driver)
- Digi International RightSwitch

- DLink DE-220P, DE-528CT, DE-530+, DFE-500TX, DFE-530TX
  - More information can be found at `http://www.dlink.ca/linux.html`.
- Fujitsu FMV-181/182/183/184
- HP PCLAN (27245 and 27xxx series)
- HP PCLAN PLUS (27247B and 27252A)
- HP 10/100VG PCLAN (J2577, J2573, 27248B, J2585) (**ISA/EISA/PCI**)
  - More information can be found at `http://cesdis1.gsfc.nasa.gov:80/linux/drivers/100vg.html`.
- ICL EtherTeam 16i/32 (**EISA**)
- Intel EtherExpress
- Intel EtherExpress Pro
- KTI ET16/P-D2, ET16/P-DC ISA (work jumperless and with hardware-configuration options)
- Macromate MN-220P (PnP or NE2000 mode)
- NCR WaveLAN
- NE2000/NE1000 (be careful with clones)
- Netgear FA-310TX (Tulip chip)
- New Media Ethernet
- PureData PDUC8028, PDI8023
- SEEQ 8005
- SMC Ultra/EtherEZ (**ISA**)
- SMC 9000 series
- SMC PCI EtherPower 10/100 (Tulip driver)
- SMC EtherPower II (epic100.c driver)
- Sun LANCE adapters (kernel 2.2 and newer)
- Sun Intel adapters (kernel 2.2 and newer)
- Schneider & Koch G16
- Western Digital WD80x3
- Zenith Z-Note/IBM ThinkPad 300 built-in adapter
- Znyx 312 etherarray (Tulip driver)

ISDN

- Linux ISDN WWW page
  - This page seems to be gone.
- ISDN4Linux tools are available from `ftp://ftp.franken.de/pub/isdn4linux/v2.0`.

- 3Com Sonix Arpeggio
  - `ftp://metalab.unc.edu/pub/Linux/kernel/patches/network/sonix.tgz`
- ASUSCOM Network Inc. ISDNLink 128K PC adapter (HiSax)
- AVM A1 (HiSax)
- AVM B1 (avmb1)
- Combinet EVERYWARE 1000 ISDN
  `ftp://metalab.unc.edu/pub/Linux/kernel/patches/network/combinet1000isdn-1.02.tar.gz`
- Compaq ISDN S0 (**ISA**) (HiSax)
- Creatix PnP S0 (HiSax)
- Dr. Neuhaus Niccy PnP/PCI (HiSax)
- Dynalink IS64PH (HiSax)
- Eicon.Diehl Diva 2.0 (**ISA/PCI**) (S0 and U interface, no PRO version) (HiSax)
- Eicon.Diehl Diva Piccola (HiSax)
- Elsa Microlink PCC-16, PCF, PCF-Pro, PCC-8 (HiSax)
- ELSA QuickStep 1000/1000PCI/3000 (HiSax)
- HFC-2BS0 based cards (HiSax)
- IBM Active 2000 (**ISA**) (act2000)
- ICN ISDN cards (icn)
- Ith Kommunikationstechnik GmbH MIC 16 (ISA) (HiSax)
- ITK ix1-micro Rev.2 (HiSax)
- Octal PCBIT (pcbit)
- Sedlbauer Speed Card (HiSax)
- Teles SO-8/SO-16.0/SO-16.3/SO-16.3c/SO-16.4 and compatible ones (HiSax)
- Traverse Technologie NETjet PCI S0 (HiSax)
- USR Sportster internal TA (HiSax)

ISDN cards that emulate standard modems or common Ethernet adapters don't need any special drivers to work.

FRAME RELAY

- Emerging Technologies Inc Synchronous Adapters (`http://www.etinc.com`)
- ET/5025 (1 port, 8-bit **ISA**)
- ET/5025-16 (2 ports, 16-bit **ISA**)
- ET/5025-25 (2 ports, 16-bit **ISA**)
- ET/5025pq (4 ports, **PCI**)

WIRELESS

- ZCOM WL2420 ISA
  - Product information can be found at `http://www.zcom.com.tw`. Object file kernel drivers are available at `www.boerde.de/~matthias/airnet/zcom_v12`.

X25

- Emerging Technologies Inc Synchronous Adapters (`http://www.etinc.com`)
- ET/5025 (1 port, 8-bit **ISA**)
- ET/5025-16 (2 ports, 16-bit **ISA**)
- ET/5025-25 (2 ports, 16-bit **ISA**)
- ET/5025pq (4 ports, **PCI**)

POCKET AND PORTABLE ADAPTERS

For more information on Linux and use of the parallel port, go to the Linux Parallel Port Home Page `http://www.torque.net/linux-pp.html` or `http://www.torque.net/parport/`. Check "Supported Parallel Port Devices" for a complete list of supported parallel port devices (excluding printers).

SLOTLESS

- SLIP/CSLIP/PPP (serial port)
- EQL (serial IP load balancing)
- PLIP (parallel port)—using LapLink cable or bidirectional cable

ARCNET

Works with all ARCnet cards.

TOKEN RING

- `http://www.linuxtr.net`
- 3Com 3C619/B/C Tokenlink 16/4 (ibmtr)
- 3Com 3C319 Velocity ISA (ibmtr)
- IBM PCI token ring adapter
- IBM Wake on Lan TR adapter
- IBM 16/4 TR PCI Adapter 2, Adapter 2 Wake on Lan, Adapter 2 Wake on Lan Special
- IBM High Speed 100/16/4 token ring
- IBM ISA 16/4, MCA 16/4 (ibmtr)
- IBM Tropic chipset cards

- Olicom RapidFire 3139, 3140, 3141, 3540
  - `http://www.olicom.com`
- Olicom OC-3136, OC-3137, OC-3138, OC-3129
  - `http://www.olicom.com`
- Madge Smart 100/16/4 PCI, 16/4 PCI Mk3, 16/4 PCI Mk2
  - `http://www.madge.com`
- Madge Presto PCI, 16/4 CardBus
  - `http://www.madge.com`
- Syskonnect TR4/16(+) SK-4190 ISA, SK-4590 PCI, SK-4591 PCI (sktr)

FDDI

- DEC DEFEA (**EISA**)/DEFPA (**PCI**) (kernel 2.0.24 and later)

AMATEUR RADIO (AX.25)

- Gracilis PackeTwin
- Ottawa PI/PI2
- Most generic 8530 based HDLC boards

PCMCIA CARDS

- See "Supported PCMCIA Cards" for a complete list or the Web pages of David Hinds at `http://hyper.stanford.edu/HyperNews/get/pcmcia/home.html`.

ALPHA, BETA DRIVERS

ETHERNET

- Racal-Interlan NI5210 (i82586 Ethernet chip). Improved support in kernel 2.2 and newer.
- Racal-Interlan NI6510 (am7990 lance chip). Starting with kernel 1.3.66 more than 16MB RAM is supported.
- Racal-Interlan PCI card (AMD PC net chip 97c970)

ISDN

- SpellCaster's Datacomute/BRI, Telecomute/BRI (**ISA**) (sc)

ATM

- Efficient Networks ENI155P-MF 155Mbps ATM adapter (**PCI**)
  `http://lrcwww.epfl.ch/linux-atm/`

FRAME RELAY

- Sangoma S502 56K Frame Relay card
  - `ftp://ftp.sovereign.org/pub/wan/fr/`

WIRELESS

- Proxim RangeLan2 7100 (**ISA**)/630x (OEM **mini-ISA**)
  `http://www.komacke.com/distribution.htm`

UNSUPPORTED

- 3Com 3C359 Velocity XL PCI
- 3Com 3C339 Velocity PCI
- IBM PCI LANStreamer, MCA LANStreamer token ring
- Intel TokenExpress PRO, TokenExpress 16/4
- Sysconnect/Schneider & Koch Token Ring cards (all of them)

SOUND CARDS

More information on sound drivers and sound cards can be found on `http://www.opensound.com/ossfree` or `http://www.opensound.com/oss.html`.

SUPPORTED

- 4Front Technology Virtual Mixer (includes SoftOSS)
- 4Front Technology Virtual Synth (SoftOSS)
- 6850 UART MIDI
- A-Plus Sound of Music (OPL3-SA)
- A-Trend Harmony 3Ds751 (**PCI**)
- AcerMagic S23
- Adlib FM synthesizer card
- Adlib MSC 16 PnP (CS4235)
- AMD Interwave reference card
- ARC Probook
- Audio Excell DSP16
- Avance Logic ALS-007 chip-based cards.
  - Code for this chip is integrated in the Sound Blaster 16 driver. Isapnptools should be used for configuration.
- AW32 Pro (R2.2-W2)
- AW35 (CS4237)

- AW37 Pro (CS4235)
- Aztech Sound Galaxy NX Pro, NX Pro 16, WaveRider 32+
- Aztech Washington
- BTC Mozart Sound System
- BTC-1831 Sound Card (Opti 1688)
- Bravo Sound Card (Opti 82C930)
- Bull PowerPc built-in audio
- CDR4235-6/-8
- CS32-3DI
- Compaq Deskpro XL integrated Business Audio
- Creative EMU8000 add on (PnP)
- Creative Phone Blaster 28.8/33.6
- Creative Sound Blaster 1.0 to 2.0
- Creative Sound Blaster Pro
- Creative Sound Blaster 16
- Creative Sound Blaster 16 ASP
- Creative Sound Blaster 16 PnP (type-1 up to type-10)
- Creative Sound Blaster 16 Vibra
- Creative Sound Blaster 2.x
- Creative Sound Blaster 32/AWE
- Creative Sound Blaster 32/AWE PnP (type-1 up to type-10)
- Creative Sound Blaster AWE64 (type-1 up to type-7)
- Creative Sound Blaster AWE64 Gold (type-1 and type-2)
- Creative Sound Blaster PCI64/128
- Creative Sound Blaster AWE64/Gold and 16/32/AWE PnP cards need to be activated using isapnptools.
- Creative ViBRA16C/CL/S (type-1 and type-2) PnP
- Creative ViBRA16X PnP (half duplex only)
- CrystaLake Crystal Clear Series 100
- Crystal Audio (CS4235)
- Crystal CRD4236B-1E
- Crystal CRD4237B-5/-8
- Crystal CSC0B35 (CS4236B)
- Crystal CX4237B-SIDE
- Crystal Onboard PnP Audio (CS4235)

- Dell Latitude built-in audio
- Diamond Crystal MM PC/104
- Digital AXP built-in audio
- ECHO-PSS cards (Orchid SoundWave32, Cardinal DSP16)
- ESS 1868, 1869 (type-1 and type-2), 1878, 1879, 1968 PnP AudioDrive
- Ensoniq AudioPCI (ES1371)
- Ensoniq AudioPCI/SoundBlaster PCI (ES1370)
- Ensoniq Soundscape Elite
- Ensoniq Soundscape PnP (model 1 and 2)
- Ensoniq Soundscape S-2000
- Ensoniq Soundscape VIVO, VIVO90
- Ensoniq ActionNote 880 C/CX
- Gallant's sound card (SC-6000 and SC-66000 based)
- Generic AD1815-based soundcard (PnP)
- Generic CMI8330-based soundcard (PnP)
- Generic Crystal CS4232-based soundcard or motherboard (non PnP)
- Generic Crystal CS4232 by Acer (PnP mode)
- Generic Crystal CS4232 type-1 up to type-3 (PnP mode)
- Generic Crystal CS4235 type-1
- Generic Crystal CS4236 (type-1 up to type-3)
- Generic Crystal CS4236-based soundcard or motherboard (non PnP)
- Generic Crystal CS4236A (type-1 and type-2), CS4236B
- Generic Crystal CS4237-based soundcard or motherboard (non PnP)
- Generic Crystal CS4237B (type-1 and type-2)
- Generic Crystal CS4238-based soundcard or motherboard (non PnP)
- Generic ESS ES688, ES1688, ES1788, ES1868, ES1869, ES1887, ES1888-based soundcard or motherboard
- Generic Jazz16-based soundcard
- Generic MAD16 (OPTi 82C928), MAD16 Pro, MAD16 Pro (duplex) (OPTi 82C929)
- Generic Mozart soundcard (OAK OTI-601 chip)
- Generic OPTi 82C924, 82C925-based sound card (PnP)
- Generic OPTi 82C924 soundcard (non-PnP mode). Use the MSS driver and the isapnp tools.
- Generic OPTi 82C930
- Generic OPTi 82C931
  - See http://spoke.nols.com/~drees/opti931.html.

- Generic Soundscape-based soundcard
- Generic Windows Sound System compatible
- Generic Yamaha OPL3-SA1 (YMF701)-based soundcard
- Generic Yamaha OPL3-SA2 (YMF711)-based soundcard (type-1, type-3, type-4)
- Generic Yamaha OPL3-SA3 (YMF715)-based soundcard
- Generic Yamaha OPL3-SAx (YMF715/YMF719) non-PnP
- Gravis Ultrasound
- Gravis Ultrasound Extreme
- Gravis Ultrasound 16-bit sampling daughterboard
- Gravis Ultrasound MAX
- Gravis Ultrasound ACE
- Gravis Ultrasound PnP (with RAM), PnP Pro
- HP OmniBook 2100 (CS4236)
- Home Studio 64 (analog audio only)
- IBM Audio Feature (CS423x)
- Logitech SoundMan Games (SBPro, 44kHz stereo support)
- Logitech SoundMan Wave (Jazz16/OPL4)
- Logitech SoundMan 16 (PAS-16 compatible)
- MED3201 audio card
- Maxi Sound 32 PnP (analog audio only)
- Maxi Sound 64 Dynamic 3D (analog audio only)
- Media Sound SW/32 (non-PnP mode)
- MediaTriX AudioTriX Pro, 3D XG
- Media Vision Premium 3D (Jazz16)
- Media Vision Pro Sonic 16 (Jazz)
- Media Vision Pro Audio Spectrum 16 (PAS-16)
- Media Vision Pro Audio Studio 16
- Media Vision Thunderboard
- Microsoft Windows Sound System board (AD1848)
- MiroSound PCM!-pro
- MultiWave AudioWave Green 16
- Music Quest MIDI connector card (MCC)
- Music Quest MQX-16, MQX-16S MIDI adapter
- Music Quest MQX-32, MQX-32M MIDI adapter
- Music Quest PC MIDI card

- NEC Harmony
- Orchid SoundDrive 16EZ
- Pine PT201
- Primax SoundStorm FM 16, SoundStorm Wave
- Pro Audio Spectrum 16, Studio 16
- RME Digi32, Digi32 Pro, Digi32/8
- Reveal SC300
- Reveal WaveExtreme Pro (with RAM)
- Roland MPU IPC-T MIDI adapter
- S3 SonicVibes
- Shark Mako
- Sharp PC8800
- Shuttle Sound System 48
- Spacewalker HOT-255 PCI 3D (**PCI**)
- TerraTec Maestro 32/96
- Terratec EWS64XL (audio only)
- Terratec Sound System Base 1 (AD1816)
- Terratec Sound System Base 64 (AD1816)
- Tomato Sound System (OPTi 82C930)
- Trust Sound Expert De Luxe Wave 32
- Turtle Beach Classic/Tahiti/Monterey
- Turtle Beach Maui
- Turtle Beach Monte Carlo 928, Monte Carlo 929
- Turtle Beach Pinnacle/Fiji
- Turtle Beach Tropez, Tropez Plus (audio only)
- Turtle Beach Daytona (audio only)
- Wearnes Classic 16
- Yamaha Sound Edge SW20-PC
- Zefiro Acoustics ZA2 (NOT RECOMMENDED)
- Zenith Z-Player
- AWE32/64 support is started in kernel series 2.1.x (check the SoundBlaster AWE mini-HOWTO by Marcus Brinkmann for installation details).
- MPU-401 MIDI Intelligent mode (don't enable blindly)
- MPU IPC-T
- MQX-32M

- MPU-401 MIDI UART only dumb port (don't enable blindly)
- Yamaha FM synthesizers (OPL2, OPL3, OPL3-SAx (since kernel series 2.1.x) and OPL4)
- OSS supports all MIDI daughter cards including Wave Blaster, TB Rio, and Yamaha DB50XG. The only requirement is that the "host" card be supported by OSS. Note that only the "host" card needs to be configured using soundconf. The daughter card will be automatically accessible through the MIDI of the "host" card.
- 13.2 Alpha, Beta drivers
- 4Front Tech. Waveloop loopback audio device
- Acer FX-3D (AD1816 based)
- AVM Apex Pro card (AD1816 based)
- Aztech AZT1008, AZT2320, AZT3000
- Aztech SC-16 3D (AD1816 based)
- Creative Sound Blaster Vibra16x
- Creative Sound Blaster Live! and Live! Value Edition
- Creative Labs has beta driver for this card. They work with kernels 2.0.36 and 2.2.5 (and most likely newer kernels in these series). The drivers can be downloaded under the software download area at http://www.creativelabs.com.
- Highscreen Sound-Boostar 32 Wave 3D (AD1816 based)
- Highscreen Sound-Boostar 16 (AD1816 based)
- HP Kayak (AD1816 based)
- IBM MWave
- Newcom SC-16 3D (AD1816 based)
- PC speaker/Parallel port DAC
  ftp://ftp.informatik.hu-berlin.de/pub/os/linux/hu-sound/
- Rockwell WaveArtist chipset
- Sonorus STUDI/O
- SY-1816 (AD1816 based)
- Terratec Base 1, Base 64 (AD1816 based)
- Terratec EWS64S (AD1816 based)
- Turtle Beach Malibu ftp://ftp.cs.colorado.edu/users/mccreary/archive/tbeach/multisound/

For the AD1816 sound chip-based sound cards, isapnptools is needed for configuration.

UNSUPPORTED

- A-Trend Harmony 3DS724 (**PCI**)
- Actech PCI 388-A3D q
- Adaptec AME-1570
- Aureal Vortex (**PCI**)
- Cardinal DSP 16
- Contributed low-level drivers
- Crystal CS4614 (**PCI**)
- Cyrix MediaGX built-in audio
- Diamond Monster Sound MX300
- Diamond Sonic Impact
- Dream 94PnP Home Studio
- EON Bach SP901 (A3D)
- ESS (**PCI**)
- ESS Maestro-1 (**PCI**), Maestro-2 (**PCI**)
- ESS Solo-1 (**PCI**)
- Echo Personal Sound System
- Generic ALS007, ALS100-based soundcard
- Orchid NuSound 3D
- Orchid SoundWave 32
- Paradise DSP-16
- Quicknet Internet LineJACK
- Terratec XLerate (A3D)
- Turtle Beach Montego
- Turtle Beach TBS-2000
- Videologic SonicStorm
- Wearnes Beethoven ADSP-16
- Western Digital Paradise DSP-16
- Yamaha YMF724 (**PCI**)

The ASP chip on Sound Blaster 16 series is not supported. AWE32's onboard E-mu MIDI synthesizer is not supported.

Nathan Laredo (`laredo@gnu.ai.mit.edu`) is willing to write AWE32 drivers if you send him a complimentary card. He is also willing to write drivers for almost any hardware if you send him free samples of your hardware.

Sound Blaster 16s with DSP 4.11 and 4.12 have a hardware bug that causes hung/stuck notes when playing MIDI and digital audio at the same time. The problem can happen with either Wave Blaster daughterboards or MIDI devices attached to the MIDI port. There is no known fix.

HARD DRIVES

All hard drives should work if the controller is supported.

(From the SCSI HOWTO) All direct access SCSI devices with a block size of 256, 512, or 1024 bytes should work. Other block sizes will not work (note that this can often be fixed by changing the block or sector sizes using the MODE SELECT SCSI command).

Large IDE (EIDE) drives work fine with newer kernels. The boot partition must lie in the first 1024 cylinders due to PC BIOS limitations.

Some Conner CFP1060S drives may have problems with Linux and ext2fs. The symptoms are inode errors during e2fsck and corrupt file systems. Conner has released a firmware upgrade to fix this problem. Contact Conner at 1-800-4CONNER (US) or +44-1294-315333 (Europe). Have the microcode version (found on the drive label, 9WA1.6x) handy when you call.

Many Maxtor and Western Digital IDE drives are reported to not happily co-exist on the same IDE cable with the other manufacturer's drive. Usually one of the drives will fail during operation. A solution is to put them on different IDE cables.

Certain Micropolis drives have problems with Adaptec and BusLogic cards. Contact the drive manufacturers for firmware upgrades if you suspect problems.

- Multiple device driver (RAID-0, RAID-1)
  ftp://sweet-smoke.ufr-info-p7.ibp.fr/public/Linux/

UNSUPPORTED

The following hard drives are mentioned as not supported by Linux. Read the bug report available.

- NEC D3817, D3825, D3827, D3847
  - These drives are slightly non-SCSI-2 compliant in the values reported in Mode Sense Page 3. In Mode Sense Page 3 all NEC D38x7 drives report their sector size as zero. The NEC drives are the first brand of drive we have ever encountered that reported the sector size as zero. Unfortunately, that field in Mode Sense Page 3 is not modifiable and there is no way to update the firmware on the D38x7 drives to correct this problem. Problems are mentioned for D3825 and D3827 (both revision 0407). Revision 0410 of these two hard drives seems to solve this problem.

TAPE DRIVES

SUPPORTED

- SCSI tape drives
    - (From the SCSI HOWTO) Drives using both fixed and variable length blocks smaller than the driver buffer length (set to 32k in the distribution sources) are supported. Virtually all drives should work. (Send mail if you know of any incompatible drives.)
- Seagate Sidewinder 50 AIT (on ICP 6527 RAID-controller)
- QIC-02 drives
- Iomega Ditto internal (ftape 3.04c and newer)

ALPHA, BETA DRIVERS

- QIC-117, QIC-40/80, QIC-3010/3020 (QIC-WIDE) drives
    - Most tape drives using the floppy controller should work. Various dedicated controllers (Colorado FC-10/FC-20, Mountain Mach-2, Iomega Tape Controller II) are also supported.

    `ftp://metalab.unc.edu/pub/Linux/kernel/tapes`
- ATAPI tape drives
    - For these an alpha driver (ide-tape.c) is available in the kernel. ATAPI tape drives supported are
    - Seagate TapeStor 8000
    - Conner CTMA 4000 IDE ATAPI Streaming tape drive

UNSUPPORTED

- Emerald and Tecmar QIC-02 tape controller cards—Chris Ulrich `insom@math.ucr.edu`
- Drives that connect to the parallel port (for example: Colorado Trakker)
- Some high-speed tape controllers (Colorado TC-15)
- Irwin AX250L/Accutrak 250 (not QIC-80)
- IBM Internal Tape Backup Unit (not QIC-80)
- COREtape Light

CD-ROM DRIVES

For more information on CD-ROM drives check the CDROM-HOWTO at `http://metalab.unc.edu/LDP/HOWTO/`.

SUPPORTED

COMMON CD-ROM DRIVES

- SCSI CD-ROM drives
  - (From the CD-ROM HOWTO) Any SCSI CD-ROM drive with a block size of 512 or 2048 bytes should work under Linux; this includes the vast majority of CD-ROM drives on the market.
- EIDE (ATAPI) CD-ROM drives (IDECD)
  - Almost all double-, quad,- and six-speed drives are supported, including:
  - Mitsumi FX400
  - Nec-260
  - Sony 55E

PROPRIETARY CD-ROM DRIVES

- Aztech CDA268-01A, Orchid CDS-3110, Okano/Wearnes CDD-110, Conrad TXC, CyCDROM CR520ie/CR540ie/CR940ie (AZTCD)
- Creative Labs CD-200 (SBPCD)
- Funai E2550UA/MK4015 (SBPCD)
- GoldStar R420 (GSCD)
- IBM External ISA (SBPCD)
- Kotobuki (SBPCD)
- Lasermate CR328A (OPTCD)
- LMS Philips CM 206 (CM206)
- Longshine LCS-7260 (SBPCD)
- Matsushita/Panasonic CR-521/522/523/562/563 (SBPCD)
- MicroSolutions Backpack parallel portdrive (BPCD)
- Mitsumi CR DC LU05S (MCD/MCDX)
- Mitsumi FX001D/F (MCD/MCDX)
- Optics Storage Dolphin 8000AT (OPTCD)
- Sanyo CDR-H94A (SJCD)
- Sony CDU31A/CDU33A (CDU31A)
- Sony CDU-510/CDU-515 (SOMYCD535)
- Sony CDU-535/CDU-531 (SONYCD535)
- Teac CD-55A SuperQuad (SBPCD)

ALPHA, BETA DRIVERS

- LMS/Philips CM 205/225/202
  `ftp://metalab.unc.edu/pub/Linux/kernel/patches/cdrom/lmscd0.4.tar.gz`

- NEC CDR-35D (old)
  `ftp://metalab.unc.edu/pub/Linux/kernel/patches/cdrom/linux-neccdr35d.patch`

- Sony SCSI multi-session CD-XA
  `ftp://tsx-11.mit.edu/pub/linux/patches/sony-multi-0.00.tar.gz`

- Parallel Port Driver
  `http://www.torque.net/linux-pp.html`

NOTES

All CD-ROM drives should work similarly for reading data. There are various compatibility problems with audio CD playing utilities (especially with newer low-end NEC drives). Some alpha drivers may not have audio support yet.

Early (single-speed) NEC CD-ROM drives may have trouble with currently available SCSI controllers.

PhotoCD (XA) is supported. The `hpcdtoppm` program by Hadmut Danisch converts PhotoCD files to the portable pixmap format. The program can be obtained from `ftp://ftp.gwdg.de/pub/linux/hpcdtoppm` or as part of the PBM utilities.

Also, reading video CD is supported in kernel series 2.1.3x and later. A patch is available for kernel 2.0.30.

Finally, most IDE CD-ROM Changers are supported.

CD-WRITERS

Linux now supports many CD-Writers. For an up-to-date list of CD-Writers supported, check the CD-Writing mini-HOWTO at `http://metalab.unc.edu/LDP/HOWTO/CD -Writing-HOWTO.html`, check `http://www.shop.de/cgi-bin/winni/lsc.pl` or check `http:// www.guug.de:8080/cgi-bin/winni/lsc.pl`. Cdwrite `ftp://metalab.unc.edu/pub/Linux/ utils/disk-management/` and cdrecord `http://www.fokus.gmd.de/research/cc/glone/ employees/joerg.schilling/private/cdrecord.html` can be used for writing CDs. The X-CD-Roast package for Linux is a graphical front-end for using CD writers. The package can be found at `ftp://metalab.unc.edu/pub/Linux/utils/disk-management/ xcdroast-0.96d.tar.gz`.

- Grundig CDR 100 IPW
- HP CD-Writer+ 7100
- HP SureStore 4020i
- HP SureStore 6020es/i

- JVC XR-W2010
- Kodak PCD 225
- Mitsubishi CDRW-226
- Mitsumi CR-2600TE
- Olympus CDS 620E
- Philips CDD-521/10,522,2000,2600,3610
- Pinnacle Micro RCD-5020/5040
- Plextor CDR PX-24CS
- Ricoh MP 1420C
- Ricoh MP 6200S/6201S
- Sanyo CRD-R24S
- Smart and Friendly Internal 2006 Plus 2.05
- Sony CDU 920S/924/926S
- Taiyo Yuden EW-50
- TEAC CD-R50S
- WPI (Wearnes) CDR-632P
- WPI (Wearnes) CDRW-622
- Yamaha CDR-100
- Yamaha CDR-200/200t/200tx
- Yamaha CDR-400t/400tx

REMOVABLE DRIVES

All SCSI drives should work if the controller is supported, including optical (MO), WORM, floptical, Bernoulli, Zip, Jaz, SyQuest, PD, and others.

Panasonic MO combines a CD-ROM drive and an optical removable disk. You must set a switch when configuring the kernel for both parts to work at the same time.

- Parallel port Zip drives
  `ftp://gear.torque.net/pub/`
- Parallel port Avatar Shark-250
  `http://www.torque.net/parport/`

Removable drives work like hard disks and floppies, just `fdisk`/`mkfs` and mount the disks. Linux provides drive locking if your drives support it. `mtools` can also be used if the disks are in MS-DOS format.

CD-R drives require special software to work. Read the CD-R Mini-HOWTO.

Linux supports both 512 and 1024 bytes/sector disks. Starting with kernel 2.1.32 Linux also supports 2048 bytes/sector. A patch to kernel 2.0.30 is available at `http://liniere.gen.u-tokyo.ac.jp/2048.html`.

The 2048 bytes/sector support is needed for

- Fujitsu magneto-optical disk drives M2513

Starting with pre-patch-2.0.31-3 IDE/ATAPI internal Zip drives, flopticals and PDs are supported.

- LS-120 floptical
- PD-CD

MOUSE DEVICES

SUPPORTED

- Microsoft serial mouse
- Mouse Systems serial mouse
- Logitech Mouseman serial mouse
- Logitech serial mouse
- ATI XL Inport busmouse
- C&T 82C710 (QuickPort) (Toshiba, TI Travelmate)
- Microsoft busmouse
- Logitech busmouse
- PS/2 (auxiliary device) mouse

ALPHA, BETA DRIVERS

- Sejin J-mouse
  `ftp://metalab.unc.edu/pub/Linux/kernel/patches/console/jmouse.1.1.70-jmouse.tar.gz`
- MultiMouse—use multiple mouse devices as single mouse
  `ftp://metalab.unc.edu/pub/Linux/system/misc/MultiMouse-1.0.tgz`
- Microsoft IntelliMouse

NOTES

Touchpad devices such as Alps Glidepoint also work, so long as they're compatible with another mouse protocol.

Newer Logitech mouse devices (except the Mouseman) use the Microsoft protocol and all three buttons do work. Even though Microsoft's mouse devices have only two buttons, the protocol allows three buttons.

The mouse ports on the ATI Graphics Ultra and Ultra Pro use the Logitech busmouse protocol. (See the Busmouse HOWTO for details.)

MODEMS

All internal modems or external modems connected to the serial port should work. Alas, some manufacturers have created Windows 95-only modems. Check "Linux-Incompatible Hardware" for Linux-incompatible hardware. Furthermore, many flash upgradable modems only have flash programs for Win95/NT. These modems cannot be upgraded under Linux.

A small number of modems come with DOS software that downloads the control program at runtime. These normally are used by loading the program under DOS and doing a warm boot. Such modems are probably best avoided because you won't be able to use them with non-PC hardware in the future.

All PCMCIA modems should work with the PCMCIA drivers.

Fax modems need appropriate fax software to operate. Also be sure that the fax part of the modem supports Class 2 or Class 2.0. It seems to be generally true for any fax software on UNIX that support for Class 1.0 is not available.

An exception to this is the Linux `efax` program, which supports both Class 1 and Class 2 fax modems. In some cases there can be a few (minor) technical problems with Class 1 modems. If you have a choice it is recommended that you get a Class 2 modem.

- Digicom Connection 96+/14.4+—DSP code downloading program
  `ftp://metalab.unc.edu/pub/Linux/apps/serialcomm/smdl-linux.1.02.tar.gz`

- Motorola ModemSURFR internal 56K. Add a couple of line to RC.SERIAL to account for IRQ and ports if they are nonstandard.

- ZyXEL U-1496 series—ZyXEL 1.4, modem/fax/voice control program
  `http://www.pe1chl.demon.nl/ZyXEL/ZyXEL-1.6.tar.gz`

- ZyXEL Elite 2864 series—modem/fax/voice control program
  `http://www.pe1chl.demon.nl/ZyXEL/ZyXEL-1.6.tar.gz`

- ZyXEL Omni TA 128—modem/fax/voice control program
  `http://www.pe1chl.demon.nl/ZyXEL/ZyXEL-1.6.tar.gz`

Also multimodem cards are supported by Linux.

- Moreton Bay RAStel multimodem card
  `Check http://www.moreton.com.au/linux.htm for Linux drivers.`

The following modem is not supported:

- Aztech MDP3858 56.6 (PCI)

PRINTERS/PLOTTERS

All printers and plotters connected to the parallel or serial port should work. Alas, some manufacturers have created Windows 95-only printers. Check "Linux-Incompatible Hardware" for Linux-incompatible hardware.

- HP LaserJet 4 series—free-lj4, printing modes control program
  ftp://metalab.unc.edu/pub/Linux/system/printing/free-lj4-1.1p1.tar.gz
- BiTronics parallel port interface
  ftp://metalab.unc.edu/pub/Linux/kernel/patches/
- misc/bt-ALPHA-0.0.1.module.patch.gz
- Epson Stylus Color 850. Use Magicfilter with one of the following filters: stylus 800-filter, stylus_color_360dpi-filter, or stylus_color_720dpi-filter.

GHOSTSCRIPT

Many Linux programs output PostScript files. Non-PostScript printers can emulate PostScript Level 2 using Ghostscript.

- Ghostscript
  ftp://ftp.cs.wisc.edu/pub/ghost/aladdin/

GHOSTSCRIPT 5.1 SUPPORTED PRINTERS

- Apple Imagewriter
- Apple Dot Matrix printer
- Apple StyleWriter 2x00 (bjc600)
- Brother HL-660 (ljet4)
- C. Itoh M8510
- Canon BubbleJet BJ10e, BJ20 (bj10e)
- Canon BubbleJet BJ100, BJ200, BJC-210 (B/W only), BJC-240 (B/W only), BJC-250 (B/W only), BJC-70 (B/W only) (bj200)
- Canon BubbleJet BJC-600, BJC-610, BJC-4000, BJC-4100 (B/W only), BJC-4200, BJC-4300, BJC-4400, BJC-4550, BJC-210, BJC-450, MultiPASS C2500, BJC-240, BJC-70 (bjc600)
- Canon BubbleJet BJC-800, BJC-7000 (bjc800)
- Canon Bubblejet BJC-610 (uniprint)
- Canon LBP-8II, LIPS III

- DEC LA50/70/75/75plus
- DEC LN03, LJ250 (decl250)
- Epson 9 pin, 24 pin, LQ series, AP3250
- Epson Stylus Color/Color II/400/500/600/800 (stcolor)
- Epson Stylus Color/Color II/500/600/800/1520 (uniprint)
- Fujitsu 3400,2400,1200
- HP 2563B
- HP DesignJet 650C
- HP DeskJet, Deskjet Plus (deskjet)
- HP Deskjet 500, Deskjet Portable (djet500)
- HP Deskjet 500C (cdeskjet)
- HP Deskjet 550C (uniprint)
- HP DeskJet 400/500C/520C/540C/690C/693C (cdj500)
- HP DeskJet 550C/560C/600/660C/660Cse/682C/683C/693C/694C/695C/850/870Cse (cdj550)
- HP DeskJet 850/855/870Cse/870Cxi/890C/672C/680/1100C (cdj850)
- HP DeskJet 500C/510/520/5540C/693C printing black only (cdjmono)
- HP DeskJet 600 (lj4dith)
- HP DeskJet 600/870Cse, LaserJet 5/5L/6L (ljet4)
- HP Deskjet 600/1200C/1600C (pjxl300)
- HP Deskjet 500/500C/510/520/540/550C/560C/850C/855C and other PCL3 printers
  `ftp:ftp.pdb.sni.de/pub/utilities/misc/hpdj-2.1.tar.gz`
- HP Deskjet 710, 720, 820 and 1000 series
  `http://www.httptech.com/ppa/`
- HP Paintjet (pjtest)
- HP Paintjet XL (pjxltest)
- HP PaintJet XL300 (pjxl300)
- HP LaserJet/Plus/II/III/4/5/6
- IBM 3853 Jetprinter color
- IBM Proprinter
- Imagen ImPress
- Lexmark Optra E+ (ljet4)
- Mitsubishi CP50 color
- NEC P6/P6+/P60
- NEC Pinwriter P2X (uniprint)

- NEC SuperScript 860 (ljetplus)
- Oki OL410ex LED (ljet4)
- Okidata MicroLine 182
- Ricoh 4081/6000 (r4081)
- SPARCprinter
- StarJet 48 inkjet printer
- Tektronix 4693d color 2/4/8 bit
- Tektronix 4695/4696 inkjet plotter
- Xerox XES printers (2700, 3700, 4045, etc.)

ALPHA, BETA DRIVERS

- Epson Stylus Color 440

SCANNERS

For scanner support there is the package SANE (Scanner Access Now Easy). Information can be found at `http://www.mostang.com/sane/`. It can be downloaded from `ftp://ftp.mostang.com/pub/sane/`. This is a universal scanner interface and comes complete with documentation and several front ends and back ends.

More information on handheld scanners can be found at `http://www.willamowius.de/scanner.html`.

Many scanners also have their own scanner-specific software packages that include drivers.

SUPPORTED

- A4 Tech AC 4096 / AS 8000P (a4scan)
  `ftp://ftp.informatik.hu-berlin.de/pub/local/linux/a4scan/a4scan.tgz`
- Adara Image Star I
  `http://fb4-1112.uni-muenster.de/ffwd/`
  `ftp://fb4-1112.uni-muenster.de/pub/ffwd/mtekscan-0.2.tar.gz`
- Conrad Personal Scanner 64, P105 handheld scanners (scan-driver)
  `ftp://tsx-11.mit.edu/pub/linux/ALPHA/scanner/scan-driver-0.1.8.tar.gz`
- Epson GT-5500 (SANE epson)
- Epson GT-6000
  `ftp://metalab.unc.edu/pub/Linux/apps/graphics/capture/ppic0.5.tar.gz`
- Escom Image Scanner 256 (SANE umax)
- Fujitsu SCSI-2 scanners
  Contact Dr. G.W. Wettstein at `greg%wind.UUCP@plains.nodak.edu`

- Genius ColorPage-SP2

  `http://fb4-1112.uni-muenster.de/ffwd/`

  `ftp://fb4-1112.uni-muenster.de/pub/ffwd/mtekscan-0.2.tar.gz`

- Genius GS-B105G handheld scanner (gs105)

  `ftp://tsx-11.mit.edu/pub/linux/ALPHA/scanner/gs105-0.0.1.tar.gz`

- Genius GeniScan GS-4500, GS-4500A handheld scanners (gs4500)

  `ftp://tsx-11.mit.edu/pub/linux/ALPHA/scanner/gs4500-2.0.tar.gz`

- HighScreen Greyscan 256 handheld scanner (BW only) (gs4500)

  `ftp://tsx-11.mit.edu/pub/linux/ALPHA/scanner/gs4500-2.0.tar.gz`

- HP ScanJet II series SCSI

  `ftp://metalab.unc.edu/pub/Linux/apps/graphics/capture/hpscanpbm-0.3a.tar.gz`

- HP ScanJet IIc, IIcx, IIp, 3c, 4c, 4p, 5p, 5pse, plus

  `http://www.tummy.com/xvscan/`

- Linotype Hell Jade, Jade2 (SANE umax)

- Logitech Scanman+, Scanman 32, Scanman 256 handheld scanners (logiscan)

  `ftp://tsx-11.mit.edu/pub/linux/ALPHA/scanner/logiscan-0.0.4.tar.gz`

- Microtek ScanMaker E3, E6, II, IIXE, III and 35t models

  `http://fb4-1112.uni-muenster.de/ffwd/`
  `ftp://fb4-1112.uni-muenster.de/pub/ffwd/mtekscan-0.2.tar.gz`

  E3 and E6 scanners are also supported by `http://www.tummy.com/xvscan/`.

- Mustek M105 handheld scanner (scan-driver)

  `ftp://tsx-11.mit.edu/pub/linux/ALPHA/scanner/scan-driver-0.1.8.tar.gz`

- Mustek HT800 Turbo, Matador 105, Matador 256 handheld scanners (scan-driver)

  `ftp://tsx-11.mit.edu/pub/linux/ALPHA/scanner/scan-driver-0.1.8.tar.gz`

- Mustek Paragon 6000CX

  `ftp://metalab.unc.edu/pub/Linux/apps/graphics/capture/muscan-2.0.6.taz`

- Nikon Coolscan SCSI 35mm film scanner

  `ftp://metalab.unc.edu/pub/Linux/apps/graphics/capture/coolscan-0.2.tgz`

- Nikon AX-210 (SANE umax)

- Pearl 256 handheld scanner (scan-driver)

  `ftp://tsx-11.mit.edu/pub/linux/ALPHA/scanner/scan-driver-0.1.8.tar.gz`

- Polaroid DMC (SANE dmc)

- Vobis/Highscreen Scanboostar Premium (SANE umax)

- UMAX SCSI scanners

  `ftp://tsx-11.mit.edu/pub/linux/ALPHA/scanner/umax-0.5.5.tar.gz`

- UMAX Vista S6, S6E, T630, Supervista S-12 (SANE umax)

- UMAX S-6E, S-6EG, S-12, S-12G (SANE umax)
- UMAX Astra 600S, 610S, 1200S, 1220S (SANE umax)
- UMAX UC 630, 840, 1200S, 1200SE (SANE umax)
- UMAX UG 80, 630 (SANE umax)
- UMAX PSD, Gemini D-16 (SANE umax)

> **Note**
>
> The Mustek drivers work only with GI1904 interface cards. Eric Chang, `eric.chang@chrysalis.org`, has created a patch to use them with IF960 interface cards.

ALPHA, BETA DRIVERS

- Abaton Scan 300/S (SANE abaton)
- Abaton Scan 300/GS (SANE abaton)
- Agfa Focus, Focus II (SANE agfafocus)
- Agfa Focus Color, Focus Color Plus (SANE agfafocus)
- Agfa Focus Lineart (SANE agfafocus)
- Agfa Arcus II (SANE microtek)
- Agfa StudioScan II, IIsi (SANE microtek)
- Agfa SnapScan 300, 310, 600 (SANE snapscan)
- Apple Scanner, OneScanner, ColorOneScanner (SANE apple)
- Artec/Ultima AT3, AT6, AT12 (SANE artec)
- Artec A6000C+ (SANE artec)
- Canon CanoScan 300, CanoScan 600, CanoScan 2700F (SANE canon)
- Genius Colorpage-Vivid+
  - Information can be found on `http://thor.prohosting.com/~chrordig/Primax/index.html`. The driver can also be found here.
- Genius GS-4000, ScanMate/32, ScanMate/GS handheld scanners (gs4500)
  `ftp://tsx-11.mit.edu/pub/linux/ALPHA/scanner/gs4500-2.0.tar.gz`
- HP ScanJet IIc, IIp, IIcx, 3c, 4c, 3p, 4p, 5p, 6100c, 6200c (SANE hp)
- HP PhotoSmart PhotoScanner (SANE hp)
- Kodak DC210 (SANE dc210)
- Kodak DC20, DC25 (SANE dc25)
- Microtek Scanmaker E2, E3, E6, II, IIG, IIHR, IISP, III, 35t+, 600Z(S), 600G(S) (SANE microtek)
- Microtek ScanMaker E3plus, 330, 630, 636, X6 (SANE microtek2)

- Microtek Phantom 636 (SANE microtek2)
- Mustek MFC-600S, MFC-600CD, MFC-800S (SANE mustek)
- Mustek MFS-6000CX, MFS-6000SP, MFS-8000SP, MFS-1200SP, MFS-12000CX (SANE mustek)
- Mustek SE-6000SP, SE-12000SP (SANE mustek)
- Mustek HT105, M800 handheld scanners (scan-driver)
  `ftp://tsx-11.mit.edu/pub/linux/ALPHA/scanner/scan-driver-0.1.8.tar.gz`
- Nework Scanny MM100

  Information can be found on `http://thor.prohosting.com/~chrordig/Primax/index.html`. The driver can also be found here.
- Nikon LS-20, LS-30, LS-1000 (SANE Coolscan)
- Plustek OpticPro 4830P, OpticPro 4831P, OpticPro 9630P/PL, OpticPro 600P, OpticPro FBIII, OpticPro FBIV (SANE plustek)
  - The sane driver can be found at `http://www.efn.org/~rick/plustek/`.
- Primax Colorado Direct 300, Colorado Direct 600/30bit, Storm Totalscan

  Information can be found on `http://thor.prohosting.com/~chrordig/Primax/index.html`. The driver can also be found here.
- Siemens S9036 (SANE agfafocus)
- Tamarack Artiscan 6000C, 8000C, 12000C (SANE tamarack)
- UMAX Vista-S8, UC-1260, Mirage IIse, PL-II (SANE umax)
- Vobis HighScan (SANE microtek2)
- Voelkner Personal Scanner 64 handheld scanner (scan-driver)
  `ftp://tsx-11.mit.edu/pub/linux/ALPHA/scanner/scan-driver-0.1.8.tar.gz`
- Vuego 310S (SANE snapscan)

UNSUPPORTED

- Acer scanners. Acer is not releasing any programming information.
- Escom 256 (Primax Lector Premier 256) handheld scanner
- Genius ScanMate/256, ScanMate/Color, EasyScan handheld scanners
- Mustek CG 8000 handheld scanner
- Primax Colorado Direct 9600, Colorado 1200p, Colorado USB 19200

  Information can be found on `http://thor.prohosting.com/~chrordig/Primax/index.html`.
- Trust Ami Scan handheld scanner
- UMAX parallel scanners

OTHER HARDWARE

AMATEUR RADIO

The following cards and so forth are supported:

- KISS-based Terminal Node Controllers
- Ottawa PI card
- Gracilis PacketTwin card
- Other Z8530 SCC based cards
- Parallel and serial port Baycom modems
- Soundblaster cards
- Soundcards based on the Crystal chipset

VESA POWER SAVINGS PROTOCOL (DPMS) MONITORS

Support for power savings is included in the Linux kernel. Use `setterm` to enable support in the Linux console, and `xset` to enable support under X.

TOUCH SCREENS

The Metro-X X-server is supporting the following touch-screen controllers:

- Carrol Touch serial touch screen
  `http://www.carrolltouch.com`
- EloGraphics
- Lucas Deeco
- MicroTouch

TERMINALS ON SERIAL PORT

Old terminals can easily be used under Linux by connecting them to the serial port of your system. All of the following terminals are supported:

- VT52
- VT100
- VT220
- VT320
- VT420

JOYSTICKS

Joystick support is in the latest XFree86 distribution (3.3.x) and in kernel versions 2.1.xx and 2.2.xx. For older kernels the following links are useful.

- Joystick driver

  For information check `http://atrey.karlin.mff.cuni.cz/~vojtech/joystick`. An FTP archive can be found at ftp://atrey.karlin.mff.cuni.cz/pub/linux/joystick.

Currently supported joysticks are the following:

- Amiga joysticks on Amiga
- CH Flightstick Pro compatibles with additional two hats and two buttons
- DirectPad Pro parallel port joystick interfaces (`http://www.ziplabel.com/dpadpro/index.html`)
- FP Gaming Assasin 3D (`http://www.fpgaming.com/portfolio/assn3d.html`)
- Gamepads with 6 and 8 buttons
- Genius Flight2000 Digital F-23 (`http://www.genius.kye.de/english/product/game.html`)
- Gravis Blackhawk Digital (`http://www.gravis.com/products/js_blackhawkdigital.html`)
- Gravis GamePad Pro (`http://www.gravis.com/products/gp_gamepadpro.html`)
- Gravis Xterminator GamePad (`http://www.gravis.com/products/xterminator.html`)
- Logitech CyberMan 2 (`http://www.cyberman2.de`)
- Logitech ThunderPad Digital (`http://www.logitech.ch/Game+Controllers/ThunderPadDigital.html`)
- Logitech WingMan Extreme Digital (`http://www.logitech.ch/Game+Controllers/WingManExtremeDigital.html`)
- MadCatz Panther (`http://www.fpgaming.com/portfolio/panther.html`)
- MadCatz Panther XL (`http://www.fpgaming.com/portfolio/panthxl.html`)
- Microsoft SideWinder 3D Pro (`http://www.eu.microsoft.com/products/hardware/sidewinder/3Dpro/default.htm`)
- Microsoft SideWinder Force Feedback Pro (`http://www.eu.microsoft.com/products/hardware/sidewinder/force-feedback/default.htm`)
- Microsoft SideWinder GamePad (`http://www.eu.microsoft.com/products/hardware/sidewinder/gamepad/default.htm`)
- Microsoft SideWinder Precision Pro (`http://www.eu.microsoft.com/products/hardware/sidewinder/precision-pro/default.htm`)
- Multisystem joysticks (Atari, Amiga, Commodore, Amstrad)
- Multisystem joysticks using 0.8.0.2 hw interface
- Nintendo Entertainment System (and clone—SVI, Pegasus ...) gamepads
- PDPI Lightning L4 gamecard (`http://www.pdpi.net`)
- Sega Genesis (MegaDrive) gamepads
- Sega Master System gamepads

- Sega Saturn gamepads
- SNESKey parallel port joystick interfaces
- Sony PlayStation gamepads
- Standard joysticks with 2, 3, or 4 axes, and up to 4 buttons
- Super Nintendo Entertainment System gamepads
- ThrustMaster FCS compatibles with additional hat
- ThrustMaster Millennium 3D Inceptor (`http://www.thrustmaster.com/products/millennium.htm`)
- ThrustMaster Rage 3D (`http://www.thrustmaster.com/products/rage3d.htm`)
- TurboGraFX parallel port joystick interface (`http://www2.burg-halle.de/~schwenke/parport.html`)

VIDEO CAPTURE BOARDS/FRAME GRABBERS/TV TUNERS

The following are programs available that support TV tuners:

- BTTV `http://www.thp.Uni-Koeln.DE/~rjkm/linux/bttv.html`
- Xawtv
- Xtvscreen
- All cards with Bt848/Bt848a/Bt849/Bt878/Bt879 and normal Composite/S-VHS inputs are supported. Teletext and Intercast support (PAL only) through VBI samples decoding in software.
- Adlink 7200 Digital I/O device
  `ftp://metalab.unc.edu/pub/Linux/science/lab/adl7200-0.60.tar.gz`
- Adlink 7300A Digital I/O device
  `ftp://ftp.systemy.it/pub/develop/adl7300-0.04.tar.gz`
- CMOS Video Conferencing Kit. The video capture card has a Bt849 chipset. It comes with a CCD camera.
- Data Translation DT2803
- Data Translation DT2851 Frame Grabber
  `ftp://metalab.unc.edu/pub/Linux/apps/video/dt2851-2.01.tar.gz`
- Data Translation DT3155
  `http://krusty.eecs.umich.edu/people/ncowan/linux/welcome.html`
- Diamond DTV2000 (based on Bt848)
- Dipix XPG1000/FPG/PPMAPA (based on TI C40 DSP). Most add-on cards are supported.
  `http://www.thp.Uni-Koeln.DE/~rjkm/linux/bttv.html` or `http://www.atlantek.com.au/USERS/wes/linux/frame.html`. The driver can be found at `ftp://ftp.atlantek.com.au/pub/ldipix`.

- Epix SVM

- Epix Silicon Video MUX series of video frame grabbing boards
  http://www.ssc.com/lj/issue13/npc13c.html

- FAST Screen Machine II
  ftp://metalab.unc.edu/pub/Linux/apps/video/ScreenMachineII.2.0.tgz

- Hauppage Wincast TV PCI (based on Bt848)
  http://www.thp.Uni-Koeln.DE/~rjkm/linux/bttv.htmlImaging Technology ITI/
  IC-PCI

  ftp://ftp.gom-online.de/pub/IC-PCI/icpci-0.3.2.tar.gz

- ImageNation Cortex I
  ftp://metalab.unc.edu/pub/Linux/apps/video/cortex.drv.1.1.tgz

- ImageNation CX100
  ftp://metalab.unc.edu/pub/Linux/apps/video/cxdrv-0.86.tar.gz

- ImageNation PX500
  ftp://ftp.systemy.it/pub/develop

- ImageNation PXC200
  ftp://ftp.systemy.it/pub/develop

- Imaging Technology Inc. IC-PCI frame grabber board
  ftp://gandalf.expmech.ing.tu-bs.de/pub/driver/icpci-0.2.0.tar.gz

- Matrix Vision MV-Delta
  http://www.matrix-vision.de/

- Matrox Meteor
  ftp://metalab.unc.edu/pub/Linux/apps/video/meteor-1.4a.tgz

- Matrox PIP-1024
  http://www.powerup.com.au/~sobeyp/pip_tar.gz

- MaxiTV/PCI (based on ZR36120)
  ftp://metalab.unc.edu/pub/Linux/kernel/misc-cards/zr36120-971127.tgz

- Miro PCTV (based on Bt848)
  http://www.thp.Uni-Koeln.DE/~rjkm/linux/bttv.html

- MuTech MV1000 PCI
  ftp://metalab.unc.edu/pub/Linux/apps/video/mv1000drv-0.33.tgz

- MuTech MV200
  `http://www.powerup.com.au/~sobeyp/mu_tar.gz`
- Philips PCA10TV (not in production anymore)
  `ftp://ftp.il.ft.hse.nl/pub/tv1000/pctv1000.02.tgz`
- Pinnacle PCTV (based on Bt848)
- Pro Movie Studio
  `ftp://metalab.unc.edu/pub/Linux/apps/video/PMS-grabber.3.0.tgz`
- Quanta WinVision B&W video capture card
  `ftp://metalab.unc.edu/pub/Linux/apps/video/fgrabber-1.0.tgz`
- Quickcam
  `ftp://metalab.unc.edu/pub/Linux/apps/video/qcam-0.7c-5.tar.gz`
- Nomadic Technologies Sensus 700
  `http://www.robots.com/` for common information. Alas, Nomadic Technologies has removed the page about the Sensus 700.
- Smart Video Recoder III (based on Bt848)
  `http://www.thp.Uni-Koeln.DE/~rjkm/linux/bttv.html`
- STB TV PCI Television Tuner (based on Bt848)
  `http://www.thp.Uni-Koeln.DE/~rjkm/linux/bttv.html`
- Tekram C210 (based on ZR36120)
  `ftp://metalab.unc.edu/pub/Linux/kernel/misc-cards/zr36120-971127.tgz`
- Video Blaster, Rombo Media Pro+
  `ftp://metalab.unc.edu/pub/Linux/apps/video/vid_src-0.7.tgz`
- VT1500 TV cards
  `ftp://metalab.unc.edu/pub/Linux/apps/video/vt1500-1.0.9.tar.gz`

DIGITAL CAMERAS

Currently five programs can be used in combination with digital cameras.

- Camediaplay (`http://www.itojun.org/itojun.html`)
  You can download it from `ftp://ftp.itojun.org/pub/digicam/C-400L/unix/`.
- Photopc (`http://www.average.org/digicam/`)
  It can be downloaded from `ftp://ftp.average.org/pub/photopc/`.
- Qvplay (`http://www.asahi-net.or.jp/~XG2K-HYS/index-e.html`)
  It can be downloaded from `http://www.asahi-net.or.jp/~XG2K-HYS/qvplay-0.93.tar.gz`.

- JCAM, a Java application which allows digital camera owners to access and download pictures from a wide variety of popular digital cameras (http://www.jcam.com).

  It can be downloaded from http://www.jcam.com/jcam/download.shtml.

- gPhoto (http://www.gphoto.org)

  It can be downloaded from http://www.gphoto.org/download.php3.

Photopc can be extended with a graphical Tk front end. This can be found at http://www.mediacity.com/~pwhite/Phototk/phototk.html. Also Qvplay can be extended with a graphical Tk front end, which can be found at http://www.bekkoame.or.jp/~tormato/pub/qvplaytk-0.73c.tar.gz.

SUPPORTED

- Agfa ePhoto line of cameras (photopc, camediaplay, JCAM)
  http://www.agfahome.com/ephoto/

- Apple QuickTake 200 (JCAM)

- Casio QV10, QV-10A, QV-11, QV-30, QV-70, QV-100, QV-200, QV-300, QV-700, QV-770 (qvplay)
  http://www.casio.com/digitalimaging/digital-results.cfm?ObjectGroup_ID=171

- Casio QV-10A, QV-11, QV-30, QV-70, QV-100, QV-300, QV-700, QV-770 (JCAM)

- Chinon ES-1000 (same hardware, protocol, and image format as Kodak DC20) (JCAM)
  http://www.planet-interkom.de/oliver.hartmann/dc20secr.htm

- Epson "Colorio Photo" CP-100 (PhotoPC) (photopc, camediaplay)
  http://www.epson.com/cam_scan/

- Epson "Colorio Photo" CP-200 (PhotoPC 500) (photopc, camediaplay, JCAM)
  http://www.epson.com/cam_scan/

- Epson "Colorio Photo" CP-200 (PhotoPC 550) (JCAM)

- Epson "Colorio Photo" CP-500 (PhotoPC 600) (photopc, camediaplay, JCAM)
  http://www.epson.com/cam_scan/

- Epson "Colorio Photo" CP-500 (PhotoPC 700) (JCAM)

- Epson PhotoPC 550 (photopc, camediaplay)
  http://www.epson.com/cam_scan/

- Fuji DS-7, DX-5 (DS-10), DX-7 (DS-20), DX-9 (DS-30), DS-300, MX-700 (JCAM)

- HP Photo Smart Digital Camera (Some people say it is supported, others say it isn't!)

- Kodak DC-20, DC-25, DC-200/210 (JCAM)
  http://www.planet-interkom.de/oliver.hartmann/dc20secr.htm

- Olympus C-300L, C-320L, C-420L, C-800L, C-840L, C-1000L, C-1400L (JCAM)
  `http://www.olympusamerica.com/digital/dhome.html`

- Olympus "Camedia" C-400L (D-200L) (photopc, camediaplay, JCAM))
  `http://www.olympusamerica.com/digital/dhome.html`

- Olympus "Camedia" C-820L (D-320L) (photopc, camediaplay, JCAM))
  `http://www.olympusamerica.com/digital/dhome.html`

- Olympus C2000Z (photocd)

- Sanyo VPC-G200/G200EX (photopc, camediaplay)
  `http://www.sanyo.co.jp/AV/CEmedia_e/products/digicam/digicam.html`

- Sanyo DSC-V1 (VPC-G200E) (photopc, camediaplay)
  `http://www.sanyo.co.jp/AV/CEmedia_e/products/digicam/digicam.html`

- Sanyo DSC-X1 (VPC-X300) (JCAM)

- Sanyo DSC-X300 (photopc, camediaplay)
  `http://www.sanyo.co.jp/AV/CEmedia_e/products/digicam/digicam.html`

- Nikon Coolpix 600/900 (Coolpix 600 untested) (photopc)
  `http://www.nikonusa.com/products/products.taf?id=128` and
  `http://www.nikonusa.com/products/products.taf?id=129`

- Sierra Imaging SD640 (photopc)
  `http://www.sierraimaging.com/support/supchimgex.html`

- Toshiba PDR-2 (not sure: photopc)
  `http://www.toshiba.com/taisisd/dsc/indexj.htm`

UNSUPPORTED

- Casio QV-120, QV-5000SX, QV-7000SX
- Kodak DC40, DC50, DC120

UPS

Various other UPSs are supported; read the UPS HOWTO.

- APC SmartUPS
  `http://www.dyer.vanderbilt.edu/server/apcupsd`

- APC-BackUPS 400/600, APC-SmartUPS SU700/1400RM
  `http://www.dyer.vanderbilt.edu/server/apcupsd`

- Fenton PowerPal

  `ftp://megatec.com.tw/Rups2/UNIX/v3.0.1` for downloads and manuals. Web site information can be found at `http://www.fentonups.com/index2.htm`.

- Fenton Tele-UPS

  `ftp://megatec.com.tw/Rups2/UNIX/v3.0.1` for downloads and manuals. Web site information can be found at `http://www.fentonups.com/index2.htm`.

- Fenton PowerOn

  `ftp://megatec.com.tw/Rups2/UNIX/v3.0.1` for downloads and manuals. Web site information can be found at `http://www.fentonups.com/index2.htm`.

- UPSs with RS-232 monitoring port (genpower package)
  `ftp://metalab.unc.edu/pub/Linux/system/ups/genpower-1.0.1.tgzMGE UPSs`

  `http://www.mgeups.com/download/softlib.htm` and `http://www.mgeups.com/download/software/linux/upsp.tgz`

- A daemon to shut down and boot up computers connected to UPSs. It's network-aware and allows server and client mode.
  `ftp://metalab.unc.edu/pub/Linux/system/ups/powerd-2.0.tar.gz`

MULTIFUNCTION BOARDS

- Pro Audio Spectrum 16 SCSI/Sound interface card

DATA ACQUISITION

The Linux Lab Project site collects drivers for hardware dealing with data acquisition and also maintains some mailing lists dealing with the subject. I have no experience with data acquisition so please check the site for more details.

- Linux Lab Project
  `http://www.llp.fu-berlin.de/`

- CED 1401

- DBCC CAMAC

- IEEE-488 (GPIB, HPIB) boards

- Keithley DAS-1200

- National Instruments AT-MIO-16F / Lab-PC+

- Analog Devices RTI-800/815 ADC/DAC board

  Contact Paul Gortmaker at `gpg109@anu.edu.au`.

WATCHDOG TIMER INTERFACES

- Berkshire Products PC Watchdog Card (ISA cards rev. A and C)

  Check `ftp://ftp.bitgate.com/pub/bitgate/pcwd` for the PC Watchdog program. A driver is included in recent kernels. More information on this product can be found at `http://www.berkprod.com/wdog.htm`.

- ICS WDT500-P

  `http://www.indcompsrc.com/products/data/html/wdt500-p.html`

- ICS WDT501-P (with and without fan tachometer)

  `http://www.indcompsrc.com/products/data/html/wdt500-p.html`

- Outsource Engineering & Manufacturing Inc. Basic Watchdog Timer Board (ISA)

  Information can be found at `http://www.ctec.net/basicwdt`. Drivers currently run on 2.0.29, 2.0.33, and 2.0.36 kernels.

MISCELLANEOUS

- Mattel Powerglove
- AIMS Labs RadioTrack FM radio card

  `ftp://metalab.unc.edu/pub/Linux/apps/sound/radio/radiotCrack-1.1.tgz`

- Reveal FM Radio card

  `ftp://magoo.uwsuper.edu/docs/radio.html`

- Videotext cards

  `ftp://metalab.unc.edu/pub/Linux/apps/video/videoteXt-0.6.tar.gz`

RELATED SOURCES OF INFORMATION

- Cameron Spitzer's hardware FAQ archive

  `ftp://ftp.rahul.net/pub/cameron/PC-info/`

- Guide to Computer Vendors

  `http://guide.sbanetweb.com/`

- System Optimization Information

  `http://www.dfw.net/~sdw/`

ACKNOWLEDGMENTS

Thanks to all the authors and contributors of other HOWTOs, many things here are shamelessly stolen from their works; to FRiC, Zane Healy, and Ed Carp, the original authors of this HOWTO; and to everyone else who sent in updates and feedbacks. Special thanks to Eric Boerner and lilo (the person, not the program) for the sanity checks. And thanks to Dan Quinlan for the original SGML conversion.

S3 Cards Supported by XFree86 3.3.x

Table B.2   S3 Cards Supported by XFree86 3.3.x.

CHIP SET	RAMDAC	CLOCKCHIP	BPP	CARD
801/805	AT&T 20C490		16	Orchid Actix GE 32 / 32+ 2MB Fahrenheit 1280(+)
801/805	AT&T 20C490	ICD2061A	16	STB PowerGraph X.24
801/805				Del S3 805 Miro Crystal 8S Orchid Fahrenheit VA VL-41
805	S3 GENDAC		16	Miro 10SD VLB/PCI SPEA Mirage VLB
801/805	SS2410	ICD2061A	8	Diamond Stealth 24 VLB/ISA
801/805	AT&T 20C490	Ch8391	16	JAX 8231/8241, SPEA Mirage
801/805	S3 GENDAC			Miro Crystal 10SD
805i				Actix GE 32i ELSA Winner 1000 ISA
928	AT&T 20C490		16	Actix Ultra
928	Sierra SC15025	ICD2061A	32	ELSA Winner 1000 ISA/ VLB/EISA
928	Bt485	ICD2061A	32	STB Pegasus VL
928	Bt485	SC11412	16	SPEA(/V7) Mercury VLB
928	Bt485	ICD2061A	32	#9 GXE Level 10/11/12
928	Ti3020	ICD2061A	32	#9 GXE Level 14/16
928				928 Movie Diamond Stealth Pro ELSA Winner 1000TwinBus ELSA Winner 1000VL ELSA Winner 2000 Miro Crystal 16S
864		ICD2061A		Miro Crystal 20SD (BIOS 2.xx)
864	AT&T 20C498	ICS2494	32	Miro (Crystal) 20SD (BIOS 1.xx)
864	AT&T 20C498/	ICD2061A/	32	ELSA Winner 1000 PRO VLB/PCI
864	STG1700	ICS9161		ELAS Winner 1000 PRO MIRO 20SD (BIOS 2.x)

Table B.2   Continued

CHIP SET	RAMDAC	CLOCKCHIP	BPP	CARD
864	STG1700	ICD2061A	32	Actix GE 64 VLB
864	AT&T 20C498/ AT&T 21C498	ICS2595	16	SPEA(/V7) Mirage P64 DRAM (BIOS 3.x)
864	S3 86C716 SDAC		32	Miro 20SD (BIOS 3.x) SPEA Mirage P64 DRAM (BIOS 4.x) Diamond Stealth 64 DRAM Genoa Phantom 64i Miro Crystal 20SD VLB (BIOS 3.xx) ELSA Winner 1000 PRO
864	ICS5342	ICS5342	32	Diamond Stealth 64 DRAM (some)
864	SDAC			Diamond Stealth 64 Graphics 2001
864	AT&T 20C498-13	ICD2061A	32	#9 GXE64 PCI
864				ASUS Video Magic PCI V864 VidTech FastMax P20
964				ELSA Winner 2000 PRO-2,4 spider Tarantula 64
964	AT&T 20C505	ICD2061A	32	Miro Crystal 20SV PCI/ 40SV
964	Bt485	ICD2061A	32	Diamond Stealth 64
964	Bt9485	ICS9161A	32	SPEA Mercury 64
964	Ti3020	ICD2061A	8	ELSA Winner 2000 PRO PCI
964	Ti3025	Ti3025	32	Miro Crystal 40SV #9 GXE64 Pro VLB/PCI
964	IBM RGB		32	Hercules Graphite Terminator 64
868	S3 86C716 SDAC		32	Miro Crystal 20SD PCI ELSA Winner 1000AVI
868	AT&T 29C409			ELSA Winner 1000AVI

TABLE B.2 CONTINUED

CHIP SET	RAMDAC	CLOCKCHIP	BPP	CARD
868				Diamond Stealth Video DRAM Diamond Stealth 64 Video 2120/2200 ELSA Winner 1000PRO/X #9 FX Motion 531 VideoLogic GrafixStar 500
968				Diamond Stealth 64 Video 3200 ELSA Gloria-4/8 ELSA Winner 2000AVI ELSA Winner 2000PRO/X-2/X-4/X-8 Genoa VideoBlitz III AV Hercules Graphite Terminator Pro 64 LeadTek WinFast S430 LeadTek WinFast S510 Miro Crystal 80SV Miro Crystal 20SV #9 FX Motion 771 VideoLogic GrafixStar 700 WinFast S430/S510
968	TVP3026		32	Diamond Stealth 64 Video VRAM ELSA Winner 2000PRO/X
968	IBM RGB		32	Hercules Terminator Pro 64 STB Velocity 64 Video #9 FX Motion 771 Diamond Stealth 64 Video 3240/3400 Genoa VideoBlitz III AVI
968	TI RAMDAC			Diamond Stealth 64 Video 3240/3400
732	(Trio32)		32	(all Trio32-based cards) Diamond Stealth 64 DRAM SE
764	(Trio64)		32	Diamond Stealth 64 DRAM Diamond Stealth 64 Graphics 2xx0 #9 FX Vision 330 STB PowerGraph 64 (all Trio64-based cards) SPEA Mirage P64 (BIOS 5.x)

TABLE B.2   CONTINUED

CHIP SET	RAMDAC	CLOCKCHIP	BPP	CARD
	(Trio64V+)			DSV3326 Diamond Stealth 64 Video 2001 DataExpert DSV3365 ExpertColor DSV3365 MAXColor S3 Trio64V+ ELSA Winner 1000TRIO/V Hercules Terminator 64/Video #9 FX Motion 331 STB Powergraph 64 Video VideoLogic GrafixStar 400
	(Trio64V2)			ELSA Winner 1000/T2D
	(ViRGE)			Canopus Co. Power Window 3DV DSV3325 DataExpert DSV3325 Diamond Multimedia Stealth 3D 2000 Diamond Multimedia Stealth 3D 2000 PRO Diamond Stealth 3D 2000 Diamond Stealth 3D 2000 PRO Diamond Stealth 3D 3000 ELSA Victory 3D ELSA Victory 3DX ELSA Winner 3000-S Expertcolor DSV3325 Hercules Terminator 64/3D LeadTek WinFast 3D S600 MELCO WGP-VG4S #9 FX Motion 332 Orchid Tech. Fahrenheit Video 3D STB systems Powergraph 3D WinFast 3D S600
	(ViRGE/DX)			Hercules Terminator 3D/DX
	(ViRGE/GX)			STB Nitro 3D
	(ViRGE/VX)			ELSA Winner 2000AVI/3D ELSA Winner 3000 ELSA Winner 3000-L-42/-M-22 MELCO WGP-VX8 STB Systems Velocity 3D

TABLE B.2	CONTINUED			
CHIP SET	RAMDAC	CLOCKCHIP	BPP	CARD
911/924				Diamond Stealth VRAM
924	SC1148 DAC			

Note

> For the ViRGE/VX,DX,GX,GX2 chipsets you need XFree86 3.3.1 or newer. You should use the XF86_SVGA server. Some Virge chip sets simply don't work and there is not much that can be done about it at this point.

SUPPORTED PCMCIA CARDS

These cards are supported by David Hinds' PCMCIA package and this list is taken from his Web page (http://hyper.stanford.edu/HyperNews/get/pcmcia/home.html).

CardBus cards are listed at the end of each section. At this time, all CardBus drivers should be treated as experimental. Beware that some cards have 16-bit and CardBus versions with very similar names. If the CardBus version is not specifically listed as supported here, then you should not expect it to work.

ETHERNET CARDS

- SMC, Megahertz, and Ositech cards use the smc91c92_cs driver.
- 3Com and Farallon cards use the 3c589_cs driver.
- Fujitsu, TDK, RATOC, CONTEC, Eagle, and Nextcom cards use the fmvj18x_cs driver.

All other cards use the pcnet_cs driver. Other NE2000-compatible cards that are not on the list are also likely to work with pcnet_cs.

- 3Com 3c589, 3c589B, 3c589C, 3c589D (3c589_cs)
- 3Com Megahertz 3CCE589E, 3CXE589D, 3CXE589EC (3c589_cs)
- Accton EN2212, EN2216 EtherCard (pcnet_cs)
- Accton SOHO BASIC EN220 (pcnet_cs)
- Addtron Ethernet (pcnet_cs)
- AIBrain EPCM-T (pcnet_cs)
- Allied Telesis CentreCOM CE6001, LA-PCM, LA-PCM V2 (pcnet_cs)
- AmbiCom AMB8002, AMB8002T (pcnet_cs)
- AnyCom ECO Ethernet (pcnet_cs)

- Apollo RE450CT (pcnet_cs)
- Argosy EN210 (pcnet_cs)
- Asante FriendlyNet (pcnet_cs) (new cards seem not to work!)
- AST 1082 Ethernet (pcnet_cs)
- Billionton LNT-10TB, LNT-10TN (pcnet_cs)
- California Access LAN Adapter
- CeLAN EPCMCIA (pcnet_cs)
- CNet CN30BC, CN40BC Ethernet (pcnet_cs)
- Compaq Ethernet Adapter (xirc2ps_cs)
- Compex/ReadyLINK Ethernet Combo (pcnet_cs)
- Compex Linkport Ethernet (pcnet_cs)
- COMPU-SHACK BASEline Ethernet (pcnet_cs)
- Connectware LANdingGear Adapter (pcnet_cs)
- Corega Ether PCC-T, PCM-T (pcnet_cs)
- CyQ've ELA-010 10baseT (pcnet_cs)
- CONTEC C-NET(PC)C (fmvj18x_cs)
- Danpex EN-6200P2 Ethernet (pcnet_cs)
- Datatrek NetCard (pcnet_cs)
- Dayna Communications CommuniCard E (pcnet_cs)
- Digital DEPCM-AA, PCP78-AC Ethernet (pcnet_cs)
- Digital EtherWORKS Turbo Ethernet (pcnet_cs)
- D-Link DE-650, DE-660 (pcnet_cs)
- DynaLink L10C Ethernet (pcnet_cs)
- Eagle NE200 Ethernet (fmvj18x_cs)
- Edimax Technology Ethernet Combo (pcnet_cs)
- EFA InfoExpress 205, 207 Combo (pcnet_cs)
- Eiger Labs EPX-ET10T2 Combo (pcnet_cs)
- Eiger Labs EPX-10BT, EPX-ET 10BT EPX-ET 10TZ (fmvj18x_cs)
- ELECOM Laneed LD-CDWA, LD-CDX, LD-CDNIA, LD-CDY, LD-CDF (pcnet_cs)
- EP-210 Ethernet (pcnet_cs)
- Epson Ethernet (pcnet_cs)
- EtherPRIME Ethernet (pcnet_cs)
- Explorer NE-10000 Ethernet (pcnet_cs)
- EZLink 4109 Ethernet (pcnet_cs)

- Farallon Etherwave, EtherMac (3c589_cs)
- Fiberline FL-4680 (pcnet_cs)
- Fujitsu FMV-J181, FMV-J182, FMV-J182A, FMV-J183 (fmvj18x_cs)
- Fujitsu Towa LA501, FMV-1080, FM50N-183 (fmvj18x_cs)
- Gateway 2000 Ethernet (pcnet_cs)
- Genius ME3000II Ethernet (pcnet_cs)
- Grey Cell Ethernet (pcnet_cs)
- GVC NIC-2000P Ethernet Combo (pcnet_cs)
- Hitachi HT-4840-11 EtherCard (fmvj18x_cs)
- Hypertec HyperNet (pcnet_cs)
- IBM CreditCard Ethernet Adapter (pcnet_cs)
- IC-Card Ethernet (pcnet_cs)
- Infotel IN650ct Ethernet (pcnet_cs)
- I-O Data PCLA/T, PCLA/TE (pcnet_cs)
- Katron PE-520 Ethernet (pcnet_cs)
- KingMax Technology EN10-T2 Ethernet (pcnet_cs)
- Kingston KNE-PCM/M, KNE-PC2, KNE-PC2T (pcnet_cs)
- KTI PE-520 Plus (pcnet_cs)
- LANEED LD-CDW Ethernet (pcnet_cs)
- LanPro EP4000A (pcnet_cs)
- Lantech Ethernet (pcnet_cs)
- Level One EPC-0100TB (pcnet_cs)
- Linksys EtherCard (pcnet_cs)
- Logitec LPM-LN10T, LPM-LN10BA, LPM-LN20T Ethernet (pcnet_cs)
- Longshine ShineNet LCS-8534TB Ethernet (pcnet_cs)
- Macnica ME-1 Ethernet (pcnet_cs)
- Maxtech PCN2000 Ethernet (pcnet_cs)
- Megahertz XJ10BT, XJ10BC, CC10BT Ethernet (smc91c92_cs)
- Melco LPC-TJ, LPC-TS, LPC-T, LPC2-T (pcnet_cs)
- Microdyne NE4200 Ethernet (pcnet_cs)
- Midori LANNER LT-PCMT (pcnet_cs)
- Micronet Etherfast Adapter (pcnet_cs)
- NDC Instant-Link (pcnet_cs)
- Network General "Sniffer" (pcnet_cs)
- New Media EtherLAN (nmclan_cs)

- New Media LanSurfer (pcnet_cs)
- New Media LiveWire (NOT the LiveWire+) (nmclan_cs)
- New Media BASICS Ethernet (smc91c92_cs)
- NextCom NC5310 (fmvj18x_cs)
- Novell/National NE4100 InfoMover (pcnet_cs)
- Ositech Four of Diamonds (smc91c92_cs)
- OvisLink Ethernet (pcnet_cs)
- Panasonic CF-VEL211P-B (pcnet_cs)
- Planet SmartCom 2000, 3500, ENW-3501-T, ENW-3502-T (pcnet_cs)
- Pretec Ethernet (pcnet_cs)
- PreMax PE-200 Ethernet (pcnet_cs)
- Proteon Ethernet (pcnet_cs)
- Ratoc REX-9822, REX-5588A/W, REX-R280 (fmvj18x_cs)
- Relia RE2408T Ethernet (pcnet_cs)
- Reliasys 2400A Ethernet (pcnet_cs)
- RPTI EP400, EP401 Ethernet (pcnet_cs)
- SCM Ethernet (pcnet_cs)
- Sky Link Express (pcnet_cs)
- SMC 8020BT EtherEZ (not the EliteCard) (smc91c92_cs)
- SMC 8022 EZCard-10 (pcnet_cs)
- Socket Communications EA LAN Adapter (pcnet_cs)
- Socket Communications LPE Low Power Ethernet (pcnet_cs)
- SOHOware Ethernet (pcnet_cs)
- SuperSocket RE450T (pcnet_cs)
- Surecom Ethernet (pcnet_cs)
- SVEC PN605C (pcnet_cs)
- TDK LAC-CD02x, LAK-CD021, LAK-CD022A, LAK-CD021AX, LAK-CD021BX (fmvj18x_cs)
- Thomas-Conrad Ethernet (pcnet_cs)
- Trust Ethernet Combo (pcnet_cs)
- UNEX NexNIC MA010 (pcnet_cs)
- Volktek NPL-402CT Ethernet (pcnet_cs)
- Xircom CreditCard CE2 (xirc2ps_cs)

FAST ETHERNET (10/100BASE-T) ADAPTERS

epic_cb and tulip_cb drivers are experimental and need a 2.2.x or newer kernel.

- 3Com 3c574TX, 3CCFE574BT (3c574_cs)
- 3Com 3c575TX, 3CCFE575BT, 3CXFE575BT CardBus (3c575_cb, performance problem)
- Abocom LinkMate FE1000 (pcnet_cs)
- Accton Fast EtherCard-16 (xirc2ps_cs)
- Accton EN2220 CardBus (tulip_cb)
- Allied Telesyn AT-2800 (tulip_cb)
- AmbiCom AMB8100 (tulip_cb)
- AnyCom ECO Ethernet 10/100 (pcnet_cs)
- Apollo Fast Ethernet (pcnet_cs)
- Argosy EN220 (smc91c92_cs)
- Compaq Netelligent 10/100 (xirc2ps_cs)
- Compex Linkport TX (tulip_cb)
- COMPU-SHACK FASTline 10/100 (pcnet_cs)
- Corega FastEther PCC-TX (pcnet_cs)
- D-Link DFE-650 (pcnet_cs)
- D-Link DFE-660TX (tulip_cb)
- Dynalink L100C (smc91c92_cs)
- EXP ThinLan 100 (pcnet_cs)
- Fiberline Fast Ethernet (pcnet_cs)
- Hamlet FE1000 10/100 (pcnet_cs)
- Intel EtherExpress PRO/100 (xirc2ps_cs, 16-bit NOT 32-bit)
- IO DATA PCET/TX (pcnet_cs)
- Kingston KNE-CB4TX (tulip_cb)
- KTI KF-C16 (pcnet_cs)
- Laneed LD-10/100CD (pcnet_cs)
- Lantech FastNet/TX (smc91c92_cs)
- LevelOne FPC-0100TX (pcnet_cs)
- LevelOne FPC-0101TX 10/100Mbps CardBus (tulip_cb)
- Linksys PCMPC100 EtherFast 10/100 (pcnet_cs)
- Linksys PCMPC200 EtherFast CardBus (tulip_cb)
- Logitec LPM-LN100TX (pcnet_cs)
- Melco LPC2-TX (pcnet_cs)

- Melco/SMC LPC-TX (smc91c92_cs)
- Microcom TravelCard 10/100 (pcnet_cs)
- Micronet EtherFast Adapter (pcnet_cs)
- NetGear FA410TXC (pcnet_cs)
- Ositech Seven of Diamonds (smc91c92_cs)
- Ositech Seven of Spades CardBus (epic_cb)
- Planet FNW-3600T (pcnet_cs)
- SMC EZ CardBus 10/100 Ethernet (tulip_cb)
- SVEC FD606 10/100 Ethernet (tulip_cb)
- TDK NetworkFlyer LAK-CB100X, LAK-CB100AX CardBus (tulip_cb)
- Toshiba IPC5008A, Advanced Network 10/100 (xirc2ps_cs)
- UMAX Technologies UMAX250 (tulip_cb)
- WiseCom WC-PC400 (smc91c92_cs)
- Xircom CBEII-10/100 (tulip_cb)
- Xircom CreditCard CE3 (xirc2ps_cs, new cards may not work!)

TOKEN-RING ADAPTERS

You should at least have kernel 1.3.72.

- 3Com 3c389 Tokenlink Velocity (ibmtr_cs)
- 3Com 3c689 TokenLink III (ibmtr_cs)
- IBM Token Ring Adapter (ibmtr_cs)
- IBM Turbo 16/4 Token Ring (ibmtr_cs)

WIRELESS NETWORK ADAPTERS

- Aironet PC4500, PC4800 wireless network adapters (airco_cs) (Ben Reed breed@almaden.ibm.com)
- AT&T/NCR/Lucent WaveLAN version 2.0 (wavelan_cs)
- DEC RoamAbout/DS (wavelan_cs)
- Harris PRISM/AM79C930 IEEE 802.11 wireless LAN http://www.absoval.com/ linux-wlan (Mark Mathews mark@absoval.com)
- Lucent WaveLAN/IEEE wireless network adapter (wavelan2_cs) (Lucent Technologies betasupport@wavelan.com)
- Raylink Wireless Network http://world.std.com/~corey/raylink.html (Corey Thomas corey@world.std.com)

- WaveLAN/IEEE wireless network adapter http://www.fasta.fh-dortmund.de/ users/andy/wvlan (Andreas Neuhaus andy@fasta.fh-dortmund.de)
- Xircom CreditCard Netwave (netwave_cs)

ISDN

- Elsa MicroLink ISDN adapter (elsa_cs) (Klaus Lichtenwalder Klaus.Lichtenwalder@WebForum.DE)
- MPS ISLINEnote ISDN adapter (mpsuni_cs) (Detlef Glaschick glaschick@mps-software.de)
- Sedlbauer Speed Star ISDN adapter (sedl_cs) (Marcus Niemann niemann@www-bib.fh-bielefeld.de)
- Teles ISDN adapter (teles_cs) (Christof Petig ea0141@uni-wuppertal.de)

MODEM AND SERIAL CARDS

Virtually all modem cards, simple serial port cards, and digital cellular modems should work. Also ISDN modems that emulate a standard UART are supported.

- Advantech COMpad-32/85 dual serial (serial_cs)
- Argosy dual serial (serial_cs)
- Black Box I114A RS-422/485 (serial_cs)
- National Instruments PCMCIA-232, PCMCIA-232/2, PCMCIA-232/4 (serial_cs)
- National Instruments PCMCIA-485, PCMCIA-485/2 (serial_cs)
- Omega Engineering QSP-100 (serial_cs)
- Quatech, IOTech dual RS-232 cards (serial_cs)
- Quatech quad RS-232 card (serial_cs)
- Socket Communications dual RS-232 card (serial_cs)
- Trimble Mobile GPS (serial_cs)

MEMORY CARDS

All SRAM cards should work. Unsupported flash cards can be read but not written.

- Epson 2MB SRAM
- IBM 8MB Flash (memory_cs)
- Intel Series 2, Series 2+ and Value Series 100 Flash (memory_cs)
- Maxtor MobileMax 16MB Flash (memory_cs)
- New Media SRAM
- RATOC SmartMedia Adapter (memory_cs)
- TDK Flash Memory SFM20W/C 20MB (memory_cs)

SCSI ADAPTERS

Be careful. Many vendors, particularly CD-ROM vendors, seem to switch controller chips at will. Generally, they will use a different product code, but not always: Older (supported) New Media Bus Toaster cards are not easily distinguishable from the current (unsupported) Bus Toaster cards.

- Adaptec APA-1450A, APA-1460, APA-1460A/B/C/D SlimSCSI (aha152x_cs)
- Adaptec SlimSCSI 1480 Cardbus (apa1480_cb, experimental, requires kernel 2.2.2.x or later)
- Digital SCSI II adapter
- Eiger Labs SCSI (qlogic_cs)
- Epson SC200 (qlogic_cs)
- Future Domain SCSI2GO (fdomain_cs)
- IBM SCSI (fdomain_cs)
- Iomega ZIP and JAZ Cards (PPA3) (aha152x_cs)
- IO-DATA PCSC-II, PCSC-II-L
- IO-DATA CDG-PX44/PCSC CD-ROM
- Logitec LPM-SCSI2
- Logitec LCD-601 CD-ROM
- MACNICA mPS110, mPS110-LP SCSI (qlogic_cs)
- Melco IFC-SC2, IFC-DC
- Midori CN-SC43 (qlogic_cs)
- NEC PC-9801N-J03R (qlogic_cs)
- New Media Bus Toaster SCSI (older cards only) (aha152x_cs)
- New Media Toast 'n Jam (SCSI only) (aha152x_cs)
- Noteworthy Bus Toaster SCSI (aha152x_cs)
- Panasonic KXL-D740, KXL-DN740A, KXL-DN740A-NB 4X CD-ROM
- Pioneer PCP-PR1W, PCP-PR2W CD-ROM
- Qlogic FastSCSI (qlogic_cs)
- Raven CD-Note 4X (qlogic_cs)
- RATOC REX-9530 SCSI-2 (qlogic_cs)
- Simple Technologies SCSI (fdomain_cs)
- Sony CD-ROM Discman PRD-250
- Taxan ICD-400PN
- Toshiba NWB0107ABK, SCSC200A, SCSC200B (qlogic_cs)

ATA/IDE CD-ROM Adapters

You should at least have kernel 1.3.72.

- Argosy EIDE CD-ROM (ide_cs)
- Caravelle CD-36N (ide_cs)
- CNF CARDport CD-ROM (ide_cs)
- Creative Technology CD-ROM (ide_cs)
- Digital Mobile Media CD-ROM (ide_cs)
- EXP CD940 CD-ROM (ide_cs, Some work, some do not)
- EXP Traveler 620 CD-ROM (ide_cs)
- H45 Technologies Quick 2x CD-ROM (ide_cs)
- H45 Technologies QuickCD 16X (ide_cs)
- IBM Max 20X CD-ROM (ide_cs)
- IO DATA CDP-TX4/PCIDE, CDP-TX6/PCIDE, CDV-HDN6/PCIDE (ide_cs)
- IO DATA CDP-TX10/PCIDE, CDP-FX24/CBIDE, MOP-230/PCIDE (ide_cs)
- IO DATA HDP-1G/PCIDE, HDP-1.6G/PCIDE (ide_cs)
- Microtech International MicroCD (ide_cs)
- Microtech Mii Zip 100 (ide_cs)
- NOVAC NV-CD410 (ide_cs)
- Sony PCGA-CD5 CD-ROM (ide_cs)
- TEAC IDE Card/II (ide_cs)

Multifunction Cards

You should at least have kernel 1.3.73.

- 3Com 3c562, 3c562B/C/D, 3c563B/C/D (3c589_cs)
- 3Com Megahertz 3CCEM556, 3CXEM556, 3CCEM556B (3c589_cs)
- 3Com Megahertz 3CCFEM556 (3c574_cs)
- 3Com 3CCFEM656B (3c575_cb, ethernet only!!)
- Accton UE2218 (pcnet_cs)
- ActionTex ComNet 33.6 (pcnet_cs)
- AnyCom Fast Ethernet + 56K Combo (pcnet_cs)
- Asus combo card (pcnet_cs)
- Billionton LM5LT-10B (pcnet_cs)
- Compaq Microcom CPQ550 Modem + 10/100 LAN (xirc2ps_cs)
- Dayna Communicard (pcnet_cs)
- D-Link DME336T, DMF560TX (pcnet_cs)

- Gateway Telepath Combo (smc91c92_cs)
- Grey Cell GCS3400 (pcnet_cs)
- GVC LAN modem (pcnet_cs)
- IBM Home and Away, Home and Away 28.8 (pcnet_cs)
- IO DATA PCEM-336T (pcnet_cs)
- Intel EtherExpress PRO/100 LAN/Modem (xirc2ps_cs)
- Linksys LANmodem 28.8 (PCMLM28), 33.6 (PCMLM336) (pcnet_cs)
- Linksys EtherFast LANmodem 56K (PCMLM56) (pcnet_cs)
- Megahertz/U.S. Robotics EM1144, EM3288, EM3336 (smc91c92_cs)
- Motorola Mariner (smc91c92_cs)
- Motorola Marquis (3c589_cs)
- Ositech Jack of Diamonds, Jack of Hearts (smc91c92_cs)
- Ositech Jack of Spades CardBus (epic_cb, experimental, requires kernel 2.2.x or later)
- PREMAX LAN modem (pcnet_cs)
- Psion V.34 Gold Card (pcnet_cs)
- Psion Gold Card Netglobal 56K+10Mb (pcnet_cs)
- Rover ComboCard 33.6 (pcnet_cs)
- TDK 3000/3400/5670 (pcnet_cs)
- Telecom Device SuperSocket LM336 (pcnet_cs)
- Xircom CreditCard CEM28, CEM33, CEM56 (xirc2ps_cs)
- Xircom RealPort REM10BT, REM56G-100 (xirc2ps_cs)
- Xircom RBEM56G-100BTX, CBEM56G-100BTX (tulip_cb, experimental, requires kernel 2.2.x or later)

ATA/IDE CARD DRIVES

These card drives are supported starting with kernel 1.3.72. Both Flash-ATA cards and rotating-media cards are supported. The very old Western Digital 40MB drives are not supported because they do not conform to the PCMCIA ATA specifications.

ATA/IDE INTERFACE CARDS

- Archos Zip100 MiniDrive (ide_cs)
- Microtech International XpressDock (ide_cs)
- DataStor Technology PCMCIA ATA/ATAPI Card (ide_cs)
- Creo DNBoy (ide_cs)

- GREYSTONE DD-25 (ide_cs)
- Shining Technology CitiDISK 250PE (ide_cs)
- Sicon Peripheral Micro Mate (ide_cs)

PARALLEL PORT CARDS

See the appendix on supported parallel port devices.

MISCELLANEOUS CARDS

- GemPlus GPR400 Smart Card Reader`http://www.linuxnet.com/smartcard/code.html` (Wolf Geldmacher `wgeldmacher@paus.ch`)
- IBM Smart Capture (iscc_cs) (Koji Okamura `oka@ec.kyushu-u.ac.jp`)
- IBM Etherjet (cs89x0_cs) (Danilo Beuche `danili@cs.uni-magdeburg.de`)
- National Instruments DAQcard700 `ftp://ftp.rtlinux.org/pub/rtlinux/sources/DAQCard700/` (Oleg Subbotin)
- Netwave AirSurfer Plus (asplus_cs) `http://ipoint.vlsi.uiuc.edu/wireless/asplus.html` (Jay Moorman `jrmoorma@uiuc.edu`)
- New Media Bus Toaster SCSI (new version) (sym53c500_cs) (Tim Corner `tcorner@via.at`)
- New Media BASICS SCSI (sym53c500_cs) (Tim Corner `tcorner@via.at`)
- Nokia/InTalk ST-500A `http://www.absoval.com/linux-wlan` (Mark Mathews `mark@absoval.com`)
- Proxim RangeLAN2 and Symphony wireless LAN cards `http://www.komacke.com/distribution.html` (Dave Koberstein `davek@komacke.com`)
- RATOC REX-9590 (iscc_cs) (Koji Okamura `oka@nanotsu.kobe-u.ac.jp`)
- Samsung MagicWave SWL-1000N `http://www.absoval.com/linux-wlan` (Mark Mathews `mark@absoval.com`)
- Silicom SPE ethernet, SEM EtherModem, SES EtherSerial `http://www.silicom.co.il/linux.htm`
- SIMA TECH SCSI9000 (sym53c500_cs) (Tim Corner `tcorner@via.at`)
- SST 5136-DN-PC DeviceNet Interface (ss5136_cs) `http://www.gnofn.org/~marksu/dn5136man.html` (Mark Sutton `Mark.Sutton@laitram.com`)
- Trimble Mobile GPS (uses serial/modem driver)
- Y-E Data FlashBuster floppy drive adapter (floppy_cs) (David Bateman `dbateman@eng.uts.edu.au`)
- Zoom Telephonics ZoomAir 4000 `http://www.absoval.com/linux-wlan` (Mark Mathews `mark@absoval.com`)

WORKING ON ...

People are working on the following cards:

- Roland SCP-55 MIDI (Toshiaki Nakatsu ir9k-nkt@asahi.net.or.jp)
- CyberRom CD-ROM (David Rowntree rowntree@dircon.co.uk)
- IO DATA PCSC-II (Katayama Nobuhiro kata-n@po.iijnet.or.jp)
- Macnica mPS-1x0 (Katayama Nobuhiro kata-n@po.iijnet.or.jp)
- Proxim RangeLAN/2 http://students.ou.edu/D/James.R.Duchek-1/rangelan2.html (Jim Duchek jimducheck@primary.net
- TView Preso (Brenden Tuck friar@zendragon.com)

UNSUPPORTED

- Adaptec/Trantor APA-460 SlimSCSI
- Eiger Labs SCSI w/FCC ID K36..
- New Media .WAVjammer and all other sound cards
- New Media LiveWire+
- Nikon CoolPix100
- Panasonic KXL-D720, KXL-D745, KXL-D783
- SMC 8016 EliteCard
- Xircom CE II Ethernet/Modem
- Xircom CE-10BT Ethernet

SUPPORTED PARALLEL PORT DEVICES

More and more, the parallel port is used to connect devices other than printers. To support this, parallel port drivers are written for the devices to work. This section presents devices for which parallel port support is written.

To be clear: Printers are not presented in this appendix because they are not supported by parallel port support projects.

Check the Linux Parallel Port support pages for more information at http://www.torque.net/parport. Here you can find

- Paride subsystem for parallel port IDE devices (http://www.torque.net/parport/paride.html)
- Support for parallel port SCSI devices (http://www.torque.net/parport/parscsi.html)

ETHERNET

- Accton EtherPocket adapter
- AT-Lan-Tec/RealTek parallel port ethernet adapter
- D-Link DE600/DE620 parallel port ethernet adapter

HARD DRIVES

- H45 Quick HD
- KingByte IDE/ATAPI disks
- KT Technologies PHd portable hard disk
- MicroSolutions backpack hard-drives
- SyQuest EZ-135
- SyQuest EZ-230
- SyQuest SparQ
- ValueStor external hard-drive

TAPE DRIVES

- Hewlett-Packard Colorado Tracker 250 tape drive (all except the T1000e)
- Hewlett-Packard HP Colorado 5GB tape drive
- Iomega Ditto tape drive
- MicroSolutions backpack 8000t, 8000td tape drives

CD-ROM DRIVES

- Freecom Power CD
- Freecom Traveller CD-ROM
- H45 Quick CD
- Hewlett-Packard HP 7100e/7200e CD-R
- KingByte IDE/ATAPI CD-ROMs
- MicroSolutions backpack CD-ROM. Models 163550 and later are supported by the paride driver. For models 160550 and 162550 separate drivers are available.
- MicroSolutions backpack PD/CD drive
- SyQuest SyJet

REMOVABLE DRIVES

- Avatar Shark 250
- Imation Superdisk
- Iomega ZIP, ZIP Plus drives

IDE ADAPTERS

- Arista ParaDrive products
- DataStor Commuter disks
- Fidelity International Technologies TransDisk products
- Freecom IQ Cable Parallel
- Shuttle Technology EPAT/EPEZ parallel port IDE adapter
- Shuttle Technology EPIA parallel port IDE adapter

SCSI ADAPTERS

- Adaptec APA-348 mini-SCSI plus adapter cable
  - Driver available at `http://www.torque.net/parpart/parscsi.html`
- Adaptec APA-358 mini-SCSI EPP adapter cable
  - Driver available at `http://www.torque.net/parpart/parscsi.html`
- Shuttle Technology EPSA-2 parallel port SCSI adapter
  - Driver available at `http://www.torque.net/parpart/parscsi.html`
- Shuttle Technology EPST parallel port SCSI adapter
  - Driver available at `http://www.torque.net/parpart/parscsi.html`

DIGITAL CAMERAS

- Connectix QuickCam

PCMCIA PARALLEL PORT CARDS

The parport_cs driver requires kernel 2.2.x or later.

- Quatech SPP-100
- IOtech DBK35, WBK20A

PLUG AND PLAY DEVICES

For people having trouble getting Plug and Play devices to work, the ISA PnP utilities written by Peter Fox are available. Quote from the README:

```
These programs allow ISA Plug-And-Play devices to be configured
on a Linux machine.

This program is suitable for all systems, whether or not they
include a PnP BIOS.
```

Commands have been taken from the Plug and Play ISA specification Version 1.0a.

More information on ISA PnP utilities can be found on the Web site of Peter Fox at `http://www.roestock.demon.co.uk/isapnptools/`.

Please let me know about hardware (not normally supported under Linux) which can be put to work with the aid of these utilities. A list of this hardware will be put in this appendix.

LINUX-INCOMPATIBLE HARDWARE

Some hardware manufacturers have created devices that are compatible with MS-DOS and Windows 95/98 only. They seem to emulate part of the normally available hardware in the devices by software packages sold together with the device. Specification on these devices is not presented to the world so it is almost impossible to write drivers for these devices. A list of devices reported as being Linux-incompatible is given in the following section.

Simply put, it is best to avoid hardware that makes statements such as "Needs Windows" or "Windows only."

PRINTERS

- Brother HL-820 printer
- Canon LBP-465 printer
- HP Deskjet 710, 720, 820, and 1000 series printers (although Windows only) are supported under Linux. Have a look at `http://www.httptech.com/ppa/`. Be warned: Support is still in early development.
- Lexmark 1000 inkjet printer
- Lexmark 3200. For windows it has an emulation driver for HP500 and HP500C. Under Linux this printer will not work using an HP500 or HP500C driver.
- Lexmark 5000 printer
- Lexmark CJ5000 (ColorJet) printer
- OkiData OkiPage 4w
- Sharp JX-9210 printer

MODEMS

- 3Com 3CXM356/3CCM356 and 3CXM656/3CCM656 PCMCIA
- AOpen FM56-P and FM56-H
- AT&T/Lucent winmodem
- Boca Research 28.8 internal modem (model MV34AI)

- Boca Research 33.6 internal modem (model MV34). (Joe Harjung has succeeded in configuring the modem under Win95 and then soft booting into Linux with the modem still working. Filippo is using this modem under Linux directly without any problems and without soft booting from Windows. I definitely need more information on these Boca Research modems.) The Boca Research 33.6 modem (model M336I) is mentioned to work with Linux. The only thing that needed to be done was to disable Plug and Play. Here are the specs of the modem:

- Three stickers saying "MC2920A-3.3," "E6030D 4035-01" and "1721 8011 A"

- Chips etc on the board

- Cirrus Logic CL-MD3450D-SC-B

- Cirrus Logic MD1724-11VC-D

- Datatronic VLM301-1??

- Omron G5V-1 (2 of them)

- AST (?) M628032-20E1

- Cirrus Logic CL-MD4450C-SC-A

- Abracon 23-040-20

- Two empty places for additional chips, one of which might be a Cirrus Logic CL-MD1724D

- 4 jumpers for COM port selection

- 10 jumpers for IRQ selection

- Other unknown jumpers

- Compaq 192 PCMCIA modem/serial card

- HP Fastmodem D4810B

- IBM Mwave ("Dolphin") card. This card is a combination of sound, modem, fax, voice control, and dictation. Software is replacing part of hardware functionality so this software should be loaded to get things working.

- Multiwave Innovation CommWave V.34 modem (`http://www.multiwave.com/`)

- Megahertz XJ/CC2560 PCMCIA

- New Media Winsurfer PCMCIA modem/serial card

- Rockwell SoftK56

- US Robotics WinModem series

- Zoltrix 33.6 Win HSP Voice/Speaker Phone modem

- Zoltrix Phantom 56K, model FM-HSP56PCI, chipset PCTel (**PCI**)

GLOSSARY

AGP: Accelerated Graphics Port. A bus interconnect mechanism designed to improve performance of 3D graphics applications. AGP is a dedicated bus from the graphics subsystem to the core-logic chipset. Information can be found at `http://www.euro.dell.com/intl/euro/r+d/r+dnews/vectors/vect_2-1/v2-1_agp.htm`.

ATAPI: AT Attachment Packet Interface. A new protocol for controlling mass storage devices similar to SCSI protocols. It builds on the ATA (AT Attachment) interface, the official ANSI Standard name for the IDE interface developed for hard disk drives. ATAPI is commonly used for hard disks, CD-ROM drives, tape drives, and other devices.

ATM: Asynchronous Transfer Mode

CDDA: Compact Disk Digital Audio. Capability of CD-ROM/Writer to read out audio tracks.

DMA: Direct Memory Access

EGA: Enhanced Graphics Adapter

EIDE: Enhanced IDE

EISA: Extended Industry System Architecture

FDDI: Fiber-Distributed Data Interface. High-speed ring local area network.

IDE: Integrated Drive Electronics. Each drive has a built-in controller.

ISA: Industry System Architecture

ISDN: Integrated Services Digital Network

MCA: Micro Channel Architecture

MFM: Modified Frequency Modulation

MMX: Multimedia Extensions. Added to the newest generation of Intel Pentium Processors. These offer better audio and video quality.

PCI: Peripheral Component Interconnect. 32-bit bus designed by Intel. Information can be found on `http://www.pcisig.com` and `http://infoserver.ee.siue.edu/~jbutter/EE580_1.html`.

PPA: Printing Performance Architecture. Protocol developed by Hewlett Packard for their series of Deskjet printers. In essence, the protocol moves the low-level processing of the data to the host computer rather than the printer. This allows for a low-cost printer with a small amount of memory and computing power and a flexible driver. However, this comes at the price of compatibility. HP's decision was to develop drivers only for Windows 95 for this printer.

RAID: Redundant Arrays of Inexpensive Disks. The basic idea of RAID is to combine multiple small, inexpensive disk drives into an array of disk drives that yields performance exceeding that of a single large expensive drive. The five types of redundant array Architectures are RAID-1 through RAID-5. A nonredundant array of disk drives is referred to as RAID-0. Some RAID systems can mix formats. Information is available at http://www.uni-mainz.de/~neuffer/scsi/what_is_raid.html.

RLL: Run Length Limited

SCSI: Small Computer Systems Interface. A standard interface defined for all devices in a computer. It makes possible the use of a single adapter for all devices.

http://www.uni-mainz.de/~neuffer/scsi/what_is_scsi.html

SVGA: Super Video Graphics Adapter

UART: Universal Asynchronous Receiver Transmitter

USB: Universal Serial Bus. Not yet supported by Linux.

VGA: Video Graphics Adapter

VLB: VESA Local Bus. Used in some 486 PCs.

WORM: Write Once Read Many

INDEX

Special Edition
Using

The One Source for Comprehensive Solutions™

The one-stop shop for serious users, *Special Edition Using* offers readers a thorough understanding of software and technologies. Intermediate to advanced users get detailed coverage that is clearly presented and to the point.

Linux, Fifth Edition
Jack Tackett, Jr. and Steven Burnett
0789721805
$49.99 US

Other *Special Edition* *Using* Titles

Caldera OpenLinux
Allan Smart et al.
0789720582
$39.99 US

KDE
Nicholas Wells
0789722143
$39.99 US

UNIX, Third Edition
Peter Kuo
0789717476
$39.99 US

TCP/IP
John Ray
0789718979
$29.99 US

Microsoft SQL Server 7.0
Stephen Wynkoop
0789715236
$39.99 US

Lotus Notes and Domino R5
Randy Tamura
0789718146
$49.99 US

NetWare 5.0
Peter Kuo, John Pence, and Sally Specker
0789720566
$39.99 US

www.quecorp.com

StarOffice
Michael Koch et al.
0789719932
$39.99 US

All prices are subject to change.

Other Related Titles

Practical KDE
Dennis Powell
078972216x
$29.99 US

Red Hat Linux Installation and Configuration Handbook
Duane Hellums
0789721813
$39.99 US

Caldera OpenLinux Installation and Configuration Handbook
Gary Wilson
0789721058
$39.99 US

C++ from Scratch
Jesse Liberty
0789720795
$29.99 US

Using Linux
Bill Ball
0789716232
$29.99 US

Platinum Edition Using HTML 4, XML, and Java 1.2
Eric Ladd
078971759X
$59.99 US

Practical Internet
Barbara Kasser
0789722267
$24.99 US

www.quecorp.com

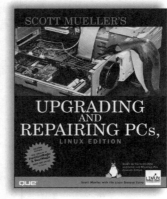

Upgrading and Repairing PCs, Linux Edition
Scott Mueller
0789720752
$59.99 US

The Concise Guide to XFree86 for Linux
Aron Hsiao
0789721821
$34.99 US

Linux Programming by Example
Kurt Wall
0789722151
$24.99 US

All prices are subject to change.